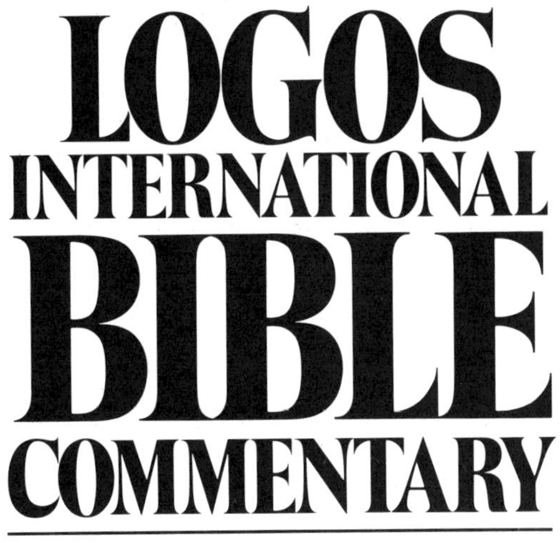

The Gospels of Matthew, Mark and Luke

With text from the New International Version Bible

Editor-in-Chief
Stephen D. Swihart, M. Div.

Logos International
Plainfield, New Jersey 07060

LOGOS INTERNATIONAL BIBLE COMMENTARY

Printed in the United States of America
Library of Congress Catalog Number: 81-80202
International Standard Book Number: 0-88270-500-8
Logos International, Plainfield, New Jersey 07060

THIS VOLUME IS DEDICATED TO THE
LORD JESUS CHRIST,
TO WHOM BELONGS ALL GLORY AND HONOR!

Advisory Consultants

David du Plessis, D.D.
Author, Bible teacher

Howard M. Ervin, Ph.D.
Author, seminary professor

Chalmer E. Faw, Ph.D.
Author, Bible teacher, professor

Lloyd B. Hildebrand, M.S.
Editor, minister

David C. Munday, B.A.
Editorial consultant

Michael Scanlan, T.O.R.
College president, author

J. Rodman Williams, Ph.D.
Author, Bible teacher, seminary president

Introductions, topical headings and commentary were prepared by Stephen D. Swihart, M.Div.

Sponsors

Without the participation of the people whose names are listed below, the *Logos International Bible Commentary* could not have been published. We wish to acknowledge their support and to express our deep appreciation for their gifts and prayers.

Mr. & Mrs. Ellis C. Adams
Aledo Christian Center
Mrs. Maude Allen
Mrs. Katherine Anderson
Mr. Paul F. Anderson
Mrs. John Anthony
Dail Applegate
Mr. & Mrs. Ralph Ascolese
Marion & George C. Ashby, Jr.
Mr. Joseph Avolese

Mr. Kenneth L. Baldner
Mr. Richard D. Baranzini
Mr. K. Barcel
Mr. & Mrs. Robert Bardwell
Mr. Walt Barfield
Mr. & Mrs. Robert W. Bargo
Ms. Lenora Barnes
Mrs. Helen Barta
Mr. R. Barthel
Dr. Stanley Beans
Mrs. John Belliotti
Mr. & Mrs. Michael S. Bender
Mr. Chuck Benedict
Mrs. Reese Bentley
Mr. Ralph Bertram
Ms. Karen Bills
Oliver Bivins
Mr. Arthur E. Bliese
Mr. Nick Boelhower
Andrew & Katherine Bogard
Mr. & Mrs. D.D. Bonner
Mr. & Mrs. Donald T. Brady
Miss Mary Brittain
Mr. Kenneth Brown
Dr. & Mrs. Robert Brown
Ms. Marilyn Bruce
Mr. & Mrs. Brian Buck
Mrs. Harold Bunkelmann
Mr. & Mrs. William S. Bunte
Mr. Joe Burke
Ms. Mary A. Burns
Mr. Jay H. Burton
Mr. & Mrs. Alfred Butler
Charles & Ruth Butler

Mr. Stanley C. Cameron
Ms. Mary Helen Capell
Joseph & Nancy Cappello
Mrs. Juanita Carlson
Ms. Alice E. Carpenter
Ms. Evelyn C. Carpenter
Mr. John Casey, Jr.
Mrs. Barbara Chambers
Mr. Nelson Channell
Mr. & Mrs. Joseph Chellis
W. Douglas & Margaret F. Childers
Mr. Cliff J. Chin
Mr. Howard L. Chin
Mr. John Christian
Mr. Jack Clark
Mrs. June B. Cohen
Mrs. G.N. Combs
Mr. Frank Compton, Jr.
Mr. Wilmer H. Comstock
Mr. S.L. Conger
Dr. & Mrs. Henry Cook
Mrs. Joyce Young Cook
Ms. Betty Cooper
Mr. Gregory Cooper
Mr. & Mrs. Ron Corbin
Ms. Ethel Corcoran
Mr. & Mrs. George Corcoran
Calvin & Judith Cornils

Mr. Richard Cowan
Mr. J.L. Cox
Mr. John Crewz
Mr. John H. Cromer
Rev. Marilyn Crown, Pastor
Mr. & Mrs. Wayne Crutchfield

Mr. & Mrs. Calvin Dahl
Mr. James Dalton
Rev. & Mrs. Michael J. D'Amico
Ms. Eleanor H. Davies
Ms. Ruth Davis
Mr. & Mrs. Thomas Dawson
Miss Jean Day
Mr. & Mrs. Donald Dean, Jr.
Mr. Oscar W. Deck
Judge F.L. Deierhoi
Mr. & Mrs. A.J. DeMarco, Sr.
Mr. & Mrs. John DePastino
Mr. & Mrs. C. Joel Dickson
Mrs. Charles W. Dickson
Mr. Eugene Dicresce
Mr. & Mrs. W. Donald Diehl
Mr. Warren Dixon
Martha L. Dobey
Mr. Dwight E. Du Bois
Mr. R.L. Dubbers
Mr. & Mrs. Joseph M. Dugan
Mr. & Mrs. A. Bailey Duncan & Wilda Lou
Ms. Betty Dunleavy
Mr. & Mrs. Dan Dunn
Mr. R.E. Dwinell
Richard Dwyer, Jr.

Mr. Mark V. Elio
Mrs. Martha Elliott
Mr. W. Ellison
Mr. B.W. Engle
Mr. & Mrs. Erickson
Mr. & Mrs. W.J. Ernest
Mrs. James Euliss
Mrs. Edith Everett

Mr. W. Richard Fabian
Oleh S. Farmiga
Mr. Roger Fearing
Mrs. Cecile Felps
Dale Fenton
Mr. & Mrs. David G. Fernald
Mr. Edward M. Fettes
Chester & Melinda Field
Major & Mrs. Peter Field
Mrs. J.V. Filsinger
First Christian Assembly
Mrs. Leo Fite
Rev. & Mrs. James Fitzhugh
Florida Wire & Rigging Works, Inc.
Mr. William Fonville & Family
Mr. James B. Ford
Mr. & Mrs. Robert Franklin
Ms. Audrey Freeman
Mr. Eugene K. Frey
Ms. Stephanie Frock
Mr. Frederick Fruehan

Mrs. Gordon Garrett
Mr. & Mrs. Harold Gassner
Mr. & Mrs. Theodore P. Gerwing
Laura Giambalvo
Mr. E.D. Gibbs
Rev. Eugene Grater
Mr. & Mrs. E.K. Gravely
Mr. & Mrs. Richard Gross
Rev. Wesley Gross
Mr. & Mrs. Willard H. Grove
Mrs. C.N. Grubbs
Mr. Mario Guarducci
Mr. W.T. Gullette
Mr. & Mrs. Wilbur Gundlach
Mr. & Mrs. C.D. Gunnoe
Patricia Guzaway

Viola Alda Haas
Mrs. Jean Hadden
Gen. & Mrs. Ralph E. Haines, Jr.
Mr. Palmer S. Haines & Children
Mr. Gerry Hamm
Mr. & Mrs. Norval Harkness
Mr. Steven D. Harmon
Mr. & Mrs. Don Harper
Mr. N.O. Hart
Mr. William Haska

Mr. & Mrs. John Hauck
James & Ruth Ann Head
Anne Heian
Frederick W. Henke, M.D.
Mary Lou Henry
Mr. Mark Hertzog
Mr. James R. Hess
Mrs. Charles Hill
Marlan & Norma Hillman
Ms. Dianne Hoard
Mr. F. Preston Hobart, Jr.
Mr. & Mrs. John Hoch
Co. Judge Ray Holbrook
Mr. Ray Holder
Mr. & Mrs. Barry J. Holloway
Mr. & Mrs. A.O. Hollis
Rev. Peter Holmes
Holy Spirit Prayer Community
Mr. Glen C. Hoover
Mr. Henry R. Hopkinson
Mr. & Mrs. George Edward Hull
Mrs. Mildred Hunt
Ms. Virginia Huntington

Ms. Aurelia Iacobelli
Mr. Roger Inbody
Mr. & Mrs. Tom L. Ingram

Ms. Donna Jacobs
Mr. & Mrs. David Janssen
Ms. Ella G. Jantzen, R.N.
Mr. & Mrs. William A. Jaworski
Mr. Alex Johnson
B.L. Johnson
Mr. Paul G. Johnson
Mr. Thomas Johnson
Mr. Milton E. Jones

Mr. John E. Karsten
Col. & Mrs. William M. Kasper
Mr. & Mrs. E.G. Kates
Mrs. June Keating
Mr. Alex D. Keller
Mr. Robert C. Kelpe
H. Jacquelyn Kennedy
Lee Killgore

Mrs. E. Kimball
Rev. & Mrs. Charles R. Kinsley
Mrs. Ruth Kirkpatrick
Mr. Chris G. Klapheke
Mrs. Dannie Kliewer
Peter Knapp
Rev. & Mrs. Roscoe A. Knapp
Mr. Stanley Kojac
Mr. & Mrs. Mike Konikowski
Miss Janice R. Konte
Audrey Louise Koustas
Mr. & Mrs. Ira L. Krammes
Ms. Dorothy Kreiger
Mr. John Kromka
Mrs. Chas. Kurrus, III

Mr. & Mrs. Vincent Laino
Gerard R.F. Landry, M.D.
Mrs. Christine Lane
Mrs. Dewey Lane
Mr. & Mrs. Jacob Lapp
Ms. Madeline Laske
Mr. Melvin Lauver
Ms. Lucille Lebeau
Mrs. Margie Leidelmeyer
Mrs. Laura Lewis
Mr. & Mrs. Hale Lichtenwalner
Ms. Eileen Limburg
Jon C. Lindgren
Mrs. Alleyne W. Little
Living Way Church
Mr. Joseph Loewy
Ms. Wilma Lombard
Rev. Ray Long
Mr. & Mrs. Richard Lopez
Dr. Joseph Lovett
Ms. Nora Lucas
Mr. George M. Lutz
Mrs. Keith Lyon
Mrs. Marjory D. Lyons
Cheryl Lytle

Angus MacDonald, D.V.M.
Mrs. Clara Maclaren
Mr. & Mrs. B.G. Malone
Mrs. Betty Maradie

Maranatha Full Gospel Church
Mr. & Mrs. Anton Marco
Mrs. Dorothy K. Marker
Donald T. & Jane Marsh
Mr. & Mrs. Richard Martin
Loretta M. Mathewson
Mr. & Mrs. Everett Matson
Mr. R.C. Matthews, Jr.
Ms. Esther L. Maurer, M.D.
Mr. Lyle May
Mr. & Mrs. D.E. McAnally
Ms. Shirley McCaleb
Mr. & Mrs. S. McClain, Jr.
Mr. A.M. McCoy
Mrs. S.W. McCreery
Mr. & Mrs. Jackie R. McDole
Mrs. C.D. McDonald
Dr. David McElroy
Mr. & Mrs. John McEwen
Mr. Ray McGregory
John B. & Helene H. McKeon
Mr. James McLaughlin, Jr.
Rev. Erin Q. McMurry
Mr. Emil W. Mehrer
Ms. Eileen L. Mendelson
Mr. Robert J. Miller, Jr.
Mr. & Mrs. John Mills
Mr. Thomas Mizeur
Mr. Conley L. Moffett
Mrs. Jane Q. Mole
Mr. & Mrs. Jim Moncrief
Ruby Lowder Moore
William M. & Carol A. Moorehad
Mr. Frank P. Morabito
Mr. & Mrs. R.E. Morrow
Mt. Zion Church
Mr. Robert R. Mueller
Mr. R. Steven Mulford
Mrs. Rubie M. Mulgrave
Mrs. Mary Musante
Ms. Maryolive W. Mygatt

Ms. Ruth Nall
Ms. Edna A. Napp
Ms. Eleanor Nappa
Mrs. Jack Neilsen
John Neufeld
Francis & Margaret Nicholson
Daniel & Millie Ninowski
Joseph & Linda Ninowski, Sr.
Diane Noerenberg
Mr. Clayton Norton

Mr. Walter D. Olmstead
Nancy M. Opsal
Ms. Barbara A. O'Reilly
Mrs. Mary Ose
Mrs. Thomas Owen

Ms. Elsie Padden
Ms. Alice Page
Mr. & Mrs. George Pallas
Mr. Nick B. Paravate
Mrs. Roy Partin
Maj. Dennis M. Patrick
Dale E. Perdue
Mr. Steven Perini
Mrs. Bessie Perry
Mr. Charles R. Peters
Grant & Donna Petersen
Mrs. Edith P. Peterson
Mrs. James Phillips
Nell M. Phillips
Mrs. William Pickett
Mrs. T.C. Pinckney
Mr. & Mrs. Earl R. Pinkston
Mr. & Mrs. H.E. Pittman
Mr. & Mrs. Roger Plumstead
Mr. & Mrs. John R. Potts
Mr. John Praktish
Mr. & Mrs. Robert Prather
Rev. Gary D. Pratt
Amy Presley
Gene & Phylene Presley
Mr. Robert Preston
John & Ernestine Priebe, Jr.
Mr. & Mrs. James Pugh

Mr. & Mrs. Louis Quagliero
Mr. & Mrs. Edward S. Quest

Ms. Carla Radloff

Mrs. A.J. Rainwater, Sr.
Mr. & Mrs. A.J. Rainwater, Jr.
Sgt. Steven Reedy
Dr. Benjamin F. Reid, Pastor
Ms. Helen Ricciardi
Mr. Leonard Rieger
Ms. Mary E. Riordan
Ms. Irene Rivais
Rivergrove Christian Ministries
Mrs. Kenneth Roach
Mr. & Mrs. Allen E. Roberts
Mrs. Grace Roberts
Mr. Rick Roberts
Ms. Joy Robinson
Mr. L.B. Robinson
Weston Robinson
Mr. & Mrs. Lester Rock
Mr. & Mrs. Rostek
Mr. David Rucker
Dr. Ross Rumph
Mr. J. Fred Rupert
William C. Rutherford

Col. & Mrs. James E. Salminen
Mrs. J. Sandy
Dolores & Milton Sauls
Mr. John Crones Sawyer
Maurice Saylor
Mrs. Virginia Scheel
Mr. Walter L. Schneider
Willard & Mildred Soper
Dr. Mervin Specht

Herbert Taylor
Mr. William S. Templeton
Mr. & Mrs. Larry Tepley
Mr. & Mrs. Ernie Tevebaugh
Mr. & Mrs. Len Thies
Mr. & Mrs. David F. Tiesma
Mr. S.A. Tilson, Jr.
Mrs. G.W. Tilton
Mr. Joseph R. Tomasso
Mrs. Ann R. Townsend
Mr. & Mrs, John Trent
Trinity Broadcasting
Mr. & Mrs. R.R. Troxell

Mr. Paul Tuchman
Ms. Naomi Tummins
Ms. Gail Turner
Mr. & Mrs. Mark Tusken

Ms. Rosemary Upton
Mr. Harold W. Uzzell

Mr. Richard VanDenBerg
Mr. Don Van Hook
Mrs. George M. Van Meter
Mrs. William Vaughan
Mr. John W. & Mary L. Vice
Mr. & Mrs. Eugene Volz

Mr. & Mrs. Lloyd & Marjorie Wakeman
Miss Loretta Wakie
Mrs. Janice Walen
Dr. & Mrs. Walter B. Wallin
Catherine Warford
Ms. Dottie Watson
Rev. Ray Weaver
Mr. James Weber
Mrs. Carol Webster
Mr. & Mrs. Fred Weck
Mrs. Ruby Welch
Mrs. Genevieve W. Welle
Mr. John P. Wenrich
Miss Helen West
Dr. & Mrs. Harry U. Whayne
Mr. Ben White
Mrs. Philip G. White
Mr. & Mrs. Roger White
Mr. & Mrs. G.H. Wicke
Mrs. W.W. Wieland
Miss Betty Wilbanks
Miss Catherine Williamson
Mr. & Mrs. David Willman
Mrs. F.E. Wilson
Mr. W.L. Witschey
Ms. Jayne Wolfe
Mrs. Jack W. Wooten
Ms. Bernadette Wozniak
Mr. Fred D. Wright
Rev. & Mrs. Latham Wright, Jr.
Mrs. W.F. Wunker, Jr.

Mr. Richard L. Yopp
Mr. Rawley L. Young
Mr. William Young
Mr. & Mrs. Edward F. Younger, Jr.

Cheryl A. Zaccardi
Mr. John A. Zachman

Mr. Robert Zellner
Mr. Randy Zemlicka
Mrs. Hazel Zieman
Mrs. Ernestine Zimmerman
Mrs. Howard Zimmerman
Donna Zito

In Memory Of

Carrie Arthur
W.H. Barfield
Charles & Margaret Benedict
Mrs. Carol Best
Daniel Burns Boles
Pocohontas Wyche R. Crews
Brandon Andrew Dice
Allen A. Dobey
Martin Dunleavy
Frank Elio
Lelia T. Fettes
William T. Flynn
Mr. & Mrs. J.E. Gunnoe, Sr.
Mrs. Martha Ann Harris
Lois June Hopkinson
Steve & Spike Johnston
Dorothy Kramer Kurland

Jeffrey S. Kojac
Mr. Frederick W. Lewis
Cathy Lima
Anne Lucas
Opal Manny
Esbelta Fazenda Matthews
Salvatore B. Messina
Michael, Daniel, Edward & Christina
Mr. Adrian I. Riordan, Sr.
Mr. Walter R. Wallin
Thelma Weber
Mr. & Mrs. O.W. West
The Parents of Dr. & Mrs. Harry Whayne
Nora L. White
Paul S. Williams
Helen D. Wright
Leonidas D. Young

Why We Choose the NIV

Welcome to a unique Bible reading experience!

After examining various renderings of Scripture, and after consulting experts in the field, we decided to use the New International Version of the Bible (NIV) for the following reasons:

1. We wanted a version of the Bible that is reliable, understandable to everyone, and true to the original meaning.
2. We wanted a version which could be read aloud in groups or silently alone.
3. We wanted a version we could recommend to families and friends.

Although several critically acclaimed translations have appeared on the market recently, none is more easily understood or more reliable than the NIV.

It is more than a paraphrase which, while attempting to make the meaning of an obscure or hard-to-understand text clear, cannot help but introduce a subjective element into the translation. What often happens is that, while rendering a passage of Scripture easy to understand, the result is the interpretation of the translator, and not always the meaning of the original Hebrew or Greek writer.

The NIV, however, is not a paraphrase. As easy as it is to understand, it is a wholly reliable and completely new translation. It is the work of over a hundred distinguished scholars working directly from the best available Hebrew, Aramaic and Greek texts—the earliest known sources. Scholars from various countries and many different denominations worked together to eliminate doctrinal bias and colloquial language. The translators represented the United States, Great Britain, Canada, Australia and New Zealand, as well as denominations such as Anglican, Assemblies of God, Baptist, Brethren, Christian Reformed, Church of Christ, Evangelical Free, Lutheran, Mennonite, Methodist, Nazarene, Presbyterian and Wesleyan.

Although the primary concern of the translators has been the accuracy of the translation, "samples of the translation were tested for clarity and ease of reading by various kinds of people—young and old, highly educated and less well educated, ministers and laymen."* The result is a highly readable, faithful and trustworthy translation—a translation we are confident you will understand, enjoy and depend on. It is recommended for use in Sunday school, church and Bible study groups—in fact, anywhere the Bible is read.

---

*The Committee on Bible Translation, *The Holy Bible: New International Version,* (Grand Rapids, Michigan: Zondervan Bible Publishers, 1978), p. viii.

Contents

How to Make This Commentary Work for You xv
Topical Index xvii
Charts and Diagrams xxi
Special Studies xxiii
Abbreviations xxv
A Capsule View of the New Testament xxvii
Introduction to the Gospels xxxi
Introduction to the Gospel According to Matthew xxxiii
Matthew 1
Introduction to the Gospel According to Mark 331
Mark 333
Introduction to the Gospel According to Luke 419
Luke 421
Selected Bibliography 591

How to Make This Commentary Work for You

A tool is only as useful as the operator's skill in knowing how to use it.

This commentary is a tool. Perhaps you are familiar with the use of commentaries. Perhaps not. In any event you can maximize your skills through the following pointers.

This book is more than an ordinary commentary. It is also a Bible dictionary, a handbook on Bible geography and culture, a Christian theology, a devotional reader and a topical fact book of vital Christian truths. Therefore, in order to make this commentary work for you, you need to make use of these two points:

1. *Textual Information.* If you are seeking comments on a particular passage, turn to that reference in this book (ready-references are placed in the upper right-hand corners of pages on the right). Now look for the specific verse or the precise words within a verse that interest you. You will find notes on virtually every significant phrase in the commentary on Matthew. If you are examining the book of Mark or Luke, you may need to refer back to the more detailed notes in Matthew where the same accounts are discussed at length (parallel references to any text are located in parentheses beneath the major titles of the sections of this commentary). For a thorough coverage of any text, the parallel passages should be read.

2. *Topical Information.* If you are seeking comments on a particular theme or word, but do not know where to find that subject in the Bible, turn to the "Topical Index" for a complete guide to all of the comments found in this particular volume on that subject. Also, consult the "Charts, Diagrams and Maps" index, and the "Special Studies" index in order to discover further available information on that theme. This approach is especially useful for answering perplexing questions or for conducting New Testament word studies.

Topical Index

Abraham, Son of—Matt. 1:1
Abraham's Side—Matt. 25:31-46; Luke 16:19-31
Abyss—Matt. 25:31-46
Adultery—Matt. 5:27-30; 10:12; Luke 18:20
Alabaster Jar—Matt. 26:6, 7
Alms/Acts of righteousness—Matt. 6:1-4
Angels—Matt. 1:19-21; 2:13, 19; 28:2, 5;
  Luke 1:11-38; 2:8-14, 21; 22:43
Anger—Matt. 5:21-26
Anna—Luke 2:36-39
Apostles—Matt. 10:1-42
Archelaus—Matt. 2:19-23
Ascension of Jesus—Mark 16:19, 20;
  Luke 24:50-53
Authority—Matt. 28:16-18
Ax—Matt. 3:7-10

Baptism
  in Spirit—Matt. 3:11, 12
  in water—Matt. 3:1-6
  of fire—Matt. 3:11, 12
  of Jesus—Matt. 3:13-17
Beatitudes—Matt. 5:1-12
Beelzebub—Matt. 12:22-37, 43-45;
  Luke 11:14-28
Bethany—Matt. 26:6,7
Bethlehem—Matt. 2:1-8; Luke 2:4
Bind and loose—Matt. 18:18-20
Blasphemy against Spirit—Matt. 12:22-37
Blood money—Matt. 27:6-10

Canaanite—Matt. 15:21-28
Capernaum—Matt. 9:1-3
Census—Luke 2:1-3
Centurion—Matt. 8:5-13
Chastity—Matt. 19:11, 12
Children—Matt. 18:10, 11; 19:13-15
Christ—Matt. 1:1; 16:15, 16
Church—Matt. 16:13-20; 18:15-20
Circumcision—Luke 1:59-66; 2:21
Cities, Sinful—Matt. 11:20-24
Cloak, Jesus—Matt. 9:20-22
Coin, Lost—Luke 15:8-10
Commandment, Greatest—Matt. 22:34-40
Commission, Great—Matt. 28:16-20
Communion of bread and cup—Matt. 26:26-30
Council, The—Luke 22:66-71a
Cross—Matt. 10:16-39; 16:24-26; 27:32
Crucifixion—Matt. 27:32-54

David, Son of—Matt. 1:1
Day of Judgment—Matt. 10:9-15
Days of Noah—Matt. 24:36-41
Demons/Demonization—Matt. 4:23-25;
  7:15-23; 8:14-17, 28-34; 9:27-34; 10:1-4, etc.
Denial of Christ—Matt. 26:69-75
Devil—Matt. 4:1-11; 12:22-37; 13:39
Disciples, Calling of—Matt. 4:18-22;
  Mark 1:16-20; Luke 5:1-11; 6:12-16
Discipleship—Matt. 8:18-22; 10:16-39;
  16:24-28; Luke 9:23-27, 57-62; 14:25-35
Divorce—Matt. 5:31, 32; 19:1-12
Dogs—Matt. 7:6; 15:26-28
Dust, Shaking off—Matt. 10:9-15

Ears to hear—Matt. 11:7-15
Elijah—Matt. 17:9-13
Emmaus—Luke 24:13-35
Epileptic—Matt. 17:14-21
Elizabeth—Luke 1:5-25, 39-56
Excommunication—Matt. 18:15-20
Eye for eye—Matt. 5:38-42
Eye of needle—Matt. 19:23-30

Faith—Matt. 9:1-3, 27-31
Fall of disciples—Matt. 26:31-35
Fasting—Matt. 6:16-18; 9:14-17
Fear—Matt. 10:16-39; 14:25-33
Fig tree—Matt. 21:18-22; 24:32-35;
  Mark 13:28-31; Luke 21:29-33
Fire—Matt. 7:15-23
First/Last—Matt. 19:23-30
Five thousand fed—Matt. 14:14-21
Flogging—Matt. 27:26

Food—Matt. 15:32-39
Forgiveness—Matt. 6:14, 15; 9:13; 18:21-35; Luke 17:3b, 4
Four thousand fed—Matt. 15:32-39
Fruit—Matt. 12:25-37

Galilee—Matt. 4:12-16
Gates—Matt. 7:13, 14
Gehenna—Matt. 25:31-46
Genealogy of Jesus—Matt. 1:1-17
Gentiles—Matt. 10:5, 6; 25:31-46
Gethsemane—Matt. 26:36-46
Golden rule—Matt. 7:12
Greatness, True—Matt. 18:1-14; 20:20-28; Mark 9:33-37; Luke 9:46-50; 22:24-30

Hades—Matt. 16:17-20; 25:31-46
Healing—See Jesus
Hell—Matt. 7:15-23; 25:31-46
Herod—Matt. 2:13-18; 14:1-13
Herodians—Matt. 22:15-17
Holy Spirit
  Available to everyone—Luke 11:9-13
  Blasphemy against—Matt. 12:31; Mark 3.29; Luke 12:10
  Dove (symbol of)—Matt. 3:16, 17; 10:16-39
  Elizabeth is filled—Luke 1:41
  Jesus' baptism—Matt. 3:11, 12, 16, 17; Luke 3:21, 22
  Jesus' birth—Matt. 1:18-25; Luke 1:28-37
  Jesus' death—Matt. 16:21-23; 17:9, 12, 22, 23; 20:17-19
  Jesus' healings—Luke 5:17-26
  Jesus' temptations—Matt. 4:1
  John's life—Luke 1:13-17
  Power of—Matt. 12:28
  Simeon, Spirit upon him—Luke 2:25-35
  Speaking words of the Spirit—Matt. 10:16-39
  Spirit baptism promised—Matt. 3:11; Mark 1:8; Luke 3:16; 24:49
  Water baptism in name of—Matt. 28:19
  Zechariah is filled—Luke 1:67-80
Hypocrites—Matt. 15:3-11; 23:1-39

Immanuel—Matt. 1:22, 23
Inn—Luke 2:5-7

Jerusalem—Matt. 24:1-31; Mark 13; Luke 13-35; 21:1ff.
Jesus
  Anointed for burial—Matt. 26:6-13
  Apostle—Matt. 10:1-4
  Arrested—Matt. 26:47-56
  Ascension—Luke 24:50-53
  Authority—Matt. 28:16-18; Luke 4:31-37
  Baptism—Matt. 3:13-17
  Betrayed—Matt. 26:14-16
  Birth—Matt. 1:18-25; Luke 1:28-37; 2:1-24
  Childhood—Matt. 3:13-17; Luke 2:40-52
  Compassion—Matt. 14:14; 15:29-39
  Crucifixion—Matt. 27:32-54
  Death is prophesied—Matt. 20:17-19; 26:20-25
  Dedication—Luke 2:22-24
  Deity—Matt. 1:22, 23; 22:41-46
  Education—Luke 2:40
  Exorcisms—See Demons/Demonization
  Family—Matt. 12:46-50
  First year of ministry—Matt. 4:12-16
  Flogged—Matt. 27:26
  Galilee ministry—Matt. 4:12-25
  Genealogy—Matt. 1:1-17; Luke 3:23-38
  Healing ministry—Matt. 4:23-25; 8:1-4, 5-13, 14-17, 28-34; 9:1-8, 18-26, 27-34, etc.
  Home in Galilee—Luke 2:40
  Judge—Matt. 25:31-33
  Knowledge of thoughts—Matt. 9:4-8; 12:25-37
  Ministry overview—Matt. 9:35-38
  Mocked—Matt. 27:27-31
  Position with God—Matt. 11:27; 12:6-8
  Prayers—Matt. 11:25-27; 14:22-24; 19:13; 26:36-46; Mark 6:46; 14:32-42; Luke 6:12; 9:28; 11:1-4; 16:27; 18:10-13; 22:32
  Preacher—Matt. 11:1-6
  Resurrected—Matt. 28:1-10
  Supported by women—Luke 8:1-3
  Teacher—Matt. 11:1-6
  Tempted—Matt. 4:1-11; Mark 1:12, 13; Luke 4:1-13
  Transfigured—Matt. 17:1-13; Mark 9:2-13; Luke 9:28-36
  Trials—Matt. 26:57-68; 27:11-25

John the Baptist—Matt. 3:1-12; 11:1-19; 14:1-13; Luke 1:8-23, 57-66, 80; 3:1-20
Jonah—Matt. 12:38-45; 16:1-4
Joseph—Matt. 1-2
Joseph of Arimathea—Matt. 27:57-61
Judea—Matt. 4:12-16
Judas Iscariot—Matt. 26:8, 9, 14-16, 20-25, 47-49; 27:1-10
Judging—Matt. 7:1-6
Judgment day—Matt. 10:9-15; 11:20-24; 25:31-46

Keys of Kingdom—1 Matt. 16:17-20
Kingdom of God/Heaven—Matt. 4:17, 23-25; 5:1-7:29; 11:7-15; 12:25-37; 13:10-17; Luke 12:22-31; 17:20-37

Lamps—Matt. 5:14-16; Mark 4:21-23; 8:16-18; 11:33-36
Last Supper—Matt. 26:17-30
Law—Matt. 5:17-20
Laying on of hands—Matt. 8:14, 15
Lazarus—Luke 16:19-31
Leper(s)—Matt. 8:1-4; Luke 17:11-19
Levi—Matt. 9:9-13
Light of the world—Matt. 5:14-16
Lord—Matt. 11:25-27
Lord's Day—Matt. 28:1
Lost—Matt. 15:23-25
Lots—Luke 1:8-23
Love—Matt. 5:43-48; 22:37-40
Lust—Matt. 5:27-30

Magi—Matt. 2:1-12
Manger—Luke 2:5-7
Marriage—Matt. 1:18; 19:1-12; 22:23-33
Mary—Matt. 1-2; Luke 1-2
Mary and Martha—Luke 10:38-42
Money—Matt. 6:19-34; 19:23-30; Luke 12:16-21; 18:23-25
Money changers—Matt. 21:12, 13
Moses' Seat—Matt. 23:1-12
Mountain—Matt. 21:21, 22
Mount of Olives—Matt. 26:36-46; Mark 14:32-42; Luke 22:39-46
Murder—Matt. 5:21-26
Mustard Seed—Matt. 13:31, 32

Nazareth—Matt. 2:19-23; 3:13-17; 4:12-16; 13:53-58; Luke 2:4, 40
Nazarene—Matt. 2:19-23
Noah, Days of—Matt. 24:36-41

Oaths—Matt. 5:33-37

Parables—Matt. 13:1-52
Paradise—Matt. 25:31-46
Passover—Matt. 26:1-5, 17-30
Peace—Matt. 10:16-39
Persistent Woman, The—Luke 18:1-8
Pharisees—Matt. 3:7-10; 16:5-12; 23:1-39
Phylacteries—Matt. 23:1-2
Pontius Pilate—Matt. 27:11-25
Prayer—Matt. 6:5-15; 7:7-11; 9:35-38; 17:19-21; 21:21, 22; 26:36-46
Priests, Chief—Matt. 2:1-8
Prophetess—Luke 2:36-39
Purse, Bag and Sword—Luke 22:35-38

Rabbi—Matt. 2:1-8; 23:1-12
Readiness—Matt. 24:36-51; 25:1-30; Luke 12:35-48; 21:34-38
Reconciliation—Matt. 5:21-26; Luke 17:1-4
Repentance—Matt. 4:17; Luke 13:1-9; 17:3b, 4
Rest—Matt. 11:28-30
Resurrection—Matt. 22:23-33; 27:51-53; 28:1-10, 11-15
Rewards—Matt. 10:40-42; 20:8-16; 25:19-30; Luke 23:41
Rich Fool, The—Luke 12:13-21
Riches—Matt. 19:16-30
Roads—Matt. 7:13, 14
Rock—Matt. 7:24-29; 16:17-20

Sabbath—Matt. 12:1-8, 9-21; Mark 2:23-28; Luke 6:1-11
Sadducees—Matt. 3:7-10; 16:5-12
Salt of the earth—Matt. 5:13
Salvation, National—Luke 1:67-75; 2:25-27
Salvation, Personal—Matt. 1:21; 10:16-39; 11:25-27; 19:16-30; Luke 13:22-30
Samaritans—Matt. 4:12-16; 10:5, 6;

Luke 9:51-56; 10:25-37
Sand—Matt. 7:24-29
Sanhedrin, The—Luke 22:66-71
Satan—See Devil
Second Coming—Matt. 24:1-25:46; Mark 13:1-36; Luke 12:49-53; 17:20-37; 21:5-28
Sermon on the Mount—Matt. 5-7; Luke 6:17-49
Serpents—Matt. 10:16-39
Servants, Wise and Wicked—Matt. 24:45-51
Seventy-two disciples—Luke 10:1-24
Sheep—Matt. 10:16-39
Sheep, Lost—Matt. 10:5, 6; 15:23-25; 18:10-14; Luke 15:1-7
Sheep and Goats—Matt. 25:31-46
Sheol—Matt. 25:31-46
Signs—Matt. 12:38-45; 16:1-4; 24:1-31; Luke 12:54-59
Simeon—Luke 2:25-35
Simon, the Pharisee—Luke 7:36-50
Sin—Matt. 18:15-20
Sin, The Unpardonable—Matt. 12:22-27
Son of God—Matt. 14:25-33; 16:15, 16
Son of Man—Matt. 8:18-20; 10:16-39
Son, Lost—Luke 15:11-32
Star, The Magi's—Matt. 2:1-12
Stone—Matt. 21:40-46
Supper, Last—Matt. 26:17-30
Synagogue—Matt. 4:23

Tabernacle—Matt. 12:1-8
Talents—Matt. 25:14-30
Tartarus—Matt. 25:31-46
Taxes—Matt. 9:9; 17:24-27; 22:15-22
Teachers—Matt. 2:1-8
Temple—Matt. 12:1-8; 21:12-17, 23-27; 24:1, 2
Temptation—Matt. 4:1-11
Theophilus—Luke 1:3, 4
Thief in the night—Matt. 24:42-44
Thrones—Matt. 19:23-30; Luke 22:22-30
Traditions—Matt. 15:1-20
Transfiguration—Matt. 17:1-13
Triumphal entry—Matt. 21:1-11

Unclean—Matt. 15:3-11

Vineyard—Matt. 20:1-16
Virgin birth—Matt. 1:18-25
Virgins, The Ten—Matt. 25:1-13

Watch and Pray—Matt. 26:36-46
Wedding banquet—Matt. 22:1-14
Wisdom—Matt. 11:16-19
Woes—Matt. 23:13-36
Wolves—Matt. 10:16-39

Yeast—Matt. 13:31-33
Yoke—Matt. 11:28-30

Zacchaeus—Luke 19:1-10
Zechariah—Luke 1:5-25

Charts and Diagrams

Divisions of the New Testament........ xxviii
Significant New Testament Dates........ xxix
Distinctiveness of the Gospels........ xxxi
Jesus' Threefold Genealogy........ 5
Angelic Appearances in the Bible........ 8
Major Prophecies Regarding Christ........ 9
The Family Tree of Herod the Great........ 16
Holy Spirit in the Two Testaments........ 22
Baptism/Baptizer/Requirements/Results........ 26
The Eight Baptisms of the New Testament........ 30
The Holy Spirit in Jesus' Life........ 31
Satan Is a Fourfold Enemy........ 35
A Chronology of Jesus' Life........ 39
Palestine in the Time of Christ........ 40
Jesus' Healing Ministry........ 44
Why Jesus Came to Earth and Why He Is Returning........ 48
The Miracles of Jesus........ 82
The Discipleship Process........ 96
Exorcism in the Bible........ 101
The Four Causes of Sickness and Their Cures........ 106
A Chronological Perspective of God's Dealings with Earth........ 129
Life's Triune Composition........ 137
The Tabernacle........ 143

The Significance of the Tabernacle's Furniture 142
The Parables of Jesus 154
The Parable of the Four Soils 157
From Caesarea to the Cross 190
The Causes and Cures of Sickness 205
Jesus' Reward System 231
Jesus' Final Week 238
A Floor Plan of Herod's Temple 241
Differing Views About Jesus' Prophecy in Matthew 24 266
The Double Fulfillment of Matthew 24 269
An Elementary Approach to the Last Days 270
A Secondary Approach to the Last Days 271
An Advanced Approach to the Last Days 272
Interpreting the Sheep-and-Goat Judgment 286
The Doctrine of Eternal Judgment 292
The Six Trials of Jesus 309
The Seven Sayings of Christ on the Cross 321
Jesus' Olivet Discourse 563
Jesus' Post-Resurrection Appearances 590

Special Studies

Apostleship 124
Baptism in the Holy Spirit 22
Blueprints for the Last Days 270
Detecting Demonization 102
Discipleship 94
Discipline in the Church 217
Fasting 110
Hell 288
Kingdom of God 43
Parables—How to Understand Them 539
Praying for the Sick 204
Salvation 135
Self-Life 197
Tabernacle and Temple Structures 142
Testing "Christian" Leadership 79

Abbreviations

The following abbreviations for the books of the Bible are used in the Commentary.

OLD TESTAMENT

Genesis	Gen.	Ecclesiastes	Eccles.
Exodus	Exod.	Song of Solomon	Song of Sol.
Leviticus	Lev.	Isaiah	Isa.
Numbers	Num.	Jeremiah	Jer.
Deuteronomy	Deut.	Lamentations	Lam.
Joshua	Josh.	Ezekiel	Ezek.
Judges	Judg.	Daniel	Dan.
Ruth	Ruth	Hosea	Hos.
1 Samuel	1 Sam.	Joel	Joel
2 Samuel	2 Sam.	Amos	Amos
1 Kings	1 Kings	Obadiah	Obad.
2 Kings	2 Kings	Jonah	Jon.
1 Chronicles	1 Chron.	Micah	Mic.
2 Chronicles	2 Chron.	Nahum	Nah.
Ezra	Ezra	Habakkuk	Hab.
Nehemiah	Neh.	Zephaniah	Zeph.
Esther	Esther	Haggai	Hag.
Job	Job	Zechariah	Zech.
Psalms	Ps. (*pl.* Pss.)	Malachi	Mal.
Proverbs	Prov.		

NEW TESTAMENT

Matthew	Matt.	1 Timothy	1 Tim.
Mark	Mark	2 Timothy	2 Tim.
Luke	Luke	Titus	Titus
John	John	Philemon	Philem.
Acts of the Apostles	Acts	Hebrews	Heb.
Romans	Rom.	James	James
1 Corinthians	1 Cor.	1 Peter	1 Pet.
2 Corinthians	2 Cor.	2 Peter	2 Pet.
Galatians	Gal.	1 John	1 John
Ephesians	Eph.	2 John	2 John
Philippians	Phil.	3 John	3 John
Colossians	Col.	Jude	Jude
1 Thessalonians	1 Thess.	Revelation	Rev.
2 Thessalonians	2 Thess.		

A Capsule View of the New Testament

The Design of the New Testament

Your New Testament may be divided into three major sections: Biographical Reading (Matthew-Acts), Postal Reading (Romans-Jude), and Prophetical Reading (Revelation). The first section possesses five books, the next one has twenty-one books, and the final unit has only one book.

1. *Biographical Reading.* The two major themes of your New Testament are the life of Jesus Christ and the life of the early church. Both of these subjects occupy a supreme position in the biographical section of your Bible. In the Gospels (Matthew, Mark, Luke and John) you will find the focus is on Christ. In the book of Acts, the attention is directed to the Church.

2. *Postal Reading.* Each of us enjoys reading letters. Within this unit of the New Testament there are various styles of letters. They were written to many different people—both churches and individuals—for a diversity of reasons. Generally, these letters are divided into two sections—those written by Paul, and those written by other men, namely James, Peter, John and Jude. The letters in the first grouping may be further subdivided between those letters addressed to churches (Romans-2 Thessalonians) and those sent to individuals (1 Timothy-Philemon). The letters in the second category are usually called "universal letters," because they are written without any specifically identified audience.

3. *Prophetical Reading.* The final unit of your New Testament is devoted to prophetic matters. Future events play a strong role in the message of the Bible. In this final book we read of the end of our present world order, and the establishment of a heavenly order on this planet. The unfolding drama of the last days is rapidly flashed before us in this thrilling book of the New Testament.

The chart entitled "The Divisions of the New Testament" will assist you in grasping the details presented above.

The Doctrines of the New Testament

The word "doctrine" means "teaching." It is the doctrine, or teaching, of your New Testament that makes it so very important. The supreme function of the Scriptures is to proclaim the message of Jesus Christ. The ultimate aim, however, is to produce converts or disciples for Christ. This is accomplished by learning and applying the teachings of the New Testament to your life. Without these doctrines there could be no conversion or spiritual development. But through these teachings our lives may become wonderfully renewed, vibrantly transformed, and productively useful for God!

When you read through your New Testament, you should be noting the different

THE DIVISIONS OF THE NEW TESTAMENT

I. Biographical

A. Life of Christ
1. Matthew
2. Mark
3. Luke
4. John

B. Life of the Church
5. Acts

II. Postal

A. Paul Writes to Churches
1. Romans
2. 1 Corinthians
3. 2 Corinthians
4. Galatians
5. Ephesians
6. Philippians
7. Colossians
8. 1 Thessalonians
9. 2 Thessalonians

B. Paul Writes to Christians
10. 1 Timothy
11. 2 Timothy
12. Titus
13. Philemon
14. Hebrews (author unknown)

C. Universal Letters
15. James
16. 1 Peter
17. 2 Peter
18. 1 John
19. 2 John
20. 3 John
21. Jude

III. Prophetical

Revelation

doctrines it discusses. Each one of them will serve you as a steppingstone in your advancement with Christ. There are ten basic doctrinal areas discussed by the biblical writers. See if your reading doesn't bear out this statement. Here are the major categories: (1) Scripture, (2) God, (3) Jesus Christ, (4) the Holy Spirit, (5) Man, (6) Sin, (7) Salvation/Sanctification, (8) the Church, (9) Angels and (10) Prophecy.

The Dates of the New Testament

The books of your New Testament are not arranged according to the dates of their writing. Instead, they are grouped according to their natural literary classifications. Although this arrangement is more meaningful for the reader, it is sometimes to our advantage to know when a book was written or when an event transpired.

Placing an exact date on the events and books of the New Testament is an impossible task. We can only approximate some of these times. The diagram entitled "Significant New Testament Dates" shows the probable dates for these various happenings.

SIGNIFICANT NEW TESTAMENT DATES

Event	Date	Writing of Books
Birth of Jesus	5 B.C.	
Baptism of Jesus	A.D. 27	
Death of Jesus	A.D. 30	
Conversion of Paul	A.D. 32	
First Missionary Journey	A.D. 47	
Second Missionary Journey	A.D. 49	1 & 2 Thess., Gal., Rom.
Third Missionary Journey	A.D. 52	1 & 2 Cor.
Paul at Rome	A.D. 59	Matt., Mark, Luke, James, Heb., (?), Eph., Phil., Col., Philem., 1 Pet., Acts, 1 & 2 Tim.,
Death of Paul	A.D. 65	Titus, 2 Pet.,
Fall of Jerusalem	A.D. 70	Jude (?)
Persecution of the Church	A.D. 80	
	A.D. 90	John's Gospel & Letters (?)
Death of John	A.D. 100	Rev. (?)

The Desire of the New Testament Writers

The writers of the New Testament obviously desired to make their writings clearly understandable and practical so their readers could reverently apply biblical truths to daily life. With this goal in mind, here are several key things to look for as you read these writings:

1. Examples to follow
2. Errors to avoid
3. Exhortations to observe
4. Promises to claim
5. Prayers to echo
6. Principles to remember
7. Truths to share

Introduction to the Gospels

The Meaning of the Gospel

The term "gospel" means "good news." The Gospels in your New Testament reveal the good news of how God sent His very own Son from Heaven to bring salvation to everyone who believes. The good news is that no one needs to be separated from God's present love or His eternal plans. The Gospels tell us how we can enter into a personal relationship with God through His Son, Jesus Christ.

The Method of the Gospel

God's good news is revealed to us through many sources throughout the universe, but the clearest expression of His plans is shown in the four books commonly called *The Gospels*—Matthew, Mark, Luke and John. These four small books tell us the story of Jesus Christ—His birth, life, death, resurrection and ascension. It is without a doubt the most remarkable story ever heard.

One might ask, after reading these accounts, why there are four Gospels instead of one large Gospel, especially since so much of the material is repeated in the other writings. The reason behind four separate accounts is a simple one—each writer had a particular point of emphasis or purpose for his document. While the four stories may seem to be much the same after one or several readings, after a more careful examination, the distinctiveness of each one becomes increasingly pronounced. The chart entitled "The Distinctiveness of the Gospels" will help you envision the unique features of each Gospel.

THE DISTINCTIVENESS OF THE GOSPELS			
Matthew	**Mark**	**Luke**	**John**
Written for Jews	Written for Gentiles	Written for the World	Written for the Lost
Jesus is: Prophesied King	Jesus is: Lowly Servant	Jesus is: Perfect Man	Jesus is: Divine Son
Son of Abraham	Son of Man	Son of Adam	Son of God
Lion-like	Ox-like	Man-like	Eagle-like

Introduction to the Gospel According to Matthew

Date: Around A.D. 50-60

Author

The author of this writing is one of Jesus' disciples; Matthew (Levi). His home was in Capernaum (Mark 2:1, 14), and his widely despised occupation involved the collection of taxes for Rome (Matt. 10:3). He abandoned the wealth of his position, however, for the privilege of following Jesus Christ (Luke 5:28). And he was pleased to introduce his spiritually lost friends to his newly found Savior and Lord (Luke 5:27-29).

Audience

Matthew wrote mainly for his countrymen, the Jews. This is shown by his frequent use of the Old Testament in his writing, which only the Jews would appreciate. Over sixty times Matthew either quotes or alludes to these ancient and sacred writings. Matthew's account would help them to understand the role of Jesus in God's plans, and how they could become His disciples (see Matt. 5-7; 11:28-30; 28:19-20).

Aim

Matthew's aim was to convince his Jewish brothers and sisters of the fact that Jesus was the One prophesied as the Messiah who would come to Israel. He wanted his kinsmen to recognize that Jesus was the Christ—the Messiah (or King) whom God had sent to fulfill the Old Testament dreams of a perfect salvation (see Matt. 1:1, 16, 17, 21). By following Jesus they could be eternally saved (see Matt. 7:21-27).

Arrangement

Matthew is not so much concerned with strict chronological order as he is with topical unity. Instead of reporting on Jesus' teachings in the order in which they were given and events in their chronological order, he groups topics together. For example, there are numerous accounts of miracles in chapters eight and nine and various parables in chapter thirteen.

One way of viewing the book of Matthew as a whole unit would be this topical arrangement: (1) The Messiah's Preparation—1:1-4:16; (2) The Messiah's Proclamation—4:17-25:46; (3) The Messiah's Passion—26:1-27:66; (4) The Messiah's Power—28:1-20.

The Roots of Jesus (Matt. 1:1-17)

(cf. Luke 3:23-38)

The Old Testament begins with a record of the *creation;* the New Testament begins with a record of the *Christ.* The first book of the Old Testament declares that a Deliverer from God *is coming;* the first book of the New Testament declares that the Deliverer *has come.* In the Old Testament there were *predictions;* in the New Testament there is the *fulfillment.*

Here we see God's method for bridging the immense chasm sin has created between heaven and earth. God will send a man. It is His intent to rule through a man, to redeem through a man, and to judge through a man. That man is Jesus Christ.

Matthew gives us "the roots" of Jesus. Among the listed names, there are prophesied persons, regal persons, Jewish persons, Gentile persons, immoral persons, moral persons, and unknown persons. Jesus identifies with each of them. For in Him there will be neither Greek nor Jew, circumcised nor uncircumcised, slave nor free (Col. 3:11).

I. *The Major Figures (1:1)*

1 A record of the genealogy of Jesus Christ the son of David, the son of Abraham:

This first verse concisely introduces the entire section under investigation, while the final verse of the section (v. 17) precisely summarizes the whole unit. The former verse draws its lead from two major figures (David and Abraham); the latter verse derives its strength from three methodical figures (three sets of fourteen generations).

The Record. In Jesus' day genealogical records were kept in the public archives and placed under the supervision of Israel's supreme court, the Sanhedrin. There are a variety of reasons for maintaining such records: (1) they provide a full, personal identification; (2) they become useful in legal cases, like inheritance claims; and (3) they give proper proof to entitle someone to the position of king or priest.

These records also demonstrate several other important practical matters—the shortness of our lives, and the brevity with which most of us will be remembered. How thankful we ought to be to know that God never forgets each thought, word and action we do in His name (Heb. 6:10; 1 Cor. 4:5).

Genealogy. Genealogies have always been significant to the Jews. After possessing the Promised Land, each family's residence was determined by genealogy (Num. 26:52-56; 33:54). Later, royal succession was attached to David's lineage (1 Kings 11:36; 15:4). Still later, after Judah's return from Babylon (536 B.C.), any person claiming priestly authority was required to prove his priestly descent by his genealogy (Ezra 2:62).

Some writers hold that the genealogy in Matthew traces Jesus' roots through Joseph, while Luke's account (3:23-38) traces Jesus' lineage through Mary. Other writers contend that both genealogies are of Joseph—Matthew showing His legal claim to the throne of David; Luke giving His actual descent. There is little room for dogmatism here.

Through the listing of these names we learn that God keeps His promises. To Abraham (Gen. 12:7, with Gal. 3:16) and to David (2 Sam. 7:12, 13; Jer. 23:5, with Luke 1:31-33) a son was promised, a unique son. That son arrived in the birth of Jesus Christ. To Israel a King was promised; He was to be the Messiah. But in order for Jesus to fulfill these promises, He had to bear the proper genealogical credentials. He had to prove himself to be a son of Abraham and a son of David. He did just that in this genealogical table.

Jesus. The name of Jesus appears 979 times in the Bible. No other name appears so frequently in the Scriptures. This name can be traced back to the Hebrew names *Joshua* and *Hosea*. It means "Yahweh is salvation."

In the Old Testament three persons bear the equivalent of the New Testament name "Jesus." They are Hosea and two men named Joshua. Each of these men foreshadow Jesus in His threefold role of *King* (seen in Joshua, who entered and conquered the Promised Land—cf. book of Joshua), *Prophet* (seen in Hosea, the prophet of grace and salvation—cf. book of Hosea), and *Priest* (seen in Joshua, the high priest who assisted in Israel's restoration after her exile—cf. Zech. 3).

"Jesus" was a popular name in the first century. Josephus, a Jewish historian of this era, mentions nineteen persons who possessed this name. Such a popularity for this name may suggest a strong interest in a Messianic hope among the people. They longed to see God deliver His people from Rome.

Christ. The term "Christ" means "anointed" (ordained, set apart or qualified). In the Old Testament, "anointed" is used of *prophets* (1 Kings 19:16), *priests* (Exod. 29:30), and *kings* (1 Sam. 9:16; 10:1). In Jesus, the Christ, may be found each of these three offices: *Prophet* (Deut. 18:15, with Acts 3:22), *Priest* (Ps. 110:4, with Heb. 7:17), and *King* (Ps. 2:6, with Matt. 28:18; Rev. 1:5).

Son of David. When Israel became a nation, she looked for a king. And many eventually ruled her people. But only one king stands at the top. The greatest leader Israel ever knew was David. The people held high opinions of this man of God. Even

God expressed His favor toward David, for through him would come earth's greatest and everlasting King, Jesus Christ (Jer. 23:5; Luke 1:31-33, 67-79).

Son of Abraham: Abraham is properly called the father of the Jewish faith and of the nation of Israel. While other godly men preceded him, he stood at the door of a new era. God placed a blessing on him—and on his seed—as on no other person prior to that time. Up to Abraham's time, God had dealt primarily with individuals. Now He would focus on a family in order to make it a great nation (Gen. 12:1-3; 17:7-8, 19; 26:4; 28:14; Gal. 3:16).

II. *The Minor Figures (1:2-16)*

2 Abraham was the father of Isaac,
Isaac the father of Jacob,
Jacob the father of Judah and his brothers,
3 Judah the father of Perez and Zerah, whose mother was Tamar,
Perez the father of Hezron,
Hezron the father of Ram,
4 Ram the father of Amminadab,
Amminadab the father of Nahshon,
Nahshon the father of Salmon,
5 Salmon the father of Boaz, whose mother was Rahab,
Boaz the father of Obed, whose mother was Ruth,
Obed the father of Jesse,
6 and Jesse the father of King David.

David was the father of Solomon, whose mother had been Uriah's wife,
7 Solomon the father of Rehoboam,
Rehoboam the father of Abijah,
Abijah the father of Asa,
8 Asa the father of Jehoshaphat,
Jehoshaphat the father of Joram,
Joram the father of Uzziah,
9 Uzziah the father of Jotham,
Jotham the father of Ahaz,
Ahaz the father of Hezekiah,
10 Hezekiah the father of Manasseh,
Manasseh the father of Amon,
Amon the father of Josiah,
11 and Josiah the father of Jeconiah[a] and his brothers at the time of the exile to Babylon.
12 After the exile to Babylon:

[a] *11* That is, Jehoiachin; also in verse 12

Jeconiah was the father of Shealtiel,
Shealtiel the father of Zerubbabel,
13Zerubbabel the father of Abiud,
Abiud the father of Eliakim,
Eliakim the father of Azor,

14Azor the father of Zadok,
Zadok the father of Akim,
Akim the father of Eliud,
15Eliud the father of Eleazar,
Eleazar the father of Matthan,
Matthan the father of Jacob,
16and Jacob the father of Joseph, the husband of Mary, of whom was born Jesus, who is called Christ.

Jesus' family record is neatly arranged into three sets of fourteen people each. This arrangement is obviously deliberate, since it leaves out some names that would normally be included in the listings.

For example, Ahaziah, Joash and Amaziah are left out of this list. They should be located between the names of Joram and Uzziah (cf. 2 Kings 8:25; 12:19-21). But these absences posed no problem for the Jewish mind, because the word "father of" (or "begat"—KJV) do not necessarily imply immediate parentage. It could be used in referring to one's grandson or great grandson, and so forth. Notice the chart entitled "Jesus' Threefold Genealogy," which briefly analyzes these personages.

The Bad Men. No man in this listing is completely free from the moral blemishes created by sin. But some were notoriously evil. Take for example Rehoboam, Abijah, and Amon. In all, at least six of Jesus' ancestors are known to be bad. Consult the chart for these names.

The Good Men. Among Jesus' ancestors numerous individuals qualify to be listed among those who chose God's way over their own. These include: Abraham, Isaac, Jacob, Judah, David, Asa and others. At least nineteen men in Jesus' family tree are known to be good. There are sixteen men who are completely unknown to us. See the diagram entitled "Jesus' Threefold Genealogy."

The Women. Rarely would you find a woman's name in any Jewish genealogy. Women were often regarded as property, not persons. They had no legal rights. But Jesus' ministry was destined to elevate them. Consider these four women from Jesus' ancestry. *Tamar* was an adulteress (Gen. 38). *Rahab* was a prostitute in Jericho (Josh. 2). *Ruth* was a despised Moabite (Ruth 1:1-3, with Deut. 23:3). *Bathsheba* was guilty of adultery (2 Sam. 11-12). Each of these women had problems, but through the grace and wisdom of God they were enabled to bring Him glory.

III. *The Methodical Figures (1:17)*

17Thus there were fourteen generations in all from Abraham to David, fourteen from David to the exile to Babylon, and fourteen from the exile to the Christ.[a]

This deliberate arrangement of three sets, each containing fourteen names, is intended, in all probability, for the purpose of easy memorization. This orderly arrangement neatly separates Israel's history into its three main political periods: Theocracy (rule by God—from Abraham to King David), Monarchy (rule by a king—from King David to the Exile), and Hierarchy (rule by a religious order—from the Exile to the coming of the Christ).

Another note of interest concerns the number fourteen. The Hebrews had no numbers that were distinct from their alphabet: they attached a numerical value to each of their letters (which were all consonants). The central name in Jesus' genealogy is "David." And the numerical value of his name (D+V+D) is precisely fourteen. This is probably no coincidence.

JESUS' THREEFOLD GENEALOGY (MATT. 1:2-16)

ABRAHAM TO DAVID	DAVID TO EXILE	EXILE TO CHRIST
+Abraham (Gen. 12—15)	+David (1-2 Sam.; 1 Chron.)	-Jeconiah (2 Kings 24; 1 Chron. 3:16,17; 2 Chron. 36)
+Isaac (Gen. 21—35)	+Solomon (1 Kings; 2 Chron.)	?Shealtiel (Luke 3:27)
+Jacob (Gen. 25—30)	-Rehoboam (1 Kings 11-15; 2 Chron. 9-12)	+Zerubbabel (Ezra 2-5)
+Judah (Gen. 29-50)	+Abijah (Kings 14-15; 2 Chron. 11-14)	?Abiud
?Perez (Gen. 46:12)	+Asa (1 Kings 15-22; 2 Chron. 14-16)	?Eliakim
?Hezron (Luke 3:33)	+Jehoshaphat (1 Kings 22; 2 Chron. 17-21)	?Azor
?Ram (Ruth 4:19)	-Joram (2 Kings 8-9; 2 Chron. 21)	?Zadok
?Amminadab (Ruth 4:19-20)	+/-Uzziah (Kings 15; 2 Chron. 26-27)	?Akim
+Nahshon (Num. 7:17)	+Jotham (2 Kings 15; 2 Chron. 27)	?Eliud
+Salmon (Ruth 4:21)	-Ahaz (2 Kings 16; 2 Chron. 28)	?Eleazor
+Boaz (Ruth 2-4)	+Hezekiah (2 Kings 18-20; 2 Chron. 29-32)	?Matthan
?Obed (Luke 3:32)	-Manasseh (2 Kings 21; 2 Chron. 33)	?Jacob
+Jesse (1 Sam. 16)	-Amon (2 Kings 21; 2 Chron. 33)	+Joseph
+David (1-2 Sam.; 1 Chron.)	+Josiah (2 Kings 22-23; 2 Chron. 34-35)	+Jesus

\+ Indicates the generally good character of the man.
\- Indicates the generally bad character of the man.
? Indicates the unknown character of the man.

a 17 Or *Messiah.* "The Christ" (Greek) and "the Messiah" (Hebrew) both mean "the Anointed One."

The Birth of Jesus (Matt. 1:18-25)

(cf. Luke 1:26-35; 2:1-7)

Before us lies the most profound story of the entire Bible. God becomes a man, and at the same time He retains His deity! Such a truth is too deep to grasp fully. We must allow our minds to respond with faith and leave the *how* to the One far more capable of performing such a miracle than ourselves.

I. *The Conception of Jesus (1:18)*

> **18This is how the birth of Jesus Christ came about. His mother Mary was pledged to be married to Joseph, but before they came together, she was found to be with child through the Holy Spirit.**

Mary Was Pledged to Be Married. The Jewish engagement process was quite different from our approach in modern America. The Jews prolonged the initiatory ceremonies and held special rites unlike our customs. There were three basic steps in their marriage process.

First, there was *engagement.* This step was frequently made by the parents of a son while he was still a young boy. The parents would select the girl they thought might become a suitable bride for their son.

Second, there was *betrothal.* In this stage engagement was ratified or made legal (prior to this stage it was possible to break the engagement). Once the betrothal was made, in the presence of witnesses, the marriage became binding. This stage was to last for one year, during which time the couple would be known as husband and wife, though they would not live together. Only a divorce could separate them at this point (cf. Deut. 22:23, 24). This is the period in which Joseph and Mary find themselves in the passage under consideration.

Third, there was the actual *marriage* itself. This was the final step. At this stage, the bridegroom would come for his wife and take her home, after a wedding supper. Joseph and Mary were apparently very near this stage.

With Child Through the Holy Spirit. The Scriptures candidly declare that Mary's pregnancy was "by the Holy Spirit." It was clearly a sovereign act of God. Jesus would be, as a result of this unprecedented union, both divine and human, simultaneously.

Here is the starting point for the role of the Holy Spirit in Jesus' life. Some authors believe that from this moment forward Jesus was indwelt and/or filled with the Spirit (though not without limits; the total action occurred at Jesus' baptism—John 3:34; cf. Isa. 11:2, 3; 42:1-4; 61:1, 2). This ministry of the Spirit, however, does not necessarily imply that the Holy Spirit was Jesus' father. Indeed, it is God, the Father, who is directly responsible for the creation of Jesus' body (Heb. 10:5). The role of the Spirit here is only to act as the agent of power in making this unique conception possible (Luke 1:35).

II. *The Communication of the Angel (1:19-21)*

19Because Joseph her husband was a righteous man and did not want to expose her to public disgrace, he had in mind to divorce her quietly.
20But after he had considered this, an angel of the Lord appeared to him in a dream and said, "Joseph son of David, do not be afraid to take Mary home as your wife, because what is conceived in her is from the Holy Spirit. 21She will give birth to a son, and you are to give him the name Jesus,[a] because he will save his people from their sins."

A Righteous Man. This is a reference to the quality of Joseph's character. To be righteous means to be in a state of right standing with God. Joseph, then, was a man who received God's approval because he followed the laws of the Old Testament with a sincere and faithful spirit.

Quiet Divorce. There were two options available to Joseph: (1) He could bring a public lawsuit against Mary, using the charge of adultery. The result of this course would be determined by the local court. (2) He could take advantage of the easy divorce laws of his day and secure a letter of divorcement, without stating the cause of the separation. Joseph favored this more gentle action.

An Angel in a Dream. Sometimes in the hustle and bustle of life God speaks to us after we close our eyes on the day and fall asleep. There are one hundred twenty-two times when the Scriptures record that God brought His word to people through dreams. An angel from the Lord appeared to Joseph in a dream that enabled him to learn God's will for his problem. (Examine the chart entitled "Angelic Appearances Recorded in the Bible.")

First, the angel assured Joseph that Mary had not been unfaithful in her love for him. Instead, it was her faithfulness to God that made her His choice in this virgin pregnancy (cf. Luke 1:26-31).

Second, the angel instructed Joseph to name the child "Jesus," indicating He would be God's instrument to bring salvation to His people (see note on Matt. 1:1). Jesus would (and will!) save them "from their sin," its penalty (Rom. 8:1-11), its power (Rom. 6:1-11), and its presence (Rev. 21:23-27).

---

a 21 *Jesus* is the Greek form of *Joshua*, which means *the Lord saves.*

ANGELIC APPEARANCES RECORDED IN THE BIBLE

Very few persons have had the privilege of seeing an angel. The following people (thirty-two individuals or groups) are said to have seen angels:

1. Hagar—twice (Gen. 16:7-11; 21:17)
2. Abraham—three times (Gen. 18:2; 22:11,15)
3. Lot (Gen. 19:1-22)
4. Jacob—three times (Gen. 28:12; 31:11; 32:1)
5. Moses (Exod. 3:2)
6. Balaam (Num. 22:22-35)
7. Joshua (Josh. 5:13-15)
8. Israel (Judge. 2:1-5)
9. Gideon (Judg. 6:11)
10. Manoah's wife (Judg. 13:3-5)
11. Manoah and his wife (Judg. 13:9-21)
12. David (2 Sam. 24:17)
13. Elijah—four times (1 Kings 19:5, 7; 2 Kings 1:3, 15)
14. Elisha and servant (2 Kings 6:16, 17)
15. Assyrians (2 Kings 19:35)
16. Shadrach, Meshach, and Abednego (Dan. 3:25)
17. Nebuchadnezzar (Dan. 3:25)
18. Daniel—five times (Dan. 6:22; 8:15, 16; 9:21; 10:5; 12:5)
19. Zechariah—six times (Zech. 1:8-19; 2:3; 3:1-6; 4:1-5; 5:5-10; 6:4, 5)
20. Joseph—three times (Matt. 1:20; 2:13, 19)
21. Mary (Luke 1:26-38)
22. Zechariah (Luke 1:11-20)
23. Shepherds (Luke 2:9-14)
24. Jesus—twice (Matt. 4:11; Luke 22:43)
25. Women at tomb (Matt. 28:1-5)
26. Disciples (Acts 1:10, 11)
27. Peter and John (Acts 5:19)
28. Philip (Acts 8:26)
29. Cornelius (Acts 10:3)
30. Peter (Acts 12:7-11)
31. Paul (Acts 27:23)
32. John (Rev. 1:1)

III. *The Completion of the Prophecy (1:22-23)*

> **22All this took place to fulfill what the Lord had said through the prophet:**
> **23"The virgin will be with child and will give birth to a son, and they will call him Immanuel"[a]—which means, "God with us."**

The Old Testament makes many predictions regarding the coming Christ. They involve His birth, life, death, resurrection, and present work. (See the chart entitled "Major Prophecies Regarding Christ".) Matthew takes full advantage of these prophecies. He quotes the Old Testament prophecies no less than sixty times to support his writings.

The Old Testament prophets often had a unique way of speaking prophetically to an immediate situation, while at the same time addressing themselves to a future fulfillment that would bring about the complete measure of the prophecy itself. Such is the case here in this prophecy taken from Isa. 7:14, and with many of the prophecies noted by Matthew.

[a] *23* Isaiah 7:14

MAJOR PROPHECIES REGARDING CHRIST

I. *His Birth*
   A. He will come from a woman's womb (Gen. 3:15).
   B. He will be born to a virgin (Isa. 7:14).
   C. He will be born in Bethlehem (Mic. 5:2).
   D. Murder will surround his birth (Jer. 31:15).
   E. He will be given the name "Immanuel" (Isa. 7:14).
   F. He will be given gifts (Ps. 72:10).
   G. He will be taken to Egypt and back (Hos. 11:1).

II. *His Life*
   A. He will be a prophet (Deut. 18:15).
   B. He will bring light to the Gentiles (Isa. 49:6).
   C. He will remove pain and disease (Isa. 53:4).
   D. He will perform miracles (Isa. 35:5, 6).
   E. He will be anointed by God's Spirit (Isa. 11:2).
   F. He will be a man of great zeal (Ps. 69:9).
   G. He will be a stumbling stone to Jews (Isa. 8:14).
   H. He will be sinless (Isa. 53:9).
   I. He will teach in parables (Ps. 78:2).
   J. He will be rejected by the Jews (Isa. 53:3).

III. *His Death*
   A. He will be forsaken by God (Ps. 22:1).
   B. He will be mocked by men (Ps. 22:6-8).
   C. He will be betrayed for silver (Zech. 11:12).
   D. He will be smitten and pierced (Zech. 12:10).
   E. He will die for the world's sins (Isa. 53:5, 10).
   F. His garments will be divided (Ps. 22:18).
   G. He will be betrayed by a friend (Ps. 41:9).
   H. None of his bones will be broken by crucifixion (Ps. 34:20).
   I. He will be beaten before His crucifixion (Isa. 50:6).
   J. He will be forsaken by His disciples (Zech. 13:7).
   K. He will be bruised in the heel (Gen. 3:15).
   L. He will be accused falsely (Ps. 35:11).
   M. He will be crucified with sinners (Isa. 53:12).
   N. He will be pierced through His hands and feet (Ps. 22:16).
   O. He will be pierced in His side (Zech. 12:10).
   P. He will be buried with the rich (Isa. 53:9).

IV. *His Resurrection and Ascension*
   A. He will rise after three days (Hos. 6:1, 2).
   B. His body will not see corruption (Ps. 16:10).
   C. He will conquer death (Ps. 22:22).
   D. He will ascend to God's right hand (Psa. 68:18; 110:1).

V. *His Present Work*
   A. As Priest (Ps. 110:4).
   B. Seated on David's throne (Amos 9:11).

Isaiah's prophecy makes two clear points about Jesus: (1) He will be miraculously born from a virgin's womb; and (2) He will be "God with us"—Immanuel.

Virgin. Mary is explicitly called a "virgin." Both the Greek word used here, and the Hebrew word from which it is quoted (Isa. 7:14), mean "a young woman." The context makes it plain that this young woman is sexually chaste. There is no room for anything shy of a miracle in this scene. Mary's baby would not have a human father responsible for his conception.

The significance of the virgin birth is at least fourfold: (1) It is a sign that God fulfills His prophecies. (2) It is a sign that no ordinary human can satisfy all the righteous demands of God and save people from their sins. (3) It is a sign that God's desire for people to be saved is beyond mere human comprehension. (4) It is a sign that Jesus previously existed in the form of God but was willing to undergo this amazing transformation in order to be our Savior (cf. Phil. 2:5-8).

Any denial of this cardinal doctrine means rejection of the trustworthiness of the

Scriptures. It may even spell out the lost spiritual condition of the one holding this position (cf. John 5:18-23; 2 John 7). We must take the virgin birth of Jesus seriously, if we are to follow Him.

Immanuel. This term means "God with us," and it provides our first glimpse of the deity of Jesus. Proofs of Jesus' deity are abundant. First, the Scriptures specifically call Him "God" (John 20:28; Titus 2:13; 2 Pet. 1:1). Second, He is able to forgive sins, an act only God can perform (Mark 2:5-10). Third, He is worshiped as God (Matt. 14:33; 28:9; John 5:23; Phil. 2:6-11; Rev. 5:12-14).

IV. *The Consecration of Joseph (1:24, 25)*

24 When Joseph woke up, he did what the angel of the Lord had
commanded him and took Mary home as his wife. 25 But he had no union
with her until she gave birth to a son. And he gave him the name Jesus.

It is easy to judge matters superficially, from only a shallow understanding or from a mere human perspective. By all natural factors Joseph had a clear case against Mary. But Joseph would not act hastily.

Joseph remained calm. He was patient and kind. No doubt this is one of the reasons why Joseph is described as a "just" man. He waited upon his Lord for a solution. And his patience was profoundly rewarded with a dream and an angelic message.

Like a solid rock Joseph stood before Mary and God. Silently and lovingly he waited. Finally God spoke, and Joseph's grief was turned into instant rejoicing. He had desired only the best for Mary, and now his prayer was abundantly fulfilled. Now he could take her home to be his faithful wife.

The Visit of the Wise Men (Matt. 2:1-12)

The Scriptures tell us very little about Jesus' infancy. The data we do possess is priceless, however, for it reveals to us the remarkable care God exercised to protect Jesus from the kingdom of darkness and the murderous hands of governmental officials before it was time for His death. We also learn here the kind of reverence we ought to have before our Savior-King.

I. *They Visit Jerusalem (2:1-8)*

2 After Jesus was born in Bethlehem in Judea, during the time of
King Herod, Magi[a] from the east came to Jerusalem 2 and asked,

[a] 1 Traditionally *Wise Men*

"Where is the one who has been born king of the Jews? We saw his star
in the east[a] and have come to worship him."
3When King Herod heard this he was disturbed, and all Jerusalem
with him. 4When he had called together all the people's chief priests and
teachers of the law, he asked them where the Christ[b] was to be born. 5"In
Bethlehem in Judea, " they replied, "for this is what the prophet has
written:

6" 'But you, Bethlehem, in the land of Judah.
are by no means least among the rulers of Judah;
for out of you will come a ruler
who will be the shepherd of my people Israel.'[c]"

7Then Herod called the Magi secretly and found out from them the
exact time the star had appeared. 8He sent them to Bethlehem and said,
"Go and make a careful search for the child. As soon as you find him,
report to me, so that I too may go and worship him."

Bethlehem. The site of Jesus' birth is significant on two accounts: (1) Micah prophesied in 735 B.C. that this city would be the place of Jesus' birth (Mic. 5:2); and (2) the name "Bethlehem" means "house of bread"—out of her would come "the bread of life," Jesus Christ (John 6:35).

Magi. The identity of the wise men (the Magi) is not stated. It is supposed by some that they may have been members of a priestly group from the Medes and Persians. Others think they may have been Jewish converts from Babylon. Perhaps the most significant note is the fact that these men are Gentiles. Matthew wanted his Jewish audience to know that God speaks to Gentiles, too.

Some legends state that there were only three wise men (note that the Scriptures do not tell us their number), and that they were kings. Even names have been ascribed to them: Melchior, Balthasar and Casper. According to tradition these men came from India, Greece and Egypt. Later, they were supposedly baptized by the Apostle Thomas. And now their bones are said to reside at the Cathedral of Cologne. These suppositions are clear examples of how legends easily grow up around biblical accounts.

Chief Priests. The term "priest" occurs nearly 800 times in the Scriptures, and for good cause. The priests were the backbone of the Jewish faith, occupying a lofty position in the operation of the Temple of God in Jerusalem.

Originally there were only three parties within the priesthood: (1) *the Levites,* who chiefly served in the manual duties of the Tabernacle and the Temple (Num. 3:5ff.); (2) *the priests,* who chiefly served in the spiritual duties of the Tabernacle and the

---

a 2 Or *star when it rose* *b 4* Or *Messiah* *c 6* Micah 5:2

Temple (Exod. 29-30); and (3) *the high priest,* who represented all of the people as he alone was granted the privilege to stand in God's presence (Exod. 28:29).

By the time of the writing of the New Testament, however, there were some fundamental alterations in the religious organization. In Jesus' day the Levites (about 10,000 in number) served on a rotating schedule, principally as guards, in the Temple (cf. John 7:32, 45-52; 18:3, 12; Acts 4:1; 5:17, 18). The priests (counting nearly 18,000 men) also served on a rotating schedule. They continued their Old Testament function of offering sacrifices in the Temple. The high priest still represented the people before God, but in addition he also served as the president of the Sanhedrin (Israel's supreme court in that day). This role made him the primary figure in Israel's dealings with Rome. He was clearly both a religious and political leader (cf. Mark 14:53, 60-64; Acts 4:6; 5:17).

In addition to these figures, two other positions are mentioned in the New Testament that were not discussed in the Old Testament. First, there was *the captain of the temple guard.* This man was second only to the high priest. His duty was to assist in the orderly oversight of all the business of the Temple (Acts 4:1; 5:24-26). Second, there were *the chief priests.* These men (mentioned sixty-four times in the New Testament) were the high-ranking administrators of the Temple treasuries. They also seem to have served as members of the Sanhedrin.

Teachers. This seems to be a general designation for those individuals who were considered to be the scholars in Israel. Their specialty was the Old Testament and the oral traditions that grew up around this writing. They did not, however, represent a united front, since some of them were liberal Sadducees and others were legalistic Pharisees. Elsewhere these men are called *rabbis* (Hebrew for "teacher").

They Were Disturbed. It seems odd to hear that King Herod and the religious personnel of Jerusalem were disturbed by the announcement concerning the Messiah. Presumably the Jews had awaited, with joyful anticipation, the arrival of this prophesied figure. But here Matthew shows us the true core of Israel's hopes. The Israelites were not seeking a Savior, but the gratification of their own appetites.

The interesting irony in this story is the fact that those who would seem to be the most unlikely candidates for knowing God's will regarding the coming Messiah were actually closer to perceiving it than those persons who had greater religious opportunities. There was more faith to be found in the remote regions than at the very heart of the Jewish capital. From this fact we learn that there may be the most profound knowledge in our heads, but until it moves our hearts and wills, we are lost persons.

The Prophecy of Micah. More than seven hundred years prior to the coming of the Christ, Micah, a prophet, was told the precise site for his birth (Mic. 5:2). This prophetic point was well understood in Jesus' time (John 7:42). From this small village would come forth the greatest of all persons. How unlikely a location for the birth of a King, but God, who ordered the event, specializes in doing things on a different plane from the logic of the natural man (cf. Isa. 55:8; Rom. 11:33-36).

The Star. A number of explanations have been suggested regarding the existence of this star: (1) it was a real star; (2) it was Jupiter and/or Saturn; (3) it was a comet; and (4) it was the star of hope within our hearts. Factual data concerning it, however, are as scarce as factual information on the Magi themselves. We only know what the Scriptures teach. And, for the Christian, this material is sufficient. In some unique manner a special star bore witness to "the bright Morning Star," Jesus Christ (Rev. 22:16).

II. *They Visit Jesus (2:9-12)*

9After they had heard the king, they went on their way, and the star
they had been in the east[a] went ahead of them until it stopped over the
place where the child was. 10When they saw the star, they were
overjoyed. 11On coming to the house, they saw the child with his mother
Mary, and they bowed down and worshiped him. Then they opened
their treasures and presented him with gifts of gold and of incense and
of myrrh. 12And having been warned in a dream not to go back to
Herod, they returned to their country by another route.

They Worship Him. There is a powerful message to be found in the story of the Magi. First, they searched for a King. Unlike the religious leaders, their faith was positive and forthright. They sought for One greater than themselves. No doubt they had learned how feeble we are to rule our own lives correctly. So they searched for a personal King to rule their affairs.

Second, they came to worship. Their motives were completely sincere. With open hearts they looked for their heavenly King that they might display their affection and worship to Him.

Third, they brought gifts to show their praise and allegiance to the King. They carried earth's treasures and laid them at His feet. The gift of gold was for a king (Gen. 41:42; 2 Sam. 12:30; Dan. 5:7, 29). The gift of incense was for a priest (Lev. 2; 1 Chron. 9:29; Luke 1:9; Rev. 5:8; 8:3). The gift of myrrh was for a man destined for a premature grave (Mark 15:23; John 19:39), though those presenting this final gift may have had only the notion of pleasing Him with a pleasant perfume (Ps. 45:8; Song of Sol. 5:13).

Wise persons still search for this personal King. And when they discover Him, they

[a] 9 Or *seen when it rose*

can only feel the desire to worship Him, and to give to Him their earthly treasures.

They Return Home. Matthew frequently mentions dreams as a source God utilizes for communicating with people (Matt. 1:20; 2:12, 13, 19, 22; 27:19). This is still a viable method through which we can hear from God (Acts 2:17).

Jesus' Family Makes Two Moves (Matt. 2:13-23)

This biblical story gives us important information regarding the nature of God. We learn that God's will can be accomplished in spite of sinful men. No weak frame so small as man can withstand the mighty hand of God (Dan. 4:35). Christians must learn to rest in this fathomless universe of tranquility. There is no trial so great that God is not greater still (1 Cor. 10:13).

I. *The Move to Egypt (2:13-18)*

13When they had gone, an angel of the Lord appeared to Joseph in a dream. "Get up," he said, "take the child and his mother and escape to Egypt. Stay there until I tell you, for Herod is going to search for the child to kill him."

14So he got up, took the child and his mother during the night and left
for Egypt, 15where he stayed until the death of Herod. And so was fulfilled what the Lord had said through the prophet: "Out of Egypt I called my son."[a]

16When Herod realized that he had been outwitted by the Magi, he was furious, and he gave orders to kill all the boys in Bethlehem and its vicinity who were two years old and under, in accordance with the time
he had learned from the Magi. 17Then what was said through the
prophet Jeremiah was fulfilled:

18"A voice is heard in Ramah,
weeping and great mourning,
Rachel weeping for her children
and refusing to be comforted,
because they are no more."[b]

During the Night. Once again special note is to be made about the nature of Joseph's

[a] *15* Hosea 11:1 [b] *18* Jer. 31:15

obedience to God. When God gave Joseph directions, he obeyed them without question and without hesitation. "In the night" he received God's orders, and "in the night" he set out to follow them. How different our lives, our homes, our churches, and even our world would be if our devotion to God were like that.

Herod. On the surface, our natural minds are inclined to imagine that man will accept whatever is best for him. But life proves this to be untrue. Men love darkness, not light (John 3:19-21). The great news of the Savior's birth did not cause men to be delighted. Instead, it resurrected a summons to kill. The natural depravity of our soul seeks consolation, not conversion. Jesus and the Church have had to learn this lesson repeatedly—in the world there will be trouble for the saints (John 15:18, 19). Purity brings with it no exemptions from problems.

Herod was a madman. Cruel. Sadistic. During his reign he killed his own wife and three sons—not to mention three hundred of his court officials, and others under his authority. At the time of his death he arranged that the high officials of Jerusalem be killed in order that someone might mourn in his hour of departure. (See the chart entitled "Family Tree of Herod the Great.")

This episode demonstrates the terrible extent to which a person may go to keep Christ from mastering his life. "Kill the infants," was his command. "Kill Jesus." A solemn truth lies beneath these words: those who reject the Lordship of Jesus are the ones who raise the hand to assist in His death.

Finally, in the person of Herod we have a perfect illustration of Satan, who operates as an angel of light. Herod said nothing negative about the Christ child; in fact, he had even stated that he wanted to worship Him. Herod consulted with religious men for his answers. Everything gave the appearance of righteousness, but that was only the external view. Inside, where reality cannot be hidden, Herod was exposed to his real self—a spiritually lost man who possessed no trace of sincere obedience to Christ.

The Prophecy of Jeremiah. Nearly six hundred years earlier, during the life of Jeremiah, Ramah was located practically on the border between the tribes of Judah and Israel. It was also in Jeremiah's lifetime that the southern kingdom, Judah, was defeated at the hands of the Babylonians (606 B.C.). The victims were apparently lodged at Ramah before being deported to their captor's domain (Jer. 31:15; 40:1).

Rachel, the mother of Joseph and Benjamin, is used here metaphorically as the mother of the two tribes comprising Judah. She cries as she sees her sons being marched off to Babylon. Matthew envisions a continuation of these tears in the slaughter of the children in this area.

II. *The Move to Nazareth (2:19-23)*

19After Herod died, an angel of the Lord appeared in a dream to
Joseph in Egypt 20and said, "Get up, take the child and his mother and

**go to the land of Israel, for those who were trying to take the child's life
are dead."**
**[21]So he got up, took the child and his mother and went to the land of
Israel. [22]But when he heard that Archelaus was reigning in Judea in
place of his father Herod, he was afraid to go there. Having been**

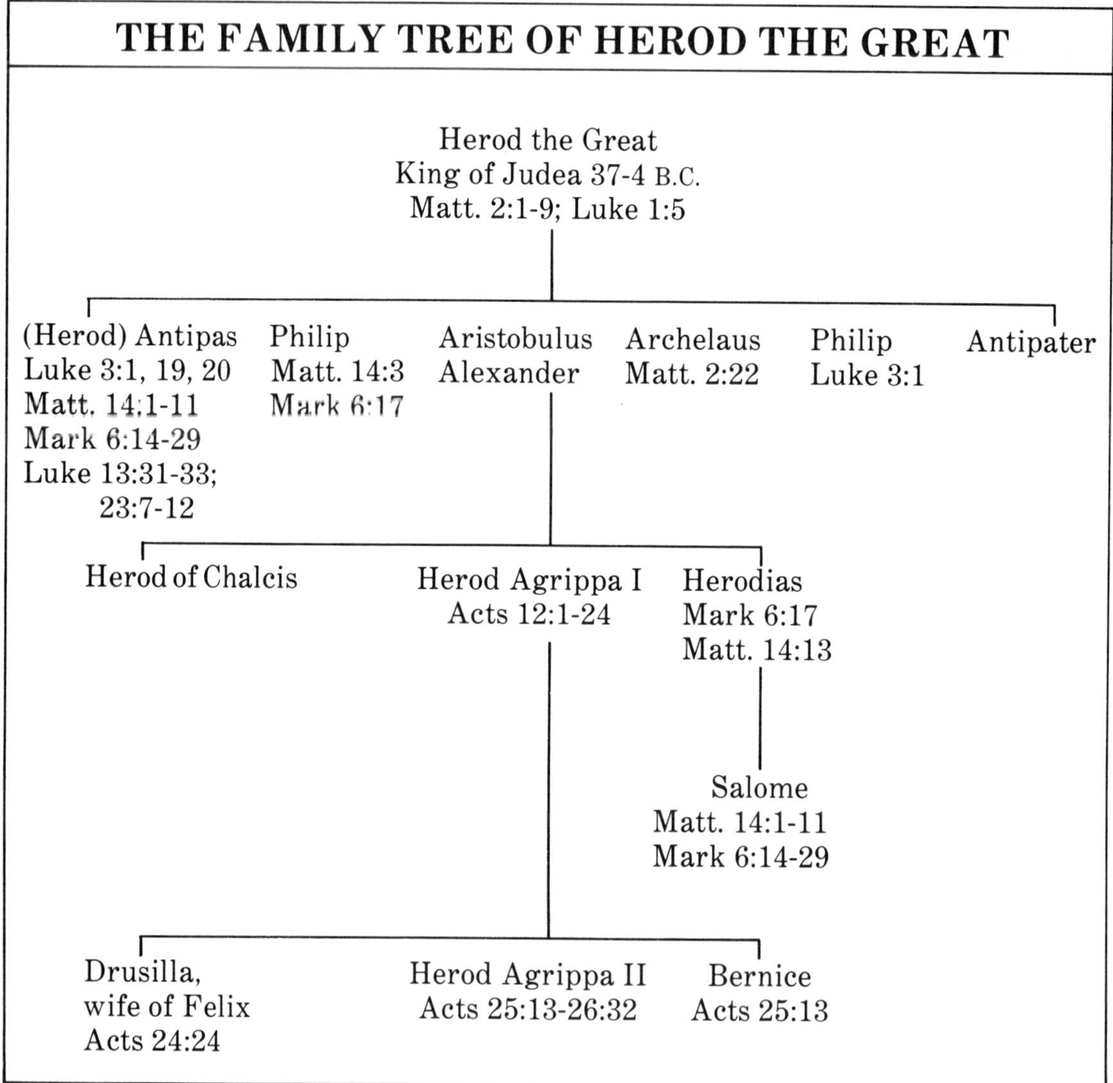

warned in a dream, he withdrew to the district of Galilee, [23]and he went and lived in a town called Nazareth. So was fulfilled what was said though the prophets: "He will be called a Nazarene."

The Enemies Are Dead. There is an end to every trial. No matter how severe, there is always a day of relief. But we must not confuse relief with retirement. The Christian is never free to stop shielding himself against the temptation to sin or to stop serving God. In the brief episode before us Joseph was released by God to leave Egypt, but the road ahead was not to be without its rough spots. He would have to be as cautious now as ever before.

Archelaus. Archelaus was an ineffective ruler. At the beginning of his domain he had three thousand of the country's men slaughtered. His administration was horribly marred. Eventually Rome had him exiled. But before his departure Joseph came back to Israel. And seeing this man on the throne caused him to settle in Nazareth, a city of Galilee under the rule of Herod Antipas. This man is the ruler who beheaded John the Baptist and assisted in the trial of Jesus (Matt. 14:1-12; Luke 23:6-12).

There are some practical matters to be learned here with regard to God's guidance. First, we see it was general in nature. He did not give Joseph a detailed blueprint. Second, we see that Joseph was to couple God's guidance with common sense. Joseph had the freedom to move with a fair amount of latitude within God's guidance.

Nazareth. Nazareth could hardly be called a significant village. It is not even mentioned once in the entire Old Testament. Even so, from her humble site the Savior-King of the world would emerge. Let us learn a lesson here. Our personal significance does not rest in our wealth or status, but solely in our obedience to the will of God!

Nazarene. It is not easy to decide precisely what prophecy Matthew had in mind here. Many scholars think a fulfillment can be located in Isaiah 11:1, or more precisely in the Hebrew word for "Branch" (*Netzer*—presumably a play on words with Nazareth, but this is uncertain). Other writers contend that Matthew's use of the plural for prophet in this passage indicates the general scorn that the prophets foresaw the Messiah receiving, including the ridicule He would receive for being from the insignificant village of Nazareth (cf. John 1:45, 46).

John the Baptist (Matt. 3:1-12)

(cf. Mark 1:1-8; Luke 3:2-17; John 1:6-8, 19-28)

There is a sudden lapse of thirty years between the close of chapter two and the start of chapter three (cf. Luke 3:23). The date is either A.D. 26 or 27. The baby John has matured and is now seen as the forerunner of the soon-to-appear Messiah. Through this bold prophet a message would echo that was destined to be the hinge between the Old Testament prophecies and the New Testament fulfillments. There would be no greater prophet in all of Israel than John the Baptist.

I. *The Man and His Message (3:1-6)*

3 In those days John the Baptist came, preaching in the Desert of
Judea [2]and saying, "Repent, for the kingdom of heaven is near."

[3]This is he who was spoken of through the prophet Isaiah:
"A voice of one calling in the desert,
'Prepare the way for the Lord,
make straight paths for him.' "[a]

[4]John's clothes were made of camel's hair, and he had a leather belt
around his waist. His food was locusts and wild honey. [5]People went out to
him from Jerusalem and all Judea and the whole region of the Jordan.
[6]Confessing their sins, they were baptized by him in the Jordan River.

John Came Preaching. The method God chose to use to motivate people was both simple and profound. He sent a holy preacher to call His people to holy living. There are several matters that should be noted about this: (1) There is nothing more effective in the arsenal of heaven than the straightforward expounding of God's clear Word. (2) The deepest problems of a troubled soul cannot be conquered by science, but they can be resolved by hearing and applying good preaching. (3) Even those quite acquainted with God's laws need to hear again and again the anointed preaching of God's servants.

The keynote in John's messages was repentance. This is the only doorway to forgiveness, to spiritual blessings, and to heaven itself. Any other approach is doomed to failure. The term "repentance" means to change your thinking, especially with regard to your spiritual life. John boldly required his converts to confess their sins (publicly!) and to start living the kind of lives that proved they were in fact children of God.

---

a 3 Isaiah 40:3

The Kingdom of Heaven/God. The motivation behind John's preaching is found in the fact that the Kingdom of Heaven was at hand, ready to be established. For John this meant that God's Messiah would soon appear and set up His kingdom of heavenly order upon the earth. (Matthew's use of the phrase, "Kingdom of Heaven," rather than, "Kingdom of God," reflects popular Jewish preference. The meaning is the same.) A detailed analysis of the Kingdom of Heaven/God may be found in this commentary in Matt. 4:17 and 5:1-7:29.

The Prophecy of Isaiah. John was not a self-appointed spokesman for God. Instead, his coming and labor were prophesied some 700 years before his birth (Isa. 40:3-5). His mission was clear—to get the people ready for the glorious appearing of the Christ, to preach to them God's will, and to set their hearts on heavenly priorities.

Observe these practical points from this portion of our text: (1) John was only a voice; God was the actual spokesman. (2) John's pulpit was made up of the desert sands; he would call people to find Christ and not some structure. (3) John's labors were essential in the preparation of the coming of the Kingdom of God; Spirit-filled people are always God's method.

John's Clothes and Food. In a day of material abundance it is easy to lose sight of God's proper estimation of the things in the world, clothes and food included. It was not a man of regal attire who introduced the coming King, but a common man with an uncommonly powerful message. Eating locusts and wild honey was not an unusual meal for simple and poor people. They would remove the wings and legs of the locusts, bake or roast them to taste, add a little salt and then eat them—much like Americans devour shrimp. The point is this: people are not moved toward Christ because of what we wear or eat, but because of our internal anointing with God's Spirit (cf. Luke 1:15).

Confession and Baptism. John convincingly linked the confession of sin with the act of baptism. In his ministry (and in the ministry of the early church—Acts 2:38; 8:12) when a person was ready to turn from his self-centered life style toward a God-centered life style, he was to be baptized in water. There seems to be no warrant for any delay in performing this action once someone confesses Christ.

II. *The Man and His Madness (3:7-10)*

[7]But when he saw many of the Pharisees and Sadducees coming to
where he was baptizing, he said to them: "You brood of vipers! Who
warned you to flee from the coming wrath? [8]Produce fruit in keeping
with repentance. [9]And do not think you can say to yourselves, 'We have
Abraham as our father.' I tell you that out of these stones God can raise
up children for Abraham. [10]The ax is already at the root of the trees,

and every tree that does not produce good fruit will be cut down and thrown into the fire.

Pharisees. The term "Pharisee" means "to separate," and it refers to a body of men who separated themselves from the masses of people who did not observe, with strict rigidity, the letter of the Mosaic Law. They traced their origins to the second century before Christ, during the rugged years of the Maccabean revolt. It was at this time, when foreign political pressures and pagan life styles were at the forefront in Israel, that the Pharisees arose in prominence. Their aim was to display a loyal faith to the God of Abraham, Isaac and Jacob.

Over the next two centuries this sect of holy men played a varying role in the politics of Israel. Progressively, however, they held less and less influence in this arena, though their popularity made them a formidable factor in governmental affairs. By the time Jesus arrived, the number of Pharisees was well over six thousand. Some estimates range as high as 5 percent of the population, which would be well over the six thousand figure.

These men were, for the most part, middle-class businessmen who had no formal training in the Mosaic Law, though there are some notable exceptions, like Gamaliel, Nicodemus and Saul. Their most basic ambition was to safeguard their religion from impurities. For a Pharisee, then, this meant there would be plenty of zeal for the *Torah* (Hebrew for "the Law"—referring to the five books of Moses: Genesis, Exodus, Leviticus, Numbers and Deuteronomy) and the prophets. Unfortunately, an equal devotion was attached by the Pharisees to the oral law, which amounted to a detailed commentary on the Torah. These lengthy explanations of the Scriptures began during the Babylonian captivity (606-537 B.C.) and grew in popularity until they finally took their place on an equal par with the Word of God. It was their proud and arrogant devotion for these unbiblical traditions that caused them to be such difficult fellows. Neither John nor Jesus would accept these men unless the Pharisees first showed the fruit of repentance in their lives.

Sadducees. While the Pharisees were gaining their strength in the second century before Christ, they were not alone in their power. The Sadducees, too, were developing into an influential body within Israel. Although the former body was largely interested in religious matters, the latter sect was more concerned with politics. The members of this organization (which were considerably smaller in number) were chiefly drawn from the well-to-do families in Israel. In time, the Sadducees became closely aligned with the high priesthood and other high-ranking members of the social world of Israel and Rome. By the New Testament period they held a position of significant power, drawn primarily from their large membership in the Sanhedrin and their almost exclusive role as chief priests.

The commonness of the Pharisees, along with their historical zeal for God, made them a rather likable group (at least in contrast to the Sadducees). But the superior stance of the Sadducees made them somewhat untouchable. They were an exclusive body, appealing only to the wealthy and powerful. This meant they maintained strong and peaceful ties with Roman officials, an action that did not rest easy with fervent Jews who desired an end to Rome's tyranny.

In theology the Sadducees were openly liberal. They denied the authority of the oral law and followed only what seemed to be convenient in the Torah. Basically, they maintained the priority of private opinion over scriptural authority. Stated differently, the Sadducees were the liberals of their day, while the Pharisees were the legalistic conservatives. In short, these two bodies were strong opposites, each holding a position of faith that was extreme. (For further information, see the Topical Index.)

Children from Stones. John does not give the customary polite greeting to the carnal religious leaders who stand before him. Rather, he calls them a "brood of vipers," a nest of poisonous snakes! He does not give them so much as a single ray of spiritual security. They need repentance and baptism as certainly as the ones they seek to influence.

You cannot trust your religious background to secure God's blessings for you. The only sure path for acceptance with God is personal repentance.

The Ax. John's message always dealt with sin. He emphatically declared the necessity of repentance in order to be saved from God's wrath. He preached this to the most common of men and to the highest officials.

There are no exceptions. Each person must choose either to repent or to perish. No one can rest on his wealth, position, ancestry or religious convictions. God's ax will remove the trees which bear no fruit of repentance.

III. *The Man and His Mission (3:11, 12)*

> **11"I baptize you with[a] water for repentance. But after me will come one who is more powerful than I, whose sandals I am not fit to carry. He will baptize you with the Holy Spirit and with fire. 12His winnowing fork is in his hand, and he will clear his threshing floor, gathering the wheat into his barn and burning up the chaff with unquenchable fire."**

Also at the heart of John's message was someone "more powerful" than himself. He never forgot this crucial point. He felt unqualified to even carry this one's sandals. For John this coming one was too great a figure to be thought of as a mere friend or a wonderful man. He would be the one before whom you could only reverently bow and receive your daily instructions.

[a] 11 Or *in*

The Fire Baptism. There are differing schools of thought on the exact nature of this baptism. One body of interpreters envisions the fire here as being a purifying agent (cf. Acts 2:3, with 1 Pet. 1:7; Rev. 3:18). The natural implication is that believers will experience the refinement of holiness once baptized in the Spirit and fire. Another body of biblical teachers is persuaded that the fire here is symbolic of a judgmental sentence (cf. Lev. 10:2; Num. 11:1; 16:35; Mal. 3:2; Matt. 13:42; 2 Thess. 1:7; Heb. 12:29). The implication in this case is that nonbelievers will taste the scorching heat that comes from the judgments of the Christ (Rev. 20:11-15). Neither position cancels out the other in reality. For God's fire will surely both refine His followers and consume His enemies, though the latter position seems more appropriate here.

The Spirit Baptism. A relatively thorough analysis of the baptism in the Holy Spirit is offered in the following special study.

Special Study: The Baptism in the Holy Spirit

1. *The Era of the Spirit*

> And I will ask the Father, and he will give you another Counselor to be with you forever—the Spirit of truth. The world cannot accept him, because it neither sees him nor knows him. But you know him, for he lives with you and will be in you. (John 14:16, 17)

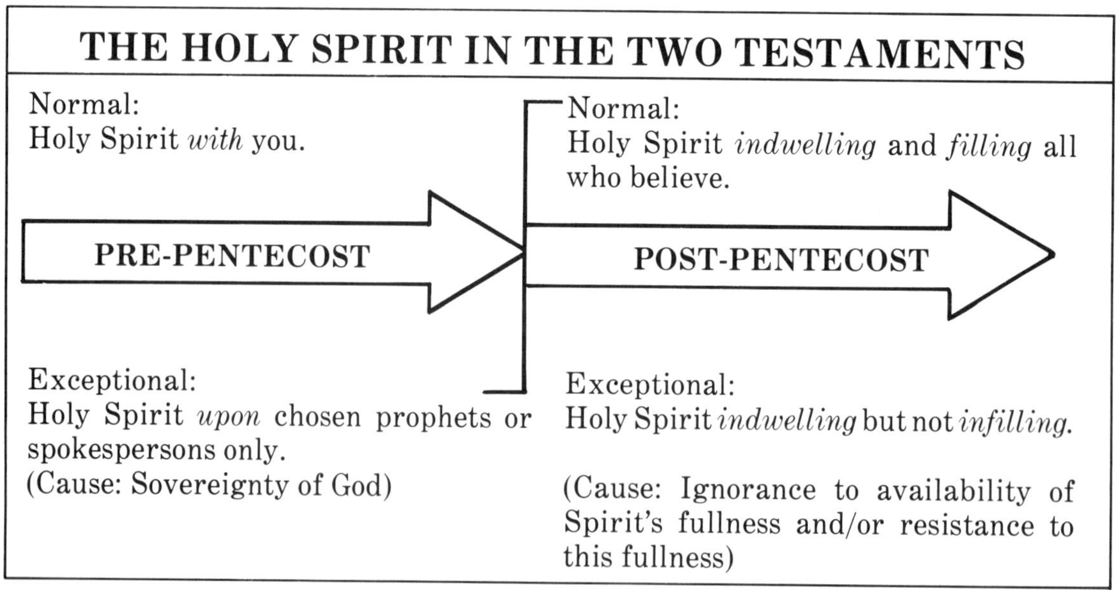

> **But I tell you the truth: It is for your good that I am going away. Unless I go away, the Counselor will not come to you; but if I go, I will send him to you. (John 16:7)**

When the disciples walked with Jesus, the Holy Spirit, too, was "with" them. They knew the presence of the Spirit. They had seen His power operate through Christ and even through themselves. But this relationship of being "with" the Holy Spirit was only temporary. It was to be replaced with a still greater intimacy—He "will be *in* you."

The turning point from "with" to "in" could only occur when Jesus went away. The ministry of the Spirit would begin after the earthly ministry of Jesus had ended. The finishing of one era would give way to the start of a new era. The members of the Godhead never compete for attention; to each is allowed a certain focus.

The independent working of each member of the Godhead is evident from the creation to the consummation of all things. While all three persons are always active, in a unique fashion one particular member is always spotlighted or emphasized in each era. In the Old Testament the Father is more pronounced; in the Gospels it is the Son; and in the book of Acts and in the letters the Spirit is more centrally focused. Once you arrive at the book of Revelation the emphasis reverses back to the Son and to the Father.

Today we live in the era of the Spirit. Jesus has gone away (John 16:7). The Spirit has come, the Spirit who desires to make His abode "in" us. Before Pentecost the Holy Spirit was largely only "with" the believer. Today He comes "in" to each believer at the precise moment of conversion (Rom. 5:5; 8:9, 11; 1 Cor. 2:12; 3:16; 6:19, 20; 2 Cor. 5:5; Gal. 3:2; 4:6; 1 John 3:24; 4:13). If you are a genuine Christian, then the Holy Spirit is dwelling in you.

2. *The Promise*

> **"I baptize you with water for repentance. But after me will come one who is more powerful than I, whose sandals I am not fit to carry. He will baptize you with the Holy Spirit and with fire." (Matt. 3:11)**

Here is a prophecy. Here is a promise. John bears the message of expectancy and hope.

Water baptism was good—as far as it went—but John knew there was more to come. Jesus would supply more. He would bring the Spirit. He would baptize us in another medium—the marvelous Holy Spirit.

You can read of this promise four times from the lips of John. It is in each of the Gospels (Matt. 3:11; Mark 1:8; Luke 3:16; John 1:33). Not very many matters are recorded by all four of the Gospel writers, but this subject finds its place of prominence at the beginning of each book.

Jesus, too, spoke prophetically of this baptism: ". . . wait for the gift my Father promised, which you have heard me speak about. For John baptized with water, but in a few days you will be baptized with the Holy Spirit" (Acts 1:4, 5). Often Jesus foretold the day when the Holy Spirit would come. Read these passages and capture the anticipation involved with each of them: Luke 24:49; John 7:38, 39; 14:16, 26; 15:26; 16:13; and 20:22.

Peter also spoke of the baptism in the Holy Spirit. In Jerusalem, before the apostles and fellow believers, he told of how the Gentiles in Caesarea received this baptism: "As I began to speak, the Holy Spirit came on them as he had come on us at the beginning. Then I remembered what the Lord had said, 'John baptized with water, but you will be baptized with the Holy Spirit' (Acts 11:15, 16).

Peter, somewhat astonished, was unable to finish his message at Caesarea, because his audience unexpectedly received the baptism in the Holy Spirit. Everyone immediately began praising God. What could Peter do? He stopped speaking and began to reflect. "Surely," he reasoned, "this baptism in the Holy Spirit which Jesus gave to us in the upper room has now been given to these too!" (Acts 10:47, paraphrased).

The baptism in the Holy Spirit has come. It came at Pentecost, while men and women prayed. It came again in Caesarea while men and women listened to Peter's preaching. And this same baptism still comes today. "This promise is for you and your children and for all who are far off" (Acts 2:39).

3. *Jesus Prays for the Spirit*

> **And I will ask the Father, and he will give you another Counselor . . . the Spirit of truth. (John 14:16, 17)**

The Holy Spirit did not accidentally *fall* from heaven. He was *sent*. There is a profound arrangement here. The Holy Spirit is under authority. He comes to earth upon the request of Jesus. He comes because Jesus prayed. Make no mistake in this matter: The Holy Spirit is in the world today because Jesus spoke to the Father. Jesus asked for the Holy Spirit.

The Holy Spirit does not arbitrarily fall from heaven upon people. He comes upon request. He comes when we pray and when we ask for Him. Jesus taught the disciples this truth.

> **If you then, though you are evil, know how to give good gifts to your children, how much more will your Father in heaven give the Holy Spirit to those who ask him! (Luke 11:13)**

Here is a principle: God's will is ready to be performed, but it awaits our invitation! We must "ask Him." Jesus asked the Father for the Holy Spirit. And we too are told to ask the Father for the Holy Spirit.

Asking. Are you asking? Are you seeking and knocking? My friend, do not assume that the Holy Spirit will *fall* upon you. He won't. He comes upon personal request. Ask.

4. *What is a Baptism?*

> **I [John the Baptist] baptize you with water, but he [Jesus Christ] will baptize you with the Holy Spirit. (Mark 1:8)**

Notice the *contrast:* "I baptize with *water* . . . He will baptize with the *Holy Spirit.*" There are two baptisms here—water and Spirit. The former came through John; the latter was yet to come through Jesus.

Notice the *comparison:* "I baptize with water . . . he will baptize with the Holy Spirit." There is one method or mode—baptism.

How did John baptize? This is important. Was it *with* water, or was it *in* water? The particular Greek term used here may be translated either way—"with" or "in." Observe the difference that is involved. If John baptized *with* water, then we can picture him drawing up some water in his hands and baptizing his candidate *with* this substance. But if John baptized *in* water, then we can envision him bringing his candidate down *into* this substance.

Which way did John baptize: *with* or *in* water? Our answer is not difficult to locate. Let's look at the baptism of Jesus by John. "As soon as Jesus was baptized, he went up out of the water." (Matt. 3:16). Jesus was baptized *in* water.

This leads us to a crucial point: John baptized the repentant person *in* water, and in like manner, Jesus was to come and baptize *in* the Holy Spirit.

Jesus, like John before Him, graciously leads us out into the deep spiritual waters and there immerses us completely into the domain of the Holy Spirit.

The following chart will aid in bringing clarity to the three baptisms God has designed for each believer.

While there is only "one baptism" (Eph. 4:5)—which is necessary for our conversion (namely, baptism into Christ's body)—there are other baptisms available to enrich our lives and service.

5. *Power*

> **I am going to send you what my Father has promised; but stay in the city until you have been clothed with power from on high. (Luke 24:49)**

Thc Baptism	The Baptizer	The Requirements	The Results
Into Christ's Body (1 Cor. 12:13)	Holy Spirit	Repentance and Faith	Salvation
Into Water (Acts 2:38)	Church	Obedience	Good Conscience
Into the Spirit (Matt. 3:11)	Jesus	Asking and Obedience	Power to Witness

Do not leave Jerusalem, but wait for the gift my Father promised, which you have heard me speak about. For John baptized with water, but in a few days you will be baptized with the Holy Spirit. . . . But you will receive power when the Holy Spirit comes on you; and you will be my witnesses in Jerusalem, and in all Judea and Samaria, and to the ends of the earth. (Acts 1:4,5,8)

What is this "promise" of the Father? What is this baptism "with the Holy Spirit?" Jesus states it most plainly: It is being "endued with power from on high;" it is "power . . . [to] witness" of Christ.

The baptism in the Holy Spirit is, more than anything else, a divine enabling or capability to speak to people unashamedly and unfearfully of Jesus Christ. This lies at the very heart of the Holy Spirit baptism: being a witness for Jesus!

6. *An Analytical Outline of the Baptism in the Holy Spirit*

I. *It Is a Conscious Experience.*
   A. The disciples were to tarry in Jerusalem until they received it—Luke 24:49; Acts 1:4, 5.
   B. The disciples at Ephesus were asked, "Did you receive the Holy Spirit when you believed?" (Acts 19:2). Their answer was to be a simple "yes" or "no."This shows the experience is knowable.
   C. If it were not a conscious experience, then you could have it and never know it and then lose it and not know that either. How absurd!

II. *It Is a Visible Experience.*
  A. The "power" of the Spirit will generate a boldness for witnessing.
  B. The fruit of the Spirit (a byproduct of the Spirit-baptism—Gal. 5:22-24) is visible fruit.
  C. The baptism (or filling) of the Spirit has the following four effects in the believer's life (see Eph. 5:18-21):
    1. Spiritual speech.
    2. Singing heart to the Lord.
    3. Thankfulness in all things.
    4. Submission to other Christians.
  D. The gifts of the Spirit are for public manifestation—1 Cor. 12:7.

III. *It Is an Audible Experience.*
  A. Elizabeth was filled and blessed the Lord—Luke 1:41, 42.
  B. Zecharias was filled and prophesied—Luke 1:67ff.
  C. Jesus was anointed and He proclaimed liberty to the captives—Luke 4:18, 19; cf. Acts 10:38.
  D. Note the experiences from the book of Acts:
    1. Acts 2:4—Tongues
    2. Acts 2:17—Prophecy, visions and dreams
    3. Acts 10:44-46—Tongues
    4. Acts 19:6—Tongues and prophecy
    (Challenge: See if you can find just one biblical illustration where someone is filled with the Spirit and nothing transpires.)

IV. *It Is Often a Post-Conversion Experience.*
  A. The disciples were saved (John 13:10; 15:1-3) but had to wait for this baptism until Pentecost.
  B. The Samaritans believed and were baptized in water, but their Spirit-baptism occurred still later—Acts 8:12-17.
  C. Paul, saved on the Damascus road, was "filled" three days later; just prior to his water baptism—Acts 9:1-17.

The Baptism of Jesus (Matt. 3:13-17)

(cf. Mark 1:9-11; Luke 3:21, 22)

We know very little of Jesus' first thirty years. Only microscopic glimpses are given here and there. The following sketch will give you a fair representation of what these nearly silent years must have been like.

Birth. The virgin birth of Jesus was prophesied over seven hundred years before, through Isaiah (Isa. 7:14). The place of His birth, Bethlehem, was also predicted in advance by the same number of years (Mic. 5:2). Joseph and Mary traveled the painstaking ninety miles to Bethlehem in order to be registered in the universal census (Luke 2:1-7). In a manger (a mere feeding trough for animals!) Jesus spent His first night. Excited shepherds looked at the baby Jesus, who was wrapped in a long linen cloth, and told a thrilling story of their encounter with angels (Luke 2:8-20).

Circumcision and Dedication. According to the Jewish custom, the son of Mary was circumcised and named on the eighth day after His birth (Luke 2:21). After forty days, the family traveled to Jerusalem to present Him to the Lord. From the start, Jesus would be dedicated to God's service (Luke 2:22, 23).

Two fowl were then sacrificed, in keeping with the Mosaic Law. Either a lamb or a fowl could be offered—the former for the wealthy and the latter for the poor (Lev. 12:6-8). Joseph and Mary were poor. During this time Simeon and Anna met Jesus. They both received a witness from the Holy Spirit that this child was indeed the long-awaited Messiah (Luke 2:25-28).

Visit from the Magi. It is uncertain when the Magi visited Jesus. Some think that they came immediately after his birth; others believe that two years may have transpired. Regardless of the timing, with deep reverence they presented to the Son of God their costly gifts.

Journey to Egypt. Shortly after the departure of the Magi, Joseph is warned in a dream of an impending danger for his baby. Under God's direction he immediately takes his wife and stepson to Egypt for safety.

Life in Nazareth. When the danger for which Joseph had been warned passed, he took his family and returned to Palestine. Apparently Joseph had planned to raise Jesus in Bethlehem, but upon discovering the cruel ruler Archelaus he decided to dwell in Nazareth. This was a small town of little significance. But because it was the childhood home of Mary (Luke 1:26-38), it was decided to become the childhood home of Jesus as well. Situated in a valley with nearby mountains and cities of substantial size, Nazareth, with its single water hole, was destined to produce "the living water," Jesus Christ (John 4:1-14; 7:37-39). Here Jesus would live in subjection to His parents and grow in favor with both God and His community (Luke 2:40, 51, 52).

Visiting the Temple at Age Twelve. Making the annual trip to Jerusalem for the Passover feast was expected of all Israel's male population (Exod. 23:14-17). But from Jesus' godly home the mother and small children would come as well. In the synagogue at Nazareth Jesus was doubtless taught the Scriptures, reading and writing. And by the age of twelve He was startling even the teachers at the temple in Jerusalem (Luke 2:41-50).

Learning a Skill. The Jewish custom was for a father to teach his son a trade. It was natural that Joseph, being a carpenter, should teach Jesus the same skill (Matt. 13:55; Mark 6:3). This meant that Jesus would have worked with His father, making such items as roofs, doors, window fittings, stairways, chairs, tables and beds.

Relating to a Family Unit. Above all else we can be assured that Jesus' parents were orthodox Jews. In their humble home Jesus would have both heard and seen in practice the principles of their faith. Jesus also shared this household with four brothers and two or more sisters (Matt. 13:56; Luke 8:19). In the beginning the family was quite critical of Jesus' ministry, but in the end they each became loyal followers (John 7:3; Acts 1:14; 1 Cor. 9:5; Gal. 1:19).

Facing a Father's Death. There is no further reference to Joseph after Jesus' twelfth year. From the cross, Jesus instructs John to provide for His mother each of her needs (John 19:26, 27). It is believed that Joseph must have died in Jesus' youth, and that Jesus must have assumed the responsibility of caring for His family until they could sustain themselves.

Now we are ready for Jesus' baptism. The King of kings has grown into adulthood. He is prepared to commence His mission.

I. *The Resistance of John (3:13, 14)*

13Then Jesus came from Galilee to the Jordan to be baptized by John.
14But John tried to deter him, saying, "I need to be baptized by you, and do you come to me?"

It is not difficult to imagine how John felt when he saw Jesus coming to be baptized by him. He knew this man was God's Messiah, and he felt it was inappropriate for him to baptize the Son of God. John felt inferior to his Lord. How often God calls the weak and unseemly to perform the most wonderful and holy tasks. Grace!

II. *The Reassurance of Jesus (3:15)*

> **15 Jesus replied, "Let it be so now; it is proper for us to do this to fulfill all righteousness." Then John consented.**

John's baptism was for sinners, and for the forgiveness of sins. Why should Jesus undergo this rite? He had no sins to be forgiven (2 Cor. 5:21; 1 Pet. 1:19). Jesus answers this inquiry by saying, "It is proper for us to do this to fulfill all righteousness." He knew that He had no need for this baptism, but He also knew that in God's plan it was His will for it to happen. So, like an obedient son before his father, Jesus willingly consented to this sacrament.

In this action we see the depth of Jesus' identification with humans. He did not come to reform the politics of Palestine, but to transform its people. Sin and its manifold effects were the Messiah's chief concern. He came to deliver people from their worst enemies—the world's life style, the flesh and the devil—by becoming one with them, even in baptism, and then dying and rising for them. (See the chart entitled "The Eight Baptisms of the New Testament.")

THE EIGHT BAPTISMS OF THE NEW TESTAMENT

1. The BAPTISM INTO WATER by John the Baptist on account of the forgiveness of sins (Matt. 3).
2. The BAPTISM INTO WATER by the disciples of Jesus on account of the forgiveness of sins (John 3:22, 23; 4:1, 2).
3. The BAPTISM INTO THE SEA by Moses (1 Cor. 10:2).
4. The BAPTISM INTO THE CLOUD by Moses (1 Cor. 10:2).
5. The BAPTISM INTO CHRIST'S SUFFERING (Luke 12:50).
6. The BAPTISM INTO CHRIST'S BODY, the universal Church (1 Cor. 12:13).
7. The BAPTISM INTO WATER by the Church (Matt. 28:19, 20; Acts 2:38).
8. The BAPTISM INTO THE HOLY SPIRIT by Jesus Christ for power to witness (Matt. 3:11; Acts 1:4-8; 11:15-18).

III. *The Responses of Heaven (3:16, 17)*

> **16 As soon as Jesus was baptized, he went up out of the water. At that**

moment heaven was opened, and he saw the Spirit of God descending like a dove and lighting on him. [17]And a voice from heaven said, "This is my Son, whom I love; with him I am well pleased."

This day marks the great turning point in Jesus' life. For thirty years He had lived an ordinary life (by way of contrast) in a simple village of Galilee. But today—at His baptism—everything is to change.

In this unique scene we see all three members of the Godhead: God the Son is baptized; God the Spirit descends like a dove upon Jesus; and God the Father brings a benediction to the service.

It is the Father who planned this route for making the redemption of the world possible; it is the Son who willingly accepted the role necessary to secure this redemption; and it is the Spirit who provided the power to make the plan work.

First, the dove appeared. This was a symbolization of the Holy Spirit, who was to play such a prominent role in Jesus' life. It cannot be stated too strongly that Jesus, as a man, needed the diverse and powerful operation of the Holy Spirit. Without the Spirit Jesus would never have been born to Mary. He needed the Holy Spirit to overcome temptations, to perform miracles, to teach as God's prophet, and to conquer death itself. Put simply, without the operation of the Spirit in Jesus' life, there would have been no miracles, no insights into God's will, no holy living, and no Calvary or resurrection! But the Spirit *did* come upon Jesus, and He was filled without measure

THE HOLY SPIRIT IN JESUS' LIFE

Event	Reference
His Birth	Luke 1:35
His maturing years	Luke 2:40, 52
His baptism	Matt. 3:16, 17; John 3:34
His power over Satan	Matt. 4:1ff.; 12:28
His miracles	Luke 5:17; Acts 10:38
His prophetic office	Luke 4:14, 15, 18
His holiness and power	Rom. 1:4
His death	Heb. 9:14
His resurrection	Rom. 8:11
His Spirit-baptizing work	John 1:32-34
His other present activities	John 16:12-15; Acts 1:1, 2

(John 3:34). (See the chart entitled "The Holy Spirit in Jesus' Life.")

Second, the voice of the Father was heard. "This is my Son, whom I love; with him I am well pleased." Thirteen simple words, but how precious they are. When our earthly father praises us, we are delighted. But when our heavenly Father gives His royal stamp of approval to us, we are doubly honored. Jesus was about to commence His public ministry. In His humanity He sensed it was time to start, but now His inner convictions were solidly confirmed.

Jesus Conquers Temptations (Matt. 4:1-11)

(cf. Mark 1:12, 13; Luke 4:1-13)

God cannot be tempted by evil (James 1:13). He is above any enticement toward sin. But this was not the case with God's Son. Jesus could be tempted, and indeed, He was tempted "in every way" (Heb. 4:15; cf. 2:18). We must occasionally remind ourselves that although Jesus' humanity never replaced His deity, neither did His deity replace His humanity. The temptations Jesus faced were real.

Before examining the details of this passage, however, there is an interesting parallel that ought to be noted between Jesus' experience and our own experience. In practically a matter of moments (actually forty days), we see four significant events occur in Jesus' life:

1. His baptism in water (Matt. 3:13).
2. His baptism in the Spirit (Matt. 3:16).
3. Divinely ordered tests presented to Him by Satan (Matt. 4:1-11).
4. His ministry begins (Matt. 4:17).

There can be no accident in this arrangement. God sent Jesus to minister to the needs of people, but before He could help people He first had to qualify for service by passing some divinely organized tests. And before Jesus could pass these tests, He had to be baptized in the Holy Spirit. But Jesus was not baptized in the Spirit until He submitted to water baptism.

These events may not occur in our own lives in the precise order shown above (for instance, points 1 and 2 may be reversed—Acts 10), but it is clear that all four of these elements in Jesus' life are common ingredients for every sincere child of God. You cannot enter into fruitful Christian work until you pass some God-ordered tests and have been baptized in the Spirit and in water!

I. *The Setting for the Temptations (4:1)*

4 Then Jesus was led by the Spirit into the desert to be tempted by the devil.

Led by the Spirit. The pattern of (a) blessing, (b) trial, and (c) triumph in Christ's life is a threefold cycle that each of His followers will discover to be a part of their experience, too. One moment the heavens are open and God is with us; the next moment it is hell that opens and we stand face to face with Satan. Life offers these extremes to us, and we cannot (nor should we will to) avoid them.

The first event in Jesus' life after being baptized, after being filled with the Spirit, and after hearing God's comforting confirmation, was a divinely appointed period of fasting and temptation. What a contrast! On the one hand, Jesus was seeking God's fellowship in the most intense method possible—a forty-day fast. On the other hand, the devil was seeking to destroy Him with the most enticing temptations possible. It is to be underscored boldly that *both* experiences were in the perfect will of God.

A person cannot be considered mature until he or she can stand up under pressures (including demonic pressure) and press on in an optimistic faith. Henry Ward Beecher states the matter graphically when he says, "An acorn is not an oak tree when it is sprouted. It must go through long summers and fierce winters; it has to endure all that frost and snow and sidestriking winds can bring before it is a full grown oak. These are rough teachers; but rugged schoolmasters make rugged pupils." Jesus was to learn this truth; we must learn it, too (cf. Heb. 5:7, 8).

Lastly, after reading that "Jesus was led by the Spirit . . . to be tempted by the devil," it might be necessary for some of us to expand our views about the nature of divine guidance. The position which states that God never wills anything other than prosperity and bliss for His children is not altogether accurate (Phil. 1:12-14; 4:11, 12; Heb. 5:7, 8; 11:32-40; 1 Pet. 4:19; Rev. 6:9-11). God may choose to perfect us with tools other than pleasure.

Tempted by the Devil. According to Webster's Collegiate Dictionary, the English-speaking world only views temptations in one fashion—enticement toward evil. We exclusively use this word in a negative manner. But this was not the case in the Greek-speaking world of Jesus' day. For those who read this account in the original language, they would know that the word "tempted" contains two possible ideas: (a) a drawing away toward sin and (b) a test for the purpose of development. Sometimes these two meanings are actually combined. Here is such an illustration. The devil attempts to lead Jesus into sin, but the Spirit uses the experience to develop even further the character of Jesus (cf. Heb. 5:8).

The nature of the tests confronting Jesus are well organized by Satan. First, Jesus would face testings that would challenge His identity, and His ability to resist food illegally gained. Second, again His identity as God's Son would be undermined, and He would be challenged about the personal applicability of God's Word. Third, He would be offered Satan's very own kingdom on earth (John 12:31; 16:11), in substitution for God's Kingdom. In brief, it is the physical, spiritual and vocational aspects of Jesus' life which seizes Satan's interest in his strategy of attack.

II. *The First Temptation (4:2-4)*

> [2]**After fasting forty days and forty nights, he was hungry.** [3]**The tempter came to him and said, "If you are the Son of God, tell these stones to become bread."**
> [4]**Jesus answered, "It is written: 'Man does not live on bread alone, but on every word that comes from the mouth of God.'[a]"**

He Was Hungry. After forty days of fasting, Jesus was hungry. That's natural. But it is precisely at this point that Satan attempted to destroy Jesus. Enticements to sin do not always appeal to our base nature. Sometimes they come along with the good and necessary functions of life, like eating. The subtle side of the test in such cases is not the need itself, but the means by which that need is satisfied. In other words, Satan's strategy here is to remedy a legitimate need (hunger) by a nonlegitimate means (supplying our own needs independent of God's timing and God's way).

The Bible mentions only three other persons who fasted for forty days: Moses (Deut. 9:9, 18, 25; 10:10); Joshua (Exod. 24:13-18; 32:15-17); and Elijah (1 Kings 19:7-18).

If You Are. Notice Satan's line of attack: (a) it was timely—at the point of Jesus' greatest hunger; (b) it was subtle—appealing to a genuine need; and (c) it was undermining—challenging the identity of Jesus. But Jesus would not allow food to distract Him (as it had Adam and Eve—Gen. 3:1-7) from believing God's Word. (Notice the chart entitled "Satan Is a Fourfold Enemy.")

Jesus trusted His heavenly Father to supply what He needed, and to do so in the proper manner and at the appropriate time. His appetite would not dictate His actions. Instead, Jesus would control the desires of His body, making them submissive to God's will.

How easily our bodies can get in the way of producing life styles that reflect Christ (cf. Ezek. 16:49, 50; Mark 9:45-47; Col. 2:20-23). We must learn, along with Jesus, to make the body our slave, rather than our lord. The success of this plan will culminate in a body that defeats the devil and renders glory to God (cf. 1 Cor. 6:19, 20; 9:24-27).

It Is Written. Here we learn the key for conquering Satanic attacks—it is the Word of God, believed and confessed. There are several reasons why our knowledge of the

---

[a] *4* Deut. 8:3

Scriptures is so critical: (a) you cannot be spiritually clean without knowing and applying God's Word—John 15:3; (b) you cannot pray effectively without God's Word abiding in you—John 15:7; (c) you cannot be sanctified without a knowledge of the Scriptures—John 17:17; (d) you cannot see through deception without knowing the Bible—Col. 2:6-8; and (e) you cannot defeat the devil without an understanding of God's written Word—Eph. 6:10-17.

Jesus used the Scriptures—as a bold verbal confession of His faith—in order to render Satan powerless against Him. We can use nothing less today if we expect to achieve any measure of spiritual success.

SATAN IS A FOURFOLD ENEMY			
1. Enemy of Jesus	**2. Enemy of Angels**	**3. Enemy of Believers**	**4. Enemy of Nonbelievers**
Matt. 4:1-10; 12:22-30 Mark 1:13; 4:15 Luke 4:1, 2; 22:3,4 John 13:27	Dan. 10:13-11:1 Jude 9 Rev. 12:7-12	Luke 13:16; 22:31 Acts 5:3 Rom. 16:20 1 Cor. 5:5; 7:5 2 Cor. 2:11; 11:3, 14 1 Thess. 2:18 1 Tim. 1:20; 5:15 Rev. 2:9, 13, 24; 3:9; 12:9	Matt. 13:4, 19 Mark 4:15 Acts 26:18 2 Cor. 4:3, 4 2 Thess. 2:9, 10 Rev. 20:7

III. *The Second Temptation (4:5-7)*

5Then the devil took him to the holy city and had him stand on the highest point of the temple. 6"If you are the Son of God," he said, "throw yourself down. For it is written:

" 'He will command his angels concerning you,
and they will lift you up in their hands,
so that you will not strike your foot against a stone.'[a]"

7Jesus answered him, "It is also written: 'Do not put the Lord your God to the test.'[b]"

It Is Written. When Satan fails at one point, he will attack at another. And the new area of concentration will frequently be at the point where we have previously expressed our strength. Jesus defeated the devil's first temptation by relying upon

[a] 6 Psalm 91:11, 12 [b] 7 Deut. 6:16

the Scriptures. So what is Satan's next tactic?—using the Scriptures in a perverted manner, just as he had done in the garden of Eden (Gen. 3:1-7). Here we see Satan using the Bible to test Jesus' understanding of, and devotion to, God's Word.

Do Not Test the Lord. Jesus did not fall for this subtle snare. The test was invalid. We cannot order God to do this or to do that. God will not protect us when we devise our own ways to test His faithfulness or love. Jesus knew this important point. So He sets the devil straight by telling him that He will not distort the true meaning of the message which is being used against Him. Psalm 91, from which Satan quotes, is not a passage that deals with God's promises for the believer so much as it is a testimony of one man's elation over his own walk with the Lord. Jesus could not (and we cannot), without some degree of qualification, claim the experiences found in this Scripture passage.

The Bible is our best weapon against Satan (Eph. 6:17). But when the Scriptures are improperly handled, they can actually work against our spiritual advancement. Truth that is distorted ceases to be truth; and nontruth can help no one. We must learn God's intended application of His Word if it is to yield fruit.

IV. *The Third Temptation (4:8-11)*

**8 Again, the devil took him to a very high mountain and showed him
all the kingdoms of the world and their splendor. 9 "All this I will give
you," he said, "if you will bow down and worship me."**
**10 Jesus said to him, "Away from me, Satan! For it is written: 'Worship
the Lord your God, and serve him only.'[a]"**
11 Then the devil left him, and angels came and attended him.

Bow Down and Worship Me. When Satan came to Eve, he promised her a wonderful life (Gen. 3:1-7). He came to Jesus with the same strategy—an offer that had the outward appearance of outshining God's promises. This is a cruel deception which has taken many as its prey. But Jesus could see through the tinsel and glitter of this scheme (though He never denies Satan's authentic claims to back up this offer). For Jesus, however, there was only one devotion in life—worship and service for God. He would not compromise this singular loyalty.

It Is Written. There may be different methods of conquering Satan's schemes, but at the heart of them all is knowing and applying the Scriptures. In each temptation Jesus replied, "It is written." How differently our lives would be lived if we frequently confessed the Scriptures as our standard and strength.

The Devil Left and the Angels Came. Satan did not constantly attack Jesus. There was relief from these assaults so that God's angels could minister to His needs.

---

a 10 Deut. 6:13

The word rendered "attend" means "to serve, to provide for one's necessities." Just precisely what the angels did for Jesus is not stated, but it is safe to assume that His body, soul and spirit were in some way strengthened. Jesus needed the help of angels (we do, too—cf. Heb. 1:14).

Jesus Starts His Ministry in Galilee (Matt. 4:12-25)

(cf. Mark 1:14-20; Luke 4:14, 15; 5:1-11; John 4:43-45)

The day arrived. Jesus, at the age of thirty, would embark on the most influential three years in the world's history. No other three-year period since the beginning of time to this present hour has had a greater impact on the character and destiny of mankind. It began with a single man in a tiny village. And His influence has resulted in a giant kingdom which spreads throughout our entire planet. Here is the account of how it all started, according to Matthew's Gospel.

I. *His Move (4:12-16)*

12When Jesus heard that John had been put in prison, he returned to
Galilee. 13Leaving Nazareth, he went and lived in Capernaum, which
was by the lake in the area of Zebulun and Naphtali— 14to fulfill what
was said through the prophet Isaiah:
15"Land of Zebulun and land of Naphtali,
the way to the sea, along the Jordan,
Galilee of the Gentiles—
16the people living in darkness
have seen a great light;
on those living in the land of the shadow of death
a light has dawned."[a]

John Is Put in Prison. Between verses eleven and twelve in this chapter a great lapse in time occurs—possibly as much as one year. Because there are no dates provided in our text, this point is easily overlooked. Let's discover what seems to have transpired during the period which Matthew chose to omit.

Once Jesus returned from His forty-day test with Satan and fellowship with God, he stayed in the presence of John the Baptist for at least two days. One day John sees Jesus coming toward him, and he announces, "Look, the Lamb of God, who takes away

a 16 Isaiah 9:1, 2

the sin of the world!" (John 1:29). On the next day John saw Jesus passing by him, and he repeated his former statement; this resulted in two disciples leaving him to follow Jesus (John 1:35-37).

After this, Andrew, one of the two disciples who followed Jesus (the other one is not named), found his brother, Simon, and informed him that they had located the Messiah (John 1:41, 42). On the next day Philip and Nathaniel were enlisted to follow Jesus (John 1:43-51). Then, later, Jesus attended a wedding in Cana (John 2:1-11), He visited in Capernaum with His family and disciples (John 2:12), He cleansed the Temple in Jerusalem during the Passover (John 2:13-25), He conversed with Nicodemus (John 3:1-21), and He ministered in Judea (John 3:22-36). After about twelve months, from the time John called Jesus "the Lamb of God," John was placed in prison (Read Matt. 14:1-12 for details regarding John's imprisonment). Now, we are up to date with Matthew's account. (See the two charts presenting chronology of Jesus' life.)

Two observations ought to be made regarding this first year that Matthew ignores: (a) It was a good year in that Jesus was gaining many converts, even more than John was winning: (b) It was a bad year in that the religious leaders in Judea were not responding positively to Jesus' message.

He Returned to Galilee, He Left Nazareth; He Lived in Capernaum. During the days in which Jesus walked among men, we see Him visiting city after city. Often, however, His travels take Him from region to region. There is as much significance in the broad settings as in the more narrow ones. An understanding of the geography discussed in the Gospels, therefore, is now in order.

When Jesus began preaching, many of the descendants of Abraham lived in a land that was either directly or indirectly governed by Roman hands. It was a divided land. In the north was the region of Galilee. South of this area was Samaria. And still further south was Judea. (See the map of Palestine in the time of Christ.)

Judea. At one time this region encompassed all of the territory discussed in the Gospels. It was governed by Herod the Great, through the appointment of Rome (from 37-4 B.C.). At his death, however, the land was divided into tetrarchies, each with its own ruler. Herod bequeathed the territory of his rule to his three sons—Archelaus receiving the region of Judea and Samaria, Antipas receiving Galilee and Perea, and Philip receiving land northeast of Galilee. Each of these areas is mentioned in your New Testament. When you read about Judea, the reference is to a relatively small body of land in the south. Its principal city is Jerusalem.

Samaria, resting between Judea and Galilee, has a tainted history. When Solomon's jealous successors fought for control of Israel, the nation split in two—ten tribes

A CHRONOLOGY OF JESUS' LIFE

Birth (December?)	B.C. 5
Visit of Wise Men (January?)	B.C. 4
Baptism by John (December?)	A.D. 26
Temptation—forty days (January?)	A.D. 27
Wedding at Cana (February?)	A.D. 27
Ministry Begins (March?)	A.D. 27
Call of First Disciples (March?)	A.D. 27
First Cleansing of Temple (March?)	A.D. 27
Ministry in Judea (April-September)	A.D. 27
Three Tours of Galilee (October-February) (Approximately seventeen months)	A.D. 27-29
Call of Twelve Disciples (July?)	A.D. 28
Period of Withdrawal (March-September?)	A.D. 29
Ministry in Judea (September-December?)	A.D. 29
Ministry in Perea (January-March?)	A.D. 30
Crucifixion (April?)	A.D. 30
Ascension (May?)	A.D. 30

Precise dates are impossible to fix in the chronology of Jesus' life. The above dates represent reasonable periods based upon the data provided in the New Testament. They are offered as a practical guideline, not as absolute or fixed dates.

A BRIEF OUTLINE OF JESUS' LIFE ACCORDING TO MATTHEW, MARK AND LUKE

The Events	Dates	Matthew	Mark	Luke
I. *Jesus' Early Years*	B.C. 5-A.D. 26			
A. Genealogy		1:1-17		3:23-38
B. Birth		1:18-25		2:1-20
C. Childhood		2:1-23		2:21-52
II. *Jesus' Ministry*	A.D. 27-30			
A. Baptism		3:1-17	1:1-11	3:1-23
B. Temptation		4:1-11	1:12, 13	4:1-13
C. Galilee Ministry	A.D. 27-29	4:12-18:35	1:14-9:50	4:14-9:50
D. Judea Ministry	A.D. 29	19:1, 2	10:1	9:51-13:21
E. Perea Ministry	A.D. 30	19:1-20:34	10:1-52	13:22-19:28
III. *Jesus' Final Week*	A.D. 30	21:1-27:34	11:1-15:23	19:29-23:33
IV. *Calvary & Ascension*	A.D. 30	27:35-28:20	15:24-16:20	23:33-24:53

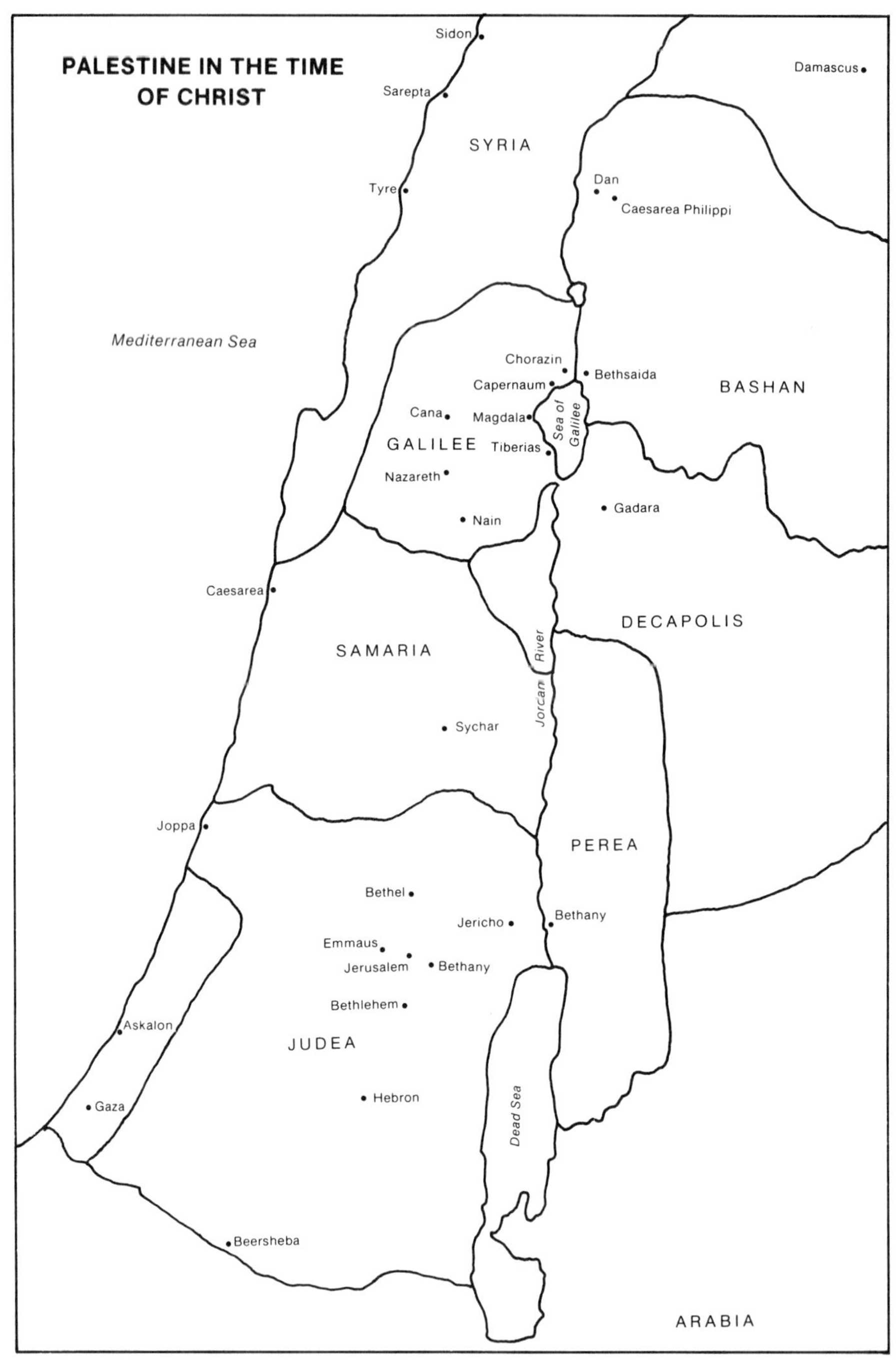
PALESTINE IN THE TIME OF CHRIST
Sidon
Sarepta
Damascus
SYRIA
Tyre
Dan
Caesarea Philippi
Mediterranean Sea
Chorazin
Bethsaida
Capernaum
BASHAN
Cana
Magdala
Sea of Galilee
GALILEE
Tiberias
Nazareth
Gadara
Nain
Caesarea
DECAPOLIS
SAMARIA
Jordan River
Sychar
Joppa
PEREA
Bethel
Jericho
Bethany
Emmaus
Jerusalem
Bethany
Bethlehem
Askalon
JUDEA
Hebron
Gaza
Dead Sea
Beersheba
ARABIA

formed a separate body with its capital in Samaria, and two tribes formed another body with its capital in Jerusalem. In 722 B.C. the ten northern tribes were conquered by Assyria. The result of this conquest brought other Assyrian captives into the region of Samaria. Soon marriages occurred between the Jews and the Gentiles—a contamination which neither the Galileans nor the Judeans found acceptable. The Samaritans' loyalty to God, as a consequence, was always challenged. They were, in the minds of the so-called orthodox Jews, physical half-breeds and spiritual renegades.

Galilee was populated by Jews chiefly during the troubled years of the second century before Christ. They were devout in their faith, but they still became the object of ridicule by the Samaritans and the Judeans.

Galilee was not large by American standards (approximately fifty miles from north to south, and twenty-five miles from east to west). But it was heavily populated. Josephus (a Jewish historian of the first century) states that there were 204 cities in Galilee, each with a population of at least 15,000. That would make a total population of about 3,000,000—a very sizable number by any standard.

The culture of Galilee was different from Judea. Being surrounded by Gentile nations and internally divided by several major trade routes, Galilee was exposed to a wide world of influences, quite unlike the somewhat closed doors found in most of Judea. In Galilee the people were accustomed to new ideas and change. Here Jesus would continue His unique ministry. But here, too, Jesus would discover much of what He found in Judea—the common people would receive Him gladly, but the leaders would often resist Him.

The Prophet Isaiah. According to the Old Testament prophet Isaiah (9:1, 2), the Messiah would have a ministry among the non-Jewish people, too. Galilee, though populated with many Jews, was also a dwelling for numerous Gentiles. As a result, the region was deemed to be somewhat barren spiritually, at least by Judean standards. In fact, the people who lived there were considered to reside in "the shadow of death." Nevertheless, into this dark territory would come a light that was destined to change the people's lives. Jesus was raised in this land, and He would give himself to these belittled people.

II. *His Message (4:17)*

> **17 From that time on Jesus began to preach, "Repent, for the kingdom of heaven is near."**

Repentance. God did not send a great general to change the lives of people. Neither did He send a rich person, nor a famous person from the halls of heaven. Instead, He sent a preacher. A common man with an uncommon message and power.

Jesus' first sermon in Galilee was entitled "Repent!" And it has not changed to this very day. No repentance means no participation in God's Kingdom.

In the original New Testament language (Greek) the word translated "repent" is a combination of two small words. The first word means "after"; the second term means "the mind," the center of our thoughts. When used together, these words mean an afterthought, a change of mind. A call to repentance, then, is a call to reconsider the state of our lives in the light of God's will. It is a call to think things over and to turn away from a self-centered life toward a God-centered/Christ-centered/Kingdom-centered life.

This turning *from* sin is often called repentance, while the turning *toward* God is often called faith. Both actions, however, are necessary for repentance or faith to be complete. Stated differently, repentance and faith are the front and back sides of the one subject known as conversion. In the Gospels of Matthew, Mark and Luke the stress is placed on *repentance*; in the Gospel of John the stress is put on *faith*. Both are necessary.

The Kingdom of Heaven. Matthew's usage of the Kingdom of heaven (rather than the Kingdom of God), is solely by personal preference. The Jews by Jesus' day had come to the place of believing that the name "God" was too sacred for mortal lips to speak. So they substituted the word "heaven" in its place.

Consult the "special study" at the close of this unit for details regarding the doctrine of the Kingdom.

III. *His Method (4:18-22)*

**18 As Jesus was walking beside the Sea of Galilee, he saw two brothers,
Simon called Peter and his brother Andrew. They were casting a net
into the lake, for they were fishermen. 19 "Come, follow me," Jesus said,
"and I will make you fishers of men." 20 At once they left their nets and
followed him.**

**21 Going on from there, he saw two other brothers, James son of
Zebedee and his brother John. They were in a boat with their father
Zebedee, preparing their nets. Jesus called them, 22 and immediately
they left the boat and their father and followed him.**

One man, working alone, no matter how ingenious he is, cannot accomplish the totality of God's will in the earth. There must be many who work together in order to achieve God's end. Jesus knew this; therefore He set out to increase His effectiveness through the labors of other spiritual men.

Selecting men for the highest positions in Jesus' ministry might seem to be quite an easy task. But consider the unorthodox choices noted here—they were fishermen. What did laymen know about the Scriptures, the Temple rules, prayer, or God's will? Were they wealthy? Probably not. Were they influential? No. Were they properly schooled in the latest theology? No. Then, with all of these negative aspects, why did Jesus choose them? The answer is both simple and profound. It was because they would follow Him; they would obey Jesus! Jesus can do more good with a single obedient person than He can with 100,000 self-willed people.

IV. *His Ministry (4:23-25)*

> **23Jesus went throughout Galilee, teaching in their synagogues, preaching the good news of the kingdom, and healing every disease and sickness among the people. 24News about him spread all over Syria, and people brought to him all who were ill with various diseases, those suffering severe pain, the demon-possessed, the epileptics and the paralytics, and he healed them. 25Large crowds from Galilee, the Decapolis,[a] Jerusalem, Judea and the region across the Jordan followed him.**

Jesus' ministry could be summed up with two words: teaching and healing. The two greatest plagues of mankind are seen here. They are ignorance and sickness. The ministry of Jesus focused on curing these all-too-common ailments.

There were three basic parts in the normal synagogue service: (1) prayers, (2) Scripture reading, and (3) a message. Since there was no official clergyman to bring the message, members or visitors of the synagogue were permitted to deliver the message, under the direction of the synagogue's president. In this very natural setting Jesus brought many of His teachings and won many of His converts.

When a teaching ends in only words, however, there will be minimal effectiveness. Words must produce works. And these works must help people who are hurting. Jesus did more than teach the people; He also touched them. His ministry would do more than enlighten the mind; it also touched the body. (See the chart outlining Jesus' healing ministry.)

Special Study: The Kingdom of God

The central message of the Bible can be stated in four simple words: "the Kingdom of God." From beginning to end this is the paramount theme of both testaments. It knows no close rival. Its importance is unsurpassed.

Oddly enough, however, this subject has been terribly abused through neglect. Too

unfortunately, more often than not, has passed over this indispensable topic. Such an

a 25 That is, the Ten Cities

JESUS' HEALING MINISTRY

Scripture	Sickness	Cause	Faith of the Sick	Jesus' Actions
Matt. 9:27-31	Two blind men		They believe Jesus is able to heal them	He touches their eyes
Matt. 9:32-34	Man is mute	Demon		Exorcism
Matt. 12:9-14 Mark 3:1-6 Luke 6:6-11	Man has a shriveled hand		Rises & stands in midst of people; stretches forth hand	
Mark 1:29-31 Matt. 8:14, 15 Luke 4:38, 39	Woman has a fever bedridden			Takes her by hand & raises her up; rebukes the fever
Mark 1:40-42 Matt. 8:2-4 Luke 5:12-16	Leper		Worships Jesus; confesses Jesus is able to heal his illness	Lays his hands on the man
Mark 2:1-12 Matt. 9:1-8 Luke 5:17-26	Man with palsy	Sin	Arises from bed at Jesus' order	Forgives sins; orders man to arise
Matt. 8:5-13 Luke 7:1-10	Man with palsy		Centurion intercedes & has great faith in Jesus' ability to heal man	
John 5:1-15	Man who has had an illness for 38 years	Sin	Arises at Jesus' order	Command: arise & walk
Matt. 9:18-26 Mark 5:21-43 Luke 8:40-56	Daughter is sick and dies			Tells her to arise; takes her by the hand & helps her up
Mark 5:25-34 Luke 8:43-48	Woman with an issue of blood		Knows if she can touch Jesus' garments she would be healed	
Matt. 15:21-28 Matt. 7:24-30	Daughter in great pain	Demon	She knew Jesus could help	
Mark 7:31-35	Man is deaf & has a speech impediment			Takes him aside privately, puts his fingers in his ears; he spits, touches sick man's tongue, looks to heaven & says, "Be opened"
Mark 8:22-26	Man is blind			Takes man by hand & leads him out of town, spits on his eyes, lays hands on eyes; after partial restoration the laying on of hands is repeated
John 4:46-54	Son is sick		Father intercedes & acts on Jesus' words	
Luke 17:11-19	Ten lepers		Cry out for mercy; obedient to Jesus' order to show themselves to the priest; healed as they go	
Matt. 17:14-20 Mark 9:14-29 Luke 9:37-43	Boy with epilepsy	Demon	Father intercedes with some faith & requests help for his unbelief	Speaks to spirit by name & commands his departure with no privilege of returning
John 9:1-41	Man is blind	Sovereignty of God	Obeys Jesus by washing his eyes at pool of Siloam	Spits on ground & makes clay, anoints his eyes, & sends him away to wash in pool of Siloam
Luke 13:10-17	Woman is crippled	Satanic spirit		Lays hands on her & pronounces her healed
John 11:1-44	Lazarus dies	Sovereignty of God		Prays aloud
Matt. 20:29-34 Mark 10:46-52 Luke 18:35-43	Man is blind		Cries out for mercy	Touches his eyes
Matt. 26:51 Mark 14:47 Luke 22:50, 51 John 18:10	Loss of ear	Severed		Restores ear

important matter must not be treated lightly.

Here then is a brief capsulization of the chief ideas entailed in the message of the Kingdom of God.

The Kingdom Is Explained

The chief idea behind the word "kingdom" is a body of people who share some common bond. The words "of God" identify the nature of that common bond. Put simply, the Kingdom of God is comprised of people who submit to God, making Him their King.[1]

From the start of creation the design was fixed. God sought to be man's King. From this position He would direct our lives, bringing to them the intended fulfillment for which they were created. In this relationship God was to be honored and obeyed, while mankind was to be rewarded and satisfied.

The only snag in the system is man's free will. God's reign is not coercive. He will not compel His subjects to submit to His kingship. That, naturally, left the first couple, Adam and Eve, along with all of their descendants, free to choose if they wanted God to be their King, or if they wanted to rule themselves. The tragic choice is all too evident. Adam and Eve resisted. They went their own way. They, in effect, dethroned God from their lives and set themselves upon this throne instead.

The effects of this original decision remain with us to this very day. Men, women, children and even complete countries have chosen to rule themselves. They want nothing to do with God's kingship or His Kingdom. They seek independence and freedom. Unfortunately, however, such persons fail to recognize that an allegiance to Him is the only source for true and lasting liberty!

After the choice of Adam and Eve to rule themselves, God renewed His Kingdom offer, though in a different format. They were given another chance, along with their descendants, to join His Kingdom. The offer was gracious—free entrance and free provisions, but you must be willing to live by the rules of the King. Nothing could be more fair or just. Still, while a handful accepted the offer, many either doubted its claims or scoffed at its declared consequences.

Today—right now—the Kingdom pledges are still in effect. They operate as they have always operated. God offers membership in His Kingdom, in which Jesus Christ is the reigning authority, and we either elect to join His nation and live by His rules, or we elect to rule ourselves and reap the consequences of being an enemy of God's Kingdom.

---

[1]The exacting details of the biblical usage for "the Kingdom of God" are quite complex. Actually, it refers to the sphere of God's rule, which embraces all of creation (Dan. 4:25, 35; Luke 1:52; Rom. 13:1,2). In our study here, however, we will only explore those areas where the kingdom relates specifically to the believer, the loyal subject in God's Kingdom.

There is no middle ground. We are either inside or outside the Kingdom. Either Jesus Christ is our personal King, or we ourselves are the king of our lives. There can be no dual kingship in our hearts. We must choose who will be number one—us or Him.

The Kingdom Is Exposed

Although the exact phrase, "Kingdom of God," does not appear in any text of the Old Testament, the concept is central to its day-to-day life and to its eschatology. Often God is seen as King of Israel (Exod. 15:18; Deut. 33:5; Isa. 41:21; 43:15; 44:6; Mal. 1:14), yet the Scriptures speak of a period when He will yet become the King of His people, in an earthly kingship (Isa. 24:23; 33:22; 52:7; Zeph. 3:15; Zech. 14:9). The throne for this reign is David's (2 Sam. 7:5-17; Ps. 89:35-49; Jer. 33:25, 26; Zech. 12:8-10), and the one seated upon it is the Son of man (Dan. 7:13, 14). It is this earthly kingdom which Israel anxiously anticipated.

After the close of the book of Malachi in the Old Testament, the prophetic voice of God was silent in Israel for nearly 400 years. Then arose a man who was to initiate the message of the Kingdom of God again—he was John the Baptist. Behind him lay the Law and the Prophets; before him was the Son of man. John was a forerunner. He was God's tool for paving the path on which this King would tread (Isa. 40:3; Mal. 3:1; Mark 1:2,3).

John taught that the Messiah, God's King, was alive and ready to establish His Kingdom. And when he had baptized Jesus, he boldly announced it was this man who would serve Israel as her King (Matt. 3:1-17; John 1:15-37; 3:22-36).

With the advent of the Son of man, Israel saw her worries as abruptly ending and her enemies being forever overthrown. It did not, however, happen the way they planned or dreamed. Jesus only continued where John left off—preaching, "The time has come. . . . The kingdom of God is near. Repent and believe the good news!" (Mark 1:15).

This approach certainly differed from Israel's radical expectations. What did Jesus mean by this unexpected announcement? Why did He preach, rather than merely organize an army and overthrow Israel's enemies? How were the Jews, and we today, to understand Jesus' teaching regarding the Kingdom of God?

Let's observe seven matters in Jesus' concept of the Kingdom of God:

1. Jesus taught that the Kingdom of God was "near" (Mark 1:15). The Greek term employed here is in the verbal tense called the consummative perfect, indicating a completed action without reference to culminating results. Therefore, the Kingdom of God was present and ready to be set up, *if* Israel would "repent and believe the good news." In other words, the establishment of God's Kingdom hinged upon obedience to the King. There would only be a kingdom for those who truly repent and follow the message of Jesus.

2. Jesus taught that the Kingdom's presence could be proven by His power over Satan (Matt. 12:28; cf. John 12:31; Rev. 12:10). Jesus came as Israel's King for the express purpose of destroying the kingdom and works of the devil (Gen. 3:15; Heb. 2:14; 1 John 3:8) of binding this strong man (Isa. 49:24,25; Matt. 12:29) and of taking away all his armor (Luke 11:21,22). Stated differently, God's Kingdom was to be fundamentally spiritual, touching the hearts of people and uprooting the hold Satan possessed over people. Unfortunately the people hated the Roman tyranny more than Satan's bondage. They were missing the point of God's Kingdom.

3. Although the Kingdom of God has always been present in the world, spiritually (as noted above), it is still to come to earth in a more direct and physical dimension. This latter phase was to be prayed for (Matt. 6:10), sought (Matt. 6:33) and waited for (Mark 15:43). Jesus taught that this ultimate aspect of the Kingdom would be inherited by the poor in spirit (Matt. 5:3; Luke 6:20), by those persecuted for the sake of righteousness (Matt. 5:10), by those who were righteous (Matt. 5:20; cf. 7:21; 21:31), converted (Matt. 18:3) and born again (John 3:3, 5). Although the Kingdom of God was more present (or "near") than ever before, it still wasn't fully present. This would occur only if Israel would repent of her many sins. Therefore, its fullest manifestation was still to be sought through prayer and holy living.

4. Jesus made it plain that the Kingdom of God would be taken away from national Israel and given to a nation (the Church—1 Pet. 2:9) who would produce its appropriate fruit (Matt. 21:33-43; 22:2-14; 23:13; 25:1-13). The time of its removal probably came at the period of Christ's Crucifixion (Dan. 9:26,27). Temporarily, then, national Israel is to be judged and withheld the full offer of the political Davidic Messiah. This suspension will continue until the time of Christ's Second Coming (Zech. 12:10-13:1; Acts 1:6; Rom. 11:1-29). It must also be stated that this momentary cessation of the fuller Kingdom offer, however, does not exclude them from God's spiritual Kingdom offer (that is, salvation). Israel can still accept God's "secret" Kingdom (Acts 2:22ff.; 3:12ff.; 5:12-14, 17-32; 6:7ff.; 9:15).

5. The Kingdom which Jesus announced was a "secret" (Matt. 13:11; cf. Eph. 3:2-6). That is, Jesus' contemporaries held views about the Kingdom that were not in full agreement with the ultimate divine plan. That gave Jesus' teaching the appearance of a secret. The Jews waited for a political kingdom from God, but Jesus seemed to offer them only a spiritual one (John 18:36,37; cf. Acts 15:14-19; Col. 1:13; 1 Tim. 6:15; 2 Pet. 1:11; Rev. 1:5). The political kingdom would only follow the acceptance of the spiritual Kingdom. God is interested in governments, but his primary interest is in people's hearts and eternal destinies. The spiritual is more crucial than the physical. And God determined there would be no earthly kingdom if there were no major acceptance of his spiritual Kingdom first. As a result, the Kingdom offer was a "mystery" to the closed minds of Israel.

6. Jesus announced that certain ones among His contemporaries would not taste death until they saw the Son of man coming to His Kingdom (Matt. 16:28; Mark 9:1; Luke 9:27). This appears to be a dual reference to Christ's Transfiguration (Matt. 17:1-8 with 2 Pet. 1:16-18) and to the destruction of Jerusalem in A.D. 70 (Luke 21:5-24). Doubtlessly there were those who questioned the reality or meaning of Jesus' statements regarding His message of the Kingdom of God. So, He told them that they themselves would see the proof of His declarations. Before their death they would see His kingship. And so they did, in His Transfiguration and in the judgment of Jerusalem.

7. The "secret" form of the Kingdom of God will come to a climax at the end of the age, in the Son of man's return to judge the nations (Matt. 25:31-46). At this point God's Kingdom will become earth-centered and Israel-centered. The political promises and expectations will then be fulfilled with an exacting accuracy (see details of this Kingdom stage below).

When all the eschatological dust has settled, it becomes evident that Jesus came to earth, and is returning to earth, for three fundamental reasons, as noted in the following self-explanatory diagram.

WHY JESUS CAME TO EARTH AND WHY HE WILL RETURN

(1) To Save the World	(2) To Sit on David's Throne	(3) To Establish the Mystery Kingdom
A. Bring salvation—Matt. 1:21; John 3:16, 17 B. Bring light to Gentiles—Matt. 12:18-21; Luke 2:32 C. Remove sin—John 1:29 D. Save world—John 5:34 E. Give life as a ransom—Matt. 20:28 F. Give abundant life—John 10:10 G. Destroy Satan's works—Heb. 2:14; 1 John 3:8 H. Fulfill Law and Pro—phets—Matt. 5:17, 18	A. Receive David's throne—Luke 1:32, 67-79 B. Be King of Jews—Matt. 2:2, 6 C. Deliver Jerusalem—Luke 2:38 D. Fulfill Law and Prophets—Matt. 5:17, 18	A. Present "mystery" kingdom—Matt. 13: 1-50; cf. Luke 4:18, 19; John 4:42; Eph. 2-3 B. Set up Church—Matt. 16:13-20 C. Fulfill Law and Prophets—Matt. 5:17, 18; cf. Acts 15:14-19

The Kingdom Is Enthroned

Finally the earthly phase of the Kingdom of God will come. This does not imply that Jesus has not been King of kings prior to this period, for indeed He has been since His birth (Matt. 2:2).At His resurrection His kingship was secured in power (Rom. 1:4; Dan. 7:13,14; Matt. 28:18; Phil. 2:8-11), and at His Second Coming His kingship will be realized in its fullest sense (Rev. 1:7; 2 Tim. 4:1).

In the garden of Eden we saw the inauguration of this earthly kingdom. But with the entrance of sin, we soon see its removal from the earth. From that time to this, the kingdom of God has been basically spiritual in nature. At the time of Jesus' return, however, God's manner of dealing with people on earth will return to the original garden state. Some day, possibly sooner than we imagine, Jesus will return and set up His earthly Kingdom.

Here are the thirteen major facets that constitute this rich future period, commonly called "The Millennium" because of its 1,000-year duration (Rev. 20:1-6; 1 Cor. 15:20-28).

1. For a thousand years Satan and his demons will be bound in the abyss (Isa. 24:21, 22; Rev. 20:1-3).

2. Jesus Christ will rule all the earth as King of kings and Lord of lords (Ps. 2:2-8; 67:4; 72:9-11; 82:8; 89:21-25,27; 96:13; 98:9; 110:1, 2; Isa. 2:4; 9:7; 25:3; 45:23, 24; 49:7; 51:5; 55:4; 66:19; Dan. 2:35, 44; 7:9-14, 25-27; Obad. 21; Mic. 4:3; 5:4; 7:15-17; Zech. 14:9; Luke 1:32; 20:43; 22:29; Acts 2:35; 3:21; 1 Cor. 15:24-28; Eph. 1:21; 2 Tim. 4:1; Heb. 1:13; 10:13; Rev. 11:15-17; 12:5; 19:6-16).

3. All those entering the Millennium will be saved and experience the fullness of the Spirit (Deut. 30:8; Isa. 4:3, 4; 32:1-5; Ezek. 36:27, 28; Jer. 31:31-34; Joel 2:28,29; Zeph. 3:10-13; Zech. 8:3, 8; 13:1-6; 14:20, 21).

4. Children will be born to those inhabiting the earth. They will be like children born today with these two exceptions: First, they will be raised in a perfect environment, permitting them an everlasting longevity, if they choose to follow Christ. Secondly, should they rebel, after the age of 100 years, they will be put to death (Isa. 65:20-23; Jer. 31:29-30; Rev. 2:26, 27).

5. The earth will be filled with the knowledge of God (Isa. 11:9; Hab. 2:14).

6. Israel will serve as the world's capital. All nations refusing to serve her will be punished (Isa. 4:4-6; 60:11, 12; Jer. 3:17; 31:35-39; Ezek. 48:35; Joel 3:17; Zeph. 3:17, 20; Zech. 8:3; 14:16-19).

7. Joy and praise will cover the earth (Isa. 12:3-6; 25:8, 9; 35:10; Ps. 98:4-9).

8. Peace will fill the earth (Isa. 2:4; 9:5, 7; 11:13; 26:12; 54:14; 60:18; Jer. 23:6; 33:16; Hos. 2:18; Joel 3:17; Zeph. 3:15).

9. All sickness will vanish (Isa. 29:17-19; 33:24; 35:5; Jer. 31:8,9).

10. Men will work, and their toil will produce a full reward (Isa. 4:2; 61:4; 62:8, 9; 65:21-23; Ezek. 34:26-29; Hos. 2:21, 22; Joel 3:18; Amos 9:13, 14).

11. There will be a temple, and sacrifices (spiritual or praise sacrifices) will be offered in Jerusalem (Ezek. 37:26-28; 40-48; Jer. 33:18, 21, 22; Zech. 14:20, 21; Mal. 3:3,4; Rev. 21:1-22:5).

12. It is my opinion that all of the above details spell out the establishment of the "new heaven and earth" (Isa. 65:17; 66:22; 2 Pet. 3:13; Rev. 21:1). Not all Bible students are agreed on the precise timing for the appearance of this new order. Some believe it will appear after the Millennium and the Great White Throne Judgment. Others believe it will appear at the beginning of the Millennium.

Those who hold that the new heaven and earth begin after the Millennium see Rev. 21:1-8 as transpiring after 1,000 years and 21:9-22:5 as millennial. The latter group takes Rev. 21:1-22:5 as referring both to the Millennium and eternity thereafter.

There is little reason to believe that the millennial reign of Christ is to be distinguished from the new heaven and earth. The only difference between the millennial kingdom and the kingdom after the Great White Throne will be the removal of all sinners (Rev. 20:11-15), and Jesus' giving the Kingdom back to His Father (1 Cor. 15:24-28).

13. At the close of the thousand years, the abyss will be opened. Coming forth from this pit will be Satan and his demons, who go forth to deceive the nations which are in the four corners of the earth (Rev. 20:7-10). Amazingly, an army shall be gathered, the number of which is compared to the sand of the sea. This army will then march to Jerusalem and surround the holy city. Next, God will cause fire to fall from heaven upon this hostile band, and they will all be devoured. This fatal conflict will end all warring, personal or otherwise, for all time!

The purpose of the Millennium is at least twofold: First, it fulfills the prophecies of an earthly kingdom. Second, it proves that people who go to hell will go there because of their own sinful ways and not because the devil made them do it!

The Kingdom Is Exclusive

The judgment of all lost men, from the time of Adam through Gog and Magog, will take place at the Great White Throne (Rev. 20:11-15). The second resurrection will bring all the guilty to this awesome day of eternal vindication. (It is probable that the fallen angels will be judged here also—Gen. 3:15; Matt. 8:29; 1 Cor. 6:3; 2 Pet. 2:4.)

The location of this judgment will neither be in heaven nor on earth. The unsaved are not qualified for either abode. They will make their home in hell—the second death.

The sole purpose of this judgment is to determine one's level of eternal punishment. The Book of Life will be opened to prove the absence of their names. The books of works will be opened to determine the degrees of their punishments.

The Kingdom Is Everlasting

Who will inherit the earth after the Great White Throne Judgment? The difficulty involved within this question focuses around the subjects of the Great White Throne Judgment. Some writers (especially amillennialists and postmillennialists) see this judgment as involving all of mankind, regenerate and unregenerate, since the creation of Adam. Such a position does not distinguish between this judgment and the judgments associated with the Second Coming of Christ (the judgment seat of Christ—for all the saved, and the judgment of the nations and Israel—to see who enters the Millennium). This view presents several insurmountable problems:

1. The rewarding of the saints is always and only identified with Christ's Second Coming (Luke 14:14; 1 Cor. 4:5; Rev. 11:18; 22:12).

2. The judgment seat of Christ is never considered as a judicial bench, but invariably a reward seat for believers (2 Cor. 5:10; cf. 1 Cor. 3:10-15).

3. Matthew distinctly states that "when the Son of Man comes . . . he will sit on his throne in heavenly glory. All the nations will be gathered before him, and he will separate the people one from another" (Matt. 25:31,32). There is no hint that any telescoping is taking place here. This judgment is clearly *not* the Great White Throne Judgment, yet its subjects, like those at the Great White Throne, are cast into the eternal fire (25:41, 46).

4. The subjects of the Great White Throne Judgment are specifically stated as being those who dwell in "death and Hades," the abode of the unrighteous dead (Rev. 20:13; cf. 6:8 with 6:9). For this reason all the participants are cast into the lake of fire (Rev. 20:14). There is no explicit statement that a single saved person will stand at this bar.

5. The location of the Great White Throne Judgment is neither in heaven nor on the earth, for no place was found for them (Rev. 20:11). The judgment of the saints and the nations, however, is clearly upon the earth.

Therefore, it seems safe to say that only the regenerate will enter the Millennium, during which they will bear children in a perfect heaven and earth. The close of this epoch will result in a great rebellion headed by Satan. Following this brief revolt, all the spiritually dead will be resurrected, judged at the Great White Throne and cast into their appropriate levels of hell.

But what happens to the righteous who entered the Millennium, or to those who were born therein and remained faithful to Christ in the period of rebellion? The solution to this dilemma seems to be as follows: There will always be nations on the earth, over whom the saints will reign "forever," (Rev. 22:5; cf. Isa. 66:22; Matt. 25:34,46; Luke 19:17; Rev. 21:24-27; 22:2).

NOTE: The preceding special study is excerpted from *Armageddon 198?* by Stephen D. Swihart (Haven Books, 1980).

The Sermon on the Mount—Part I
The Character of Kingdom Life (Matt. 5:1-16)

(cf. Luke 6:20-23)

The Sermon on the Mount, extending through three chapters, represents the longest single teaching we have from Jesus. Here we find the very core of Jesus' doctrine. No one can learn about the Christian life and skip these chapters. They are the framework around which all of our spirituality and maturity is constructed.

It is never enough to say we are made members of God's Kingdom because we believe such and such. It takes more than convictions to be admitted. These convictions must be coupled with an appropriate character. Jesus' principal interest here is to show the kind of character God is interested in developing within those who occupy His Kingdom.

I. *The Beatitudes (5:1-12)*

5 Now when he saw the crowds, he went up on a mountainside and
sat down. His disciples came to him, 2and he began to teach them,
saying:

3"Blessed are the poor in spirit,
for theirs is the kingdom of heaven.
4Blessed are those who mourn,
for they will be comforted.
5Blessed are the meek,
for they will inherit the earth.
6Blessed are those who hunger and thirst for righteousness,
for they will be filled.
7Blessed are the merciful,
for they will be shown mercy.
8Blessed are the pure in heart,
for they will see God.
9Blessed are the peacemakers,
for they will be called sons of God.
10Blessed are those who are persecuted because

of righteousness,
for theirs is the kingdom of heaven.

11"Blessed are you when people insult you, persecute you and falsely
say all kinds of evil against you because of me. 12Rejoice and be glad,
because great is your reward in heaven, for in the same way they
persecuted the prophets who were before you.

The word "beatitude" means "perfect blessedness or happiness." The aim of the gospel of the Kingdom is to bless people, to fill them with joy. Jesus came to bless us. The blessed life is the inheritance of each disciple of the Messiah.

Beatitudes appear throughout the Bible. In the Old Testament the blessed person is the one whom God calls (Ps. 65:4; Isa. 51:2) and forgives (Ps. 32:1). It is the one who has the Lord as his God (Ps. 144:15), who places his trust in God (Ps. 2:12), who reverently fears Him (Ps. 112:1), who hears and keeps God's Word (Ps. 119:2), who waits for the Lord (Isa. 30:18), and who avoids the wicked in preference for God's laws (Ps. 1:1-3).

In the New Testament the blessed person is also the one whom God calls (Eph. 1:3, 4; Rev. 19:9) and forgives (Rom. 4:7), who believes (John 20:29; Gal. 3:9), who hears and keeps Christ's words (Matt. 13:16; Rev. 1:3), who endures temptations for Jesus' sake (James 1:12), who watches for the Lord's return (Luke 12:37), and who participates in the first resurrection (Rev. 20:6).

There are eight beatitudes given in Matthew 5. Before we examine them in detail, several introductory matters should be understood.

First, there are numerous paradoxes in these beatitudes: the rich are the poor, the comforted are the mourners, the overcomers are the nonaggressors, the filled are the hungry, and the joyful are the persecuted. To the natural eye none of this makes much sense, but to the spiritual eye, to the one who walks in the Spirit, it not only makes sense, it is the absolute truth.

Second, it must not be assumed that this abundant joy is poured out upon everyone without qualification. This clearly is not the case. There are some stipulations for receiving the blessings of the Kingdom of God. In these eight beatitudes we discover the type of person who is truly touched with the spirit of heaven.

Third, there are specific promises offered to each person who qualifies as a "blessed" person. These promises include the Kingdom itself, comfort, the earth, righteousness, mercy, seeing God, the position of becoming a son or daughter of God and rewards in heaven. From this listing it would appear that the blessings being offered are available today but will not be completed in this present life time. In other words, God's blessings begin today and then last forever. They are for this world and the world to come as well.

Now let us consider the beatitudes individually:

1. *Blessed are the poor in spirit.* It is a miserably shallow life that believes itself to be "good enough" to make it through this world with only a little help from above. Jesus pronounces a blessing on the "poor in spirit"—that is, on those who feel so ill-supplied to manage their own affairs and to please God that they humbly bow with the deepest respect and awe in His presence. Such persons are humble, teachable, dependable, appreciative and wise. They are moved to repentance upon the first trace of sin in their hearts. They are not proud, but broken. These, alone, are worthy of the Kingdom.

2. *Blessed are those who mourn.* There are many things about which we may mourn, but the idea this verse conveys is mourning over our own sinfulness. There should be no room in our souls for any lighthearted feelings about sin. Our own inadequacies deserve far more than a mere flippant mental assent. We must acknowledge, to the fullest possible measure, our paramount need for divine forgiveness in order to be justified in God's presence (cf. James 4:6-10; 1 John 1:7-10).

John Knox, the great reformer, was heard to say this in his final prayer: "I now weep for my corruption; I can only rest on your mercy." St. Francis of Assisi, founder of the Franciscan Order, used to refer to himself as the greatest sinner who ever lived, because he maintained that anyone who had received all the graces he had been given would have to be a much better person than he was. John Bunyan, author of *Pilgrim's Progress*, wrote these insightful comments: "Since I repented last time, another matter has given me great sorrow, which is, that if I rigorously scrutinize the best of what I now do, I discover sin." Jonathan Edwards, the famous preacher, has left us these solemn words: "Often do I sense how full of sin and uncleanness I am." May the Holy Spirit show us our sins, too, until we acknowledge them, hate them, and fully appreciate our Savior who died because of them!

3. *Blessed are the meek.* The meek are those persons who possess patient and self-controlled spirits. They are like the deepest waters of the ocean—they are silent and unmoved. They do not retaliate when wronged, but instead, they stand up under offenses and respond with a firm, but gentle, character. It is for these persons that the earth's ownership has been reserved.

4. *Blessed are those who hunger and thirst for righteousness.* To experience hunger and thirst is one of life's worst possible conditions. Yet it is this penetrating figure of speech which Jesus uses to show us how desperately we ought to desire righteousness for ourselves and for our society. A righteous person is someone who earnestly seeks to align himself and others with the will of God. For those who desire this type of daily walk, God promises a full measure of satisfaction.

5. *Blessed are the merciful.* For those who show mercy (compassion and tenderness), the same shall be shown to them in return. We get what we give. Blessed are those who bless. All of life is a two-way street. Rub perfume on another and you are bound to get some on yourself too.

6. *Blessed are the pure in heart.* How easy it is to merely appear pure—outwardly. But Jesus calls His hearers to be pure (or without offense) internally. Our thoughts and attitudes must withstand God's tests for holiness as much as our words and actions. If we are to see God, we must keep our hearts in tune.

7. *Blessed are the peacemakers.* Personal squabbles and global wars have been with us since the beginning. Some people have abandoned any hope for improvement of this situation. But this is not the case with the children of God. They lead the world in unifying, uniting, arbitrating, peacemaking—between individuals and nations—whenever possible. They carry the tools for making peace wherever they go.

8. *Blessed are those who are persecuted for righteousness.* Being a member of the Kingdom of God brings no exemption from troubles. Each one who seeks to follow the King will be the subject of verbal assault (and possibly even the subject of physical abuse). But the reward for living righteously (or rightly) far outweighs any expenses we might pay here and now. Our lot will not differ from that of the prophets. They were often belittled, but they were more often blessed by God. Therefore, let us rejoice to walk in the company of such distinguished persons.

In this beatitude is Matthew's first of thirteen uses of the term "reward" (cf. 5:46; 6:1,2,4,5,6,16,18; 10:41 (twice), 42; 16:27). There are many other references, however, which embrace this theme of reaping what you sow (5:25, 26; 7:13,14,24-27; 10:11-15; 11:20-24; 25:31-46). The concept of retribution (whether it be good or bad) plays an important role in the gospel message.

II. *The Salt of the Earth (5:13)*

> **13"You are the salt of the earth. But if the salt loses its saltiness, how can it be made salty again? It is no longer good for anything, except to be thrown out and trampled by men.**

Jesus may have had in His mind three concepts when He used salt to teach a spiritual lesson.

First, salt was associated with purity in Jesus' day. The Romans held salt to be the purest of all things. In the sacrifices offered to the Lord, salt was often included, being worthy of His standards (Lev. 2:13; Ezra 6:9). Jesus, therefore, is telling His audience to keep up their guard, to shield their thoughts, words and actions from all impurities. If they are to function properly in God's Kingdom they must be pure in character.

Second, salt was the most common of all preservatives. It kept meat from spoiling. Members in God's Kingdom, then, must function as preservers of the virtues of life and of the divine doctrines. They are to hold back the corruptive forces, to restrain the advance of the destructive elements of society. How rotten this world would be if there were no Kingdom of God present.

Third, salt provided a special flavor for foods. Without salt, food is often quite bland to the taste. But a little seasoning brings foods to life. In the same manner, those who are members of God's Kingdom are to add a unique spice to the life we live in this world. The character of the Kingdom makes the world a better place in which to live.

It must also be observed that Jesus did *not* say you can spread salt around, much like you would shake it from a canister. Rather, He declared, "You *are* salt." The matter, in Jesus' mind, is clear-cut. Either you are salt, or you are not. You are either in the Kingdom and the character of the King is in you, or you are outside of the Kingdom altogether. In brief, we are either saved or we are lost. There is no other alternative.

There is, however, another side to the salt story. Salt may lose its powers. Salt was used in the Temple and added to sacrifices as a symbol of incorruption (Lev. 2:13; Mark 9:49). But when the salt became unfit for use, it was sprinkled on the steps of the Temple in wet weather so no one would slip. Naturally, the salt was tramped on by men. Likewise, members of God's Kingdom can lose their purity, preservative influence and flavoring work. Through compromise, lukewarmness and general passivity, the disciples of the Messiah can lose their saltiness. In such a case the party involved is useless to God. How deplorable this state is.

III. *The Light of the World (5:14-16)*

> **14"You are the light of the world. A city on a hill cannot be hidden.**
> **15Neither do people light a lamp and put it under a bowl. Instead they put it on its stand, and it gives light to everyone in the house. 16In the**
> **same way, let your light shine before men, that they may see your good deeds and praise your Father in heaven.**

Elsewhere in the Scriptures "light" is a symbol of glory, truth and holiness (1 Tim. 6:16; 1 Pet. 1:19; 1 John 1:5). But here it is a bright symbol of "good works," which are to characterize Kingdom life.

Notice that this light does not speak—it shines. Lighthouses do not blow horns or ring bells to attract attention to their light. They just shine, shine, shine. Neither do lights hide themselves. Instead, they operate in the open "before men." Light is meant to be seen. And the result of these open works of light will bring praises for God.

Light cannot save anyone, but it can shine on people and their paths so that they might see the facts regarding themselves and their course. Light can expose dangers and the way of escape, but beyond this it is helpless. Jesus did not call us to save the world. Our mission, as members of His Kingdom, is to light the steps that people can use to avert their spiritual peril.

Light speaks of our outward lives; salt speaks of our inward lives. With light we protect others; with salt we preserve ourselves.

The Sermon on the Mount—Part II
The Commandments of Kingdom Life (Matt. 5:17-48)

The doctrines of the New Testament may ring with the notes of grace, but they will never become harmonious without the melody of strict obedience. The ministry of Christ did not abolish the Old Testament; it fulfilled it.

There are more than 2,200 imperatives found in the twenty-seven books of the New Testament. While many of these exhortations are not offered as being crucial commandments for each believer to follow, over 750 imperatives do possess a definite force and solemnity for each disciple of Christ. When the final tally has been made, we might surprisingly notice that there are more orders to obey in the New Testament than there are to follow in the Old Testament Law.

Jesus begins this section of His discourse by introducing us to the subject of the Law, which He states He came to fulfill and which He expects each of His disciples to obey. He proceeds to itemize six specific examples from the Mosaic Law and teaches how the Law is to be kept. The popular notions about these laws were superficial. Jesus would show their deeper meanings, their broader implications.

Naturally, no one in himself can be expected to keep these laws. Our wills are too weak and too corrupted to adhere to all of God's rules for our lives. We desperately need God's help if we are to keep these commandments. The practice of prayer and the power of the Holy Spirit are essential in doing God's will.

Finally, these laws should never be viewed as some legalistic code dispatched from heaven for the slaves in God's Kingdom to follow. Rather, these are guidelines that bring safety and joy to life. These laws do not confine a person; rather, they liberate the individual. They are designed to bring order and character to our otherwise chaotic lives.

I. *The Law (5:17-20)*

17"Do not think that I have come to abolish the Law or the Prophets; I have not come to abolish them but to fulfill them. 18I tell you the truth, until heaven and earth disappear, not the smallest letter, not the least stroke of a pen, will by any means disappear from the Law until everything is accomplished. 19Anyone who breaks one of the least of these commandments and teaches others to do the same will be called

least in the kingdom of heaven, but whoever practices and teaches these commands will be called great in the kingdom of heaven. [20]For I tell you that unless your righteousness surpasses that of the Pharisees and the teachers of the law, you will certainly not enter the kingdom of heaven.

Do Not Think That I Came to Abolish. Suspicion is a natural response whenever you hear someone teach things that are out of the ordinary. Certainly Jesus' sermons were raising peoples' eyebrows. Even so, He wanted to give His audiences the total scriptural basis for His comments. Although Jesus' insights seemed novel, He was actually merely restating God's original will, which popular religious traditions had kept the people from understanding.

The Jews were generally quite zealous in keeping the laws laid down by Moses (John 9:28, 29; Rom. 10:1,2). Unfortunately, this zeal was misdirected. They became so intent on keeping the laws of Moses that they eventually convinced themselves that salvation was solely based upon an external conformity to these regulations. They failed to discern that no matter how diligently they pursued this course, they would still fall short of a perfect obedience (Rom. 3:9-21; 10:1-3). Only one person ever obeyed all of Moses' laws. That person was Jesus, and He came to show how these laws were to be followed.

I Came to Fulfill. There seems to be a twofold sense in which Jesus came to fulfill the writings of the Old Testament (here called the Law and the Prophets). First, there was the moral (or spiritual) aspect. In this area Jesus demonstrated the perfect behavior God sought in all who belong to His family or Kingdom. Jesus was a flawless model of righteousness. Second, there were the national (or physical) aspects. In this vein Jesus, as the Messiah, was to usher in and establish God's Kingdom among men. It was to be a global kingdom, with Israel at its core (Isa. 2:2-4; Zech. 14:9-21). Jesus recognized these prophecies, too (Matt. 4:17). Regrettably, as we shall learn in Matthew's account, too few Jews were willing to accept the moral/spiritual terms that were necessary for the manifestation of the Kingdom to become a present and full reality (Matt. 21:43; Rom. 11:13-32).

Anyone Who Breaks the Least of the Commandments. There are several items to be learned here about the members of the Kingdom.

First, we discover that some members of the Kingdom are less than or greater than other members. It should be obvious that the people who occupy the Kingdom are not all on the same spiritual level. Some are considered the least (or least significant) because of their disobedience to God's will. Others are deemed the greatest (or most significant) because of their obedience to God's will.

Second, we discover it is possible to sin and still be a part of the Kingdom. No one in the Kingdom is perfect all of the time (except Jesus, of course).

Third, we discover that the commandments are not equal in weight. The Jews often debated which commandments were the greatest or the least. It was generally agreed that the greatest law was to love God with all your heart, soul and strength (Deut. 6:5). The least law was not to take a mother bird, together with her eggs, for your possession (Deut. 22:6). There were 613 commandments in the writing of Moses. None were to be neglected, but certain ones possessed more significance than others.

Anyone Who Practices and Teaches These Commandments. It is safe to say that some members of the Kingdom of God, because of their obedience, *are* greater than other members who are less obedient. Some persons *do* exercise a degree of discipline and godliness that is greater than that of others. Corresponding to the varying levels of obedience and involvement will be appropriate rewards (1 Cor. 3:10-15; 2 Cor. 5:10). The way we live today plays a direct role in our reward status, both now and in the world yet to come (Matt. 5:12; 19:27-30; Luke 6:35; 19:11-27; Rev. 22:12).

Unless Your Righteousness Surpasses That of the Pharisees. The Pharisees followed a *form* of righteousness, but Jesus was not impressed with their particular form. He called people to conform to *God's* laws, and not to the nonscriptural traditions taught by the Pharisees. The Pharisees concentrated on external righteousness, but Jesus required an internal harmonizing of the heart with God's will, too. Unless this happened, there would be no participation in the benefits of the Kingdom of God. Genuine righteousness is more than outward behavior; it also must involve inward and personal attitudes. The Pharisees lacked these latter ingredients.

II. *Murder, Anger and Reconciliation (5:21-26)*

21"You have heard that it was said to the people long ago, 'Do not murder,[a] and anyone who murders will be subject to judgment.' 22But I tell you that anyone who is angry with his brother[b] will be subject to judgment. Again, anyone who says to his brother, 'Raca,'[c] is answerable to the Sanhedrin. But anyone who says, 'You fool!' will be in danger of the fire of hell.

23"Therefore, if you are offering your gift at the altar and there remember that your brother has something against you, 24leave your gift there in front of the altar. First go and be reconciled to your brother; then come and offer your gift.

25"Settle matters quickly with your adversary who is taking you to court. Do it while you are still with him on the way, or he may hand you over to the judge, and the judge may hand you over to the officer, and you may be thrown into prison. 26I tell you the truth, you will not get out until you have paid the last penny.[d]

a 21 Exodus 20:13 b 22 Some manuscripts *brother without cause* c 22 An Aramaic term of contempt d 26 Greek *kodrantes*

You Have Heard. . . but I Tell You. These were powerful words. Jesus taught with overwhelming authority. In effect, Jesus is placing himself on the same level as Moses, the great lawgiver of the Old Testament. Thus, Matthew is presenting Jesus as the new Moses, the new lawgiver or interpreter of the old Law. The fact that Jesus is delivering this sermon on a mountain is also interesting, because Moses, too, went up to a mountain to obtain the Law from God.

Do Not Murder. The Law stated, "You shall not murder" (that is, commit premeditated murder—Exod. 20:13). Later, someone added the phrase, "and anyone who murders will be subject to judgment." This was not a part of the original statement, though the addition does not violate the consequences suggested by the Scriptures (Gen. 9:6). The point Jesus stresses is the fact that too many of His contemporaries were overlooking the root causes that bring about this ugly fruit of murder in the first place. Beneath this external action resides an internal state which is every bit as lethal. The diseased roots of anger, expressed in calling people irritating names (such as *Raca*—empty-head/"fool"—idiot, moron) are as evil, says Jesus, as first-degree murder.

Settle Matters Quickly. The repercussions of an anger that is out of control are plainly stated here. First, there is the loss of fellowship with God. Offering gifts to God, while anger burns in your heart toward someone, is a valueless exercise of worship. You cannot be wrong with people and be right with God. Reconciliation, whenever possible, is mandatory. Second, there is the real threat of a lawsuit. If you want to keep your shirt, keep your mouth shut when angry. Learn to build bridges, not walls.

III. *Adultery, Lust and Dismemberment (5:27-30)*

> **27"You have heard that it was said, 'Do not commit adultery.'[a] 28But I tell you that anyone who looks at a woman lustfully has already committed adultery with her in his heart. 29If your right eye causes you to sin, gouge it out and throw it away. It is better for you to lose one part of your body than for your whole body to be thrown into hell. 30And if your right hand causes you to sin, cut it off and throw it away. It is better for you to lose one part of your body than for your whole body to go into hell.**

But I Tell You. The seventh commandment (in the listing of the Ten Commandments) regards the matter of adultery (Exod 20:14). This seems to be simple enough to grasp—do not commit the physical act of sexual immorality; that is, remain sexually faithful to your mate for the duration of your life. This is how Jesus' audience had been

a 27 Exodus 20:14

taught to follow this law. But this interpretation lacked depth. It only related to the surface situation. It did not embrace the root factors.

According to Jesus, there are two types of adultery: (1) physical adultery and (2) mental adultery. This commandment, then, not only forbids the action of adultery with the body, but the lustful passion for it as well.

The words translated, "anyone who looks at a woman lustfully," mean much more than a mere glance at a woman. This passage conveys the idea of feeding our minds with lust, of prodding it along in order to deliberately commit mental adultery. It has been said, "you cannot keep the birds from flying overhead, but you can keep them from building a nest in your hair." Likewise, you may not be able to prevent an initial thought or two from passing through your mind, but you certainly can decide whether you will provide them with a comfortable lodging or with a one-way ticket out of your mind.

Better to Lose One Part. It is obvious that Jesus' orders here are not to be taken literally, but figuratively. In other words, Jesus' instruction is to cut yourself free from every possible association, picture or word that might lead to any kind of adultery—mental or physical. How carefully each of us ought to shield our eyes and ears from unwholesome movies, television programs, music, books, magazines, friendships and business enterprises. (For a study on the word "hell," see comments following Matt. 25:31-46.)

IV. *Divorce (5:31, 32)*

> **31"It has been said, 'Anyone who divorces his wife must give her a certificate of divorce.'[a] 32But I tell you that anyone who divorces his wife, except for marital unfaithfulness, causes her to commit adultery, and anyone who marries a woman so divorced commits adultery.**

Certificate of Divorce. In Jesus' day the marital union had its difficulties, too. Mates became disgusted with each other. A certificate of divorce would be obtained, presumably dissolving the marriage bond. Jesus, however, did not accept this all-too-common practice. God's plan was (and is): one mate, one marriage, for life. The only possible exception offered is "unfaithfulness" (usually interpreted to mean adultery). Anyone who divorced his or her mate for another cause, or married an illegally divorced person, was guilty of adultery.

Marital Unfaithfulness. It must be underscored that this teaching from Jesus was never intended to be an encyclopedic statement. That is, these very few words (which essentially focus on "marital unfaithfulness") do not represent all God has said or wills regarding the matter of divorce. There is much more to the subject than is revealed in

a 31 Deut. 24:1

the scope of these particular comments. Therefore, to build a formal and closed case about divorce from these words alone is to lock oneself in a very tight and unbiblical straightjacket. These comments must be seen in the light of other passages on the same subject. (For instance, read Matt. 19:3-12 and 1 Cor. 7:1-40.) The whole matter of repentance and forgiveness is ignored here. Presumably the case under consideration involves no change of heart—there is mention of only an apparently swift divorce and remarriage. When there is godly sorrow for marital sins, however, surely God's grace must enter the picture to forgive and to help those who have suffered the torment of a broken marriage.

V. *Oaths (5:33-37)*

**[33]"Again, you have heard that it was said to the people long ago, 'Do
not break your oath, but keep the oaths you have made to the Lord.'
[34]But I tell you, Do not swear at all: either by heaven, for it is God's
throne; [35]or by the earth, for it is his footstool; or by Jerusalem, for it is
the city of the Great King. [36]And do not swear by your head, for you
cannot make even one hair white or black. [37]Simply let your 'Yes' be
'Yes,' and your 'No,' 'No'; anything beyond this comes from the evil one.**

The Law required that no one swear falsely (that is, God forbade anyone to use His name in a statement or a promise that was not true or would not be kept—Exod 20:7; Deut. 23:21, 22). By Jesus' day the making of oaths had simply gotten out of hand. People were making ridiculously intricate and meaningless oaths. Presumably, if you swore by the name of the Lord, or heaven, or some other weighty matter, then you were fully obligated to keep the oath. But if you did not invoke these persons, places or objects, then you were not bound to perform your promises. In this light, Jesus proposed a remedy—tell the truth, period. Forget the ceremony. Let your words be found true, without all the fuss of making detailed oaths (cf. James 5:12).

VI. *An Eye for an Eye (5:38-42)*

**[38]"You have heard that it was said, 'Eye for eye, and tooth for tooth.'[a]
[39]But I tell you, Do not resist an evil person. If someone strikes you on the
right cheek, turn to him the other also. [40]And if someone wants to sue
you and take your tunic, let him have your cloak as well. [41]If someone
forces you to go one mile, go with him two miles. [42]Give to the one who asks
you, and do not turn away from the one who wants to borrow from you.**

Eye for Eye. The teachers of Jesus' generation displayed no difficulty in quoting God's laws; their unfortunate shortcomings came in misunderstanding the meaning

a 38 Exodus 21:24; Lev. 24:20; Deut. 19:21

of the laws they quoted. The popular idea behind this particular order was the false opinion that each person could take the matter of vengeance and justice into his own hands. But this interpretation is precisely the opposite of its original meaning.

The purpose for this law was to prevent private retaliation, not to promote it (Lev. 19:18; Prov. 24:29). The Old Testament states that if someone hits you in the eye, then you can take him to court and have justice rendered in your behalf (Exod. 21:23-25). Individuals were not to take matters into their own hands. The whole intent in giving this commandment was to keep justice both fair and public.

Turn the Cheek. This passage does not teach, as some suppose, that we are to allow just anyone to clobber us at will. God forbid this! Instead, the intention of the verse is to calm us down when confronted with people who display disrespect for us. Notice that the evil person here is not actually hitting anyone with the intent to harm him; rather, he is slapping (with the back of the hand) someone's "right cheek." This is not a fist fight, but a gesture of disrespect. A vengeful spirit would return this insulting slap, but Jesus can see the fruitlessness of such a reaction. No one wins by fighting back. Sometimes those who deserve our love the least really need it the most. Our aim must be to win them, not to conquer them.

Let Him Have Your Coat. Here is a second example of a nonaggressive and loving reaction when one is personally wronged. If someone sues you, resolve to approach the suit with a nonretaliating disposition. This certainly cannot mean that members of God's Kingdom are to cast justice to the winds as long as we live in this world, but it does seem to imply that whether we win the case or not we ought to make the most of the situation by being a witness of God's love (cf. 1 Cor. 6:1-11). Also, these words display the radical indifference we ought to possess towards possessions. Christians should not be overly concerned when someone robs them of things that will pass away, such as clothing.

Go Two Miles. The Roman mile was 4,860 feet long (or 1,000 paces). Milestones were placed at various intervals to indicate distances to towns and other sites. Since the Jews were the conquered servants of Rome, any soldier or official could require a Jew to carry baggage for a mile along one of these routes.

There were two ways this service could be given—either with resentment or with love. The former type of external obedience would yield only a burning disgust, while the latter type of internal obedience would produce satisfaction and opportunities to witness for God's Kingdom. Jesus plainly states the need for a second-mile disposition among His followers. Certainly this is our Lord's attitude toward us. Can we do less for others?

Give to Those Who Want to Borrow. We can either be possessive or generous with our material goods. Let us remember that all we have comes from God. It is not the getters who are blessed, but the givers (Acts 20:35). Lend things to people.

VII. *Love Everyone (5:43-48)*

43"You have heard that it was said, 'Love your neighbor[a] and hate your enemy.' 44But I tell you: Love your enemies[b] and pray for those who persecute you, 45that you may be sons of your Father in heaven. He causes his sun to rise on the evil and the good, and sends rain on the righteous and the unrighteous. 46If you love those who love you, what reward will you get? Are not even the tax collectors doing that? 47And if you greet only your brothers, what are you doing more than others? Do not even pagans do that? 48Be perfect, therefore, as your heavenly Father is perfect.

You Have Heard. Nowhere is there any commandment that says, "Hate your enemy." This concept was concocted solely by hateful men. God's Law has always been love—love for everyone (Lev. 19:18). The Jews were a very prejudiced people. They hated the Jewish tax-gathering traitors, the Samaritan half-breeds, and the Roman Gentiles. There was much bitterness and resentment in their hearts. Jesus, therefore, informed His listeners that God lets the sun shine and the rain fall upon everyone, without any prejudice. He loves everyone. And we must also, if we are to prove to be His children. Again, this is not an injunction to become everyone's doormat. Instead, it is a call to cleanse our hearts of an attitude of hate toward anyone. The only spirit worthy of the members of the Kingdom of God is love. Let us ask God to be filled with this profound love (Eph. 3:14-21).

Be Perfect. In lifting this verse from its context, some teachers have seen this exhortation as a call to sinlessness. But this is not intended. No one in this life (excluding Jesus) will ever attain to a state of flawlessness (1 John 1:7-10). This is wholly impossible.

The sense of the passage is this—make your *love* perfect (or complete)—by loving both those who love you and those who do not love you. Be like your Father, who loves both the lovely and the not so lovely.

---

a 43 Lev. 19:18 *b 44* Some late manuscripts *enemies, bless those who curse you, do good to those who hate you*

The Sermon on the Mount—Part III
The Conduct of Kingdom Life (Matt. 6:1-7:12)

(cf. Luke 6:37-42; 11:1-4, 9-13; 12:22-31)

In the first division of this sermon (5:1-16) the stress is placed upon the general character of the members of God's Kingdom. In the second unit (5:17-48) the emphasis is given to the specific commandments that kingdom people are to observe. In this third part (6:1-7:12) the focus is drawn to the conduct of the adherents of the Kingdom. The first section deals with us personally; the second deals with our relationship to the Law and the Prophets; the third deals with our relationship to people, God and things.

I. *Acts of Righteousness (6:1-4)*

6 "Be careful not to do your 'acts of righteousness' before men, to be
seen by them. If you do, you will have no reward from your Father
in heaven.
2"So when you give to the needy, do not announce it with trumpets, as
the hypocrites do in the synagogues and on the streets, to be honored by
men. I tell you the truth, they have received their reward in full. 3But
when you give to the needy, do not let your left hand know what your
right hand is doing, 4so that your giving may be in secret. Then your
Father, who sees what is done in secret, will reward you.

Acts of Righteousness. The King James Version of the Bible translates this phrase with these words, "Do . . . your alms." This latter word, "alms," is often translated from the Greek language as "righteousness." For the Jew, the act of giving to the needy was one of the highest acts of righteousness anyone could perform. Every member of the nation of Israel was to pity the poor and to help relieve their condition (Deut. 15:11; Matt. 19:21; cf. Rom. 12:13; James 2:16). Through this service a person could exercise the reality of his righteousness.

Your Reward. Contributing to the needs of the poor is to be a private matter. Bragging and showing off have no place in the proper dispensing of good-will gifts. Jesus strongly renounces this hypocrisy. If the giving is done to be seen and appreciated, then the giver receives his full reward at the moment he makes his contribution. But if the gift is done without anyone's notice, then God will see to it that a full reward will be sent to this selfless giver.

The specific rewards associated with proper acts of righteousness are most generous. Prosperity (Prov. 11:24, 25; 19:17), physical protection (Ps. 41:1, 2), and a good name of dignity and honor (Ps. 112:9) will accompany those who truly support the efforts that relieve the hurts of suffering people.

The words of George Mueller are most appropriate here: "God judges what we give by what we keep." When it is our turn to die, we will only be able to take with us what we have given away for the good of others and for the glory of God. There will be no regrets in heaven that we gave away things to help people.

II. *Praying (6:5-15)*

5"But when you pray, do not be like the hypocrites, for they love to pray standing in the synagogues and on the street corners to be seen by men. I tell you the truth, they have received their reward in full. 6When you pray, go into your room, close the door and pray to your Father, who is unseen. Then your Father, who sees what is done in secret, will reward you. 7And when you pray, do not keep on babbling like pagans, for they think they will be heard because of their many words. 8Do not be like them, for your Father knows what you need before you ask him.

9"This is how you should pray:

" 'Our Father in heaven,
hallowed be your name,
10your kingdom come,
your will be done
on earth as it is in heaven.
11Give us today our daily bread.
12Forgive us our debts,
as we also have forgiven our debtors.
13And lead us not into temptation,
but deliver us from the evil one.[a]'

14For if you forgive men when they sin against you, your heavenly Father will also forgive you. 15But if you do not forgive men their sins, your Father will not forgive your sins.

Do Not Be Like the Hypocrites. A hypocrite's prayers avail nothing. They are spoken to men, and not to God. So it follows that their complete reward comes from those to whom they pray.

---

a 13 Or *from evil;* some late manuscripts *one, / for yours is the kingdom and the power and the glory forever. Amen.*

There were three times each day that the Jews set aside for formal prayer—9:00 A.M., 12 noon and 3:00 P.M. (cf. Ps. 55:17; Dan. 6:10; Acts 3:1). Regardless of the place or circumstances, the devout Jew was to drop everything and pray. It was commonly believed (though scripturally unsupportable) that the prayers offered in the Temple were the most effective; next in line came the prayers made in the synagogue. If neither of these places were convenient, the individual could pray wherever he found himself. It seems that numerous Jews, especially the Pharisees, found themselves wherever the largest audience was.

There is a proper place for public prayer in the will of God (Acts 3:1; 4:24-31) but here Jesus emphasizes our need also to pray privately. This is secret prayer—unannounced and unattended, except for the appointment you have made with God.

Do Not Be Like the Pagans. The problem with the praying habits of the pagans (other than the fact that they prayed to demons—cf. 1 Cor. 10:20) is that they felt their prayers would be more effective if they were lengthy utterances. The notion was that if you droned on in prayer long enough, you would eventually get whatever it was you requested. Unfortunately, this false idea of merit through duration has crept into the prayer habits of various disciples of Christ, too. Jesus soundly rejects the opinion that in order to be effective our petitions must be long or loud. No. The longest recorded prayer in the New Testament comes from Jesus and lasts approximately two minutes (John 17). Many others are only one sentence long (Matt. 14:30; Luke 18:13; 23:42; Acts 7:60; Eph. 3:14-19). God is more concerned with the content of the prayer and the attitude of the petitioner than with the duration of the petition.

Your Father Knows. God knows our need before we utter a single syllable. Praying does not bring God up to date with our condition. Rather, it gives us an opportunity to participate in those works of God that will satisfy our needs. Prayer is a way of expressing our confidence in the love and provisions God has for us personally.

This Is How You Should Pray. After specifying the wrong ways to pray, Jesus proceeds to give a sample of the right way to pray. Every necessary element for a richly spiritual life is contained in these few words. First, as ought to be expected, God and His Kingdom are given the initial place in the prayer. Second, our own needs—both physical and spiritual—are mentioned in the spirit of expectancy. (Observe that Christ's disciples do not hoard things—"*daily* bread.") Third, our relationship to people is covered with the grace of forgiveness. Finally, in the fourth position, the desire for protection from Satanic forces is confidently expected.

Forgiveness. This word (in its various forms) is one of the most significant and practical terms found in the entire Bible. From Genesis to Revelation it appears nearly 120 times. It is found in twenty-three of the Bible's books. And, appropriately enough, it is located more often in the gospels than anywhere else (forty-four times).

Here is a classic passage which, unfortunately, has been the object of much misunderstanding. These words appear to be self-explanatory and self-sufficient. But herein lies the root of the problem. These verses, in order to be properly understood, need to be seen in the light of a passage from Luke, namely 17:3. Here, Jesus says, "If your brother sins, rebuke him, and if he repents, forgive him."

Forgiveness is not something God gives to everyone without qualification. Instead, He makes forgiveness available to everyone, and upon the individual's repentance He instantly bestows this grace. But if there is no repentance, there can be no forgiveness. The same method of dealing with people may be applied to ourselves. We cannot forgive someone when God himself has not yet forgiven them. On the other hand, at the first trace of repentance, our hearts must open wide so that the flow of forgiveness will be both free and abundant.

III. *Fasting (6:16-18)*

> **[16]"When you fast, do not look somber as the hypocrites do, for they disfigure their faces to show men they are fasting. I tell you the truth, they have received their reward in full. [17]But when you fast, put oil on your head and wash your face, [18]so that it will not be obvious to men that you are fasting, but only to your Father, who is unseen; and your Father, who sees what is done in secret, will reward you.**

A few observations regarding the overall context of verses 1-18 now deserve attention.

First, the three subjects addressed here (acts of righteousness, prayer and fasting) represent the three pillars upon which maximum kingdom living stands. Caring for the needs of people marks the pinnacle of good works; prayer is the vital link between earth and heaven; and fasting is the fuel that gives power both to our good works and our prayers.

Second, each of these grand virtues can be rendered useless by performing these duties with improper motives (vv. 2, 5, 16).

Third, a rich reward awaits each one who practices these graces in a proper spirit of selflessness.

When You Fast. In both Hebrew and Greek the term translated "fast" means abstinence from food. When the abstinence is involuntary, the idea behind the term is "hunger" (and is sometimes rendered in this fashion—2 Cor. 6:5). But when the abstinence is voluntary, for spiritual purposes, then the idea of "fasting" is implied.

There are three types of fasts discussed in the Scriptures: (1) a *complete* fast, in which case no food or drink is taken into the body—Deut. 9:9, 18; Esther 4:16; Acts 9:9; (2) a *partial* fast, when certain unnecessary items are deleted from one's menu—Dan. 10:3; and (3) a *common* fast, where all foods are skipped, though water (or some other mild drink) is permitted.

The purpose of fasting is generally threefold: (1) to produce piety, (2) to perfect prayer, and (3) to penetrate problems. These points are clearly established in these passages: 2 Sam. 12:16-23; Ezra 8:21; Dan. 10:3; and Acts 14:23.

Do Not Look As the Hypocrites. God only required the Jews to fast one day each year—on the Day of Atonement (Lev. 16:29-34; Num. 29:7-11; cf. Acts 27:9). All other fasting was to be a matter of private devotion. The Pharisees, however, boasted that they denied themselves and fasted twice each week—Monday and Thursday, the two chief market days, of course (Luke 18:12). So that no one would overlook their devotion, they would not bathe, or anoint themselves with any perfumes, or comb their hair, or smile. They even disfigured their faces with a whitening solution in order to appear all the more holy. Naturally, Jesus rebuked such ridiculous fasts. There would be no reward in this, beyond whatever people might give to them in their passing. True fasting, says Jesus, has its place and its proper reward from God. But first, the exercise of self-denial is to be a private matter, and not a public display.

IV. *Money Matters (6:19-34)*

[19]"Do not store up for yourselves treasures on earth, where moth and
rust destroy, and where thieves break in and steal. [20]But store up for
yourselves treasures in heaven, where moth and rust do not destroy,
and where thieves do not break in and steal. [21]For where your treasure
is, there your heart will be also.
[22]"The eye is the lamp of the body. If your eyes are good, your whole
body will be full of light. [23]But if your eyes are bad, your whole body will
be full of darkness. If then the light within you is darkness, how great is
that darkness!
[24]"No one can serve two masters. Either he will hate the one and love
the other, or he will be devoted to the one and despise the other. You
cannot serve both God and Money.
[25]"Therefore I tell you, do not worry about your life, what you will
eat or drink; or about your body, what you will wear. Is not life more
important than food, and the body more important than clothes? [26]Look
at the birds of the air; they do not sow or reap or store away in barns, and
yet your heavenly Father feeds them. Are you not much more valuable
than they? [27]Who of you by worrying can add a single hour to his life[a]?

a 27 Or *single cubit to his height*

[28]"And why do you worry about clothes? See how the lilies of the field grow. They do not labor or spin. [29]Yet I tell you that not even Solomon in all his splendor was dressed like one of these. [30]If that is how God clothes the grass of the field, which is here today and tomorrow is thrown into the fire, will he not much more clothe you, O you of little faith? [31]So do not worry, saying, 'What shall we eat?' or 'What shall we drink?' or 'What shall we wear?' [32]For the pagans run after all these things, and your heavenly Father knows that you need them. [33]But seek first his kingdom and his righteousness, and all these things will be given to you as well. [34]Therefore do not worry about tomorrow, for tomorrow will worry about itself. Each day has enough trouble of its own.

In the preceding section (6:1-18) Jesus discusses losing God's reward as a result of seeking the praise of men; in the present passage Jesus examines losing God's reward as a result of seeking this world's possessions. Life's ultimate issues are based on this question: "Where is my heart?" The things I treasure reveal the direction of my love; and either I love the things of earth, or I love the things of heaven.

Store Up for Yourselves Treasures. Jesus contrasts the two kinds of treasures which are available to us. First, He says there are "treasures on earth." A person may accumulate untold earthly possessions. He may be the wealthiest person on the block or in the city or even in the world, but what has he gained? Certainly he may have momentary satisfactions (though he may not). But when the moment of pleasure has ended, when the treasure is no longer a personal joy (due to natural erosion, or thieves, or even sickness and death) what happens then?

Jesus shows us how shortsighted we can be. We tend, by our very natures, to think of *now* and only of now. Everything is geared to today, to this present life. But what of tomorrow, when the "now" is forever gone? What will we think of our self-centered getting on the day when all of our earthly accumulations vanish before our eyes and we face God? What will we think then?

Second, Jesus says there is a way to store up "treasures in heaven." We can make deposits in the world yet to come. By putting our time, talents and finances into spiritual interests, we are actually investing in a brighter future for ourselves. This includes not only heaven itself, but personal rewards to accompany our eternal life with Christ and God (1 Cor. 9:25; 2 Cor. 5:10; 2 Tim. 4:8; Rev. 2:10; 3:11).

Good and Bad Eyes. Earthly treasures blur heavenly light. Our eye acts like a window, and through clear windows much light comes. But if the window is cluttered with the things of this world, then the amount of light permitted to enter is hindered proportionately. How little light is to be found in some persons because of their interest in temporal pleasures and earthly goods. For them, the treasures of heaven are meaningless. They are altogether blinded by the excessive attention they have given to the things of this world.

God and Money. Our wills are capable of only one ultimate loyalty. Though we live in the world, the world is not to live within us. That is, we cannot serve God and money simultaneously. The decision facing each member of the Kingdom of God in this regard is "either/or." Either the King will be honored with first-place devotion, or money will be given this supreme position. This does not mean all of the members of God's Kingdom must be poor in order to be spiritual. Rather, it means there is not enough room in our hearts to be in love with each of these masters (cf. 1 Tim. 6:10; Heb. 13:5). We must choose to love one or the other.

Do Not Worry About Life. There is a common tendency to worry about the supply of our basic needs (cf. 6:25, 31, 34). Jesus discerns this common trait of people, and He assures everyone that of the two alternatives before us—worry or faith—worry will yield nothing (unless maybe more of the same). Worry cannot add a single moment to our life. To allow this fruitless, faithless and material-centered disposition to develop within us is to be abandoned forever.

Telling someone not to worry, however, means little until there is a channel in which faith can operate. Clear reasoning helps us not to worry. The reasoning Jesus provides is fourfold.

First, Jesus brings our attention to the physical body (v. 25). Is not this wonderful body of ours (which is made in God's image—Gen. 1:26) more important than the fuels that run its parts? That is, don't our bodies deserve a higher rating in our minds, by the very nature of things, than food and clothes? First things first. Won't He care for you?

Second, Jesus shows us the birds of the air (v. 26). They have no savings plan, yet they are fed by the Father of the Kingdom. Won't He also care for you?

Third, Jesus directs us to the beautiful lilies of the field, which do not worry, because God cares for them (vv. 28-30). Won't He care for you?

Fourth, Jesus reminds us that it is the pagans, who do not know God, who run around attempting to get more and more (v. 32). Won't He care for you, His children?

Children of God have as their responsibility to seek first the Kingdom of God and His righteousness—which is to say, we are to promote the advancement of God's will in all the earth. And if we will do our part (of seeking God's Kingdom and His righteousness), then God will do His part—which is to supply all of our needs (cf. Phil. 4:19). It is not the children's responsibility to provide for their needs; this is the Father's role. And God gladly assumes His duty. So, let us do our part and cease our worrying. Our reserves are as big as God himself.

A brief note should be added here regarding the phrase, "all these things." Some teachers have taken this verse out of context and built an elaborate system of prosperity promises for each believer. This manipulation of the text is plainly unjustified. The promise here is not for untold wealth, but for food, drink and clothing—nothing less, and nothing more (vv. 25, 31, 32; cf. 1 Tim. 6:6-10). God's promises are glorious enough; we do not need to enlarge upon them in order to make them appear all the more sensational.

Do Not Worry About Tomorrow. Finally, with regard to finances, Jesus instructs His audience not to worry about tomorrow. The Lord makes only one day for us at a time, and we are to rejoice and be glad in each one as it arrives (Ps. 118:24). There will be enough matters in each day to keep us busy, so we will not need to pick up another day and attempt solving its difficulties, too.

V. *Judging (7:1-6)*

7 "Do not judge, or you too will be judged. 2For in the same way you
judge others, you will be judged, and with the measure you use, it
will be measured to you.
3"Why do you look at the speck of sawdust in your brother's eye and
pay no attention to the plank in your own eye? 4How can you say to your
brother, 'Let me take the speck out of your eye,' when all the time there
is a plank in your own eye? 5You hypocrite, first take the plank out of
your own eye, and then you will see clearly to remove the speck from
your brother's eye.
6"Do not give dogs what is sacred; do not throw your pearls to pigs. If
you do, they may trample them under their feet, and then turn and tear
you to pieces.

Do Not Judge. Jesus commanded, "Do not judge." Regrettably, this is about all of the passage that many people remember. They never read (or remember) the next five verses. But these latter verses give us the proper understanding of the three opening words.

First, we need to consider what Jesus did *not* mean. Certainly He could not have meant that it was wrong to pass judgment (or to render a decision) against sin. For Jesus himself spoke out sharply against the evil practices of His day (Matt. 5:17-6:34; 19:8, 9; etc.). Neither could He have meant it was wrong to render a guilty verdict against sinners. For, again, Jesus often confronted sinners with a crisp note of judgment. Listen to this: "Woe to you, teachers of the law and Pharisees, you hypocrites! You travel over land and sea to win a single convert, and when he becomes one, you make him twice as much a son of hell as you are" (cf. Matt. 23:13-33)! In the mind and ministry of Jesus it was never wrong to judge sin and sinner alike. They come together; they are inseparable. The early church, likewise, did not experience any difficulty in judging people in this twofold manner (Acts 5:1-11; 8:18-23; Rom. 16:17, 18; 1 Cor. 5; Gal. 2:11-14; etc.).

It is only a half-truth to say that God hates sin, but He loves sinners. Yes, Jesus died for everyone in the entire world (1 John 2:1, 2). Yes, all may be forgiven. But until we repent of our sins and turn our wills over to God, we are children of Satan (1 John 3:8-10), God's enemies (James 4:4), and condemned to an everlasting judgment (John 3:18; Eph. 2:1-3). This must never be forgotten.

Second, we must consider what Jesus *did* mean. In reading the entire context (vv. 1-6), it becomes very plain that Jesus is denouncing (or judging!) the person who has a critical, fault-finding attitude. No one has the right to pick at the minor faults ("the speck of sawdust") in others, says Jesus, when he has not yet dealt with his own major blemishes ("the plank").

In effect, Jesus is saying, "Repent of your own gross sins before you point your finger at someone else's sin." Then, Jesus states something that is often ignored. He declares that once you clean up your own spiritual life, then you are to go help others clean up theirs, too. Do you see it? It is not wrong to find sins in others. It is only wrong to use your index finger in pointing out these flaws when you have equivalent or even worse sins yourself. Jesus teaches that you should get rid of your own sins first, and then lend a hand (not a stiff, pointed finger) to help others put their lives together.

In the Way You Judge, You Will Be Judged. Sowing and reaping—it's a natural law. You get back what you give out. If you give out gentleness, you will get back gentleness. If you serve meanness to others, you will be served the same. It is the boomerang principle. Whatever you throw out will return unchanged.

This is the lesson Jesus sought to convey to His hearers. If you judge others severely, you can expect the same kind of judgment in return. But if you will judge them with mercy and compassion, then this will be the standard by which you are judged. Put simply, you get what you give. It naturally follows, then, that you ought to treat others the way you desire to be treated.

Dogs and Pigs. These animals represent two of the most common, yet detested, animals found in Palestine (Lev. 11:7; Prov. 26:11; 2 Pet. 2:22). These terms also represent those persons who hear the sacred message (or "the pearl") of God's Kingdom but are disposed to reject it, and even to harm those who bring it to them.

Not everyone is open or receptive to the gospel story. Some persons love their sins too dearly to listen to any words of correction. In hearing the message of repentance, they feel compelled to cling even more tightly to their own vices. Therefore, Jesus orders His listeners not to waste their time with such persons. There are plenty of others who will listen; speak to them instead (Matt. 10:14, 15, 23; 11:23; Rom. 16:17, 18; 1 Cor. 5).

VI. *Ask, Seek, Knock (7:7-11)*

7"Ask and it will be given to you; seek and you will find; knock and the door will be opened to you. 8For everyone who asks receives; he who seeks finds; and to him who knocks, the door will be opened.

9"Which of you, if his son asks for bread, will give him a stone? 10Or if he asks for a fish, will give him a snake? 11If you, then, though you are evil, know how to give good gifts to your children, how much more will your Father in heaven give good gifts to those who ask him!

Ask, Seek, Knock. Here is a compounding of prayer encouragements and prayer promises. These three words in the original Greek are written as present tense imperatives. The idea behind the present tense is that of continuation. And the thought behind the imperative mood is that of a command, an order. When put together, Jesus is basically saying, "God so greatly enjoys your requests that He commands you to continuously ask, seek and knock. Never tire of going to Him with everything that concerns you."

Your Father Gives Good Gifts. Here Jesus compares the admirable qualities of earthly fathers (who, by nature, are morally blemished or evil) with the unsurpassed qualities of our heavenly Father (who, by nature, is impeccable). The logic is crystal clear: if evil fathers give good gifts to their children, how can a loving God do any less? What an encouragement this is to pray and to expect results. God will always give something good to those children who come to Him and ask for good things in faith (Heb. 11:6; James 4:2). Never be afraid to ask for things when you pray. God encourages it.

VII. *The Supreme Code of Conduct (7:12)*

12In everything, do to others what you would have them do to you, for this sums up the Law and the Prophets.

In the Kingdom of God there is no higher code of ethics than the Golden Rule. The entire teaching of the Old Testament on conduct, in capsule form, is contained in this single sentence. It is the Golden Rule for Kingdom life. In the world you are taught to get; in the Kingdom you are taught to give. In the world you are taught to look out for yourself; in the Kingdom you are taught to look out for others. Treat others as you would like to be treated.

The Sermon on the Mount—Part IV The Confirmation of Kingdom Life (Matt. 7:13-29)

In this final section of the Sermon on the Mount we are directed by Jesus through the doorway of eternal life (7:13,14), beyond the obstacle of false teachers (7:15-23), and finally through the tests that befall everyone (7:24-27).

Here is a threefold message that takes us by the hand and leads us triumphantly from our first trial to our final trial as believers. First, there is the test of whether or not we will enter God's Kingdom at all. Second, there is the test of detecting and avoiding false prophets or teachers. Third, there is the test of living a life of continuing obedience. Those who pass these tests display for everyone a true confirmation that they are indeed members of God's dynamic Kingdom on earth.

I. *Narrow and Wide Approaches to Life (7:13, 14)*

> **[13]"Enter through the narrow gate. For wide is the gate and broad is the road that leads to destruction, and many enter through it. [14]But small is the gate and narrow the road that leads to life, and only a few find it.**

The Two Gates. There are two different gates by which we enter into our daily activities. First, there is the *narrow* or *small* gateway. In order to get through this tiny passageway we must detach ourselves from every possession. There is room enough only for us and nothing else. Second, there is the *wide* gate. Through this gate you can carry many possessions—all you can hold. There is no limit here. Each person on this planet has chosen one of these two gates—either the one requiring self-denial, or the one allowing self-indulgence.

The Two Roads. Beyond each gate is a corresponding road. On the other side of the wide gateway is a super highway with broad lanes for easy travel. There are very few restrictions—just plenty of room to roam. Behind the small gate, however, is an equally narrow road. The word translated "narrow" here is elsewhere translated "tribulation" and means "pressed in." The narrow road is, therefore, very limited in its flexibility. You cannot roam wherever you wish if you select this small lane. Only God's will is to be found in the narrow road.

The Two Destinations. At the end of each road there is a destination. The termination of the broad way is destruction in eternal hell. But the end of the narrow way is eternal life in God's presence. It is impossible for these roads to lead their travelers to other destinations.

The Few Who Find It. The gate to eternal life is "small," the road is "narrow," and only a few bother to "find it." How horrible and frightening this declaration is. The majority of the world's occupants are contented as they unknowingly walk off to their eternal destruction. They care too little for matters that will affect their eternal destiny.

Which of these two ways have *you* chosen? What confirmation is there that you have chosen the narrow path of the few? Does your life reflect the marks of one who has decided to take the straight-and-narrow path in following Jesus? These are the true tests, and you must answer them honestly.

II. *True and False Prophets (7:15-23)*

**15"Watch out for false prophets. They come to you in sheep's clothing,
but inwardly they are ferocious wolves. 16By their fruit you will
recognize them. Do people pick grapes from thornbushes, or figs from
thistles? 17Likewise every good tree bears good fruit, but a bad tree
bears bad fruit. 18A good tree cannot bear bad fruit, and a bad tree
cannot bear good fruit. 19Every tree that does not bear good fruit is cut
down and thrown into the fire. 20Thus, by their fruit you will recognize
them.**

**21"Not everyone who says to me, 'Lord, Lord,' will enter the kingdom
of heaven, but only he who does the will of my Father who is in heaven.
22Many will say to me on that day, 'Lord, Lord, did we not prophesy in
your name, and in your name drive out demons and perform many
miracles?' 23Then I will tell them plainly, 'I never knew you. Away from
me, you evildoers!'**

Watch Out. A person is never to be evaluated by his external reputation; instead, he should be evaluated on the basis of the fruit of his daily life. Not everyone who wears sheep's clothing is actually a sheep. Not all who profess Christ possess Christ. Unfortunately, some prophets, pastors, elders, evangelists, teachers, deacons and church leaders are not what they claim to be. Speaking religious words and performing religious works do not necessarily imply real inner conversion to God's will. We must examine the fruit—the spiritual character—of those who declare they are walking in the narrow way, the will of God.

Leaders must pass rigid tests before they should be considered worthy of our following them. Their lives must produce an evidence (or fruit) of sincere devotion to God. They cannot speak one thing and then live another. Each disciple of Christ must carefully examine the true character of his or her church leaders. Many of these persons will be found true to God, but some will fail the tests. Such persons should be advised of their crucial shortcomings, and then they should be informed that you will no longer submit to their presumptuous authority. (See the "Special Study" at the close of this unit.)

No less than sixteen times, the Gospel writers record that Jesus warned His audience to watch out (Matt. 7:15; 10:17; 16:6,11; 24:4,23,26; Mark 4:24; 8:15; 12:38; 13:5; Luke 8:18; 12:1; 17:23; 20:46; 21:8). The threat of being deceived is real, and we must take it seriously even today.

Thrown into the Fire. Someday Jesus will deal with these false personalities (see Matt. 25:31-46; Rev. 20:11-15). Their characters will be revealed. And their punishment will be set. They will be cut down like rotten trees, and thrown into the fire to be consumed. Separated from Christ, they will spend eternity reaping the fruits of their corrupt characters. What a tragic end to life!

The biblical doctrine of divine justice and eternal judgment is revealed throughout the sixty-six books that constitute the sacred Scriptures. This subject cannot be rejected or neglected if a proper perspective of God and people is to be maintained. The severe nature of this subject demands both our sober attention and full acceptance.

Arguments against the doctrine of hell usually revolve around this sort of question: "If God is love (and He is!), then how can He send anyone to an everlasting hell?" Three things should be remembered in attempting to answer this question.

In the first place, God's love does not overlook sin or the punishment sin deserves. Instead, it is God's love that offers an escape from hell. It is God's love that offers forgiveness. God's love sends no one to hell.

In the second place, it is often wrongly assumed that because no earthly father would ever send one of his children to hell, neither will God treat His children in this manner. The problem with this logic, however, is to be found in the identity of God's children. Certainly God does not send any of His children to hell! Never! It is those, instead, who are *not* His children who are appointed a place in hell. The Bible teaches that every person on this earth is either a child of God or a child of Satan (1 John 3:8-10). Those, and only those, who fail to follow God and Jesus Christ will be sentenced to hell.

In the third place, this question is misleading. God does not send anyone to hell. Heaven and hell are a conscious choice. *We* choose either heaven or we choose hell. We do this in our daily decisions. God does not force anyone to go to heaven or to hell. That decision is ours (John 3:16-21; Rom. 1:18-32).

Only He Who Does God's Will. Entrance into heaven will not be based upon our confessions, our good works, our miraculous gifts, nor any other such matter. Heaven is reserved for the obedient—period.

Some persons will be greatly shocked to discover that despite their religious fervor, they will not be qualified for entrance into God's Kingdom. We, too, might be surprised to note that some professing Christians (with a supernatural ministry of prophesying, exorcising demons, and miraculous signs) will not be accepted by God. Again, it is not our words or works that interest Him, but our wills. Do we delight in obeying Him? This is the true test. It is a one-point examination which will separate the true Christian leaders from the false ones. Only those who have been obedient will be permitted to stay in His presence.

III. *Wise and Foolish Builders (7:24-29)*

24"Therefore everyone who hears these words of mine and puts them
into practice is like a wise man who built his house on the rock. 25The
rain came down, the streams rose, and the winds blew and beat against
that house; yet it did not fall, because it had its foundation on the rock.
26But everyone who hears these words of mine and does not put them
into practice is like a foolish man who built his house on sand. 27The rain
came down, the streams rose, and the winds blew and beat against that
house, and it fell with a great crash."

28When Jesus had finished saying these things, the crowds were
amazed at his teaching, 29because he taught as one who had authority,
and not as their teachers of the law.

Jesus starts this lesson (verse 13) by dividing the human race into two groups—a broad group that goes the way of the world, and a narrow group that goes the way of God's will. Next, He analyzes some of those who presumably have taken the narrow route, and finds in her ranks certain "false prophets," false Christian leaders. Now he further examines the so-called members of this narrow group and finds still more "foolish" persons. This time the guilty people are the common persons who "hear" God's will but fail to practice it.

Obedience does more than unlock the door to heaven for church leaders. It is this very same key that must be used by each individual Christian if we expect to be saved and to enjoy the benefits of God's Kingdom.

Building for a Storm. Jesus uses a simple illustration to make His point clear. Those who hear and do God's will are compared to a person who builds his house upon a rock. Then comes the rain, the rising streams and the winds to pound vehemently against the structure. But these fierce elements are incapable of ruining the house. Why? Because it is built on a secure foundation. In other words, the person who builds his life around the deliberate hearing and doing of God's will shall stand forever. The bitter enemies of life (symbolized in the rains, rising streams and winds) will touch everyone, including the faithful disciples. But in the end, those who are obedient will emerge safe and solid.

Those who hear, but fail to put Jesus' words into practice, are like a person who builds his house (or life) on sand. When this house (or life) is tested, it will collapse.

There is a subtle distinction to be made here between these two parties. Both individuals hear the same message, and both know what should be done, but only one applies the message to himself. Here lies the vast difference between people, religious people—the matter of obedience to the will of God. Both parties may hear and both may agree, but only the one who applies the words personally will be safe in the time of judgment and will be permitted entrance into the Kingdom of God.

The Authority of Jesus. Jesus certainly did not preach like His contemporaries. His teachings were different. They were never dull or evasive. Instead, they were always straightforward and practical. Jesus didn't resort to quoting other teachers in order to support His claims. He simply stated that what He said was God's will, and everyone was left to receive it as such. This excited the people. And they were left amazed at His profound authority.

Special Study: Testing "Christian" Leadership

1. *The validity of a testing process.* There are some persons who will object to any form of testing. They feel confident that they are able to detect the difference between a spiritual or nonspiritual person solely by some mystical alarm system within themselves. They are also quick to point out that believers are not to judge anyone. But these statements, despite their sincerity, are inadequate responses.

The Scriptures provide strong counsel to "test everything [not just a few matters, but everything, and then to] hold on to the good" (1 Thess. 5:21). "The spiritual man," says Paul, "makes judgments [evaluations, appraisals, discernments] about all things" (1 Cor. 2:15). Unfortunately, people who *do* evaluate the measure of the "Spirit" in a person or experience are often considered to be doubters of God and quenchers of miraculous faith. But this is not the case at all.

No less than forty-two times the New Testament instructs us to beware of accepting teachings, experiences and people as being spiritual when in fact they are not spiritual. This repeated advice makes several points abundantly clear:

(a) Deception is everywhere, including in Christian circles;

(b) Christians can be deceived in varying degrees; and

(c) Wise believers will properly evaluate what they hear, see and feel before they accept anything as coming from God. (See Matt. 7:15; 10:17; 16:6, 11; 24:4, 23, 26; Mark 4:24; 12:38; Luke 11:35; 17:3; 21:36; Acts 13:40; 1 Cor. 6:9, 10; 8:9; 15:33; Gal. 5:15; Eph. 5:6; Phil. 3:2; Col. 2:8; 1 Thess. 5:21; Heb. 3:12; 1 John 5:21; 2 John 8; and so forth.)

2. *The testing process.* When you listen to someone, how can you know what to accept and what to possibly discard as sensational, an immature misunderstanding or blatant deception? How can you, a spiritual person, "test everything [and] hold on to the good" (1 Thess. 5:21)? Here are several points to remember in making your evaluation fair and scriptural:

(a) *Discern the person's humanity.* At the start it should be established that no human being possesses the totality of spiritual truth (Phil. 3:12-15). That means, in practical terms, no one can avoid error altogether. There are some flaws in the best person's theology. Advanced age and profound godliness do not guarantee perfection. No human being carries this warranty. Don't ever expect to find someone with all the answers. There is no such person.

(b) *Discern the person's level of maturity.* Not all Christians are the same—obviously. We are at different levels of spiritual development (Heb. 5:11-6:[illegible]). Some persons, because they have walked on the road of spiritual obedience longer than others, are more advanced in both the breadth and depth of truth.

When I first became a pastor (at the age of twenty), it wasn't long before I became painfully aware of my immaturity. At the start, I thought everything about life was either black or white. But with the passing of time I came to realize there are exceptions, too. The wise person, I discovered, can see the gray areas.

For instance, we have the promise from Paul's pen that God will meet all our needs (Phil. 4:19). Yet, in the very same paragraph, Paul states that at times (and in accordance with God's will) he had suffered need (Phil. 4:11-13). Only a mature person can discern and apply matters like these. Do not expect more from a person than his level of maturity will allow.

(c) *Discern the person's reputation.* You can learn a great deal about someone by exploring their recent past. Have they demonstrated trustworthiness, reliability, consistency or stability? Avoid the temptation to place much stock in the conversation of wavering persons (James 1:5-8).

(d) *Discern the person's character.* Look for the fruit of the Spirit (Gal. 5:22, 23). If love, joy, peace, patience, kindness, goodness, faithfulness, gentleness and self-control are absent, then so is the Spirit filling. Be certain to carefully filter whatever you may hear from such people.

(e) *Discern the person's teachability.* Very few things are more lethal to a person than an unteachable attitude. People who do not want to be confused with the facts because their minds are already made up are in serious trouble (2 Tim. 2:23-26).

Detect harpers who grind out the same message again and again. Shield yourself from those persons who are always placing a pound of stress on an ounce of truth, or those who are placing an ounce of stress on a pound of truth. A teachable person will have a keen sense of proportion and balance. He is neither rigid nor uncompromising. The genuine Christian leader is open to scriptural correction and change.

(f) *Discern the person's level of reliance upon the Scriptures.* This is the key issue. Does the leader base the whole of his or her faith solely on the Old and New Testaments? Further, are this person's views compatible with those of historical Christianity—that is, does he hold to a doctrinal view that is acceptable to general orthodox Christianity? Whenever anyone teaches views that are opposed to those of the universal church, it is a clear signal to avoid such persons.

(g) *Discern the person's motives.* True Christian leaders will always seek to do these things: honor Christ above all else, edify the church, and convert the lost. False ministers do not have these three objectives as fixed priorities; true ministers do.

A Leper Is Healed (Matt. 8:1-4)

(cf. Mark 1:40-45; Luke 5:12-16)

Matthew begins his Gospel by outlining the steps that brought Jesus into this world, along with the accompanying results of His entrance (1:1-2:23). Then, he tells us about John and how he baptized Jesus in the Jordan River (3:1-17). We see Jesus tested, yet triumphant in each ordeal (4:1-11). Following this we both hear and see Jesus teaching, healing and inviting His first disciples to follow Him (4:12-25). Next, we read a lengthy discourse of Jesus' theology—three sparkling chapters on how to live a heavenly life in an earthly environment (5:1-7:29). Before us now are two chapters that are devoted almost exclusively to Jesus' healing ministry.

You cannot miss this deliberate ordering of events by Matthew. His intent is far more than merely to bring information to his reading and listening audience. He also seeks their transformation. In order to achieve this goal he first sets forth the Messiah's words; now he displays the Messiah's works. (Note the following chart, entitled "The Miracles of Jesus.")

THE MIRACLES OF JESUS

The Miracles	Matthew	Mark	Luke	John
Leper cured	8:1-4	1:40-42	5:12-16	
Centurion's servant cured	8:5-13		7:1-10	
Peter's mother-in-law cured	8:14, 15	1:30, 31	4:38, 39	
Storm stilled	8:23-27	4:37-39	8:22-25	
Demonized men cured	8:28-34	5:1-17	8:26-39	
Paralytic cured	9:2	2:3-12	5:18-26	
Jairus's daughter cured	9:18-26	5:22-43	8:41-56	
Woman with hemorrhage cured	9:20-22	5:25-34	8:43-48	
Two blind men cured	9:27-31			
Demonized man cured	9:32, 33			
Withered hand cured	12:10-14	3:1-6	6:6-11	
5000 fed	14:15-21	6:30-44	9:10-17	6:1-15
Christ walks on water	14:25	6:48		6:16-21
Syro-Phoenician's daughter cured	15:21-28	7:24-30		
4000 fed	15:32-38	8:1-9		
Demonized boy cured	17:14-18	9:14-27	9:37-43	
Tax money in fish	17:24-27			
Two blind men cured	20:29-34	10:46-52	18:35-43	
Fig tree cursed	21:18, 19	11:12-21		
Dumb and deaf man cured		7:31-35		
Blind man cured		8:22-26		
Large catch of fish			5:1-11	
Widow's son restored to life			7:11-17	
Woman's infirmity cured			13:11-17	
Man with dropsy cured			14:1-4	
Ten lepers cured			17:11-19	
Malchus's ear restored			22:50, 51	
Water turned into wine				2:1-11
Nobleman's son is cured				4:46-54
Sick man cured				5:1-15
Blind man cured				9:1-41
Lazarus raised from dead				11:1-45
Catching 153 fish				21:1-6
Demonized man		1:23-28	4:33-37	

I. *The Request of the Leper (8:1, 2)*

8 When he came down from the mountainside, large crowds followed him. 2A man with leprosy[a] came and knelt before him and said, "Lord, if you are willing, you can make me clean."

A Man with Leprosy. Leprosy (or as it is often called now, Hansen's disease) is one of the most terrible diseases of all times. No other sickness can draw life from a person with such calculated cruelty. First, a patch of skin becomes discolored and numb, usually somewhere on the face. From there the patch may spread and grow into thick, glossy, tumorlike welts. Next, the disease advances to the hands and feet. The fingers and toes commonly shrink and lose their usefulness. As the external tumors grow, they leak and discharge a very unpleasant odor. Finally, the disease will work internally, affecting the larynx (or voice box). Slowly, inch-by-inch, the victim dies over a span of ten to twenty years.

Probably of equal torment to the victim of this disease was the social and spiritual side-effects caused by the disease. The leper was banned from his community and from the Temple. He was compelled to leave his home and friends, to dwell in a special area set apart exclusively for lepers. Banished. Unclean. Defiled. These are the horrors attached to such a disease in the biblical period and for some time thereafter.

The Leper Came to Jesus. This is always the first step in the healing process—desire. Many would prefer the attention they receive in sickness over the benefits of health. Their real sickness is in their attitude. But this leper came to be cured. Healing begins with a desire to get well. And the first place we should express that desire is before Jesus.

The Leper Knelt. There was no cure for leprosy in Jesus' day (though there is a cure today). The situation was hopeless, humanly speaking. But this leper knew a greater power than the current medical remedies. He knew of Jesus' power to heal the sick, and he came and knelt before Him. Here is the second step in this man's approach—a deep reverence for Jesus Christ.

The Leper Said, "You Can Make Me Clean." First, there was desire. Second, there was reverence. Now we see his faith. The leper called upon Jesus with the confidence that He could work a miracle of healing in his sick body. No wavering. The leper had a steadfast confidence in the power of Jesus over diseases.

II. *The Responses of Jesus (8:3, 4)*

3Jesus reached out his hand and touched the man. "I am willing," he said. "Be clean!" Immediately he was cured[b] of his leprosy. 4Then Jesus

a 2 The Greek word was used for various diseases affecting the skin—not necessarily leprosy. b 3 Greek *made clean*

said to him, "See that you don't tell anyone. But go, show yourself to the priest and offer the gift Moses commanded, as a testimony to them."

Jesus Said, "Be Clean." Immediately the cruel disease was gone. The marks indicating leprosy had totally disappeared. There would be no sickness in the presence of Jesus for those who met the prerequisites of desire, reverence and faith. Healing was very much a part of Jesus' ministry. He delighted in healing the sick as much as the sick delighted in being healed.

"Don't Tell Anyone. . . . Show Yourself to the Priest." Jesus instructs this former leper to do two things. First, he was to tell no one of his miracle. Various reasons are proposed as to why Jesus made this charge. Possibly it is due to the fact that people tend to overemphasize the physical miracles, and in so doing they undercut the spiritual miracles of repentance and forgiveness. Jesus wanted to maintain a sharp focus on the primary intent of His mission—spiritual healing. Also, it is equally likely Jesus gave this command because He wanted to avoid sensationalism. His audience might have tried to sweep Him into the popular role of an exclusively political Messiah.

Second, Jesus tells the man to fulfill Moses' law for healed lepers (Lev. 13, 14). There were proper channels for the confirmation of a healing in the biblical period. In this case it was confirmed by visiting the priest and undergoing an examination. Healings today, through prayer, ought also to be checked out through proper medical channels as a witness to God's love and power. (For specific details regarding Jesus' healing ministry, see the following two accounts and the Subject Index.)

Jesus Heals a Centurion's Servant (Matt. 8:5-13)

(cf. Luke 7:1-10)

In the previous story we saw the drama of a *personal petition* to Christ for healing (8:1-4). Here is a story of an *intercession* to Christ for the healing of a friend.

The major elements involved in this healing are very much like the ones demonstrated in the preceding episode. Note the centurion's desire. He *came* to Jesus. Observe his reverence. He said, "I do not deserve to have you come under my roof." Notice his faith. He told Jesus, "Just say the word." Jesus' response was simple and direct: "I will go and heal him." The persons are different, but the principles and results remain unchanged.

I. *The Dialogue of the Centurion with Jesus (8:5-9)*

5When Jesus had entered Capernaum, a centurion came to him, asking
for help. 6"Lord," he said, "my servant lies at home paralyzed and in
terrible suffering."
7Jesus said to him, "I will go and heal him."
8The centurion replied, "Lord, I do not deserve to have you come
under my roof. But just say the word, and my servant will be healed.
9For I myself am a man under authority, with soldiers under me. I tell
this one, 'Go,' and he goes; and that one, 'Come,' and he comes. I say to my
servant, 'Do this,' and he does it."

A Centurion. The Roman army was composed of large units called legions, which usually enlisted 6,000 men. Rome had twenty-five legions in her total army. Each legion was subdivided into ten smaller units, called cohorts, consisting of 600 men each. The leader of these individual groups was called a tribune. The next level was a sixfold division of the cohort (a group of 100 men each). This body was appropriately called a century and was commanded by a centurion. The number of troops assigned by Rome to the region of Judea was five cohorts, or about 3,000. This means there would have been approximately thirty centurions in the area where Jesus ministered.

My Servant. Servants (or slaves) in the Roman world were usually considered to be less than human. They were thought of as being possessions, mere tools for the master's convenience. A slave had no rights of his own. He could be used, abused, sold or even killed without any action from the state. But in this account we read of an exception to this rule of society. Here we find two men—Jesus and a centurion—who appreciate and respect the worth of individuals, regardless of their particular status in life.

Jesus Said, "I Will Go and Heal Him." The compassion of Christ is readily displayed by His willingness to help the centurion's servant. The confidence of Jesus is evidenced in His assertion that the servant will be healed (and not merely prayed for). These two ingredients—compassion and confidence—are distinctive traits that always graced the character of Jesus.

Just Say the Word. The centurion had to earn this rank by being a proven soldier. He had to be well-groomed in the art of receiving orders before he would be permitted to issue them. Apparently this centurion had learned this aspect of leadership with rare perfection, because it is from this experience that he displayed his remarkable faith. Whenever the centurion gave an order, those under his authority were expected to do as he commanded. In like manner, He expected that Jesus could order diseases to depart and that they would simply go at His command.

Observe that the distance between him and the expected miracle did not trouble him. He believed that Christ's authority knew no fixed boundaries. Neither did the method—a mere word—bother him. The centurion did not ask for medicine; he sought only a word from Jesus' lips. How confident he was in Jesus' power over sickness.

II. *The Delight of Jesus (8:10-12)*

10When Jesus heard this, he was astonished and said to those following
him, "I tell you the truth, I have not found anyone in Israel with such
great faith. 11I say to you that many will come from the east and the
west, and will take their places at the feast with Abraham, Isaac and
Jacob in the kingdom of heaven. 12But the subjects of the kingdom will
be thrown outside, into the darkness, where there will be weeping and
gnashing of teeth."

The Feast with Abraham. A saving faith in God was not confined to the Jews. Gentiles could also believe and share in the benefits of God's Kingdom. This centurion is clear proof of this truth (cf. Acts 17:24-30).

The actual identity of this feast is debated. Some scholars see in this description a symbolic feast which depicts the fellowship that will be shared by all believers throughout all of eternity. Other persons envision a literal meal that will be enjoyed by all believers, probably to be eaten shortly after the time of Jesus' Second Coming (Rev. 19:9, 17). Possibly there is merit in believing that Jesus had both of these views in mind when He spoke of this festive occasion.

The Subjects Will Be Thrown Outside. The word translated "subjects" here is more literally rendered "sons." The sons of Abraham, the natural heirs of the Kingdom, will be expelled from God's blessings because they have not received Jesus' message. Naturally, this does not imply that every Jew will be eliminated from the presence of God's light throughout eternity, but only those Jews who refuse to receive God's revelation in Jesus Christ. These Jews (and Gentiles, too—cf. Matt. 25:31-46) will be sentenced to an eternal darkness, where only bitter tears and tormenting anguish will forever grip them (Dan. 12:2; Mark 9:45-48; Rev. 20:10-15).

There is much talk in theological circles today that eliminates the prospect of a literal hell for non-Christians. But this line of argumentation is based solely upon human wishes, and not upon divine revelation. Jesus offers no hope to the person who dies in a state of rebellion against God's laws (Matt. 3:12; 18:8; 25:41-46; Jude 6, 7; Rev. 14:9-11; 20:11-15).

III. *The Deliverance of the Servant (8:13)*

[13]Then Jesus said to the centurion, "Go! It will be done just as you believed it would." And his servant was healed at that very hour.

It Will Be Done Just As You Believed It. The faith of the centurion was met with a corresponding healing. The language used here, upon a first reading, suggests that faith alone was responsible for this healing miracle. In fact, if you go one step farther, you might conclude (as some have done) that you can get whatever your faith desires. In other words, if you exercise proper faith, then you can be healed of all sicknesses all of the time. This line of reasoning, however, has at least four crucial shortcomings.

1. It assumes it is always God's will to heal everyone, if they only believe God for it. This all-too-common presentation of total health for the total person for the totality of time is an oversimplification of the healing issue. What about Paul's poor eyesight (Gal. 4:13-15), Timothy's frequent stomach ailments (1 Tim. 5:23) and Trophimus, whom Paul left sick in Miletus (2 Tim. 4:20)?

2. It assumes that all illness is Satanic. But this is only partially true. Illness may also have a natural cause (Gen. 27:1), a sovereign purpose (John 9:1-3) or a basis in chastisement (1 Cor. 11:27-32).

3. It assumes God never uses sickness, and that illness cannot have any redemptive value. But again, this is only partially true. The Scriptures are quite plain in stating that God can and does use sickness in accomplishing some of His plans (Deut. 28:15-68; Mic. 6:13; 1 Cor. 11:27-32; Gal. 4:13-15).

4. It assumes that the only reason people are not healed when they are sick is because they fail to exercise their God-given faith. What a terrible burden of guilt is carried by someone who believes this teaching, but is ill and unable to get well. Such persons are often urged to ignore their symptoms and to confess their healing, as though it were actually present. Regrettably, some people have actually died because they supposed this healing formula was comprehensive and correct. Again, however, this position is only partially correct.

Jesus *does* heal today. And faith *is* the key to these healings. But these two statements do not present the total picture. For instance, should the person who is sick because of chastisement pray to be healed, or should he repent of the sin that is actually causing the illness in the first place? He should repent, obviously. What about the person who "claims" he is healed, but still manifests the symptoms of very poor eyesight? Should he use his glasses when he drives his family to the store, or should he throw his glasses away? Obviously, he should keep his glasses and wear them!

Jesus never tested people in order to qualify them to receive His healing power. Neither were any of His miracles of healing delayed beyond a matter of a few minutes, though today some people are injected with guilt if they fail to "claim" their healing and act as though they had it, even if it means months or years of nagging discomfort. This kind of so-called healing doctrine is nonscriptural.

If you are going to be healed through the prayer of faith, then you must: (1) be certain you are in right relationships with God and people—Matt. 5:23, 24; 1 John 1:9; and (2) be certain you are confident of Christ's power to heal you—Matt. 9:28-30. Jesus said you only need to believe He is *able* to heal you, if you are to be healed by Him. This does not require a mountain of faith, but a mere mustard-seed level; yet it is enough if you are going to be healed.

If you are not healed immediately or within a reasonable span of time, do not give up on your healing. Continue to "abide in Him" (John 15:7). There will be other days and circumstances for healing possibilities. Call for the prayers of the elders, as well as those of your friends (James 5:14-16). Attend a service where a person with a respected healing ministry is present. Ask for your miracle. Expect it. Rejoice if it comes in this day. Rejoice if it does not come in this present hour (Phil. 4:11-13). Press on! (For further comments, see the Topical Index, under the heading "Jesus—Healing Ministry.")

He Was Healed at That Very Hour. Each healing from Christ, with three known exceptions, was received immediately (Matt. 8:3, 13, 15; 9:6, 7, 22, 29, 30; 15:28, 30, 31; 17:18; 20:34; Mark 3:1-6; 7:33-35; Luke 13:13; John 4:53, 5:8, 9). In the three exceptions to this rule, the delay only lasted for several minutes (Mark 8:22-26; Luke 17:11-19; John 9:1-7). In all cases the healing was total; that is, the sick person was completely restored to perfect health. This is the way Jesus heals; and many thousands of people today attest to this type of healing.

It would be inaccurate to state that a gradual healing (for instance, a healing that requires six months of recuperation) is purely miraculous. Such a healing is certainly under God's attention and care; still, it is not a supernatural healing in the same sense healings in the Gospels are. A gradual healing is probably more accurately a natural healing—a healing which God has, by creation, designed into the body itself. Both non-Christians and Christians alike share in this type of healing.

Jesus Heals Many Persons (Matt. 8:14-17)

(cf. Mark 1:29-34; Luke 4:38-41)

Jesus' healings were both private (8:14, 15) and public (8:16, 17). He always managed to bring help, whether there was a crowd present or only one at hand. There was no showmanship—only compassion—in Jesus' miracles.

The leper petitioned Christ for his own needs (Matt. 8:1-4). And the centurion interceded for the needs of another (Matt. 8:5-13). But in this passage Jesus heals with no apparent call for help. From His own heart He moves to touch the sick.

I. *The Mother-in-Law of Peter (8:14, 15)*

> **[14]When Jesus came into Peter's house, he saw Peter's mother-in-law lying in bed with a fever. [15]He touched her hand and the fever left her, and she got up and began to wait on him.**

Peter's House and Mother-in-Law. There are three considerations about the life of Peter to be gained from this single account: (1) He had a home. (2) He may have had two homes. Either Peter sold his home in Bethsaida in order to be closer to Jesus' home in Capernaum, or this home was his second one (John 1:44; Mark 1:21, 29, 30). (3) He had a wife, one who later accompanied him on his missionary travels (1 Cor. 9:5).

He Saw Her. The cause for Jesus coming to Peter's house is not stated here, though in Luke's account the intent seems to be traced to a concern for Peter's mother-in-law. Although He does not seem to be directly guided to her, and though she did not call out to attract His attention, He found her. Our Lord knows when we are down. He sees us. Nothing that touches us can ever escape His compassionate attention (cf. 2 Cor. 1:2-4).

He Touched Her. Jesus often touched people with His hands and expected a miracle to happen. There are no fewer than nine such examples recorded in the Gospels (Matt. 8:3, 15; 9:18, 25, 29; 17:7; 20:34; Luke 7:14; 22:51).

This physical contact may represent the clearest example of the role Jesus served as the God-man. In His deity He would touch God, and in His humanity He would touch people. Together, the God-man served as a two-way channel: one way for the blessings of heaven to flow to people, and the other way for people to cross from this temporal world into God's everlasting Kingdom.

II. *The Masses of the Community (8:16)*

> **[16]When evening came, many who were demon-possessed were brought to him, and he drove out the spirits with a word and healed all the sick.**

He Drove Out the Spirits. Jesus came into this world to defeat the devil (Heb. 2:14, 15; 1 John 3:8-10). He was to gain back what people lost when Adam and Eve rebelled in the garden (Gen. 3). Proof of this fact is no more clearly seen than in Jesus' ministry of commanding demons to depart from people. The chart at the conclusion of Matt. 8:33, 34 shows an analysis of this work of Jesus.

He Healed All the Sick. No sickness was too small or too large for Jesus' compassion and power. No person was too young or too old to be qualified to receive His miracles. Everyone, on this evening, without any exceptions, was to be healed.

Of the thirty-five recorded miracles in the ministry of Jesus, 74 percent, or twenty-six of them, are healings of some form of sickness. He cured a leper (Matt. 8:1-4), a paralytic (Matt. 9:1-8), two blind men (Matt. 9:27-30), and a woman suffering from hemorrhaging (Matt. 9:20-22). Others had a fever (Matt. 8:14, 15), were crippled, dumb and lame (Matt. 15:30, 31), or suffered from intense pain (Matt. 4:23, 24). Regardless of the symptoms, Jesus could heal all of them.

On the other side of the coin we see that not every person who was ill throughout Jesus' ministry received a healing. In Nazareth, for instance, "he could not do any miracles there, except lay his hands on a few sick people and heal them" (Mark 6:5). Why was this the case here? Because "they took offense at him" (Mark 6:3). Neither did Jesus indiscriminately heal everyone (John 5:1-15). There were conditions to be satisfied. If these prerequisites were not met, then there could be no healing.

III. *The Message of the Prophet (8:17)*

17This was to fulfill what was spoken through the prophet Isaiah:

"He took up our infirmities
and carried our diseases."[a]

He Took Our Diseases and Carried Our Illnesses. Here is a quotation from Isa. 53:4. This Old Testament prophet envisioned a time when the Messiah would come and remove all illness and suffering. The actual fulfillment of this verse has been a debated topic by many scholars. Some see the realization in Jesus' hanging on the cross. Others picture the fulfillment taking place prior to the cross, in Jesus' earthly ministry. It is this latter position that receives Matthew's support.

This verse raises an important issue that must now be discussed. Did Jesus pay for our healing on the cross? That is, did Jesus take our sicknesses upon himself on the cross in the same manner that He took our sins upon himself? In other words, if healing is in the Atonement (or if healing is as much a part of Christ's work on the cross as forgiveness), then can we expect to be restored to health physically in the same manner that we are restored to spiritual health each time we repent of our sins?

Jesus fulfilled the prophecy of Isaiah 53:4 during His earthly ministry. Therefore, He did not make provision on the cross for the removal of our sicknesses *in the same manner* in which He made provision for the continuous removal of our sins. Here is a four-point itemization of this reasoning.

(1) The work of Jesus on the cross of Calvary is discussed no less than 175 times in the New Testament. In each case *sin* is the key issue (see Matt. 20:28; 26:28; John 1:29;

[a] *17* Isaiah 53:4

Rom. 3:25; 4:25; 5:18; 1 Cor. 5:17; 15:1-4; 2 Cor. 5:21; Gal. 1:4; 3:13; 4:4, 5; Eph. 2:14-16; Col. 1:20-22; 2:14; 1 Tim. 2:6; Titus 2:14; 1 Pet. 3:18; 1 John 1:7-10; 2:1, 2; 4:10; etc.). There is not a single reference that includes physical healing as a part of Jesus' work on the cross. (Isa. 53:4 and 1 Pet. 2:24 could be considered to be exceptions; these two verses will be discussed below.)

(2) There are forty-three separate items discussed in the twelve verses of Isa. 53. This complexity cannot be overlooked in attempting to interpret its various parts. The topics discussed include these matters (arranged chronologically):

Jesus' appearance—v. 2
Jesus' reception and rejection—vv. 3, 4
Jesus' reputation—v. 9
Jesus' healing ministry—v. 4; cf. Matt. 8:17
Jesus' trial—vv. 7, 8
Jesus' death—vv. 5, 6, 10, 11, 12
Jesus' burial—v. 9

Because this passage covers the whole scope of Jesus' life—from birth to death—we must be careful in choosing which verses to apply to His specific work on the cross; namely, these are verses 5, 6, 10-12. Special note ought to be made regarding the fact that these verses exclusively relate to *spiritual* healing. Jesus' work on the cross, according to Isa. 53, related only to sin, to building a highway from earth to heaven. The only clear reference to Jesus' healing ministry (v. 4) is interpreted by Matthew as being fulfilled during His earthly ministry, not on the cross.

(3) 1 Pet. 2:24, which is a partial quotation of Isa. 53:5, has been suggested as a possible fulfillment of Jesus taking our sicknesses on the cross, along with our sins. Supposedly, Jesus' blood atoned for our sins, but His stripes paid for our physical healing. According to Peter, however, it is the body of Jesus—including both blood and stripes—that paid our *sin* debt. Additionally, even a casual reading of Isa. 53:5 leaves one with the impression that the reference here to healing is spiritual in nature.

No other reference in the entire Bible suggests that Jesus' stripes were for our physical healing. Since any interpretation of a passage must be supported by at least one other clear passage of Scripture, it seems unlikely that physical healing is the proper meaning behind Peter's wording.

The word translated "healed" in 1 Pet. 2:24 is used twenty-seven other times in the New Testament. Often the term is used of a literal, physical healing (Matt. 8:8, 13; etc.). But no less than five times the term is also used of spiritual healing (Matt. 13:15; Luke 4:18; Acts 28:27; Heb. 12:13; James 5:15. This final reference is used of both a physical healing and a spiritual healing). It seems probable that Peter had *spiritual* healing in view in the use of this quotation, especially since the context would not indicate otherwise.

(4) This distinction between Jesus' earthly ministry and His ministry on the cross (the former being physical and spiritual, the latter being essentially spiritual) explains why some people are not instantly (or even eventually) healed as a result of the prayer of faith. We cannot expect to receive healing in the same totality or swiftness as we can expect to receive forgiveness from our sins.

Those persons who state that healing is in the cross also usually believe that the absence of faith is the sole cause for the absence of a healing (or constant health for that matter). An emphatic stress, therefore, is placed upon a strong verbal confession of faith. And this is good, but it must not be stretched beyond its intended usage. A sick person, for instance, is sometimes instructed never to say that he is sick. They see a confession of sickness as being a denial of 1 Pet. 2:24, where the Word is presumably saying that you "were" physically healed on the cross. But this conclusion is unfounded, as shown above.

Additionally, this type of so-called faith teaching only results in generating massive guilt feelings in the one who wants to be healed but just cannot seem to generate enough obedience or faith in order to secure God's promise. This is not a healthy teaching on healing! It lacks a degree of balance and appreciation for any exceptions in the matter of sickness

When it *is* God's will to heal you (and it often *is* His will), how much faith is actually required for this miracle to happen? Does it take tons of faith and weeks of a positive confession in order to receive a miracle? No. Jesus only requires this much faith: "Do you believe I am able to do this" (Matt. 9:28-30)? That is all. And that is enough! Praise the Lord. (Consult the Topical Index for other passages and comments on healing.)

Call to Discipleship (Matt. 8:18-22)

(cf. Luke 9:57-62)

The greatest privilege given to mortals is the opportunity to follow and serve Jesus Christ! People cannot know a greater honor.

Here is a story of two persons who sought to follow Jesus. They were full of noble pledges and sincerity. But they each lacked one basic ingredient: a proper knowledge of what it means to follow Jesus Christ. Their minds were filled with fantasies and false notions about discipleship.

How shallow are some of the decisions we make in life. With a single impulse we are inclined to do something, and just as quickly we are apt to change our minds in order to do something else. Too many decisions for Christ have been made in this same fashion.

I. *The First Invitation (8:18-20)*

[18]When Jesus saw the crowd around him, he gave orders to cross to the other side of the lake. [19]Then a teacher of the law came to him and said, "Teacher, I will follow you wherever you go."

[20]Jesus replied, "Foxes have holes and birds of the air have nests, but the Son of Man has no place to lay his head."

In the parallel account of this episode (Luke 9:57-62) we learn that Jesus extends an invitation to no less than three persons. The responses He receives reflect the differing attitudes Jesus received from His audiences. The first person is eager, but naive. The second individual is reluctant and perhaps insecure. And the third person (only recorded by Luke) has divided interests. These reactions are not at all unlike those we hear today from people who listen to the gospel message and the call to discipleship.

I Will Follow You. Here is a person filled with zeal. He is eager to obey before he even knows the command. Just say the word and he is ready to get on with the task—or so he says. But Jesus could detect the fact that this scribe (or teacher/theologian) was missing a certain aspect in his understanding of discipleship, namely its negative side. His quick response certainly demonstrated his sincerity, but it also displayed his lack of familiarity with the life Jesus lived. Foxes and birds had a place to call home, but Jesus had none. To follow Jesus, therefore, meant more than the joy of seeing crowds and miracles. There also had to be the selfless devotion to a spiritual kingdom that may yield few personal worldly possessions.

It is not stated if Jesus' response to this prospective disciple dampened his spirit or whetted his spiritual ambition still further. Many writers feel this disciple turned away from Jesus at this point, but there is not a single indication that he did so. Rather, because of his fervent desire to follow Jesus, he may have received the total package of discipleship joyfully. Let us hope he did.

The Son of Man. In Jesus' reaction to this man's enthusiasm, He calls himself by His favorite title—"the Son of Man." Only Jesus designates himself thusly and the Gospel writers record Him doing so some sixty-five times.

There are three ways in which Jesus uses this title: (1) it depicts His humanity, especially as a servant—Matt. 20:28; (2) it depicts His suffering, especially on the cross—Mark 8:31; and (3) it depicts His glory, especially as the future King of all the earth—Matt. 26:64. Here, Jesus uses this title to depict His humanity.

II. *The Second Invitation (8:21, 22)*

> 21**Another man, one of his disciples, said to him, "Lord, first let me go and bury my father."**
> 22**But Jesus told him, "Follow me, and let the dead bury their own dead."**

Let Me Go. If the first prospective disciple is overzealous, then this one is clearly overly hesitant. He says he wants to be Jesus' disciple, but he reveals his reservations when he announces his desire to go home. There are always those who say they want to follow Jesus, but only after they have gotten everything squared away first.

Let the Dead Bury Their Own Dead. These words strike us as being quite strong. But just precisely what did Jesus mean by this response? Two acceptable interpretations are offered for properly understanding what Jesus said.

First, Jesus may have meant that this disciple was to leave the burial of his spiritually dead father to the care of other equally spiritually dead persons.

A second interpretation, the more probable one, sees Jesus as having meant that *now* was the time for this disciple to follow Him and that he was not to wait for the death of his father or the settling of his father's estate. Actually, the expression used here ("let me go and bury my father") is common in the Middle East as a way of stating that one is obligated to care for the necessities surrounding death. There is no reason to believe, from this usage, that the father was dead or even near death. Rather, this disciple merely expresses what he feels to be his natural obligation, while Jesus rearranges his priorities.

Again, we are not told of the effect produced by Jesus' words. The counsel may have been too much to bear. Perhaps he went home. But it is likely that these words are just what the disciple wanted to hear. Perhaps this confirmation of his desire enabled him to be free to serve the Christ he loved.

Special Study: The Doctrine of Discipleship

Discipleship is surely one of the most vital themes of the New Testament. No Christian or church can mature properly without an understanding of the term "disciple." Therefore, this extra study is included here in order to enrich your understanding and appreciation for this doctrine.

1. *A Hebrew Word Study.* The Hebrew term for discipleship is *lamad.* This word

means to be a learner or follower. Therefore, it depicts the deliberate process of making God's will one's own. For the Old Testament Jew, a disciple was a person who lived with the constant mental attitude of obedience in his whole being to God's will.

There are numerous examples of disciples in the Old Testament. Consider these: The training of Joshua and other men under Moses (Exod. 17:8-14; 24:13; 32:15-18; 33:9-11; Num. 11:28; 27:15-23; Deut. 1:38; 3:21-28; 31:1-8, 14-23; 34:9; John 9:28); Samuel's training under Eli (1 Sam. 1-3); the prophets' training under Samuel and other prophets (1 Sam. 10:5-13; 19:20; 1 Kings 20:35; 2 Kings 2:3-7, 15; 4:1, 38; 6:1; 9:1; Isa. 8:16; Jer. 45:1); Elisha's training under Elijah (1 Kings 19:15, 16, 19-21; 2 Kings 2:1-11); and the training of all Jewish children under their parents (Gen. 18:17-19; Exod. 12:26, 27; 13:14, 15; Deut. 4:9, 10; 6:1-15; 11:18-21; Ps. 78:4-6).

2. *A Greek Word Study.* The New Testament word for disciple is *mathetes* (math-ā-taś). It means to be a pupil, a learner, a scholar, an apprentice, or one who submits to teaching. The concept of teaching and learning is paramount in discipleship. If there is no instruction, then there can be no legitimate discipleship.

But what type of instruction is involved in Christian discipleship? Is a disciple to regard his mind as a vessel for accumulating much knowledge? Should he expend his every free moment in study, reading, memorizing, and the like? Is the disciple's goal to reach a predetermined level of biblical education? No, not at all. Discipleship is more than education; it is also sanctification.

How dreadfully inadequate is a form of discipleship that requires that the "disciple" only acquire a certain quota of facts. The goal of discipleship is not *learning* all of God's Word, but *doing* all of God's will. It is the formation of life, not simply information about life, that depicts the core of Christian discipleship. The objective is not to acquire mere facts *about* God, but to reach a firm commitment to follow Him. In a capsule form, the purpose of discipleship is to produce the character and works of Christ throughout one's entire being—in thought, word and deed.

According to Jesus, a disciple of His is recognizable by these ten things: (1) preeminently in love with Him—Luke 14:26; (2) committed to loving the brethren—John 13:34, 35; (3) a good steward of all his possessions—Luke 14:33; (4) crucified to self—Luke 9:23; 14:27; (5) devoted to prayer—Matt. 6:5-13; 9:37, 38; Luke 11:1ff; (6) disciplined in fasting—Matt. 9:15; (7) skilled in Bible knowledge—John 8:31; 15:7, 8; (8) a bearer of much fruit—John 15:1-8, 16; (9) able to exercise authority over demons and disease—Matt. 10:1, 8; and (10) a maker of other disciples—Matt. 28:19, 20.

Possibly the best single English word for "disciple" is "apprentice." An apprentice is someone who is bound by contract to another party for a prescribed period for the purpose of learning an art or trade. In Christian usage, then, an apprentice or disciple is someone bound by agreement (formal or informal) to another party for a period of time for the purpose of learning how to live the mature Christian life.

3. *Various Types of Disciples.* The New Testament mentions disciples of Moses (John 9:28), the Pharisees (Matt. 22:16), John the Baptist (Matt. 9:14), and Jesus. The disciples of Jesus fall into three categories: (1) in a broad sense it applies to those who followed Him—John 6:66; (2) in a narrow sense it applies to the Twelve whom He chose to be with Him—Matt. 10:1; and (3) in a particular sense it applies to all who are genuine Christians—John 15:8; Acts 6:1, 2, 7; 14:20, 22, 28; and so forth. Within this latter group there is a still further distinction.

Two types of disciples are discussed in regard to the New Testament church. The first group was relatively free from home responsibilities and therefore able to travel any distance with great men of the faith. The second group of disciples, however, was bound by home ties and unable to travel any substantial distance.

Those disciples who were free from home obligations were discipled on the job.

THE DISCIPLESHIP PROCESS

The Savior is not looking for men and women who will give their spare evenings to Him—or their weekends—or their years of retirement. Rather, He seeks those who will give Him first place in their lives. (William MacDonald)

1. Salvation: Birth—Upward Aspects of Discipleship
   a. Hearing and Receiving God's Word—John 20:30, 31; Rom. 10:14-17; James 1:21; 1 Pet. 1:23-25
   b. Submitting to Jesus—Matt. 11:28-30; Luke 14:25-27; John 14:6; Acts 4:12; Rom. 10:9-13
2. Sanctification: Growth—Inward Aspects of Discipleship
   a. Learning and Practicing God's Word—John 17:17, 19; Eph. 5:25, 26; 2 Tim. 2:15; 3:16, 17; 2 Pet. 2:2
   b. Submitting to Disciple Maker(s)—1 Cor. 4:15, 16; 11:1; Phil. 3:17; 4:9; 1 Thess. 3:7-9; 5:12, 13; Heb. 13:7, 17
3. Perfection: Maturity—Outward Aspects of Discipleship
   a. Sharing God's Word—John 15:7-14; Heb. 5:12; 1 John 2:3-5; 3:18
   b. Leading Others—Matt. 4:19; 28:19, 20; John 20:21; 1 Thess. 1:6-8; 2 Tim. 2:2; 1 Pet. 3:15

To obtain God's best, we must give our best. (Oswald J. Smith)

They learned to teach from teachers; they learned to evangelize from evangelists; they learned to shepherd from shepherds; and so forth. This group was discipled by the simple, yet profound and biblical, method of show and tell and do. Any institution today which seeks to equip its students without an intensive and extensive on-the-job training is destined to produce weak and unbalanced disciples.

On the other hand, those disciples who were bound by home obligations usually were discipled through two different methods: large church meetings and small home fellowships. When the early church began, they met in the Temple (Acts 2:42, 46; 5:20, 42) and on Solomon's porch (Acts 5:12, 13) for their large gatherings. There were also many small meetings in homes (Acts 2:42-47; 4:23-31; 5:10, 42; 8:3; 12:5, 12; 20:20). The early church recognized something from which we could greatly profit—neither a large group meeting nor a small group meeting is complete in itself. Both are vital to the full development of a disciple.

Please study the chart entitled "The Discipleship Process." It gives an analytical outline of the discipleship process.

Jesus Calms a Storm (Matt. 8:23-27)

(cf. Mark 4:35-41 and Luke 8:22-25)

Sometimes we are inclined to believe if we could only live in the presence of Jesus there would be no further trials. We dream of undisturbed peace and joy. But this was not the case with the disciples. They had much to learn, and often the tests were difficult.

The disciples had to learn how to face storms and to sail through them. And they did not learn this art at Jesus' feet alone, or in some comfortable upper room. This kind of knowledge only came through rugged life experiences.

Some things cannot be taught in the classroom. They must be branded into us through the rough experiences of everyday life. Each of us must learn this truth if we are to make sense of our walk with Christ. Some days we will be found picking up full baskets; but on other occasions we will find ourselves practically overcome by some storm of life and crying out desperately for divine assistance. Both types of experience are integral to God's plan for our discipleship.

I. *Anxiety (8:23-25)*

23Then he got into the boat and his disciples followed him. 24Without

warning, a furious storm came up on the lake, so that the waves swept over the boat. But Jesus was sleeping. 25The disciples went and woke him, saying, "Lord, save us! We're going to drown!"

Genuine faith always must work its way from deep within our being to our exterior life. Discipleship is much more than spiritual ideas or doctrinal beliefs. It is faith, put to practice, in the real world of everyday events. Until we are tested, what we say is only theory, a mere internal idea. God must bring our beliefs to actualization. And to do so requires testing.

There is nothing wrong with going to Christ with your problems. In fact, He expects us to come; He even delights in our coming to Him with our difficulties. But we must not come to Him full of doubts and fears. We must come with faith (Heb. 11:6). It may be easy to say that God's provisions are bigger than mankind's problems, but our Lord expects us to see God's power as being intensely personal. He honors this type of faith.

II. *Authority (8:26)*

26He replied, "You of little faith, why are you so afraid?" Then he got up and rebuked the winds and the waves, and it was completely calm.

You of Little Faith. The disciples failed their test, and Jesus rebuked them for their small faith. But He did not give up on them. He still loved them. And He continued to teach them, so their beliefs would be transformed from mere theories into personalized truths. The goal of Jesus was to get the disciples' head-faith into a practicing faith in the world of real problems. He wanted them to apply their spiritual authority as He would apply it at the point of adversity.

He Rebuked the Winds. Some people see in these words Jesus' authority over the elements of nature. This authority may stem from His possessing the gift of miracles (cf. 1 Cor. 12:10). Others see a Satanic source behind this storm—a source over which Jesus possessed total control. Either position seems realistic.

III. *Amazement (8:27)*

27The men were amazed and asked, "What kind of man is this? Even the winds and the waves obey him!"

Naturally, the disciples were amazed at Christ's powerful and practical authority. They wondered if there was any limit to His miracles. Interestingly, those who knew Him best were constantly amazed by Him. The more they knew Him, the more they marveled. Can anyone say anything less today? Indeed not!

Jesus Heals Two Demonized Men (Matt. 8:28-34)

(cf. Mark 5:1-20 and Luke 8:26-39)

It must have been a pathetic sight to see two men separated from their families and living in the tombs because of demonic problems. Their home was a mere cave. Hiding from people, like criminals, this desperate pair of men sought Jesus for help. In a prolonged encounter, each is set free to return home as a transformed man. How desperately Jesus longs to heal people of such demonic bondage and to reestablish them in their homes and communities.

Here are ten surface matters which everyone ought to see in this account (including the parallel descriptions in Mark and Luke): (1) evil spirits are a terrible reality which Jesus never denied; (2) evil spirits can enter a human body and distort its normal functions; (3) evil spirits are quite capable of speaking through the mouth of the one they indwell; (4) evil spirits recognize the superiority of Jesus over them; (5) evil spirits know their destiny is fixed, and that they will be sent to a place of torment; (6) Jesus could command the demons to depart and to go elsewhere; (7) once the demons leave an individual, that person will return to a normal physical and mental state; (8) people will frequently fail to understand or appreciate the ministry of exorcism; (9) when someone is delivered from demonic bondage, he will desire to testify for Christ; and (10) the best place to share a genuine spiritual experience is at home and with those who can see the transformation firsthand.

I. *The Encounter (8:28)*

> **28When he arrived at the other side in the region of the Gadarenes,[a] two demon-possessed men coming from the tombs met him. They were so violent that no one could pass that way.**

Region of Gadarenes. The precise site of this story is uncertain, though a location on the southeast edge of the Sea of Galilee is the most popular suggestion. See the map in the section of the commentary that covers Matt. 4:12-16; the Gadarenes will be found in the region of Decapolis.

Demon-Possessed Men. Most authors who write today on the subject of demons are careful to point out that the traditional rendering of "demon possession" is better

---

a 28 Some manuscripts *Gergesenes;* others *Gerasenes*

understood by the translation, "demonized." This latter term simply denotes demonic influence or control, without any thought of ownership (or possession).

This translation also serves to clear up another problem. For a long period it has been taught that some people are *oppressed* by demons, others are *obsessed* by them, and still others are *possessed* by these evil spirits. Again, the pure language of the Bible is against this trilevel gradation of demonization. According to the Scriptures a person is either demonized or he is not demonized. No thought is given to degrees of demonization.

Five terms are used in the King James Version of the Bible to refer to demonic influence:

1. You can be *vexed* by demons (Matt. 15:22; Luke 6:18; Acts 5:16).
2. You can be *oppressed* by demons (Acts 10:38).
3. You can be *with* (Greek: *en*) a demon; that is, you can be within the scope of a demon's influence or control (Mark 1:23; 5:2).
4. You can *have* a demon indwelling your body (Matt. 11:18; Mark 7:25; 9:17; Luke 4:33; 8:27; 13:11; John 7:20; 8:48, 49, 52; 10:20, 21).
5. You can be demon *possessed*/demonized; that is, under demonic influence or control, to varying degrees (Matt. 4:24; 8:16, 28, 33; 9:32; 12:22; Mark 1:32; 5:15, 16, 18; Luke 8:36).

These five usages are synonymous. To *have* a demon is the same as being *vexed* by a demon. And so forth.

A careful examination of these passages will disclose to you the fact that no distinction is made between internal activities (supposedly possession) and external activities (supposedly oppression). In each instance the demonic work occurs *within* the person under attack.

II. *The Exchange and Exorcism (8:29-32)*

> **29"What do you want with us, Son of God?" they shouted. "Have you come here to torture us before the appointed time?"**
> **30Some distance from them a large herd of pigs was feeding. 31The demons begged Jesus, "If you drive us out, send us into the herd of pigs."**
> **32He said to them, "Go!" So they came out and went into the pigs, and the whole herd rushed down the steep bank into the lake and died in the water.**

Have You Come to Torture Us? The demon's speech displays the uniqueness of Jesus in two ways: (1) they address Him as the Son of God—indicating His position as the God-man; and (2) they acknowledge Him to be the one who can cast them into the abyss—indicating His power over the demonic world.

Further, the awareness of the demons regarding prophetic matters is fascinating. First, they know there is a fixed time for them to be sentenced (cf. Matt. 25:41, 46; Jude 6). Second, they know their judgmental sentence will result in "torment"—that is, retribution for their offenses against God (cf. Rev. 20:1-10).

The Demons Begged Jesus. We see several interesting points in this episode: (1) Demons can speak through the ones they indwell. In fact, they can even present a verbal fight in order to keep from being cast out of their body-home. (2) There were many demons in these two persons (a "legion," or more than 6,000, according to the

EXORCISM IN THE BIBLE

Scripture	Victim(s)	Key Phrase (KJV)	Believer or Unbeliever	Symptom(s)
Matt. 4:24	All	Possessed	?	Sickness
Matt. 12:22	Man	Possessed	?	Blindness and muteness
Matt. 15:22-28 Mark 7:25	Daughter	Vexed with Had	?	Suffering
Mark 1:23-26 Luke 4:33-35	Man	With Had	?	Uncleanness Impurity
Luke 4:40, 41 Matt. 8:16	All	Came out Possessed	?	Sickness
Luke 6:17, 18	Multitude	With	?	Vexation
Luke 8:26-39 Matt. 8:28-34 Mark 5:2-20	Man	Had Possessed With	?	Extraordinary strength, wild, screaming self-torture, nakedness, mental disorder
Luke 9:38-42 Mark 9:14-29 Matt. 17:14-18	Son	Has	?	Fear, screaming pain, foaming at mouth, uncontrolled body movement, muteness, grinding teeth, suicidal impulses
Luke 11:14	Man	Gone out	?	Muteness
Luke 13:10-16	Woman	Had/Bound	Believer	Crippled body
Acts 5:14-16	All	With	?	Sickness/Vexation
Acts 8:5-7	Many	Possessed	?	Sickness
Acts 16:16-18	Woman	Possessed	?	Fortunetelling
Acts 19:11, 12	?	Went out	?	Sickness

parallel accounts!). Some were exceedingly powerful, while others were clearly intelligent. (3) Even Jesus could not expell these demons with a single, calm, authoritative command. Instead, at least in this case, it required some time and work in order to remove the demons from the bodies of these men.

They Went into the Pigs. Why did Jesus honor the request of the demons to be cast into the herd of swine? Several answers have been offered: (1) The Jews (assuming the herd was owned by Jews) had no business raising swine, since God's law forbade eating them (Lev. 11:7). Even if the herd of pigs was not owned by Jews, however, it would be appropriate for Jesus to cast out the demons into animals that Jews considered unclean. (2) Jesus could not cast them into hell because it was not yet time, just as the demons had indicated. This will not occur before Jesus' Second Coming. Apparently, persons today who teach that demons can be cast into hell are a bit premature in their sentencing. (Note the chart entitled "Exorcism in the Bible.")

III. *The Excitement (Matt. 8:33, 34)*

> **33Those tending the pigs ran off, went into the town and reported all this, including what had happened to the demon-possessed men. 34Then the whole town went out to meet Jesus. And when they saw him, they pleaded with him to leave their region.**

Sometimes divine miracles frighten people more than demonic madness. The people could see the complete restoration of the formerly demonized men (they were fully clothed and in their right mind), but their hearts could not accept the cost for these healings—a herd of pigs. Somehow it struck them as being too high a price. How pathetic the logic of certain self-centered people is. They always prefer their earthly goods to heavenly blessings. Tragically, they ask Jesus to leave them alone, and so He departs.

Special Study: Detecting Demonization

Just as demons vary in their degrees of wickedness, (Matt. 12:43-45), so too, demonic victims will yield varying manifestations. Some persons will seem perfectly normal, while others will express themselves as madmen. The reason for this difference is traced to the kind and number of demons actually exercising influence in a given person.

Perhaps the chief characteristic of demonization is the projection of a new personality in the victim. Whenever a person begins to exhibit a "Dr. Jekyll and Mr. Hyde" personality, this is a clue to demonic activity.

When a believer is habitually plagued with uncontrollable thoughts, speech, worry, resentment, hatred, doubts, indecision, lust, lying, addictions, or other sinful inclinations, then the source of these forceful compulsions may be demonic. The body, too, is quite capable of manifesting these traits without Satan (Gal. 5:19-21; Col. 3:5-9; Rom. 1:24-32). Still, the possibility of a demonic base must not be ruled out.

If a believer's problem is not demonic, but fleshly, then it will yield to sincere prayer and submission to God. For example, fear, if it is fleshly, will disappear when filled with the Holy Spirit (2 Tim. 1:7; 1 John 4:18). If the fear, however, is demonic, then an exorcism may be required.

The most certain method for detecting demonic activity is through the gift of the Spirit called "the discerning of spirits" (1 Cor. 12:10). Any person with this gift is capable of distinguishing between that which is from ourselves and that which is from God or from Satan. Naturally, any person with this gift should be sought out if a demonic problem is considered to be likely and no relief from the problem has yet been secured.

A Paralytic Is Forgiven and Healed (Matt. 9:1-8)

(cf. Mark 2:1-12 and Luke 5:17-26)

We observe three of Jesus' miracles in this scene: (1) the forgiveness of sins; (2) the reading of people's minds; and (3) the healing of a sick man.

It is sometimes stated that Jesus could perform such miraculous feats because He was God. But this line of reasoning ignores certain teachings of the Scripture. When Jesus became a human being, He emptied himself of His divine prerogatives (though He did *not* empty himself of His deity—Phil. 2:5-8).

Stated differently, Jesus, of himself, could heal no one. He needed to rely upon the Holy Spirit as much as any other person. This is why Luke says, in his parallel account of this episode, that "the power of [or from] the Lord was present for him to heal the sick" (5:17).

It is inaccurate to believe that whenever Jesus desired to do so He could switch over to His divine nature. This is not the case. There is little virtue in stating that Jesus became a man if He could, at any moment, retreat to His divine refuge for help. Jesus was a man, through and through (Heb. 2:14, 15; 4:14-16). The miracles He performed were accomplished in the same manner that the church (the mystical body of Christ) brings miracles to its needy people today—by the gifts of the Holy Spirit (Rom. 12:4-8; 1 Cor. 12-14).

I. *The Forgiving (9:1-3)*

9 Jesus stepped into a boat, crossed over and came to his own town.
2 Some men brought to him a paralytic, lying on a mat. When Jesus
saw their faith, he said to the paralytic, "Take heart, son; your sins are
forgiven."
3 At this, some of the teachers of the law said to themselves, "This
fellow is blaspheming!"

His Own Town. Jesus' home at this time was Capernaum (Matt. 4:12-13). We know very little about this city; even its location is a subject of debate. A modern site called Tell Hum serves as the most popular location—on the northwestern side of the Sea of Galilee. This must have been an important city in Jesus' day. It had its own tax office (Matt. 9:9) and a hundred Roman soldiers (Matt. 8:5). It was also the home of James and John (Matt. 4:21; Mark 1:19). Jesus performed numerous miracles here (Matt. 9:1-26; 17:24-27; John 4:46-53; 6:17-25, 59). On the whole, however, its residents were unresponsive, and as a result, they were subject to Jesus' strong prophetic rebuke (Matt. 11:23).

Jesus Saw Their Faith. One of the beautiful facets of this story is the fact that genuine faith can be *seen*. Jesus did not *hear* their faith or *feel* their faith—He could *see* it. Real faith is visible to the human eye. It is not something private or mystical. Rather, it is open, public and active (cf. Acts 14:9; James 2:18).

Matthew does not record what Jesus saw in these men that caused Him to proclaim the presence of their faith. But Mark and Luke each relate how these men had to carry their friend upon the roof of the house and then remove the roofing in order to lower him before Jesus. The typical home of Palestine had a flat roof of wooden beams, covered with brushwood and clay. It was easy to maintain, and provided a comfortable place for rest and reflection. Access to the roof was usually gained either through a ladder (for the poor people) or an attached stairway (for the wealthy).

It is sometimes stated that the faith of the sick man's friends was responsible for the miracle of forgiveness and healing. But this position is improbable. With few exceptions, Jesus only forgave and healed those who personally exercised faith in Him (Matt. 9:22, 29; etc.). It is more reasonable to assume that the word "their" includes the one who was sick.

Your Sins Are Forgiven. It is not stated why these four men brought their friend to Jesus. It is probable that they had heard of Jesus' healing power and, therefore, they sought Him to heal their companion. Regardless, Jesus' wisdom penetrates beyond the visible symptoms of being a paralytic. He sees a deeper malady in need of attention—the healing of forgiveness.

This profound illustration serves us notice that before we jump into prayer for what appears to be a problem, we should first investigate the matter more closely. Jesus was mature. He did not allow His senses to govern His decisions. Instead, He patiently got to the root of things before He spoke or acted. Naturally, we ought to do the same.

Jesus' response nearly brought the house down. It was unheard of to tell someone that his sins were forgiven. According to the narrow-mindedness of certain Jews, it was left up to God to decide whether or not anyone's sins should be forgiven. No one, they thought, could ever pronounce another person's sins forgiven. But Jesus wanted to assure this person that because of his faith he was placed in right relationship with God. By faith he was made a member in good standing among the citizens of the Kingdom.

II. *The Healing (9:4-8)*

4Knowing their thoughts, Jesus said, "Why do you entertain evil thoughts in your hearts? 5Which is easier: to say, 'Your sins are forgiven,' or to say, 'Get up and walk'? 6But so that you may know that the Son of Man has authority on earth to forgive sins. . . ." Then he said to the paralytic, "Get up, take your mat and go home." 7And the man got up and went home. 8When the crowd saw this, they were filled with awe; and they praised God, who had given such authority to men.

Knowing Their Thoughts. Jesus was apparently given a word of knowledge from the Holy Spirit about the thoughts of certain ones present in the house (cf. 1 Cor. 12:8). He was made aware of their mental anger. Although their faces and tongues made them appear to be innocent, it was their evil thoughts that betrayed them. We must never evaluate others, or even ourselves, by how we look or speak, but by how we think in our hearts.

Which Is Easier. It was a common theology in Jesus' day for people to associate sickness with sin. In other words, it was believed that people were made ill as an act of divine chastisement because of their sins. Only through forgiveness could the chastisement (or sickness) be removed. So, if Jesus pronounced a person forgiven, then, in order to support His assertion, the individual had to rise and be healed. While Jesus sometimes rejected this exclusive type of logic because of its narrowness (cf. John 9:1-3), He never discarded it altogether (cf. John 5:14). In this particular case, the cause for the man's sickness probably was sin. Therefore, after seeing the faith of this man, Jesus knew he would be both forgiven and healed.

In order to better understand the nature of sickness and healing, a chart showing the four causes for illness, along with varying cures, is provided. (See the chart entitled "The Four Causes of Sickness and Their Cures.") A balanced knowledge of these matters is indispensable in providing a proper discernment and remedy for each situation.

THE FOUR CAUSES OF SICKNESS AND THEIR CURES

I. People Become Sick Because of Sin

Scriptures	Symptoms	Specific Sins	Cures
1. Lev. 26:14-46	Consumption, fever that wastes away the eyes and soul	Disobedience	Confession of iniquity
2. Deut. 28:15-68	Consumption, fever, inflammation, boils, hemorrhoids, scab, itch, madness, blindness, bewilderment of heart, miserable and chronic sicknesses	Disobedience; service without joy and service without a glad heart	
3. Num. 16:41-50	Plague	Grumbling against God's leaders	Prayer and atonement
4. Num. 21:4-9	Snake bites	Grumbling against God's leaders	Intercessory prayer and personal faith
5. 1 Cor. 11:17-34	Weakness, sickness, and death	Improper treatment of the Lord's body (Christians), and failure to examine oneself	Considerateness
6. James 5:14-16	Weakness/sickness	Failure to confess faults	Calling for elders' prayers, repentance, calling for Christians' prayers

II. People Become Sick Because of Natural Factors

Scriptures	Symptoms	Specific Factors	Cures
1. [illegible]	Blindness	Old Age	Not cured
2. Gen. 48:10	Blindness	Old Age	Not cured
3. 1 Sam. 3:2; 4:15	Blindness	Old Age	Not cured
4. 1 Kings 14:4	Blindness	Old Age	Not cured
5. Phil. 2:26-30	Near death	Overworked	Prayer (and rest?)
6. 1 Tim. 5:23	Frequent weaknesses	Unknown	A little wine (cf. Prov. 31:6)

III. People Become Sick Because of God's Sovereign Activity

Scriptures	Symptoms	Specific Causes	Cures
1. John 9:1-3	Blindness	To glorify God in the healing	Mud pack on eyes and washing
2. John 11:1-4	Sick to death	To glorify God in the healing	Jesus prays
3. Job 2:1-7; 31:35-37; 38:1-42:6	Boils	To demonstrate God can do anything with his own, and to teach Satan certain principles	Unknown

IV. People Become Sick Because of Satan's Activity

Scriptures	Symptoms	Specific Reasons	Cures
1. Matt. 12:22	Blind and Deaf	Unknown	Not stated
2. Matt. 17:14-18	Epileptic	Unknown	Rebuking the demon
3. Mark 5:1-20	Mental disorder	Unknown	Commanding demons to leave, after getting their name
4. Luke 13:10-16	Crippled body	Unknown	Pronouncement of faith
5. Acts 5:14-16	Sick/Afflicted	Unknown	Peter's shadow
6. Acts 19:11, 12	Various illnesses	Unknown	Handkerchiefs and aprons taken to sick after they had touched Paul

The Calling of Matthew (Matt. 9:9-13)

(cf. Mark 2:13-17 and Luke 5:27-32)

Matthew writes few words about himself. He humbly notes only that Jesus kindly invited him—a hated tax collector—to follow Him, and that he accepted this gracious invitation.

At least two practical matters should be noted in this episode. One, Matthew had to leave certain things behind in order to follow Jesus. The tax collector's trade was not without its rewards. There was money and a degree of authority. But Jesus told Matthew that these rewards of ambition were to be abandoned. It cannot be said that following Jesus is free from changes. Indeed, living for Jesus may require many personal alterations. Two, Matthew gave up nothing that was not replaced with something still greater. His surrender to Jesus meant gaining a new life of honor, dignity and fulfillment.

I. *The Meeting (9:9)*

> **9 As Jesus went on from there, he saw a man named Matthew sitting at the tax collector's booth. "Follow me," he told him, and Matthew got up and followed him.**

The Tax Collector's Booth. It was a common custom in biblical times for countries that were in subjection to greater military powers to be taxed. The Jews frequently found themselves being taxed, especially under the rule of Rome. The purpose of the taxation was simple—to deplete the captives' resources in order to keep them weak, and to enrich the empire's reserves in order to keep it strong. Naturally, these tax gatherers were most hated men. Matthew (also called Levi) was such a man.

Rome had a tax for everything imaginable. There were taxes on property, animals, real estate and slaves. Taxes were due on both imports and exports. Even crops, income, the use of some roads and entering towns were taxed. Collecting these various fees required a massive staff of tax agents. In order to most efficiently handle the situation, tax franchises were sold to the highest bidders. These men were then given a certain amount to collect. Exactly how much should be collected from the individuals to be taxed were decisions left to the tax collectors. Injustice was inevitable. The tax gatherers got rich, and the citizens were robbed.

Matthew collected taxes from a booth along the main road between Acre and Damascus. His specific duty was to collect taxes on the goods that were being transported on this road. From this rather simple labor Matthew probably made a lucrative income.

Follow Me. It is probable that Matthew had both seen and heard quite a bit of Jesus, since his tax booth was so close to Jesus' home in Capernaum. Perhaps Matthew had listened to Jesus on numerous occasions. Regardless of the exact details, Matthew was now ready to be Jesus' disciple.

The brevity of the account is striking—"he got up and followed." There is no resistance, no debating, no questioning—just obedience. It is as if Matthew had been waiting for this priceless opportunity. When it arrived, he did not negotiate, but he simply accepted Jesus' terms unconditionally. How our lives ought to reflect this same excellent disposition.

II. *The Dining (9:10-13)*

> **10While Jesus was having dinner at Matthew's house, many tax collectors and "sinners" came and ate with him and his disciples. 11When the Pharisees saw this, they asked his disciples, "Why does your teacher eat with tax collectors and 'sinners'?"**
>
> **12On hearing this, Jesus said, "It is not the healthy who need a doctor, but the sick. 13But go and learn what this means: 'I desire mercy, not sacrifice.'[a] For I have not come to call the righteous, but sinners."**

Why Does Your Teacher Eat with Tax Collectors and "Sinners"? The Pharisees could find fault with everything and everyone, especially with Jesus. In this case, they thought He was overdoing it by associating with those who neither profess a faith nor prove the presence of any faith by their actions. Jesus, on the other hand, retorted with a sharp but subtle bit of irony: "It is not the healthy who need a doctor, but the sick." In other words, "Since you Pharisees are so healthy (or you believe yourselves to be so healthy) that you have no need of my words or works, I will minister to those who do need them and who will receive them."

I Desire Mercy, Not Sacrifice. What a sting! Jesus announced to His critics the need to go and learn the meaning of Hos. 6:6. They probably could have quoted this passage, but Jesus told them they were yet unable to live it. So, He instructed them to go and take a serious look at the Scriptures, and to see if their lives measured up.

How pitiful a religious life is if it follows all the rules by the letter but never learns the inner quality of mercy. The Pharisees specialized in rituals, but they failed in relationships. God is not nearly so interested in our sacrifices as He is in our attitude and service toward others (cf. Ps. 51:16, 17).

---

a 13 Hosea 6:6

Facts About Fasting **(Matt. 9:14-17)**

(cf. Mark 2:18-22 and Luke 5:33-39)

Within Jewish society there was a diversity of convictions and practices concerning their faith. The Sadducees, the Pharisees, the Zealots, the Essenes and the disciples of John the Baptist each held to differing points of view. Jesus' teachings differed from each of these existing groups, at least to some degree. It was natural, therefore, that Jesus and His disciples would set the pace for a whole new slant to the Jewish faith.

I. *The Immediate Problem (9:14)*

> **14 Then John's disciples came and asked him, "How is it that we and the Pharisees fast, but your disciples do not fast?"**

John's disciples were confused about the actions of Jesus' disciples. While the disciples of both the Pharisees and John the Baptist fasted twice a week, Jesus' disciples did not fast at all. John's adherents thought this common tradition ought to be observed by every spiritual person.

II. *The Present Picture (9:15)*

> **15 Jesus answered, "How can the guests of the bridegroom mourn while he is with them? The time will come when the bridegroom will be taken from them; then they will fast.**

Jesus said, in effect, that everything has a proper timing. He revealed that the time while He walked on earth was the wrong time to fast. His period of ministry on earth was a time for rejoicing. It was the time the prophets had longed to see. Later, after His departure, however, the time would come when it would be appropriate to fast. (A brief doctrinal sketch on the subject of fasting is included at the close of this study. Also refer to the notes on Matt. 6:16-18.)

III. *The Eternal Principle (9:16, 17)*

> **16 "No one sews a patch of unshrunk cloth on an old garment, for the patch will pull away from the garment, making the tear worse.**
> **17 Neither do men pour new wine into old wineskins. If they do, the skins**

will burst, the wine will run out and the wineskins will be ruined. No, they pour new wine into new wineskins, and both are preserved."

Jesus' words and works were not traditional, to say the least. In fact, Jesus' ideals were often completely new to the current trends of the religious people. Jesus was quite aware of this situation. He knew His practices would be considered radical by some, but He was determined not to affix His new message to the old traditions of religious rituals, even though it meant occasional confusion and hostility.

The Christian message was revolutionary. It still is, especially for those who are willing to act upon its message.

Special Study: The Doctrine of Fasting

1. *Perception of Fasting.* The Hebrew (or Old Testament) term for fasting means "to completely abstain from food." Sometimes the phrase "to afflict one's soul" (KJV) was used instead of fasting, but the result was the same—abstinence from food (Lev. 16:29). The Greek (or New Testament) term for fasting means "not to eat." It is used of involuntary abstinence, in which case hunger is in view (2 Cor. 6:5; 11:27); and it is used of voluntary abstinence, in which case fasting is in view.

2. *Practice of Fasting.* The Bible mentions the practice of fasting no less than eighty-one times. It was practiced by Abraham's servant (Gen. 24:33), Moses (Exod. 34:28), all of Israel on the Day of Atonement (Lev. 16:29, 31), each Nazarite (Num. 6:3, 4), Hannah (1 Sam. 1:7, 8), Jonathan (1 Sam. 20:34), Saul (1 Sam. 28:20), David (2 Sam. 1:12), Uriah (2 Sam. 11:11), Elijah (1 Kings 19:8), Ahab (1 Kings 21:27), Ezra (Ezra; 10:6), Nehemiah (Neh. 1:4), Esther (Esther 4:16), Daniel (Dan. 9:3), Darius (Dan. 6:18), Joel (Joel 1:14), Jesus (Matt. 4:2), John the Baptist (Matt. 11:18), Anna (Luke 2:37), certain prophets and teachers in the church at Antioch (Acts 13:1-4), Paul (Acts 27:21, 33) and others.

3. *Purpose of Fasting.* There seem to be three essential purposes for which a person may fast. First, to produce power—Matt. 4:2. Second, to perfect prayer—Mark 9:29. Third, to penetrate problems—2 Sam. 12:16-23. Actually, each of these purposes overlaps and no sharp line of separation can be drawn between them.

4. *Publicity of Fasting.* Fasting is never to be done in order to show off before people. Jesus denounced this hypocritical manner of fasting (Matt. 6:16-18). This does not mean, however, that all fasting must be kept a tight secret in order to be effective. Often all of Israel was called to fast together (Joel 2:15, 16). We may tell others if we are fasting, as long as it is done in the spirit of humility and edification.

5. *Prolongation of Fasting.* There is no fixed duration for a fast. A fast may involve

only a meal, or it may be stretched out over several weeks. The important point to remember is that duration does not necessarily imply greater spirituality or better chances for success in prayer. *The key is personal obedience to the voice of God.* If He instructs you to fast for a day, then adding another day is valueless (if not counter-productive). The discernment of another mature Christian should be sought to determine whether to undertake a prolonged fast.

6. *Promises of Fasting.* In Isaiah 58 there is a nine-point list of the blessings that accompany spiritual fasting. See if you can locate them. They will be found in verses 8 through 11.[1]

Jesus Heals a Girl and a Woman (Matt. 9:18-26)

(cf. Mark 5:21-43 and Luke 8:40-56)

The subject of healing is a matter that lies near to the heart of God. The Scriptures state that Jesus came to reveal the Father (John 1:18; 14:9). To look upon and to listen to Jesus, then, is to fix your attention on God himself. Of Jesus it is said, "he had compassion on them and healed their sick" (Matt. 14:14). Healing was important in Jesus' ministry because it was (and is) important to God.

Jesus was eminently practical. His doctrines were not farfetched, nor did they rest solely in some distant tomorrow after death. Rather, Jesus ministered directly to the needs of everyday people. In these stories we see two remarkable healings. They show us how much Jesus is concerned with the typical troubles that touch each of us.

I. *The Information (9:18, 19)*

> **18While he was saying this, a ruler came and knelt before him and said, "My daughter has just died.[a] But come and put your hand on her, and she will live." 19Jesus got up and went with him, and so did his disciples.**

The synagogue was ruled by a board of elders. It was their duty to give guidance and maintain order in their meetings. It was the daughter of one of these officials who was sick. Illness is a stranger to no one. It visits the rich and the poor, the mighty and the weak, the spiritual and the carnal.

[1]This information on fasting has been taken from *The Victor Bible Source Book* by Stephen D. Swihart (Wheaton, Ill.: Victor Books, 1977), pp. 145-151.

a 18 Or *daughter is now dying*

This leader had strong faith. He was confident that Jesus could help him and his family. He did not approach Jesus declaring his status, but he came confessing his faith. This is the only acceptable approach we have to Jesus.

II. *The Interruption (9:20-22)*

20Just then a woman who had been subject to bleeding for twelve
years came up behind him and touched the edge of his cloak. 21She said
to herself, "If I only touch his cloak, I will be healed."
22Jesus turned and saw her. "Take heart, daughter," he said, "your
faith has healed you." And the woman was healed from that moment.

A Woman Touched the Edge of His Cloak. In the process of traveling to Jairus's home, Jesus is momentarily interrupted by a desperate woman. Her action may seem a bit bizarre. Still, she knew that Jesus, and only Jesus, held the answer to her prolonged and frustrating illness.

"If I can only touch him," she reasoned, "then my sickness will disappear." What faith! She worked her way through the crowd until she got near Jesus and touched the edge (or hem) of His cloak. The Mosaic Law stipulated that each Jew was to wear a tassel on the four corners of his outer garment. The purpose of these tassels was to remind the wearer, as well as those who saw them, to keep God's laws (Num. 15:38, 39; Deut. 22:12). Certainly this woman could see an obedient walk in Jesus, and she, too, desired to be pure before God. So, she touched the hem of His garment, where the tassels would be attached.

Notice the two effects of this miracle from the parallel accounts: (1) The woman knew she was immediately healed. (2) Jesus instantly sensed the departure of power from His body. In the former instance there is the reception of a medical transformation; in the second instance there is the release of a healing transfusion. Like the mysterious contact between the north and south poles of a magnet, so there was a distinct contact between Jesus and this woman.

Jesus Turned. Jesus sought out the identity of this woman. The cause for this was an important matter—to show that faith caused her healing, not the touching of His garment. To state this may sound overly simplistic and unnecessary, but the fact is that too many persons place the mechanics of the miracle on a higher plane than the faith that brought it about.

How little Jesus requires of us in order to receive a miracle. We must merely touch Him with our faith. That is all. He is not concerned about our positions or possessions. He simply wants to know that we have faith (cf. Heb. 11:6).

III. *The Incomprehension (9:23-26)*

23When Jesus entered the ruler's house and saw the flute players and
the noisy crowd, 24he said, "Go away. The girl is not dead but asleep."
But they laughed at him. 25After the crowd had been put outside, he
went in and took the girl by the hand, and she got up. 26News of this
spread through all that region.

The people and circumstances which surround us play such active roles in shaping our current level of faith. Jesus knew this. It is natural then, after observing that many thought the girl to be dead, that He reassured Jairus so he would continue in his faith. How essential it is for each of us to persevere in our faith—unhindered by voices and situations that lead in opposite directions. In the end there was a miracle, just as Jesus had promised. We must keep from wavering until we hear the final words from Christ himself.

The Blind and Dumb Are Healed (Matt. 9:27-34)

The Gospels are filled with fascinating and miraculous stories. Why? Because Jesus wants you and me to understand that He is vitally interested in real, everyday people who have real, everyday problems. He wants us to know He can do something for us, if we will only believe He is able to help us.

The story of Jesus healing the two blind men may be viewed as follows: their cry (v. 27), their confession (v. 28), their cure (vv. 29, 30a), their charge (v. 30b), and their communication (v. 31).

The story of Jesus healing the man who could not speak may be summarized as follows: the demonization of the man (v. 32), the departure of the demon (v. 33a), the delight of the crowd (v. 33b), and the deception of the Pharisees (v. 34).

I. *The Blind Men Are Healed (9:27-31)*

27As Jesus went on from there, two blind men followed him, calling
out, "Have mercy on us, Son of David!"
28When he had gone indoors, the blind men came to him, and he asked
them, "Do you believe that I am able to do this?"
"Yes, Lord," they replied.
29Then he touched their eyes and said, "According to your faith will it

be done to you"; [30]and their sight was restored. Jesus warned them
sternly, "See that no one knows about this." [31]But they went out and
spread the news about him all over that region.

Son of David. See notes on Matt. 1:1 for details.

Do You Believe I Am Able? First, notice what Jesus did *not* say. He did not ask, "Do you believe it is my *will* to heal you?" Second, notice what Jesus *did* say. He asked, "Do you believe I am *able* to heal you?" It was not a matter of Jesus' *will* but of His *ability* that is focused here for us. Which is easier to believe in—His will or His ability? His ability, naturally. You cannot know Jesus' will for everyone all of the time, but you can always know His power, His ability. This is all Jesus asks from us in order to receive whatever His will is for us.

According to Your Faith. For comments on these words, see Matt. 8:13.

See That No One Knows About This. The reason behind this stern advice is not stated. There are several possible explanations for His words here. Jesus may have been concerned that spreading the news regarding this miracle would result in (1) a misplaced emphasis on physical miracles, (2) a closed door in other communities because of the jealousy of its religious leaders, and/or (3) a premature and misunderstood ambition on the part of the crowds to make Him their king by sheer force. One, two or all three of these ideas may have been in Jesus' mind (cf. Matt. 16:1-4; John 6:14, 15; 7:6-8).

II. *The Dumb Man Is Healed (9:32-34)*

[32]While they were going out, a man who was demon-possessed and
could not talk was brought to Jesus. [33]And when the demon was driven
out, the man who had been dumb spoke. The crowd was amazed and
said, "Nothing like this has ever been seen in Israel."
[34]But the Pharisees said, "It is by the prince of demons that he drives
out demons."

Demon-Possessed. See Matt. 8:28 for comments.

The Prince of Demons. This is a designation for Satan. The Pharisees were not content to disagree with Jesus; they also sought to ridicule His works by calling them miracles performed by the power of Satan. This is an unthinkable accusation, but some people still falsely charge today's miracles to the same source. We must not make hastily drawn conclusions about the supernatural, lest we join hands with the Pharisees in a presumptuous and critical spirit. The attitude of our heart must be one of charity, not vindictiveness. There will always be some people with whom we do not fully agree; yet, if they reside under the banner of Christ's Lordship, we must receive them as brothers and sisters in the faith.

Praying for More Workers (Matt. 9:35-38)

Jesus was consumed with a passion for transforming lives. What a need there is today for people with an identical passion—people who will join Jesus as a disciplined worker in meeting the needs of people. Many persons are content to sit and leave this work for others to do. But Jesus' model life constantly challenges us to be more and more devoted to His cause. And our prayer is that others will capture this grand vision and give themselves to the task of introducing people of all ages to God's glorious Kingdom of righteousness, peace and joy (cf. Rom. 14:17).

I. *Declaration of Power (9:35)*

> **35Jesus went through all the towns and villages, teaching in their synagogues, preaching the good news of the kingdom and healing every disease and sickness.**

Jesus came to teach and to heal people. His ministry was profound, powerful and, most of all, it was people-centered. No one could come into contact with Jesus and be left the same. Fortunately, His labors were conducted tirelessly. Jesus traveled to every town and village possible—both large and small. He went to everyone. How this illustration ought to burn deeply and brightly in the spirit of each one who calls himself a disciple of Christ.

II. *Demonstration of Pity (9:36)*

> **36When he saw the crowds, he had compassion on them, because they were harassed and helpless, like sheep without a shepherd.**

Beyond all the obvious things that can be noted about Jesus, there is something that goes far deeper, into His very heart. Jesus was stimulated and driven by a heart full of compassion. He could look at the face of each member of His audiences and see people who were "harassed and helpless." This condition greatly disturbed Jesus. He labored relentlessly to provide the leadership, the wisdom, the truth and the miracles that were necessary to help these spiritually impoverished people. He gave them himself, without compromise and without conditions.

III. *Determination in Prayer (9:37, 38)*

[37]Then he said to his disciples, "The harvest is plentiful but the workers are few. [38]Ask the Lord of the harvest, therefore, to send out workers into his harvest field."

Jesus made three powerful statements about His ministry. The principles found here can be (indeed, they must be) applied to each Christian and to every local church.

First, Jesus said, "the harvest is plentiful." There is an abundance of available crops. Hurting people can be found everywhere. Needs must be satisified everywhere. There is no shortage of work.

Second, Jesus said, "the workers are few"—in number. The demand is greater than the supply. There are more people with needs than there are people to help meet the needs. The amount of work to be done is great, but the need for more workers is even greater. There must be more workers if Jesus' job—the Church's job—is to be fully accomplished.

Third, Jesus said, we must ask "the Lord of the harvest to send out workers." The solution to the problem of needing more workers is prayer—earnest and specific petition. The desire of God's heart is exposed here. He sees the problem. And He is willing to commission more laborers. But we must ask; we must pray them into this service.

These three points cannot be stressed too strongly. They must be taught again and again. And they must be practiced until Jesus comes!

The Twelve Disciples: Their Call and Commission (Matt. 10:1-42)

(cf. Mark 6:7-13; 13:9-13; and Luke 9:1-16; 21:12-19)

It has been observed that flash powder will make a more brilliant light than the arc lamp, but you cannot use it to light your home, for instance, because it does not last long enough to be of any value. This passage teaches us that consistency, stability and steadfastness are more vital to success than brilliancy.

The same principle can be applied to Christian service. Eager beginners are desirable, but in the end it is the consistently faithful worker who gets the job done. It is not necessarily the dynamic worker who is truly used of God, but the person who never misses a beat in Christ's cadence call.

I. *Their Call (10:1-4)*

10 He called his twelve disciples to him and gave them authority to drive out evil[a] spirits and to heal every disease and sickness.
2These are the names of the twelve apostles: first, Simon (who is called Peter) and his brother Andrew; James son of Zebedee, and his brother
John; 3Philip and Bartholomew; Thomas and Matthew the tax collector;
James son of Alphaeus, and Thaddaeus; 4Simon the Zealot and Judas
Iscariot, who betrayed him.

Twelve Disciples/Twelve Apostles. Many people followed Jesus. His words and works won scores of people (John 4:1, 2). These adherents were called "disciples." This is a general designation for a learner and follower. (See Matt. 8:18-22 for a more thorough discussion on the subject of discipleship.)

Among Jesus' disciples a few men were selected to be called His "apostles." An apostle is someone who is *sent forth* with a special mission to accomplish. Twelve men were called into this unique service. The importance and complexity of this term merits amplification; therefore a "special study" has been prepared at the close of this unit.

The Men. The twelve men whom Jesus chose were unimpressive persons. None were abundantly rich. None were famous or had secular powers at their command. They were a rather simple lot. Perhaps their most redeeming quality was the fact that they listened to Jesus with a teachable spirit (excluding Judas Iscariot). Their minds and characters were not so fixed that they could not be changed or improved. They were willing to obey. Without any doubt, these qualities made them the best choices possible for such an important appointment.

Simon Peter, the impulsive leader who denied Christ, was a fisherman (Matt. 26:31-35, 69-75; Mark 1:16). Andrew, a follower of John the Baptist, and a fisherman by trade, was Simon's brother (John 1:40).

James, one of the sons of Zebedee, worked with his father in a fishing enterprise. John, who was James's brother and fellow worker, is believed to be the author of the Gospel and the letters that bear his name. Both James and John are addressed by Jesus as "sons of thunder," indicating their quick ability to be rough and tough (Mark 3:17).

Philip was a naive, shy, searching and sincere man (John 1:45; 6:5-7; 14:8). His vocation is not stated. Bartholomew (also called Nathaniel) was Philip's brother, and was praised by Jesus as having no deceit or falsehood (John 1:47).

Thomas was always direct, honest, devoted, and yet often perplexed, even doubting

---

a 1 Greek *unclean*

(John 11:16; 14:5; 20:24, 25). It is this apostle who has caused us to develop the phrase, "doubting Thomas." Matthew, the despised tax collector, became the author of the first Gospel. Interestingly, we do not possess a single word from Matthew's lips, but we hold a book from his pen.

James, the son of Alphaeus, is unknown in the Scriptures beyond his mention in the listings of the twelve disciples. Thaddaeus's life is equally obscure with that of James.

Simon, called the Zealot, is so designated because he belonged to a party of enthusiastic men who sought to overpower Rome and to deliver Israel from her political enemies. Judas Iscariot, the treasurer for the twelve, betrayed Christ (John 12:1-6).

There they are—diverse in their backgrounds, but devoted in their common mission. These men were destined to change the course of the whole world for the rest of time.

II. *Their Commission (10:5-42)*
A. *Its Sphere (10:5, 6).*

5These twelve Jesus sent out with the following instructions: "Do not go among the Gentiles or enter any town of the Samaritans. 6Go rather to the lost sheep of Israel.

The Gentiles. This is a general designation for any body of people who are not Jews. Stated in geographic terms, the twelve apostles were instructed in their witnessing campaign to go only to the territories of Galilee and Judea (and probably only to the former area, since they were already there, and because Samaria was located between them and Judea).

The Samaritans. When King Solomon died, the nation of twelve tribes became divided. Two tribes in the South (then collectively called Judah) kept their capital in Jerusalem. The ten tribes in the North (then collectively called Israel), forming an independent nation, chose Samaria as its capital city. In 722 B.C. these northern tribes were conquered by the Assyrians. At that time more than 27,000 Jews were deported to other lands, while other captives of Assyria were imported to this territory. The result was intermarriage between Jews and Gentiles, a condition frowned upon by practically every Jew.

Lost Sheep of Israel. Sheep, the most common of all Israel's animals, are frequently employed in the Scriptures as being symbolic of the Jews (Ps. 74:1; 78:52; 79:13) and of Christians (John 10:7-30; 21:16, 17; Heb. 13:20; 1 Pet. 5:2). Here, the attention is drawn to those sheep of Israel who have gone astray and become spiritually dead (cf. Ps. 119:176; Isa. 53:6; Ezek. 34:16; Luke 15:4-7).

Jesus instructed His disciples to devote their present labors only to these individuals. Before you work in the areas of broad circumference, you must first work in the hub. The hub was Israel; the circumference was Samaria and the nations in the rest of the world. The restriction Jesus placed upon His disciples here was only temporary (cf. Matt. 28:19, 20). Once their training was completed it would be lifted. First things first. Today, Israel; tomorrow, the world.

B. *Its Service (10:7, 8).*

7As you go, preach this message: 'The kingdom of heaven is near.' 8Heal the sick, raise the dead, cleanse those who have leprosy,[a] drive out demons. Freely you have received, freely give.

The mission of the apostles involved both words and works. The words were to be *convicting*—God's Kingdom (or rule among men) is near. The works were to be *convincing*—the sick and the dead are to be restored.

The fact that this miraculous ministry continued throughout the entire period of the New Testament (and beyond) is undeniable. But it must also be remembered that the bestowal of these gifts upon the twelve apostles was not intended to represent a power that all believers could exercise at will (cf. Acts 4:33; 5:12; etc.). The ministry of these men was decidedly unique.

C. *Its Simplicity (10:9-15).*

9Do not take along any gold or silver or copper in your belts; 10take no bag for the journey, or extra tunic, or sandals or a staff; for the worker is worth his keep.

11"Whatever town or village you enter, search for some worthy person there and stay at his house until you leave. 12As you enter the home, give it your greeting. 13If the home is deserving, let your peace rest on it; if it is not, let your peace return to you. 14If anyone will not welcome you or listen to your words, shake the dust off your feet when you leave that home or town. 15I tell you the truth, it will be more bearable for Sodom and Gomorrah on the day of judgment than for that town.

The Worker Is Worth His Keep. The disciples had seen God provide for each need of Jesus; now they were to trust Him to meet their own needs. They were to take no money, only a message. Their ministry was to reflect utter sincerity and complete dependency. This was not a money-making venture. The purpose was simple—to help people find God's Kingdom.

Shake the Dust Off. The grace of showing hospitality to strangers was an expected courtesy in Jesus' day. It was not uncommon for unknown people to be taken in and

---

a 8 The Greek word was used for various diseases affecting the skin—not necessarily leprosy.

welcomed. But there are always exceptions to any rule. Sometimes the warmth of a heart grows cold, and the showing of hospitality disappears.

Whenever Jesus' disciples were refused the courtesy of a place to lodge and food to eat, they were to shake the very dust from their feet that came as a result of entering that village. The symbolism here is quite dramatic. The Jew commonly believed Gentiles were so detestable that even the dust of their territory was defiling. So, as an act of cleansing themselves, they would shake the dust from themselves after any encounter with a Gentile. Jesus turns the tables here by stating that those who refuse His message should have their dust removed from the disciples' feet. The effect of the gesture must have been next to enraging.

The Day of Judgment. Jesus declared that the residents of classically evil Sodom and Gomorrah will be given a less severe sentence on the Day of Judgment than the residents of the cities who resist the witness that is brought to them by Jesus' disciples. The reason for this is simple—the more light anyone receives, the greater his responsibility becomes for acting in accordance with the revelation he has (Luke 12:47, 48; Rev. 20:11-15).

D. *Its Severity (10:16-39).*

16"I am sending you out like sheep among wolves. Therefore be as
shrewd as snakes and as innocent as doves. 17But be on your guard
against men; they will hand you over to the local councils and flog you in
their synagogues. 18On my account you will be brought before governors
and kings as witnesses to them and to the Gentiles. 19But when they
arrest you, do not worry about what to say or how to say it. At that time
you will be given what to say, 20for it will not be you speaking, but the
Spirit of your Father speaking through you.

21"Brother will betray brother to death, and a father his child;
children will rebel against their parents and have them put to death.
22All men will hate you because of me, but he who stands firm to the end
will be saved. 23When you are persecuted in one place, flee to another. I
tell you the truth, you will not finish going through the cities of Israel
before the Son of Man comes.

24"A student is not above his teacher, nor a servant above his master.
25It is enough for the student to be like his teacher, and the servant like
his master. If the head of the house has been called Beelzebub,[a] how
much more the members of his household!

26"So do not be afraid of them. There is nothing concealed that will not
be disclosed, or hidden that will not be made known.27 What I tell you in

[a] 25 Greek *Beezeboul* or *Beelzeboul*

the dark, speak in the daylight; what is whispered in your ear, proclaim from the housetops. 28Do not be afraid of those who kill the body but cannot kill the soul. Rather, be afraid of the one who can destroy both soul and body in hell. 29Are not two sparrows sold for a penny[a]? Yet not one of them will fall to the ground apart from the will of your Father. 30And even the very hairs of your head are all numbered. 31So don't be afraid; you are worth more than many sparrows.

32"Whoever acknowledges me before men, I will also acknowledge him before my Father in heaven. 33But whoever disowns me before men, I will disown him before my Father in heaven.

34"Do not suppose that I have come to bring peace to the earth. I did not come to bring peace, but a sword. 35For I have come to turn

" 'a man against his father,
a daughter against her mother,
a daughter-in-law against her mother-in-law—
36a man's enemies will be the members of his
own household.'[b]

37"Anyone who loves his father or mother more than me is not worthy of me; anyone who loves his son or daughter more than me is not worthy of me; 38and anyone who does not take his cross and follow me is not worthy of me. 39Whoever finds his life will lose it, and whoever loses his life for my sake will find it.

In this speech of Jesus we see prophetic notes that go beyond the scope of this single mission (cf. v. 23, especially). Here are problems and promises that are to be remembered for future witnessing campaigns, too. There also seems to be a distinct note of expansion, beyond the duty of the twelve apostles, to all who dare to live fully open lives for Christ (see vv. 21, 22, 32-39).

It is important to note that the report of Jesus' warnings in this section are influenced by the actual experience of the community to whom Matthew was writing. They were actually experiencing being taken before civil authorities and the division of families, and so Matthew put special emphasis on this (cf. Acts 3-8).

Sheep and Wolves. By nature, sheep are weak, harmless and defenseless. Wolves, on the other hand, are strong, dangerous and aggressive. The contrasts are evident. Jesus' point is to warn His disciples of the vast difference between those who are inside God's Kingdom and those who are outside of it. In other words, Jesus is counseling us not to be naive.

Serpents and Doves. The serpent illustrates the devil, and the dove depicts the Holy

a 29 Greek *an assarion* b 36 Micah 7:6

Spirit (Matt. 3:16; Rev. 12:9). The disciples, in order to keep from being devoured by the wolves, must be as wise as Satan and as pure as the Spirit. It is not always easy or safe to present the gospel of the Kingdom of God. Some will hear it gladly, while others will seek to put an end to its proclamation. Therefore, the servant of the Lord must be exceptionally cautious not to unnecessarily offend anyone.

Be on Your Guard: No one is guaranteed deliverance from trouble—in fact, the opposite is promised to each faithful disciple (cf. Acts 8:1; 13:50; 16:23; 2 Tim. 3:12). But the power from the Holy Spirit to face these tests (whether they come from the synagogue [or church] or governmental officials or even one's very family) will be immediately available to each and every devoted disciple of Jesus Christ (cf. Rom. 8:28-39; 2 Cor. 4:9; 2 Tim. 3:11).

He Who Stands Firm Will Be Saved. Jesus' charge to stand firm to the end of life, despite the harassment of irritating people and circumstances, is emphatically strong. Only those who remain true to Christ will, in the end, be saved. The rewards of heaven are not for the compromising disciple, but for the triumphant overcomer (Rev. 2:7, 11, 17, 26; 3:5, 12, 21; 21:7, 8).

A similar note is sounded a few verses later when Jesus says, "Whoever disowns me before men, I will disown him before my Father in heaven" (v. 33). Still later, Jesus talks of being "worthy" to be considered a true disciple of His (vv. 37-39). The language is straightforward and penetrating. There is no hope offered to the casual disciple. Instead, the point of follow-through is made absolutely explicit—either you are a serious disciple of Jesus or you are not a disciple at all.

Two practical matters need to be observed at this point. One, the Bible never teaches that a person can become saved solely through an approach of "easy believism" (that is, a faith that only touches the mind and not the heart or the will). Two, the Bible never teaches that a person can remain saved if he fails to stand firm on the essentials of the faith (cf. John 15:1-6; 1 Cor. 15:1, 2; Col. 1:21-23; 1 Tim. 1:18-20; 2:15; 4:1, 16; 6:20, 21; 2 Tim. 2:17, 18; Heb. 6:4-9; James 5:19, 20; Rev. 3:4, 5; 21:7, 8; etc.) Such sober passages ought to cause each one to examine himself to see if he is truly saved (2 Cor. 13:5).

Flee. Jesus did not call His disciples to be persecuted, but to preach. When a certain community is hostile to the gospel message, it is time to move to a new community. There is no sense in casting pearls before a herd of swine (Matt. 7:6).

You Will Not Finish Before the Son of Man Comes. This statement clearly transcends the boundary of the apostles' initial mission. It refers to the totality of their work—before they end their lives, and before they have had a chance to bring the gospel message to every city in Israel. Before this happens the Son of Man will have returned. The precise meaning of these words is debated. Some believe Jesus is referring to His exalted encounter with God, Moses and Elijah on the mountain where He would be transfigured with radiant glory (Matt. 17:1-13; 2 Pet. 1:16-18). Others hold to the position that Jesus is referring to His personal (though indirect) campaigns against rebellious Israel through the military conquests by Rome upon Israel's cities in 66-70 A.D. (Matt. 16:27, 28; 19:28; 24:1-28). Some even see a reference here to the Day of Pentecost (Acts 2). There can be little room here for dogmatism.

A Student Is Not Above His Teacher. Jesus tells His disciples to take a close look at how people treat Him because they can expect to receive no lighter considerations themselves. If the master is abused, so will be his servants. It ought to come as no shock then to discover that verbal and physical persecution against Christians is more the norm than the exception throughout the world.

Do Not Be Afraid. The fear of men brings with it an ineffective witness for Christ. Our words are snared when our hearts are in a state of trembling. Jesus, knowing this truth, assures His followers of four matters that are directly aimed at resolving these natural concerns: (1) there is coming a day when every secret sin and sinner will be exposed—justice will prevail in the end; (2) no one can kill your soul or cast it into hell—you are safe in God's hands; (3) the practically worthless sparrow is even under God's guardianship—you, being infinitely more valuable, will have no incident disturb you that does not first pass through God's hands; and (4) God's knowledge and concern for you is so thorough that even the individual hairs of your head have not escaped His attention or involvement (cf. Rom. 8:28-39).

I Will Acknowledge Him/I Will Disown Him. The thought of a private faith is foreign to the teachings of Jesus. You cannot be one kind of person in public and another in secret. Jesus calls for a bold openness among His disciples. If you are a Christian, say so "from the housetops" (v. 27). If you are not, admit it. But never fall prey to the temptation to keep your religion a matter solely between yourself and God—this passive position either borders upon or actually enters the domain of disowning Jesus Christ!

I Did Not Come to Bring Peace. This statement must be understood in the light of its context. Surely "the Prince of Peace" (Isa. 9:6) is not promoting hostility. Instead, He is notifying His disciples of the fact that just as His life produced enemies, so their lives would yield a company of enemies, too. No one can live the Christian life and fail to become alienated from certain people. In fact, the sword (a symbol of division and persecution) will be used against the believer by the members of his very own household (cf. Mark 13:9-13). Yet, Jesus charges these disciples to hold fast to their faith and not to give in to family pressures. Otherwise, they will not be fit to be called true disciples of Christ.

The Cross. Taking up the cross, by design, promises no earthly pleasures. It is solely a picture of rejection, suffering and death. To come and pick up a cross is an unappealing invitation. No one delights in the prospect of suffering. But this is Jesus' offer. He does not extend fancy promises to us (as is so commonly done today). Instead, He merely invites us to follow Him, knowing full well that His road would lead directly to Calvary.

Finding Life. The only way anyone can truly find himself is by losing himself in Christ (cf. Phil. 1:21; 3:1-15). Through surrender we win. Life is in Christ, and the persons who find Him also find meaningful, productive and eternal life. Think of it as an equation. Jesus, plus zero, equals a wonderful life. It is only when the "zero" is replaced with things that life becomes dull and carnal. All we truly need is Jesus.

E. *Its Sweetness (10:40-42)*

> [40]**"He who receives you receives me, and he who receives me receives the one who sent me. [41]Anyone who receives a prophet because he is a prophet will receive a prophet's reward, and anyone who receives a righteous man because he is a righteous man will receive a righteous man's reward. [42]And if anyone gives a cup of cold water to one of these little ones because he is my disciple, I tell you the truth, he will certainly not lose his reward."**

There is much more than a sword and a cross to the Christian life. There is also the joy of making converts and the knowledge that they will receive God's best rewards for their obedience (2 Cor. 5:10; Rom. 8:17; Rev. 22:12; etc.).

Leaders need to occasionally remind themselves that while they may occupy positions of apparent supremacy over their followers, the appearance is not actual. Those who accept and support Christ's leaders will themselves be rewarded equally with the men to whom they submit. What honor Christ has given to each one who receives His word and His servants.

Special Study: Apostleship

1. *Jesus: The Apostle*—"When the time had fully come, God *sent* His son" (Gal. 4:4). Jesus was God's representative (John 14:9). He was *sent* out from heaven to accomplish the will of the One sending Him (John 4:34). Frequently Jesus referred to God, especially in the Gospel according to John, as the One who *sent* Him (3:17, 34; 4:34; 5:23, 24, 30, 36, 37, 38; 6:29, 38, 39, 44, 57; 7:16, 18, 28, 29, 33; 8:16, 18, 26, 29, 42; 9:4; 10:36; 11:42; 12:44, 45, 49; 13:20; 14:24; 15:21; 16:5; 17:3, 18, 21, 23, 25; 20:21—forty-one times!).

Jesus did not hastily decide one day to leave heaven and visit earth. No. He was *sent*.

There was a design of the most minute detail which had been prepared beforehand. The Father *sent* Him forth according to His schedule and according to His purposes.

The scriptural title for someone who is *sent forth in behalf of another* is "apostle." The word means "one who is sent forth as a messenger or agent, a bearer of a commission." It is for this reason that Jesus is addressed as "the apostle" (Heb. 3:1).

2. *The Twelve Apostles*—Once Jesus began His earthly ministry, He chose twelve men whom He would disciple (or teach). These twelve disciples were also called "apostles" once Jesus *sent* them out (Matt. 10:2).

Observe that these men were not self-appointed. They were chosen. They did not volunteer for this position, but by special selecting, after a night in prayer, Jesus called twelve men to His side to serve in this capacity (Luke 6:12, 13).

Apostleship is never the product of personal talents (regardless of how numerous and refined they may be) or popularity. Men's minds will almost invariably select the wrong person for the wrong calling. Being an apostle is entirely the Lord's doing. An eager worker may leave his home and friends in order to follow Jesus and be His ambassador, but unless Jesus has done the choosing and the sending, such a person could never be a true apostle.

These twelve apostles played a significant role in Jesus' earthly ministry and in the affairs of the early church. The corporate identity of this unique group is of no minor importance, for they will "sit on thrones, judging the twelve tribes of Israel" (Luke 22:30; cf. Rev. 20:4). Further, they will have their names engraved on the twelve foundation stones of the new Jerusalem (Rev. 21:14).

The number and calling of this select group is forever established. Their role as apostles is unquestionably special (Acts 2:43; 4:33; 5:12; etc.). Just as there were twelve sons of Jacob who formed the twelve tribes of Israel, so there would be twelve apostles to form the foundation for the new Israel of God (Eph. 2:19ff.). Matthias is the twelfth apostle, replacing Judas (Acts 1:26).

3. *Additional Apostles*—Until the thirteenth chapter of Acts (around 46 A.D.), there seem to have been only twelve recognized apostles in the early church. At this point, however, others began to be divinely called to this position. In this particular chapter we read of how Barnabas and Saul were called by the Holy Spirit to fulfill this role (13:1-3; cf. Acts 14:4, 14; 1 Cor. 9:5, 6; 15:9; Gal. 1:1).

Other apostles mentioned in the Scriptures include Andronicus and Junias (Rom. 16:7), Apollos (1 Cor. 4:6-9), James, the Lord's brother (Gal. 1:19), Silas and Timothy (1 Thess. 1:1; 2:7), Titus (2 Cor. 8:23) and Epaphroditus (Phil. 2:25). In all, eleven new names (including Matthias—Acts 1:26; 2:14) are added to "the twelve" whom Jesus chose. It is highly probable that others were commissioned, but were never recorded in the Scriptures.

Jesus and John the Baptist (Matt. 11:1-19)

(cf. Luke 7:18-35)

No Christian has ever been exempt from asking honest, soul-searching questions about his faith. Each of us has inquired about matters that have troubled us. But this need not be confused with doubt. To doubt something is to reject it. Faith, on the other hand, inquisitively turns certain matters over and over in order to inspect them more closely and to gain a better understanding. This is precisely what occurred with John the Baptist and his disciples.

I. *John Asks About Jesus' Identity (11:1-6)*

11 After Jesus had finished instructing his twelve disciples, he went
on from there to teach and preach in the towns of Galilee.[a]
2When John heard in prison what Christ was doing, he sent his disciples
3to ask him, "Are you the one who was to come, or should we expect
someone else?"
4Jesus replied, "Go back and report to John what you hear and see: 5The
blind receive sight, the lame walk, those who have leprosy[b] are cured, the
deaf hear, the dead are raised, and the good news is preached to the poor.
6Blessed is the man who does not fall away on account of me."

Jesus Teaches and Preaches. Jesus was both a teacher and a preacher. These two words have been carefully studied in recent years, and the results are worth our investigation.

A *preacher* is a herald. In ancient times a herald was a man of great importance. He was hired by either a ruler or the state in order to make public proclamations in a clear voice. Preaching, then, is the act of heralding an understandable message to some audience. The message of Jesus centered in the fact that God's Kingdom had now invaded the earth (Matt. 4:17). Jesus preached about God—His works and His will.

A *teacher* is an interpreter. He draws practical and personal applications from the objective revelation of God and His will. He calls his audience to understand and to apply these revelations. Jesus, therefore, preached the nearness of God's Kingdom among people, while at the same time, He taught them the implications of this

a 1 Greek *in their towns* b 5 The Greek word was used for various diseases affecting the skin—not necessarily leprosy.

Kingdom news. Naturally, these words were intended to both evangelize and to edify His listeners.

John in Prison. A total of seven different Greek words are translated into our one English term "prison." The particular word used here means to be imprisoned in a "place of bonds." The site of this dungeon was at Herod's castle in Manchaerus (in the territory of Perea, east of the Dead Sea).

Imprisonment for the cause of Christ is not new, either to the New Testament or to our own current events (Luke 21:12; Acts 4:3; 5:18; 8:3; 12:3; 16:22-34; 22:23-29; 28:16; 2 Cor. 6:5; 11:23). There is little glamour in being thrown into jail, but every disciple of Christ must accept this possibility as one of the costs of faithful discipleship.

Are You the One? John had been imprisoned for boldly speaking out against a ruler's sins (Matt. 14:1-12). It was here, in the confinement of a prison cell, that John began to question his previous convictions. How easy it is to have a dynamic faith when you are busy serving God on the front lines of action, like John had done. But when the activity ceases and the mind is free to roam, how easy it is for us to submit our faith to some hard, but sincere, questions.

John was no exception to this kind of thinking. He actually wondered if Jesus were really "the One," or if he should be expecting someone else. There is no doubt here—only an intense questioning from a devoted servant of God.

In John's mind the coming of the Christ meant an end to Roman tyranny and to all other forms of unrighteousness. Through this figure would come a powerful social and political fire that would consume wickedness in its entirety (Mal. 3:1-3; 4:1, 2; Matt. 3:11; 4:17). But after reflecting upon these convictions in the light of Jesus' ministry of preaching, teaching and healing, he became confused.

Here is a straightforward example of how even the godliest of men are incomplete in themselves. No one has all the answers. The very best among God's servants only see a portion of all God's dealings or plans (1 Cor. 13:12).

Report to John. Jesus did not rebuke John or his disciples for this questioning. In fact, he calls John "more than a prophet" (v. 9), and the greatest man ever born to a woman up to that time (v. 11). We must never think our questions are too silly or too dumb to ask. There is no ridiculous question we can ever ask, if we will but ask it from a heart of honesty and sincerity. This is an integral part of a real, living faith.

The Old Testament envisioned a coming Christ who would reign as King over all the earth (Ps. 9:8). This King would establish His throne in Jerusalem, and every nation on the planet would render to Him their loyalty (Ps. 96:13; 98:9; Isa. 2:2; Zech. 14:16-21). At the appearance of this figure, the end of death and suffering would come (Isa. 25:8), and the formation of a new heaven and earth (Isa. 65:17; 66:19-24).

At long last the saints would be vindicated and be given full authority over the management of the earth (Dan. 7:27). This is what John, along with many of his contemporaries, expected to see.

Unfortunately, the popular opinions regarding the works of the Christ neglected to see other Old Testament prophecies. These prophecies included Jesus' mission as a Prophet and Priest (Deut. 18:15; Isa. 42:1-9; 61:1-3). They also included his suffering, atoning death and, after that, His victorious resurrection (Ps. 2; 22; Isa. 53; Hos. 6:1, 2; Zech. 11:12; 1 Cor. 15:1-3). It is these latter prophecies that Jesus, in effect, tells John's disciples to remember.

II. *Jesus Reveals John's Identity (11:7-15)*

7As John's disciples were leaving, Jesus began to speak to the crowd about John: "What did you go out into the desert to see? A reed swayed by the wind? 8If not, what did you go out to see? A man dressed in fine clothes? No, those who wear fine clothes are in kings' palaces. 9Then what did you go out to see? A prophet? Yes, I tell you, and more than a prophet. 10This is the one about whom it is written:

" 'I will send my messenger ahead of you,
who will prepare your way before you.'[a]

11I tell you the truth: Among those born of women there has not risen anyone greater than John the Baptist; yet he who is least in the kingdom of heaven is greater than he. 12From the days of John the Baptist until now, the kingdom of heaven has been forcefully advancing, and forceful men lay hold of it. 13For all the Prophets and the Law prophesied until John. 14And if you are willing to accept it, he is the Elijah who was to come. 15He who has ears, let him hear.

Jesus Began to Speak About John. John was far more than just *a* prophet; he was *the* prophet who had been prophesied to come by both Isaiah (40:3, 4) and Malachi (3:1). To be even more precise, he was "the Elijah" whom Malachi predicted would come before the great day of the Lord appears (Mal. 4:5, 6 with Luke 1:17). No woman ever gave birth to a greater son, yet the least person in the Kingdom is greater than he. What a contrast. How can John be at one and the same time both the greatest and less than the least?

The solution to this problem is more simple than might be imagined. John was the hinge between the old dispensation under the Law and the Prophets, and the new dispensation under Jesus, the Christ. In a sense, he belonged to both ages, and to neither period. (See the diagram entitled, "A Chronological Perspective of God's Dealings with Earth.") While John prepared the way for Jesus' ministry, because of his

a 10 Mal. 3:1

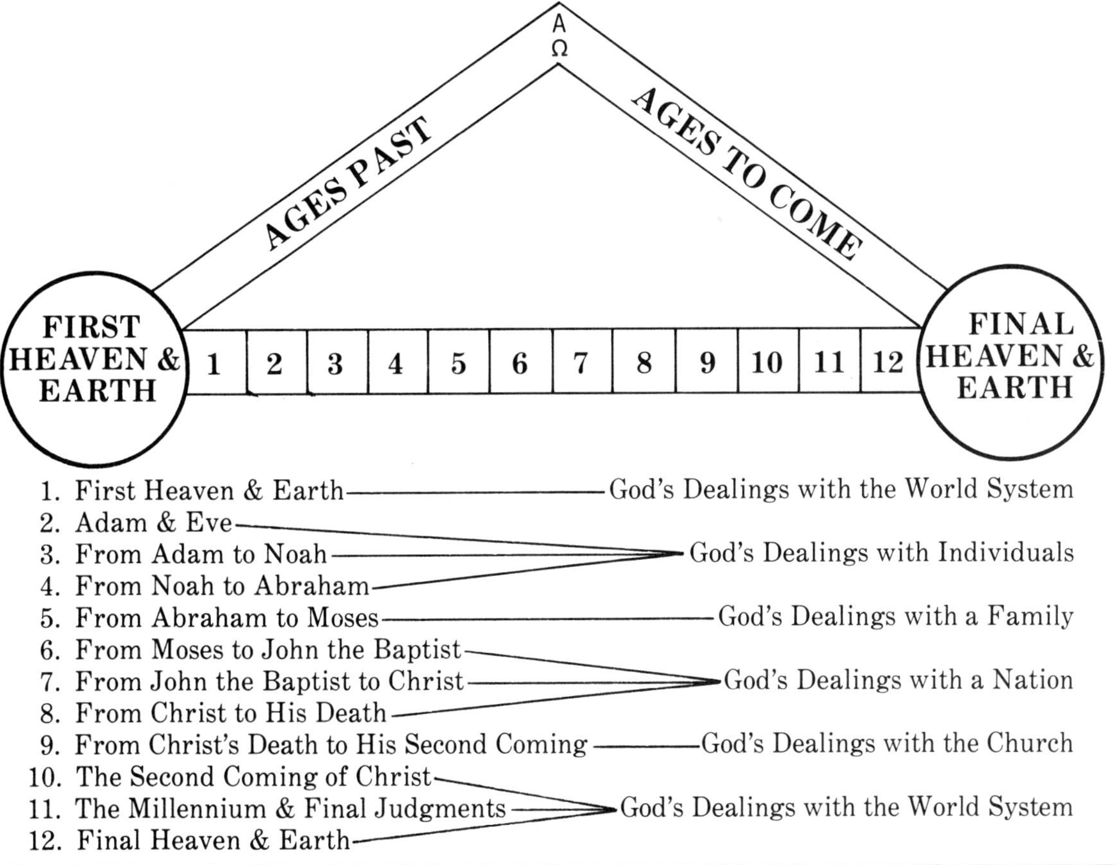

A CHRONOLOGICAL PERSPECTIVE OF GOD'S DEALINGS WITH EARTH

imprisonment, he never shared in it directly. He did not hear Jesus teach or see Him perform miracles, yet virtually everyone else had access to these privileges. In other words, John's low status was not due to his spiritual state, but to his particular confining circumstances in history (Matt. 13:16, 17). Jesus is pointing out to His audience how privileged they ought to consider themselves. By virtue of their circumstances they could hear and see more than John—in this sense they were greater than John.

The Kingdom of Heaven Has Been Forcefully Advancing, and Forceful Men Lay Hold of It. These words have received opposite interpretations by various commentators. The general cause for this difference is due to the first Greek verb in this passage (here rendered, "forcefully advancing"). In the original language it is uncertain whether this term is a passive verb (in which case the Kingdom would receive the action of the verb, thereby implying that the Kingdom suffers violence because of violent men in the world) or a middle-voice verb (in which case the Kingdom participates in the action of the verb, thereby implying that the Kingdom is advancing because of the forceful people who dwell within). The New International Version selects the latter interpretation, which favors the context here and elsewhere (Luke 16:16; Acts 14:22).

The thought behind this passage must not escape us. There is a solemn note here regarding who enters the Kingdom of God. It belongs only to the "forceful"; that is, only to the eager and sincere person who is qualified to be enlisted in this body. No one drifts into the Kingdom or rides in on the train of another. Each of us must diligently seek entrance if we are to be a part of God's family (Luke 13:24). The professing Christian who is lukewarm, casual and undisciplined in his faith, is, at best, walking on dangerously thin protection.

He Who Has Ears. People may listen without hearing. This was the case with numerous ones in Jesus' audiences (cf. 13:9, 43; Mark 4:9, 23; Luke 8:8; 14:35; Rev. 2:7, 11, 17, 29; 3:6, 13, 22; 13:9). They could repeat what Jesus said, but somehow they could not bring themselves to apply it. The words were too radical to accept. Only those who were spiritually tuned in to God's frequency would believe these statements of Jesus.

To the natural ear what Jesus said did sound a bit farfetched. Imagine hearing these words about John and the Kingdom for the first time. From this vantage point we can at least partially understand the negative reaction Jesus received. The natural ear never believes in the supernatural. The heart must be converted to God's will before the ear will accept God's words (John 7:17).

III. *Jesus Rebukes His Generation (11:16-19)*

16"To what can I compare this generation? They are like children sitting in the marketplaces and calling out to others:

17" 'We played the flute for you,
and you did not dance;
we sang a dirge,
and you did not mourn.'

18For John came neither eating nor drinking, and they say, 'He has a
demon.' 19The Son of Man came eating and drinking, and they say, 'Here

is a glutton and a drunkard, a friend of tax collectors and "sinners." ' But wisdom is proved right by her actions."

This Generation. Many who heard Jesus were like some children who are never satisfied. If you played dancing music, they would want something else. If you sang to them a dirge (or funeral hymn), they would not appreciate this either. No matter what you did, they would never be satisfied. They would always want something else.

When John came, he was ridiculed for his habits. When Jesus came, He, too, was belittled for His practices. No matter what they did, there were always those who found fault.

Wisdom Is Proved Right. The ministries of John and Jesus were scorned, but the wisdom of their works is undeniable. Each of these men was responsible for turning people to God. The resultant transformed lives is proof that their labors were wise indeed.

Danger for Sinful Cities (Matt. 11:20-24)

(cf. Luke 10:12-15)

Jesus worked many miracles in the cities of Israel, but in the places where the greatest number of miracles occurred there was no evidence of repentance. The cities were spiritually callous. They would not use such words as these: "I am wrong." "Please forgive me." "Teach me more." They were dead to God. So, Jesus informed them that their unresponsiveness, in the face of such miracles, would guarantee them a drastic judgment from God.

**20Then Jesus began to denounce the cities in which most of his miracles
had been performed, because they did not repent. 21"Woe to you,
Korazin! Woe to you, Bethsaida! If the miracles that were performed in
you had been performed in Tyre and Sidon, they would have repented
long ago in sackcloth and ashes. 22But I tell you, it will be more bearable
for Tyre and Sidon on the day of judgment than for you. 23And you,
Capernaum, will you be lifted up to the skies? No, you will go down
to the depths.[a] If the miracles that were performed in you had been
performed in Sodom, it would have remained to this day. 24But I tell
you that it will be more bearable for Sodom on the day of judgment than
for you."**

a 23 Greek *Hades*

They Did Not Repent. Here is a shocking account of the ineffectiveness of miracles in converting the hearts of sinners. It is practically unthinkable that someone, much less the majority of the people in a whole city, would not repent after seeing Jesus' supernatural ministry. Still, the bulk of the people remained unchanged after hearing and seeing Jesus.

Jesus' miracles were specifically designed to authenticate His message (Matt. 11:2-5; Mark 2:9-12; Luke 5:24-26; 18:42, 43; John 2:11; 4:48; 5:36; 11:4, 40-42; 14:11; 15:24). Certainly they glorified God (Luke 5:26; John 11:4). But the masses who saw them were unmoved. Their hearts were cold. Their minds were filled with skepticism. And they would not change. Unfortunately there are many such persons today who spurn testimonies of the miraculous.

Woe to Korazin, Bethsaida and Capernaum. The city of Korazin is only mentioned in the Bible with regard to receiving Jesus' anger and pity (or woe). Bethsaida is the original home of three of Jesus' disciples—Philip, Andrew and Peter (John 1:44; 12:21). And Capernaum, the second home of Jesus (Matt. 4:13), was the site of much spiritual activity (Matt. 17:24-27; Mark 2:1-12; 9:33-37; Luke 4:23; John 4:46-54).

Each of these cities, located within a couple of miles of each other on the northern shores of the Sea of Galilee, received much of Jesus' attention. But the abundance of opportunities yielded very little fruit. Today these sites are forever buried in ruins, except for the few remains archaeological teams have uncovered.

Tyre, Sidon and Sodom. Why did Jesus select these particular cities to say that their inhabitants would have repented if they had been shown what Korazin, Bethsaida and Capernaum had seen? In the mind of the Jew, few favorable comments could be made about these notorious centers of evil. Even the prophets denounced them (Isa. 23; Ezek. 16; 26-28). They were wicked, to be sure, but they had never received the tremendous privileges of seeing and hearing the Son of God. And if they had had this opportunity, says Jesus, they would have repented to the full, in sackcloth and ashes. Yet, those cities who did have this privilege were too carnal to receive Him. What an insult!

The Day of Judgment. How often Jesus and the Scriptures speak of a day of reckoning, a day when every sin will be exposed before sinners (Eccles. 12:14; Mal. 4:1, 2; Matt. 7:22, 23; 12:36, 37; 25:41-46; Jude 6; Rev. 20:11-15). In that day Jesus Christ will judge people according to their spiritual opportunities (Matt. 10:11-15; Luke 11:31, 32; 12:47, 48). Those who did not know God's special revelation will be judged altogether differently from those who had received but rejected it (Rom. 2:1-16). The greater the light, the graver the responsibility.

Jesus Praises His Father (Matt. 11:25-27)

(cf. Luke 10:21, 22)

How few and precious are the prayers we possess from the lips of Jesus. We know Jesus was deeply devoted to prayer, yet we have only the words from seven of His prayers (1. Matt. 11:25-27; 2. John 11:41, 42; 3. John 17:1-26; 4. Matt. 26:36-46; 5. Luke 23:34; 6. Mark 15:34; 7. Luke 23:46). Most of these prayers are but a sentence long. One prayer fills an entire chapter; even so, it is only a couple of minutes in duration.

In the prayer before us now we see the spirit of celebration. Jesus is full of joy. He rejoices in seeing God at work. Also in this prayer are some weighty statements about Jesus' relationship to the Father.

I. *Praise to the Father (11:25, 26)*

> **25At that time Jesus said, "I praise you, Father, Lord of heaven and earth, because you have hidden these things from the wise and learned, and revealed them to little children. 26Yes, Father, for this was your good pleasure.**

Lord of Heaven and Earth. When the term "Lord" is applied to God, it generally refers to His role as the supreme authority in life. The scope of this authority is here revealed as being universal, everywhere, in heaven and in earth. Stated differently, Jesus praises God because He is sovereign over every affair that happens in space and time. Nothing is outside His jurisdiction or oversight.

You Have Hidden and Revealed. The meaning of these words has been intensely debated for centuries. Three views occupy the chief positions. On the one side it is argued that God sovereignly reserves the right to select the ones to whom He will reveal the things necessary for becoming a member of the Kingdom of saved persons. On the other hand, it is offered that God's plan of salvation is extended to everyone, though the self-conceited, the so-called wise and learned, exempt themselves from these insights. Still others hold to a position that is somewhere between these views.

The adherents of the first view are often called Calvinists, because they essentially follow John Calvin's line of logic here. The members of the second position are usually addressed as Arminians, because they pretty much subscribe to the reasonings of Jacob Arminius. The followers of the third position prefer to go under no particular heading. Here is an overview of these three theological interpretations.

Calvinism

1. *Total Depravity.* Man cannot save himself through his moral conduct or good works. His will is in total bondage, not permitting him the ability to choose God's will (John 6:44; Rom. 7:18, 19; 8:7, 8; 1 Cor. 2:14).

2. *Unconditional Election.* God chooses who will be and who will not be saved by an act of His own will (Eph. 1:3-14).

3. *Limited Atonement.* Christ died only for the elect (those whom the Father decides will be saved) and no one else (John 10:11; 17:9; Acts 20:28).

4. *Irresistible Grace.* What God wills to transpire in a person's life cannot be resisted or altered. Those whom God selects cannot escape accepting His salvation (Rom. 8:29, 30).

5. *Perseverance.* Those whom God chooses cannot lose their salvation (Phil. 1:6; 2 Thess. 3:3; Heb. 6:4-9).

Arminianism

1. *Partial Depravity.* Man cannot save himself through his moral conduct or good works. His will is in partial bondage, permitting him to choose either God's will or Satan's will (John 3:16-21; 7:17; Rom. 10:13-17).

2. *Conditional Election.* God chooses only those whom He foreknows will exercise faith in Christ and obey His will (1 Pet. 1:2).

3. *Unlimited Atonement.* Christ died for everyone—none excluded—although only believers will be saved in the end (John 3:16; 1 Tim. 2:4; 4:10; 2 Pet. 2:1; 1 John 2:1, 2).

4. *Resistible Grace.* What God wills to transpire in a person's life can be resisted. While God's will is that everyone be saved, His offer may be rejected (Ps. 107:11, 12; Matt. 22:14; Matt. 23:37; Acts 7:51).

5. *Conditional Security.* A Christian can lose his salvation through disobedience (Exod. 32:30ff; Ps. 69:20-28; 1 Cor. 9:27; Rev. 3:5; 13:8; 17:8).

Other scholars state that the above line of reasoning is either too extreme to the left side or to the right side. They prefer a less absolute and a more balanced view. In other words, while these interpreters may not possess a neat system for presenting their position, they feel there is sufficient scriptural evidence to give the appearance of supporting *both* the Calvinistic and the Arminian points of view. Therefore, rather than choosing between one or the other of these arguments, they prefer to see a measure of truth in both camps. This particular variety of logic is intentionally nonprecise. They are content to leave the black and white with God, while they settle for seeing things as being gray from the human perspective. They contend that the matter cannot be grasped with the finite mind; so they leave the "how to" with God.

II. *Position of the Son (11:27)*

[27]"All things have been committed to me by my Father. No one knows the Son except the Father, and no one knows the Father except the Son and those to whom the Son chooses to reveal him.

All Things Have Been Committed to Me. In the hands of Jesus rests the governorship of everything in heaven and earth (Matt. 28:18; John 3:35; 5:21-29; 13:3; 17:2; 1 Cor. 15:25-27; Eph. 1:20-23; Heb. 2:8-10; 1 Pet. 3:22). While the Father is still above this level (1 Cor. 15:27, 28), it is the Son, Jesus, who serves at the Father's right hand. Through Jesus alone comes all authority. At His command are all the angels (Matt. 26:53; Col. 1:16; 2:10, 15). He reigns over all the rulers of the earth (Rev. 1:5). Life and death are in His grip (Heb. 2:14, 15; Rev. 1:18). Regardless of its microscopic or telescopic size, nothing is outside his immediate control. Jesus is the Lord of everything, everywhere, in all of space.

No One Knows the Son/No One Knows the Father. Is the knowledge of the Son and of the Father to be understood from a Calvinistic perspective? An Arminian perspective? Some other angle? Teachers are not agreed, and there is small hope in finding a theological solution that will satisfy everyone.

The following analysis of the salvation process is offered with the intent of making the fundamental elements of sovereignty and free will as clear and as balanced as possible.

Special Study: Salvation

1. *God's Offer of Salvation—A Historical Perspective.* In the very beginning, Adam and Eve were the only people on the earth. God placed them in a wonderful garden and gave them commands to obey by personal choice and free will. They could either obey and live or rebel and die (Gen. 2:15-17). They chose disobedience (Gen. 3:1-7; 2 Cor. 11:3; 1 Tim. 2:9-14).

God created Adam as a free moral agent, knowing He would be rejected by this creation. So God sovereignly designed the road that would lead people back into fellowship with himself. He made this plan before He made the earth or anything else (Rom. 16:25, 26; Eph. 1:3-11; 3:9-11; Col. 1:25-27; 2 Tim. 1:9, 10; Titus 1:1-3; 1 Pet. 1:17-21; Rev. 13:8).

The moment Adam fell, God promised to bring forth a Savior through Eve's seed (Gen. 3:15). In His own sovereign way, God chose the pattern through which deliverance would come. Soon Eve bore two sons—Cain and Abel. Both recognized their need for salvation, and both were given ample instructions on how to secure it (Gen. 4:1-7). But, by an act of his own will, Cain rejected God's will and killed his brother. God, then, judged Cain by dismissing him from the presence of those through whom He would chiefly work and dwell. This physical and spiritual separation from the chosen seed-line gave rise to the pagan world (Gen. 4:8-14; Rom. 1:18-32). God gave Eve another son, Seth, and he served as the cornerstone for God's chosen seed genealogy (Gen. 4:25, 26; contrast Gen. 4:16-24 with 5:6-32).

Out of the chosen seed-line of Seth, God called faithful Abraham to be the father of a nation, Israel (Gen. 12:1-3; Neh. 9:7, 8; Acts 7:2-6; Heb. 11:8). This nation would serve God and give birth to the Savior.

Israel was not to save the world, but to be the tool for bringing into the world its Savior. This national distinction further accented the division God made between the line of His chosen seed and the surrounding nations. This national election, however, did not automatically mean all Jews were saved (Rom. 9-11) or that all pagans were lost. Israel had God's special revelation either to accept or to reject. The nations had God's natural (or general) revelation either to accept or to reject (this includes *nature:* Ps. 8; 19:1-6; 29:1-10; 93:1-4; 104:24; Isa. 40:26; Acts 14:15-17; Rom. 1:19, 20, 32; 2:14, 15; 10:16-18; *history:* Acts 17:24-29; and *conscience:* Eccles. 3:11; Rom. 2:14-16). Additionally, during the Old Testament period God often overlooked the ignorance of the Gentile masses (Acts 17:30 with Acts 14:16; Rom. 3:25; 4:8, 15; 5:13; 7:7, 8).

In the dispensations from Adam to Christ it was not God's immediate intention to proclaim the gospel to the whole world. This was to be done later, in full harmony with His sovereign, redemptive design. In the fullness of God's perfect time, Christ came into the world (Gal. 4:4). Today, as it has always been, people must still choose to accept or reject God's way of salvation. As a result of this choice, the world is still divided between those who are saved and those who are lost (John 3:16-21; 2 Cor. 4:3-7).

2. *The Process of Conversion.* Salvation is a two-way affair. God plays a part; you play a part. The role of the Father is to *design* the plan (Eph. 1:3-11); the role of the Son is to *discharge* the plan (Matt. 20:28); and the role of the Holy Spirit is to *declare* the plan (John 16:8-11). It is our job to receive personally this complete plan (John 1:12).

Questions are now raised over whether or not the Trinity extends this plan to everyone and whether or not people are, in themselves, even capable of receiving this plan due to their depravity. The diagram entitled, "Life's Triune Composition" will serve to explain the author's view in this matter.

3. *The Desire of God and the Faith of People.* God does not delight in seeing even one human miss His plan of salvation (Ezek. 18:23, 32; 2 Pet. 3:9). This is why He offers His plan of salvation to everyone, everywhere (Isa. 45:22; 49:6; 55:1-3; Ezek. 33:11; Matt. 28:19; John 3:14-17; 6:33, 51; 7:37; Acts 17:24-28; 2 Cor. 5:17-19; Eph. 3:6-10; Col. 1:6, 23; 1 Tim. 2:4-6; 4:10; 2 Tim. 4:17; Titus 2:11; Rev. 22:17).

The Scriptures repeatedly and explicitly imply an inherent ability within people to respond to the Spirit's wooings (Matt. 8:10; John 1:7; 3:14-18; 5:44-47; 7:17; 8:24; 10:37,

38; Rom. 3:21ff.; 16:25, 26; I Thess. 2:13; Heb. 3:1-4:16; 11:1-40; James 1:21; Rev. 22:14-19). If anyone dies and goes to hell, it is not because God failed to give him a fair chance, but because he spurned the opportunities offered to him. No one *has* to go to hell. It is a choice we each make. No one *has* to go to heaven. Again, it is a decision from our own wills in response to God's plan for our salvation. We either reject or accept His offer.

LIFE'S TRIUNE COMPOSITION

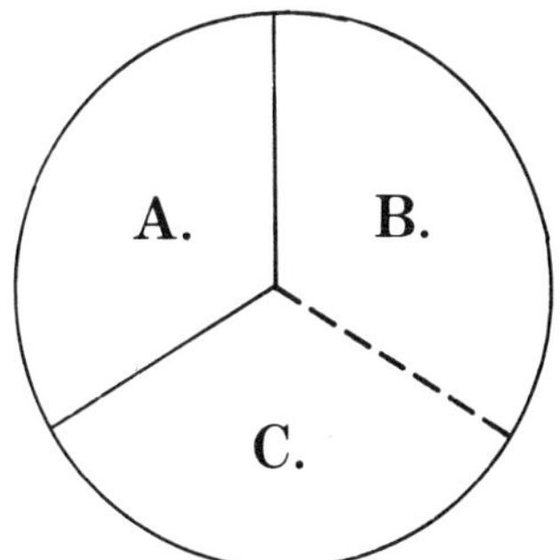

A. *God's Decrees of Sovereign Will.* In this dimension of life, God executes His own will in our behalf, and no one thwarts His purposes in this realm (Ps. 33:9-11; 37:23; Prov. 16:1-4, 9, 33; 19:21; 20: 24 with Gen. 45:4-8; 50:20; 2 Sam. 17:14; Rev. 17:17). It is incorrect to say God never intervenes in the intimate affairs of man. He surely does!

B. *God's Decrees of Positive Free Will.* In this part of life we have a free will to enter into God's salvation covenant and into His perfect plans for our daily life (Ps. 25:14; Prov. 3:32; Rom. 12:1-22; Eph. 5:17; Col. 1:9; etc.). We *can* obey God, if we want to do so. God desires for us to choose to live in this area. We have no control over area "A," but we can elect to live in area "B."

C. *God's Decrees of Negative Free Will.* In this section of life we may resist and spurn God's nonsovereign will for our lives (area "B"). That is, we can choose to live and to die in sin (Ps. 106:13; 107:11; Luke 7:30; Acts 7:51). God does not desire for us to live in this section. Although each of us lives in this section from time to time, we can repent of our sins and be restored to section "B."

Rest for the Weary (Matt. 11:28-30)

When the Christian life is lived as it ought to be lived, it will produce rest. The disposition of composure and tranquility is a certain mark of those who have learned to follow Jesus. The path marked *self-made religion* is full of lifeless duties, rituals and regulations; but the road marked *genuine Christianity* is filled with the kind of obligations that yield a restful fruit.

> **28"Come to me, all you who are weary and burdened, and I will give**
> **you rest. 29Take my yoke upon you and learn from me, for I am gentle**
> **and humble in heart, and you will find rest for your souls. 30For my yoke**
> **is easy and my burden is light."**

Come to Me. Here are three simple words that carry a message never to be forgotten. Notice the simplicity of the invitation—*come.* It is an invitation that is within everyone's reach. We can each come. Notice the thrust of the call—*come to me.* Jesus does not offer us a program, but himself. Salvation is not centered in following a plan, but in following a Person (Phil. 1:21; Heb. 12:1, 2)! We must never remove our attention from Jesus Christ, for in Him is rest and life.

The Weary and Burdened. Jesus addresses an audience that is exhausted from a meaningless pursuit after God. How exasperating man-made religion (including any false imitation of Christianity) always is. Additionally, the more diligently one applies himself to a pseudofaith, the more separated he becomes from spiritual reality. The Christian way is not arrived at through hard work, constant exertion and intense searching.

Numerous Jews in Jesus' day were legalistic. They followed the laws of Moses to the letter (Matt. 23:4). Unfortunately, they missed the chief point of the law—it was intended to lead a nation to finding Christ, and not to be an end in itself. The law only revealed more and more of one's personal shortcomings. No one was ever set free through a study of or an application of the law, because no one could perfectly follow its many commandments (Rom. 3:9-20; 7:7-25). Naturally, this fact would leave the seeker only frustrated, especially in light of the law's legalistic misinterpretation by the Jewish leaders.

I Will Give You Rest. The promise Jesus offers is most practical. It is not theoretical, philosophical or futuristic. It is personal, and it is for *now.* The term translated "rest" does not mean the ceasing of labor or involvement in spiritual pursuits, but the finding of peace, security and contentment. Jesus offers the kind of mental and emotional rest that makes life fulfilling (John 10:10; 14:27; Phil. 4:7-9). Jesus offers rest that is not only for the body, but "for the soul" (v. 29; that is, it is for the intellect, the emotions and the will).

Take My Yoke. The religious leaders offered their adherents a yoke, a backbreaking yoke (Matt. 23:4). Their interpretations of Moses' laws put the people in constant bondage. There were more rules to keep, under the teachings of the Pharisees, than there was power to keep them. There was some rule to be kept for almost everything one did. In all of these duties, there was little sight of God himself. There was only the constant vision of His commandments to be borne.

Jesus offered another type of yoke. His yoke would reveal God. His yoke would be based upon a proper interpretation of the laws of Moses. It was the spirit of the law and not the letter of the law that Jesus taught. It was this yoke that would produce rest for those who wore it.

This sounds like a strange paradox: "Take my yoke upon you . . . and you will find rest." Normally you would never combine the thought of a yoke with the promise of rest, but this is Jesus' solution. Here is a profound insight for our spiritual development—there can be no rest apart from proper conformity to God's will. There are millions of other suggested plans for finding lasting peace and contentment, but only this formula has the endorsement of Jesus. Until we come to Jesus and perform His will, we will never know genuine rest.

Learn from Me, for I Am Gentle and Humble. How differently Jesus must have taught from many of His contemporaries. Jesus did not seek to impress His audience with His knowledge or to sway His listeners with neat plans for success. Neither did He attempt to elevate himself above His hearers. Instead, He considered himself to be a man who experienced what He himself taught. He loved people, and He was confident He could help them find what they needed and wanted.

We, too, must learn this style of leadership if we are to be agents of transformation and rest. First, we must take up the Lord's yoke ourselves. Second, we must experience the rest that is offered by Him. Third, we must speak from a confident, but gentle and humble, heart.

My Yoke Is Easy and My Burden Is Light. There are some persons who would say it is difficult to be a true follower of Jesus Christ or God. But this is not the testimony of Jesus. He boldly states that life, when lived in accordance with God's will, is easy and light (cf. 1 John 5:3). It is not hard to obey God. His rules for us are not unrealistic. They are just the opposite—realistic, practical and very achievable. It is self-made expectations or man-made regulations that place a strain on us and rob us of God's rest. When Jesus is followed, there will be an abundance of rest and fulfillment (cf. Heb. 3:7-4:13).

Lord of the Sabbath (Matt. 12:1-8)

(cf. Mark 2:23-28 and Luke 6:1-5)

The Bible clearly states, from the opening days of creation forward, that one day out of seven was to be a unique day for rest. The interpretations of what is meant by this rest, however, have caused controversy. The Jews, by Jesus' day, had devised numerous absurd restrictions. They had succeeded in capturing the legality of the principle, but they had missed the spirit of it altogether.

The crux of this story is found in the contrast between the trifles of self-made religion and the truth of a God-made relationship. The Pharisees saw only the legislation, but Jesus envisioned the exception to the rule. The Sabbath was not intended to rule people, but to serve them. It was to be a day of restoration, not restrictions.

I. *The Immediate Problem (12:1, 2)*

**12 At that time Jesus went through the grainfields on the Sabbath.
His disciples were hungry and began to pick some heads of grain
and eat them. 2 When the Pharisees saw this, they said to him, "Look! Your
disciples are doing what is unlawful on the Sabbath."**

The Sabbath. The word "sabbath" comes from the Hebrew language, and it means "to refrain from work, to rest." It is used to designate the seventh day in each week, the day when everyone in Israel was instructed by God to rest.

In six days God made the universe. On the seventh day He rested from all His labors. God then blessed the seventh day and made it holy (Gen. 2:2, 3). He declared that just as He had worked for six days and rested on the seventh, so, too, all people ought to work six days and rest on the seventh day (Exod. 20:8-11; Lev. 19:3, 30). Neither was there to be any buying or selling of items on this day (Neh. 10:31; 13:15-22). It was to be a day of worship (Deut. 5:12-15; Ezek. 46:3). The Jews celebrated this holy day from Friday evening at sundown until Saturday evening at sundown. Failure to keep this ordinance was a capital offense (Exod. 31:14, 15).

Your Disciples Are Doing What Is Unlawful on the Sabbath. The Old Testament provides few stipulations for observing the Sabbath. Beyond the restrictions of not working, buying or selling (Exod. 20:10; Neh. 10:31), there were no other obligations. By the period of the New Testament, however, many more man-made rulings had been established. Between the close of the last book of the Old Testament and the appearance of Jesus' ministry, more than 400 years had transpired. Numerous changes in worship can be seen during this period. Among these changes was the development of a series of new and hairsplitting traditions that everyone was to follow on the Sabbath day.

For instance, we read in the New Testament that picking grain (Matt. 12:2), healing the sick (Mark 3:2), carrying your mat (John 5:10), and walking more than 2,000 steps on this holy day (Acts 1:12) were strictly forbidden. The Jews had devised a thirty-nine-point list of major Sabbath offenses. Beneath each of these major headings were many additional smaller matters that were also forbidden.

II. *The Past Picture (12:3-5)*

**[3]He answered, "Haven't you read what David did when he and his
companions were hungry? [4]He entered the house of God, and he and his
companions ate the consecrated bread—which was not lawful for them to
do, but only for the priests. [5]Or haven't you read in the Law that on the
Sabbath the priests in the temple desecrate the day and yet are innocent?**

The practice of the disciples was not without precedent. David, much earlier, had done virtually the same thing when he and his men ate the bread in the Tabernacle that was intended to be eaten only by the priests (1 Sam. 21:1-6). Jesus shows these critics that God's laws, therefore, have exceptions. They are guidelines for normal conditions, but when unusual circumstances arise, then unusual alternatives must be considered without any guilt feelings. This point is clearly displayed in the Temple itself when the priests are kept busy on the Sabbath (contrary to Sabbath law—Exod. 20:10), yet they are innocent. In other words, the Sabbath laws, like all the others, must be viewed with a degree of perspective, proportion and grace. There is an exception to every rule, and here are two perfect cases in point.

III. *The Eternal Principle (12:6-8)*

**[6]I tell you that one[a] greater than the temple is here.[7] If you had known
what these words mean, 'I desire mercy, not sacrifice,'[b] you would
not have condemned the innocent. [8]For the Son of Man is Lord of the
Sabbath."**

One Greater than the Temple Is Here. The Temple signified the presence of God. In the Holy of Holies (the most sacred chamber of the Temple) the visible glory of God could be found (Exod. 40:34 with 1 Kings 8:1-13). It was during the days of Solomon that the

---

[a] 6 Or *something*; also in verses 41 and 42   [b] 7 Hosea 6:6

Lord's glory filled the innermost sanctuary, but in Ezekiel's day, this glory departed because of Israel's many sins (Ezek. 9:3; 10:1ff.). It did not return again until Jesus appeared. In Him was the glory of God (John 1:14); in Him was the fullness of the Godhead bodily (Col. 2:6); and in Him was the fulfillment of all the Temple types (that is, in Jesus' body and mission was the fulfillment of all the ceremonies of the Temple, all the servants of the Temple, and all the physical parts of the Temple. See the special study at the close of this unit).

I Desire Mercy, Not Sacrifice. Whenever God's laws are viewed as a mere legalistic code to be followed, then the virtue of mercy is abandoned. This is precisely what happened to the Pharisees. They were quick to point their fingers in accusation. But Jesus charges these proud and pitiless men to reexamine the meaning of Hos. 6:6. In effect, Jesus rebuked these callous men for their condemning attitudes. They should be looking for ways to help people, not ways to hinder them.

The Son of Man Is the Lord of the Sabbath. The Pharisees had reversed the original meaning of the Sabbath ordinance. Although there were divinely ordered restrictions to be kept on this day, the thrust behind these guidelines was to yield a blessing for its adherents. On this day people could relax, enjoy their families and friends, and most of all, they could worship the Lord without any needless interruptions. Indeed, the Sabbath was made for people, and not people for the Sabbath, as the Pharisees had made it (Mark 2:27).

Special Study: The Tabernacle and Temple Structures

Originally, God spoke to people either directly or through dreams, visions, angels and the like. After Israel was miraculously rescued from Egypt, however, God added another dimension to His communication process—the Tabernacle. This elaborate tentlike structure was constructed during the days of Moses in the wilderness (Exod.

THE SIGNIFICANCE OF THE TABERNACLE'S FURNITURE

Objects	Symbolical Meaning	Christological Meaning
Brazen Altar	Atonement by sacrifice	Atonement through Jesus
Brazen Laver	Cleansing from world	Holiness through Jesus
Table of Showbread	Spiritual food	Life through Jesus
Candlestick	Spiritual illumination	Light through Jesus
Altar of Incense	Prayer	Prayer through Jesus' name
Ark of Covenant	God's covenant through Moses	God's covenant through Jesus
Mercy Seat	Acceptance through lamb's blood and God's mercy	Acceptance through Jesus' blood and God's mercy

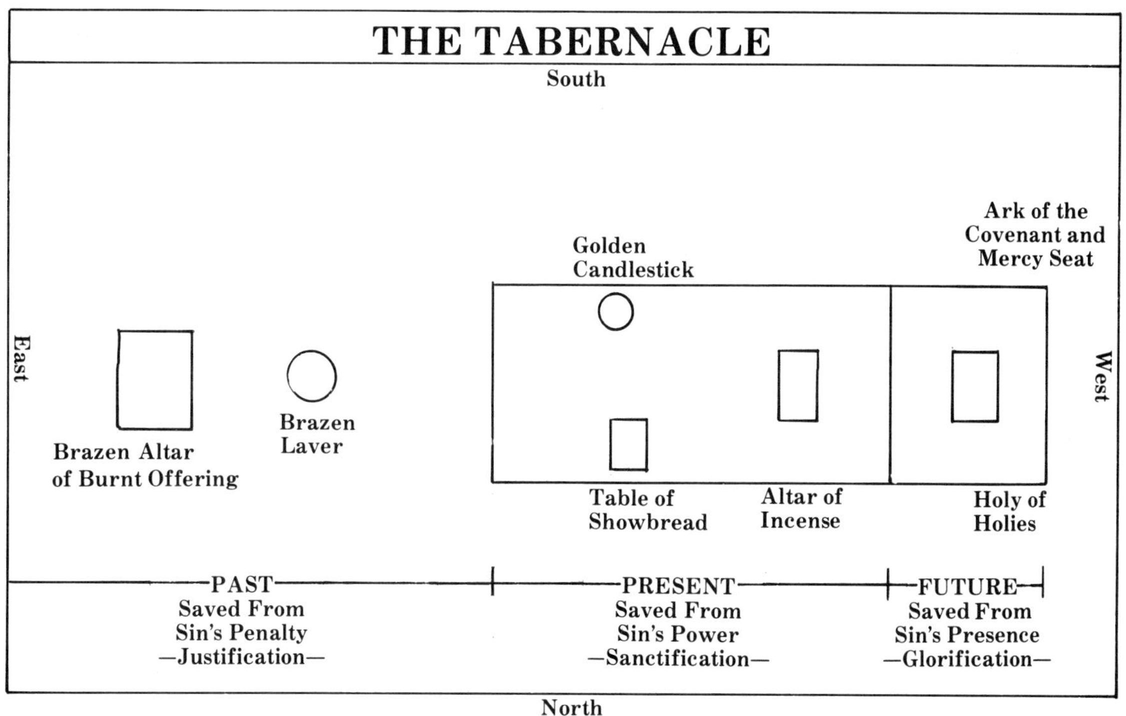

25-27; 30-31; 35-40). The purpose of the Tabernacle was to demonstrate God's presence among His people (Exod. 40:34). It also provided a number of sacrificial ceremonies which displayed how sinful people could be forgiven by a holy God (cf. Lev. and Heb.). Later, in the days of Solomon, this structure was superseded by a permanent structure called the Temple. The Temple greatly resembled the Tabernacle, and the same essential services were continued here.

There are two charts in this special study that describe the original Tabernacle, along with the prophetic significance of its various elements. It should be remembered that throughout the life and ministry of Jesus we see the fulfillment of the prophetic aspects of this structure. It has been a principle with God to speak with Israel through spiritual types (or prophetic symbols, like the Tabernacle and the Temple), and then to speak with them through the fulfillment of those types (called antitypes). Jesus is the culmination of all God's previous type-communications. It should be noted, however, that the exact meaning of each of these types is not always certain. Several options are equally viable. The above interpretations are not offered as being the only possible meanings.

Healing on the Sabbath (Matt. 12:9-21)

(cf. Mark 3:1-12 and Luke 6:6-11, 17-19)

The services in the synagogues of Jesus' day were much like our church services today. They sang, prayed, read the Scriptures and brought a teaching. The purpose was to reflect the atmosphere that was believed to be present in heaven. The synagogue was to be a place where people could find hope for conquering their troubles. It was to be a haven, a place of love and faith. Here people would unite to hear God's will explained. Here people would find answers for their problems. Here would be the spirit of expectancy.

Regrettably, actual experience often falls short of theory, and such was the case in the synagogue as well. As we see in this passage, the synagogue often displayed the weaker side of its potential. But in spite of the carnality that permeates these episodes, there is also the spiritual element that succeeds in keeping God's work marching forward.

I. *Inside the Synagogue (12:9-13)*

> **9Going on from that place, he went into their synagogue, 10and a man**
> **with a shriveled hand was there. Looking for a reason to accuse Jesus, they asked him, "Is it lawful to heal on the Sabbath?"**
>
> **11He said to them, "If any of you has a sheep and it falls into a pit on the**
> **Sabbath, will you not take hold of it and lift it out? 12How much more**
> **valuable is a man than a sheep! Therefore it is lawful to do good on the Sabbath."**
>
> **13Then he said to the man, "Stretch out your hand." So he stretched it out and it was completely restored, just as sound as the other.**

Is It Lawful to Heal on the Sabbath? It is almost impossible to imagine they would raise such a question. In many synagogues of Jesus' day the programs of the institution took priority over the problems of the individuals. Such a lopsided and inflexible situation had to be addressed. And Jesus would not waste a second before setting the record straight.

It Is Lawful to Do Good on the Sabbath. Jesus had a unique ability for locating persons with deep hurts. Jesus desired to help such people and not merely to maintain some purely human, religious order of service. The synagogue was to be a place where people's needs could be met. And the Sabbath day was to be a day for helping those who suffered. The Jewish leaders, however, had developed such a rigid interpretation of the Sabbath rest that they missed its purpose altogether (see details in Matt. 12:1-8). Apparently, they deemed it appropriate to help a fallen sheep, but not to help a crippled man. Jesus would not tolerate this distorted order of values.

Hand Was Completely Restored. Notice the simplicity of this healing—"Stretch out your hand." There were no academic tests to pass and no standard of perfection to be attained first. Jesus looked only for public obedience. Jesus wanted the man to express his faith openly and without shame or embarrassment. The requirements were well within this man's abilities. He met the conditions and was completely restored to health.

They Plotted How They Might Kill Jesus. The natural mind reasons that the appearance of a miracle will produce a most positive result, but you cannot use the natural mind to predict people's responses. The Bible tells us, again and again, that our hearts are corrupt, impure and prone toward evil (Mark 7:20-23). Here we see clear proof of the sordid condition of the human heart. The healing of a crippled man did not convert these sinners, but instead it further irritated their own self-righteousness (cf. Matt. 11:21-23; 12:38-45; Luke 10:12-15; John 3:16-21). Let us learn a practical lesson from this episode—if people will not listen to Jesus' words, it is highly unlikely they will heed His miracles either (Luke 16:30, 31)!

II. *Outside the Synagogue (12:14-21)*

14But the Pharisees went out and plotted how they might kill Jesus.
15Aware of this, Jesus withdrew from that place. Many followed him,
and he healed all their sick, 16warning them not to tell who he was. 17This
was to fulfill what was spoken through the prophet Isaiah:

18"Here is my servant whom I have chosen,
the one I love, in whom I delight;
I will put my Spirit on him,
and he will proclaim justice to the nations.
19He will not quarrel or cry out;
no one will hear his voice in the streets.
20A bruised reed he will not break,
and a smoldering wick he will not snuff out,
till he leads justice to victory.
21In his name the nations will put their hope."[a]

[a] 21 Isaiah 42:1-4

Jesus Withdrew from That Place. There is an unspoken rule that has always been in the synagogue (and in the Church, too). It goes something like this, "You must help people, but you must not rock the boat in the process." Rocking the boat means doing something that might upset certain persons. Jesus knew this unspoken guideline. But His interest was centered on helping people who hurt, regardless of the cost. Here the cost was excommunication. Jesus seemed to be rejected after only one exposure to the people. There was no room for this kind of person in this synagogue.

Observe that Jesus departed without offering any resistance. Still, "many followed him, and he healed all their sick." There is a wonderful word of encouragement here. Even when Jesus was expelled from a synagogue, still He was found and followed. He was never far from those who earnestly desired to be His true disciples, wherever they were. This is true today as well.

Warning Them Not to Tell Who He Was. See notes on Matt. 9:30 for comments.

The Prophet Isaiah. Matthew, who sees so many fulfillments of Old Testament prophecies in the life of Jesus, finds here another prediction about Jesus. This one is taken from Isa. 42:1-4. In these verses we see four prophecies regarding Jesus: (1) His unique relationship to God (He is chosen, beloved and anointed by Him), (2) His special mission (He is to be a proclaimer of justice), (3) His unusual character (He does not argue and He is full of gentleness), and (4) His certain success in doing God's will (He will rally many about himself, including Gentiles, and give them the hope of eternal life).

The Unpardonable Sin (Matt. 12:22-37)

(cf. Mark 3:20-30 and Luke 11:14-23)

There are many kinds of sins for which we may be found guilty. One person has noted there are more than seven hundred sins recorded in the Bible. But for each of these violations there is divine forgiveness available through repentance and obedient faith in the Lord Jesus Christ (1 John 1:7-2:2).

Yet there remains one sin for which there is absolutely no forgiveness, "either in this age or in the age to come" (Matt. 12:32). It is often called "the unpardonable sin." This is a horrible sin to commit, for all who commit it shall be cast into the torments of hell forever. Let us earnestly learn, then, the nature of this sin and how we can avoid committing it.

I. *The Charge (12:22-24)*

[22]Then they brought him a demon-possessed man who was blind and mute, and Jesus healed him, so that he could both talk and see. [23]All the people were astonished and said, "Could this be the Son of David?"

[24]But when the Pharisees heard this, they said, "It is only by Beelzebub,[a] the prince of demons, that this fellow drives out demons."

How shallow and off the track are some people's assessments of spiritual matters. And how hardened is their speech against the genuine works and workers of God. There seems to be no limit to the extent to which some persons will go in attempting to discredit God-anointed ministries.

The Pharisees could not see the hand of God in this miracle. In fact, their carnal eyes were so perverted to spiritual realities that they actually attributed this supernatural healing to the leader of the demonic host, Beelzebub (another title for Satan). Associating Jesus with this name, which means "lord of the dung hill" (a place for garbage and human excrement) was a most thoughtless act.

II. *The Countercharges (12:25-37)*

[25]Jesus knew their thoughts and said to them, "Every kingdom divided against itself will be ruined, and every city or household divided against itself will not stand. [26]If Satan drives out Satan, he is divided against himself. How then can his kingdom stand? [27]And if I drive out demons by Beelzebub, by whom do your people drive them out? So then, they will be your judges. [28]But if I drive out demons by the Spirit of God, then the kingdom of God has come upon you.

[29]"Or again, how can anyone enter a strong man's house and carry off his possessions unless he first ties up the strong man? Then he can rob his house.

[30]He who is not with me is against me, and he who does not gather with me scatters. [31]And so I tell you, every sin and blasphemy will be forgiven men, but the blasphemy against the Spirit will not be forgiven. [32]Anyone who speaks a word against the Son of Man will be forgiven, but anyone who speaks against the Holy Spirit will not be forgiven, either in this age or in the age to come.

[33]"Make a tree good and its fruit will be good, or make a tree bad and its fruit will be bad, for a tree is recognized by its fruit. [34]You brood of vipers, how can you who are evil say anything good? For out of the overflow of the

a 24 Greek *Beezeboul* or *Beelzeboul;* also in verse 27

heart the mouth speaks. 35 The good man brings good things out of the good stored up in him, and the evil man brings evil things out of the evil stored up in him. 36 But I tell you that men will have to give account on the day of judgment for every careless word they have spoken. 37 For by your words you will be acquitted, and by your words you will be condemned."

Jesus Knew Their Thoughts. No less than five times the Scriptures attest to the ability of Jesus to know the thoughts of others (Matt. 9:4; 12:25; Mark 2:8; John 2:24, 25; Rev. 2:23). Such insights were doubtlessly imparted by God (1 Cor. 12:8). Today, Jesus knows every secret thought of everyone. Because of His divine state of exaltation, nothing is hidden from Him. He knows everything there is to know about each of us.

Here we notice Jesus hearing the thoughts of His critics. Jesus responds boldly to His assailants. His words are sharp and direct. He will leave no room for doubt as to who is the real servant of Satan.

Every Kingdom Divided Against Itself Will Be Ruined. If homes, cities and nations cannot stand up under internal division, how can Satan withstand such a division? He cannot. Therefore, Jesus points out, it is ridiculous even to think He could be a servant of Satan and, at the same time, cast out demons from people. Satan does not cast himself out or revoke his own works. Such a practice would be foolish on his part. It would divide his kingdom and render him powerless. No, Satan does not work to inhabit someone only to have one of his associates cast him from that residence.

By Whom Do Your People Cast Out Demons? Jesus stated that other Jews were doing the same thing He had just done, and without the condemnation of the Pharisees. Jesus' actions were not unprecedented. If His actions were wrong, then so were theirs. If He were a disciple of Satan, so were they. This perfect logic drew no response.

The Kingdom of God Has Come upon You. Jesus declares that His power over Satan actually proves God's Kingdom is presently active among men. Satan's hold on people, says Jesus, can be revoked because he has been defeated through the invasion of God's Kingdom in the earth. Men, women and children can be set completely free from all demonic harassment because God's power is far greater than Satan's grip (cf. Mark 16:17; James 4:7; 1 John 4:4).

Further, Jesus announces that even as a thief must tie up the owner of a household before he can steal his property, so He has bound Satan in order to snatch back the souls he has ensnared. Satan's reign over men has now come against a dramatic confrontation. No longer will his powers be awesome (Heb. 2:14, 15; Col. 2:15). Through the power of the Holy Spirit in the Kingdom of God, Satan must flee from even the youngest Christian (James 4:7)!

He Who Is Not With Me Is Against Me. How swiftly Jesus reverses the accusation of who is truly guilty of sin. The Pharisees are placed in an awkward position by His statement. Jesus makes it abundantly plain that if anyone does not positively unite with Him and His mission, then that person is a hindrance to the advancement of God's Kingdom. There can be no neutrality. It is an either-or decision. *Either* we are actively following Jesus and doing His will, *or* we are actively following the interests presented by self, sin and Satan (1 John 3:8, 9). There is no other option available in the light of this context.

Blasphemy Against the Spirit. There are innumerable sins for which divine forgiveness is available. Even sins that are directed at Christ can be forgiven. Both Peter, in his denials of Christ (Matt. 26:74, 75), and Paul, in his persecution of Christ and His church (Acts 9:1ff.), experienced pardon. There are no sins too wretched for the grace and love of God to forgive—except one. The only exception to this rule is that sin which is called the "blasphemy against the Spirit." How should we understand the nature of this unique sin?

First, notice the party who is potentially guilty of this horrible offense. Jesus tells the Pharisees it is *they* who are candidates for committing this unpardonable sin. The disciples do not receive this threat, but the callous, arrogant and unrepentant Pharisees are its recipients.

Second, notice the person against whom this offense is committed. It is the Holy Spirit. The Pharisees not only rejected the message of Jesus, they also resisted the miracles which the Holy Spirit brought through Jesus. This is a double denial and rejection of God's witness. With closed ears they refused to receive heaven's double call to repentance and salvation. As a result of casting aside the work of the Holy Spirit, they were actually refusing God's final offer to make Jesus' words plain. As a result, they were actually sealing their own doom.

The unpardonable sin, then, is the *continued rejection* of the Holy Spirit's witness to the ministry of Christ's love and salvation. There is only one sin that sends anyone to hell—closed minds and hearts—closed to God's plan of eternal life through Jesus Christ. This single sin knows no forgiveness, and naturally, only a spiritually lost person is capable of committing it. On the other hand, if a person desires to repent, this is evidence that he or she has not committed this sin.

A Tree Is Recognized by Its Fruit. Lastly, Jesus renounces the Pharisees for their hypocrisy. He tells them that trees are known by their fruit—good trees will invariably yield good fruit, while bad trees will always produce bad fruit. There is no possibility for any exceptions here. In like manner, Jesus shows that a person's heart is exposed by the words of his mouth. It is by these words that a person is either justified or condemned. And the words of the Pharisees, calling Jesus a companion of Satan, left no question about the nature of their hearts and the absence of personal salvation in their lives.

The Sign of Jonah (Matt. 12:38-45)

(cf. Luke 11:29-32)

Once Jesus had completed His stunning rebuke of the Pharisees (Matt. 12:25-37), they immediately changed the subject. This is a common tactic. If one fails with one line of attack, frequently he will attempt another approach with a different angle. But Jesus would not be trapped by these spiritually hollow persons.

I. *The Carnal Request (12:38)*

> **38 Then some of the Pharisees and teachers of the law said to him, "Teacher, we want to see a miraculous sign from you."**

These religious men now demanded a sign from Jesus in order to prove the veracity of His words, as if what they had already seen was insufficient evidence (Matt. 12:28). They wanted more. This is one of the traits of spiritually weak persons. They always want more evidence in order to be persuaded. They are never content with what they have. In a pretense of interest, they seek still further convincing proofs.

II. *The Careful Response (12:39-45)*

> **39 He answered, "A wicked and adulterous generation asks for a miraculous sign! But none will be given it except the sign of the prophet Jonah. 40 For as Jonah was three days and three nights in the belly of a huge fish, so the Son of Man will be three days and three nights in the heart of the earth. 41 The men of Nineveh will stand up at the judgment with this generation and condemn it; for they repented at the preaching of Jonah, and now one greater than Jonah is here. 42 The Queen of the South will rise at the judgment with this generation and condemn it; for she came from the ends of the earth to listen to Solomon's wisdom, and now one greater than Solomon is here.**
>
> **43 "When an evil[a] spirit comes out of a man, it goes through arid places seeking rest and does not find it. 44 Then it says, 'I will return to the house I left.' When it arrives, it finds the house unoccupied, swept clean and put in order. 45 Then it goes and takes with it seven other spirits more wicked than itself, and they go in and live there. And the final condition of that man is worse than the first. That is how it will be with this wicked generation."**

---

a *43* Greek *unclean*

A Wicked and Adulterous Generation. What a rebuke! The word "wicked" refers to one who is morally or ethically bankrupt. It is used of persons who bring pain, sorrow and evil to others. The word "adulterous" is used here in its figurative sense, meaning those who enjoy intimate relationships with the world when they should be showing this affection toward God (cf. Matt. 16:4). Jesus could detect the carnal intent of His inquirers, and He is soundly disturbed by their unbelief. He will not permit these frauds to escape without a statement accusing them of their guilt.

The Sign of Jonah. Jesus, then, gives His hearers a sign, a prophetic sign (though they probably sought more tangible evidence). The sign was Jonah. Just as he had spent three days and nights in a great fish before being restored to dry land, so Jesus would be encased by the earth for the same period before He would be resurrected. This was a terrific sign, but unless you were one of Jesus' disciples (or unless you had heard these words after the Resurrection, as we have been so privileged), then the practicality of this sign would have been missed. It is as if the teachers of the law and the Pharisees received what they asked for without getting what they expected or wanted. How common this disappointment is, especially among those who will not accept what is placed before them. God always gives us enough of His grace to allow us to be abundantly blessed. It is when we want more and more that we get into trouble (Luke 1:5-22; 1 Cor. 10:1-13).

The Men of Nineveh/The Queen of the South. If the citizens of Nineveh accepted the words of the reluctant prophet, Jonah, and if the Queen of Sheba received the words of Solomon, Jesus asked, how can you expect them not to condemn those who reject the witness of the Son of God? The people of Nineveh (see the book of Jonah) and the Queen of the South (see 1 Kings 10:1-13) listened attentively to a lesser figure than Jesus. Yet the generation of Jesus' day would not, to a large degree, listen to Him. Even though they received the greater light, they refused to accept its illumination. Surely they will be judged more severely than any other generation of people on the earth (Matt. 10:11-15; 11:20-24).

An Evil Spirit Comes Out and Returns. In a final note of correction, Jesus turned to the subject of unclean spirits (or demons). How subtly, yet soberly, Jesus tells His audience that whereas they were once on the right path, now they have stopped in their spiritual journey. They had been delivered from a demonic grip (probably through hearing and following the counsel of John the Baptist). They were now clean and orderly, but their hearts were left "unoccupied." In other words, many in Jesus' hearing had turned from sin, but they had not yet turned toward Christ. We must remember it is never enough for a person to stop sinning; he must also start serving Christ. Conversion is not complete until a sinner turns from his own self-willed life and surrenders himself to Jesus (Matt. 10:39). To be caught between these two stations is a dangerous trap. In this place we are neither friends with the world nor friends of Jesus. As a result of such lukewarmness, our doorway is open to even worse demonic harassment.

The point Jesus makes is tremendously useful to everyone. Receive all God has for you. Do not resist any of His offerings. It is not enough to be void of negative traits; we must also be filled with positive virtues. We must permit the Holy Spirit to have full and free access to every facet of our lives.

Jesus' Fuller Family (Matt. 12:46-50)

(cf. Mark 3:31-35 and Luke 8:19-21)

Sometimes it is those nearest to us who unintentionally hinder God's works in our lives. Many persons have yielded to the sincere, but misunderstanding, voices of their families. Consequently, they have bypassed the full measure of God's will for them. Home, as important as it is—even to God—cannot replace the value of God's Kingdom. Jesus would not fall to the undiscerning concern of his family.

46While Jesus was still talking to the crowd, his mother and brothers stood outside, wanting to speak to him. 47Someone told him, "Your mother and brothers are standing outside, wanting to speak to you."[a]

48He replied, "Who is my mother, and who are my brothers?" 49Pointing to his disciples, he said, "Here are my mother and my brothers. 50For whoever does the will of my Father in heaven is my brother and sister and mother."

It must have been extremely difficult for Jesus to withstand the bitter attacks that came from so-called spiritual leaders of His day. Such insults always bring pain and a burden. His own family, too, came to speak with Him. The contents of what they wanted to say are not stated. But it is not difficult to imagine that they thought Jesus had spoken a bit too harshly and should now come home for a while to rest and possibly to reconsider His ideas (Mark 3:21; John 7:5).

Jesus asks, "Who is my mother, and who are my brothers?" He then answers His own question by stating it is those who do God's will that are members of His family. How difficult it must have been for Him to say this. Yet, Jesus knew there could be no compromise in His mission. The family of Christ would be made up of those who could accept His message and who could dedicate themselves to following each of His footprints.

a 47 Some manuscripts do not have verse 47.

The Parable of the Four Soils (Matt. 13:1-23)

(cf. Mark 4:1-20 and Luke 8:4-15)

The eight parables found in Matthew 13 are all alike in that they share the same theme—the Kingdom of heaven (or of God). This explains why they are sometimes called "the Kingdom parables." They are different in their stress upon varying aspects of God's Kingdom. Some of the parables focus upon the King. Others concentrate on the subjects of the King. Still others look more sharply at the Kingdom's realm or character. And some blend each of these elements together.

Perhaps the key thread in these parables that probably shocked many in Jesus' audience was His continuous downplay of an immediate, full and climactic establishment of God's Kingdom. This was the prevailing opinion regarding the Kingdom—it would appear suddenly, abolish all unrighteousness and enthrone an earthly messiah as king over all the earth. But this notion was not in accord with God's timing. And the parables here show how the Kingdom was (and is) to enter and spread throughout the entire world first. Then would come the climactic aspects of the Kingdom. This point is the chief "secret" of all the parabolic teachings (Matt. 13:11).

One of the most loved and frequently quoted stories of Jesus is this one now before us. It is a simple message taken from the world of farming, but its truths are applicable for all people the world over and for all of time.

There are several lessons to be learned in this parable. First, we see the Word of God. Acting as a seed, it can grow in our lives and produce wonderful fruit. Second, we notice the devil—the one who can remove the Word of God from us, if we do not properly understand it (this underscores the need for a strong, systematic teaching ministry in the local church). Third, we observe the shallowness of some who profess a Christian faith—they have no roots. Fourth, we perceive the natural enemies of God's Word—worry, riches and pleasures. Fifth, we see the the qualifications for bearing spiritual fruit—a noble, good and persevering heart. Sixth, we understand that only a few who hear God's Word (one out of four) retain it to the extent that they are truly saved. The remainder may profess faith, but they do not possess it.

I. *The Information (13:1-9)*

13 That same day Jesus went out of the house and sat by the lake.
2Such large crowds gathered around him that he got into a boat
and sat in it, while all the people stood on the shore. 3Then he told them

**many things in parables, saying: "A farmer went out to sow his seed. 4As
he was scattering the seed, some fell along the path, and the birds came
and ate it up. 5Some fell on rocky places, where it did not have much soil. It
sprang up quickly, because the soil was shallow. 6But when the sun came
up, the plants were scorched, and they withered because they had no root.
7Other seed fell among thorns, which grew up and choked the plants.
8Still other seed fell on good soil, where it produced a crop—a hundred,
sixty or thirty times what was sown. 9He who has ears, let him hear."**

The term "parable" means the placing of things side by side for the sake of making a comparison. It is the art of telling a story through the use of earthly objects. It is the skill of using visible things to convey invisible realities. Some people call parables eternal (or heavenly) messages from temporal (or earthly) objects. In short, a parable is the communication of a spiritual truth through the use of physical objects. Parables, then, turn the abstract into the concrete. They open our eyes, spark our attention and fill our souls with grand truths.

For a listing of Jesus' parables, see the chart entitled "The Parables of Jesus."

THE PARABLES OF JESUS

I. Plant Parables

1. Fig tree—Matt. 24:32-35
2. Tree known by its fruit—Matt. 12:33-37
3. Vineyard—Matt. 21:33-46
4. Mustard seed—Matt. 13:31, 32
5. Tares—Matt. 13:24-30
6. Yeast—Matt. 13:33
7. Seed-sower—Matt. 13:1-23

II. Animal Parables

1. Lost sheep—Matt. 18:12-14; Luke 15:3-7
2. Sheep and goats—Matt. 25:31-46

III. People Parables

1. Unmerciful servant—Matt. 18:23-35
2. Laborers in the vineyard—Matt. 20:1-16
3. Two sons—Matt. 21:28-32
4. Ten virgins—Matt. 25:1-13
5. Master takes a far journey—Mark 13:34-37
6. Two debtors—Luke 7:41-43
7. Good Samaritan—Luke 10:30-37
8. Persistent friend—Luke 11:5-10
9. Rich fool—Luke 12:16-21
10. Wise stewards—Luke 12:42-48
11. King goes to war—Luke 14:31-33
12. Prodigal son—Luke 15:11-32
13. Unjust steward—Luke 16:1-13
14. Persistent woman—Luke 18:2-8
15. Pharisee and Publican—Luke 18:10-14
16. Lazarus and the rich man—Luke 16:19-31

IV. Object Parables

1. Hidden treasure—Matt. 13:44
2. Pearl—Matt. 13:45, 46
3. Fish net—Matt. 13:47-51
4. Marriage feast—Matt. 22:2-14; Luke 14:16-24
5. Talents—Matt. 25:14-30
6. Unfinished tower—Luke 14:28-30
7. Rewards—Luke 19:11-27
8. House on rock and sand—Matt. 7:24-27
9. Yeast—Matt. 13:33
10. Candle under bushel—Matt. 5:15, 16
11. New cloth and old garment—Matt. 9:16
12. New wine and old skins—Matt. 9:17

II. *The Implications (13:10-17)*

[10]The disciples came to him and asked, "Why do you speak to the
people in parables?"
[11]He replied, "The knowledge of the secrets of the kingdom of heaven
has been given to you, but not to them. [12]Whoever has will be given more,
and he will have an abundance. Whoever does not have, even what he
has will be taken from him. [13]This is why I speak to them in parables:

"Though seeing, they do not see;
though hearing, they do not hear or understand.

[14]In them is fulfilled the prophecy of Isaiah:

" 'You will be ever hearing but never understanding;
you will be ever seeing but never perceiving.
[15]For this people's heart has become calloused;
they hardly hear with their ears,
and they have closed their eyes.
Otherwise they might see with their eyes,
hear with their ears,
understand with their hearts
and turn, and I would heal them.'[a]

[16]But blessed are your eyes because they see, and your ears because they
hear. [17]For I tell you the truth, many prophets and righteous men
longed to see what you see but did not see it, and to hear what you hear
but did not hear it.

The Secrets of the Kingdom. The reasons Jesus provides for speaking in parables are twofold: (1) to reveal the secrets of the Kingdom to serious seekers; (2) to conceal the secrets of the Kingdom from carnal inquirers.

There were two sets of people listening to Jesus as He taught. One group was eager and responsive. The other group was closed-minded and critical. The purpose of the parabolic approach was to reveal truths to simple folks, while actually concealing the same truths from the so-called wise people (cf. Matt. 11:25, 26).

Furthermore, Jesus states that those who are open and responsive will be given even greater insights into the things of God (1 Cor. 2:9-11). But those who are stubborn of heart will remain confounded and even lose what little bit of spiritual reality they do possess.

The Prophecy of Isaiah. Jesus quotes Isa. 6:9-10, and in so doing, He announces that the less positive members among His audiences are actually fulfilling this prophecy.

[a] *15* Isaiah 6:9, 10

There is nothing secretive in these words. They are so easy to understand that His point cannot be missed. Jesus saw that His audiences included spiritually blind persons. And they were blind to His message because they chose to close their eyes and ears to God's truth.

Blessed Are Your Eyes. The believers of the Old Testament era desired earnestly to see the day when the Messiah would walk on the earth. Noah, Abraham, Moses, Samuel, David, Isaiah, Daniel and thousands (if not millions) of others looked forward to this period, but none lived to see it (Heb. 11:13, 39, 40; 1 Pet. 1:10, 11). Only one generation would know this honor of honors. The disciples of the first century were to know and to marvel at this rare privilege (John 1:1-14; 1 John 1:1-3).

III. *The Interpretation (13:18-23)*

18"Listen then to what the parable of the sower means: 19When anyone
hears the message about the kingdom and does not understand it, the
evil one comes and snatches away what was sown in his heart. This is the
seed sown along the path. 20What was sown on rocky places is the man
who hears the word and at once receives it with joy. 21But since he has
no root, he lasts only a short time. When trouble or persecution comes
because of the word, he quickly falls away. 22What was sown among the
thorns is the man who hears the word, but the worries of this life and the
deceitfulness of wealth choke it, making it unfruitful. 23But what was
sown on good soil is the man who hears the word and understands it. He
produces a crop, yielding a hundred, sixty or thirty times what was
sown."

There are few teachings that are more practical to the growing Christian than those found in this parable. There are three major elements that demand our most sincere attention.

1. *The Sower.* "A farmer went out to sow" (v. 3). That is all. Jesus may have seen a farmer planting seeds in a field and used him as an illustration. The identity of the farmer is not important. Anyone can sow. Rich or poor; professional or amateur; strong or weak. Any individual can plant seeds.

2. *The Seed.* This is the "message about the kingdom" (v. 19). It is that message of heaven which reveals God's presence and power in the world. No greater seed has ever been planted. It is a seed of faith, of hope, of love, of eternal life. This seed defeats Satan and ushers in the Kingdom of God and the era of the Holy Spirit.

3. *The Soils.* There are four different soils: the soil of a roadway or trodden path

(v. 4), a rocky soil (v. 5), a thorny soil (v. 7) and a good soil (v. 8). The four soils represent four kinds of people who hear the words of God's Kingdom and the effects that can be expected when they hear this message.

If the ratios used here are not accidental, then it can be said that approximately one quarter of those persons who hear the teaching of God's Word will "not understand it" (v. 19). Naturally, there will be no results produced by such a situation. In fact, Satan will see to it that those who lack spiritual understanding will remain in darkness, even though they may come and listen to the Word of the sower. How important it is for people to ask questions and get answers for their faith. The only poor question is the one we fail to ask. The first step in defeating the devil comes by understanding the message of the Bible.

Another quarter of those hearing the biblical message will immediately receive it with joy (v. 20). But before long, these shallow persons discover that those who live according to the principles of the Kingdom will receive a variety of pressures because

THE PARABLE OF THE FOUR SOILS

	Conditions of the Soils/People	Tests	Results
Soil 1	Trodden soil No understanding	Birds devour them Trodden under foot	Satan removes the Word No belief and no salvation
Soil 2	Rocky soil Received with joy No depth	Not much earth or moisture No root/scorched by the sun Persecution arises over the Word	Immediate growth Endures for a while, then withers Believes for a while, then falls away
Soil 3	Thorny soil	Cares of this world/life Deceitfulness of riches Lust of things Pleasures of this life	Word is choked to death No fruit/no fruit that lasts
Soil 4	Good soil Understands the Word Accepts the Word Holds on to the Word Honest and good heart	(not stated)	Yields fruit: one-hundred-fold, sixtyfold, thirtyfold Bears fruit with patience

of it (v. 21). As a result of this pressure they will fall away without producing any "crop." The meaning of "crop," in this usage, is probably the natural byproducts that accompany an individual's Spirit-filled walk with Jesus Christ.

The next quarter of listeners also receive the Word of God, but soon they abandon it for the material possessions of this present world (v. 22). The spiritual lifespans of such people are too short to bear any lasting fruit.

The final quarter hear God's message, understand it and hold on to it with perseverance until they bear lasting fruit (v. 23). The reference to three different sizes of crops (one-hundredfold, sixtyfold and thirtyfold) may suggest the different levels of obedience found in Christ's disciples. Some live up to their full potential, while others live at about one-half or one-quarter of their real potential.

One final observation deserves a special comment. It is appropriate to look intensely at the seed (the Word of the Kingdom) in each of these four parties. This may be more important than anything else. Notice that both our conversion and our fruitfulness depend upon how we respond to the Word of God. When it is not understood, or when it is only given a shallow treatment, it produces nothing that will last. It seems fair (even necessary!) to ask ourselves, then, what role the Scriptures play in our own daily lives. Surely, if we are not in God's Word, His Word cannot be in us. And if His Words do not dwell richly in us, we cannot bear any fruit (John 15:1-8).

Examine the chart entitled "The Parable of the Four Soils." It analyzes this parable with the full revelation that is given in the three Gospel records.

The Parable of the Weeds (Matt. 13:24-30)

(cf. Matt. 13:36-43; Mark 4:26-29)

Just as there is an appointed time for reaping the harvest in the farmer's field, so there is an appointed time in God's Kingdom for gathering the fruit. Someday—sooner than we might imagine—God will say the time is finished. It's harvest time!

> **24Jesus told them another parable: "The kingdom of heaven is like a**
> **man who sowed good seed in his field. 25But while everyone was**
> **sleeping, his enemy came and sowed weeds among the wheat, and went**
> **away. 26When the wheat sprouted and formed heads, then the weeds**
> **also appeared.**
> **27"The owner's servants came to him and said, 'Sir, didn't you sow**
> **good seed in your field? Where then did the weeds come from?'**
> **28" 'An enemy did this,' he replied.**
> **"The servants asked him, 'Do you want us to go and pull them up?'**

29" 'No,' he answered, 'because while you are pulling the weeds, you may root up the wheat with them. 30Let both grow together until the harvest. At that time I will tell the harvesters: First collect the weeds and tie them in bundles to be burned, then gather the wheat and bring it into my barn.' "

The telling of this parable (vv. 24-30) and the explaining of this parable (vv. 36-43) are separated by two short stories (also parables). In the interest of convenience, the interpretation of these parables is included in the following comments.

For such a short parable there are plenty of significant details. And each of them is clearly spelled out for our understanding. Here, then, are a few highlights that capture the essence of this illustration.

First, we learn that the Kingdom will infiltrate the whole world and claim it for God. Nevertheless, as long as this phase of the Kingdom age exists, there always will be the presence of God's children and the devil's children in the same world. Evolution can offer us no hope of eliminating the weeds of society. Until the Son of man sends out His angels to separate the wheat from the weeds, the present order of things will continue. This dual existence of good and evil certainly did not conform to the Jew's opinions about the Kingdom.

Second, we learn it is not our mission to remove the weeds from the world. This would be an impossible task—both from the perspective of discerning precisely who is a weed, and from the angle of knowing how to remove such an overwhelming number of weeds. Our task is not condemnation; our labor of love is reconciliation (2 Cor. 5:17-21). We are not to consume the world, but to convert it to Christ! This, too, differed greatly from popular Jewish teachings.

Third, we learn that a time has been appointed when the Son of man will send out His angels in order to remove all the weeds from the earth. They will then cast these weeds—non-Christians—into a fiery furnace of great discomfort. No one who fails to follow Christ can escape this appointment. Every sinner will be exposed. And the wages for his sins will be paid in full. The time of this judgment is set at "the end of the age" (v. 39). The Jews thought and hoped it would happen immediately. But they must wait until Jesus' Second Coming.

Fourth, we learn that a time has also been appointed when all the sons of the Kingdom—all the Christians—will live together in a world of sinless bliss. God has not forgotten His people or His promises. Everyone who has lived for Him will be gloriously rewarded, but they must wait for its proper timing.

The whole world is headed down a dead-end street. Someday everyone will come face to face with the Son of man, Jesus. Those who have followed Him will enjoy His presence and a sinless environment forever. But those who have not joined Him will face a just retribution. What a choice! The decision is mine—and yours!

The Parables of the Mustard Seed and Yeast (Matt. 13:31-35)

(cf. Mark 4:30-32 and Luke 13:18-21)

A picture, it has been said, speaks a thousand words. But the thousand words so spoken are not always the same for each person. That makes quite a few different words coming forth from the same picture.

What is true of pictures is equally true of Jesus' parables. They each speak a thousand words. But these words are not the same for each Bible interpreter.

While Jesus explained the first two parables in this series of eight parables, He did not explain the remaining six. As a result, differing interpretations have emerged. And perhaps, if one's point of view is not altogether incompatible with the Scriptures, there may be merit found in a number of varying interpretations.

The two parables now before us have been placed together in this study because of their apparent similarities (this dualistic tendency is characteristic of Matthew's writing [5:13-16; 13:44-46]). Both illustrate a pattern of growth—the former being external in nature and the latter being internal in nature.

I. *The Parable of the Mustard Seed (13:31, 32)*

> **31He told them another parable: "The kingdom of heaven is like a mustard seed, which a man took and planted in his field. 32Though it is the smallest of all your seeds, yet when it grows, it is the largest of garden plants and becomes a tree, so that the birds of the air come and perch in its branches."**

The obvious sense of this story is to be found in the immediate size of God's Kingdom and its contrasting size in subsequent years. Although its dimensions are small and unimpressive at the start, its end will be most notable. The Kingdom originates in only one person, Jesus Christ; but it will spread until it encompasses people throughout the entire world.

Take courage. We must not measure things by first appearances. Little is much, when God is in it. Small things can become big things. God can greatly multiply seemingly insignificant matters and turn them into matters of global importance.

The Jews who sought an immediate and climactic kingdom were to learn in this parable (and the previous ones as well) that God's plan was less dramatic than they had anticipated. His Kingdom would grow gradually through those who received its message. Further, His Kingdom would invade all the world, not confining itself to the borders of Israel.

The reference to "the birds of the air" that perch in the branches of the mature plant may refer to the shelter and rest that the Kingdom will provide for its members. Others see in these birds the operation of demonic forces in the domain of the Kingdom. Neither of these possibilities adds to or distracts from the basic teaching of the story. The Scriptures refer to birds in both a positive manner (Matt. 6:26) and a negative manner (Matt. 13:4, 19). Either position is defendable.

II. *The Parable of the Yeast (13:33)*

> **33He told them still another parable: "The kingdom of heaven is like yeast that a woman took and mixed into a large amount[a] of flour until it worked all through the dough."**

This parable seems to stress the same fundamental points found in the preceding parable. Although some teachers have seen the yeast (or leaven), as it is used here, as representing evil doctrines that will eventually permeate the whole church (Matt. 16:6, 12; 1 Cor. 5:6-8; Gal. 5:8, 9), this negative interpretation is unprovable, since leaven is also used in positive ways (Lev. 7:13; 23:17).

There is one clear contrast that ought to be noted between these two parables. In the former illustration the growth of the Kingdom is externally visible. In this story, however, the growth is internal and not so easily perceived. Perhaps the point to this contrast is found in the fact that wherever the Kingdom may be seen, its works go beyond immediately visible considerations. Men, women, children, and even complete communities and nations, have been internally transformed by the message and power of the Kingdom of heaven. The Kingdom of heaven is more than God's rule among men; it is also His power in them for the sake of transforming them.

III. *The Fulfillment of a Prophecy (13:34, 35)*

> **34Jesus spoke all these things to the crowd in parables; he did not say anything to them without using a parable. 35So was fulfilled what was spoken through the prophet:**
>
> **"I will open my mouth in parables,**
> **I will utter things hidden since the creation of**
> **the world."[b]**

It should be understood that Jesus did not always speak in parables. A few persons have stretched these words to such an extreme length that they actually believe Jesus

---

a 33 Greek *three satas* (probably about ½ bushel or 22 liters) b 35 Psalm 78:2

only spoke in parables. But this is not the case at all. Jesus certainly used parables, and on at least one occasion (cited here), He taught only by parables, but He generally used other, more direct, methods (cf. Matt. 5-7 for a combination of methods). This fact should be clear to all, but some have missed it.

On this unusual day of parabolic teachings, Matthew became aware that here was another prophetic fulfillment in Jesus' life. This time the prophecy was taken from Ps. 78:2. There are two items to note in this prophecy. First, there is the declaration that the Messiah would teach in parables. Second, there is the announcement that the Messiah would disclose matters that had previously been veiled. Certainly Jesus' teachings about the gradual expansion of the Kingdom through personal acceptance is one illustration of such a previously unknown matter. Everyone was expecting an immediate overthrow of the kingdoms of the earth, followed by the full establishment of God's Kingdom among people. Jesus, however, taught that the Kingdom would develop gradually.

The Parable of the Weeds Is Explained (Matt. 13:36-43)

(cf. Matt. 13:24-30 and Mark 4:26-29)

**36Then he left the crowd and went into the house. His disciples came to
him and said, "Explain to us the parable of the weeds in the field."
37He answered, "The one who sowed the good seed is the Son of Man.
38The field is the world, and the good seed stands for the sons of the
kingdom. The weeds are the sons of the evil one, 39and the enemy who
sows them is the devil. The harvest is the end of the age, and the
harvesters are angels.
40"As the weeds are pulled up and burned in the fire, so it will be at the
end of the age. 41The Son of Man will send out his angels, and they will
weed out of his kingdom everything that causes sin and all who do evil.
42They will throw them into the fiery furnace, where there will be
weeping and gnashing of teeth. 43Then the righteous will shine like the
sun in the kingdom of their Father. He who has ears, let him hear.**

For comments see Matt. 13:24-30.

The Parables of the Hidden Treasure and the Fine Pearl (Matt. 13:44-46)

Just as the two former parables possessed similar messages about the Kingdom of heaven, these two illustrations also share a common truth—there is great value in being a part of God's Kingdom.

Being a part of the Kingdom of heaven is like owning a priceless treasure or a magnificent pearl. Such an experience cannot be measured in earthly terms. But it can be said concerning this experience that it is worth giving up everything for. The result of such a wise trade is fullness of joy.

I. *The Parable of the Hidden Treasure (13:44)*

> **44"The kingdom of heaven is like treasure hidden in a field. When a man found it, he hid it again, and then in his joy went and sold all he had and bought that field.**

Some teachers of the parables will have no rest until they find a significance for every person, place or thing mentioned in every parable. Others content themselves with the discovery of the central aim of the story, believing that the rest is insignificant. Perhaps a moderate stance between these two extremes is the safer approach for interpreting the parables. (Notice that Jesus explained many of the details in His parables, though there was no apparent significance to some of the items He mentioned—Matt. 13:1-9 with 13:18-23; and Matt. 13:24-30 with 13:36-43.)

In this parable the hidden treasure is the Kingdom of heaven. It is a hidden treasure (or a secret—Matt. 13:11) because the Jews were expecting a much more obvious kingdom than the one Jesus presented. The person discovering this truth is not disappointed, however. Indeed, he is overjoyed to participate in the Kingdom, regardless of the form it takes. Surely no human expense is too great for being a part of God's Kingdom.

II. *The Parable of the Fine Pearl (13:45, 46)*

> **45"Again, the kingdom of heaven is like a merchant looking for fine pearls. 46When he found one of great value, he went away and sold everything he had and bought it.**

There is a single, major difference between this parable and the parable of the hidden treasure—the one who makes the discovery. The first one to find a great treasure was an unsuspecting landowner (possibly a farmer). The second one to locate a great treasure is a searching merchant. The first person was not seeking any fortune, while the second person is seeking diligently. Both, nevertheless, find the dream of their lifetimes. Can there be a note here (as is characteristic in Matthew's Gospel) of hope for both the ignorant Gentile and the eager Jew? Maybe so.

Finally, it should be observed that these important parables put the sacrifice required to follow Jesus in its proper perspective. Following Jesus results in such joy and fulfillment that a person undertakes it willingly and gladly. The sacrifice is immeasurably outweighed by the rewards of discipleship.

The Parable of the Fish Net (Matt. 13:47-50)

This parable, for all practical purposes, is almost identical to the parable of the wheat and the weeds (Matt. 13:24-30, 36-43). Here the illustration of a huge fish net is used to depict the final day when God will gather up everyone and separate the good fish from the bad. At the Second Coming of Jesus Christ this act will find its literal fulfillment.

> **47"Once again, the kingdom of heaven is like a net that was let down into the lake and caught all kinds of fish. 48When it was full, the fishermen pulled it up on the shore. Then they sat down and collected the good fish in baskets, but threw the bad away. 49This is how it will be at the end of the age. The angels will come and separate the wicked from the righteous 50and throw them into the fiery furnace, where there will be weeping and gnashing of teeth."**

Once again we are introduced to the fact that during this Kingdom age both good and bad people will be present. In this phase of God's Kingdom there will be no separation of the righteous from the unrighteous, until the end of the age.

Special emphasis is given in this parable to the punishment of the "bad fish," the spiritually dead people of this world. God looks differently at the unconverted than we do. On the one hand, He views them with profound redemptive love, but on the other hand, He sees them as being "wicked," and deserving of severe punishment (suggested in the words "fiery furnace," "weeping" and "grinding of teeth").

It must never be forgotten that a great and awesome day is rapidly approaching when the Judge of the universe will no longer tolerate sin. A so-called good life, or a mere profession of Christ, will not sustain us in that hour. Outward conformity, with inward lukewarmness, will be revealed in its fullness. Then it will be too late to change. In that moment our destinies will be forever sealed.

By every means, then, let us humble ourselves. Let each of us throw aside any shallow or self-centered interests. Let us turn wholly toward Christ and make Him the very purpose and joy of our daily lives!

The Parable of the House Owner (Matt. 13:51, 52)

This is the eighth and final parable in a series of illustrations given by Jesus. As such, it appropriately climaxes Jesus' teachings with the kind of remarks you might expect to hear after a teaching. Here we see Jesus trying to determine His pupils' level of understanding and comprehension of His teachings. Also, here is an exhortation for each student to share wisely the knowledge he has gained.

I. *The Inquiry (13:51)*

> **51"Have you understood all these things?" Jesus asked.**
> **"Yes," they replied.**

Within Jesus' question can be seen His personal desire to be effective. How useless a teaching is, regardless of its profoundness, if it goes beyond the grasp of the listeners. Jesus did not seek to be profound, but to be understood (yet He always spoke profound truth).

No teacher or leader should assume that his audience is totally comprehending what he is saying. This would be a naive assumption. Even Jesus, the greatest teacher of all time, had to explain His point occasionally because His disciples did not understand what He was talking about (Matt. 13:36; 15:15; Mark 7:17; John 16:17-19). It would be a good practice for pastors to quiz church members from time to time in order to discover if they are actually grasping the message being delivered to them.

II. *The Exhortation (13:52)*

> **52He said to them, "Therefore every teacher of the law who has been instructed about the kingdom of heaven is like the owner of a house who brings out of his storeroom new treasures as well as old."**

For the first time Jesus calls His disciples "teachers." This was Jesus' ambition from the start—to turn His followers into leaders, to convert His students into teachers (Matt. 5:19). How important it is for this goal to be the aim of each church (Eph. 4:11-16; 2 Tim. 2:2).

Next, Jesus compares His new teachers to the owner of a house who possesses valuables that are both old and new. When the disciples came to Jesus, they brought a knowledge of the Law and the Prophets with them. But Jesus gave them new insights on these old truths. They, in turn, were to teach their audiences both the old and the new truths.

How much we ought to learn from this statement. Truth is not to be found solely in the ancient past, nor in the technological present hour either. We must live and learn from both the past as well as the present. Our teachings must possess ingredients that provide the soundness of the past and the freshness of the present.

Jesus Goes Home (Matt. 13:53-58)

(cf. Mark 6:1-6 and Luke 4:16-30)

Jesus had many troubles. Rough times come to everyone, sooner or later. Jesus was no exception. He felt everything you and I feel. His life was not without its valleys.

The thought of going home usually strikes a note of joy within us. There is something special about home. But there are occasional exceptions to this feeling; Jesus' return to His home town did not result in the usual cordial exchanges. Instead, the people were first amazed, and then they became disgusted with Him.

I. *The Resistance of the People (13:53-57a)*

> **53When Jesus had finished these parables, he moved on from there.**
> **54Coming to his home town, he began teaching the people in their synagogue, and they were amazed. "Where did this man get this wisdom and these miraculous powers?" they asked. 55"Isn't this the carpenter's son? Isn't his mother's name Mary, and aren't his brothers James, Joseph, Simon and Judas? 56Aren't all his sisters with us? Where then did this man get all these things?" 57And they took offense at him.**

His Home Town. Jesus' home, for about thirty years, was Nazareth. It was a rather insignificant town of Galilee—not mentioned even once in the entire Old Testament, the Apocrypha, the Talmud or by the historian Josephus (cf. John 1:45, 46). Lodged in a high valley of 1,300 feet, and surrounded by hills reaching upwards to 1,600 feet, this town could easily peek down on nearby trade routes, though it enjoyed little commerce itself.

Here Jesus was raised and taught a carpenter's trade (the skill of His father). But around the age of thirty He left this village and His family to be baptized by John and to start His special ministry. Later, Jesus was to move His entire family from this doubting town to the city of Capernaum (Matt. 4:13).

He Began Teaching; They Were Amazed; They Took Offense at Him. Jesus was the perfect teacher. His words revealed the absolute will of God. Certainly no one could challenge His love or zeal. Still, in spite of theological accuracy and compassionate fervor, the crowds of Nazareth were content to remain unchanged. Here we learn that even the very best teacher and teachings will not convert some people.

Where Did This Man Get These Miraculous Powers? They Took Offense at Him. Whenever people reject Jesus' marvelous words, they usually reject His miraculous works, too. Healing the sick, setting free the demonized, and even raising the dead will not save everyone, not even the majority. Miracles are important, but for many persons they only breed further questions and opposition.

They Took Offense at Him. The word "offense" means "to cause to stumble." In other words, the citizens of Nazareth stumbled over Jesus. With their natural eyes they could see and remember that He was a carpenter's son, the son of Mary, the brother of James, Joseph, Simon and Judas (and certain unnamed sisters). It was these natural factors that blinded them. They could not imagine God using someone they knew. So, they doubted (v. 58). Certainly this account reveals how a prejudiced heart can keep a person from receiving things from God.

II. *The Response of Jesus (13:57b, 58)*

> **But Jesus said to them, "Only in his home town and in his own house is a prophet without honor."**
> **58 And he did not do many miracles there because of their lack of faith.**

A Prophet Without Honor. For one reason or another, it is usually those with whom we are close who are hardest to influence and change. They listen to us, but they are not moved.

Lack of Faith. The reason for Jesus' poor reception was due to the people's lack of faith. Jesus was willing, but the people were stubborn. Jesus was ready, but the people were defiant. Jesus was able, but the people stopped His works with their unbelief. How easily and frequently doubt keeps us from miracles (cf. Heb. 12:1, 2; "the sin" that so easily entangles us is doubt). It should be noted that "faith" here is not restricted to a narrow doctrinal usage, but to the whole character of one's life.

John Is Beheaded (Matt. 14:1-13)

(cf. Mark 6:14-29 and Luke 9:7-9)

Death is inevitable. It comes to everyone—rich or poor, intelligent or ignorant, spiritual or carnal. We all know this. Yet, somehow it is never easy to face, especially if it is the horrible death of an outstanding spiritual friend.

John the Baptist was Jesus' cousin. There was a natural bond between these men. But more importantly, John was the one who paved the way for the start of Jesus' ministry. It was John who called Israel to repentance and to expect the arrival of God's Messiah. It was also John who baptized Jesus and gladly pointed people to follow Him. Now John was dead, killed by a wicked and fickle ruler.

The reality of such an event must be faced, and the work of the Kingdom must continue. The answer to why such things happen is plain—in this dispensation God will permit wicked men to practice evil. Our mission is to confront, convict and convert such persons.

I. *Herod's Conscience (14:1, 2)*

14 At that time Herod the tetrarch heard the reports about Jesus,
2and he said to his attendants, "This is John the Baptist; he has
risen from the dead! That is why miraculous powers are at work in him."

Herod the Great ruled as king of the Jews from 40-4 B.C. (see notes on Matt. 2:1-19). He was a most aggressive, innovative and despised ruler. In his death his kingdom was divided and given to three of his sons. The Herod referred to here (also called Herod Antipas) reigned as tetrarch (a ruler of a section of a country, a governor) of Galilee and Perea. He was a weak leader—governed by his own carnal lusts and the domineering pesonality of his second wife, Herodias.

The conscience of Herod would not rest in the face of his personal sins. In a most careless and drunken moment, Herod permitted a dancer (his adopted daughter,

Salome) to ask him for anything. After she consulted with her mother, she decided to ask to have John's head delivered to her on a platter. The request jolted Herod. He could not imagine such a request. Nevertheless, he regretfully consented. The thoughts of this stupid decision were to haunt him relentlessly.

II. *Herod's Carnality (14:3-5)*

**3Now Herod had arrested John and bound him and put him in prison
because of Herodias, his brother Philip's wife, 4for John had been saying
to him: "It is not lawful for you to have her." 5Herod wanted to kill John,
but he was afraid of the people, because they considered him a prophet.**

John soundly rebuked Herod Antipas for his second marriage, calling it unlawful. And so it was, as far as the Mosaic law was concerned (Lev. 18:16; 20:21). Herodias had been married to Herod Philip (the half-brother of Herod Antipas). Through this union she gave birth to a daughter named Salome. Antipas was married to the daughter of Aretas, the king of the Nabatean Arabs. But once Antipas and Herodias met, they set their hearts on marrying each other. So they secured divorces from their mates and then married each other. Somehow all of this immoral romance does not sound too far removed from our own contemporary scene.

Here we learn that speaking God's will against arrogant sinners can cause martyrdom. There is no promise in God's Word that will assure anyone of absolute physical safety. In certain instances, life and death rest in the choice of words we use. John cared little for his physical safety. His sole ambition was to boldly proclaim God's message to sinful men. And the core of that message was "Repent!" The cost meant his death. Can our word be any less straightforward?

III. *Herod's Craziness (14:6-11)*

**6On Herod's birthday the daughter of Herodias danced for them and
pleased Herod so much 7that he promised with an oath to give her whatever she asked. 8Prompted by her mother, she said, "Give me here on a
platter the head of John the Baptist." 9The king was distressed, but
because of his oaths and his dinner guests, he ordered that her request
be granted 10and had John beheaded in the prison. 11His head was
brought in on a platter and given to the girl, who carried it to her mother.**

The Daughter of Herodias Danced. On the surface this appears to be a natural occurrence, but this is not the actual case. It would be quite rare for a princess to dance before anyone. Generally, the dancers of that era performed in a manner designed to arouse sexual lust; therefore, the thought of a ruler's daughter dancing in this manner would have been quite unusual. But, being prompted by her mother, the teen-ager gave Antipas the performance he desired. In fact, he so enjoyed its sensuality that he unthinkingly offered her anything she wanted, up to half of his kingdom (Mark 6:23)!

Prompted by Her Mother. Herodias hated John the Baptist, and she was determined to nurse a bitter grudge against him for his insults. She knew Herod would not kill this man, because deep inside she knew Herod felt John was a holy man (Mark 6:20). Herodias, however, did not share this opinion of concern for his life. Subtly, she schemed and devised a plan for John's death. On the ruler's birthday she instructed her daughter to appeal to Herod's base nature through a sensual dance. (Did she know Herod already had his eyes on this young and attractive adopted daughter?) Herodias was confident that her fickle husband would be aroused and, therefore, would offer her a great request. When this happened, she was ready to ask for John's head. The incredible plot worked!

He Ordered That Her Request Be Granted. Herod made an unthinkable mistake, and he knew it. But a man with a weak moral nature is destined to repeatedly follow the course of immoral and stupid decisions. Herod could have admitted his ridiculous error, but in order to keep from losing face with his friends, he consented to worse folly—John's execution.

The disciples of John must have been deeply shocked and crushed at the news of John's death, especially when they heard the details surrounding his cruel execution. They might have asked if there would be any retribution from God for such gross injustice. Indeed, their desire for justice was carried out in two events which followed.

First, Aretas, whose daughter Antipas divorced in order to marry Herodias, engaged in war with him. The result was the utter defeat of Herod's army.

Second, Herodias persuaded Antipas to seek the title of king from the emperor in Rome (a title which Philip, Herodias's first husband, now held). Philip, in learning of these plans, sent messages ahead to advise the emperor of the treacherous nature of Antipas. When Antipas and Herodias appeared before the emperor (Gaius Caesar, or as he is more commonly known, Emperor Caligula), he was not given the desired title of king, but was instead sent to Gaul to live the rest of his life in exile with his wife.

IV. *Christ's Consciousness (14:12, 13)*

12 John's disciples came and took his body and buried it. Then they went and told Jesus.

13 When Jesus heard what had happened, he withdrew by boat privately to a solitary place. Hearing of this, the crowds followed him on foot from the towns.

Here is a simple, yet moving, phrase—"they went and told Jesus." When tragedy strikes, there is only one sure refuge—Jesus. When you do not know which way to turn, it is time to turn to Jesus. And when you feel hurt or perplexed, go and tell Jesus your story. You will find Him to be the most understanding and comforting friend you will ever meet.

Observe, too, that Jesus is moved by this report about John. He is not without the deepest feelings of sympathy, compassion and grief. Jesus could hurt and be moved to sorrow. We must never forget that our wonderful Savior and Lord is sincerely touched by the concerns and problems that touch us.

Jesus Feeds the Five Thousand (Matt. 14:14-21)

(cf. Mark 6:30-44; Luke 9:10-17 and John 6:1-15)

No one can be a Christian and doubt the miraculous, for it is woven so carefully into the messages of the Bible that to remove all the supernatural accounts would mean doing away with the Christian faith altogether. Assuredly, we are not Christians simply because we believe in miracles. But there is no Christian, ever so weak in his faith, who does not have a strong faith in the reality of miracles.

We believe in miracles because we believe in God. Should God not exist, then there would be no accounts of miracles. But because He does exist, and because He does intervene in the affairs of our lives, we read of numerous miracles. In fact, we are bold to assert that miracles are still among us today, for God has changed neither His character nor His address!

I. *The Compassion of Jesus (14:14)*

14 When Jesus landed and saw a large crowd, he had compassion on them and healed their sick.

Here is the scene of a large crowd of people from various towns, following Jesus into a remote place. It was Jesus' custom to come to the people. He would visit their synagogues to teach and to work miracles there. But progressively Jesus' entrance into these centers was being shut off. This often compelled Him to work outside the city limits. Fortunately, many people were not so narrow in their faith that they confined their religious experience to a certain synagogue. They wanted more. And if they could not find it there, they would seek it elsewhere. May we learn this lesson, too.

We must not overlook Jesus' reaction to the crowd. He had compassion on them, and He healed their sick. Here is the probable cause behind their following Jesus. They could perceive His profound love for them, and His supernatural power with God. They wanted more than religious-sounding words; they wanted help. They wanted to be touched. And they knew Jesus would not disappoint them.

II. *The Concern of the Disciples (14:15-17)*

15 As evening approached, the disciples came to him and said, "This is a remote place, and it's already getting late. Send the crowds away, so they can go to the villages and buy themselves some food."

16 Jesus replied, "They do not need to go away. You give them something to eat."

17 "We have here only five loaves of bread and two fish," they answered.

Both the disciples and Jesus had a concern for the crowd's need for food, but here we notice the contrast between Jesus' approach to decision making and that of His disciples. The circumstances seemed to indicate that Jesus ought to send the crowd back to their homes, since it was getting late and the people were hungry. There was no food where they were, so the decision, in the mind of the disciples, appeared to be an obvious one.

Jesus, on the other hand, disregarded what came so easily. The facts were clear enough, but the solution for this particular situation was not to be satisfied in the customary manner. God had a miracle in store for this event. So, Jesus prayed.

How different would be the solutions to many of our problems if we only went beyond the obvious factors and consulted with God. There just might be miracles earmarked for each of us.

III. *The Contentment of the Crowd (14:18-21)*

**18 "Bring them here to me," he said. 19 And he directed the people to sit
down on the grass. Taking the five loaves and the two fish and looking
up to heaven, he gave thanks and broke the loaves. Then he gave them
to the disciples, and the disciples gave them to the people. 20 They all ate
and were satisfied, and the disciples picked up twelve basketfuls of
broken pieces that were left over. 21 The number of those who ate was
about five thousand men, besides women and children.**

When God does something, He does it right. When He answers a prayer, He supplies more than just enough to get by on; He gives graciously and abundantly. You can count on being fully satisfied when God answers your requests.

Jesus and Peter Walk on Water (Matt. 14:22-36)

(cf. Mark 6:45-52 and John 6:15-21)

Jesus was intensely spiritual. He was also eminently practical. In His relationship with God, He never lost touch with people, and in His relationship with people, He never overlooked God. Jesus saw life as a single unit—God and man were inseparable. Every situation, then, presented itself with an opportunity for God's involvement. This fact is seen nowhere more clearly than in the story of Jesus and Peter walking on the water.

I. *Jesus Hears God (14:22-24)*

22Immediately Jesus made the disciples get into the boat and go on
ahead of him to the other side, while he dismissed the crowd. 23After he
had dismissed them, he went up into the hills by himself to pray. When
evening came, he was there alone, 24but the boat was already a consider-
able distance[a] from land, buffeted by the waves because the wind was against it.

He Dismissed the Crowd. After Jesus had prayed and miraculously fed the five thousand with only five loaves and two fish, He dismissed the crowd. On the surface (at least in Matthew's account) there is nothing peculiar about sending these people home. But in John's record of this story, we discover that Jesus told the crowd to go home because they intended to "make him king by force" (John 6:15). The people had been dramatically aroused by Jesus' miracles. They were flooded with fantasies of how Jesus could resolve their difficulties, if only He would become their king. But Jesus had to quench these incomplete ideas, so He ordered them to go home.

There is an all-too-common flaw evidenced in these people—they drew inappropriate conclusions from Jesus' miracles. Their eyes became so attached to the physical aspects of Jesus' works that they altogether missed their more important spiritual dimensions. The issues of repentance and holiness were not a serious part of their considerations. Their minds were fixed on the physical miracles, and this lack of balance in their perception of Jesus' mission caused them to become sidetracked; instead of understanding His mission, they developed an altogether carnal (though probably sincere) ambition to make Jesus their king. In short, they were blessed, they

a 24 Greek *many stadia*

misinterpreted the cause for their blessings, and they got ahead of God. This still happens today. We must not permit the glorious light that emanates from miracles to overshadow the remainder of God's purposes for us and for His Church.

He Went to Pray. Here is a delightful glimpse into the spiritual priorities that motivated Jesus' life. Let's notice several truths concerning this period of prayer. First, Jesus must have been extremely tired, but His physical weariness would not keep Him from a conversation with His Father. Second, Jesus wanted to be alone; He sought a private audience with God. Third, Jesus came to God *after* a marvelous and miraculous time with a huge crowd; now He would express His appreciation and continued reliance upon God's will. Also, He would ask God to reveal the full intent of His mission to the impulsive crowd as they journeyed home.

Buffeted by the Waves. We must never think obedience to Christ will exempt us from having problems. Consider the disciples. They followed Christ's orders to the letter. And what happened? They found themselves battered by the waves and shaken by the winds. Yes, the path of obedience is sometimes paved with trials. But obstacles can be turned into opportunities. Trials are not sent to make us weak, but to show us our weakness, so we might trust God and Christ for the miracles we need. The disciples were having great difficulty in rowing their boat across the sea, but when Jesus appeared, the trouble was resolved (John 6:21).

III. *Jesus Helps Peter (14:25-33)*

25 During the fourth watch of the night Jesus went out to them, walk-
ing on the lake. 26 When the disciples saw him walking on the lake, they
were terrified. "It's a ghost," they said, and cried out in fear.
27 But Jesus immediately said to them: "Take courage! It is I. Don't be
afraid."
28 "Lord, if it's you," Peter replied, "tell me to come to you on the water."
29 "Come," he said.
Then Peter got down out of the boat and walked on the water to Jesus.
30 But when he saw the wind, he was afraid and, beginning to sink, cried
out, "Lord, save me!"
31 Immediately Jesus reached out his hand and caught him. "You of
little faith," he said, "why did you doubt?"
32 And when they climbed into the boat, the wind died down. 33 Then
those who were in the boat worshiped him, saying, "Truly you are the
Son of God."

The Fourth Watch. The first watch ran from 6:00 to 9:00 P.M.; the second went from

9:00 P.M. to 12:00 midnight; the third lasted from midnight to 3:00 A.M.; and the fourth watch ran from 3:00 to 6:00 A.M. Assuming Jesus dismissed the crowd during the later afternoon or early evening (possibly as late as the early portion of the first watch), then the disciples must have been fighting the sea and wind for approximately ten hours. Who can say it is always smooth sailing when you follow Jesus? This is not true. Jesus' disciples (both then and today) must face adverse elements, too.

Jesus Went Walking on the Lake. This event, as sensational as it is, cannot be considered any more miraculous than Jesus' other miracles. If the Holy Spirit can flow through Jesus in order to heal the sick and to raise the dead, then that same Spirit can cause Jesus to walk on the surface of the sea. Although Jesus was (and is) divine, there is no evidence that He used these powers to produce this miracle. In fact, if Jesus had utilized His deity, there would be no miracle here at all. God can do anything. Walking on the water requires no miracle for God. Jesus, however, walked as a man upon this "floor" of water. And He did so in the same manner as Peter did—by faith.

They Were Terrified. This is understandable. Most people might react in a similar fashion. The disciples had been rowing almost fruitlessly for nearly ten hours. They were completely exhausted. In a predawn hour their eyes caught a figure approaching their boat. And since no mortal had ever managed to walk on water, they assumed it had to be a ghost (that is, a spirit-appearance of God or an angel).

Don't Be Afraid. Jesus could understand the disciples' alarm in seeing Him walk on the water. So he revealed His identity to them. How kind our Lord is to bring peace to us when we face the supernatural. There should never be any fear when God is responsible for a miracle. It is only fraudulent and demonic types of miracles that ought to trigger a warning in our spirits.

Peter Walked on the Water. Peter wanted proof. It was not enough that his eyes could see a blurred image of a man walking on the water. It was not enough that his ears could hear the muffled voice of Jesus through the raging sea. He must know for certain. Peter wanted a confirmation. And Jesus was ready to yield to him this additional proof.

Peter certainly was not divine. Yet, look at him get out of the boat and walk on the water to Jesus! How could he do this? Did he possess a mountain of faith? No, Peter's faith was far more common than that. Then how could he walk on water?

This is an important question, because some people actually teach that each believer can do *anything,* if only he has enough faith. But this statement is only partially true. It was not Peter's faith that caused him to leave the boat; it was Jesus' invitation for him to come to Him. Here, then, is the crucial key to miracles—first, we must hear the voice of Jesus; then we must follow His orders. Faith that acts without hearing Jesus' voice (or the Word of God) is not faith at all, but presumption (and presumption can lead you into water that is over your head!). Peter did not start to get out of his boat before he heard the will of Jesus. In effect, there was as much obedience in Peter's actions as there was faith. Peter would have never jumped into the water without first getting clearance from Jesus—otherwise he would have sunk immediately. The first key to miracles, then, is a knowledge of God's will. The next key is an obedient faith. Working together, knowledge, obedience and faith can produce the miraculous.

Peter Saw the Wind. How quickly we can lose our miracles through distractions! Peter saw the heavy seas tossed by the winds, and he became fearful. The precise moment that he became afraid, he doubted and began to sink. Peter was a sincere disciple. But he was also human. And sincere humans can take their eyes off Jesus. No one's faith is perfect all the time. Not even Jesus' choice disciples were flawless. That same fact applies to disciples today, too.

Lord, Save Me. The instant we take our eyes off Jesus and begin to sink, we need to do exactly what Peter did—to cry out to Jesus for help! It would have been senseless for Peter to struggle and attempt swimming back to the boat, especially when the waves were so rough and when Jesus was so near. So he asked for help. And he no sooner made his need known than Jesus reached out His hand to pull him up. Jesus rebuked Peter for his doubting; still, they walked together on the water to the boat!

Son of God. Jesus never calls himself the Son of God, although God (Mark 1:11), Satan, (Matt. 4:3, 6) and the disciples (Matt. 14:33) address Him with this title. In fact, it is the most common title for Jesus in the New Testament letters (though not in the Gospels). The meaning of the expression seems to be at least twofold: (1) it is an equivalent expression for the Messiah; and (2) it is a reference to Jesus' deity—God the Son.

III. *Jesus Heals People (14:34-36)*

> **34When they had crossed over, they landed at Gennesaret. 35And when the men of that place recognized Jesus, they sent word to all the surrounding country. People brought all their sick to him 36and begged him to let the sick just touch the edge of his cloak, and all who touched him were healed.**

Often we read of how Jesus touched people and cured them. Here is the reverse of that order—people touch Jesus and are healed. In the one case it is Jesus who takes the initiative; in the other, it is the people who take it. In both instances the result is the same.

Here can be found the superabundant compassion of Jesus. There is a high level of compassion shown in the action of touching others at one's own will. But there is a greater level of mercy shown when an individual permits others to touch him at their own will. Jesus was both approachable and touchable.

We must do more than touch people in Jesus' name. We must permit them to touch us, too. This latter action requires much more grace from us. But we could never do less than follow our Lord and copy His pattern for our lives.

The Danger of Bad Traditions (Matt. 15:1-20)

(cf. Mark 7:1-23)

There is no small number of wrong religious convictions. For instance, some people feel there are no absolutes, no black-and-white issues in life. For them, everything is relative, conditional and subjective. This is the very opposite of Christianity.

Other people are committed to values and religious beliefs, but they do not feel it is necessary for everyone else to accept their own standard in order to be correct. They are flexible and tolerant, feeling no need to persuade others over to their views. This is the general position of liberal religion in the world.

Still other people are to be found with false positions. These are the legalists. They contend that everything is to be done in a certain way and that only their unique convictions are to be accepted as truth. Such persons are narrow-minded and highly critical of all who differ from them. This kind of person is merely attempting to imitate the truth.

Throughout Jesus' ministry He was confronted with a broad variety of people. But perhaps the most difficult people with whom Jesus worked were the legalists—the Pharisees and the so-called teachers of God's law. These religious leaders were almost always prone to challenge the truth of God with their petty, man-made traditions. In the story before us we see such an example.

I. *The Challenge of the Pharisees and Teachers (15:1, 2)*

15 Then some Pharisees and teachers of the law came to Jesus from Jerusalem and asked, [2]"Why do your disciples break the tradition of the elders? They don't wash their hands before they eat!"

Why Do Your Disciples Break the Tradition? Here is the major drawback of legalism—its adherents are always pointing accusing fingers at others when they themselves are guilty of far more serious offenses. It is always easier to find faults than it is to find remedies.

The Pharisees did not seek to help Jesus or His disciples. Their attitude was bitter and negative. Their hearts were not warm or soft. Instead, they sought only to find blemishes in others, and then to accuse others of improper living. How pathetic (and unfortunately common) this type of religious faith is.

The Tradition of the Elders. The term "tradition" means "that which is handed down from one generation to the next." Here it refers to those teachings of Israel's leaders that emerged from the time of her captivity in Babylon (587 B.C., forward). These oral interpretations of the Old Testament Scriptures grew more and more popular, until they were eventually placed on a par alongside the biblical text itself. In the mind of many Jews (especially those who were born long after the traditions had become generally accepted) these additional interpretations of the Mosaic Law were absolutely binding (although the more critical Sadducees rejected these oral and largely legalistic rulings).

When the Jews returned from Babylon (537 B.C.), it was necessary for the laws of Moses to be read and explained. These explanations (or verbal commentaries on the sacred text) later became formalized and widely accepted. During Jesus' day these added comments were collected and carefully organized. By the middle of the second century these oral traditions were collected and put into a book. Eventually (about 500 A.D.) a writing called the Talmud emerged. In these pages are found the oral traditions, the legal (or binding) interpretations of the Mosaic law, and the nonlegal (or nonbinding) interpretations, too. Today, for the Orthodox Jew, the writings of the Talmud represent the law code for his faith. Liberal Jews (which by far are the more numerous) do not accept the Talmud as their authority.

The charge the Pharisees brought to Jesus was the failure of His disciples to wash their hands before they ate. How keen the eyes of these critics were. They could instantly detect a minute violation in their presumptuous traditions, while overlooking the more serious flaws in themselves. And how bold were their mouths. They would not bite their tongues in silence. No. Instead, they would open their mouths wide in order to release poison through their tongues.

One could surely hope that in the two-thousand years since these words were written we would have evolved into more sensible, flexible and spiritual people. But hopeful evolutionists have been left keenly disappointed. People have not changed. Our hearts are made of the same material today as they were then. There have always been, and always will be, those who find more value in past traditions than in God's truth. Jesus constantly encountered this type of situation; we will too.

II. *The Charge of Jesus (15:3-11)*

[3]Jesus replied, "And why do you break the command of God for the sake of your tradition? [4]For God said, 'Honor your father and mother'[a] and 'Anyone who curses his father or mother must be put to death.'[b] [5]But you say that if a man says to his father or mother, 'Whatever help you might otherwise have received from me is a gift devoted to God,' [6]he is not to 'honor his father[c]' with it. Thus you nullify the word of God for the sake of your tradition. [7]You hypocrites! Isaiah was right when he prophesied about you:

[8]" 'These people honor me with their lips,
but their hearts are far from me.
[9]They worship me in vain;
their teachings are but rules taught by men.'[d] "

[10]Jesus called the crowd to him and said, "Listen and understand. [11]What goes into a man's mouth does not make him 'unclean,' but what comes out of his mouth, that is what makes him 'unclean.' "

You Nullify the Word of God. If Jesus had been a liberal religionist or a nonreligionist, then He probably would have ignored the accusations brought by the Pharisees. But Jesus was deeply committed to God and to His truth. He could not stand by passively and allow some ridiculous, man-made tradition to supersede the real Word of God.

As quickly as the Pharisees handed out their medicine, they were compelled to take it themselves. In essence, Jesus asked them, if their traditions are so important, then why do they violate God's commands? Next, Jesus called His accusers "hypocrites." Finally, the explosion occurred when Jesus told them that their worship of God was in vain because it represented a man-made religion rather than a God-made relationship!

The illustration Jesus used to prove His point was taken from the Ten Commandments. The Law stated that a child was to honor his parents (Exod. 20:12). But the tradition of the elders reversed this ruling by stating that if a parent had a need of some possession his son had, he could not have it if the son would simply say it belongs to God (even if the son were to keep and use the object himself!).

Jesus could not have been more direct or candid. He found the faith of these Pharisees pitifully shallow, and He told them so. There are people who feel we should never evaluate other people's religious faith, but the example of Jesus indicates otherwise. Our Lord Jesus Christ challenged, rebuked and pointedly criticized these presumptuous persons.

There are people today who, like the Pharisees, believe in God but worship Him in

---

a 4 Exodus 20:12; Deut. 5:16 *b 4* Exodus 21:17; Lev. 20:9 *c 6* Some manuscripts *father or his mother* *d 9* Isaiah 29:13

vain. They possess a form of godliness—they follow the traditions of their church—but they are spiritually dead. We must, like Jesus, pinpoint the errors of clearly detrimental traditions.

You Hypocrites. Several hundred years before Jesus lived, the Greek theater provided a popular source of entertainment. Often in this early theatrical period there would be only one actor, who played the part of every person in the play. He would assume the differing roles by holding up different masks (or faces) and speaking through the holes provided for his mouth. The person who played each of these differing roles was called a "hypocrite" (or play-actor). Later, by Jesus' time, the word "hypocrite" had come to be used negatively in reference to anyone who pretended to be something he was not. Naturally, no one would appreciate being called a hypocrite. It amounted to being called a phony, a fake, a fraud.

The unfortunate side to all of this seems to stem from the fact that some hypocrites are actually devout and sincere. They do not recognize their role playing. They have played the part for so long that their hearts are deceived by their very own mouths.

Isaiah Prophesied About You. This speech from Isa. 29:3 was a stinging rebuke. It cut through the facade of the Pharisees' religious words and exposed a barren heart. Jesus never hesitated to reveal carnal religious leaders. His words blasted holes in their superficial teachings, so everyone could see the inadequacy of their life styles based on false traditions. Jesus came to teach us how to walk in the Spirit. And there was no way for a person to embrace both human traditions and divine promises at the same moment.

What Comes out of His Mouth Makes Him Unclean. When absurd traditions become the standard of the day, then what had been naturally clear becomes hopelessly blurred. The laws of Moses required the priests to wash before performing their duties (Lev. 15:5-27); they even required anyone (priest or otherwise) to wash himself and his clothes if he had had contact with someone who possessed an open and pus-filled sore (Lev. 15:11). The tradition of the elders, however, had taken these rulings and grossly elaborated upon them until their original intent had been bent out of shape altogether. They insisted that *everyone* should *always* wash himself before *every* meal. Clearly these restrictions went far beyond the Law. But this is always at the heart of legalism or Pharisaism—demanding more external conformity than God himself requires! This false holiness would not find Jesus' approval.

III. *The Conversation with the Disciples (15:12-20)*

12Then the disciples came to him and asked, "Do you know that the Pharisees were offended when they heard this?"

[13]He replied, "Every plant that my heavenly Father has not planted will be pulled up by the roots. [14]Leave them; they are blind guides.[a] If a blind man leads a blind man, both will fall into a pit."

[15]Peter said, "Explain the parable to us."

[16]"Are you still so dull?" Jesus asked them. [17]"Don't you see that whatever enters the mouth goes into the stomach and then out of the body? [18]But the things that come out of the mouth come from the heart, and these make a man 'unclean.' [19]For out of the heart come evil thoughts, murder, adultery, sexual immorality, theft, false testimony, slander. [20]These are what make a man 'unclean'; but eating with unwashed hands does not make him 'unclean.' "

The disciples wanted Jesus to know that His speech really offended these church officials. But Jesus was fully aware of the results of His words, and He had no apology to offer. Rather, He would take the opportunity to teach His disciples three lessons, concerning salvation, discernment and spiritual character.

1. *Salvation.* Jesus uses the illustration of a plant and says that only those whom the Father plants will not be uprooted and destroyed. All others, however, will be pulled up by the roots someday and judged. Put simply, the man-made religion of the Pharisees (and any other self-made person or groups today) presents a false hope that will ultimately taste God's vengeance. Only those who follow God's will are secure.

2. *Discernment.* Jesus instructs His followers to forsake the directions of the Pharisees. This may have been difficult for some of His listeners to understand, since they had been raised to be loyal to these persons. But Jesus knew that blind guides cannot lead anyone into God's light. Such persons, both then and now, are to be abandoned.

3. *Spiritual character.* How subtly we can be snared into believing that by doing certain things, or by not doing certain things, we are thereby made spiritual. But God looks beyond the obvious external appearances of our lives. He explores our hearts, too. Ceremonies, rituals and traditions will help no one if his heart is not pure and abiding in the truth.

a 14 Some manuscripts *guides of the blind*

The Canaanite Woman (Matt. 15:21-28)

(cf. Mark 7:24-30)

What kind of people catch Jesus' attention? Do you have to be a Christian superstar or a great financial supporter of His church? Do you have to be a world-famous evangelist? A television clergyman? A bishop or cardinal? How can you get Jesus to look your way? Must you do good works? Must you be a nearly sinless person? Honestly, what does it take to get Jesus to display an interest in your life? The answers to these questions are found in this text.

I. *Her Revelation (15:21, 22)*

21 Leaving that place, Jesus withdrew to the region of Tyre and Sidon.
22 A Canaanite woman from that vicinity came to him, crying out, "Lord, Son of David, have mercy on me! My daughter is suffering terribly from demon possession."

Tyre and Sidon. When Jesus withdrew to the region of Tyre and Sidon, He may have thought that here, in Gentile territory, he could relax (Mark 7:24). Also, Jesus knew the time for His final trip to Jerusalem was soon to occur. He probably wanted time alone in order to prepare and to pray about these matters. But before He could fulfill these wishes, there would be several significant interruptions. The Gentiles needed the touch of Jesus as critically as anyone. And one mother in particular determined that she would not leave Jesus' presence until He granted her request.

A Canaanite Woman. The Canaanites had descended from a grandson of Noah bearing this name (Gen. 9:18). They were a cursed people, from the time of their origins (Gen. 9:25-27). They were known for their corrupt idolatrous practices, and Israel was to destroy them without mercy when entering their land (Deut. 7:1-5, 24; 9:4; 20:10-18). A few Canaanites, however, continued to maintain their national identity until Jesus' day. Here, then, is a perfect sneak preview of Jesus' ultimate involvement with Gentiles, even the most defiled among their company—the Canaanites.

Lord, Son of David, Have Mercy on Me. This desperate mother knew to whom she was speaking. He was the "Lord" (or Master/King) and "Son of David" (see note on

Matt. 1:1). She was not merely addressing some compassionate gentleman, but the Messiah. He was no ordinary person who walked in her territory. No. This was the one who had been prophesied; and this was her chance—possibly her only chance—of getting His attention.

II. *Her Relentlessness and Reverence (15:23-25)*

23Jesus did not answer a word. So his disciples came to him and urged him, "Send her away, for she keeps crying out after us."
24He answered, "I was sent only to the lost sheep of Israel."
25The woman came and knelt before him. "Lord, help me!" she said.

She Keeps Crying Out. When you are on the right road, never stop or turn around. Here is a most important matter in the discipline of prayer. Never give up. Always persevere! This mother was jeered by the disciples, but she continued despite the resistance. She even was strongly tested by Jesus. Still, she persisted until she won the battle in determined faith.

I Was Sent to the Lost Sheep of Israel. There are several matters requiring attention in this statement. First, these words are directed to the disciples. It is they who are to learn a lesson here. Second, there words reveal the order of priorities for the proclamation of God's Kingdom message—Jews first, Gentiles second (Acts 3:26; Rom. 1:16). Third, these words show the discipline of Jesus in following God's plans (even though we eventually see that there is elasticity in God's orders). Fourth, these words tell us that in Israel (the land of God's people) are those who need to be found and saved from spiritual destruction (because they are lost in a maze of spiritually dead religious restrictions and regulations).

The Woman Came and Knelt. Jesus has little to do with proud, self-sufficient people (and they have little to do with Him). But this woman did not address Jesus with these attributes. Her heart and speech were clothed in reverence. She recognized her lowly position before the flawless Son of God. So she asked for mercy and help. Without these ingredients, there could have been no miracle for her. She knew this. Reverence must be displayed and mercy must be received before the stage can be set for the supernatural to occur.

III. *Her Reasoning and Results (15:26-28)*

26He replied, "It is not right to take the children's bread and toss it to their dogs."
27"Yes, Lord," she said, "but even the dogs eat the crumbs that fall from their masters' table."

28Then Jesus answered, "Woman, you have great faith! Your request is granted." And her daughter was healed from that very hour.

Children's Bread, Dogs and Crumbs. At first it appeared that Jesus was not the slightest bit interested in this very troubled mother. He even went so far as to say He was not sent by God to help her. But the mother was not to be deterred. She continued her pleadings. And again Jesus indicated to her that He was not sent to help the Gentiles (or puppies), but Israel. Nevertheless, this mother of undaunted faith did not tire in asking for her miracle.

This mother did not come to Jesus for herself. She came on behalf of another, her daughter. Her pleading was not selfish. She wanted to touch the one she loved, even if she were "only a mere dog" begging for the extras from the table of the master. She would not be annoyed by this designation; neither would she be arrogant or proud. She only wanted help—the kind of help she knew Jesus could perform.

A comment needs to be made regarding Jesus' use of the word "dog." There are two Greek words translated "dog" in the New Testament. One of these terms means a full-grown dog that walks the streets looking for garbage. The other of these terms means a small dog, a puppy, a house pet. It is this latter, nonoffensive term that Jesus employed here. Jesus was not belittling this woman for her race, but explaining his God-ordained priorities. It was not yet time, explained Jesus, for a Gentile ministry. This was to come later. Still, the mother insisted that even puppies, while not getting the main meal, do at least get some crumbs. There is a strong feeling of warmth in this intense conversation. The mother expected a miracle—a single crumb—for her daughter. And she was not disappointed.

Finally, the barrier was broken wide open, and the mother's request was granted. In fact, Jesus congratulated the mother for her great faith. The reverence, intercession and persistence of this remarkable lady had won her a place in Christ's heart and a deliverance for her tormented daughter!

The Compassion of Jesus (Matt. 15:29-39)

(cf. Mark 7:31-8:9)

For three days the crowds continued to besiege Jesus with their needs, and for three days Jesus tirelessly resolved their problems. In the beginning, the needs were of a permanent nature. The people were physically handicapped. But later the needs were of only a temporary nature. The people were hungry.

What a marvelous Lord we have in Jesus. He cares for both the major problems and the minor issues that touch each one of us.

I. *He Heals the Helpless (15:29-31)*

29 Jesus left there and went along the Sea of Galilee. Then he went up
into the hills and sat down. 30 Great crowds came to him, bringing the
lame, the blind, the crippled, the dumb and many others, and laid them
at his feet; and he healed them. 31 The people were amazed when they
saw the dumb speaking, the crippled made well, the lame walking and
the blind seeing. And they praised the God of Israel.

Who were in the crowds that came to Jesus? What kinds of people would listen and be transformed by His words? Were they church officials? Some were. Were they professional persons? A few were. Were they critical spectators who went for "the show"? Several perhaps. But the majority were simple people, little people with big needs.

They came from everywhere. Yet there was a common bond that drew them to Christ, much like a powerful magnet draws a handful of steel nails. These people had hurts, and they believed Jesus could help them. Some were blind or lame. Others were crippled and mute. They were people with real problems. They knew the meaning of pain. And they were confident that Jesus would see their sorrows and supply a cure for their many ailments. How fitting are these words of the songwriter: "What a friend we have in Jesus!"

No one can go to Jesus with a sincere heart and leave empty-handed (Heb. 11:6). It is an impossibility. You can no more stand in the rain and not get wet than you can humbly stand in Jesus' presence and not get help. Jesus is there when you need Him.

II. *He Helps the Hungry (15:32-39)*

32 Jesus called his disciples to him and said, "I have compassion for
these people; they have already been with me three days and have
nothing to eat. I do not want to send them away hungry, or they may
collapse on the way."

33 His disciples answered, "Where could we get enough bread in this
remote place to feed such a crowd?"

34 "How many loaves do you have?" Jesus asked.

"Seven," they replied, "and a few small fish."

35 He told the crowd to sit down on the ground. 36 Then he took the
seven loaves and the fish, and when he had given thanks, he broke them
and gave them to the disciples, and they in turn to the people. 37 They all
ate and were satisfied. Afterward the disciples picked up seven
basketfuls of broken pieces that were left over. 38 The number of those

who ate was four thousand, besides women and children. [39]After Jesus had sent the crowd away, he got into the boat and went to the vicinity of Magadan.

It is interesting to observe how frequently the subject of food and eating is brought up in the New Testament. In the Gospel of Matthew alone we have already noted seventeen references (either implicit or explicit) that talk about this matter (3:4; 4:3, 4;5:6; 6:1-4, 11, 16-18, 25-34; 7:9, 10; 9:10, 11, 14, 15; 10:9-15, 42; 11:18, 19; 12:1-8; 14:13-21; 15:2, 26, 27). You cannot get away from food; and neither should you attempt to do so.

These people experienced a wonderful retreat. Their souls were filled with praise, but soon their stomachs were hungry. We cannot live on blessings alone. We must have bread also. And Jesus desires for us to have both—food for the body and food for the soul.

The Signs of the Times (Matt. 16:1-4)

(cf. Mark 8:11-13)

Many of the Pharisees and Sadducees could not manage to see beyond the ends of their noses when it came to spiritual matters. They were quite capable of properly interpreting the physical phenomena, yet they were unable to accurately assess spiritual phenomena. They were spiritually bankrupt. So, instead of assisting Jesus, they tested Him with the hope He would fail. But Jesus never fails. *Never!*

16 The Pharisees and Sadducees came to Jesus and tested him by asking him to show them a sign from heaven.

[2]He replied,[a] "When evening comes, you say, 'It will be fair weather, for the sky is red,' [3]and in the morning, 'Today it will be stormy, for the sky is red and overcast.' You know how to interpret the appearance of the sky, but you cannot interpret the signs of the times. [4]A wicked and adulterous generation looks for a miraculous sign, but none will be given it except the sign of Jonah." Jesus then left them and went away.

Pharisees and Sadducees. It is rare to ever find the Pharisees and Sadducees together. They were opposites in almost every way. But they did have this much in common—they wanted to rid themselves of Jesus and His teachings. It is ironic how arch-rivals can somehow find a note of unity in fighting Christ. (For details on these two sects, see the Topical Index.)

a 2 Some early manuscripts do not have the rest of verse 2 and all of verse 3.

They Tested Him. The first thing these religious people demanded was a sign. But the real barb is revealed in the fact that their desire was insincere. They did not seek a sign in order to be convinced, but merely to test Jesus. Their hearts were not filled with faith or hope, but with poison.

You Know the Sky, but Not the Times. The average person is perceptive of natural phenomena. He observes what is going on around him. He can articulate the contemporary conditions fairly accurately. He reads the headlines and watches the news. He is informed. Still, something is missing. He is unable to relate all of these happenings to what God is doing. Somehow, in his reasoning, God is the least understood.

This is precisely the condition Jesus encountered with the Pharisees and Sadducees. They could understand the sky:

> Red sky in the morning—sailors' warning
> Red sky at night—sailors' delight

But in spiritual matters they were still in the dark. Their natural perception was terrific, but their spiritual perception was terrible. God's very own Son stood within an arm's distance, and yet they could not see Him. How regrettable this problem of divine insight was and is (John 3:16-21; 7:17; 2 Cor. 4:3, 4).

The Sign of Jonah. In a previous discourse this very same sign was offered to the Pharisees, along with an identical rebuke (see notes at Matt. 12:38-42). How undeserving are narrow-minded, religious people. They are wicked and guilty of spiritual adultery, says Jesus. They refuse to believe what is set before them. They always want more proofs, more signs. But their hearts are insincere and they will not be given any further proofs. Enough has already been given to make Jesus' mission clear to them.

We must come to Jesus with open hands if we are to come away full (Heb. 11:6). There are no great secrets for receiving things from God or for understanding His messages. We can only approach Him with purity and teachability. And these are enough. Praise God, these are enough (1 Cor. 2:9-14; 1 John 2:20, 27)!

The Yeast of the Pharisees and Sadducees (Matt. 16:5-12)

(cf. Mark 8:14-21)

Jesus taught something here that was difficult for even His closest followers to grasp. And today it remains a hard lesson for many to receive. The message is this: the convictions of certain religious (or so-called Christian) leaders is like yeast, spreading a subtle, but lethal, cancer throughout the listener's entire soul, until it captures and destroys the victim.

Many fine people attend church services, or even preside over churches as pastors, elders or deacons, who are not Christians (2 Cor. 11:13-15). These are often moral persons. Respected persons. Loving persons. But persons who, like the Pharisees and Sadducees, can only see the obvious facts of the natural life, while their eyes are shielded to the true message of the Scriptures.

> **5When they went across the lake, the disciples forgot to take bread.**
> **6"Be careful," Jesus said to them. "Be on your guard against the yeast of**
> **the Pharisees and Sadducees."**
> **7They discussed this among themselves and said, "It is because we**
> **didn't bring any bread."**
> **8Aware of their discussion, Jesus asked, "You of little faith, why are**
> **you talking among yourselves about having no bread? 9Do you still not**
> **understand? Don't you remember the five loaves for the five thousand,**
> **and how many basketfuls you gathered? 10Or the seven loaves for the**
> **four thousand, and how many basketfuls you gathered? 11How is it you**
> **don't understand that I was not talking to you about bread? But be on**
> **your guard against the yeast of the Pharisees and Sadducees." 12Then**
> **they understood that he was not telling them to guard against the yeast**
> **used in bread, but against the teaching of the Pharisees and Sadducees.**

Be on Your Guard. No less than twelve times does Jesus instruct His followers to beware of accepting teachings, experiences or people as being spiritual when in fact they are not spiritual at all (Matt. 7:15; 10:17; 16:6, 11; 24:4, 23, 26; Mark 4:24; 12:38; Luke 11:35; 17:3; 21:36). This reechoing caution must open our eyes to at least two practical realities: (1) true believers can be deceived; and (2) wise believers will properly evaluate what they hear, see and feel before they accept it as coming from God.

The Yeast/Teaching of the Pharisees and Sadducees. The following itemization has been prepared in order to capture an overview of the temperament and the theology of the Pharisees and Sadducees as presented in the New Testament (naturally, there are individual exceptions to these points).

Pharisees

1. Legalistic observers of the Mosaic Law (Acts 26:5)
2. Zealous for the oral traditions (Matt. 15:1-9)
3. Belief in the Resurrection (Acts 23:6-9)
4. Belief in angels and spirits (Acts 23:6-9)
5. Eager to make converts to their blindness (Matt. 23:15)
6. Generally rejected John's message and baptism (Luke 7:30)
7. Generally rejected Jesus' message and mission (Matt. 12:14, 34; John 7:32, 45)
8. Extremely proud and self-righteous (Matt. 23:6-12)
9. Hypocritical (Matt. 3:7; 12:34; 23:13-36)
10. Ready to persecute opponents (Acts 9:1-2)

Sadducees

1. Conservative observers of the Mosaic Law
2. Rejected the oral traditions
3. Disbelief in the Resurrection (Matt. 22:23; Acts 23:6-9)
4. Disbelief in angels and spirits (Acts 23:6-9)
5. Exclusivists
6. Generally rejected John's message and baptism (Matt. 3:7)
7. Generally rejected Jesus' message and mission (Matt. 16:6, 12)
8. Extremely proud and self-righteous (Acts 5:17; 23:6-10)
9. Hypocritical (Matt. 3:7)
10. Ready to persecute opponents (Acts 4:1; 5:17, 18, 33, 40)

The Foundation of the Church (Matt. 16:13-20)

(cf. Mark 8:27-30 and Luke 9:18-21)

Jesus' discussions with His disciples at Caesarea Philippi represent the apex of His ministry. Up to this point Jesus had prepared His audience to receive and to enter the Kingdom of God; from now on He will be seen preparing His disciples for His crucifixion in Jerusalem.

Three years have passed now. Only six months remain in the earthly ministry of Jesus. During the early period the disciples were hoping to see Jesus wear a regal crown; they will now be repeatedly taught that Jesus must first bear a rugged cross. It was for this hour that Jesus Christ came into the world—to die in our place (Rom. 5:12-21; 2 Cor. 5:18-21).

The four Gospels are so aware of this divinely ordered mission of Jesus that more space is devoted to the six months following Caesarea Philippi than to the thirty-three years preceding it. In fact, an overwhelming and deliberately disproportionate amount of space is devoted to these closing days, especially the final seven days—from the triumphant entry forward. The chart entitled "From Caesarea to the Cross" will assist you in appreciating these facts.

FROM CAESAREA TO THE CROSS

Book	Ministry Begins	Six Months to Live: Pivoting Point: Caesarea Philippi	Six Days to Live Triumphant Entry
Matt.	4:12	16:13 (43 percent of Matthew remaining)	21:1 (25 percent of Matthew remaining)
Mark	1:14	8:27 (50 percent of Mark remaining)	11:1 (32 percent of Mark remaining)
Luke	4:14	9:18 (62 percent of Luke remaining)	19:29 (21 percent of Luke remaining)
John	2:13	Omitted	12:12 (43 percent of John remaining)

Note: By combining these statistics we learn that 52 percent of the Gospel writing is devoted to events at and after Caesarea Philippi. Some 30 percent of the Gospel message is devoted to the final six days of Jesus' mission.

This information leads us to make several observations:

1. The principal interest of the Gospels is to proclaim Jesus' death and resurrection. Good Friday and Easter are the biggest days on the calendars of the Gospel writers. Jesus' substitutionary death for you and me is at the heart of the biblical message.
2. Jesus knew He was going to die at least six months before the Crucifixion. God did not keep it a secret from Him.
3. Jesus discussed the matter of His death with the disciples no less than three times before the triumphant entry (Matt. 16:21-23; 17:22, 23; 20:17-19). Even in the face of death good words can be spoken. Jesus did more than prepare himself for this day and hour; he also prepared those nearest to Him for it as well.

I. *The First Test (16:13, 14)*

13When Jesus came to the region of Caesarea Philippi, he asked his disciples, "Who do people say the Son of Man is?"

14They replied, "Some say John the Baptist; others say Elijah; and still others, Jeremiah or one of the prophets."

In a short while Jesus would be killed. And as the time for His death approached, Jesus was compelled to test the effectiveness of His ministry on the lives of those upon whom the destiny of Christianity rested—the twelve disciples.

Did they understand? Was their thinking clear? Would they carry on the ministry Jesus had only begun? These questions crossed Jesus' mind. Were they really ready to go on without Him? In the region of Caesarea Philippi, Jesus decided to give His most loyal pupils their final exam. There were only two questions. One would be easy; the other would be more difficult.

The question expressed in the above passage was easy. People speculated that Jesus was John the Baptist or Elijah. Some thought He was Jeremiah or another prophet. The disciples answered this question correctly. They were now set for the next inquiry.

II. *The Second Test (16:15, 16)*

15"But what about you?" he asked. "Who do you say I am?"
16Simon Peter answered, "You are the Christ,[a] the Son of the living God."

What About You? This question is identical to the former one, with one major exception. The question now became intensely personal. "What about *you?*" Our relationship with Jesus Christ is far more than formal and abstract; it is direct, warm and concrete. Jesus works with us personally, and we, in turn, must respond to Him individually.

It should be noted also that Jesus is emphatic about this. His identity must be known. There must be no doubts left in His disciples' minds regarding His uniqueness among men. If anyone else had asked these questions or had anticipated these responses, He would have been considered immeasurably deceived, proud and arrogant. But when the Son of God appears among men, He must be recognized and understood completely. This is the purpose of Jesus' inquiries.

The Christ. The Greek word "Christ" (like the Hebrew word "Messiah") means anointed or ordained. The Jews used this word as a title to refer to the One God would send into this world to establish peace, order and righteousness. As such, this person was to be a prophet, priest and king, simultaneously (see notes on Matt. 1:1).

This was not the first time these disciples associated Jesus with the title of "Christ." Much earlier, Jesus had repeatedly made His identity known to them and to others (Matt. 11:3-6; John 4:25, 26; 5:31-40; 8:14-28). John the Baptist called Jesus the Christ (John 3:28); so did Andrew (John 1:41) and Martha (John 11:27). But now it was time

a 16 Or *Messiah*; also in verse 20

to seal His identity once and for all. The matter was to be absolutely settled in each disciple's mind.

Son of the Living God. Each disciple of Jesus is called a son of God (John 1:12; Rom. 8:14-19; 1 John 3:1, 2). There is, however, a special sense in which this designation is applied to Jesus. The intent here is to refer to Jesus as being the very offspring of God, making Him the God-man (John 5:16-30; Luke 1:32, 35).

Peter's twofold designation of Jesus, then, describes Him in His mission and in His majesty. In Jesus' Christhood we see His relationship to the world—his mission. In Jesus' Sonship we see His relationship to the Father—His majesty.

III. *The Final Results (16:17-20)*

**17Jesus replied, "Blessed are you, Simon son of Jonah, for this was not
revealed to you by man, but by my Father in heaven. 18And I tell you
that you are Peter, [a]and on this rock I will build my church, and the gates
of Hades[b] will not overcome it.[c] 19I will give you the keys of the kingdom
of heaven; whatever you bind on earth will be bound in heaven, and
whatever you loose on earth will be loosed in heaven." 20Then he
warned his disciples not to tell anyone that he was the Christ.**

Revealed to You by My Father. If intelligence could bring us to a proper understanding of Jesus' identity, then every intelligent person in this world would be a Christian. But the identity of Jesus cannot be known through human reasoning. This is proven in Jesus' first question to His disciples. The general public has opinions about Jesus, but these ideas are incorrect. No one can truly know the genuine identity of Jesus without a revelation being given to him from God (see notes on Matt. 11:25-27). And God is quite willing to make this insight available to everyone who will seek for it with a pure desire (John 3:16-21; 7:17).

On this Rock. Much debate has been offered over these very few words. The three major views are offered for your consideration:

1. Peter is the rock, the first pope, upon whom Jesus built His Church. In Peter, then, rested the greatest degree of spiritual authority in the early church. He alone held such an honored distinction or authoritative position.
2. Peter is a *petros* (Greek: a detached stone) and upon the *petra* (Greek: a mass of rock) the Church will be built. According to this view, the *petra* stands for Peter's confession of Jesus as the Christ. Peter is only made a *petros* because of his confession. Anyone making this same confession automatically becomes a *petros*, too. Thus, Jesus is enabled to build His Church upon such individuals.
3. Peter is the rock upon whom Jesus began to erect His Church, though Peter is not

a 18 *Peter* means *rock*   *b 18* or *hell*   *c 18* Or *not prove stronger than it*

to be viewed as a pope. Neither is he to be seen as the only rock in the foundation of the Church. Each apostle and prophet (including the twelve—Matt. 18:18; John 20:23—and others with these offices—Eph. 2:19ff.) share this distinction.

I Will Build My Church. Five simple English words, each containing only one syllable. One sentence. Still, they hold incredible importance. Repeat them to yourself. Each time you say them, stress a different word, until all five words have been emphasized. There is a special message in each word.

First, we perceive it is Jesus who will build this Church. It will not be man-made, but Jesus-made. There have been attempts to duplicate this structure. Satan has used men to erect man-centered or problem-centered churches, but Jesus has not authorized or energized such constructions (2 Cor. 11:13-15). There is but one true Church, and Jesus is both its architect and its builder (Eph. 4:1-16; Col. 1:18).

Second, we note the certainty of the establishment of this Church. It *will* be built, despite the attacks it will receive from hell's trenches.

Third, we see that the Church will be constructed gradually. It will be built, piece by piece, generation after generation. And it will not be completed before Jesus' Second Coming.

Fourth, we observe the ownership of the Church. It belongs to Jesus. No one can say "my" church, except Jesus. We, as His disciples, are servants in *His* Church.

Fifth, we notice the construction itself—a Church. This word, in the Greek language, is a compound of two terms: "out of" and "calling." The Church, then, is an assembly of people who have been *called out* of the world and *united together* around the Lordship of Jesus Christ. This idea was, to state it mildly, a radical departure from the popular Jewish expectations of the coming Messiah.

This is the first appearance of the term "Church" in the Gospels. In fact, it is only used twice by Jesus in the Gospels (Matt. 16:18; 18:17). The nation of Israel always stood for God's choice, God's people. It had been His focal point for revelation and works for nearly two thousand years. But Jesus announced a new focal point, an institution called the "Church." It was to supersede, and even to temporarily replace, God's dealings with national Israel (Matt. 21:42-45; Rom. 9-11; 1 Pet. 2:9, 10)!

The Gates of Hades. Hades is the temporary abode of every spiritually and physically dead man or woman (Luke 16:19-31; Rev. 20:11-15). When an unrighteous person dies, this becomes his or her new home, until the day of the Second Resurrection (at the end of the Millennium). Since everyone who goes to this place is a child of Satan (1 John 3:8-10), Jesus is stating, in a figurative way, that no one—not even Satan and his companions—will be able to halt the development of His great Church.

The Keys of the Kingdom. In the literature of the rabbis that surrounded this era, we discover that the practice of binding and loosing was relatively common. There are three ways in which the rabbis exercised this authority:

1. *Doctrinal*—in this case he would either prohibit (bind) or permit (loose) a certain practice, based upon its place in the Mosaic Law.
2. *Disciplinary*—in this case he would either remove (bind) or reinstate (loose) someone of the congregation.
3. *Occult*—in this case he would either present someone to (bind someone to) or deliver someone from (loose someone from) the powers of Satan.

In the New Testament all three of these ideas are present. It is the responsibility of each Christian, and church leader in particular, to perform the following binding and loosing duties.

1. Assure doctrinal purity and practice in the Church (Matt. 16:18; 1 Cor. 4:1, 2; Gal. 1:6-10; Titus 1:5-9; Jude 3, 4).
2. Purify the church of unrepentant, so-called Christians (Matt. 18:15-20; 1 Cor. 5:1-13), and to receive back into fellowship those who truly repent of their sins (2 Cor. 2:6-8).
3. Turn unrepentant believers over to Satan (probably through the action of removing someone from a congregation/excommunication—1 Cor. 5:1-5; 1 Tim. 1:20), and to deliver repentant believers from Satan's clasp (Mark 16:17; Acts 8:7; 16:16-18; Rom. 16:20; Eph. 6:10-18; etc.).

Finally, it should be noted that only Peter is here addressed as holding these keys, but in a short while all of Jesus' disciples will be seen holding these keys (Matt. 18:15-20; John 20:23). Some teachers contend that Peter's initial hold on these keys set him apart from his peers. Other teachers hold that these same keys became the property of each local church (see references in the above three points for support of this claim).

Jesus Predicts His Death (Matt. 16:21-23)

(cf. Mark 8:31-33 and Luke 9:22)

The account of Jesus' death and resurrection struck a bitter note with the disciples, especially with Peter. He told the Lord plainly that such an event would never happen, not in his presence. But the Lord rebuked Peter, because he did not discern the way God was working.

It is a humbling note to consider that the one who had only moments earlier received the Father's words now spoke Satan's speech. But this is precisely what happened. How swiftly our minds may depart from spiritual truth! There is never a safe moment to trust in our own natural reasoning or abilities to accomplish God's will.

I. *The Report (16:21)*

21From that time on Jesus began to explain to his disciples that he must go to Jerusalem and suffer many things at the hands of the elders, chief priests and teachers of the law, and that he must be killed and on the third day be raised to life.

Here is an odd mixture of words that must have puzzled the disciples. First, Jesus announced His death, or more specifically, His execution. And notice who is to be responsible for this murder—the so-called spiritual leaders in Jerusalem! It is a sad and shocking comment on the state of Judaism at that time. The self-made religionists had so twisted God's revelations to them that their professions are here proved to be utterly void of their claims. We see from this passage that a religious person—unless he is sincerely submitted to the truth of the Scriptures—can be no more discerning, and no less dangerous, than a convicted murderer!

Second, Jesus states that He will be resurrected from the dead on the third day. On several prior occasions Jesus told the Pharisees that Jonah's three-day experience in the belly of the large fish foreshadowed his own three-day and three-night experience in the earth (Matt. 12:38-42; 16:1-4). Naturally, the Pharisees did not understand this statement. But it is equally unlikely that Jesus' own disciples grasped His point either. Even here, with the use of plain terms, it seems improbable that these words really registered with them (cf. Matt. 28:17; Mark 16:9-14; Luke 24:13-35). Their emotions would not permit their ears to hear anything after Jesus had announced His imminent murder. Truth is not always easily received or understood.

II. *The Rebuke (16:22)*

22Peter took him aside and began to rebuke him. "Never, Lord!" he said. "This shall never happen to you!"

There is an enriching lesson in these words: God's thoughts are not our thoughts, and neither are His ways our ways (Isa. 55:8). When we attempt to be guided by our own assessment of things, even if that assessment is filled with compassion, there is a high probability of error. God's plans, perspective and power are infinitely greater than ours. This is why human reasoning and divine logic are often in conflict. It is much wiser to take God at His Word (even when His Word seems unclear or impractical) than it is to try alternate solutions. God always knows best. Always.

III. *The Reprimand (16:23)*

[23]Jesus turned and said to Peter, "Out of my sight, Satan! You are a stumbling block to me; you do not have in mind the things of God, but the things of men."

What a correction! Only moments earlier Peter had received and declared God's revelation. Now he unknowingly receives and announces Satan's plans to keep Jesus from the cross. Therefore, Jesus sternly reprimands Peter for his lack of discernment and his misguided words.

Peter should have known better. Jesus had just announced that He "must" experience this murder and resurrection. Unfortunately, Peter, like so many of us would have done, reacted before he thought. His words revealed sincerity and total devotion, but they also exposed his carnal nature. Actually, Peter's virtues got in his way, because he permitted his zeal to have priority over God's revelation.

This is an all-too-common snare. We want what is best for someone, and because of this, we start to define what we think would be best, without first consulting God. Peter cared for Jesus' physical protection, and normally this would be appropriate. But Peter failed to discern that here was an exception to the rule. Jesus' death was in God's plans, and Peter must accept it as a divine purpose.

Before we rush to conclusions about a person's condition, let us wait on the Lord. Let us hear from heaven before we boldly (and possibly inaccurately) open our mouths to speak.

Call to Discipleship (Matt. 16:24-28)

(cf. Mark 8:34-38 and Luke 9:23-26)

If anyone desires to follow Jesus and become His disciple, he can count on this one inevitable fact—there is a price for this grandest of all privileges. Before we quickly volunteer to become a Christian, we must recognize the cost involved.

I. *Its Responsibilities (16:24-26)*

[24]Then Jesus said to his disciples, "If anyone would come after me, he must deny himself and take up his cross and follow me. [25]For whoever wants to save his life[a] will lose it, but whoever loses his life for me will

a 25 The Greek word means either *life* or *soul*; also in verse 26.

find it. [26]What good will it be for a man if he gains the whole world, yet forfeits his soul? Or what can a man give in exchange for his soul?

There are many who profess a belief in Christ. They say He is the greatest teacher who ever lived. They love His life. But such noble statements as these do not necessarily make one a genuine disciple. More than praise for Christ is required in order to become His disciple. There also must be personal denial, a personal bearing of the death-to-self cross, and a personal allegiance of obedience to follow wherever He leads. This alone is true discipleship. (See the special study at the close of this unit, plus other specific comments in the notes on Matt. 10:34-39.)

II. *Its Rewards (16:27, 28)*

[27]For the Son of Man is going to come in his Father's glory with his angels, and then he will reward each person according to what he has done. [28]I tell you the truth, some who are standing here will not taste death before they see the Son of Man coming in his kingdom."

Jesus spoke these same words earlier in His ministry. Now, near its climax, He repeats them. Great truths are not always simple to apprehend. They must be repeated frequently, in the hope that they will find a permanent lodging in the hearts of those who hear them. (See Matt. 10:23 for comments on these precise words.)

Special Study: The Self-Life

1. *The Root of the Problem.* It is not enough to confess our sins. We must also deal directly with the source of our sins—self (Matt. 10:37, 38; Luke 9:23, 62; 14:26, 33; 17:10).

It was Thoreau who correctly stated, "There are an hundred men hacking at the branches of evil, to one who is striking at the root." This imagery provides a perfect picture of the association that exists between sins and self.

When any of the roots of the self-life (such as self-will, self-justification, self-efficiency, self-pity, self-made ambition and so forth) are alive, they will always yield corrupt fruit—that is, sin.

Self is the disciple's greatest foe—not Satan, not people and not circumstances. We are our own worst enemies.

2. *Brokenness.* Often we hear the exhortation to rededicate our lives, to start over with a fresh determination to do better. But usually this is not our actual need. Instead, our deeper need is brokenness—the annihilation of each trait of the self-life. A person may rededicate his life to Christ at every invitation, but too frequently the result is only the futile turning over of "a new leaf" with hopes for a better tomorrow. This approach to discipleship, however, is incomplete and woefully inadequate.

We must learn the critical fact that spiritual life does not flow from a strong, self-willed determination to serve Christ, but rather it flows from a broken self (Ps. 34:18; 51:17)! God only uses those who are broken.

It is easy to fall into the snare of believing that hyperactivity in Jesus' name is synonymous with spirituality, but it is not. It is not any flurry of works that pleases the Lord, but a denial of self and an obedient spirit that He honors.

3. *Things Broken.* The Bible often speaks of broken things. Let us consider just three items:

(a) *Broken Bread.* Jesus once fed a crowd of five thousand with only five loaves of bread (Matt. 14:15-21). But how could five loaves possibly feed such a large audience? Here is the answer. Jesus took the loaves into His hands, prayed over them, and then He broke them for distribution. Those five broken loaves then supplied the needs for thousands of hungry people.

Broken things can always be multiplied in Jesus' hands. When we allow Him to break us (and *not* when we strive to break ourselves), we can be used to meet people's needs. In fact, the greater the degree of brokenness to self, the greater our measure of fruitfulness for God.

On another occasion Jesus fed four thousand by utilizing the same method—breaking bread (Matt. 15:32-38). Jesus always feeds His followers with broken things—broken pastors, broken laymen, broken missionaries, broken singers and so forth.

A third time Jesus broke bread. It was during the night of His betrayal. After breaking it, Jesus said, "Take and eat; this is my body" (Matt. 26:26). Today we celebrate Communion because of this event in the upper room. Some people believe this element in the Communion service represents the broken will of Jesus, that He did not possess a single trace of the self-life. He was utterly broken. He gave himself without reservation or compromise.

(b) *Broken Grain.* On one occasion Jesus spoke to His listeners about grain. He said that unless it falls into the ground and dies, it will bring forth no fruit at all. But if it will die, then it will yield much fruit (John 12:24).

The lesson here is easy to grasp. Within every disciple of Christ is the potential to bring forth spiritual fruit. But there is a problem—each disciple must die to self before that life can burst forth. Without this element, there can be no productivity.

(c) *Broken Alabaster Jar.* Several days before Christ's Crucifixion, He was eating in Simon the leper's home, when Mary came to anoint His head and feet (Matt. 26:6-13). Carefully, she "broke the jar" and poured out all of its contents (Mark 14:3). For this wonderful act Jesus declared that Mary would be spoken of throughout the whole world.

Why should this single service draw such attention? What was so unique about this action? Consider for a moment the perfume which Mary used. It was no ordinary, inexpensive balm. This perfume was priced at the equivalent of a year's salary! Nevertheless, despite the cost, Mary was delighted to surrender her best, and she did this by breaking the jar which held her treasure. In like manner, inside every disciple of Christ is a most precious treasure (2 Cor.4:6, 7), but until its shell is broken, the contents remain valueless. Only in brokenness can the sweet fragrance come forth.

4. *Two Principles.* Here are two important principles worth remembering. First, our effectiveness before men is equivalent to our brokenness before God. This is vertical brokenness, and it has to do with our sins. We must confess them, all of them, and stay up-to-date with our Lord. Second, we are only as effective before God as we are broken before men. This is horizontal brokenness, and it has to do with our relationships with people. We must work diligently to maintain an open communication with every person we know.

It is not when we are strong in intellect, emotions or will that God uses us. It is when we are weak—broken—that God's power actually flows through us (2 Cor. 12:9, 10).

Jesus Is Transfigured (Matt. 17:1-13)

(cf. Mark 9:2-13 and Luke 9:28-36)

Wonderful days under God's blessings are sometimes followed by horrible days under Satan's attacks. No Christian—not even Jesus—is exempt from such a combination of opposites. The life of a disciple is strangely mixed with great highs and terrible lows. Each one who walks with Christ knows these two occasional extremes.

The episode before us now unveils a terrific moment in Jesus' life. It is a mountaintop experience of the highest caliber. His entire countenance is brightly illuminated. But at the heart of this awesome experience is a penetrating dark spot. There is the irreversible revelation that at the bottom of this same mountain awaited the men who would bring about His cruel death.

I. *A Mountain of Glory (17:1-8)*

17 After six days Jesus took with him Peter, James and John the
brother of James, and led them up a high mountain by them-
selves. 2There he was transfigured before them. His face shone like the
sun, and his clothes became as white as the light. 3Just then there
appeared before them Moses and Elijah, talking with Jesus.
4Peter said to Jesus, "Lord, it is good for us to be here. If you wish, I

will put up three shelters—one for you, one for Moses and one for Elijah."
[5]While he was still speaking, a bright cloud enveloped them, and a voice from the cloud said, "This is my Son, whom I love; with him I am well pleased. Listen to him!"
[6]When the disciples heard this, they fell facedown to the ground, terrified. [7]But Jesus came and touched them. "Get up," he said. "Don't be afraid." [8]When they looked up, they saw no one except Jesus.

There can be no doubt that Jesus needed spiritual renewal at this point. He felt the weighty pressures growing heavier. So He went to the mountain to pray, to talk things over with God (Luke 9:28).

The need for Jesus to get away from the crowds was real. And it is one we need to recognize, too. It is impossible to give, give, give without recharging our spiritual cells. Our internal motors and gears were not made for giving only. Our minds and hearts also need to receive, to be renewed and to be refreshed. There come times when we must drop what we are doing and follow Jesus up the mountainside to do nothing but pray. This is a need we each share. Our spiritual strength and freshness depend upon it.

Jesus Took Peter, James and John. Jesus was exceedingly wise. He not only recognized His own need to prepare for the days immediately ahead, but He also knew His disciples would need a special miracle to withstand the shock they must face. If these three men could share this glorious moment with Jesus, they would be far better equipped to face the worst trial of their lives—the crucifixion of Jesus. With the support of this mountaintop experience these most intimate friends of Jesus could comfort and support the other disciples in their soon-coming valley of terrible grief.

He Was Transfigured. The Greek term translated "transfigured" is a form of the verb *metamorphoomai,* from which we derive the word "metamorphosis." It denotes a change in form. Jesus, then, experienced a dramatic metamorphosis, a striking alteration in appearance. His entire body and clothes became radiant (glorified). The reason, meaning and implications of this experience are uncertain. We simply do not understand the depths of this miracle. But we can surmise at least this much—Jesus needed a special spiritual experience in order to face the trials soon to strike Him in Jerusalem, and God would provide Him with such a stabilizing miracle. God gives to no one more pressure than he can bear (1 Cor. 10:13).

Moses and Elijah. These two men respectively represent the Law and the Prophets of the Old Testament. Together, they bear witness of the future course Jesus must tread, particularly in His soon-to-occur crucifixion at Jerusalem (Luke 9:31). Jesus knew He had been sent to fulfill all of the Old Testament prophecies (Matt. 5:18), and here is a profound revelation of how these prophecies would culminate in His death. Perhaps we also see here a remarkable confirmation of Jesus' desire to be certain He is on track with God's plan. Each of us needs this sort of reassurance from time to time. Whatever the cause for the appearance of these two men, their ministry helped in preparing Jesus to face a bleak immediate future.

I Will Put Up Three Shelters. Here again we see how Peter's zeal gets in his way (cf. Matt. 16:21-23). His offer was well-intended, though foolish. He had a good, generous heart, but he was impetuous and failed to think through the implications of his statements.

We must also note that Peter's ambition was not altogether unlike many people's ambitions today. Once Peter experienced this terrific spiritual encounter, he immediately wanted to house it in a physical (or permanent) structure. Today there are many who feel that the supernatural can be placed in some kind of box. Further, they seek to forever encamp themselves on this mountain's peak. But all of this commotion results in few spiritual results. God will not be confined by our physical structures or by our self-made plans. He transcends the elements of space and time. Temples are obsolete; God works in and through *people* today. We must not attempt to confine His presence to a certain place or to a particular group (John 4:20-24).

A Bright Cloud and a Voice. The words of the Law and the Prophets (personified in Moses and Elijah) are now given a final and authoritative endorsement by God himself. At the start of Jesus' ministry the Father spoke these essential words to inaugurate Jesus' mission (Matt. 3:17); now the same words would be repeated to culminate His work in the earth. How pleased Jesus must have been to know that His life and labors were in thorough accordance with God's will. Who today does not need a similar occasional sign of approval from God? We do not need to fret for a sign, though; God will give signs as we need them, as we remain faithful in obedience and prayer.

II. *A Valley of Agony (17:9-13)*

9As they were coming down the mountain, Jesus instructed them, "Don't tell anyone what you have seen, until the Son of Man has been raised from the dead."

10The disciples asked him, "Why then do the teachers of the law say that Elijah must come first?"

11Jesus replied, "To be sure, Elijah comes and will restore all things.
12But I tell you, Elijah has already come, and they did not recognize him, but have done to him everything they wished. In the same way the

Son of Man is going to suffer at their hands." [13]**Then the disciples understood that he was talking to them about John the Baptist.**

Don't Tell Anyone. How we each love to tell of our rare and precious moments in life. No doubt these disciples could hardly wait to tell everyone of their priceless encounter with God and the two glorified prophets on the mountain peak. But their story would have to wait.

Intimate moments are sometimes meant to be kept a secret. There is a proper time and place for such inspirational messages, and neither situation was now conducive for the expressing of their experience. The disciples would have to wait until after Jesus' death and resurrection (2 Pet. 1:16-18).

Elijah Must Come First. As ought to be expected, there were questions in the minds of the disciples. They struggled to reconcile what they were taught by the scribes with what they had experienced with Jesus. This is a common occurrence. Spiritual experiences always open new doors of inquiry and quest.

The question foremost in the disciples' minds was about the appearance of Elijah. Wasn't he to come again to this earth before the manifestation of the Messiah (Mal. 4:5)? Yes, and he did come, says Jesus, in the spirit and power of John the Baptist (Luke 1:17).

With that statement, the disciples were content to rest their busy minds. It was an unforgettable episode. Their mental diaries would never forget this incredible experience.

An Epileptic Is Healed (Matt. 17:14-21)

(cf. Mark 9:14-29 and Luke 9:37-43)

No one of us likes to think that we, or our children, have a demon problem, but such a possibility can exist. We must never overlook all the possible causes for our problems. And the threat of a demon being responsible for our problems must be considered.

I. *The Report (17:14-16)*

[14]**When they came to the crowd, a man approached Jesus and knelt before him.** [15]**"Lord, have mercy on my son," he said. "He is an epileptic**

and is suffering greatly. He often falls into the fire or into the water. [16]I brought him to your disciples, but they could not heal him."

First, notice who brought this request to Jesus. It was the demonized boy's father. This, in itself, seems not worthy of note. Yet it *is* a good reminder of how fathers ought to be the spiritual leaders in their homes, and how they ought to carry their family members to Jesus. The need for this type of spiritual father is evident everywhere. May more and more fathers assume their duties as steadfast men of God.

Second, notice the condition of the father's son. He was epileptic, behaving at times very normal, and behaving at other moments very abnormally. This feature—sudden abnormal behavior—is one key sign of demonic influence. Such actions are not certain proof that a demon is at the root of the situation, but neither can this possibility be ignored. The immediate projection of new and different personality traits is a tip-off that more than natural factors may be involved.

Several times in Jesus' ministry He was confronted by parents who had children with a demon (Matt. 15:22-28; Luke 9:38-42). This is a sobering thought. Our children may need a demonic exorcism. Let's learn, then, how it can be solved today.

II. *The Rebukes (17:17, 18)*

[17]"O unbelieving and perverse generation," Jesus replied, "how long shall I stay with you? How long shall I put up with you? Bring the boy here to me." [18]Jesus rebuked the demon, and it came out of the boy, and he was healed from that moment.

Here is a double rebuke. First, Jesus rebukes the crowd—including His own disciples—for their shallow faith. After three years of public ministry and private training, Jesus hoped for a more mature faith from His audience and disciples. How often we, too, labor relentlessly to make some point perfectly understood, only to discover that our efforts are but partially effective. Naturally, we are disappointed, just as Jesus was upset, but we press on and make our point again and again. Jesus was disturbed, but He was not defeated. He would heal the boy and teach His disciples another lesson. What patience Jesus has with slow learners!

Second, Jesus rebuked the demon. The cause for the son's epilepsy was a demon that indwelt the boy. This fact does not require us to draw the conclusion that all epilepsy has a demonic base, but it does challenge us to see demons as a possible cause for this (or any other) illness. *If* the sickness is caused by demons, then an authoritative command for their departure (by any spiritual Christian—Mark 16:17) will result in their leaving. If there is no change in the ill party, then the cause may involve other factors (such as natural malfunctions or God's chastisement or sovereign plans. See the discussion at the close of this chapter on "Praying for the Sick").

III. *The Reason (17:19-21)*

[19]Then the disciples came to Jesus in private and asked, "Why couldn't we drive it out?"

[20]He replied, "Because you have so little faith. I tell you the truth, if you have faith as small as a mustard seed, you can say to this mountain, 'Move from here to there' and it will move. Nothing will be impossible for you.[a]"

Once Jesus exorcised the demon, the disciples wanted to know why their attempts had been unsuccessful. They had expelled demons before; what hindered them in this particular case?

Jesus merely stated that their faith was weak. Exorcisms are not identical. Some situations demand more faith and more prayer (possibly even fasting). One almost wonders if the disciples were becoming a little self-confident due to their past success record with demons. Maybe they were leaning more upon their own experience than upon the Holy Spirit's power. Such a situation certainly quenches the fullest potential of the Spirit's work in our lives.

Demons are not more powerful than a Christian. But fears, doubts and self-conceit will always cripple us. Believe God. Resist Satan, and he will flee (James 4:7; 1 John 4:4).

Special Study: Praying for the Sick

Imagine, for a moment, that you've been asked during a church service to pray for the healing of a Christian who is blind. You rise from your seat and come to the microphone slowly. You stand in silence. Everyone is waiting—listening. Now it is time to pray. What will you say? How will you pray for this blind person's healing?

Will you say, "Thy will be done"? Or will you say, "By the stripes of Jesus you were healed"? Or will you rebuke Satan? What will you say? Certainly you possess no mystical powers to heal blindness yourself; so, how will you pray a genuinely spiritual prayer?

Would you like some help for your prayer? Some guidance? *Before you pray for the sick, remember the four causes of sickness.* It's practically impossible to prescribe the proper remedy when the cause is never considered first. You need to know *why* people become sick before you request *what* you want God to do for them.

Four Causes of Blindness

I would like to introduce you to four persons. Each person is blind. And each case of blindness has a different cause.

First, meet Isaac, the patriarch. He was blind because of old age (Gen. 27:1). Then there was an unnamed Jew in the wilderness. He was blind (or more specifically, he was threatened by God with blindness) because of sin (Deut. 28:15; 27, 28). After him,

---

a 20 Some manuscripts *you.* *[21]But this kind does not go out except by prayer and fasting.*

meet another unnamed man who was in a synagogue. His blindness was due to a demon (Matt. 12:22). The last person I want you to meet is also anonymous. This man was in the area of Jerusalem's Temple, and he was blind because of God's sovereignty (John 9:1-3).

Now let's go back to our opening question. You have been asked to pray for a blind person's healing. Imagine that the cause of this person's blindness is due to purely natural factors (like Isaac's). With this additional insight, how will you now pray? Or I could ask, how will you not pray? Certainly you will not need to pray about sin, sovereignty or Satan. These are irrelevant factors, because they do not touch upon the cause of the man's blindness.

But suppose the person for whom you are about to pray is blind because of sin (like the person in the wilderness). How will you pray in this case? Obviously exorcism is not the cure. Medicine is a poor solution. The need in this case is repentance.

Sometimes the four potential causes for our ailments team up together to cause an affliction. For instance, the road of sin can easily lead a person into a great variety of natural factors that will contribute largely to his illness. Even doors of Satanic sickness are opened when the sin route is taken. In cases like these our praying must encompass more than just a single cause. Each element will require attention. Notice the chart entitled "The Causes and Cures of Sickness."

THE CAUSES AND CURES OF SICKNESS			
Ailment	**Scripture**	**Causes of Ailments**	**Cures for Ailments**
Blind	Gen. 27:1	Natural factors	None in Genesis record (Prayer? Medicine?)
Blind	Deut. 28:15; 27, 28	Disobedience to God's Word	Obedience to God's Word
Blind	Matt. 12:22	Demon	Exorcism
Blind	John 9:1-3	Sovereignty of God	Sovereignty of God

You Can Pray for the Sick

Maybe what has been said above sounds like it would be impossible for you ever to pray effectively for the sick. But this is not true! You can pray for the sick. Indeed, you must! People who are suffering from varying ailments need your prayers. And most of all, they need you to pray a prescription that will effectively touch the cause of their sickness. This manner of praying is not beyond your grasp at all. Never withdraw from praying for the sick. God has healing miracles stored in heaven that await your spiritual prayers.

Below are six basic principles to help you approach praying for the sick with wisdom. These steps possess no magic. Neither is their application always successive, as this logical progression might suggest. God will not be cornered into some closed system of rules for healing the sick. He is God, and as God, He always allows himself sufficient room for exceptions. God loves you, and He will always give you His best, when you give to Him your best (Rom. 8:28). Pray believing. Ask your Father for a miracle. Ask to know how to pray in each individual case. Expect an answer. God will not disappoint you (Heb. 11:6).

PRINCIPLE NUMBER ONE: Confess All Known Sins

The first step toward healing is to draw so near to God that you can actually sense His presence. Open your heart fully before His search light. Ask Him to reveal anything which might have been offensive to His will—in thought, word or deed.

It is not uncommon for our Father to bring some of the following items to our attention: a critical attitude, negative speech, self-centeredness, lack of love, worry, impatience, gossiping, bitterness, unforgiveness, resentment, complaining, temper, lack of submission, lack of self-discipline, lack of faithfulness to God's Word and so forth. The only thing left to do is to repent. We must first acknowledge our shameful spiritual condition if God is to heal our ailing physical condition.

PRINCIPLE NUMBER TWO: Mend All Relationships Where Possible

This principle actually belongs under point number one, but because of its monumental significance it is listed separately. Rare is the case when God heals someone who is not properly related with all other persons. God does not forgive those sins which we have committed against others until we first have made a confession of our guilt to the party (or parties) we have sinned against (Matt. 5:23, 24; James 5:14-16; cf. Acts 24:16).

Here is an important rule for our confessions: Private sins need only private confessions to God, but the extent to which our sins are public, an equally public confession is required. This failure to deny self and make a public apology has stopped many Christians from enjoying the fuller benefits of health in Christ. You must mend all relationships, as far as possible. Go the second mile. Forgive. Forget. Say, "I'm sorry. Forgive me." Be humble. And the Lord, at the right moment, will raise you up again.

Revival of an entire church is a very rare sight. Honestly, I doubt that few people truly grasp what a revival is. I confess I did not understand it until I saw it for myself.

Foremost to revival is the confession of sin, especially the ones that have been too long overlooked. And high in the listing of these sins is the unmended relationships we have neglected. Resentment. Bitterness. Gossiping. Hate. Lies. Lukewarmness. Grudges. All of these must be confessed.

PRINCIPLE NUMBER THREE:
Resist Satan

The key which unlocks the door to conquering Satan is very simple. Merely stand your ground in Christ, confess God's promises as your sole provision for life, refuse to experience a standard of life which is less than God's standard, and boldly command the devil to flee from your presence (James 4:6, 7).

Remember this point—Christians never fight *for* victory; we fight *from* victory! There is no demon or circumstance which is capable of defeating the Christian who keeps his sins confessed, his relationships unbroken, and his eyes fixed on the risen Jesus (Heb. 12:1, 2; Rom. 8:31-39; 2 Cor. 2:14).

So, if Satan is attempting to place a plague of sickness upon you or your family or upon another believer, tell him in audible speech that he can't do it because he is a defeated foe. Tell him that you, as a follower of Christ, have been granted authority over his evil works (Mark 16:17). Be bold. He will leave you alone.

PRINCIPLE NUMBER FOUR:
Trust God, Completely

It is one thing to commit the matter of illness (or anything else) to the Lord. It is another matter to leave it there. This is trust—leaving the method and the timing of our healing in the hands of God.

The writer to the Hebrews makes this point of trust clear when he says we inherit the promises of God through "faith *and* patience" (6:12). Prayer for healing must stand on the promise that God, in the person of Jesus Christ, is the Great Physician. Then it must rest its case there. Trust does not take back what it commits.

PRINCIPLE NUMBER FIVE:
Call for the Prayers of Others

There are generally four spheres of faith when praying for healing. The *first sphere* is usually exhibited by the sick party. This sphere is most often the weakest. The *second sphere* of faith comes from the support of Christian friends who intercede on our behalf. It is always easier to pray for healing if you are presently in health. The *third sphere* comes from the elders of the local church. The faith of these men for divine healing ought to be an example for all (James 5:14, 15). The *fourth sphere* comes from someone with the gift of healing. It may be that you will need to utilize all four of these spheres before healing occurs.

Don't overlook the possibility of being healed through prayer. There are many skeptics—both in and out of the church. Jesus had His critics when He healed the sick.

Doubters have always existed. It is true that, although many Christians with healing ministries are sincere, others are clearly insincere. Regardless, there is nothing to lose, and everything to gain, in putting God first and seeking someone who has a proven ministry in the area of healing. Attend a service. It may be that God has a miracle in store for you.

PRINCIPLE NUMBER SIX:
Check With a Physician

The Bible does not forbid Christians from going to doctors, but neither does it insist upon it. Here then is a most important guideline: Faith has a place in God's plan for our health, and so does medicine. It is our responsibility to discover from God which prescription He has signed for our particular situation.

Let me explain. There are four possible sources for all of our problems: sovereignty, sin, natural factors and Satan. If the immediate source of an ailment is sovereignty, sin or Satan, then it is clear that applying medicine as a sole remedy would be drastically insufficient (1 Kings 15:11-14, 23, 24; 2 Chron. 16:12). Getting a shot for a demon-caused illness will have little (if any) effect on the actual problem. Or taking pills for a sovereignly caused illness will have little or no effect on God's sovereignty. On the other hand, if our sickness is natural, then we are often wise to prayerfully consider the best medical resources available.

"But," you ask, "how can we know whether our sickness is natural or something else?" There is a workable solution to this problem. Follow the principles laid forth in points one through five, above. If the sickness is caused by sin, sovereignty or Satan, then it will either be cured in these steps, or God will reveal to you why your efforts are, for the moment, ineffective. If, however, the sickness is natural, then follow step six, above. See a good physician.

The overriding principle is this: *Seek God first.* Put your trust in Him. Do not lean upon your own understanding (Prov. 3:5, 6). Wait for God's prescription. He will not leave you comfortless. God cares about your health, too. Give it to Him. He will carry you through whatever comes.

So, before you rush to apply a remedy to the symptoms, open your heart fully to the Lord, and seek the source or cause of the problem. It may well be that the voice of God is speaking to you. Listen. Don't be afraid to stand on the ground of faith. And don't be ashamed to see a doctor. Follow God's directions, and you will receive what is best for you.

Jesus Predicts His Death (Matt. 17:22, 23)

(cf. Mark 9:30-32 and Luke 9:43-45)

Sometimes if a problem is yet to be endured, there is small consolation in knowing the positive fruit it will produce. Here Jesus attempts to comfort His disciples by telling them that He will arise from the dead on the third day. But what sticks in the minds of His loyal followers is the grief that comes from knowing he must be killed.

Is the result worth the cost? Calvary is the most glorious event in the totality of history. What results! But what a price! A part of us grieves sorrowfully at the cost of Jesus' life. But somehow a greater part of us rejoices that His death means our everlasting life!

> **22When they came together in Galilee, he said to them, "The Son of**
> **Man is going to be betrayed into the hands of men. 23They will kill him,**
> **and on the third day he will be raised to life." And the disciples were**
> **filled with grief.**

In this passage, there is but one item on Jesus' mind—His betrayal and crucifixion. He knew how people (including his very own disciples) can become easily distracted; so He reminds them a second time of the suffering He must soon endure. Again, the disciples are perplexed by His statements. Here is clear proof that without divine enablement, spiritual truths merely enter one ear and pass through the other one (1 Cor. 2:9-14).

There were three events awaiting Jesus at Jerusalem: (1) His betrayal, (2) His death and (3) His resurrection. Certainly these first two items were painful to consider, but the final promise doubtlessly provided Him with the stamina He needed to face the bitter hours ahead (Heb. 12:2).

Jesus Pays Taxes (Matt. 17:24-27)

Jesus and His disciples had just spent approximately six months in Gentile territory. Their reception and experiences there had been highly positive. Now Jesus returns to His own community, and as soon as He steps foot into town, He is approached to pay back taxes, or more specifically, temple dues.

I. *The Collectors Talk with Peter (17:24-25a)*

[24]After Jesus and his disciples arrived in Capernaum, the collectors of the two-drachma tax came to Peter and asked, "Doesn't your teacher pay the temple tax[a]?"

[25]"Yes, he does," he replied.

The taxes discussed here are unique. They are not payments required by Rome. Instead, they are dues owed to God by every male Jew who was twenty years of age or older. The purpose of this tax was to maintain the many functions of the Temple in Jerusalem (Exod. 30:11-16; 2 Chron. 24:6, 9).

There were animals to purchase for daily sacrifices; incense, grain and wine were also in frequent use in the Temple. Additionally, there were garments and utensils to replace. And the Temple's many servants must be provided for. All this was costly. So, a tax was imposed by God to meet these needs.

The cost of this annual tax was two drachma. This amounted to about two days' wages. Apparently, Jesus had not paid this fee because of His extended stay away from Jewish soil. Now He would satisfy this ruling from Moses' writings.

II. *Jesus Talks with Peter (17:25b-27)*

When Peter came into the house, Jesus was the first to speak. "What do you think, Simon?" he asked. "From whom do the kings of the earth collect duty and taxes—from their own sons or from others?"

[26]"From others," Peter answered.

"Then the sons are exempt," Jesus said to him. [27]"But so that we may not offend them, go to the lake and throw out your line. Take the first fish you catch; open its mouth and you will find a four-drachma coin. Take it and give it to them for my tax and yours."

Jesus did not mind paying this tax, but He did want to teach Peter a lesson or two in its payment. First, Peter was to learn that while kings do not require a tax from their own households, so Jesus did not actually need to pay a tax for His Father's house. Nevertheless, Jesus consented to this custom. He would not usurp Peter's answer to the collectors with His own rights. Certainly this action displays His patient handling of our immaturity. Peter (and the tax collectors in particular) could not understand Jesus' teaching, so Jesus bypassed His own privilege in order to keep them from being offended by Him (cf. Rom. 14-15).

Second, Peter was to learn that miracles can happen in the most unexpected places and ways. Jesus might have pulled a coin out of the thin air, but instead He instructed Peter to find the necessary money in the mouth of a fish! Why was the miracle to occur

a 24 Greek *the two drachmas*

in this peculiar fashion? Perhaps the nature of this miraculous event was to dramatize to Peter (and to us, too) how limitless are the ways in which God can satisfy our needs. Peter may have thought at first that such an order was ridiculous, but he consented anyway. And at the end of his obedience was the miracle Jesus promised. Certainly it can be stated here that God's ways are not man's ways. The miraculous defies human understanding. Let's be certain that we never limit God to our own level of reasoning.

Who Is the Greatest? (Matt. 18:1-14)

(cf. Mark 9:33-37 and Luke 9:46-48)

Great men never feel great.
Small men never feel small. (Ancient proverb)

The greatest men and women of this world are those who have not lost their child's heart. The childlike (not the childish) are those who best please God.

I. *The Standard for Greatness (18:1-5)*

18 At that time the disciples came to Jesus and asked, "Who is the greatest in the kingdom of heaven?"
2He called a little child and had him stand among them. 3And he said: "I tell you the truth, unless you change and become like little children, you will never enter the kingdom of heaven. 4Therefore, whoever humbles himself like this child is the greatest in the kingdom of heaven.
5And whoever welcomes a little child like this in my name welcomes me.

Who Is the Greatest? God measures greatness in a way that is different from the ways of men. His standards are altogether different. You cannot use the criteria of our society and equate these with greatness in God's Kingdom.

Competition is an odd thing. There is something about us which enjoys defeating someone else. We practically revel in being better than another. This self-centered mentality is in each of us, and especially in our culture at large. Teams strive for the number-one position. Individuals strain for the highest score. Businesses work every angle to be bigger and better. And on it goes—seemingly without end.

Unless You Change. Where does all this competitiveness stop? The answer is this: in the Kingdom of God. Here is the only place on our planet where competition and winning do not make one the greatest. Here greatness is not measured by our success records, but by our dispositions, our attitudes, our characters.

In the Kingdom of God you cannot race anyone to any spiritual goal line, for the very moment you attempt to compete, you are automatically disqualified. In the Kingdom no one compares himself with others. Rather, his delight is to actually elevate others above himself (Phil. 2:1-5). The aim is to make others greater than ourselves. One can only wonder how God feels, for instance, about the self-elevating contests that are sometimes used today supposedly to promote His Kingdom work.

The disciples of Jesus' day, and those who follow Him today, must learn this crucial lesson. Trying to be great or to do great things for God's sake are very self-centered enterprises. God does not want us to be great or to do great things. Instead, He only wants us to be childlike, humble, teachable and obedient.

II. *The Snares to Greatness (18:6-9)*

> **6"But if anyone causes one of these little ones who believe in me to sin,**
> **it would be better for him to have a large millstone hung around his**
> **neck and to be drowned in the depths of the sea. 7Woe to the world**
> **because of the things that cause people to sin! Such things must come,**
> **but woe to the man through whom they come! 8If your hand or your foot**
> **causes you to sin, cut it off and throw it away. It is better for you to enter**
> **life maimed or crippled than to have two hands or two feet and be**
> **thrown into eternal fire. 9And if your eye causes you to sin, gouge it out**
> **and throw it away. It is better for you to enter life with one eye than to**
> **have two eyes and be thrown into the fire of hell.**

Anyone Who Causes One of These to Sin. The opposite of a great person is one who causes another person to stumble, to sin. Personal sin is bad enough, but one who makes other disciples sin (consciously or unconsciously) is the lowest person of them all (Rom. 1:28-2:2). The destination for such a person is the fires of hell. Certainly it would have been better, when viewed from the eternal perspective, if such a person had never been born.

Woe to the Man. Humility and childlikeness are never automatic. *Believing* in Christ and *acting* like Christ are not synonymous. If we are to become mature, we must first recognize the obstacles that immediately confront us. Then, we must act responsibly to remove those obstacles that hamper our full communion with and commitment to Christ.

First, there are the obstacles that come from people. Whether they be well-meaning or malicious, people can block our path to pleasing the Lord. It is all too easy to compromise our convictions when we are under pressure from people. We must learn never to allow people to occupy a higher throne in our hearts than Christ's throne—regardless of the cost.

Second, there are the obstacles that come directly from ourselves. There are the misguided and lustful hand, foot and eye. These members of our bodies must be managed well if we are to enjoy the beauties of heaven. Mastering our fickle whims and evil tendencies is one of the most spiritual tasks we can ever pursue.

III. *The Surety of Greatness (18:10-14)*

> **10"See that you do not look down on one of these little ones. For I tell you that their angels in heaven always see the face of my Father in heaven.[a]**
>
> **12"What do you think? If a man owns a hundred sheep, and one of them wanders away, will he not leave the ninety-nine on the hills and go to look for the one that wandered off? 13And if he finds it, I tell you the truth, he is happier about that one sheep than about the ninety-nine that did not wander off. 14In the same way your Father in heaven is not willing that any of these little ones should be lost.**

Their Angels in Heaven. It is sometimes difficult for our human reasoning to understand how a God of infinite abilities can be interested in little children—but He is! In fact, He has even assigned angels to watch over these little ones (as well as over all adult believers—Heb. 1:14). These angels patiently wait in God's presence until He sends them on assignments in behalf of earth's children. Then they return to await further orders. It is also quite probable that at least one angel is always in the immediate (though invisible) presence of every child (and believing adult) in the whole world, while other angels stand before God to receive His next orders.

These little kids do not merit this angelic guardianship. Instead, it is God's delight to watch over them. It is not because of their greatness that God cares for them. No one will ever be great enough to merit such attention. But He sends His angels to them because of the greatness in a child's simplicity, singleheartedness and vulnerability.

A Sheep Wanders Away. Sheep are often pictured in the Scriptures as people because of their proneness to wander (Ps. 119:176; Isa. 53:6; Ezek. 34:16). And just as frequently God the Father (Ps. 77:20; 80:1) and Jesus (Ezek. 34:12, 23; Zech. 13:7; John 10:14; Luke 15:2-7; Heb. 13:20) are portrayed as Shepherds who seek the safety (or salvation) of the huge flock of sheep all over the earth. The supreme interest of God and Jesus is that each person, in all of time, be rescued and restored to God's family.

---

a 10 Some manuscripts *heaven.* [11]*The Son of Man came to save what was lost.*

Dealing With Sin in the Church (Matt. 18:15-20)

This is a highly controversial subject. Some people will not talk about it at all. Others get an introduction to the topic and then stop far short of a balanced understanding. But we must press on, all the way to the end of this theme, because this teaching can save a local church from the fatality of unchecked sin.

There are extremists in every phase of life, including the church. In the issue before us, there are those people who adamantly resist the very notion of ever speaking to any persons about sin in their lives. At the opposite end from this spectrum are people who almost ceaselessly point an accusing index finger at those who fail to measure up to their own opinionated standards. But truth is to be found somewhere between these two extremes, as we shall discover in Jesus' teaching.

I. *Dealing with the Problem (18:15-17)*

> **15"If your brother sins against you,[a] go and show him his fault, just between the two of you. If he listens to you, you have won your brother over. 16But if he will not listen, take one or two others along, so that 'every matter may be established by the testimony of two or three witnesses.'[b] 17If he refuses to listen to them, tell it to the church; and if he refuses to listen even to the church, treat him as you would a pagan or a tax collector.**

Jesus faced people—church people—very realistically. He knew they would sin. There has never been a Christian who did not sin (1 John 1:10). Each of us commits sins. And through confession to God, these sins are forever blotted out of God's sight (1 John 1:9). Our lives can be kept clean by simply repenting at the precise moment we commit a known sin. But what about the Christian who sins and does not confess or repent? Where does he stand? What happens to him?

Jesus knows the nature of people. He anticipated that there would be people in the church who would get entangled in sin, and who would not stop practicing it. How are we to react to such persons? What is our Lord's prescription?

Whenever a fellow Christian wrongs you, you should turn immediately to this passage and follow its instructions. Here is Jesus' four-step approach to dealing with people who sin and do not repent.

---

a 15 Some manuscripts do not have *against you.* *a 16* Deut. 19:15

Step One: Go and show him his fault. There is a natural tendency within each of us to make two mistakes when someone sins against us. First, we are inclined to pray and to leave the matter with God (and perhaps to dwell on it in our minds or even to confess the flaw to others—to gossip). Second, we are inclined to say nothing, or even to avoid the sinning Christian. Sometimes we reason that we are just as human as they, so we drop it altogether. But not one of these approaches, no matter how righteous or sincere they may sound to our ears, is given to us from Jesus.

Certainly our Lord knows more about us than anyone else. Then He must also know how to best help us when we fall into sin. If we fail to follow His instructions, we are actually failing to do what is best for our Christian friends.

What does Jesus order us to do when we have been wronged by a Christian who is living in sin? He instructs us to go to him and to correct him. The approach is to be direct, and the conversation is to be specific.

There is not to be any beating around the bush when you talk to another Christian about his sin. This does not, in any degree, imply that you ought to be sarcastic, negative or rude. God forbid (Gal. 6:1, 2)! Our tones, though piercing, must be spoken with the deepest level of our love.

If the erring one listens and heeds the counsel given to him, the mission is a success, and it can be forgotten. But if the sin continues, then you must advance to the next step.

Step Two: Take others along and repeat step one. Sometimes your personal efforts will be brushed aside. When this happens, you must not stop. Find several of your most mature Christian friends, and take them along with you. Repeat your efforts. Sin can be a nasty trap, requiring the aid of several persons in order to make the rescue effective.

Again, if the sinning brother or sister repents of his or her sinful practice, then the person has been delivered from a fruitless Christian life. But what if this step fails in yielding any results? Then press on to step number three.

Step Three: Tell the church. No one enjoys telling or hearing about the sin of another Christian, especially a Christian from within our very own membership. Nevertheless, despite the discomfort it causes, it is a much less painful experience than the hurt that is caused by ignoring the sin (1 Cor. 5:5-7)!

Neglect never stopped the spreading of sin or healed an ailing church. Confrontation hurts, but it is the best cure. The church must be told the story. And the church must act competently upon the issue. A warning—firm, yet compassionate—must be delivered. Rights may be suspended. Privileges may be revoked—whatever the church deems appropriate for the matter at hand. Even these dealings, however, are sometimes futile.

Step Four: Excommunication. There will be cases where all of the above approaches fail to produce positive results. Sin can grip a man or woman very tightly at times. And if the offender remains obstinate, there is only one recourse—excommunication (1 Cor. 5:1-13). Such persons are to be expelled from the rolls of the church and regarded like any other spiritually lost human being (illustrated here as the characteristically unregenerated pagans and tax collectors). Their names must be dropped from the rolls of the church. The membership list of the local church must reflect, as best as possible, the list compiled in heaven by God himself. Let us, then, neither add to it, nor take from it, with any degree of haste. (See the special discussion on this topic at the close of this unit.)

II. *Discovering the Power (18:18-20)*

18"I tell you the truth, whatever you bind on earth will be bound in
heaven, and whatever you loose on earth will be loosed in heaven.
19"Again, I tell you that if two of you on earth agree about anything
you ask for, it will be done for you by my Father in heaven. 20For where
two or three come together in my name, there am I with them."

Bind and Loose. These terms have been discussed earlier (see notes on Matt. 16:19). The idea presented here is the fact that the church possesses the authority to extend or withhold membership from anyone.

Two or Three. The all-too-common application of this passage to the general principles of prayer is an unfortunate misunderstanding (or overlooking) of the context. Jesus makes it clear that these comments are intended to reemphasize and reconfirm His previous statements on binding and loosing when He says, "*Again,* I tell you." In other words, the prayer promises supplied here pertain specifically to those petitions that focus on the matter of church discipline. God will hear anything regarding these kinds of prayers, and Jesus will even guarantee His presence during such proceedings. We must not fear, then, to exercise our authority in the process of disciplining a sinning brother or sister.

Any other application of these words will culminate in bitter disappointment and confusion. For instance, numerous ones have supposed that because they agreed in prayer for some matter that their request was incapable of going unanswered. They "claimed" it together, and now God "must" supply it. But this practice has not been proven to work always. Many sincere Christians have found their prayers harmonizing with other Christian's prayers, but in the end the results were not what they had prayed about. They followed this single verse as closely as possible, still the results were nonproductive. Why? Because the broader context for this verse was ignored. This is not a formula for general prayer, but for prayer that pertains to the matter of church discipline.

Special Study: Church Discipline

Introduction

In numerous respects the local church is like many secular organizations. We are designed to accomplish certain objectives and to maintain a certain level of discipline in our membership. These two fundamentals are necessary for all organizations.

Anyone is eligible to join the church, if he or she meets the requirements of being a genuine Christian. But attached to this stipulation are the reasonable expectations that once one joins the church, he or she will maintain a respectable Christian life. Should anyone fail to keep his or her personal life style in tune with the standards required by the Bible, then his or her membership is subject to review.

We believe these principles are biblical. The church must clearly define its objectives and the standards it expects of its members. If anyone should fall short of these basic qualifications, then some action must be taken—in love—to rectify the problem.

The purpose of this particular study is to expose the biblical procedure for handling major problems that occasionally befall church members.

The Place of Discipline in the Bible

A. *God Disciplines Directly.*

The theme of direct disciplinary action from God runs throughout the Bible.

In the third chapter of Genesis the Lord excommunicated Adam and Eve from the Garden of Eden (vv. 22-24). And in the final chapter of Revelation, Jesus threatened that all the curses of this highly judgmental book will rest upon anyone who tampers with its message. Between these two points, the Bible is replete with illustrations of disciplinary actions that fall directly from God on the sinful individuals (see Gen. 6, 7; 19:23-25; Exod. 7-14; Lev. 10:1-3; Num. 12:1-15; 25:4-9; Acts 5:1-11; 1 Cor. 11:17-34; Rev. 2:18-29; etc.).

B. *God Disciplines Indirectly.*

As often as not, God delegates His authority to exercise discipline to His own people. One of the most serious tasks of Christians is to "judge those inside" the church (1 Cor. 5:12). It is *our* responsibility as well as God's to handle matters requiring discipline.

Discipline at the hands of humans is not strange to the Scriptures. Often God instructed His people to deal with those who were not living in accordance with His commandments.

Israel was rewarded for stoning Achan and his family for stealing (Josh. 7); the sons of Levi were honored for killing Jewish idolators, including their own brothers, friends and neighbors (Exod. 32); Phinehas was highly commended for driving a spear through a man and woman who were guilty of sexual immorality (Num. 25:6-13); Elijah was never challenged for calling down fire upon the servants of an ungodly king (2 Kings 1); Nehemiah, in an outrage over the lukewarmness in Israel, "rebuked them and called curses down on them. . . . beat some of the men and pulled out their hair. . . . made them take an oath in God's name" (Neh. 13:25). And on it goes (see Exod 30:33; Lev. 13:46; 17:4; Num. 5:2, 3; 12:14, 15; Ezra 7:26; 10:8; etc.).

The New Testament picture is much the same, though excommunication replaces the death penalty for certain sins. Jesus gives clear-cut statements regarding the procedure for excommunication (Matt. 16:19; 18:15-18; John 20:23). And Paul steadfastly reinforces Jesus' words (1 Cor. 5; Titus 3:10). Also see Luke 6:22; John 9:22; 12:42; 16:2; 1 Cor. 16:22; 2 Cor. 2:5-7; 2 Thess. 3:14, 15; 1 Tim. 5:19, 20.

There can be left no question in the mind of the sincere Christian regarding discipline through human instrumentality. God both authorizes and demands that we deal with sin in the local church.

The Purpose of Discipline

All discipline—whether it comes directly or indirectly from God—is "for our good, that we may share in his holiness" (Heb. 12:10).

There is no malice or revenge in any Christian disciplinary action—not even a trace. The goal is solely that the erring party may come to see his or her sin, repent of it and be "saved on the day of the Lord" (1 Cor. 5:5). All discipline is designed to be corrective, never destructive (1 Tim. 1:18-20).

The only desire of those making the decision to discipline is that their efforts will produce "a harvest of righteousness and peace for those who have been trained by it" (Heb. 12:11).

Also, it is through this procedure that the rest of the congregation is made fearful of sinning (1 Tim. 5:20). Church discipline prevents sin from spreading.

When properly administered, disciplinary actions not only "get rid of the old yeast" (1 Cor. 5:7) from the membership, and put a fear of sinning in the whole congregation, but they also uphold the righteousness of God. The church must not allow unwholesome living to bring disgrace to the name of Jesus Christ.

The Importance of Remaining Objective

There is nothing more detrimental to correct discipline than allowing our emotions to guide our thoughts and decisions. Feelings must never be permitted to sway us into a decision that is too strong or too weak.

The only guide in matters of discipline is the objective Word of God. The Bible is the single source for all decision making.

What the Bible condemns we must condemn. What the Bible condones we must condone.

We are to say what the Bible says—nothing more, nothing less and nothing else!

The Sins Counted Worthy of Excommunication

Sins differ in their degrees of evil (Luke 12:45-48; etc.). As is true in society at large, some crimes carry greater penalties than others.

There are two major categories into which the sins of excommunication may be classified: (1) immorality and (2) heresy. Here is an explanation of these important terms.

(1) *Immorality* encompasses a broad variety of serious sins. In Paul's excommunication address to the Corinthians he lists six specific offenses that the church today must use as a standard or guideline for determining those sins worthy of excommunication. They are these: sexual immorality, greediness, idolatry, slander, drunkenness and swindling.

Another explicit collection of serious sins is found in Rev. 21:8. The persons listed here are said to have their part "in the fiery lake of burning sulfur." They are "the cowardly, the unbelieving, the vile, the murderers, the sexually immoral, those who practice magic arts, the idolators and all liars."

(2) *Heresy* is that activity which leads to divisiveness or an unhealthy split in the local church (Titus 3:10). Such persons are heretics (dividers), and they should be properly excommunicated (see also 1 Tim. 1:19, 20). The heretic often demonstrates his divisiveness through false teaching.

Two Kinds of Excommunication

Because not all offenses (or sins) are the same, not all church discipline is the same. Whenever any matter requires the action of the church, it must be viewed as a serious offense. But the church recognizes that there are two kinds of actions it may elect to utilize in order to correct the offending member.

(1) *Partial Excommunication*

In a partial excommunication, the guilty person is one who "does not obey our instruction" (that is, the instruction of the apostles or the Scriptures—2 Thess. 3:14). The disobedience here is not as major as some other sins, but it is serious enough to merit a church action (in the Thessalonian context, for instance, the erring parties were refusing to work). In such instances the church must instruct its members to "not associate with him" (the erring person—2 Thess. 3:14). Also, the church must "not regard him as an enemy, but warn him as a brother" (2 Thess. 3:15).

In other terms, a partial excommunication maintains that the erring party is a Christian, but that his (or her) rights and privileges in the church and among Christians are being revoked until such a time that he (or she) should repent.

(2) *Total Excommunication*

In a total excommunication the guilty person is one who "refuses to listen to the church" when repeatedly reproved for a clear offense against another Christian (Matt. 18:17). After a continual refusal to repent, the church must regard such a party as "a pagan and a tax collector" (Matt. 18:17). In other words, they should be considered as spiritually lost and in need of salvation. Naturally this means the removal of their names from the church rolls, along with all privileges of membership.

The Procedure for Excommunication

The ultimate step in the church's disciplinary authority is excommunication.

Excommunication is the act of separating a person from all the privileges of the local church. Hopefully the duration of this decision will only be temporary, because of a change of heart in the erring party (see 1 Cor. 5:1-13 with 2 Cor. 2:5-8). Regrettably, in instances where there is no change, the excommunication becomes permanent.

Here are the steps that are to be followed before any excommunication proceedings are to be made final. These guidelines are based on Jesus' words in Matthew 18:15-18.

(1) If you are aware of sinful practices in the life of a brother or sister, go—in private—and correct him (or her).

(2) If your private counsel does not work, then take one or two others with you and bring the correction again.

(3) If your collective efforts still produce no positive effect, then bring the matter to the whole church for their action.

(4) If the erring party refuses to hear the counsel of the church, then let that person be removed from all church privileges and rights.

Restoration to Fellowship and to the Church

The goal of church discipline is to convey the serious consequences sin produces in the life of an unrepentant person. The action of the church in warning and disciplining its members only serves to visibly display what, in fact, has already transpired in heaven (Matt. 18:18).

But this is only half of the story. The aim of all excommunication is restoration, not unending punishment.

When the church excommunicates one of its members, it is with the clear and unhesitant understanding that complete restoration is both possible and desirable.

No person who shows clear proof of repentance should be chastened any longer by the church. Once an erring person stops the practice for which he or she was excommunicated, and once he or she expresses a desire for forgiveness, then the church will lovingly return the individual's name to the church rolls as a member in good standing and renew to him or her all the former rights and privileges.

Ground Rules for Forgiveness (Matt. 18:21-35)

How can we cultivate a forgiving attitude? By frequently going to Calvary and seeing the high price that was paid to secure our own forgiveness!

It is significant that immediately following Jesus' teaching on discipline and excommunication, Matthew now includes a lengthy section on mercy and the need for continuous forgiveness.

I. *Peter's Question (18:21)*

21Then Peter came to Jesus and asked, "Lord, how many times shall I forgive my brother when he sins against me? Up to seven times?"

Peter raises a most practical question, especially in light of Jesus' previous discussion on disciplining your brother in the faith (18:15-20). Suppose your brother sins against you, repents of his wrongs and then repeats the process a half a dozen times. When do you draw the line? When do you say, "enough is enough?"

II. *Jesus' First Answer (18:22)*

22Jesus answered, "I tell you, not seven times, but seventy-seven times.[a]

How often should you forgive a sinning and repenting fellow believer (cf. Luke 17:3, 4)? The New International Version records Jesus as saying the number should be seventy-seven (an alternate translation of this figure, however, could be seventy times seven, or 490 times—in either case the fundamental meaning is the same). Peter reasoned that there must be a limit somewhere in the extending of this forgiving grace. But Jesus sets no boundaries at all. Forgiveness is always available for those who repent. This is the way God forgives us, and it must be the way we forgive others.

III. *Jesus' Second Answer (18:23-35)*

**23"Therefore, the kingdom of heaven is like a king who wanted to
settle accounts with his servants. 24As he began the settlement, a man
who owed him ten thousand talents[b] was brought to him. 25Since he was
not able to pay, the master ordered that he and his wife and his children
and all that he had be sold to repay the debt.**

---

a 22 Or *seventy times seven* *b 24* That is, several million dollars

26“The servant fell on his knees before him. ‘Be patient with me,’ he
begged, ‘and I will pay back everything.’ 27The servant’s master took
pity on him, canceled the debt and let him go.
28“But when that servant went out, he found one of his fellow servants
who owed him a hundred denarii.[a] He grabbed him and began to choke
him. ‘Pay back what you owe me!’ he demanded.
29“His fellow servant fell to his knees and begged him, ‘Be patient with
me, and I will pay you back.’
30“But he refused. Instead, he went off and had the man thrown into
prison until he could pay the debt. 31When the other servants saw what
had happened, they were greatly distressed and went and told their
master everything that had happened.
32“Then the master called the servant in. ‘You wicked servant,’ he
said, ‘I canceled all that debt of yours because you begged me to.
33Shouldn’t you have had mercy on your fellow servant just as I had on
you?’ 34In anger his master turned him over to the jailers until he should
pay back all he owed.
35“This is how my heavenly Father will treat each of you unless you
forgive your brother from your heart.”

In this parable Jesus illustrates His first answer. Then He adds one further note. Anyone who does not sincerely forgive someone who repents will himself not be forgiven by God (Matt. 6:14; Mark 11:25)! In this passage one of the chief causes for stunted spiritual growth in numerous Christians is revealed. By harboring grudges, resentment and bitterness (each being a mark of unforgiveness), believers have sealed the door to further progress in spiritual matters. Not until a forgiving attitude replaces a negative spirit will they start to advance again. Unfortunately some believers have died as mere infants in the faith because they stumbled over this prerequisite for continued growth.

Divorce (Matt. 19:1-12)

(cf. Mark 10:1-12)

God’s plan for marriage is oneness until death separates this bond. But too frequently there are other considerations that terminate this union.

“Divorce” is a painful word. It smarts deeply in each one who cherishes the sanctity

a 28 That is, a few dollars

of marriage. But it is a word that cannot be ignored. It will not go away. And we must learn to face it and to handle it with much wisdom.

Jesus skirted no issue—regardless of its touchiness—including divorce. His speech is straightforward. And His teaching on the subject remains our standard to this very hour.

I. *The Law of Creation (19:1-6)*

19 When Jesus had finished saying these things, he left Galilee and
went into the region of Judea to the other side of the Jordan.
2Large crowds followed him, and he healed them there.
3Some Pharisees came to him to test him. They asked, "Is it lawful for
a man to divorce his wife for any and every reason?"
4"Haven't you read," he replied, "that at the beginning the Creator
'made them male and female,'[a] 5and said, 'For this reason a man will
leave his father and mother and be united to his wife, and the two will
become one flesh'[b]? 6So they are no longer two, but one. Therefore what
God has joined together, let man not separate."

The matter of divorce was a bone of contention among the Jews. For some, the thought of dissolving a marriage, except for the cause of adultery, was not even to be contemplated. But for others, the possibility of a legal divorce hinged on the smallest offense of a wife—including such items as yelling, spoiling a meal, speaking disrespectfully and losing eye appeal.

Unfortunately it was this shallow position on marriage that received the highest acceptance in Jesus' day. And with this cockeyed notion in their minds, the Pharisees set out to test Jesus. Possibly here, they reasoned, Jesus could be trapped, and thereby His credibility as a teacher of God's law could be destroyed.

Here comes the barbed question: "Does God permit a man to divorce his wife *for any reason at all?"* In other words, which current position—the conservative or the liberal view—is correct?

If Jesus wanted to win votes, He could have easily done so here. But He did not come to earth to make God popular. Jesus came to show men and women the entrance to the Kingdom of God and how to be holy citizens within that kingdom. There would be no compromise to this call. Jesus would declare God's will and challenge each one to live inside its borders.

In the mind of Jesus the Scriptures long ago revealed the forever settled will of God on the subject of divorce. The disclosure came in the opening pages of the Bible—Genesis, chapter two (verses 23, 24). Jesus did not bite the bait offered by the Pharisees. Instead, He simply quoted God's clear position. Marriage was (and is!) to

---

a 4 Gen. 1:27   *b 5* Gen. 2:24

be the most intimate union found on earth. Here, one plus one equals one. The husband and wife are joined together in marriage to form a unique and single expression of life, with each member complementing and fulfilling the other member. And no one is granted permission to sever this lifelong attachment.

II. *The Law of Moses and Jesus (19:7-9)*

> **7"Why then," they asked, "did Moses command that a man give his wife a certificate of divorce and send her away?"**
> **8Jesus replied, "Moses permitted you to divorce your wives because your hearts were hard. But it was not this way from the beginning. 9I tell you that anyone who divorces his wife, except for marital unfaithfulness, and marries another woman commits adultery."**

Once the Pharisees had received Jesus' reply, they were swift to point out to Him how Moses had permitted his people to write out a certificate of divorce (Deut. 24:1-4). With this statement, the Pharisees figured Jesus was now trapped. He had committed himself to being conservative, while Moses, they reasoned, was a great deal more lenient. Surely, they thought, Moses was more accurate than Jesus.

But Jesus' insights into the meaning of the Scriptures were exceedingly profound. And again His critics would be shamed for their shallow and distorted understanding of the divine laws, which they falsely claimed to love and to follow.

Moses did not favor divorce any more than Jesus favored divorce. It was due to the hardness of the hearts of the people that Moses permitted this to happen. Such an occurrence did not please God at all. In other words, the views of Moses and Jesus on divorce were quite likely identical.

Based upon the above scriptural text, and the words of Jesus located in the other Gospels (Mark 10:2-12; Luke 16:18), the following points should be noted:

1. The only justified basis for a divorce, in Jesus' teaching, was adultery. Although divorce is permissible in this case, it is not required. Repentance, forgiveness and renewed love can rectify any otherwise hopeless marriage. The innocent party may choose to divorce the mate, however, and in such cases is free to remarry.
2. If a person divorces someone without proper justification, then, any remarriage constitutes adultery.
3. While the weight of the discussion on divorce often falls on guilty women, Jesus also taught that the same principles for divorce apply to guilty men as well. Women, even in Jesus' day, could complete a divorce against their sinning male mate.

The above statements represent, in capsule form, the entire teaching of Jesus regarding the matter of divorce. There is a subtle danger about these words, however, that is easily overlooked. In a sincere attempt to both understand and apply Jesus' teaching, we can fail to remember that this very brief discussion by Jesus is not intended to be an exhaustive treatment on the subject of marriage and divorce. These statements on divorce must be examined in the broader scope of the total Bible. Here, then, are four vital items that Jesus did not find necessary to include in these particular discourses.

1. There is a second legitimate grounds for divorce—the departure of one's unbelieving mate (1 Cor. 7:15).

2. A Christian is not to separate from (or divorce) his or her mate, but if he or she does do this, then the departing party is not to remarry (1 Cor. 7:10, 11).

3. Widows may remarry (1 Cor. 7:8, 9, 39).

4. Any divorce—legitimate or otherwise—by any person (Christian or non-Christian) is a forgivable sin (1 John 1:9). There is only one unforgivable sin, and it is not divorce (Matt. 12:31, 32)! A second marriage is capable of receiving God's blessing, if the mates are sincerely repentant and desirous of making Christ the Lord of their lives. Such parties are to be treated by us and the local church as Christians in a spiritual state with God. We must not shun or deprive them of our love and fellowship.

III. *The Law of Chastity (19:10-12)*

> **[10]The disciples said to him, "If this is the situation between a husband and wife, it is better not to marry."**
>
> **[11]Jesus replied, "Not everyone can accept this teaching, but only those to whom it has been given. [12]For some are eunuchs because they were born that way; others were made that way by men; and others have renounced marriage[a] because of the kingdom of heaven. The one who can accept this should accept it."**

Marriage is a common union in our world, but chastity, for the sake of God's Kingdom, is an equally acceptable state. Some men and women have turned aside the pleasures of a family life. They have abandoned domestic interests because of a special burden and love for their Lord's work. Such persons are truly gifted of God to perform this role of single adulthood (1 Cor. 7:7, 32-34).

---

a 12 Or *have made themselves eunuchs*

Jesus Blesses the Children (Matt. 19:13-15)

(cf. Mark 10:13-16; Luke 18:15-17)

There is not a little child in the world who would not come to Jesus if given the opportunity. Children love Jesus because Jesus loves them.

> **[13]Then little children were brought to Jesus for him to place his hands on them and pray for them. But the disciples rebuked those who brought them.**
>
> **[14]Jesus said, "Let the little children come to me, and do not hinder them, for the kingdom of heaven belongs to such as these." [15]When he had placed his hands on them, he went on from there.**

There are four items of interest in this episode. Each of them teaches us an important lesson.

First, we notice there are wise and loving parents who want to bring their children to Jesus for His blessing. What a weighty responsibility it is to raise children. This is not an easy duty. So, mature parents take their little ones to meet Jesus. No other encounter in a child's life is as important as this. The highest goal of each parent ought to be the privilege of introducing their sons and daughters to Jesus Christ.

Second, we notice that some people (including the followers of Christ) have low opinions of children. Little people are not important to them. They believe Jesus is too busy to permit "simple-minded young people" to get under His feet. Jesus only has time for, and an interest in, adults, or so some have falsely conjectured.

Third, we notice that Jesus not only loves little children, He even teaches that God's Kingdom is specifically designed to include them. Children are significant to God and Jesus. They are worthy of our attention, time, prayers and blessings, too.

Fourth, we notice how Jesus blessed the children—He laid His hands on them and prayed for them. If you want blessed kids (or kids that are a blessing to your home, church and community), then you must pray for them. Touch them. Pick them up in love and ask God to grant them a prosperous and holy journey throughout life.

The Rich Young Man (Matt. 19:16-30)

(cf. Mark 10:17-31 and Luke 18:18-30)

When everything has been said and done, there is only one really important goal in life—obtaining eternal life. This objective ought to be at the top of everyone's priority list.

I. *Jesus' Dialogue with the Man (19:16-22)*

16Now a man came up to Jesus and asked, "Teacher, what good thing must I do to get eternal life?"

17"Why do you ask me about what is good?" Jesus replied. "There is only One who is good. If you want to enter life, obey the commandments."

18"Which ones?" the man inquired.

Jesus replied, " 'Do not murder, do not commit adultery, do not steal, do not give false testimony, 19honor your father and mother,'[a] and 'love your neighbor as yourself.'[b]"

20"All these I have kept," the young man said. "What do I still lack?"

21Jesus answered, "If you want to be perfect, go, sell your possessions and give to the poor, and you will have treasure in heaven. Then come, follow me."

22When the young man heard this, he went away sad. because he had great wealth.

We may glean many practical lessons from this common drama of life. Here are a few items that should speak to each of us.

First, we learn that morality is not a synonym for salvation. We may be innocent of many offenses, but we will never be good enough to merit or earn our salvation. There is only one truly good person, and He is the Lord God. No one else (excluding Jesus) is free of faults and blemishes. We each fall short of God's standards for pure thoughts, words and actions (Rom. 3:23).

Second, we learn that neither morality nor riches can satisfy a person's desire for salvation. How frequently we are seduced to believe that a certain life style, accompanied with lots of money and things, will quench the emptiness in our hearts. But such solutions will never fulfill our deepest hungers.

---

a 19 Exodus 20:12-16; Deut. 5:16-20 *b 19* Lev. 19:18

Third, we learn that the things we often consider to be the desired luxuries of life are actually stumbling blocks to salvation. It is difficult for many rich persons to decide between treasures on earth and treasures in heaven. The magnetic attraction of temporal items is great—and the higher their abundance, the stronger their pull becomes. Each of us must carefully guard his heart to maintain a divine perspective on earth's material possessions.

II. *Jesus' Dialogue with the Disciples (19:23-30)*

23Then Jesus said to his disciples, "I tell you the truth, it is hard for a
rich man to enter the kingdom of heaven. 24Again I tell you, it is easier
for a camel to go through the eye of a needle than for a rich man to enter
the kingdom of God."
25When the disciples heard this, they were greatly astonished and
asked, "Who then can be saved?"
26Jesus looked at them and said, "With man this is impossible, but with
God all things are possible."
27Peter answered him, "We have left everything to follow you! What
then will there be for us?"
28Jesus said to them, "I tell you the truth, at the renewal of all things,
when the Son of Man sits on his glorious throne, you who have followed
me will also sit on twelve thrones, judging the twelve tribes of Israel.
29And everyone who has left houses or brothers or sisters or father or
mother or children or fields for my sake will receive a hundred times as
much and will inherit eternal life. 30But many who are first will be last,
and many who are last will be first.

The Eye of a Needle. In one sense the easiest thing anyone can do is enter God's Kingdom (that is, become a Christian—Matt. 11:28-30; John 1:12). In another sense it is the most difficult task that some people will ever pursue (Matt. 7:13, 14; 11:12; Luke 13:24). In fact, it is so hard for some—especially the rich people—that it would be easier for the largest animal known to the Jews, the camel, to first pass through the small eye of a mending needle. (A few commentators believe this eye of the needle may refer to a small passageway into a walled city through which a camel could pass only after it removed all of its burdens and crept through on its knees. There is, however, no evidence to support this particular notion.)

Who Can Be Saved? If a large camel can pass more readily through the small opening at the end of a needle than a rich person can be saved, then, the disciples reasoned, how can anyone ever be saved? Everyone who truly wants to receive eternal life can receive it, says Jesus. But the success of getting it does not rest within our own abilities. Rather, it rests in God's grace toward each one of us. Here we learn that no obstacle to salvation is so big that God's love and power are not still greater. No one can offer an excuse for his condemnation, for God always stands ready to make a path possible so that anyone can be saved who really wants to be saved.

At the Renewal of All Things. This is a reference to the Second Coming of Jesus Christ, at which time He will purge the earth of every sin and sinner (Mal. 3:1-3; 4:1; Matt. 25:31-46). There is good reason to believe that this is another way of referring to the new heaven and earth (Isa. 65:17; 66:22; 2 Pet. 3:13; Rev. 21, 22).

Twelve Thrones. After Jesus' Second Coming, he will inaugurate His thousand-year reign over all the nations. At the core of this rule will be earth's capital—Jerusalem (Zech. 14:16-21). Presiding over the affairs of this city and the national interests of Israel will be Jesus' twelve closest disciples (the twelfth disciple being Matthias—Acts 1:15-26). The precise duties of these disciples are not spelled out, though it is reasonable to assume that they will assure continued righteousness and peace for everyone living within Jewish borders (cf. Rev. 2:26, 27; 19:11-16; 20:4).

A Hundred Times As Much. Here the promise shifts from the immediate band of disciples to every past, present and future Christian. The profits for following Christ are one hundred times greater in this life (Mark 10:30—including persecutions) and in the life to come than what we would have received had we not chosen to become Christians. There is no loss in making Jesus Christ our Lord and Savior. Indeed, the very opposite is the actual case. Those who surrender everything to follow Jesus are abundantly rewarded. The richest people in this world are those who have given their all to Jesus!

First Will Be Last/Last Will Be First. Many of those people who are first in line today for success, status and earthly goods will be at the last of the line when Jesus returns. And those persons who are at the bottom of the social and political lists today may very well be at the top of the list at the Second Coming. Jesus does not see us as other people see us. His eye is not flattered by what we hold in our hands, but by what we possess in our hearts.

Workers in God's Vineyard (Matt. 20:1-16)

During the fall of the year in Israel it is harvest time for the vineyards. The grapes are ripe. And they must be gathered in before the rainy season comes and the grapes spoil on the vines. That means hiring numerous workers to gather in the crops quickly, now at the peak moment of their ripening.

It was not at all uncommon for people in Jesus' lifetime to go to the marketplace looking for work. Here the employers would come to seek workers for their daily needs. Often men would be selected for tasks early in the morning. But others would have to wait until noon, or possibly even later, for their employment.

From this typical first-century scene Jesus draws a wonderful illustration about the employment and payment God offers to those who will labor in His vineyard. The truths from this short story will profit each one who hears with an open mind and heart.

I. *Recruiting the Workers (20:1-7)*

20 "For the kingdom of heaven is like a landowner who went out ear-
ly in the morning to hire men to work in his vineyard. [2]He agreed
to pay them a denarius for the day and sent them into his vineyard.
[3]"About the third hour he went out and saw others standing in the
marketplace doing nothing. [4]He told them, 'You also go and work in my
vineyard, and I will pay you whatever is right.' [5]So they went.
"He went out again about the sixth hour and the ninth hour and did
the same thing. [6]About the eleventh hour he went out and found still
others standing around. He asked them, 'Why have you been standing
here all day long doing nothing?'
[7]" 'Because no one has hired us,' they answered.
"He said to them, 'You also go and work in my vineyard.'

Like all parables, this one conveys an earthly story with spiritual implications. In this opening section we discover that the Lord's harvest is ripe, ready to be reaped. But the Master will not harvest alone; He will enlist workers (you and me) to assist in His tremendous works (Matt. 9:35-38).

In the Kingdom of God no one is unemployed (though some, regrettably, are lazy). Everyone has a job. From the youngest right up through the oldest, there is a task for each member of God's family. There is no place for retirement or idleness in God's plans.

Further, it should be noted that the workers are signed up at all hours of the day. Likewise, some believers serve Christ faithfully for nearly a century, while others serve Him for only seconds before their deaths. There is a vast difference between the number of hours people put in for Christ; still, each one agrees to the same pay—eternal life.

II. *Rewarding the Workers (20:8)*

[8]"When evening came, the owner of the vineyard said to his foreman,

'Call the workers and pay them their wages, beginning with the last ones hired and going on to the first.'

Some people have worked for Jesus for many years, while others have labored in His service for only a few days or hours. Between these two extremes are multitudes of people who have entered God's Kingdom at every conceivable juncture. But whether the duration has been for only several minutes, or for many faithful decades, the pay is the same. Adoption into God's family is finalized the moment we come to Christ in repentant faith. We will never be any more saved ten years after our conversion than we were ten seconds after that first step. Our level of maturity and the number of our good works will have increased greatly, but we can never be more saved.

Some persons have drawn the conclusion that this story teaches an across-the-board equality in heaven. It does no such thing. We will not all share the same position, nor will we all receive the same rewards in our eternal dwelling (see Dan. 12:2, 3; Matt. 25:14-30; 1 Cor. 3:10-15; 2 Cor. 5:10). The reward in this particular episode is heaven itself. We will each, as Christians, share equally in this grand reward. But once we step our first foot through the gates of pearl, we will immediately perceive that those who have honored Christ the most while here on this earth will be the most honored in the holy city. (See the chart entitled, "Jesus' Reward System.")

JESUS' REWARD SYSTEM

For Saints:		For Sinners:	
Everlasting life	Luke 18:30; John 6:40	Judgment	Rev. 20:11-15
Glorification	Rom. 8:29, 30; 1 Cor. 15:35-37	Torment	Luke 16:19-24
Joint heirship with Christ	Rom. 8:17	Darkness	Matt. 8:12
Reigning with Christ	2 Tim. 2:12; Rev. 2:26, 27	Smoke	Rev. 14:9-11
Crowns	1 Cor. 9:25; 2 Tim. 4:8; James 1:12; 1 Pet. 5:4; Rev. 2:10	Fire	Isa. 33:14; 66:24
Rest	Heb. 4:9; Rev. 14:13	Weeping and wailing	Matt. 13:42
Fullness of joy	Ps. 16:11	Grinding of teeth	Matt. 22:13
		No rest	Rev. 14:9-11
		Remembrance	Luke 16:19-31
		No escape	Luke 16:19-31
		Everlasting	Rev. 20:10; 2 Thess. 1:7-10

III. *Reminding the Workers (20:9-16)*

**[9]"The workers who were hired about the eleventh hour came and
each received a denarius. [10]So when those came who were hired first,
they expected to receive more. But each one of them also received a
denarius. [11]When they received it, they began to grumble against the
landowner. [12]'These men who were hired last worked only one hour,'
they said, 'and you have made them equal to us who have borne the
burden of the work and the heat of the day.'**

**[13]"But he answered one of them, 'Friend, I am not being unfair to you.
Didn't you agree to work for a denarius? [14]Take your pay and go. I want
to give the man who was hired last the same as I gave you. [15]Don't I have
the right to do what I want with my own money? Or are you envious
because I am generous?'**

[16]"So the last will be first, and the first will be last."

For one reason or another we are often jealous. There is a petty kind of rivalry in us that says we are better than so-and-so and we are more deserving than another. We look at our records, our expenditures of time, talents and tithes, and we conclude that we are at least one notch above someone else.

This truth requires our full attention. You cannot build a life or a church on the basis of seniority. This kind of attitude only leads to exclusivism—*my* church, *my* classroom, *my* material, *my* teacher, *my* pew and so forth. Work in God's vineyard is for everyone. And no one has a corner on a certain section of it. Teamwork and the joy of service please God. Let us rejoice that God is forever hiring more people to accomplish His great work. Our principle of operation must be one of grace, not legalistic justice. Otherwise, we who are first (or prominent) now may end up being last (or the least prominent) later!

Jesus Predicts His Death (Matt. 20:17-19)

(cf. Mark 10:32-34 and Luke 18:31-34)

Benjamin Franklin keenly observed a flaw of preparedness in many persons, so he wrote this wise note: "By failing to prepare, you are preparing to fail."

Jesus never failed to prepare. From His birth He was in a constant state of preparation. As a youth, He grew in stature, wisdom and favor with God and men.

As a man He learned obedience through the things He suffered (Heb. 5:7, 8). No experience ever touched Jesus which He did not use as another steppingstone toward His final and most tremendous work at Jerusalem.

For Jesus, Jerusalem meant the end. Here He would be put to death. And here He would be resurrected. Jerusalem represented the worst ordeal of His entire life, as well as the grandest blessing the world would ever know.

> **17Now as Jesus was going up to Jerusalem, he took the twelve disciples
> aside and said to them, 18"We are going up to Jerusalem, and the Son of Man will be betrayed to the chief priests and the teachers of the law.
> They will condemn him to death 19and will turn him over to the Gentiles
> to be mocked and flogged and crucified. On the third day he will be raised to life!"**

The thought of what awaited Jesus in Jerusalem must have been an immense burden to Him. This is the fourth time Jesus discussed the matter with His disciples (Matt. 16:21; 17:9, 12, 22, 23). He could not put the issues out of His mind.

What can we learn from the repeated occurrences of this theme in our Savior's life?

First, we learn that our Savior was human. Trials for Jesus were no easier to face than they are for us. Jesus did not wear some unique shield over His mind or heart to keep them from aching. No. He hurt—and just as deeply as you or I could ever hurt. Jesus (though God incarnate) was completely human.

Second, we learn that our Savior was undeterred. How easily it seems that we can be distracted from our spiritual priorities, especially if there are pressures confronting us. But Jesus would not be sidetracked. He knew His mission, and He would see it to the end. There was no wavering or turning aside in Jesus' steps.

Third, we learn that our Savior's heart was full of love. Jesus was not going to die for a noble idea. He was going to die for people—past, present and future. Jesus thought of you and me as He prepared to go to Jerusalem. It was His heart that carried Him through the rugged journey. It was love—sacrificial and undeserved love—that made Jesus face those who would require His death.

Fourth, and last, we learn that our Savior possessed a knowledge of His future. God had told Jesus what was to occur in Jerusalem. There would be no surprises. The facts were open before His eyes. Certainly this prophetic revelation assured Jesus of God's will and interest. Jesus could be confident that God had gone before Him to prepare the events. There would be no accidents, despite the agony of the trial itself.

Two Ambitious Disciples (Matt. 20:20-28)

(cf. Mark 10:35-45)

Ambition can be a fine thing, if it is properly motivated. The desire to be more spiritual, mature and fruitful is an excellent aim. But it is carnal to seek to be more spiritual, mature or fruitful than some other person. There is no room for this kind of ambition in the Kingdom of God. James and John learned that such a status in the Kingdom is decided solely by God, and not by our ambitious goals.

I. *The Request (20:20, 21)*

20Then the mother of Zebedee's sons came to Jesus with her sons and,
kneeling down, asked a favor of him.
21"What is it you want?" he asked.
She said, "Grant that one of these two sons of mine may sit at your right and the other at your left in your kingdom."

If Jerusalem marked the end of the road, then the establishment of God's political kingdom upon the earth must be just around the corner—or so the disciples reasoned, especially the mother of the sons of Zebedee. So she came to Jesus with the kind of request one might expect to hear from a proud mother. She wanted her two boys, James and John, to occupy the lead positions in the Kingdom when it arrived in full blossom.

No doubt she had learned of Jesus' teaching about how her sons, along with the other disciples, would sit on thrones and reign over Israel (Matt. 19:28-30). So, she made a sincere request that her sons' thrones be situated next to Jesus' throne. It would have required a bold faith to make this petition, especially in light of how unrealistic a militaristic kingdom appeared. Jesus was no soldier, and He enlisted no men of arms to work for Him; still this mother was persuaded that somehow Jesus would overthrow the Roman powers and establish His own throne in Jerusalem. What confidence!

Apparently this mother's zeal was not any greater than the two disciples' desire. They accompanied her and stood ready to hear Jesus' decision. They had talked it over. They wanted to be Jesus' best men.

How noble our desires can be; and how equally undiscerning our ambitions can be.

Still, our Lord does not rebuke these men or their mother; rather, He simply instructs them.

II. *The Response (20:22, 23)*

> **22"You don't know what you are asking," Jesus said to them. "Can you drink the cup I am going to drink?"**
> **"We can," they answered.**
> **23Jesus said to them, "You will indeed drink from my cup, but to sit at my right or left is not for me to grant. These places belong to those for whom they have been prepared by my Father."**

Jesus could not promise these disciples any future position in the Kingdom. That was a matter left up to the Father. The only thing Jesus could offer them was a drink from the same cup that He would soon drink. It was an offer of martyrdom. Doubtlessly this was not what James and John wanted to hear, but their profound allegiance to Jesus Christ would make them willfully share this tragic cup.

We learn here how easy it is to permit our zeal and devotion for Jesus Christ to get us ahead of God's will. Our motivation pushes us forward more and more, until we find ourselves moving faster than God intends for us to move. In the end we need to be stopped and to be confronted with the more realistic will of God for our lives. It is a difficult lesson to learn, but those who receive it are certain to remain stable, balanced and fruitful, because their point of focus is not their position in the Kingdom; it is, rather, the Kingdom's work in the earth.

III. *The Repercussions (20:24-28)*

> **24When the ten heard about this, they were indignant with the two brothers. 25Jesus called them together and said, "You know that the rulers of the Gentiles lord it over them, and their high officials exercise authority over them. 26Not so with you. Instead, whoever wants to become great among you must be your servant, 27and whoever wants to be first must be your slave— 28just as the Son of Man did not come to be served, but to serve, and to give his life as a ransom for many."**

It isn't our position in life that makes us great, said Jesus. Instead, it is whether we use our life to serve people that counts as greatness. No one is greater than he who gives his life for the salvation of others. It was to this end that Jesus was born, and to this same end the disciples must devote their lives.

Two Blind Men Receive Sight (Matt. 20:29-34)

(cf. Mark 10:46-52 and Luke 18:35-43)

One of the most important elements in the occurrence of a miracle is seizing the right moment. Put another way, miracles are not always as close to us in one instance as they might be in another. So, we must capture them when they are within our grasp.

This is exactly the testimony of these two blind men. Probably their blindness extended back into their past lives for numerous years, maybe even to birth. But in one brief moment, all of their darkness could be turned into light, for Jesus was passing by their way. This was the opportunity of a lifetime. There would never be a moment like this again.

Jesus was not everywhere at once. He was confined to one place at a time. Those who had the privilege to see Him or to hear Him had to seize that opportunity before it left them.

Today Jesus is in heaven. Fortunately He has sent His ambassadors into all the world; still, these servants of Christ are not everywhere. They, too, are restricted to one location at a time. So we must hear their message and follow their counsel while it is within our grasp. Some opportunities come only several times throughout an entire lifetime. Let us pursue them and grab hold of them when they pass our way.

> **29As Jesus and his disciples were leaving Jericho, a large crowd followed him. 30Two blind men were sitting by the roadside, and when they heard that Jesus was going by, they shouted, "Lord, Son of David, have mercy on us!"**
>
> **31The crowd rebuked them and told them to be quiet, but they shouted all the louder, "Lord, Son of David, have mercy on us!"**
>
> **32Jesus stopped and called them. "What do you want me to do for you?" he asked.**
>
> **33"Lord," they answered, "we want our sight."**
>
> **34Jesus had compassion on them and touched their eyes. Immediately they received their sight and followed him.**

Persistently, these men cried out for the Lord to show them mercy. This was the rarest day in their lives. Jesus was passing by! They cried still louder—repeatedly—until Jesus saw them and was moved with compassion to restore their sight. They refused to listen to the people surrounding them. Public opinion was against them, but they knew Jesus' opinion was what they needed.

Don't let people pull you down. Pray. Speak out. Do whatever is necessary, but do not allow your faith in personal miracles be snatched away by thoughtless people, even if it is a large crowd that resists you. Press on. Persist until you hear from Jesus for yourself.

The Triumphal Entry (Matt. 21:1-11)

(cf. Mark 11:1-11; Luke 19:8-44 and John 12:12-19)

The day is Sunday. The place is Jerusalem. And the event is the jubilant triumphal entry of Jesus. For three and a half remarkable years Jesus has been ministering in the public's sight. Today He will start His final ministry. It will only last six days. Everything looked very promising at the start, but at the end of the road was to be a cross. (Notice the chart entitled "Jesus' Final Week" for a complete listing of the events of His final week on earth.)

I. *The Preparation (21:1-5)*

21 As they approached Jerusalem and came to Bethphage on the
Mount of Olives, Jesus sent two disciples, [2]saying to them, "Go to
the village ahead of you, and at once you will find a donkey tied there,
with her colt by her. Untie them and bring them to me. [3]If anyone says
anything to you, tell him that the Lord needs them, and he will send
them right away."
[4]This took place to fulfill what was spoken through the prophet:

[5]"Say to the Daughter of Zion,
'See, your king comes to you,
gentle and riding on a donkey,
on a colt, the foal of a donkey.' "[a]

Prophecy is a marvelous ingredient in the Scriptures. It is also a very common element. Over 25 percent of the Bible is written in the form of prophecy.

It is not difficult for God to tell His prophets what will happen in the future. Before Him lies all of time in a single glance. The future, from God's vantage point, is no less present and fulfilled than the present moment is to us now.

---

a 5 Zech. 9:9

JESUS' FINAL WEEK

	HARMONY OF THE GOSPELS			
	Matthew	**Mark**	**Luke**	**John**
Sunday				
The Triumphal Entry	21:1-11	11:1-11	19:28-44	12:12-19
Monday				
Cursing the Fig Tree	21:18-22	11:12-14, 20-25		
Cleansing the Temple	21:12, 13	11:15-17	19:45, 46	
Healing in the Temple	21:14			
Tuesday and Wednesday				
His Authority Questioned	21:23-27	11:27-33	20:1-8	
Parable of the Two Sons	21:28-32			
Parable of the Wicked Landowner	21:33-46	12:1-12	20:9-19	
Parable of the King's Son	22:1-14			
The Question of the Tribute Money	22:15-22	12:13-17	20:20-26	
The Sadducees' Question	22:23-33	12:18-27	20:27-40	
The Great Commandment	22:34-40	12:28-34		
Jesus' Question	22:41-46	12:35-37	20:41-44	
Woes Pronounced Against the Pharisees	23:1-39	12:38-40	20:45-47	
The Widow's Offering		12:41-44	21:1-4	
The Visit of the Greeks				12:20-36
Discourse on Unbelief				12:37-50
Prophecies of Coming Calamities	24:1-51	13:1-37	21:5-36	
Parable of the Ten Virgins	25:1-13			
Parable of the Talents	25:14-30			
Discourse on the Judgment Day	25:31-46			
The Plot of Judas	26:1-5, 14-16	14:1, 2, 10, 11	22:1-6	
Thursday				
The Preparation for the Passover	26:17-19	14:12-16	22:7-13	
The Passover Meal	26:20	14:17, 18	22:14-18	13:2
Strife Among the Disciples			22:24-30	
Washing the Disciples Feet				13:1-17
The Traitor Designated	26:21-25	14:18-21	22:21-23	13:21-30
The Lord's Supper	26:26-30	14:22-26	22:19, 20	
Jesus' Parting Words				14:1-31
Parable of the True Vine				15:1-11
The Promise of the Holy Spirit				16:7-15
The Intercessory Prayer				17:1-26
The Agony in the Garden	26:36-46	14:32-42	22:39-46	18:1
The Betrayal	26:47-56	14:43-52	22:47-53	18:3-13
The Healing of Malchus' Ear			22:50, 51	
Good Friday				
Jesus Before the High Priest	26:57	14:53	22:54	18:13, 14
Peter's Denial of Jesus	26:58, 69-75	14:54, 66-72	22:54-62	18:15-18, 25-27
Jesus Before the Council	26:59-68	14:55-65	22:66-71	18:19-24
Jesus Before Pilate	27:1, 2, 11-14	15:1-5	23:1-5	18:28-38
Jesus Before Herod			23:6-12	
Pilate's Attempt to Release Jesus	27:15-26	15:6-15	23:13-24	18:38-40
The Appeal of Pilate's Wife	27:19			
Pilate Washes His Hands	27:24-26			
Pilate Gives the Death Sentence	27:26-30	15:15	23:24	19:1-16
Jesus Mocked	27:27-30	15:16-20	22:63-65	19:1-3
Suicide of Judas	27:3-10			
Jesus Led Away to be Crucified	27:31-33	15:20-22	23:26	19:16, 17
Weeping of the Women			23:27-31	
Jesus Is Offered Wine	27:34	15:23		
The Crucifixion	27:35-38	15:24-28	23:33-38	19:18-24
Casting Lots for His Garments	27:35	15:24	23:34	19:23, 24
The Jews Mock Him	27:39-43	15:20, 29-32	23:35	
The Dying Thief's Confession			23:39-43	
Jesus Commends His Mother to John				19:25-27
Darkness Prevails, Jesus Expires	27:45-50	15:33-37	23:44-46	19:28-30
The Veil of the Temple Rent, and Graves Opened	27:51-53	15:38	23:45	
The Centurion's Confession	27:54	15:39	23:47	
The Descent from the Cross	27:57, 58	15:42-46	23:50-53	19:31-38
The Burial	27:59-61	15:46, 47	23:53	19:39-42
The Watch at the Sepulchre	27:62-66			

It is only for our benefit—our amazement and reverence toward the Lord—that He has placed in the Scriptures these astonishing predictions. The completion of one such startling prophecy is seen here.

In approximately 520 B.C. the prophet Zechariah was told how Israel's greatest King would someday enter Jerusalem upon a young donkey (Zech. 9:9). Naturally, liberal commentators view this passage with a critical eye. They cannot bring themselves to accept the possibility that such exacting predictions can be so minutely fulfilled. So, they dismiss its supernatural character altogether. And they do this by stating that Jesus, being a prophetic mastermind, set up the whole parade in order to "fulfill" the people's expectations for the coming King of Israel. Such a shallow view of God and Christ, however, is to be soundly rejected.

Jesus' knowledge of Messianic prophecies was unquestionably astute. But He could no more manipulate God's plans than you or I can manipulate them. Jesus was in continuous communion with His Father. And whatever the Father said He was to do, He did exactly as He was told (John 5:30; 8:26-28; 12:49; 14:10). That alone caused Jesus to fulfill over one hundred unique prophecies during His first coming.

II. *The Presentation (21:6-11)*

6The disciples went and did as Jesus had instructed them. 7They brought the donkey and the colt, placed their cloaks on them, and Jesus sat on them. 8A very large crowd spread their cloaks on the road, while others cut branches from the trees and spread them on the road. 9The crowds that went ahead of him and those that followed shouted,

"Hosanna[a] to the Son of David!"
"Blessed is he who comes in the name of the Lord!"[b]
"Hosanna[a] in the highest!"

10When Jesus entered Jerusalem, the whole city was stirred and asked, "Who is this?"

11The crowds answered, "This is Jesus, the prophet from Nazareth in Galilee."

Long ago God promised Israel a King from heaven (2 Sam. 7:4-13; Isa. 24:23; 33:22; Dan. 9:24-27; Zeph. 3:15; Zech. 14:9-21). And the people anxiously awaited this glorious moment. Unfortunately, what God promised and what the people hoped for were not in agreement.

The people's expectation for this king was a strong, aggressive and capable man who would crush all of Israel's *political* foes, forever. But God's King—Jesus—was preeminently interested in crushing Satan, Israel's *spiritual* foe. Put in capsule form,

a 9 A Hebrew expression meaning "Save!" which became an exclamation of praise; also in verse 15 *b 9* Psalm 118:26

the people were looking for a military King, but God sent them a spiritual King. (God promised Israel a military King, too, but His appearance was to follow the manifestation of this spiritual King. In Jesus' Second Coming the people's political expectations will be fulfilled.)

Despite these differences, the people were joyous. They cried, "Hosanna" (meaning, "Save us now"). They were desperately looking for God's King, the Messiah. Jesus seemed to be the most likely candidate to accomplish their dreams. So they honored Him with the highest of praises and reverence.

It is doubtful that very many of those who were shouting praises really understood what was happening. For in only five days their words of exaltation would be reversed to a chant of murder—"crucify him" (Matt. 27:15-26).

Even the twelve disciples would become befuddled at what was to occur inside Jerusalem (Luke 24:13-32). But in spite of all this seeming confusion, God was at work accomplishing His prophesied plans.

Jesus Enters the Temple (Matt. 21:12-17)

(cf. Mark 11:15-19 and Luke 19:45-48)

The Temple in Jerusalem was meant to show the way a sinner could find peace with God. It was to be a citadel for the true faith. But in this religious capital there was corruption instead. Jesus recognized this condition, and He would not tolerate this spiritual pollution of God's house, even if it meant His death.

I. *His Courage (21:12, 13)*

> **12Jesus entered the temple area and drove out all who were buying and selling there. He overturned the tables of the money changers and the benches of those selling doves. 13"It is written," he said to them, "'My house will be called a house of prayer,'[a] but you are making it a 'den of robbers.'[b]"**

Jesus Entered the Temple. This is the second time Jesus avenged the Lord's house by removing the profit-making moneychangers. The first time He did so was at the beginning of His ministry (John 2:13-17). Now He must do it again in the last week of His ministry. (See the floor plan of the Temple in the diagram entitled "A Floor Plan of Herod's Temple.")

---

a 13 Isaiah 56:7 *b 13* Jer. 7:11

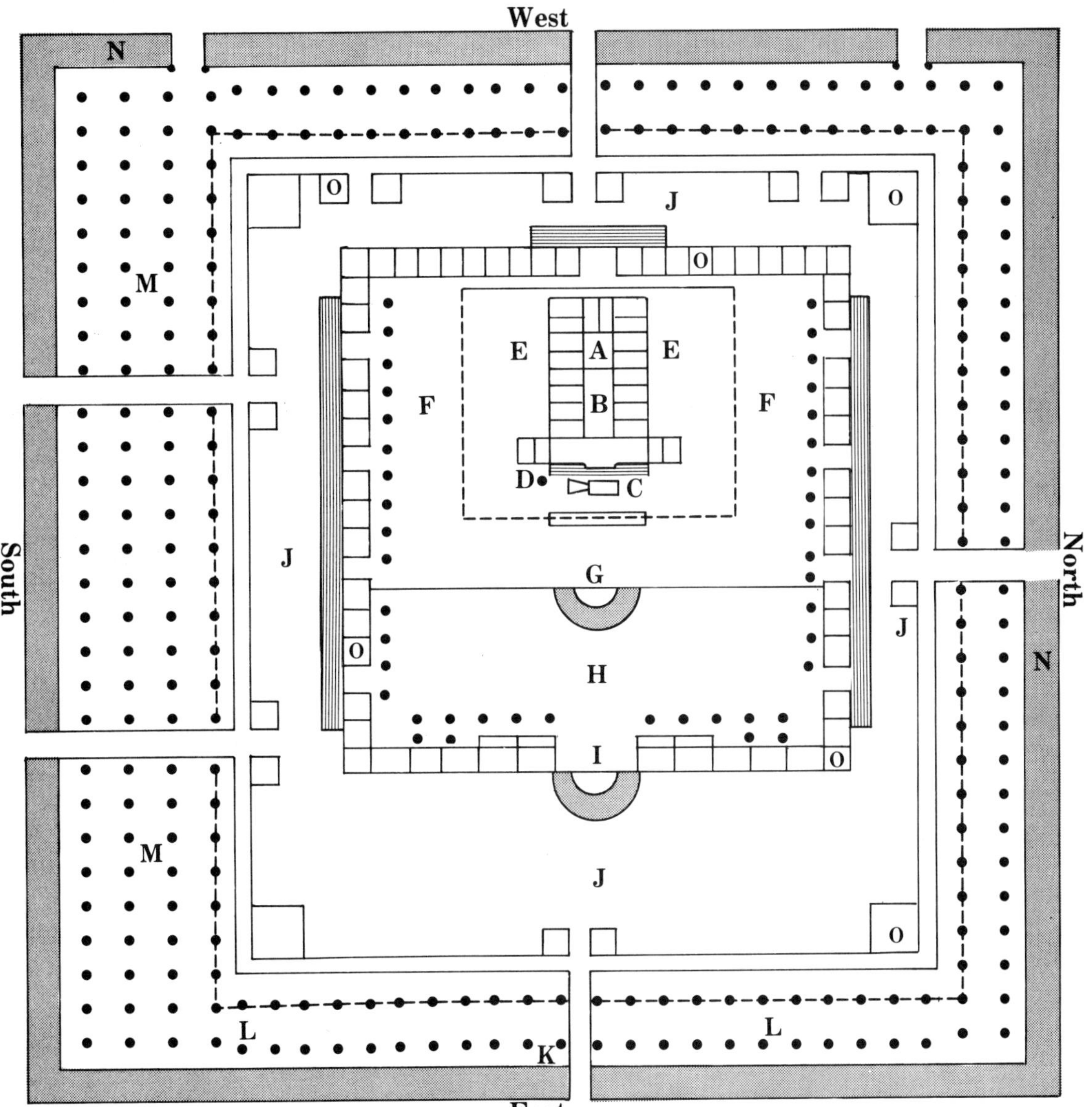

PLAN OF THE TEMPLE IN THE TIME OF CHRIST.

A. The Holy of Holies.
B. The Holy Place.
C. The Altar of Burnt-offerings.
D. The brazen Laver.
E. The court of the Priests.
F. The court of Israel.
G. The gate of Nicanor.
H. The court of the Women.
I. The gate Beautiful.
J. The court of the Gentiles.
K. The Eastern or Shushan gate.
L. Solomon's Porch, or colonnade.
M. The Royal Porch.
N. The outer Wall.
O. Apartments for various uses.

How sad it must have made Jesus to see this dead religious activity in the heart of Israel. Surely here you would expect to find the purity of the faith. Equally regrettable is the reappearance of the evil men whom Jesus had removed earlier. Bad persons, however, always return to bad practices. They are like weeds—forever coming up in the midst of the finest crops. We must not walk past these truths with haste. They are practical in this very hour, too.

Moneychangers. According to God's commandments, every Jew twenty years of age was to pay an annual Temple tax of a half-shekel of silver (Exod. 30:11-15). This very modest fee served to help pay the expenses incurred in the daily maintenance of the holy structure.

Since many Jews lived in places where a half-shekel silver coin was not available, a large group of moneychangers were assigned the duty of exchanging the people's foreign currency into the only acceptable religious currency for payment of this tax. Naturally, they charged a fee for this service. Apparently their price was equivalent to thievery.

Actually, there never was a Jewish half-shekel coin. A shekel is a measurement of weight (probably just less than a half ounce). Nevertheless, the moneychangers would exchange the worshipers' foreign coins for half-shekel silver coins from Tyre (which bore the image of their local god—Baal Melkart!). Here is a clear illustration of how ridiculous people can become when attempting to merely externalize God's commandments. The law specified a particular amount, but the ambitious and greedy moneychangers saw an opportunity to presumably keep the law and make a fast dollar at the same time.

Those Selling Doves. The worship functions of the Temple largely revolved around animal sacrifices. A person would bring in his ox, sheep or doves for sacrifice, but here he would be told that his animals were unacceptable and that he must purchase the more holy animals conveniently provided by the Temple itself. The price for these animals was extremely inflated, and naturally, they were no more pure than any other animal. Still, the system seemed to be unchallenged—at least until Jesus entered the temple.

A House of Prayer. This is a quote from Isa. 56:7, which concludes with the words, "for all nations" (cf. Mark 11:17). The Temple in Jerusalem was intended by God to stand for a house where anyone—Jew or Gentile—could find Him and have his sins forgiven. But the profiteering Jews had perverted this house into a den for robbers to steal from sincere believers.

II. *Jesus' Compassion (21:14-17)*

14 The blind and the lame came to him at the temple, and he healed

them. [15]But when the chief priests and the teachers of the law saw the
wonderful things he did and the children shouting in the temple area,
"Hosanna to the Son of David," they were indignant.
[16]"Do you hear what these children are saying?" they asked him.
"Yes," replied Jesus, "have you never read,

" 'From the lips of children and infants
you have ordained praise'[a]?"

[17]And he left them and went out of the city to Bethany, where he spent
the night.

He Healed Them. Wherever there are people, there are numerous needs. Jesus would not concentrate on the negative aspects of Jerusalem alone. There was much positive work to be done, too. So, in the middle of spiritual impurity, Jesus reached out to touch and heal the sick. There will always be roses among the thorns. We must not overlook them. They deserve and require our attention.

The Chief Priests and Teachers Were Indignant. These religious leaders were envious of Jesus (Matt. 27:18). They burned with rage to see Him do the things they could not do. They had been successful in wringing the people's purses, but had failed at winning their hearts, as Jesus had done. So they became utterly flushed with their own anger. In a fit they approached Jesus and rebuked Him for permitting the people to speak so highly of Him. Jesus, on the other hand, put these accusers in their place by quoting Ps. 8:2, which, in effect, says that His admirers were only revealing the truth (a truth the accusers should have recognized!).

Jesus Withers a Fig Tree (Matt. 21:18-22)

(cf. Mark 11:12-14, 20-25)

Every fruit farmer has the same goal—fruitfulness. If there is no fruit, then there is trouble. The farmer must have fruit in order to survive.

In a sense, God is like a fruit farmer. He waits patiently for fruit to come forth from His vineyards. But when there is none, season after season, then He must make some practical, though critical, decisions regarding His farm.

God wants fruit. That is, He expects to see His professing followers walking obediently in His will. This is natural and just. But if God does not see this happening,

a 16 Psalm 8:2

sooner or later, judgment must come, and God's wrath will descend upon these self-willed persons like a crushing flood. This, too, is natural and just. In this lesson we find the terrible price that is to be paid for being fruitless "believers" in God.

I. *The Act (21:18, 19)*

18Early in the morning, as he was on his way back to the city, he was hungry. 19Seeing a fig tree by the road, he went up to it but found nothing on it except leaves. Then he said to it, "May you never bear fruit again!" Immediately the tree withered.

On the day before this episode occurs—Sunday—Jesus entered Jerusalem with loud shouts of "Hosanna!" coming from the people. Today, however, there would be a radical change of attitude. There would be no praises echoing in the air. Instead, the atmosphere would be sharply tense from start to finish.

As Jesus journeyed to Jerusalem to begin His day's work, He noticed a fig tree in the distance. Being hungry, He decided to stop there and eat some of its fruit. But upon examining the tree, He discovered it was fruitless. Jesus then did something we might not have expected to occur. He cursed the tree, and it died!

There is an unforgettable lesson here, for in that tree is found the condition of depraved Israel (as well as many professing Christians today). There were leaves on this fig tree. This covering served as a signal that beneath her foliage should be precious fruit. But the appearance was deceptive. There was no fruit as promised in her leaves. And Jesus would not tolerate such hypocritical barrenness.

Jesus came to bless Israel, but He found little that was worthy of a blessing. There was a great profession of faith, but only a very small possession of faith. He was left with no alternative. He could not bless fruitlessness; he had to curse it.

II. *The Amazement (21:20)*

20When the disciples saw this, they were amazed. "How did the fig tree wither so quickly?" they asked.

Naturally, the disciples were both shocked and amazed. Immediately, they asked Jesus for an explanation, and He was ready to provide one. Here is an important point we must never forget—when you need an explanation of any supernatural event, ask Jesus. Friends may attempt to rationalize God's miracles, but Jesus will work on building up your faith in order to produce miracles in your very own life.

III. *The Answer (21:21, 22)*

21Jesus replied, "I tell you the truth, if you have faith and do not doubt,

not only can you do what was done to the fig tree, but also you can say to this mountain, 'Go, throw yourself into the sea,' and it will be done. [22]If you believe, you will receive whatever you ask for in prayer."

I Tell You the Truth. What Jesus was about to speak would be so incredible that He felt it was necessary to preface His statements with a note of assurance. Believing in miracles is one thing, but being responsible for producing a miracle is quite another. Jesus wants His disciples to know that they, too, could actually perform such a miracle. In fact, they could perform even greater miracles than withering a mere fig tree.

If You Have Faith. To have faith is to expect, and the opposite of expectation is doubt. Doubt is that wavering uncertainty which only hopes for the best and has little steadfast confidence in receiving what it has specifically requested of God. It is a most unrewarding state. One may confess that he has earnestly prayed, but he may also confess, by his lack of anticipation, that he is not certain how God will respond to what he has sought. That is doubt, and it will secure nothing from God (Heb. 11:6; James 1:5-8). The person who prays in faith, however, rests assured that his mountain will indeed be removed, and he spares no speech to tell others of his yet-to-arrive answer.

Say. Faith does more than believe in the heart; it also speaks a positive expectation with the mouth. There is always something verbal about faith.

Never underestimate the power of your speech. Death and life are in the power of the tongue (Prov. 18:21). This is potency plus. The Scriptures go so far as to teach that nothing comes into existence apart from speech. For example, six times in Genesis, chapter one, we read, "God *said* . . . and it was so" (vv. 3, 6, 9, 14, 20, 24). It was God's speech that brought creation into being (Ps. 33:6-9; John 1:1-3; Heb. 1:1-3; 11:3). It is also His speech which brings healing (Ps. 107:20), the weather (Ps. 147:15-18), the Scriptures (2 Tim. 3:16), physical and spiritual life (Deut. 8:3; John 6:63; Eph. 5:25, 26; James 1:18; 1 Pet. 1:23), and His will through all things that exist (Ps. 29:4-9; 46:6; Isa. 55:11). There is a force of energy in the spoken word.

It is our speech more than anything else, which hinders the removal of the obstructing mountains which are before us. If we are going to learn how to pray in faith, we must first learn how to guard our speech from negative confessions. Complaining must cease; anxieties must be replaced with divine promises; fears must be surrendered to God's trust. Watch what you say; it can make the difference between answered and unanswered prayer.

This Mountain. The illustration of casting mountains into the sea was a common Jewish phrase for removing one's difficulties. Jesus uses this imagery to teach a lesson about prayer. His impelling point is this—there is no problem too large for the prayer and confession of faith to remove.

Whatever. In a nutshell, "whatever" means anything, but not everything. That is, we may ask for anything in keeping with God's will (1 John 5:14, 15), but this certainly does not include everything of which we could dream. Our requests must meet with God's approval, and this may be ascertained by embracing a promise He gives to us from the Bible.

Ask. Let's learn something wonderful here that will give great confidence to our prayers. Asking is as important an ingredient in prayer as praise or confession or intercession (see Matt. 6:8; 7:7, 8, 11; 18:19; 21:22; Mark 11:24; Luke 11:9, 10, 13; John 11:22; 14:13, 14; 15:7, 16; 16:23, 24; Eph. 3:20; Col. 1:9; James 4:2, 3; 1 John 3:22; 5:14-16). There is absolutely no shame in coming to God with requests. Not once, in all of Scripture, does God belittle His precious children for coming to Him with their earnest petitions. Quite the contrary, God delights in hearing about everything that touches our lives.

Jesus' Authority Is Challenged (Matt. 21:23-27)

(cf. Mark 11:27-33 and Luke 20:1-8)

Jesus always rubbed the religious officials in Jerusalem the wrong way. Everything He did seemed to undermine their authority. So, they set out to know by whose authority He thought He operated. Obviously, it was another insidious and vain attempt to destroy Jesus' credibility. The end can be anticipated from the start. Those who set out to challenge Jesus' authority are themselves challenged and discredited.

I. *The Challenge (21:23)*

> **23 Jesus entered the temple courts, and, while he was teaching, the chief priests and the elders of the people came to him. "By what authority are you doing these things?" they asked. "And who gave you this authority?"**

The Temple Courts. The courts of the Temple structure were incredibly immense. The less distinguished corridor on the eastern side of the Temple was called Solomon's Porch. Here rested two parallel series of Corinthian columns, rising thirty-five feet into the air and proportionately spaced over a distance of about 1,500 feet. These beautiful marble columns then turned west for approximately 1,050 feet beside the court of the Gentiles, and finally south for another 1,500 feet. The more elaborate set of columns, called the Royal Porch, stood at the southern end of the Temple. There were four rows of white marble columns in this area. Each pillar was thirty feet high and six feet in diameter. It was in these areas that the teachers of the law conducted their classes and held debates. Here they found Jesus and entered into a discussion with Him.

By What Authority. Once Jesus had arrived at the Temple and had begun to teach, He was immediately challenged by the religious leaders. They wanted to know just who He thought he was, since Jesus always appeared to have all the answers. After all, they were the real authorities in Israel, or so they supposed.

II. *The Counter-Challenge (21:24-27)*

24Jesus replied, "I will also ask you one question. If you answer me, I
will tell you by what authority I am doing these things. 25John's
baptism—where did it come from? Was it from heaven, or from men?"
They discussed it among themselves and said, "If we say, 'From
heaven,' he will ask, 'Then why didn't you believe him?' 26But if we say,
'From men'—we are afraid of the people, for they all hold that John was
a prophet."
27So they answered Jesus, "We don't know."
Then he said, "Neither will I tell you by what authority I am doing
these things.

Jesus asked these so-called spiritual heads by whose authority John the Baptist was appointed to preach. Was it by man or by God? Now the leaders did not want to answer that question, because no matter what they would say, it would mean their embarrassment. If they said John was sent from God, then they must answer for their neglect in obeying his speech. And if they said John was not sent from God, then the people would disrespect them and even hate them for being so stupid. So, they declined to answer Jesus' inquiry. And in like manner Jesus declined to answer their silly challenge, because both He and John had been sent by God.

Jesus was smart. He knew when people asked loaded questions. And He also knew that straightforward, honest answers to such questions would solve nothing in the end. Jesus did not need to defend himself. Teaching and living the truth were a sufficient defense. Adding more to this would be meaningless.

The Parable of the Two Sons (Matt. 21:28-32)

Those who teach and supposedly defend God's written Word are not necessarily *doers* of His Word. It is always easier to proclaim something than it is to perform it. Jesus' critics were long on finger-pointing speeches, but short on personal application. They could call others to repent, though somehow they found it convenient not to repent.

28"What do you think? There was a man who had two sons. He went to the first and said, 'Son, go and work today in the vineyard.'

29" 'I will not,' he answered, but later he changed his mind and went.

30"Then the father went to the other son and said the same thing. He answered, 'I will, sir,' but he did not go.

31"Which of the two did what his father wanted?"

"The first," they answered.

Jesus said to them, "I tell you the truth, the tax collectors and the prostitutes are entering the kingdom of God ahead of you.
32For John came to you to show you the way of righteousness, and you did not believe him, but the tax collectors and the prostitutes did. And even after you saw this, you did not repent and believe him.

Jesus asked the Jewish leaders who does God's will—the person who resists at first but later consents, or the person who consents at first but later resists? The leaders answered correctly that it is the first person, the one who, in the end, obeys the Father. Then, Jesus pointed out, it is the so-called nobodies, His many disciples, who are accepted by God, for they have obeyed Him, and not them.

The Parable of the Landowner (Matt. 21:33-46)

(cf. Mark 12:1-12 and Luke 20:9-19)

Jesus asked His critics a pointed question: "What should be done to tenants who beat, stone and kill the master's servants, including his very own son?" The religious officials, who seemed to specialize in putting their feet in their mouths, answered that those wretched tenants should be put to death. "Precisely," exclaims Jesus, "*you* are those tenants!"

I. *The Parable Is Told (21:33-39)*

**33"Listen to another parable: There was a landowner who planted a
vineyard. He put a wall around it, dug a winepress in it and built a
watchtower. Then he rented the vineyard to some farmers and went
away on a journey. 34When the harvest time approached, he sent his
servants to the tenants to collect his fruit.**

**35"The tenants seized his servant; they beat one, killed another, and
stoned a third. 36Then he sent other servants to them, more than the first
time, and the tenants treated them the same way. 37Last of all, he sent his
son to them. 'They will respect my son,' he said.**

**38"But when the tenants saw the son, they said to each other, 'This is
the heir. Come, let's kill him and take his inheritance.' 39So they took him
and threw him out of the vineyard and killed him.**

Vineyards were sometimes surrounded by a wall of stone, or a large hedge of thorny plants, or both. A wine press consisted of two structures. The first one served as a container for the grapes, along with room for two to seven men who would walk over the grapes, releasing their juice. The second structure would catch the juice from the trodden grapes. The watchtower, ranging in height from fifteen feet to fifty feet, housed a guard who would protect the vines from thieves or hungry animals. Normally, this poorly constructed tower would last only one season. Some, however, have been discovered which were made of stone and were intended to house the owner of the vineyard during the harvest season.

From this natural setting Jesus drew a sharp message for His audience. The owner of the vineyard has made a substantial investment in this property, and he naturally expects a fair return. The return, however, is the chief problem. Those running the farm are totally disinterested in the owner's investment. So, they spurn his appeals. The owner is finally compelled to deal a severe blow to the stubborn tenants. This response was expected, but Jesus' application was totally unexpected. He called the Jews, those directly in front of Him, the unfaithful tenants!

II. *The Parable Is Applied (21:40-46)*

**40"Therefore, when the owner of the vineyard comes, what will he do
to those tenants?"**

41"He will bring those wretches to a wretched end," they replied, "and

he will rent the vineyard to other tenants, who will give him his share of the crop at harvest time."

[42]Jesus said to them, "Have you never read in the Scriptures:

> **" 'The stone the builders rejected**
> **has become the capstone[a];**
> **the Lord has done this,**
> **and it is marvelous in our eyes'[b]?**

[43]"Therefore I tell you that the kingdom of God will be taken away
from you and given to a people who will produce its fruit. [44]He who falls
on this stone will be broken to pieces, but he on whom it falls will be crushed."[c]

[45]When the chief priests and the Pharisees heard Jesus' parables, they
knew he was talking about them. [46]They looked for a way to arrest him,
but they were afraid of the crowd because the people held that he was a prophet.

The chief priests and Pharisees by this time had had it. They wanted Jesus to be locked up, but the people thought He was absolutely correct, thus making such an arrest impossible. Their plans would have to wait. And in the meanwhile they would have to hear Jesus teach the people that, because of fruitless living, the Kingdom of God would be given to other people (Gentiles!) who would bear fruit responsibly.

Have You Never Read? These words cut deeply into the already raging pot of irritated emotions of the chief priests and Pharisees. They prided themselves as being knowledgeable in the Scriptures. But the constant problem with the knowledge of proud persons is that they never manage to see themselves as the possible object of God's wrath. They are forever neglecting or misunderstanding the passages that apply to themselves.

The Stone the Builders Rejected. Jesus envisions himself here as being the personal fulfillment of Ps. 118:22. In Him is the builder's best stone, but, for reasons of greed and self-made ambition, the builders chose to discard this rare and precious stone. The point Jesus makes from all of this symbolism is that once He is rejected by Israel (in His crucifixion), He will start a new work by offering the Kingdom promises to the Gentiles.

The implications of this removal of the Kingdom offer from Israel has received at least two differing interpretations:

(a) One view is to conclude that God has forever finished His dealings with *national* Israel. According to this position, God's interest is solely resting in a new people (or nation—1 Pet. 2:9) called spiritual Israel (for the Church—Gal. 6:16).

---

[a] *42* Or *cornerstone* [b] *42* Psalm 118:22, 23 [c] *44* Some manuscripts do not have verse 44.

(b) Another view is to state that God has only temporarily suspended His dealings with *national* Israel. For the moment God is at work with spiritual Israel, the Church. In the future, however, God will reactivate His Kingdom offer for ethnic Jews, especially to those living in the Promised Land (Zech. 12:10-13:1; Rom. 11).

Broken to Pieces/Crushed. A person may stumble over Jesus and His teachings, resulting in the brokenness of his understanding. But if that person does not, in the end, respond positively to Jesus' words, then that person will be crushed to powder in the hour of His judgment. Many people have taken offense at Jesus' stern, rocklike statements, and those who reject them will only discover that the stone they threw aside has come back to destroy them.

The Parable of the Wedding Banquet (Matt. 22:1-14)

(cf. Luke 14:15-24)

A wedding, for the Jews, was a great celebration. The host would invite many guests to join in this festive ceremony. For a whole week the groom would be a king—wearing special clothes and doing no labor at all. His friends would join him with tambourines and singing. Speeches would be made, and great feasts would be eaten. It was a wonderful event. But Jesus tells us of a particular wedding where a certain portion of the joy is missing.

I. *The King's First Appeals (22:1-4)*

22 Jesus spoke to them again in parables, saying: [2]"The kingdom of
heaven is like a king who prepared a wedding banquet for his
son. [3]He sent his servants to those who had been invited to the banquet to
tell them to come, but they refused to come.
[4]"Then he sent some more servants and said, 'Tell those who have been
invited that I have prepared my dinner: My oxen and fattened cattle
have been butchered, and everything is ready. Come to the wedding
banquet.'

Just as any father would desire a fine wedding for his son, so this king seeks to honor his son with a grand and festive wedding. To the dismay of the king, however, his invitation to come to the wedding is rejected—and not once, but twice!

In like fashion the King of the universe—God—issued invitation after invitation to the people of Israel through His servants, the prophets. But again and again His gracious offerings have been cast aside. How gracious God is to patiently and relentlessly reissue His grace to us. What pathetic and callous persons are those who resist His biddings to be saved and blessed.

II. *The King's First Anger (22:5-7)*

> **5"But they paid no attention and went off—one to his field, another to his business. 6The rest seized his servants, mistreated them and killed them. 7The king was enraged. He sent his army and destroyed those murderers and burned their city.**

The king, by this time, has had it with those he invited. And he sends an army to destroy the people and the city who mistreated his servant. The reference here is obviously to Jerusalem. Her destiny was fixed—she would fall under the Roman legions in A.D. 70 (see Matt. 24; Mark 13; Luke 21).

III. *The King's Further Appeals (22:8-10)*

> **8"Then he said to his servants, 'The wedding banquet is ready, but those I invited did not deserve to come. 9Go to the street corners and invite to the banquet anyone you find.' 10So the servants went out into the streets and gathered all the people they could find, both good and bad, and the wedding hall was filled with guests.**

If the Jews will not accept God's invitation, then the king will extend his offer to the Gentiles. They will come. Some of them will be sincere, while others will be insincere; still, many come in response to the offer. Today, in the church, are numerous ones who have responded to the gospel—many are true converts, but some remain spiritually lost.

IV. *The King's Final Anger (22:11-14)*

> **11"But when the king came in to see the guests, he noticed a man there who was not wearing wedding clothes. 12'Friend,' he asked, 'how did you get in here without wedding clothes?' The man was speechless.**
>
> **13"Then the king told the attendants, 'Tie him hand and foot, and throw him outside, into the darkness, where there will be weeping and gnashing of teeth.'**
>
> **14"For many are invited, but few are chosen."**

In biblical times the host would often provide special garments for a wedding ceremony. It would have been considered quite rude for someone not to wear the clothing that had been prepared for the occasion. In like manner, God has prepared a robe of righteousness for each of us—through faith in Jesus Christ (Rom. 13:14; Gal. 3:27). Attempting to come to God in our own clothing, that is, in our own righteousness, would be no more effective than the approach of Adam and Eve to God in their own self-made leaf coverings (Gen. 3:8-24). We must wear Jesus' righteousness if we are ever to escape the horrible consequences of hell.

Should We Pay Taxes? (Matt. 22:15-22)

(cf. Mark 12:13-17 and Luke 20:20-26)

When love is thin, fault finding is thick. There seems to be a built-in mechanism in each of us that is more likely to judge a tree by its leaves than by its fruit. The short of it is this—if we would spend more time improving ourselves, there would be little time left to criticize others. Unfortunately, the Pharisees had not yet learned this virtue.

I. *The Anticipated Trap (22:15-17)*

15Then the Pharisees went out and laid plans to trap him in his words.
16They sent their disciples to him along with the Herodians. "Teacher," they said, "we know you are a man of integrity and that you teach the way of God in accordance with the truth. You aren't swayed by men, because you pay no attention to who they are. 17Tell us then, what is your
opinion? Is it right to pay taxes to Caesar or not?"

Plans to Trap Him. The Pharisees sought a plot that would openly trap Jesus. They decided to attempt trapping Him in His teaching. If they could find a flaw in His doctrine, they reasoned, then they could denounce Him publicly. How subtle certain opponents of the truth are. They use every trick at their disposal (religion, the Bible, tradition, personality and so forth) in order to ensnare their prey.

Their Disciples and the Herodians. The Pharisees had been embarrassed enough. They were not about to be humiliated endlessly. Therefore, they sent their younger disciples to Jesus in order to try out another test. If it failed, it would not be a personal blow to their egos. Naturally, if it succeeded, they would be quick to take the credit. The Herodians (whose identity is somewhat incomplete) seem to be a party of Jews who, for one reason or another, favored the political dynasty of the Herods. They certainly were enemies of Jesus, probably because they feared He represented a threat to their position in Herod's empire (Mark 3:6; 12:13).

We Know You Are. When these men approached Jesus, they were polite, even complimentary. Their lips voiced words of praise, but their hearts were laced with bitterness and malice. Often the words one speaks do not expose the true state of his heart. We are not always safe to measure another's sincerity by what he or she might say. Compliments are no foolproof sign of love or loyalty.

Is It Right to Pay Taxes. There were four main taxes imposed on the Jews: (1) tax on their land, (2) tax on their personal property, (3) tax on any import or export and (4) a poll tax from every adult male. It was this latter tax that occupied the interest of these men.

It was disgusting to the Jew to pay any foreign ruler a tax. They considered such a payment a mark of personal slavery. They wanted to be the servants of no one, except God. So, paying taxes meant the continuation of foreign dominion; not paying taxes meant breaking the law.

Now comes the barbed inquiry: "Should we or should we not pay poll taxes to Caesar?" The Pharisees could hardly wait for Jesus' reply. For if He said yes to the poll tax, then His followers would resent His loyalty to the pagan Roman lords. But if He said no to the tax, they could report Him to the Roman officials for instigating rebellion among the people. Either way, he was trapped, or so they imagined.

II. *The Actual Truth (22:18-22)*

> **18But Jesus, knowing their evil intent, said, "You hypocrites, why are**
> **you trying to trap me? 19Show me the coin used for paying the tax."**
> **They brought him a denarius, 20and he asked them, "Whose portrait is**
> **this? And whose inscription?"**
>
> **21"Caesar's," they replied.**
>
> **Then he said to them, "Give to Caesar what is Caesar's, and to God what is God's."**
>
> **22When they heard this, they were amazed. So they left him and went away.**

Jesus' reply was brilliant. He instructed them to find a denarius (a coin equivalent to about a day's pay). Then He asked them whose face and inscription appeared on it. Naturally, it was Caesar's image. Well, said Jesus, give to Caesar what belongs to him, but don't forget to give to God what is His, too.

Perfect! Rome was satisfied. God was honored. And the befuddled critics were left speechless—the way they should have been from the start.

Sometimes there is a fine line between obeying the state and obeying God. Here Jesus demonstrates that a believer must give to the state its tolls, without any hesitation. Yet, in this compliance there is to be no jeopardizing of God's rules. We must live in this world in peace, even if there is no peace from the world toward us personally.

No Marriage in Heaven (Matt. 22:23-33)

(cf. Mark 12:18-27 and Luke 20:27-38)

The next group to plot against Jesus were the Sadducees. While the Pharisees represented the theologically broad-minded, middle-class businessmen, the Sadducees stood for the theologically narrow-minded ruling class.

The beliefs of the Sadducees were extremely limited. They refused to believe the teachings of any of the books of the Old Testament except the Torah (Genesis, Exodus, Leviticus, Numbers and Deuteronomy). Because they rejected more than they accepted, there was little real substance to their faith.

I. *The Anticipated Trap (22:23-28)*

**23That same day the Sadducees, who say there is no resurrection,
came to him with a question. 24"Teacher," they said, "Moses told us that if
a man dies without having children, his brother must marry the widow
and have children for him. 25Now there were seven brothers among us.
The first one married and died, and since he had no children, he left his
wife to his brother. 26The same thing happened to the second and third
brother, right on down to the seventh. 27Finally, the woman died. 28Now
then, at the resurrection, whose wife will she be of the seven, since all of
them were married to her?"**

One of the cardinal points of rejection among the Sadducees was the notion of any future resurrection from the dead. For them, life was here and now only. They cast away every idea that suggested there was life after death. And, as might be expected, they held to their view adamantly.

With this self-concocted position on no life after death firm in hand, they approached Jesus with their absurd question. They wanted Jesus to tell them who a woman will be married to in heaven if she has had more than one husband on earth.

Actually, they are not interested in knowing the truth, but in settling their convictions about the supposed perverted doctrines of Jesus. His answer will give them the ammunition they need to clearly renounce Him, along with His theology, they reasoned.

II. *The Actual Truth (22:29-33)*

> **[29]Jesus replied, "You are in error because you do not know the Scriptures or the power of God. [30]At the resurrection people will neither marry nor be given in marriage; they will be like the angels in heaven. [31]But about the resurrection of the dead—have you not read what God said to you, [32]'I am the God of Abraham, the God of Isaac, and the God of Jacob'[a]? He is not the God of the dead but of the living."**
> **[33]When the crowds heard this, they were astonished at his teaching.**

The Sadducees had no sooner asked their question before Jesus sent back a lightning-bolt response. First, He delivered a staunch rebuke by accusing them of knowing neither God's Word nor His power! He flatly told them they were in error. Few would dare to challenge the highest professors in the Jewish state, but Jesus met the task squarely and without any flinching.

Second, He corrected their mistaken view of equating life on earth as being parallel to that in heaven—there will be no marriages there.

Third, He informed them that life after death *is* true, and that it can be found in the Torah they claimed to believe.

Shocked, the Sadducees departed in disgrace. They had set a trap, only to find themselves caught in it. This is always the lot of those who seek to elevate themselves at the expense of others.

Perhaps here, too, we ought to learn the lesson that looking critically for holes in someone's theology (when it does not fully agree with our own set of convictions) is dangerous business. If we looked for ways to be united, rather than divided, the body of Christ would certainly display a far better witness of God's love and grace.

The Two Greatest Commandments (Matt. 22:34-40)

(cf. Mark 12:28-34)

This is the third time in a day that Jesus was presented with a trick question. Actually, Jesus was asked the most difficult questions the religious leaders could

a 32 Exodus 3:6

create, because the opinions of the leaders themselves were divided regarding each question. We should be thankful that they asked these tough questions, because Jesus' answers were very illuminating. While our motives may be better than those of the men who sought to trap Jesus, our questions are often the same. We, too, want to know which of all the commandments is the greatest. Jesus' answer opens our eyes to the profound simplicity involved in pleasing God.

I. *The Anticipated Trap (22:34-36)*

[34]Hearing that Jesus had silenced the Sadducees, the Pharisees got together. [35]One of them, an expert in the law, tested him with this question: [36]"Teacher, which is the greatest commandment in the Law?"

This trap came from a lawyer. He was supposedly an expert or a scholar in interpreting the meaning of the Scriptures. But even this so-called man of the Word had little genuine love in his heart for divine matters.

The question from the lawyer was a fundamental one. He asked which was the greatest of all the commandments (there were 613 laws in the Old Testament, or more specifically, in the writings of Moses).

II. *The Actual Truth (22:37-40)*

[37]Jesus replied: " 'Love the Lord your God with all your heart and with all your soul and with all your mind.'[a] [38]This is the first and greatest commandment. [39]And the second is like it: 'Love your neighbor as yourself.'[b] [40]All the Law and the Prophets hang on these two commandments."

Jesus' answer was profound. He reduced the essence of the entire Old Testament to one commandment, a commandment with two sides. Side one is to love God with maximum intensity. Side two is to love people even as you love yourself.

How delightfully simple the Christian faith is. And how warmly positive its requirements are. There is only loyalty and love at its core.

---

a 37 Deut. 6:5 *b 39* Lev. 19:18

Jesus Stumps the Pharisees (Matt. 22:41-46)

(cf. Mark 12:35-37 and Luke 20:41-44)

If you question God, someday He will question you. It is better to submit to God with a few questions puzzling your mind than to resist Him until all your inquiries are resolved.

41 While the Pharisees were gathered together, Jesus asked them,
42 "What do you think about the Christ[a]? Whose son is he?"
"The son of David," they replied.
43 He said to them, "How is it then that David, speaking by the Spirit,
calls him 'Lord'? For he says,

44 " 'The Lord said to my Lord:
"Sit at my right hand
until I put your enemies
under your feet." '[b]

45 If then David calls him 'Lord,' how can he be his son?" 46 No one could
say a word in reply, and from that day on no one dared to ask him any
more questions.

Now Jesus turns the tables. He takes the offense. And He asks His inquirers a perplexing question: "Whose son is the Messiah?"

Jesus knew how they would respond. "He is the son of David," they said. But Jesus knew that this answer was memorized and delivered without a proper understanding. So He then asks them, "Why does David himself call the Messiah 'Lord'?" Surely it should be considered unusual for a father to call his son "Lord." In other words, David recognized that the Messiah was the Son of God, so why didn't the Pharisees recognize this, especially since that Son stood in their very presence and performed countless miracles attesting to that very truth?

This was too much for Jesus' critics. They could not handle His wisdom. His deity was irrefutable. The Pharisees were afraid to say any more, lest they would become still deeper over their heads in embarrassment.

---

[a] *42* Or *Messiah* [b] *44* Psalm 110:1

Jesus Renounces the Religious Leaders (Matt. 23:1-39)

(cf. Mark 12:38-40 and Luke 13:34, 35; 20:45-47)

When Jesus entered the Temple on Tuesday, He was quickly confronted and challenged. First, His authority was questioned by the chief priests and elders (Matt. 21:23ff.). Second, the Herodians and the disciples of the Pharisees attempted to trap Him in His teaching (Matt. 22:15ff.). Third, the Sadducees took a turn at attempting to belittle His theology (Matt. 22:23ff.). Fourth, a Pharisee tried his skills in stumping Jesus (Matt. 22:34ff.). Finally, Jesus turned the tables and took the offensive position (Matt. 22:41ff.). Jesus asked a question, but His critics were unable to answer His inquiry. So they departed from His presence.

It is after these repeated ordeals that Jesus delivered His longest discourse against the carnal religious leaders. His early remarks were somewhat calm; His later points were penetratingly specific and sharp; and His concluding words were choked with tears of sorrow.

I. *Severe Wrongs (23:1-12)*

23 Then Jesus said to the crowds and to his disciples: 2"The teachers
of the law and the Pharisees sit in Moses' seat. 3So you must obey
them and do everything they tell you. But do not do what they do, for
they do not practice what they preach. 4They tie up heavy loads and put
them on men's shoulders, but they themselves are not willing to lift a
finger to move them.

5"Everything they do is done for men to see: They make their phylac-
teries[a] wide and the tassels of their prayer shawls long; 6they love the
place of honor at banquets and the most important seats in the syna-
gogues; 7they love to be greeted in the marketplaces and to have men
call them 'Rabbi.'

8"But you are not to be called 'Rabbi,' for you have only one Master
and you are all brothers. 9And do not call anyone on earth 'father,' for
you have one Father, and he is in heaven. 10Nor are you to be called
'teacher,' for you have one Teacher, the Christ.[b] 11The greatest among
you will be your servant. 12For whoever exalts himself will be humbled,
and whoever humbles himself will be exalted.

---

a 5 That is, boxes containing Scripture verses, which were worn on the forehead and arms   b 10 Or *Messiah*

Moses' Seat. In this period each town had its own synagogue and favorite teacher of the law. It is believed that within each of these synagogues was a special seat that was reserved for the gifted teacher. He would sit there and proclaim the will of God from the writings of Moses. Here, Jesus seems to indicate that the entire body of Pharisees acted as though they occupied this special seat, and in a sense they did sit in this chair as teachers.

Obey Them/Do Not Do What They Do. A proper understanding of these words is derived from the context itself. Certainly Jesus is not placing an all-encompassing stamp of approval upon the teaching of the Pharisees (Matt. 5:21-48; 15:3-11). However, neither is He stating that every word coming from their mouths is the exact opposite of the truth. Sometimes they would do justice to Moses' seat, and when they did, they were to be obeyed. Regrettably, when they managed to rightly interpret Moses' words, they failed to apply it to themselves.

The Pharisees were hypocrites (or playactors). They preached by the mile, but only practiced by the inch. They believed in law and order—as long as they could lay down the law and give the orders. Real faith is a show-and-tell affair. The Pharisees, however, were content only to "tell."

Tie Up Heavy Loads. The Pharisees were specialists in giving orders. Because they accepted the oral traditions (or interpretations) of the Law, they were obligated to keep hundreds of new and minute details not found in Moses' writings. It was supposed that the more regimented life became, the more holy the person became who followed these strict rules. But this is far from the truth. Legalistic bondage to insignificant codes results in guilt and despair, not freedom or discovery (Matt. 11:28-30). Ironically, while the Pharisees were quick to give commandments for supposed holy living, they were slow in keeping the regulations themselves. Somehow they managed to find exceptions to their rules, though they would not do even so little as lift a finger to communicate these exceptions to others.

Done for Men to See. Jesus pointedly denounced the vanity and pride of the Pharisees. Their arrogance was public, and Jesus made His critical observations of them equally public. He exposed their faulty characters through several of their favorite practices (see the following).

Phylacteries. These were small leather boxes (between one-half inch and one and one-half inches long) into which various Scripture passages were placed (usually Exod. 13:1-10, 11-16; Deut. 6:4-9; 11:13-21). These boxes were then attached to leather straps and bound to the left hand (the one nearest the heart) and on the forehead, between the eyes (Exod. 13:9, 16; Deut. 11:18). The purpose for wearing these Scripture "promise boxes" was to remind the wearer to keep God's laws. In Jesus' day there was little evidence that the common people ever wore the phylacteries. They seem to have been used exclusively by the Pharisees. And as might be expected, they proudly widened the straps that held the phylacteries in place so that no one could miss seeing them.

Tassels. See notes on Matt. 9:20-22.

Place of Honor at Banquets and in the Synagogue. At a banquet it was considered an honor to sit close to the host, and in the synagogue the preferred seats were up front. Naturally, the Pharisees sought these prominent seats for themselves. They wanted to be noticed. They enjoyed the attention they received.

There are people like this today. If they were ever placed off in some corner to labor without any spotlight of attention, they would quickly resign and seek service wherever they could be noticed. The spirit of the Pharisees has not left us.

Rabbi. This title was bestowed upon Jewish men who had been elevated in the public eye as respected teachers of God's law. The Pharisees would parade about in the marketplaces in the hope that they might be given this formal greeting. But Jesus strongly condemns this practice of gloating over titles. Unfortunately there were many who relied so much on the words of these rabbis that these words were practically considered to be the source of the people's faith. Jesus annihilates this notion, however, by stating that there is only one ultimate Master or Father—God—and that there is only one Teacher—Christ. Everyone else is a brother or sister in the faith.

Our task, then, is not to elevate ourselves or others through the use of big-sounding titles, but humbly to serve people (Matt. 18:1ff.; 20:20ff.). Therefore, let us beware of how we use such titles as "pastor," "reverend," "priest," "father," "evangelist" and the like.

II. *Serious Woes (23:13-36)*

13"Woe to you, teachers of the law and Pharisees, you hypocrites! You shut the kingdom of heaven in men's faces. You yourselves do not enter, nor will you let those enter who are trying to.[a]

15"Woe to you, teachers of the law and Pharisees, you hypocrites! You travel over land and sea to win a single convert, and when he becomes one, you make him twice as much a son of hell as you are.

16"Woe to you, blind guides! You say, 'If anyone swears by the temple, it means nothing; but if anyone swears by the gold of the temple, he is bound by his oath.'
17You blind fools! Which is greater: the gold, or the temple that makes the gold sacred?
18You also say, 'If anyone swears by the altar, it means nothing; but if anyone swears by the gift on it, he is

a 13 Some manuscripts *to.* [14]*Woe to you, teachers of the law and Pharisees, you hypocrites! You devour widows' houses and for a show make lengthy prayers. Therefore you will be punished more severely.*

**bound by his oath.' 19You blind men! Which is greater: the gift, or the
altar that makes the gift sacred? 20Therefore, he who swears by the
altar swears by it and by everything on it. 21And he who swears by the
temple swears by it and by the one who dwells in it. 22And he who
swears by heaven swears by God's throne and by the one who sits on it.**

**23"Woe to you, teachers of the law and Pharisees, you hypocrites! You
give a tenth of your spices—mint, dill and cummin. But you have neglected the more important matters of the law—justice, mercy and faithfulness. You should have practiced the latter, without neglecting the
former. 24You blind guides! You strain out a gnat but swallow a camel.**

**25"Woe to you, teachers of the law and Pharisees, you hypocrites! You
clean the outside of the cup and dish, but inside they are full of greed
and self-indulgence. 26Blind Pharisee! First clean the inside of the cup
and dish, and then the outside also will be clean.**

**27"Woe to you, teachers of the law and Pharisees, you hypocrites! You
are like whitewashed tombs, which look beautiful on the outside but on
the inside are full of dead men's bones and everything unclean. 28In the
same way, on the outside you appear to people as righteous but on the
inside you are full of hypocrisy and wickedness.**

**29"Woe to you, teachers of the law and Pharisees, you hypocrites! You
build tombs for the prophets and decorate the graves of the righteous.
30And you say, 'If we had lived in the days of our forefathers, we would
not have taken part with them in shedding the blood of the prophets.'
31So you testify against yourselves that you are the descendants of those
who murdered the prophets. 32Fill up, then, the measure of the sin of
your forefathers!**

**33"You snakes! You brood of vipers! How will you escape being condemned to hell? 34Therefore I am sending you prophets and wise men
and teachers. Some of them you will kill and crucify; others you will flog
in your synagogues and pursue from town to town. 35And so upon you
will come all the righteous blood that has been shed on earth, from the
blood of righteous Abel to the blood of Zechariah son of Berakiah,
whom you murdered between the temple and the altar. 36I tell you the
truth, all this will come upon this generation.**

The Greek word for "hypocrite," which appears seven times in this passage, means to play the role of another person. It is a word that comes from the Greek theater. When an actor put on a mask and played a role, he was called a hypocrite. A "good" hypocrite would play many different roles. In the time of Jesus, several hundred years later, the word "hypocrite" was used quite negatively of people who acted in a "spiritual" way when they were actually living in a carnal manner. Jesus hated the sin of hypocrisy, so He spoke out against it boldly and openly. This is His longest discourse on the subject.

In Matthew's writing there are no less than thirty-five teachings that are specifically directed at carnal Jews whose profession of faith was one thing but whose possession of faith was another thing altogether. In a valid sense, then, this Gospel is heavily embedded with accounts that are designed to expose the shallowness (and even the falseness) of numerous Jewish persons, especially among the religious leaders.

Pretending to be spiritual, when you are not spiritual, is a serious offense, so far as Jesus is concerned. Here Jesus pronounces eight woes upon these religious actors.

The term "woe" has several meanings. First, it expresses divine displeasure, even divine wrath. It indicates inevitable chastisement or judgment upon those who bear it. Second, it expresses divine sorrow or grief. God does not delight in having to discipline people. He dislikes it, and He administers it with sorrow. The Pharisees and scribes were living in the sin of hypocrisy. God had to punish them for this; His wrath would fall on them swiftly and thoroughly; still He regrets that it is necessary. Below are the eight woes Jesus pronounced upon this self-righteous body of men.

1. *Roadblocking (v. 13).* Hypocrites love company. They detour people from the truth and shuttle them off into their own practices. They shall not see heaven. Neither shall the ones whom they prevent from receiving the truth. How dangerous it is to allow false spirituality to go unchecked!

2. *Deceiving (v. 14).* Hypocrites can pray beautiful prayers, especially if they can be worked to their own advantage. They approached unsuspecting women in order to devour them of their possessions. Such persons do not mind "living it up," and doing so at another's expense. Money, and the things money can buy, are imposing priorities in the hearts of most hypocrites.

3. *Evangelizing (v. 15).* Evil begets evil. Hypocrites reproduce their own kind. You cannot make a spiritual man from a carnal instructor. The pupil will be like his teacher. Converts to mere religion are not truly saved. Instead, they are spiritually crippled.

4. *Swearing (vv. 16-22).* If a person's word is not trustworthy, then swearing on a stack of Bibles, or on the gold of the Temple, or on anything else, really does not matter. How swiftly a hypocrite will run to mere symbols to convey his supposed faith. But it is our deeds, and not our swearing, that gives us honor and respect. If you make a promise, keep it. If you make a statement, tell the truth. You don't need to make long or formal oaths.

5. *Tithing (vv. 23, 24).* Hypocrites are specialists at majoring in minor issues and minoring in major issues. For instance, tithing is a minor issue, but displaying justice, mercy and faithfulness is a major issue. Both are to be done, but the stress is to be placed upon the latter virtues. The Pharisees reversed this order. They were always placing a pound of emphasis upon an ounce of truth, and vice versa.

6. *Cleaning (vv. 25, 26).* Another distinctive mark of hypocrisy is the exaltation of ritual to the neglect of more practical matters. The Pharisees could sometimes follow the strict rules of their man-made faith, like washing dishes in a prescribed manner, but when it came to cleansing their own lives, they ignored the dirt found there. This reversal of the trivial and the urgent is a common practice among hypocrites.

7. *Pretending (vv. 27, 28).* Hypocrites enjoy showing off, while inside (behind the exterior of their display) they are empty of real virtues. They are like freshly painted tombs—pretty to look at but filled with decay on the inside.

8. *Venerating (vv. 29-36).* Finally, hypocrites look back into the past with rose-colored glasses. They speak reverently of the past religious leaders, while scowling at those who persecuted them. In reality, however, hypocrites do not defend the saints but join in harming them and their work. Today there are those among us who would give the appearance of supporting certain spiritual projects, only to defeat them when called upon to personally support them, or when such projects conflict with their own self-made interests.

Jesus climaxed this portion of His discourse by stating that His followers would continue to receive harsh treatment from these so-called men of God. But in the end these persecutors would receive the fruit of their unjust actions. In fact, the judgment would come during that very generation. This was clearly fulfilled in A.D. 70, when the Roman soldiers utterly demolished the city of Jerusalem and crushed the entire nation of Israel (see notes on Matt. 24).

III. *Sincere Wooings (23:37-39)*

37"O Jerusalem, Jerusalem, you who kill the prophets and stone those sent to you, how often I have longed to gather your children together, as a hen gathers her chicks under her wings, but you were not willing. 38Look, your house is left to you desolate. 39For I tell you, you will not see me again until you say, 'Blessed is he who comes in the name of the Lord.'[a]"

God is not some cosmic monster with a club—always ready to bash those who get out of line. He is exceedingly patient. He waits. He woos. He is willing to forgive and to restore. But if He is continuously resisted, then the hammer must fall, and the sparks will fly.

a 39 Psalm 118:26

Jerusalem had stiff-armed God for years. Stubborn. Self-made. Proud. Content. Religious. These were her markings. Now she would suffer for her insubordination. The city and the nation would crumble to the ground. Disgraced and ruined, she would be scattered among the nations. Her inhabitants would become a people without a country. And this was to be just the earthly phase of her punishment for committing the sin of hypocrisy. Beyond this is hell, too (see Topical Index for references to comments on "hell").

The End of the Age (Matt. 24:1-31)

(cf. Mark 13:1-27 and Luke 21:5-28)

The end was near for Jesus and for Jerusalem. Israel would destroy the Son of Man. And the Son of Man would return in A.D. 70 to destroy Jerusalem (Matt. 16:27-28; 21:42-44).

In these dark hours, only a few days before the Crucifixion, Jesus attempted to persuade Jerusalem's inhabitants to abandon their spiritual folly. But she would not heed His words. He pleaded. He prayed. He rebuked. But they remained unmoved in their humanly devised religious piety. So, God would execute His justice against her. And she would be terribly humbled.

Here, Jesus tells the future. He speaks of Jerusalem's fall in A.D. 70, and He talks, at the same time, of His return at the end of the age. However, it is difficult, if not impossible, in this passage to separate definitively between these two predicted events. The reason for this inability is seen in the fact that these predictions present a unique double exposure of the Second Coming laid over the much earlier events of A.D. 70. Note the chart entitled "Differing Views About Jesus' Prophecy in Matthew 24."

Stated differently, in Jesus' words are a deliberate, yet ambiguous, double fulfillment. In His prophecies are a dual expectation—the destruction of Jerusalem in A.D. 70 and His own Second Coming. The reason behind this overlapping type of prophetic presentation can be found in the fact that both events are so similar in nature that one prediction is capable of describing two events.

I. *Disgust in the Temple (24:1-2)*

24 Jesus left the temple and was walking away when his disciples
came up to him to call his attention to its buildings. 2"Do you see
all these things?" he asked. "I tell you the truth, not one stone here will be
left on another; every one will be thrown down."

DIFFERING VIEWS ABOUT JESUS' PROPHECY IN MATTHEW 24		
	24:4-14	24:15-28
View 1	Everything pertains to A.D. 70.	
View 2	Everything pertains to the Second Coming.	
View 3	Everything pertains to both A.D. 70 and the Second Coming.	
View 4	Pertains to A.D. 70.	Pertains to the Second Coming.
View 5	First Half of the Tribulation	Second half of the Tribulation.
View number three is the more probable meaning of the passage, though there is little room for dogmatism in the matter.		

How differently do the disciples perceive the things of this world, compared to the way Jesus sees them. The attention of the disciples was fixed on the temple's marvelous construction. The attention of Jesus, however, was set on the temple's soon-to-happen destruction.

The temple was a wasteful achievement. Literally thousands of men had worked for more than forty years to erect one of the most beautiful structures to be found anywhere in the world. But despite the splendor, it would be judged by God and left in a disgraceful heap of rubble. How well this account pictures the futility of human achievements in glorifying God. When the glitter is only external, there is a certain destiny with judgment.

II. *Discussion Outside the Temple (24:3-31)*

1. *First Cycle of Signs (24:3-8)*

3 As Jesus was sitting on the Mount of Olives, the disciples came to him
privately. "Tell us," they said, "when will this happen, and what will be
the sign of your coming and of the end of the age?"
4 Jesus answered: "Watch out that no one deceives you. 5 For many will
come in my name, claiming, 'I am the Christ,[a]' and will deceive many.
6 You will hear of wars and rumors of wars, but see to it that you are not
alarmed. Such things must happen, but the end is still to come. 7 Nation

[a] 5 Or *Messiah*; also in verse 23

**will rise against nation, and kingdom against kingdom. There will be
famines and earthquakes in various places. 8All these are the beginning of birth pains.**

2. *Second Cycle of Signs (24:9-14)*

**9"Then you will be handed over to be persecuted and put to death, and
you will be hated by all nations because of me. 10At that time many will
turn away from the faith and will betray and hate each other, 11and
many false prophets will appear and deceive many people. 12Because of
the increase of wickedness, the love of most will grow cold, 13but he who
stands firm to the end will be saved. 14And this gospel of the kingdom
will be preached in the whole world as a testimony to all nations, and
then the end will come.**

3. *Third Cycle of Signs (24:15-28)*

**15"So when you see standing in the holy place 'the abomination that
causes desolation,'[a] spoken of through the prophet Daniel—let the
reader understand—16then let those who are in Judea flee to the
mountains. 17Let no one on the roof of his house go down to take
anything out of the house. 18Let no one in the field go back to get his
cloak. 19How dreadful it will be in those days for pregnant women and
nursing mothers! 20 Pray that your flight will not take place in winter or
on the Sabbath. 21For then there will be great distress, unequaled from
the beginning of the world until now—and never to be equaled again.
22If those days had not been cut short, no one would survive, but for the
sake of the elect those days will be shortened. 23At that time if anyone
says to you, 'Look, here is the Christ!' or, 'There he is!' do not believe it.
24For false Christs and false prophets will appear and perform great
signs and miracles to deceive even the elect—if that were possible. 25See,
I have told you ahead of time.**

**26"So if anyone tells you, 'There he is, out in the desert,' do not go out; or,
'Here he is, in the inner rooms,' do not believe it. 27For as the lightning
comes from the east and flashes to the west, so will be the coming of the Son
of Man. 28Wherever there is a carcass, there the vultures will gather.**

4. *Final Sequence of Signs (24:29-31)*

29"Immediately after the distress of those days

**" 'the sun will be darkened,
and the moon will not give its light;**

---

[a] 15 Daniel 9:27; 11:31; 12:11

the stars will fall from the sky,
and the heavenly bodies will be shaken.'[a]

[30]"At that time the sign of the Son of Man will appear in the sky, and all the nations of the earth will mourn. They will see the Son of Man coming on the clouds of the sky, with power and great glory. [31]And he will send his angels with a loud trumpet call, and they will gather his elect from the four winds, from one end of the heavens to the other.

Once the disciples learn of Jesus' prophecy, they are quick to ask three short questions:

1. When will these things be?
2. What will be the sign of your coming?
3. What will be the sign of the end of the age?

In these inquiries we are capable of discerning the thoughts that the disciples had for the end of God's prophetic clock. They viewed everything as coming to an abrupt conclusion. They looked for God's earthly kingdom to be established practically overnight. There was no doubt in their minds that they would see it all happen in their own life spans.

Jesus was aware of the disciples' dreams. They were ambitious men, full of zeal and eagerness. So Jesus delivers a lengthy answer for their three questions. The contents of his answer reveals a two-phase fulfillment. The first installment would occur in A.D. 70, when the magnificent temple would be completely flattened. The second installment, being very much like the first, would come at His own second descent.

It is quite probable that the greater bulk of these prophecies were *literally fulfilled* in A.D. 70, when the Roman General Titus captured, desecrated and destroyed the city of Jerusalem (see details in Luke 21). There remains, however, a *typological or ultimate fulfillment* for these same prophecies. In other words, the events of A.D. 70 serve as a shadow of those events that will occur immediately prior to Christ's Second Coming. What happened in A.D. 70 will happen again, allowing for minor differences, before Christ comes to earth to rule the world. Observe the diagram on the following page, which depicts this dual-type prophecy.

Here is an itemized listing of Jesus' predictions. Details regarding these events will be discussed in Luke's account of these prophecies.

1. Religious deception—vv. 4, 5, 11, 23, 24, 25, 26
2. Wars and rumors of wars—vv. 6, 7a
3. Famines—v. 7b
4. Earthquakes—v. 7c

---

a 29 Isaiah 13:10; 34:4

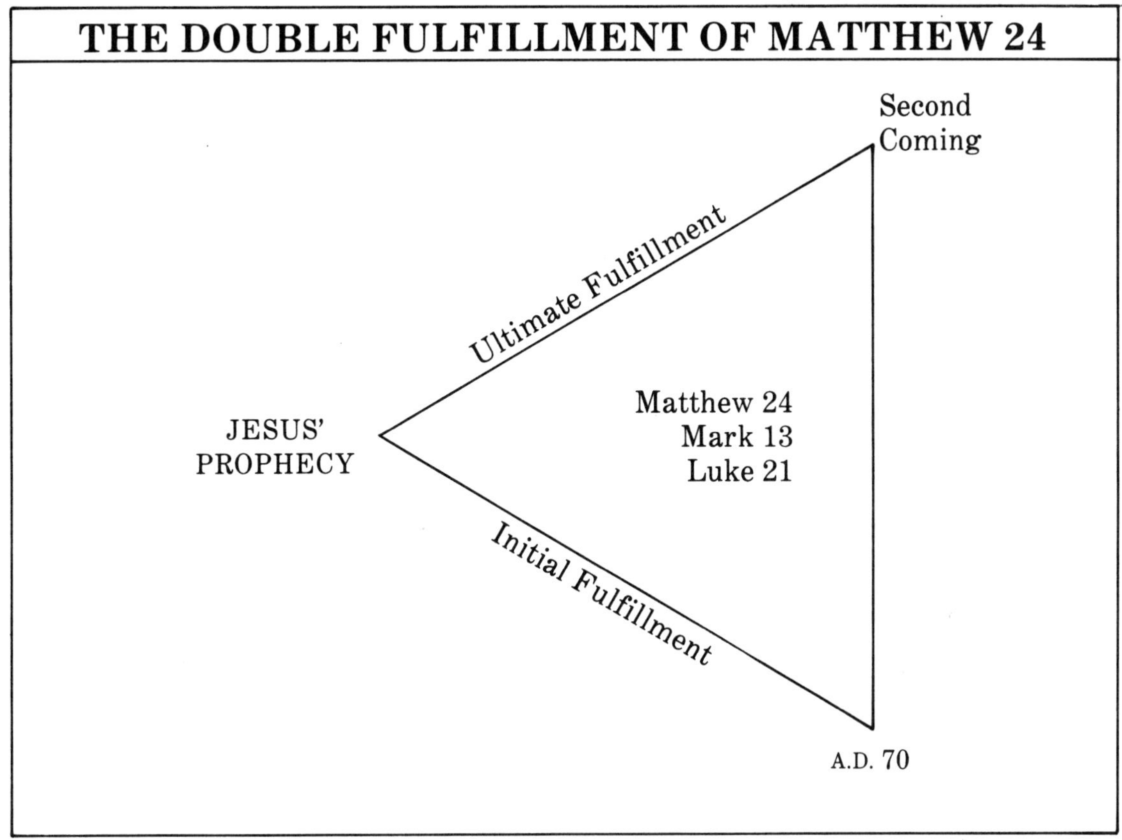

5. Persecution and hate—v. 9
6. Departure from the faith—v. 10a
7. Betrayal, hate and increased carnality—vv. 10b-12
8. Gospel preached in whole world—v. 14
9. Abomination of desolation—v. 15
10. Exodus from Jerusalem—vv. 16-20
11. Unequalled distress—vv. 21, 22
12. Divine judgment—vv. 27-31

Finally, it should be noticed that Jesus' answer takes on a series of cycles. That is, no less than four times Jesus introduces a series of signs and then culminates each series with words that sound climactic. Each of these series (except for the last one) seems to share a common starting point and ending point in time. It is as if Jesus were repeating himself, except for a particular item which he seeks to highlight in each cycle.

In the first cycle the emphasis is on worldwide signs; in the second cycle the emphasis is on believer signs; in the third cycle the emphasis is on Jerusalem signs; and in the fourth cycle the emphasis is on heavenly signs. In other words, the period under discussion will affect the whole earth, though the people of Israel and believers in particular are at the focal points. Nevertheless, there will be an end to these signs at the appearance of the ultimate and final sign—Jesus' return to earth. The special study below will assist you in understanding the broader scope of these and other related prophecies for the last days.

Special Study: Blueprints for the Last Days

An Elementary Approach to the Last Days

Our understanding of prophecy should begin at a very simple stage. The two major events of the last days are the first and second comings of Jesus Christ. (See the chart below.)

1. *First Coming.* In a study of the first coming of Christ we learn about the Savior's birth, ministry, death and resurrection. Here we focus intently on how Jesus paid the price at Calvary for our sins—past, present and future (1 John 2:1, 2). This is simple enough to excite each of us, and yet it is quite profound.

2. *Second Coming.* In a study of the Second Coming of Christ we learn that at this event Jesus will exercise His kingship to the fullest degree. Sin will be punished, and righteouness will be rewarded. It will be a vastly different world after Jesus comes to earth again (Rev. 19:11-16).

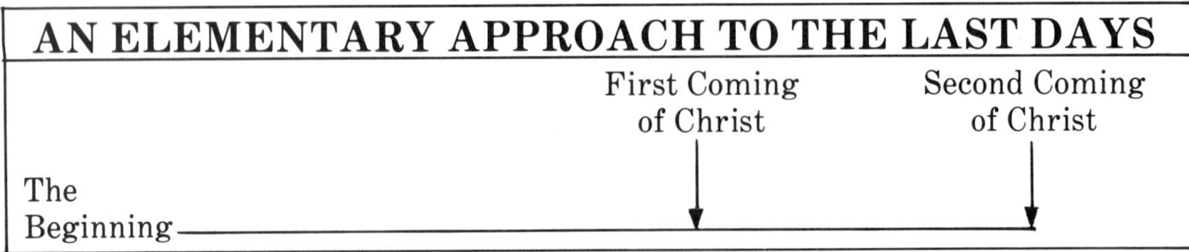

This is an elementary approach to the study of the last days. It is enriching, but it does lack an obvious degree of finesse. There is a great deal more that should be said regarding the end of this world system as we presently know it.

A Secondary Approach to the Last Days

In the secondary approach to prophecy of the last days we start to pick up a few of the fine points. Here are four additional notes. (Notice the diagram.)

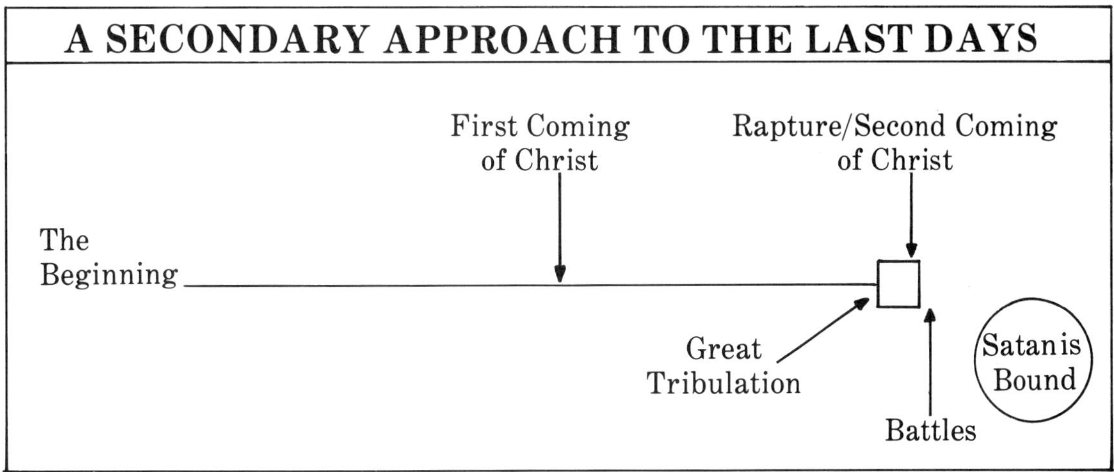

1. *Great Tribulation.* Before Jesus returns to reign on this planet, there will be a terrible period of political, economic, demonic and natural unrest, such as has never existed. Paradoxically, it will also be a time of massive evangelization. The duration of this upheaval and revival will be three and a half years.

2. *The Rapture.* The Rapture is that stupendous time when all true Christians—whether they be dead and in the grave, or alive and on the earth—will be caught up into the sky to meet the Lord Jesus Christ (1 Thess. 4:13-18). Various views are held regarding the precise time when it is believed the Rapture will occur. At this present level, however, we only need to recognize that prior to Jesus' return to earth all Christians will be caught up to meet Him in the sky.

3. *Battles.* At the Second Coming of Christ there will be three battles. One battle will involve the rescuing of Jews in the ancient territory of Edom, just south of the Dead Sea (Isa. 34:6-15; 63:1-6). Another battle will deliver Jerusalem from her hostile enemies (Joel 3; Zech. 12:9). And the final battle, at Armageddon, will bring an end to all earth's wars, at least for a thousand years (Rev. 16:16-21; 19:11-21).

4. *Satan Is Bound.* Once Jesus returns, there will be no room left on earth for Satan, nor for his fallen companions. This diabolic company will be rounded up and dumped into the abyss (Isa. 24:21-23; Rev. 20:1-3). No longer will we, or the nations of the

world, be deceived. No longer will satanic temptations distract us from a pure walk of obedience to earth's greatest King—Jesus Christ.

An Advanced Approach to the Last Days

There are other matters to be learned in the advanced study of prophecy. Here are four more items that need to be added to your chart of the last days. (See the following chart.)

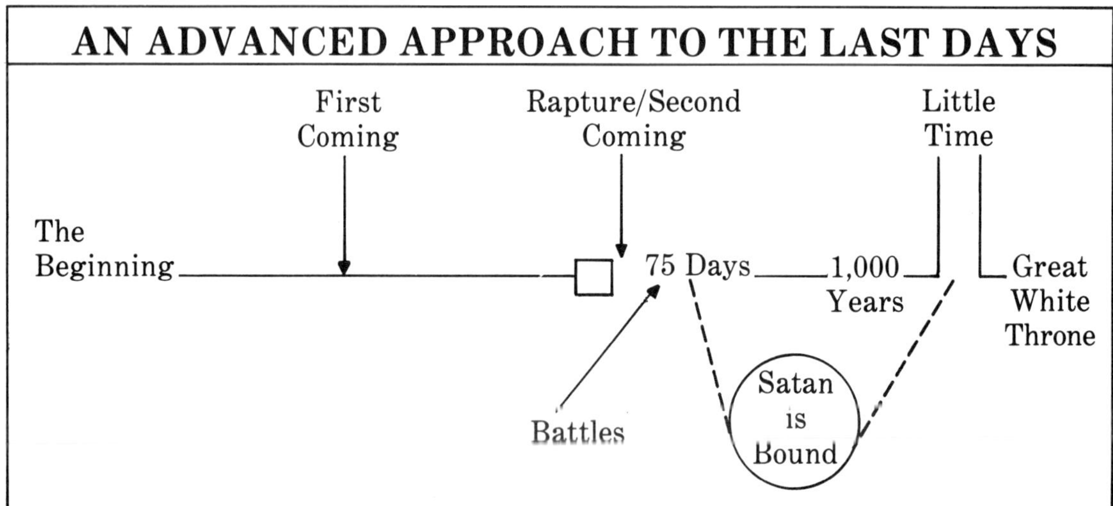

1. *Seventy-Five Days.* After the Second Coming of Christ that ends the Tribulation period, seventy-five days will transpire before the Millennium begins. (Rev. 12:6 says the Great Tribulation will be "1260 days." Dan. 12:11, 12 speaks of "1290 days"—an extra thirty days—and "1335 days"—forty-five additonal days—from the beginning of the Tribulation to a future point that can be seen as the beginning of the Millennium. Therefore we have seventy-five days between the Second Coming and the beginning of the Millennium. Cf. Dan. 12:7; Rev. 11:2.) It is difficult to determine with any degree of dogmatism what occurs during this period. The following events are offered as suggestions of what could possibly fill this time span.

a. The judgment of unbelieving Jews (Ezek. 20:33-38; Zeph. 3:11).
b. The salvation of believing Jews (Zech. 12:10-13:1; Rom. 11:25-29).
c. The witnessing of the converted Jews to Gentiles who have not heard of Christ (Isa. 2:2-4; 66:18-21; Zech. 2:11; Rom. 11:12).
d. The judgment of unbelieving Gentiles (Matt. 25:31-40).
e. The rewarding of all resurrected believers (Luke 14:14; 2 Cor. 5:10).
f. The marriage supper (Rev. 19:9; Matt. 22:1-14; Luke 14:15-24).

g. The inauguration of the new heavens and new earth (2 Pet. 3:10-14; Rev. 21, 22).

2. *A Thousand Years.* This millennial period refers to that time when Christ will rule the whole earth, allowing for no resistance to His will (Ps. 2; 110:1, 2; Dan. 2:44, 45; Rev. 20:1-6).[1]

3. *Little Time.* At the close of the thousand-year reign of Christ upon the earth, the abyss will be opened, releasing Satan and his host to prey one final time upon the inhabitants of this planet. He will go out to deceive the people. In ambitious haste he will gather together a feeble army of supporters. These pathetic soldiers will march to Jerusalem for earth's final war. God will consume them instantly and put an everlasting seal on any further such disturbances on the earth.

4. *Great White Throne Judgment.* The very last act of God against sinners is viewed here at this terrible and awesome judgment seat. All those who have stiff-armed Christ out to the maximum limits of their life—those who have resisted God's offer of salvation through Christ—will be resurrected, sentenced to their appropriate level of punishment, and cast into the lake of unending fire (Rev. 20:11-15). The sad facts of this event will be discussed at length in another chapter.

NOTE: The preceding special study is excerpted from *Armageddon 198?* by Stephen D. Swihart (Haven Books, 1980).

The Parable of the Fig Tree (Matt. 24:32-35)

(cf. Mark 13:28-31 and Luke 21:29-33)

Once Jesus told His disciples of Jerusalem's destruction and of His own return to earth, they were quite anxious to know when all of this would transpire. They sought a prophetic time clock in order to discern when these events would happen.

Jesus accommodates this desire with a parable from the fig tree. He tells His disciples that even as a fig tree gives signs in the twigs and leaves that notify us of the approach of summer, so too, the fulfillment of all the previously mentioned twelve

[1]The position of this book is premillennial (that is, the belief that Jesus will return to the earth and set up a kingdom, over which He will rule for 1,000 years). Some scholars follow an amillennial approach (which holds that Christ will not reign on the earth for a thousand years—instead, the number is symbolic, they say, and refers to His heavenly reign). Others are postmillennial (believing the Church will, in effect, establish the Kingdom on the earth, after which Christ will return in final judgment). For a detailed analysis of these views see *The Meaning of the Millennium,* edited by Robert G. Clouse (InterVarsity Press, 1977).

signs (Matt. 24:1-31) mark the period when Jerusalem would collapse and when He would return to earth.

> **32"Now learn this lesson from the fig tree: As soon as its twigs get**
> **tender and its leaves come out, you know that summer is near. 33Even so,**
> **when you see all these things, you know that it[a] is near, right at the door.**
> **34I tell you the truth, this generation[b] will certainly not pass away until**
> **all these things have happened. 35Heaven and earth will pass away, but**
> **my words will never pass away.**

Scholarship is divided over the interpretation of these words. The first problem comes from the meaning of the term "generation." It can mean "all people living in a certain period," or it can mean "a certain race of people," in which case the Jewish race would be intended. Each translation/interpretation has its merits.

The second problem regards time—when did Jesus see "all these things" happening? Did Jesus mean A.D. 70 or His Second Coming or both? The charts in the previous section (Matt. 24:1-31) illustrate the various views people have taken on the chronology of this issue.

Although no single position will satisfy everyone, still a stance can be taken. There *is* a right answer to these inquiries, whether we are personally capable of discerning it or not.

The prophecies of Matthew 24 clearly appear to have a double fulfillment. In other words, in the first sense of the word "generation" (all people living in a certain period), the prophecy *was* fulfilled by the generation which witnessed the destruction of Jerusalem, and the prophecy *will be* fulfilled by the generation which will witness the Second Coming of Christ. In the second sense of the word "generation" (a certain race of people), it is referring to the *race* of Jews, who will remain until Christ's Second Coming.

Being Ready When Jesus Returns (Matt. 24:36-51)

(cf. Mark 13:32-37 and Luke 21:34-36)

No one can tell, with absolute precision, the exact time when the Son of man will return. We must remember that Jesus only gave us signs, not a prophetic stopwatch. Neither He nor the angels know the precise moment when this will occur. Only the Father knows.

We should take little stock in writings or in teachers who seem compelled to fix a

a 33 Or *he* *b 34* Or *race*

specific time for the climax of these prophetic matters. Doubtlessly, it is much more important for you to be ready whenever it occurs than it is for you to be able to say you know when it will happen.

I. *The Days of Noah (24:36-41)*

> **36“No one knows about that day or hour, not even the angels in heaven, nor the Son,[a] but only the Father.37 As it was in the days of Noah, so it will be at the coming of the Son of Man. 38For in the days before the flood, people were eating and drinking, marrying and giving in marriage, up to the day Noah entered the ark; 39and they knew nothing about what would happen until the flood came and took them all away. That is how it will be at the coming of the Son of Man. 40Two men will be in the field; one will be taken and the other left. 41Two women will be grinding with a hand mill; one will be taken and the other left.**

The Days of Noah. While Jesus was teaching about the last days, the days of Noah impressed him as being a perfect parallel. In the days of Noah people were primarily interested in satisfying their bodily lusts—food, drink and marriage/sex. They were blinded by these desires. They made them their gods and devoted themselves to full indulgence in these areas (Gen. 6).

There is nothing wrong with these desires, in themselves, but in Noah's day they were totally out of proportion with God's intent. As a result, the appetites of the bodies became masters of the people.

They Knew Nothing About What Would Happen. This is an odd statement, because it gives the impression that the people in Noah's day had never heard about the coming judgment. But they had heard—for 120 years (Gen. 6:1ff.)! Noah preached righteousness (the right way to live) for over a century to these people (2 Pet. 2:5; Gen. 6:3). The people were not ignorant of the approaching doom. Instead, they were so resistant to its message that they let it pass right by them, leaving no impression whatever of Noah's message.

Certainly these words deserve our careful attention. Today there are more than twice the number of evangelical Christians in the world than there were only twenty-five years ago. There are more genuine believers alive now than at any other period of history. Nevertheless, the impact of Christian influence on the amoral revolution in our society is almost imperceptible. People's lusts for physical pleasures are seemingly undistracted by righteous preaching. The days of Noah and our own are, pathetically, very similar.

The Flood Took Them Away/One Will Be Taken. Some writers see the Rapture of

a 36 Some manuscripts do not have *nor the Son.*

the believer in this "taken" scene. But it is much more consistent with our Lord's parallel point to believe that the ones being taken are those who are swept away in divine judgment. The theme here is judgment, not a rescue plot. The illustration of the flood depicts God's wrath. Those taken in the flood (or those taken in the field or at the mill) are those who are guilty of spurning God's call to righteous living.

II. *The Thief in the Night (24:42-44)*

[42]"Therefore keep watch, because you do not know on what day your Lord will come. [43]But understand this: If the owner of the house had known at what time of night the thief was coming, he would have kept watch and would not have let his house be broken into. [44]So you also must be ready, because the Son of Man will come at an hour when you do not expect him.

Because the hour of our Lord's return is not knowable, we are again challenged to live in such a way that we will be ready at any moment for His coming. We must not take this lightly, lest we be found shamefully unprepared when He returns—like the person who is unprepared for the sudden appearance of a thief in the night (1 Thess. 5:1-4; 2 Pet. 3:10; Rev. 3:3; 16:15).

When a person truly believes Jesus could return to earth in his own lifetime, he is certain to prepare himself for this glorious event. But if there is any doubt about the reality or the nearness of Christ's coming, then that person will relax and live as he pleases.

III. *The Wise and Wicked Servants (24:45-51)*

[45]"Who then is the faithful and wise servant, whom the master has put in charge of the servants in his household to give them their food at the proper time? [46]It will be good for that servant whose master finds him doing so when he returns. [47]I tell you the truth, he will put him in charge of all his possessions. [48]But suppose that servant is wicked and says to himself, 'My master is staying away a long time,' [49]and he then begins to beat his fellow servants and to eat and drink with drunkards. [50]The master of that servant will come on a day when he does not expect him and at an hour he is not aware of. [51]He will cut him to pieces and assign him a place with the hypocrites, where there will be weeping and gnashing of teeth.

In the audiences who followed Jesus there were two kinds of servants: (a) those who were faithful workers and lovers of people and (b) those who were unfaithful workers and abusers of people. The former group, declares Jesus, will be abundantly rewarded when He returns. They will be put in charge of many possessions. But the latter group, those who think that Jesus' return is off in the distant future, will grow lax in their standard of living. When Jesus returns, these persons will be utterly consumed and thrown into hell.

There *is* an association between the way we view Jesus' Second Coming and the way we live. Those who take Him seriously also live seriously. Those who take Him lightly also live lightly. Take note of how you live, for it reflects how you truly believe.

The Parable of the Ten Virgins (Matt. 25:1-13)

The details in the parable before us are numerous. There are five wise virgins, five foolish virgins, lamps, oil, a bridegroom, a midnight call, a wedding banquet and a shut door. Eight images in all. And not even so much as one of them is explained. We only know that all of this information relates to the return of Jesus Christ and to the subsequent establishment of God's Kingdom on the earth.

It would be easy to read into this story an interpretation that is not actually there. We could give precise definitions for each of the parable's articles of interest. But this apparently is not necessary. Otherwise Jesus would have explained each aspect for us. Therefore, we are left with a main lesson that is unmistakable, surrounded by a company of miscellaneous details.

The main lesson is this: be ready—now—for the Second Coming of Christ, and you will join in the joyful celebration of that event. But if you are not ready when it occurs, you will taste the bitter consequences of God's rejection.

**25 "At that time the kingdom of heaven will be like ten virgins who
took their lamps and went out to meet the bridegroom. 2Five of
them were foolish and five were wise. 3The foolish ones took their lamps
but did not take any oil with them. 4The wise, however, took oil in jars
along with their lamps. 5The bridegroom was a long time in coming,
and they all became drowsy and fell asleep.**

**6"At midnight the cry rang out: 'Here's the bridegroom! Come out to
meet him!'**

**7"Then all the virgins woke up and trimmed their lamps. 8The foolish
ones said to the wise, 'Give us some of your oil; our lamps are going out.'**

9" 'No,' they replied, 'there may not be enough for both us and you.

Instead, go to those who sell oil and buy some for yourselves.'
10"But while they were on their way to buy the oil, the bridegroom arrived. The virgins who were ready went in with him to the wedding banquet. And the door was shut.
11"Later the others also came. 'Sir! Sir!' they said. 'Open the door for us!'
12"But he replied, 'I tell you the truth, I don't know you.'
13"Therefore keep watch, because you do not know the day or the hour.

In the traditional wedding ceremony the bride would leave her father's home with a large escort of family and friends. They would all travel to some previously appointed place where they were to meet the groom and his numerous friends. At this place there was to be the wedding ceremony and many related ceremonies, such as singing, dancing, the reciting of love poems and banqueting. In this parable we see that the bridal party had arrived at the destination, but the groom and his party had not yet arrived. It is with this traditional setting that Jesus taught one of His most forceful messages on the necessity of constant preparedness on the part of the bride.

There are two points in this episode that should be discovered and firmly grasped.

First, we ought to notice the similarity of the virgins. From all human appearances, the ten virgins looked alike. Their interest in the coming of the bridegroom seemed to be identical, too. Each carried a lamp, and each heard the midnight call of the groom. How united they appeared on the surface.

But the similarity ceases after the surface appearances. These girls were not the same at all. There was one all-important matter that made them dramatically and drastically different from each other. Some were truly ready for Christ's sudden coming; some were not ready at all.

In the church there are many who profess a common doctrinal position, and who adopt a common life style on the exterior. But on the inside, where truth cannot be concealed from God, they are vastly different. We cannot always tell if someone is a genuine Christian by outward appearances. Let us never forget that among the members of the church there are those whom God considers to be wise and those whom He designates as being foolish. The difference is in their degrees of preparedness.

But how can *we* today get ready and stay ready for the Second Coming of Jesus Christ? To prepare ourselves means we must align ourselves with God's priorities. There can be no adequate readiness until we set our lives in tune with God's will. This means our interests and devotions should be firmly planted in these four priorities:

1. Jesus and His Body, the Church (Eph. 4:11-16)
2. Personal holiness (Eph. 4:17-5:21)
3. Family life (Eph. 5:22-6:4)
4. Our jobs (Eph. 6:5-9)

God's will for the believer is that he should harmonize himself with these divine interests. This is the manner by which God unfolds His priorities to us (as revealed in the book of Ephesians). We ought to be committed to them utterly and in the successive order in which God has revealed them to us.

Second, we ought to notice the separation of the virgins. The time of the bridegroom's return was unknown. The virgins probably anticipated his immediate appearance, but much time had passed, and they all fell asleep. No one knows the hour of Christ's Second Coming. It may be near, or it may be far away. Nevertheless, He is coming, and whether we be awake or asleep, we can still be ready in our hearts for His marvelous return.

Once Jesus returns, there will be a separation between His wise and foolish followers. We must never forget that this world, in the mind of God, is only composed of two kinds of persons—those who are ready to face Him and those who are not ready.

Once the bridegroom appears, it will be too late to change your past mistakes and get ready on the spur of the moment. Neither can another person's readiness be of any assistance to the unprepared. The Second Coming of Jesus Christ will be intensely personal. We cannot depend upon anyone else to get us ready. We must do it ourselves. And we must do it now, before it is forever too late. This is the paramount lesson Jesus sought to convey in this parabolic teaching.

The Parable of the Talents (Matt. 25:14-30)

Laziness and Christianity do not mix. They are bitter enemies. Christian service can be neither passive nor casual. It must be active and aggressive. The lukewarm person has no place in God's Kingdom (Rev. 3:14-21).

Henry Van Dyke has stated the matter succinctly: "It is better to burn the candle at both ends, and in the middle too, than to put it away in the closet." This is the essence of Jesus' teaching in this lesson.

I. *Giving Out Responsibilities (25:14-18)*

14"Again, it will be like a man going on a journey, who called his servants and entrusted his property to them. 15To one he gave five talents[a] of money, to another two talents, and to another one talent, each according to his ability. Then he went on his journey. 16The man who had received the five talents went at once and put his money to work

a 15 A talent was worth more than a thousand dollars.

and gained five more. [17]So also, the one with the two talents gained two more. [18]But the man who had received the one talent went off, dug a hole in the ground and hid his master's money.

A Man Going on a Journey. The shape that the Kingdom of God was to take under Jesus' teaching differed radically from popular Jewish expectations. With the advent of the Christ—heaven's King on the earth—the Jews envisioned an immediate and thorough political overthrow of all Israel's enemies. But Jesus taught that before heaven's throne would appear on the earth, there must be much work accomplished. The political dimensions of the Kingdom were not to be imminent, as they supposed. So, Jesus talked of His own departure in the terms of a man who was to take a journey, the trip referring to Jesus' ascension into heaven.

He Entrusted His Property to Them. Jesus' work was not to end with His absence. Instead, it was (and is) to continue in a full-scale measure (or even a greater measure!—Matt. 28:19, 20; John 14:12). For about three and a half years, Jesus prepared His followers for this endowment. In a matter of a few days it would soon be theirs.

Talents. A talent is a measurement of weight (in the same way an ounce is a measurement of weight). The talent was commonly used in measuring sums of money, like silver and gold, in order to determine their value. Here the term seems to take on the additional meaning of spiritual gifts or responsibilities.

According to His Ability. Several truths ought to be noted regarding the bestowal of these talents.

First, the giving of the talents to the servants is a sovereign action. The master was not obligated to distribute anything to anyone. No one could order him to give them these gifts or responsibilities. The disbursement rested solely within his own grace. In like fashion, no one can demand anything from God. He gives freely, but He also gives sovereignly (1 Cor. 12:11, 18). It is by grace that we have what we have.

Second, each servant receives something—no one is excluded. Every servant has worth and ability. In God's Kingdom, too, everyone has been given talents and certain skills in order to best serve one another (1 Cor. 12:7, 11). No one can say he is not important, for this is not the case at all (1 Cor. 12:12-27).

Third, the number of talents distributed to each servant is unequal. That is, some workers are more talented (here shown as much as five times more talented) than other workers. This uneven gifting is also to be found in God's Kingdom. We are not all the same—otherwise, we would have need of no one else. But the fact is that we do need the services and gifts of others (1 Cor. 12:12-27). Some persons may possess many talents, while others may have only a few, but no one has all the talents and no one is empty-handed.

This fact is an obvious, though often neglected, statement. We must not think we can do, or are expected to do, what every other Christian can accomplish. Neither can we ask or expect others to do what God has specifically enabled us to perform. It is imperative for us to see this. In this point we discover the extreme importance of each believer fulfilling his or her role in the Kingdom of God. Only to the degree that each person uses his abilities, then, is God's full work actually accomplished.

Fourth, the distribution of the talents is based upon each person's abilities. Some persons, by virtue of their make-up, are incapable of competently handling more than a few talents. Giving riches, for instance, to an indiscriminate spender, is a sad mistake. In the Kingdom, then, the distribution of gifts and responsibilities is according to our abilities to properly manage them. This message of personal limitations ought to cause each of us to prayerfully evaluate our God-given abilities before assuming responsibilities that lie beyond our present skills.

II. *Giving Out Rewards (25:19-30)*

19"After a long time the master of those servants returned and settled
accounts with them. 20The man who had received the five talents
brought the other five. 'Master,' he said, 'you entrusted me with five
talents. See, I have gained five more.'
21"His master replied, 'Well done, good and faithful servant! You have
been faithful with a few things; I will put you in charge of many things.
Come and share your master's happiness!'
22"The man with the two talents also came. 'Master,' he said, 'you
entrusted me with two talents; see, I have gained two more.'
23"His master replied, 'Well done, good and faithful servant! You have
been faithful with a few things; I will put you in charge of many things.
Come and share your master's happiness!'
24"Then the man who had received the one talent came. 'Master,' he
said, 'I knew that you are a hard man, harvesting where you have not
sown and gathering where you have not scattered seed. 25So I was
afraid and went out and hid your talent in the ground. See, here is what
belongs to you.'
26"His master replied, 'You wicked, lazy servant! So you knew that I
harvest where I have not sown and gather where I have not scattered
seed? 27Well then, you should have put my money on deposit with the
bankers, so that when I returned I would have received it back with
interest.
28" 'Take the talent from him and give it to the one who has the ten

talents. 29For everyone who has will be given more, and he will have an abundance. Whoever does not have, even what he has will be taken from him. 30And throw that worthless servant outside, into the darkness, where there will be weeping and gnashing of teeth.'

After a Long Time the Master Returned. If this parable teaches us certain matters about God's Kingdom—and it does—then we ought to observe here that Jesus wanted His disciples to know there would be no immediate establishment of His rule on the earth. The master (Jesus) must first go on a journey (to heaven), and then, after an extended stay, He will return. While the disciples felt assured that this earthly phase of the Kingdom was just around the corner (Acts 1:6), Jesus sought to convey the idea that His return would not be at any second. Peter, for instance, was told by Jesus that he must die before the Kingdom would come (John 21:18, 19). Paul, too, knew that certain events must transpire before Jesus would return to earth (2 Thess. 2:1-12).

Settled Accounts. It is certain that we will each be rewarded or judged according to how we have used or misused our abilities. An awesome day of reckoning is coming, when faithful ones will be blessed and lazy ones will be cursed. We can be certain there is a direct relationship between the way we live today and the way God will treat us on that day. Each diligent laborer for Christ will be paid in full. And each delinquent laborer will be terribly shocked and punished.

I Will Put You in Charge of Many Things. Responsibility and service will not cease after Jesus' Second Coming. There will be much to do then also, and those who have faithfully fulfilled God's will in today's world will be correspondingly compensated in the world of tomorrow. The specific duties are not itemized, but it is reasonable to state (if you are a premillennialist) that Christians will assist Christ in His one-thousand-year earthly reign of all the nations (Rev. 2:26, 27; 19:11-20:6).

You Wicked, Lazy Servant. On the day of judgment it appears there may be excuses offered in defense of a fruitless life, but none of these will alter the final verdict one iota. Spiritual laziness cannot be excused. Burying one's talent in the sands of idleness, rather than investing it in the soils of eager service, will bring disaster. You cannot coast into God's Kingdom. You must be involved, otherwise you will be rejected (James 2:14-26).

Separating the Sheep and Goats (Matt. 25:31-46)

When Jesus Christ returns to earth, He will come as a roaring lion, not as a gentle lamb. The clock of patience will have run its course, and punishment for sin will take its place. It will be an awesome thing to be alive in the day when our Lord comes again.

Possibly the most outstanding details of this judgment scene are the following:

1. Everyone will be surprised at their judgment (vv. 37, 44). The subjects in this account are not informed Christians, but Gentiles who are unaware of their impending judgments.

2. The basis of the judgment is works (vv. 35, 36, 42, 43). Those who are alive at the time of the Second Coming of Christ and who enter the Millennium will do so because of their sensitivity to Christ's brothers. In fact, Jesus states that any good work performed to one of His disciples is equivalent to doing that work to Jesus himself (v. 40)!

Further, what is *not* said in the following Scripture text is as important as what has been directly revealed. Matthew's interest is not to present an exhaustive account of the events occupying the space known as the final days. Rather, he selects several key events and, for one reason or another, skips over the broader picture of last-day prophecy. Within the following pages a commentary on these topics is presented, and a few expanded notes are given to help clarify the broader context in which these events occur.

I. *The Judge and the Judgment (25:31-33)*

> **31"When the Son of Man comes in his glory, and all the angels with
> him, he will sit on his throne in heavenly glory. 32All the nations will be
> gathered before him, and he will separate the people one from another
> as a shepherd separates the sheep from the goats. 33He will put the sheep
> on his right and the goats on his left.**

The Son of Man. Jesus used this title in three different ways (see notes on Matt. 8:18-20). Here He alludes to a popular passage in the book of Daniel (7:13, 14) that His disciples would have immediately understood. In this reference, the Son of man is seen receiving absolute authority from "the Ancient of Days" (or God the Father). From the moment of this transfer of authority the Son of man is empowered to rule every nation on the face of the earth, without any threat of being overthrown in His authority.

Jesus is more than the divine son of God; He is also the human son of Mary. It is this human being, now glorified, who will sit on the throne and judge us. God the Father will not judge us. He has given this task to Mary's son—the son of earth, of pain, of temptations and vexing trials (John 5:22). No one is more qualified to know how to evaluate human ability and responsibility than this Son of man, Jesus.

He Will Sit on His Throne. At this moment Jesus is seated on a heavenly throne at the right hand of the Father (Acts 7:55; Heb. 1:3; 8:1). From this position He exercises a role of supreme authority in both heaven and earth. In fact, it can be said that Jesus is currently the King of all the earth (Matt. 28:18; 2 Tim. 5:15; Rev. 1:5). But it must also be acknowledged that the fullness of His rule has yet to be displayed. This absolute realization of Christ's Lordship over the inhabitants of the earth will become vividly manifested at the time of His Second Coming.

The location of this throne is not stated, though an indication is made in the phrase, "in heavenly glory." Unfortunately, this is a rare, but interpretative, translation of the original Greek text. There is little to support this idea. The phrase should read, "on His throne of glory," as stated earlier in the same verse. The word "heavenly" is not in the Greek manuscript. The text makes it clear that the glory is the Son's, and that the throne is on the earth (in Jerusalem—Zech. 14:16ff.).

The Nations Will Be Gathered Before Him. At the Second Advent of Christ there will be numerous judgments, possibly as many as seven:

1. Judgment upon unbelieving Jews (Ezek. 20:33-38; Zeph. 3:11; Mal. 3:1; 4:1)
2. Judgment upon residents of Edom (Isa. 34:8-15; 63:1-6)
3. Judgment upon armies holding Jerusalem (Joel 3; Zech. 8; 12:9)
4. Judgment upon armies at Armageddon (Rev. 16:16-21; 19:11-21)
5. Judgment upon Satan and his host (Rev. 20:1-3)
6. Judgment upon the Gentiles (Matt. 25:31-46)
7. Judgment upon the glorified saints (1 Cor. 3:11-15; 2 Cor. 5:10)

These Second Coming judgments are not simultaneous, but successive, following one another over a span of possibly seventy-five days (Dan. 12:12, 13). The particular judgment that captures Matthew's interest here is number six, the judgment of the Gentiles.

This judgment is one of the largest. Here each *living* Gentile (or non-Jew) will stand before the Lord Jesus Christ and be classified as either a goat (someone unworthy of the Kingdom of God) or a sheep (someone worthy of the Kingdom of God).

Two questions ought to be answered at this juncture:

1. How do we know only Gentiles will be included in this judgment? Because Matthew writes that only the "nations" will be gathered before Jesus in this particular judgment. The word translated "nations" is elsewhere rendered "Gentiles." It is another way of referring to all the non-Jewish people on the earth.

2. Why does Matthew focus upon the Gentiles? Actually, Matthew is neither playing favorites nor showing prejudice. If you look carefully at the Scriptures that precede this section, you will notice passages that emphasize the judgment of the Jews and Jerusalem (24:1-35), and (probably) professing Christians (25:1-30). In other words, Matthew focuses on three major parties who will be affected at the Second Coming—the unprepared Jews, the unprepared "Christians," and the unprepared Gentiles.

II. *The Judgment of the Sheep (25:34-40)*

34"Then the King will say to those on his right, 'Come, you who are
blessed by my Father; take your inheritance, the kingdom prepared for
you since the creation of the world. 35For I was hungry and you gave me
something to eat, I was thirsty and you gave me something to drink, I
was a stranger and you invited me in, 36I needed clothes and you clothed
me, I was sick and you looked after me, I was in prison and you came to
visit me.'

37"Then the righteous will answer him, 'Lord, when did we see you
hungry and feed you, or thirsty and give you something to drink?
38When did we see you a stranger and invite you in, or needing clothes
and clothe you? 39When did we see you sick or in prison and go to visit
you?'

40"The King will reply, 'I tell you the truth, whatever you did for one of
the least of these brothers of mine, you did for me.'

Interpreting the sense of this passage is difficult. A person's beliefs regarding the nature of the Millennium and the timing of the Rapture play inescapable roles in the understanding of events. The chart entitled, "Interpreting the Sheep and Goat Judgment" serves to clarify the general positions held by the major schools of thought on this subject.

The chronological aspects of last-day prophecy are extremely complicated. We may never fully agree on the details of this teaching. Still, we study, we remain open to more complete prophetic insights, and we grow accordingly.

When Christ returns to earth, His primary intent will be to set up His own Kingdom of universal righteousness and peace. Since the very beginning, God has desired for us to live together harmoniously, in a garden of bliss.

INTERPRETING THE SHEEP AND GOAT JUDGMENT

Various Positions	Identity of Judgment	Meaning of Sheep	Meaning of Goats	Meaning of Brothers
1. Amillennial.	This is the same judgment as Rev. 20:11-15.	All saved persons from the very beginning—living and dead.	All lost persons from the very beginning—living and dead.	Saints in general.
2. Postmillennial.	Same as above.	Same as above.	Same as above.	Same as above.
3. Premillennial; Pretribulational (Dispensational).	This is *not* the same judgment as Rev. 20: 11-15. It occurs 1,000 years before this passage .	Only living Gentiles who become saved during the seven year Tribulation; these are *not* Christians in any formal way.	Only living Gentiles who remain lost by the time of the Second Coming.	Ethnic Jews who are alive during the tribulation period.
4. Premillennial; Pretribulational (Nondispensational).	Same as # 3.	Same as # 3, except that they are considered to be Christians.	Same as # 3.	Either ethnic Jews or Christians who suffer greatly because of the Tribulation—thus, they are called "the least."
5. Premillennial; Posttribulational.	Same as # 3.	Only living Gentiles who become saved after the Second Coming and before the start of the Millennial Kingdom. They are saved through the witness of Jews who are converted at the Second Coming.	Only living Gentiles who remain lost by the time of this judgment—which is probably seventy-five days after the Second Coming.	Same as # 4.

This is still God's plan. And it will be fulfilled. But in order to create this new Kingdom, there must first be some judging of earth's peoples and powers. Initially this will include a judgment to be executed against the Jews. The essence of the judgment will be the examination of all living Jews by Christ to determine if their hearts are still hard toward Jesus, or if they have yielded their hearts to Him. Those who have not become Christians will be cast into hell at the time of the Second Coming. And those who become Christians will be privileged to enter the Kingdom (or the Millennium).

Paradox plays a significant role in Scripture. Initially, we find the judgment of the unbelieving Jews. But we also know from other Scriptures that this time marks the greatest period of Jewish salvation ever known (Rom. 11:1-36). Many will be saved, and many will be lost.

There are numerous Scriptures which teach that the Jews will be restored to their land (Isa. 11:11, 12; 35:8-10; Jer. 3:18, 19; Ezek. 36-38; Zeph. 3:9-13, 18-20; etc.). This regathering process will take place prior to the Second Coming and will have its climax with Israel's judgment at Christ's return (Ezek. 20:33-38; Zeph. 3:11). This judgment on Israel will purge all unbelievers from among them, so that only the saved will enter the promised land and the millennial period.

Zechariah writes of a day when God will pour out the Spirit of supplication and prayer upon all the house of David and the inhabitants of Jerusalem (12:10-14). It is in that day when the Lord will remove the sin of the Jews. All Jerusalem will be saved in that day (Zech. 12:10-13:1). When will all of this happen? At the precise moment of the Second Coming of Jesus Christ. In other words, there will be numerous conversions of Jews to Jesus in the hour of His Second Advent. At this time they will have their blindness removed, and they will be converted.

These converted Jews will then be sent into all the world to declare the glory of Jesus among the nations and to invite them to the marriage supper (Isa. 2:2-4; 66:18-21; Zech. 3:8-10; Rev. 19:9). Apparently, there will be people on the earth, even after Armageddon, who have not so much as heard of the Lord's fame nor seen His glory (Isa. 66:19). The result of this witnessing will be numerous conversions. In fact, it seems to be one of the most successful evangelistic campaigns ever conducted (Isa. 66:18-21; Zech. 2:11; Rom. 11:12). Nevertheless, some will not hearken to the call from the Jews, while others will give only an outward gesture (Matt. 22:1-14; Luke 14:15-24).

Finally, all the nations (that is, all the Gentiles) will be gathered before Christ. Some will be considered sheep (saved); others will be goats (lost). The sheep of this judgment probably become such through the witness of the Jews who are converted at the Lord's return. (One must remember that if the posttribulational view of the Rapture is correct—and this is highly likely—there will be no saved person on the earth when Jesus returns, for all the Christians are raptured. Therefore, the sheep of this judgment apparently were not sheep at the time of the Rapture, only days earlier. They will have become sheep (or will have been saved) some time shortly *after* Christ's return.)

III. *The Judgment of the Goats (25:41-46)*

41"Then he will say to those on his left, 'Depart from me, you who are

**cursed, into the eternal fire prepared for the devil and his angels. 42For
I was hungry and you gave me nothing to eat, I was thirsty and you gave
me nothing to drink, 43I was a stranger and you did not invite me in, I
needed clothes and you did not clothe me, I was sick and in prison and
you did not look after me.'**

**44"They also will answer, 'Lord, when did we see you hungry or
thirsty or a stranger or needing clothes or sick or in prison, and did not
help you?'**

**45"He will reply, 'I tell you the truth, whatever you did not do for one of
the least of these, you did not do for me.'**

**46"Then they will go away to eternal punishment, but the righteous to
eternal life."**

Apparently, the only ones who will face this particular judgment will be those who will be alive at the time of Christ's Second Coming. The rest, those in the grave who are spiritually lost, will be resurrected and judged 1,000 years later. The chief reasons for not seeing this judgment of the lost as that judgment of the lost mentioned in Revelation 20:11-15 may be itemized as follows:

1. This Scripture does not mention a one-thousand-year interval of Christ's reign prior to this judgment, as does the book of Revelation (20:1-9).
2. This Scripture does not mention any resurrection of the dead, as does the book of Revelation.
3. This Scripture does not mention any celestial setting for this judgment, as does the book of Revelation.
4. This Scripture does not mention any opening of books, as does the book of Revelation.

One final note remains regarding the specific judgment mentioned in Matthew's account. Observe the descriptions of the place where the guilty before Christ are sentenced:

1. It is a place that is eternal (vv. 41, 46).
2. It is a place of fire and punishment (vv. 41, 46).
3. It is a place especially designed for Satan and his angels—not humans—though those humans who chose to follow Satan will end up going there (v. 41).

Special Study: Hell

Jesus called hell a place of "eternal punishment" (Matt. 25:46), and "darkness" (Matt. 8:12). He also called it "a fiery furnace," where there would be "weeping and gnashing of teeth" (Matt. 13:42). Elsewhere Jesus called it an "eternal fire, prepared for the devil and his angels" (Matt. 25:41; *also see* Matt. 5:22, 29, 30; 8:12; 10:28;

11:22-24; 12:31, 32; 13:40-42; 18:6-9; 22:13; 23:15, 33; 25:30; 26:24; Mark 12:40; 16:16; Luke 12:47, 48; 16:19-31; John 3:16, 17; 5:28, 29; 8:21, 24; 15:6; 17:12). In brief, Jesus not only believed in the doctrine of hell, He actually taught on the subject more than anyone else in the Bible. He discussed it more frequently than the topic of heaven.

The following is a short discussion on the seven major biblical words that must be understood in order to grasp the doctrine of hell:

1. *Sheol*—occurs sixty-five times and is translated with these two words: "grave" and "death." The general meaning is "the place of the dead." It has reference to both the righteous dead (Ps. 16:10; 30:3; Isa. 38:10; etc.) and the wicked dead (Num. 16:33; Job 24:19). It is a place of conscious existence (Deut. 18:11; 1 Sam. 28:11-15; Isa. 14:9). It was regarded as being temporary, a place from which the righteous ones were to be resurrected (Job 14:13, 14; 19:25-27; Ps. 16:9-11; 17:15; 49:15; 73:24). *Sheol* is said to be located "beneath the waters [oceans]" (Job 26:5), and in the "depths of the earth" (Ps. 63:9).

2. *Hades*—occurs eleven times and is translated "depths" (Matt. 11:23; Luke 10:15), "Hades" (Matt. 16:18; Rev. 1:18; 6:8; 20:13, 14), "hell" (Luke 16:23) and "grave" (Acts 2:27, 31). *Hades* is the temporary or intermediate abode of only the unrighteous dead. It is located in "the depths" of the earth (Matt. 11:23; Luke 10:15), "in the heart of the earth" (Matt. 12:40).

3. *Tartarus*—occurs only once (2 Pet. 2:4) and is translated "hell." It is probably another word for the "abyss," since fallen angels reside there (cf. 1 Pet. 3:19; Jude 6, 7).

4. *Abyss*—occurs nine times and is translated "abyss" (Luke 8:31; Rev. 9:1, 2, 11; 11:7; 17:8; 20:1, 3), and "deep" (Rom. 10:7). With the possible exception of Rom. 10:7 this is a reference to the abode of imprisoned fallen demons. This pit will be opened during the tribulation period to release a host of these evil spirits.

5. *Gehenna*—occurs twelve times and is only translated "hell" (Matt. 5:22, 29, 30; 10:28; 18:9; 23:15, 33; Mark 9:43, 45, 47; Luke 12:5; James 3:6). *Gehenna* is the Greek form of the Hebrew *hinnom,* the Valley of Hinnom. This valley encompasses Jerusalem on its western side.

In the southern section of the Hinnom Valley the Jews worshiped Molech (2 Kings 23:10; 2 Chron. 28:3; 33:6; Jer. 7:31; 19:2-6). This god, who was worshiped by the Moabites and Ammonites, was a fire god of the Assyrians and Canaanites. Jewish tradition describes this deity as being hollow and made of brass. Its appearance was like a huge man with the face of a calf, with his hands stretched out. The worship of Molech consisted of casting little children into a fiery furnace. King Josiah attempted to put an end to this abominable worship by destroying the altars and making it a place where dead bodies were thrown and burned (2 Kings 23:13, 14). Later it became the refuse center for Jerusalem. Its furnace fires were always burning in order to consume what was dumped there.

Gehenna is identical in meaning with the "lake of fire" (Rev. 19:20; 20:10, 14, 15) and the "second death" (Rev. 20:14; 21:8).

The distinction between *hades* and *gehenna* is found in their duration. *Hades* is the temporal or intermediate state, while *gehenna* is eternal. All those in *hades* will be resurrected at the close of the Millennium, judged and cast into their everlasting abode, *gehenna* (Rev. 20:11-15).

Lastly, *gehenna* has been "prepared for the devil and his angels" (Matt. 25:41). That is, it was originally designed only to house the Satanic host but has been enlarged to include those humans who fail to choose the way God has made available to them.

6. *Abraham's side*—occurs twice (Luke 16:22, 23). The righteous dead, *before* Christ's resurrection, went to a separate abode in *sheol* bearing this name. Between the righteous dead and the unrighteous was a "great chasm" which could not be crossed.

7. *Paradise*—occurs three times (Luke 23:43; 2 Cor. 12:4; Rev. 2:7). Paul was "caught up to the third heaven . . . . up to Paradise." Paradise is obviously in the immediate presence of God. If "Abraham's side" is to be identified with paradise, then it can be said that at Christ's ascension the location of the righteous dead shifted from within the earth to God's presence (Eph. 4:8-10). All who die "in Christ" today go immediately to be with Christ in heaven or paradise (2 Cor. 5:8; Phil. 1:23).

Only one additional matter needs attention: the scriptural descriptions of hell. Below, in outline fashion, are seven basic aspects of this terrible site.

1. *Vision*—Luke 16:23
2. *Torments*—Luke 16:23
   a. *levels of hell*—Matt. 23:14; Luke 12:47, 48; Rom. 2:5, 6; 2 Cor. 11:15; 2 Tim. 4:14; Rev. 2:23; 20:11-15.
   b. *darkness:*
      1) darkness—Matt. 8:12; 22:13; 25:30; Jude 6
      2) chains of darkness—2 Pet. 2:4
      3) blackest darkness—2 Pet. 2:17; Jude 13
   c. *prison:*
      1) gates—Job 17:16; Isa. 38:10; Matt. 16:18
      2) chains—Jude 6; Rev. 20:1, 2
      3) keys—Rev. 1:18
   d. *smoke:*
      1) rises for ever—Rev. 14:9-11
      2) burning sulfur—Rev. 14:9-11; 19:20
   e. *fire:*
      1) fire—Luke 16:24

2) everlasting burning—Isa. 33:14
3) unquenchable—Isa. 66:24; Matt. 3:12
4) fiery furnace—Matt. 13:42
5) eternal fire—Matt. 18:8
6) lake of fire—Rev. 20:14-15

f. *no rest*—Rev. 14:9-11
g. *weeping and wailing*—Matt. 22:13
h. *gnashing of teeth*—Matt. 22:13
i. *place of wrath*—Deut. 32:22
j. *naked before God*—Job 26:6; Prov. 15:11; Ps. 139:8
k. *eternal/unending*—Dan. 12:2; 2 Thess. 1:8, 9; Rev. 20:10
l. *worm dies not*—Isa. 66:24; Mark 9:44-48

3. *Speech*—cf. Matt. 22:13
4. *Remembrance*—cf. Isa. 65:17; Luke 16:28
5. *Great chasm*—Luke 16:26
6. *Ineffective prayer*—Luke 16:27
7. *Sorrow for lost souls*—Luke 16:28

If you were to die in five minutes, where would you go—to heaven or to hell? Would you consider your death to be a personal blessing or a personal judgment? What would you want to do over? What would you wish to have erased from your past?

Regrettably, our minds have been so overexposed to sin in our world (through television, newspapers, radio, movies, magazines) that the threat of hell's fires seems unreal to many of us. We must guard ourselves from this threat of casual belief! The reality of eternal judgment must awaken each of us to the seriousness of how we live our daily lives. Jesus put it this way:

> If thy hand offend thee, cut it off: it is better for thee to enter into life maimed, than having two hands to go into hell, into the fire that never shall be quenched: where their worm dieth not. . . .
>
> If thy foot offend thee, cut if off: it is better for thee to enter half into life, than having two feet to be cast into hell, into the fire that never shall be quenched: Where their worm dieth not. . . .
>
> If thine eye offend thee, pluck it out: it is better for thee to enter into the kingdom of God with one eye, than having two eyes to be cast into hell fire: Where their worm dieth not and the fire is not quenched. (Mark 9:43-48, KJV)

NOTE: The preceding special study is excerpted from *Armageddon 198?* by Stephen D. Swihart (Haven Books, 1980).

THE DOCTRINE OF ETERNAL JUDGMENT

Analyzed	Visualized
1. *Sheol* (Hebrew: the place of the dead). Originally housed all the dead—now only used for unrighteous dead (Job 14:13, 14). 2. *Hades* (Greek: invisible, gloomy). Temporary dwelling of unrighteous dead (Luke 16:23). 3. *Abyss/Pit* (Greek: unfathomable pit). Temporary dwelling of fallen angels and unrighteous dead (Rom. 10:7; Rev. 20:1). 4. *Tartarus* (Greek: the place of deepest judgment). Temporary dwelling of fallen angels (Pet. 2:4). 5. *Gehenna* (Greek: Valley of Hinnom, southeast of Jerusalem, used as fiery refuse center). Permanent dwelling place for fallen angels and unrighteous dead (Rev. 20:11-15).	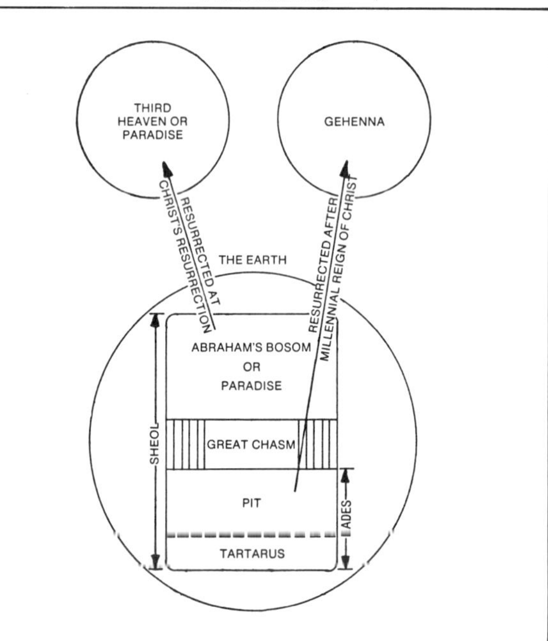

The Plot Against Jesus (Matt. 26:1-5)

(cf. Mark 14:1, 2 and Luke 22:1, 2)

In the preceding two chapters of Matthew's Gospel, Jesus announced His sovereign rule as King and Judge. The spirit of these prophecies is exhilarating. Hope fills the atmosphere with a refreshing anticipation of these long-sought promises. But how swiftly the tempo shifts here to His cruel death. Before He could wear the crown of glory, He first had to wear the crown of thorns. Before exaltation, humiliation must come. And Jesus had to die before He could truly conquer every enemy that opposes God's perfect will.

**26 When Jesus had finished saying all these things, he said to his
disciples, [2]"As you know, the Passover is two days away—and the
Son of Man will be handed over to be crucified."**
**[3]Then the chief priests and the elders of the people assembled in the
palace of the high priest, whose name was Caiaphas, [4]and they plotted
to arrest Jesus in some sly way and kill him. [5]"But not during the Feast,"
they said, "or there may be a riot among the people."**

Passover (also called the Feast of Unleavened Bread) traces its origin to the days of Moses, when God's children were enslaved in Egypt (Exod. 12). God instructed Moses to have every family kill an unblemished lamb. They were then to sprinkle the blood from the lambs upon the two doorposts and on the lintels of their homes. Following this, they were told to eat these lambs with unleavened bread and bitter herbs. This was to be no leisurely meal. Instead, it was to be eaten with haste, being fully prepared to leave their dwellings at a moment's notice.

In the night when the first Passover meal was consumed, there was much weeping in Egypt, for the Lord had sent a destroyer through the land to kill the first-born children of the houses where there was no blood on the doorposts or on the lintels. Those families who had applied the blood, however, were protected from this plague of death.

With a cry of grief ringing in their ears, the Pharaoh finally released Israel so the Israelites might be able to return to their homeland and worship their God. It was an unforgettable night. The melody of victory was soon hummed throughout the entire Jewish camp. And with great haste they shuttled themselves out of the land of bondage.

This event occurred on the fourteenth day of the first month of the Jewish calendar, Nisan (which corresponds to our calendars as being the period between March 15 and April 15). From that day until our own, the Passover is still remembered and celebrated by the Jews. Its fuller significance, however, can only be appreciated through an understanding of the life and death of Jesus Christ, God's Passover Lamb. In this first Passover is a prepicturing of Jesus' death on Calvary for the sins of the entire world.

Jesus shed His blood so we might personally apply its atoning virtues to the doorways of our own lives. Christ is the Passover, says Paul (1 Cor. 5:7). We do not need to be annihilated (spiritually or physically) by the destroying angel (that is, by Satan). We can be rescued (or saved) by the blood of God's Lamb, Jesus.

The chief priests should have known what God's Word teaches about this. But their hearts were cold and unteachable. They were not looking for God's Passover Lamb; they were only looking for a way to kill this menace who continually disrupted their hypocritical religious system. They were shrewd. Scheming and plotting, they were determined to kill Jesus, while maintaining a popular public image.

Jesus Is Anointed (Matt. 26:6-13)

(cf. Mark 14:3-9 and John 12:1-8)

The proper perspective is an integral part of our understanding of Scripture. Seeing things from a poor vantage point will always result in distorted and incomplete knowledge. We must see the whole picture related to a concept before we are enabled to evaluate it properly.

The disciples were often quick to misinterpret a situation, because they frequently assessed matters from only a temporal or human perspective. They failed to see things from Jesus' point of view. Here is an instance of such a poor perspective. A fine woman was about to honor her Lord, Jesus, but the disciples only envisioned a waste of money in her actions.

We must learn to see everything from every possible angle before we pass judgment. A quick response from a distorted perspective will always require a later alteration. Let us, therefore, be clear about a matter before we draw hasty conclusions.

I. *The Anointing (26:6, 7)*

6While Jesus was in Bethany in the home of a man known as Simon the Leper, 7a woman came to him with an alabaster jar of very expensive perfume, which she poured on his head as he was reclining at the table.

Bethany. This was a small village, located about two miles southeast of Jerusalem. It probably served as Jesus' main residence while He ministered in Judea (Matt. 21:17; Mark 11:11). This village was the home of Mary, Martha, Lazarus and Simon the Leper (John 11:1ff.; Matt. 26:6, 7). It is also from this site that Jesus ascended into heaven (Luke 24:50, 51). The town still exists today, and has a population of less than a thousand persons.

Simon the Leper. Simon was, in all probability, a healed leper. Jesus could always find a place in His heart for those who suffered from physical ailments. And those whom Jesus touched were always eager to open their homes to Him in return. Spiritual experiences seem to possess a way of being mutually rewarding.

A Woman with an Alabaster Jar. A woman named Mary was in Simon's house (John 12:2-8). But because seven women named Mary are mentioned in the Gospels, it is impossible to know which one is in view here. It doesn't really matter. What counts is this woman's devotion to Christ. There were no less than sixteen people invited to this house for supper, but only this one lady was spotlighted.

We must never consider our lot in life as being insignificant. This lady, for instance, has been mentioned many thousands of times throughout the entire world because of her love of Christ. Anointing Him with costly perfume (probably worth a whole year's pay!) was her way of displaying her devotion. And for this action Jesus applauded her (and rebuked those who thought she was going a bit overboard in her manner of showing affection).

II. *The Argument (26:8, 9)*

> **8When the disciples saw this, they were indignant. "Why this waste?" they asked. 9"This perfume could have been sold at a high price and the money given to the poor."**

The chief critic in this episode is Judas Iscariot (John 12:6). And from John's account we also learn he was not really interested in poor people at all, but in how he might profit from such a tempting sum of money. Judas was the treasurer for the disciple band. He was also a thief! His fingers enjoyed the jingle of money, and Mary's cash would have suited his cravings a great deal.

III. *The Answer (26:10-13)*

> **10Aware of this, Jesus said to them, "Why are you bothering this woman? She has done a beautiful thing to me. 11The poor you will always have with you, but you will not always have me. 12When she poured this perfume on my body, she did it to prepare me for burial. 13I tell you the truth, wherever this gospel is preached throughout the world, what she has done will also be told, in memory of her."**

How quickly we might be tempted to criticize any substantial outlay of money for a single moment's pleasure—even if that joy is spiritual in nature. Mary's action seemed to be too extravagant to be practical; at least this is what the disciples thought. But Jesus thought otherwise.

It may be that Mary was the only one present who truly believed Jesus when He said He would be killed in a short while. Realizing this, she may have anointed Him with her treasured perfume in preparation for His death. In any case, Jesus thought her motives and actions were quite fitting for the occasion. There would be other times to care for the poor; now it was time to prepare Jesus' body for burial.

Judas Agrees to Betray Jesus (Matt. 26:14-16)

(cf. Mark 14:10, 11 and Luke 22:3-6)

Everyone has his price, or so they say. Judas certainly had his price—thirty pieces of silver (equivalent to five weeks' pay, or more, depending on the particular silver coins that were offered him).

[14]Then one of the Twelve—the one called Judas Iscariot—went to the chief priests [15]and asked, "What are you willing to give me if I hand him over to you?" So they counted out for him thirty silver coins. [16]From then on Judas watched for an opportunity to hand him over.

What made Judas betray Jesus? As treasurer of the disciple party, was he hungry for money? Yes, the Scriptures even call him a thief, being without compassion (John 12:2-6; 13:29). What about bitterness? Did he resent being rebuked by Jesus? Yes, immediately after being told to leave Mary alone in her anointing of Jesus, he went to the chief priests to offer his services in trapping Jesus (Matt. 26:6-16).

Was Judas ever really saved? Was he a true disciple of Christ? Probably not, for the scriptural record states that Judas was influenced by the devil (John 13:2), indwelt by the devil (John 13:27) and even called a devil (John 6:70). Nevertheless, none of the other disciples were apparently able to detect any demerits in this disciple until after Jesus' betrayal (Matt. 26:20-22).

There are some who see in Judas a man who was predestined to betray Christ. It is supposed that he had no other choice, no alternative, except to turn Jesus over to the authorities. It was "in the cards," so to speak, for him to do this. But this kind of reasoning makes God the ultimate author of evil. Judas was not coerced or persuaded by God to harm Jesus Christ. It is God's will that none should perish, including Judas (2 Pet. 3:9). Jesus' atonement was extended to him as it is to all other persons (2 Pet. 2:1; 1 John 2:1, 2). Judas sinned because he chose to do so on his own accord (though, certainly, he did follow the wishes of Satan in doing so).

The Last Supper (Matt. 26:17-30)

(cf. Mark 14:12-26; Luke 22:7-23 and John 13:1-30)

The day was Thursday. It must have been a sober day. The morning was spent in preparation for the Last Supper. Now the time had arrived for their final meal together. It would be the most informative, inspiring, penetrating and mysterious meal they would ever eat.

I. *Preparations (26:17-19)*

17On the first day of the Feast of Unleavened Bread, the disciples came to Jesus and asked, "Where do you want us to make preparations for you to eat the Passover?"
18He replied, "Go into the city to a certain man and tell him, 'The Teacher says: My appointed time is near. I am going to celebrate the Passover with my disciples at your house.' " 19So the disciples did as Jesus had directed them and prepared the Passover.

Feast of Unleavened Bread/Passover. The Passover was the first and greatest holiday in the Jewish calendar (occurring on the fourteenth day of the first month in their year).

First, there was the giving of a perfect lamb to the priest in the Temple. They would kill the lamb, catch its blood in a gold or silver bowl, and then pass the blood along a row of priests until it came to the priest nearest the altar. He would then sprinkle the blood at the altar's base.

Second, the lamb would be flayed and cooked.

Third, as the lamb was being roasted, those preparing the Passover meal would purchase unleavened bread, bitter herbs, wine and sauce. Once all these matters were finished, they would take the lamb, along with all the other ingredients, to the room they had selected for eating this meal.

The Passover meal was eaten leisurely, while the Jews reclined on cushions of straw, hay, leaves or wool (though the wealthy probably lined their cushions with feathers). These cushions were placed around a square table in the center of the room. The participants in the meal would then rest their weight on their left arms and elbows, allowing their right arms freedom to reach the food. When they grew tired of this position they could easily lie on their chests and continue with the feast.

Go to the City. It was the custom in Jerusalem during the Passover season for everyone to open his home to the visitors who would come to celebrate this feast from outside Israel. If any person, family or group of people asked for a room, they were to be given space for this celebration, without charge. The disciples were instructed to request a room in the home of a man whom they would see carrying water (probably in a jar on his head) to his home (Mark 14:13).

There is a certain degree of mystery in this command. First, it was quite uncommon to see a man carrying water to his home—this was a woman's responsibility. Second, how would Jesus know this person's home would be large enough to accommodate thirteen guests? Perhaps Jesus knew this man and his custom of fetching water for his household. Or, it is just as likely that God supernaturally revealed this particular man and his home to Jesus. Regardless of the exact source for this selecting process, it is clear that Jesus had the matter well in hand.

My Appointed Time Is Near. The death of anyone is no accident. The number of our days rests in the hands of God, who orders them according to His infinite wisdom and sovereignty (Deut. 32:39; cf. Rev. 1:18). God may prolong our lives because of obedience (Exod. 20:12) or prayer (Isa. 38:1-21); or He may shorten our lives because of our sinfulness (Gen. 9:6; 1 Cor. 11:27-32). Whatever the case, the ultimate time for our departure is in the control of the Lord of heaven and earth. Jesus knew this truth. He would not attempt to resist God's decision about the hour of His appointed death. The timing was fixed in heaven. God had determined it, and it would not be altered.

II. *Proclamations (26:20-25)*

20When evening came, Jesus was reclining at the table with the
Twelve. 21And while they were eating, he said, "I tell you the truth, one
of you will betray me."
22They were very sad and began to say to him one after the other,
"Surely not I, Lord?"
23Jesus replied, "The one who has dipped his hand into the bowl with
me will betray me. 24The Son of Man will go just as it is written about
him. But woe to that man who betrays the Son of Man! It would be
better for him if he had not been born."
25Then Judas, the one who would betray him, said, "Surely not I,
Rabbi?" Jesus answered, "Yes, it is you."[a]

One of You Will Betray Me. In the midst of the meal, Jesus made the most shocking announcement of His ministry—one of His very own disciples would betray Him!

a 25 Or *"You yourself have said it"*

Quickly, the disciples, including Judas, defended themselves. They could hardly believe such a statement would ever be made. But Jesus knew the hearts of each disciple, as well as the prophecies requiring His death by a traitor. So, He stated candidly that such an event would happen.

The One Who Has Dipped His Hand into the Bowl with Me. Here is the deepest agony of the betrayal. It will come at the hands of one who had eaten with Jesus, the host of the disciples at the Passover meal. In the Middle East there was a strong tradition that you never harm the one who hosts you. This was an unthinkable offense. Still, in Jesus' inner circle there was one who would abandon even the most reasonable courtesy and betray Him.

Just As It Is Written. Jesus was bold in His statements because He knew the Scriptures must be fulfilled. Notice the following prophecies that speak directly of Jesus' death:

Gen. 3:15	Satan will strike Jesus' heel.
Ps. 22:1	Jesus will be forsaken by God.
Ps. 22:6-8	Men will mock Him in His final hours.
Ps. 22:11, 14-18	He will be crucified, experience terrible agony and see men gamble for His garments.
Ps. 22:19	God will hear His prayer on the cross.
Ps. 34:20	His bones will not be broken.
Ps. 35:11	He will be falsely accused.
Ps. 41:9	He will be betrayed by a friend.
Isa. 50:6	He will be spit upon.
Isa. 52:13-15	He will be horribly disfigured by men.
Isa. 53:3	He will be despised and rejected by men.
Isa. 53:5-11	He will carry our sins in his body.
Isa. 53:9	He will die with the wicked and be buried with the rich.
Dan. 9:26, 27	He will be cut off (killed) in the midst of Israel's seventy weeks.
Hos. 6:2	On the third day He will be raised from the dead.
Zech. 11:12	He will be betrayed for thirty pieces of silver.
Zech. 12:10	He will be pierced.

Better for Him If He Had Not Been Born. What is true for Judas here is equally true for everyone who rejects Jesus. The end of life for those who fail to surrender themselves to Jesus' love is a pitiful destiny—eternal hell (Rev. 20:11-15). To live without Christ means incomplete fulfillment; but to die without Christ means utter loss. Hell, in short, is total separation from Jesus and the glories that accompany His presence. In hell there is only the dark side of existence—pain, sorrow and hopelessness. It is better, indeed, to have never lived, than to live and die without giving Jesus a proper place in your priorities.

III. *Presentations (26:26-30)*

26While they were eating, Jesus took bread, gave thanks and broke it,
and gave it to his disciples, saying, "Take and eat; this is my body."
27Then he took the cup, gave thanks and offered it to them, saying,
"Drink from it, all of you. 28This is my blood of the[a] covenant, which is
poured out for many for the forgiveness of sins. 29I tell you, I will not
drink of this fruit of the vine from now on until that day when I drink it
anew with you in my Father's kingdom."
30When they had sung a hymn, they went out to the Mount of Olives.

Jesus now inaugurates a new covenant, a new Passover. It must have been quite mysterious to hear Jesus talk of His body and blood as the elements necessary for the forgiveness of sins. Then to eat the bread and to drink the cup must have only added to the already tense atmosphere. No doubt the disciples had many questions zooming through their minds, but these would all be answered in proper time.

Take and Eat; This Is My Body. What is the significance of Jesus' body, as displayed in the bread? Is there a special reason for two elements being presented to the disciples, rather than only one? Perhaps so. The body of Jesus is never, in itself, said to atone for our sins—this is the work of Jesus' blood. But how can Jesus sacrifice His blood if He does not first surrender His body to Calvary's cross? The body of Jesus, which is to be eaten, then, may be intended to represent and transmit His selfless spirit, His brokenness before God, His utter willingness to do God's will by representing us on the hill of judgment. No one could take Jesus' life by force; instead, He laid it down by His own selfless will (John 10:17, 18).

Drink, This Is My Blood. There is only one cure for sin—the blood of Jesus. "Without the shedding of blood there is no forgiveness" (Heb. 9:22). Until Jesus had shed His blood in our place, we were without any hope in the world (Eph. 2:1-3, 12). Here is a three-point list of the results that are produced by Christ's blood atonement: (1) God-ward—it cancels our sins (Rom. 3:25; 5:9; Eph. 1:7; Col. 1:14); (2) self-ward—it cleanses our consciences (Heb. 10:22); and (3) Satan-ward—it conquers our chief enemy (Rev. 12:9-11).

These two elements—the body and the blood—are the Christian's food and drink. There is no more hungering or thirsting from either the inner man or the outer man for the one who truly draws his sustenance from Christ.

---

a 28 Some manuscripts *the new*

Jesus Predicts the Fall of the Disciples (Matt. 26:31-35)

(cf. Mark 14:26-31 and Luke 22:31-34)

How well our Lord knows our many weaknesses, including those we have not manifested yet. We often think of ourselves as being adequate for the tasks that are set before us, but how little do we recognize our limitations and needs for God's grace in the simplest act. There would be no church at all today if it were not for the operation of the Holy Spirit to keep us on track. Like the disciples, we confidently announce our faithfulness; yet our record shows moments of hesitation and even refusal to comply with God's total wishes. Oh, the matchless patience of God and Christ, who know our shortcomings and yet still love us!

I. *Jesus Addresses the Disciples (26:31, 32)*

31Then Jesus told them, "This very night you will all fall away on account of me, for it is written:

" 'I will strike the shepherd,
and the sheep of the flock will be scattered.'[a]

32But after I have risen, I will go ahead of you into Galilee."

You Will All Fall Away. In the night when the disciples boasted they would never be unfaithful to Christ, they did, nevertheless, fall far short of their self-confident declarations. Notice, this is not the testimony of spiritually lost men, but of saved persons, genuine disciples. And what is true of them is sometimes true of us, too. Our expectations are occasionally greater than our abilities, and we fall down for a moment. This has happened to the most sincere Christians; none are excluded (2 Cor. 1:8-11). We are not perfect, and we might wisely admit it—both to ourselves and to Christ.

For It Is Written. This quotation from Zech. 13:7 provides two insights regarding Jesus' soon-to-occur ordeal in Jerusalem. In the first place, we see who it is that will strike the shepherd. It is God the Father! While it is our sins that killed Jesus, it is still God's initiative that carries the plan along, from start to finish. He is the ultimate author of Jesus' crucifixion (Acts 4:28; Eph. 1:1-11). In the second place we see God's all-embracing knowledge of future events. He can foresee the dispersing of the

a 31 Zech. 13:7

shepherd's sheep (that is, the scattering of Jesus' disciples). Before Him lies all of time; in a single glance He can envision all of the past, the present and the future (Ps. 139:15, 16; Isa. 41:26; 42:9; 44:7; 46:10).

I Will Go Ahead of You. God's prophecies will be fulfilled, regardless of how much we set our wills against them. The Word of God is always right. None of the disciples thought they would ever reduce their loyalty to Jesus. But sometimes we do fail our Shepherd. Still, he informs us that he will go ahead of us and meet us farther down the road—just as He met the disciples in Galilee after His resurrection. Jesus does not reject us for our momentary weaknesses. We can be eternally thankful for this grand fact.

II. *Jesus Addresses Peter (26:33-35)*

33Peter replied, "Even if all fall away on account of you, I never will."
34"I tell you the truth," Jesus answered, "this very night, before the rooster crows, you will disown me three times."
35But Peter declared, "Even if I have to die with you, I will never disown you." And all the other disciples said the same.

When we think we are at our highest tide, we are sometimes about to walk into our lowest ebb. We must not place any confidence in our flesh (that is, in our own natural abilities). Many persons have found themselves to be their own very worst enemies (2 Cor. 12:1-10; Phil. 3:4-7). Our pride, self-confidence and past victories have each paved a subtle path that we occasionally walk unknowingly upon. These are weak materials to rely upon for support. We cannot trust ourselves or count on circumstances or rely exclusively upon others. Rather, we must put all our faith in the changeless Lord Jesus Christ. We must believe Him and trust Him—moment by moment. There is no other way we can faithfully serve Him. It is not our brilliance or zeal that expands God's Kingdom, but Christ's power working through humble and obedient vessels with pliable spirits.

Gethsemane (Matt. 26:36-46)

(cf. Mark 14:32-42 and Luke 22:39-46)

There is a crucial lesson that God seeks to teach us. It is profound, and far too few will learn it. Still, our heavenly Father attempts to show each of us this principle and to make it plain. It is a truth about the nature of His dealings with us. And for those who learn it, it is a fountain of unending joy and power.

Stated simply, the lesson is this: God delights in using those who are broken. Spiritual life does not flow from a strong, self-willed determination to serve Christ. Often we are exhorted to rededicate ourselves, but how fleshly and unrewarding this self-exerted attempt to do better can be. Our real need may not be rededication, but death to self-will. Death to self-ambition, self-pity, self-righteousness, self-justification and every other trait in the carnal hierarchy of the self-life.

And how does God bring us to this place of self-denial and death? What are His tools? The answer is (among other things) suffering and trials. Jesus, for instance, "learned obedience from what he suffered" (Heb. 5:8). In the account before us we see one of Jesus' worst trials. It is also one of the highest points in His ministry to the world—to you and to me, personally.

I. *The First Prayer Cycle (26:36-41)*

**36Then Jesus went with his disciples to a place called Gethsemane, and
he said to them, "Sit here while I go over there and pray." 37He took
Peter and the two sons of Zebedee along with him, and he began to be
sorrowful and troubled. 38Then he said to them, "My soul is overwhelmed
with sorrow to the point of death. Stay here and keep watch with me."**

**39Going a little farther, he fell with his face to the ground and prayed,
"My Father, if it is possible, may this cup be taken from me. Yet not as I
will, but as you will."**

**40Then he returned to his disciples and found them sleeping. "Could
you men not keep watch with me for one hour?" he asked Peter.
41"Watch and pray so that you will not fall into temptation. The spirit is
willing, but the body is weak."**

A Place Called Gethsemane. Interestingly, the word "Gethsemane" means "oil press." It was a small garden (or grove) of olive trees, beyond the Kidron Valley, near the Mount of Olives, where Jesus retired to pray. Josephus (a first-century historian) states that General Titus had these trees cut down in his A.D. 70 campaign against Jerusalem. Today, however, olive trees adorn this site, along with the Church of St. Mary, in memorial of the time Jesus spent there.

I Go and Pray. Jesus took prayer seriously. It was not merely "devotions." Jesus needed help, divine help. And prayer was the only way He could get it, so He prayed. God is delighted when we pray. But He is much more pleased when we are prayerful persons. Jesus was a prayerful man. But even being full of prayer is no guarantee against tests; in fact, it practically assures they will come, because God knows He can use the prayerful person to advance the cause of His Kingdom and to overthrow the powers of Satan.

He Took Peter and the Two Sons of Zebedee (James and John). Jesus asked his nearest disciples to join Him in prayer. Severe trials are not meant to be endured alone. We must ask our friends to unite with us in the struggle of prayer. There is no shame in requesting this prayer support. In fact, the wise person knows the importance of another's prayers, and he requests them (Eph. 6:19).

My Soul Is Overwhelmed. Jesus hurt deeply. In fact, the intensity of the ordeal was so extreme that He felt He could have died right there in the garden. A false notion is sometimes taught that the Christian life is designed to be only mountaintop living, with an unbroken chain of sheer joy and victory. This is a deception, a mere half-truth (cf. Eccles. 3). Jesus would have found no comfort at all in such a doctrine at this juncture in His life. His trial was real, and so was His smarting soul. And there is no disgrace or spiritual shallowness in any part of this episode. Indeed not. We must recognize that suffering *is* sometimes a part of God's will for us (1 Pet. 4:19; Ps. 119:67, 71). Jesus knew this, and we must know it, too.

If It Is Possible, Yet Not As I Will. The cup of martyrdom is not easy to drink from, not even for Jesus (this is especially true for the sinless Jesus). In fact, Jesus asked God to remove it from Him. This is not a note of weakness, but reveals, in the fullest measure, the humanity of Christ. His feelings toward suffering were no different from our own. He sought to escape the crushing pain of the moments that loomed before Him. This is natural—and it is a sinless petition, too.

On the reverse side of this very same petition, Jesus' deep inner man desired conformity to God's will. This is the key to Jesus' praying. He never bargained with God. He always wanted to obey His Father. So, He would bear the sorrow, the shame, the torture and the distress. He would be willing to do whatever God required of Him.

Here is the model prayer. It is searching, personal, penetrating, postulating and submissive. It is the kind of prayer we each ought to remember, copy and teach others to follow.

Watch and Pray. The three disciples were mildly chided by Jesus for falling asleep. He hoped they would have joined Him in His restless prayer, but their tiredness was greater than the critical circumstances they failed to perceive around them. So, He instructed them to watch (that is, to stay awake) and to pray. Jesus knew what was about to happen. The temptations that were about to befall the disciples would be most difficult; they needed to prepare for these moments ahead with prayer.

There is a very practical note in this address for each of us. Temptations are all about us. But we can overcome them by prayer. In fact, we can build up a resistance or a spiritual defense system in advance of the temptation itself by simply praying. Through the powerful channel of prayer we can shield ourselves from would-be destructive temptations.

II. *The Second Prayer Cycle (26:42, 43)*

> **42He went away a second time and prayed, "My Father, if it is not possible for this cup to be taken away unless I drink it, may your will be done."**
> **43When he came back, he again found them sleeping, because their eyes were heavy.**

Jesus learned another painful lesson in the garden. He discovered the grief of being let down by His best friends during His most vexing test. Their hearts were sincere, but their bodies were weak. Jesus now knew that He must resolve this trial by himself. No one could bear it for Him (not even *with* Him!).

III. *The Third Prayer Cycle (26:44-46)*

> **44So he left them and went away once more and prayed the third time, saying the same thing.**
> **45Then he returned to the disciples and said to them, "Are you still sleeping and resting? Look, the hour is near, and the Son of Man is betrayed into the hands of sinners. 46Rise, let us go! Here comes my betrayer!"**

Jesus found that doing God's will is sometimes a difficult matter. Three times Jesus prayed the same prayer. He wanted to be absolutely sure of God's will. There is no shame, in the midst of a serious trial, in talking to God about the same matter on several occasions. Those who teach that there is no need for more than one prayer about anything have yet to visit the Garden of Gethsemane in their experience. Some trials require more than a bold confession of faith; they require a determined and sustained wrestling with God, like Jacob with the angel (Gen. 32:22-32). This was Jesus' experience, and it may well be ours too.

Jesus Is Arrested (Matt. 26:47-56)

(cf. Mark 14:43-50; Luke 22:47-53 and John 18:1-11)

We can withstand assaults from our enemies, but a cruel attack from a supposed friend is exceedingly hard to handle. Still, it happens, and sometimes it happens to Christians. It even happened to Jesus.

I. *The Arrangement of Judas (26:47-49)*

**[47]While he was still speaking, Judas, one of the Twelve, arrived. With
him was a large crowd armed with swords and clubs, sent from the
chief priests and the elders of the people. [48]Now the betrayer had arranged a signal with them: "The one I kiss is the man; arrest him."
[49]Going at once to Jesus, Judas said, "Greetings, Rabbi!" and kissed him.**

Judas was a disciple. He followed Jesus. He preached, exorcised demons and healed the sick. He looked like the rest. No one suspected Judas of treachery. Not Judas. He was one of the chosen twelve who was closest to Jesus. Yet here, in the small circle of Jesus' most intimate followers, was a cold-hearted traitor.

What had happened? Where did Judas go wrong? How could a person in such a high spiritual position go astray?

The answer from the Scriptures is candid. Judas loved money (Matt. 26:14-16). But we must also recognize that Judas loved Jesus, too. There is no evidence to the contrary. Now comes the practical lesson in this sad episode. You cannot be like Judas, loving both Jesus and money, and expect to be a true disciple. Christ requires an either-or loyalty at this point (Matt. 6:24). It isn't difficult for each of us to imagine that we can somehow love both money (or the things money secures) and at the same time love Jesus, and be fair to each interest. Judas thought so, and he died a mistaken man. Many are attempting to copy Judas today, and they, too, regardless of their outward appearances, are on the dreadful road of betrayal and spiritual death!

II. *The Action of Peter (26:50, 51)*

**[50]Jesus replied, "Friend, do what you came for."[a]
Then the men stepped forward, seized Jesus and arrested him. [51]With**

a 50 Or *"Friend, why have you come?"*

that, one of Jesus' companions reached for his sword, drew it out and struck the servant of the high priest, cutting off his ear.

As might be expected, it was Peter who hastily pulled out his sword and took a swipe at a man's head, managing to remove only an ear (John 18:10)! We might commend Peter for his zeal, but we must certainly condemn him for his impulsive and carnal action. God requires far more than fervent spirits in our service for Him. We must also discern His will and walk in it, and these were two steps Peter completely overlooked.

III. *The Addresses of Jesus (26:52-56)*

52"Put your sword back in its place," Jesus said to him, "for all who
draw the sword will die by the sword. 53Do you think I cannot call on my
Father, and he will at once put at my disposal more than twelve legions
of angels? 54But how then would the Scriptures be fulfilled that say it
must happen in this way?"
55At that time Jesus said to the crowd, "Am I leading a rebellion, that
you have come out with swords and clubs to capture me? Every day I sat
in the temple courts teaching, and you did not arrest me. 56But this has
all taken place that the writings of the prophets might be fulfilled."
Then all the disciples deserted him and fled.

First, Jesus addressed His disciples. He informed them that the tools of force will not accomplish God's will. If this were the case, then He would have called upon 72,000 angels to achieve this goal (a legion was composed of 6,000 members; twelve legions would have been 72,000). God's plan was the cross, not the sword. He had stated that it would be this way in the prophecies regarding the coming Christ (Dan. 9:26, 27), and that is the way it would be.

The reference to "all who draw the sword will die by the sword" has been understood in two different ways. One view is that all acts of war (symbolized here in the sword) are to be condemned. The most dramatic implications of this view are seen in pacifist bodies who refuse to use any weapons in a time of military conflict (these persons are often called conscientious objectors). Various Christian denominations use passages like this one to support their nonaggressive positions.

The other view states that this passage only has reference to the immediate context, in which case such an action was neither necessary (for Jesus could have called upon the angels for assistance) nor prophetically appropriate (for the prophets predicted Jesus' crucifixion). According to this second view, there are times when the use of the sword *is* justified (Gen. 9:6; Rom. 13:4).

Second, Jesus addresses His arresters. He asked them to give the cause for their sudden interest in His arrest, and why they felt it was necessary to come adorned with swords and clubs. Jesus knew the answer to His own inquiry: prophecy. This must occur as the prophets revealed it would. Jesus must exhaust the fulfillment of their predictions—and so He would, indeed.

Jesus Stands Before the Sanhedrin (Matt. 26:57-68)

(cf. Mark 14:53-65)

William Boetcker warns us of seven mischievous "misses" who are responsible for most of our troubles: Miss Information, Miss Quotation, Miss Representation, Miss Interpretation, Miss Construction, Miss Conception and Miss Understanding. In the story before us we see all of these "misses," and more.

I. *The Assembly (26:57, 58)*

[57]Those who had arrested Jesus took him to Caiaphas, the high priest, where the teachers of the law and the elders had assembled. [58]But Peter followed him at a distance, right up to the courtyard of the high priest. He entered and sat down with the guards to see the outcome.

The chronology offered here of Jesus' trials is incomplete. Therefore, it is necessary that the accounts from the other Gospels be joined together in order to present a unified, whole picture. Once this is achieved, it becomes evident that Jesus was actually tried on six different occasions. Notice the sequence below and in the chart entitled "The Six Trials of Christ."

A. *Three Trials by the Jewish Church*
1. Before Annas (John 18:12-24)
2. Before Caiaphas (Matt. 26:57-68)
3. Before chief priests and elders (Matt. 27:1, 2)

B. *Three Trials by the Roman State*
1. Before Pontius Pilate (Matt. 27:11-14)
2. Before Herod (Luke 23:8-12)
3. Before Pontius Pilate (Matt. 27:15-26)

THE SIX TRIALS OF CHRIST

1. *Before Annas,* the father-in law of the high priest, Caiaphas, immediately after His arrest—John 18:12-24. This trial was illegal, held contrary to Jewish law; no indictment was made; it was conducted at night; no witnesses were presented; and no counsel was provided for the defendant.
2. *Before Caiaphas,* the high priest immediately after leaving Annas—Matt. 26:57-68; Mark 14:53-65. Two false witnesses were raised, but their testimonies contradicted one another. In answering the question of whether He was the Christ, Jesus affirmed it.
3. *Before chief priests and elders,* in the morning—Matt. 27:1, 2; Mark 15:1; Luke 22:66-71. Here, Jesus admits to His deity, resulting in His being convicted and referred to Pilate. This session was probably conducted in order to conform to the daylight ruling in Jewish law.
4. *Before Pontius Pilate*—Matt. 27:11-14; Mark 15:1-5; Luke 23:1-7; John 18:28-38. Accusations are made here of Christ's disloyalty to Rome, claiming to be King of the Jews. Pilate refers the case to Herod.
5. *Before Herod*—Luke 23:8-12. Jesus is silent in this trial. Herod had cut off God's voice through beheading John the Baptist; Jesus was to continue this silence. Here, the soldiers mock Christ.
6. *Before Pontius Pilate*—Matt. 27:15-26; Mark 15:6-15; Luke 23:13-25; John 18:39-19:16. Pilate offers to scourge and release Jesus, but the crowd demands His crucifixion, and Pilate succumbs to their cry.

Taken from *The Victor Bible Source Book* by Stephen D. Swihart (Wheaton: Victor Books, 1977) pp. 86, 87.

II. *The Accusations and Anger (26:59-68)*

59The chief priests and the whole Sanhedrin were looking for false
evidence against Jesus so that they could put him to death. 60But they
did not find any, though many false witnesses came forward.
Finally two came forward 61and declared, "This fellow said, 'I am able
to destroy the temple of God and rebuild it in three days.' "
62Then the high priest stood up and said to Jesus, "Are you not going
to answer? What is this testimony that these men are bringing against
you?" 63But Jesus remained silent.
The high priest said to him, "I charge you under oath by the living
God: Tell us if you are the Christ,[a] the Son of God."

[a] 63 Or *Messiah;* also in verse 68

64"Yes, it is as you say," Jesus replied. "But I say to all of you: In the future you will see the Son of Man sitting at the right hand of the Mighty One and coming on the clouds of heaven."

65Then the high priest tore his clothes and said, "He has spoken blasphemy! Why do we need any more witnesses? Look, now you have heard the blasphemy. 66What do you think?"

"He is worthy of death," they answered.

67Then they spit in his face and struck him with their fists. Others slapped him 68and said, "Prophesy to us, Christ. Who hit you?"

Looking for False Evidence. According to the rules established by the Jewish supreme court (called the Sanhedrin) it was illegal to hold any trial at night. Furthermore, it was written in their laws that no one could be tried during the Passover season. Another of their rules required them to conduct their transactions in a special hall of the Temple; otherwise, all decisions were rendered invalid.

So much for regulations. When men's hearts are bent on destruction, there is no room for equality or justice. The Jews broke practically every rule in the book, but somehow, in their perverted minds, the end justified the means.

You can never reason with the unreasonable, or teach the unteachable. Whenever truth is resisted, you may rest assured that people will find a way to justify their carnal activities.

Tell Us If You Are the Christ. This court had some time earlier decided to rid themselves of Jesus (Matt. 26:4; John 11:49, 50). This was merely the so-called official process for the advancement of their past plots.

Since the actual evidence against Jesus was both scarce and distorted, everything hinged upon one crucial issue—Jesus' identity. Everyone present had heard that Jesus was acclaimed as being the long-desired Messiah. But now they wanted to hear Jesus make this claim himself. And they sought to hear it with their own ears. Jesus unhesitatingly satisfied their diabolic appetites. He candidly announced that He is indeed the Messiah, and more. Jesus further elaborated that He is also the one who will rule all of the earth and sit at God's right side, the position of supreme authority (Dan. 7:13, 14).

This was too much—to the delight of the scheming leaders. Caiaphas tore his robe in disgust, called Jesus a horrible blasphemer, dismissed any need for further witnesses, and called on his audience for the same assessment, which he wholeheartedly received. The stage had been fixed, the trap had worked (or so they reasoned), and the only thing left to do was to have the state pass the sentence of death. This would happen tomorrow, but in the meanwhile they would quench their base desires by tormenting and taunting Jesus.

Peter Denies Christ (Matt. 26:69-75)

(cf. Mark 14:66-72; Luke 22:54-62 and John 18:15-18, 25-27)

Great men are never invulnerable. They sin, too. Peter is such an example. He knew no rival for being the most outspoken on the subject of faithfulness. But even strong men have weak spots. And Peter had his before the public eye. He denied Jesus—not once, but three times. This was a horrible sin, being committed at the worst possible moment in Jesus' life. Yet it is, like all other sins, a forgivable offense (Luke 22:31, 32; 1 John 1:9). We can certainly be thankful for this knowledge.

I. *The First Denial (26:69, 70)*

69 Now Peter was sitting out in the courtyard, and a servant girl came to him. "You also were with Jesus of Galilee," she said.
70 But he denied it before them all. "I don't know what you're talking about," he said.

II. *The Second Denial (26:71, 72)*

71 Then he went out to the gateway, where another girl saw him and said to the people there, "This fellow was with Jesus of Nazareth."
72 He denied it again, with an oath: "I don't know the man!"

III. *The Third Denial (26:73-75)*

73 After a little while, those standing there went up to Peter and said, "Surely you are one of them, for your accent gives you away."
74 Then he began to call down curses on himself and he swore to them, "I don't know the man!"
Immediately a rooster crowed.
75 Then Peter remembered the word Jesus had spoken: "Before the rooster crows, you will disown me three times." And he went outside and wept bitterly.

This is a classic presentation of grace. In this particular account we read only of Peter's miserable failure and of his utter shame for it. But elsewhere we read how Jesus told him, "I have prayed for you, Simon, that your faith may not fail. And when you have turned back, strengthen your brothers" (Luke 22:32). Peter was no different from the other disciples—the hearts of each of them turned to water at the moment of Jesus' betrayal. Jesus knew this would occur. Prophecy had foretold this event (Matt. 26:31). But Jesus could look beyond this momentary lapse in obedience. He could see a man who truly loved Him. He could see a man who would face his sins, turn from them and then be used in helping other fallen people. So, Jesus prayed, being confident that Peter, in the end, would not let Him or the other disciples down.

Judas Hangs Himself (Matt. 27:1-10)

(cf. Acts 1:16-20)

Sin is never a light matter. The degree and number of our sins may vary greatly, but the result is always the same—guilt.

Once Judas saw the full result of his sin, he felt terrible. He even confessed his mistake to the religious leaders, and returned the betrayal money, but the consequences were unalterable. No amount of grief could rectify the problems.

There is a deep discovery to be made here. It is this: once a sin is committed, its effects are not always easily erased. Our sins may be forgiven, if we truly repent, but the scars created by our sins will remain with us (and possibly with others, too).

I. *Jesus' Condemnation (27:1, 2)*

27 Early in the morning, all the chief priests and the elders of the people came to the decision to put Jesus to death. 2They bound him, led him away and handed him over to Pilate, the governor.

This is the third trial in a series of six (Matt. 26:57-68). It must have been a short session, since the night before they had reached the conclusion to seek Jesus' death. This meeting involved nothing more than making the prior decision official.

Under Roman law the Jews could not exercise the right of capital punishment (death—John 18:31). So, they now bound Jesus' hands and led Him away to be tried in Pilate's court (Matt. 27:11-26).

II. *Judas' Conscience (27:3-5)*

3When Judas, who had betrayed him, saw that Jesus was condemned, he was seized with remorse and returned the thirty silver coins to the

chief priests and the elders. [4]"I have sinned," he said, "for I have betrayed innocent blood."

"What is that to us?" they replied. "That's your responsibility."

[5]So Judas threw the money into the temple and left. Then he went away and hanged himself.

Did Judas die a saved man or a lost man? The unanimous verdict of Bible students is that he died in his sins, a spiritually lost man. The reasons for this conviction are well-founded:

1. Though Judas confessed his sin before men, there is no proof of a genuine repentance before God. We must not evaluate a person by his speech alone, even if it be lined with tears of remorse (Heb. 12:14-17).
2. Judas hung himself (Matt. 27:5). Had Judas found forgiveness, there would have been no more guilt or desire to destroy himself.
3. Jesus said of Judas that it would have been better for him if he had never been born than to live and betray the Christ (Matt. 26:24). Certainly these are not the kinds of words you would expect to hear spoken to a saved person.
4. Jesus called Judas "the one doomed to destruction," and then He plainly distinguished between the salvation of the other disciples and the lost condition of Judas (John 17:12).

There can be little room for doubt. Judas died the way he lived—straddling the fence between a devotion to Christ and a love for money. Those who die in this state will not see heaven (Matt. 6:24).

III. *Judas's Coins (27:6-10)*

[6]The chief priests picked up the coins and said, "It is against the law to put this into the treasury, since it is blood money." [7]So they decided to use the money to buy the potter's field as a burial place for foreigners. [8]That is why it has been called the Field of Blood to this day. [9]Then what was spoken by Jeremiah the prophet was fulfilled: "They took the thirty silver coins, the price set on him by the people of Israel, [10]and they used them to buy the potter's field, as the Lord commanded me."[a]

Blood Money. The supreme hypocrisy of the religious leaders is shown at its worst in this revealing episode. First, they persuaded Judas to betray Jesus for thirty pieces of silver—this was premeditated-murder money. Second, they refused to minister to Judas's remorse—this is irresponsibility in the duty of their profession. Third, they "reverently" kept the Law which forbade the taking of any money that had been gained immorally (Deut. 23:18)—this set a double standard because just hours before

---

a 10 Zech. 11:12, 13; Jer. 32:6-9

they had used that same money to fund the plot they now rejected!

Burial Place for Foreigners. Judas's coins were used to buy a field from a potter (who probably had depleted the land of its productive resources). This site, just outside the city's southern wall, would then be used as a cemetery for foreigners (or for Jews who died while visiting Jerusalem, leaving no indication of any existing relatives or friends).

Jeremiah the Prophet. This quotation from Jeremiah is actually located in the book of Zechariah (11:12, 13). The probable reason for Matthew referring to Jeremiah is due to the fact that all the writings of the prophets may have been copied originally on only one scroll, beginning with the prophet Jeremiah (not Isaiah, as is done now). In such a situation it would have been natural to refer to all of these words by the name of the first prophet in the series.

Jesus Stands Before Pilate (Matt. 27:11-25)

(cf. Mark 15:1 15; Luke 23:3-25 and John 18:28-40)

There were, in all, six trials of Jesus—three before Jewish rulers and three before Roman rulers. None were conducted legally. Each succeeding trial manifested the depraved and determined nature of men who had set themselves to get their own way.

The extent to which Jesus lowered himself for us is staggering. He left the glories of heaven for a humble home on earth. He departed from the sound of angelic praises to hear the curses of men. He left behind immortality to wear the garments of human flesh, which sadistic men would nail to a cross!

There is no device capable of measuring such love. Let us rejoice at this revelation of our Savior. Let Him be praised forever, for He is worthy indeed!

I. *Pilate's Impression (27:11-14)*

11Meanwhile Jesus stood before the governor, and the governor asked him, "Are you the king of the Jews?"

"Yes, it is as you say," Jesus replied.

12When he was accused by the chief priests and the elders, he gave no
answer. 13Then Pilate asked him, "Don't you hear how many things they
are accusing you of?" 14But Jesus made no reply, not even to a single
charge—to the great amazement of the governor.

The Governor. Pontius Pilate was a powerful governor. Appointed to his position by the Emperor Tiberius in A.D. 26, Pilate had command of approximately 120 cavalry troops and 2,500-5,000 infantrymen. His position provided him with the authority to take men's lives or to pardon them at will. The Sanhedrin had no such authority (John 18:31), so they sent Jesus to Pilate to ratify their sentence for His execution.

Are You the King of the Jews? When the Jewish leaders sentenced Jesus to death, His alleged crime was blasphemy (Matt. 26:65, 66). But when they brought Him to Pilate, they charged Him with treason—a crime that was doubtlessly calculated to bring a sharper ring to Pilate's ears (Luke 23:2). But Pilate could see through this false accusation. These men were jealous; it was out of envy that they brought Jesus to him (Matt. 27:18).

Nevertheless, Pilate asked Jesus if He was a king. And Jesus responded affirmatively, but He qualified His answer by stating that His Kingdom was not of this world (John 18:36). Jesus posed no threat to Rome, and Pilate knew it. Therefore, Pilate was prepared to drop the matter, though he finally concluded it would be best to send Him to Herod, since Jesus, being a Galilean, belonged to Herod's jurisdiction (Luke 23:6, 7).

Jesus Made No Reply. Jesus would not answer the Jews who falsely accused Him. There was no purpose in speaking to those who would not listen. You cannot reason with the unreasonable or defend yourself before those whose minds are already made up. Such was the case that presented itself before Jesus. He would not waste His time answering their irreconcilable charges.

This strong and controlled temperament impressed Pilate. He had tried many men, but none had been like this one. His composure was radiating; His silence was compelling. Pilate could find no fault with Him (Luke 23:4).

II. *Pilate's Intention (27:15-18)*

> **15Now it was the governor's custom at the Feast to release a prisoner chosen by the crowd. 16At that time they had a notorious prisoner, called Barabbas. 17So when the crowd had gathered, Pilate asked them, "Which one do you want me to release to you: Barabbas, or Jesus who is called Christ?" 18For he knew it was out of envy that they had handed Jesus over to him.**

Pilate was moved to release this man. He could see clearly that Jesus had been "framed." Jesus posed no military or political threat to Rome. Therefore, Pilate offered the release of a notorious criminal, Barabbas, in exchange for the death penalty of Jesus, thinking (presumably) that the people would have enough sense to seek justice on the part of a known prisoner (or at least pity on the part of a known innocent man,

Jesus). But his plan failed. The people wanted Barabbas to be freed and Jesus to be crucified. How distorted our logic can become when it is motivated by childish stubbornness and envy (v. 18)! Further, we see how easily some are influenced by religious leaders, even though the influence they present is evil in nature (Matt. 27:20).

III. *Pilate's Interruption (27:19)*

> **19While Pilate was sitting on the judge's seat, his wife sent him this message: "Don't have anything to do with that innocent man, for I have suffered a great deal today in a dream because of him."**

While the evidence is not complete, it is at least reasonable to state that Pilate's wife may have been a Jewish convert and therefore understood that Jesus could have easily been the prophesied Messiah. The Greek Orthodox Church today includes this woman in their listing of saints. But, when one looks solely upon the evidence presented in the Scriptures, no such decision is possible. We only know she had a dream (the contents of her dream being unknown) and that she wanted her husband to release Jesus because of His innocence.

IV. *Pilate's "Innocence" (27:20-25)*

> **20But the chief priests and the elders persuaded the crowd to ask for Barabbas and to have Jesus executed.**
>
> **21"Which of the two do you want me to release to you?" asked the governor.**
>
> **"Barabbas," they answered.**
>
> **22"What shall I do, then, with Jesus who is called Christ?" Pilate asked.**
>
> **They all answered, "Crucify him!"**
>
> **23"Why? What crime has he committed?" asked Pilate.**
>
> **But they shouted all the louder, "Crucify him!"**
>
> **24When Pilate saw that he was getting nowhere, but that instead an uproar was starting, he took water and washed his hands in front of the crowd. "I am innocent of this man's blood," he said. "It is your responsibility!"**
>
> **25All the people answered, "Let his blood be on us and on our children!"**

There are two parties claiming innocence here, but neither of them were free from guilt. First, there was the guilt of Pilate. No less than three times Pilate sought the release of Jesus (Luke 23:4, 14-16, 20-22), but in the end he surrendered to the pressures of the mob that had gathered outside his residence. Pilate was weak—spiritually, morally, ethically and judicially. He was a coward who sought to wash away his irresponsible action in a basin of water (a symbol which the Jews would have easily understood—Exod. 30:17-21). But no such magic was possible. He condemned Jesus by his incompetent handling of the whole ordeal. Before God Pilate stands guilty (Acts 2:23; 4:27).

Second, there is the guilt of the Jewish crowd. They, too, believed themselves to be innocent, declaring, "Let His blood be on us and on our children," as though putting Jesus to death were an action that would have no personal repercussions. Little did they realize that they had spelled out their own just curse (Matt. 23:30ff.; Acts 5:28; 1 Thess. 2:14-16; Heb. 10:28-31). The Jew's persistent resistance to the gospel message meant that they would soon taste God's most severe wrath (Matt. 23:37ff.).

Jesus Is Flogged, Mocked and Crucified (Matt. 27:26-56)

(cf. Mark 15:16-41; Luke 23:26-49 and John 19:17-37)

The life of Christ may be summarized by these five brief captions: His Virgin Birth, His Virtuous Life, His Vicarious Death, His Victorious Resurrection and His Visible Return. We have come through the first two of these in Matthew's Gospel; now we are ready for the third—Jesus' Vicarious Death.

The events leading to Jesus' death present a horrible scene. He was flogged, mocked, crucified and rejected by nearly everyone. The only positive note in the entire episode is the fact that this was all in God's plan and that the Gospel does not end here. Actually, it might be rightly stated that it is here where the gospel of our salvation begins. In this story we have the beginning of our deliverance from self, sin and Satan (Rom. 5:6ff.; 2 Cor. 5:14ff.; Col. 1:13ff.; Heb. 9:11ff.; etc.).

I. *Jesus Is Flogged (27:26)*

> **26Then he released Barabbas to them. But he had Jesus flogged, and handed him over to be crucified.**

Flogging was an exceedingly painful beating with a leather whip which had pieces of bone or metal imbedded in its cord. Two soldiers would stand on either side of the bent and bare victim. They would then exchange blows. This cruel act was used only on traitors and murderers. No more than forty blows were to be inflicted, since it was believed that no one could survive a larger number of blows. Not infrequently, a flogging would open the tissues of the back to such an extent that even arteries would be lacerated and organs would be exposed.

This flogging came as no surprise to Jesus. He knew Roman procedures, and He knew God's prophecies predicting this event (Isa. 53:5). Unquestionably, there is no limit to the extent that Jesus was willing to suffer for us. Let us never forget this fact, for it was *our sins* that killed Him (Rom. 5)!

II. *Jesus Is Mocked (27:27-31)*

[27]Then the governor's soldiers took Jesus into the Praetorium and gathered the whole company of soldiers around him. [28]They stripped him and put a scarlet robe on him,[29] and then wove a crown of thorns and set it on his head. They put a staff in his right hand and knelt in front of him and mocked him. "Hail, King of the Jews!" they said. [30]They spit on him, and took the staff and struck him on the head again and again. [31]After they had mocked him, they took off the robe and put his own clothes on him. Then they led him away to crucify him.

Jesus was stripped of His own clothing and given a scarlet robe to wear, a crown of thorns for His head and a reed for His hand. He was then spat upon, hit upon the head and mocked. Isaiah describes Jesus at this juncture as being more marred than any other human (Isa. 52:14). The torments were so severe that Jesus would be incapable of carrying His own cross the full distance to Golgotha, just outside the city walls (vv. 32, 33).

III. *Jesus Is Crucified (27:32-54)*

1. *Rejected by People of the State (27:32-38)*

[32]As they were going out, they met a man from Cyrene, named Simon, and they forced him to carry the cross. [33]They came to a place called Golgotha (which means The Place of the Skull). [34]There they offered him wine to drink, mixed with gall; but after tasting it, he refused to drink it. [35]When they had crucified him, they divided up his clothes by casting lots.[a] [36]And sitting down, they kept watch over him there. [37]Above his head they placed the written charge against him: THIS IS JESUS, THE KING OF THE JEWS. **[38]Two robbers were crucified with him, one on his right and one on his left.**

Once the soldiers finished flogging and mocking Jesus, they now took Him to Golgotha to crucify Him. This was a merciless crew. To them Jesus was just another enemy of the State. He was to die like every other convicted criminal. There was no pity in their hearts, no softness in their words and no grace in their duty. They were rugged, tactless and callous.

The journey to Golgotha was exhausting for the tortured body of Jesus. With the

a 35 A few late manuscripts *lots that the word spoken by the prophet might be fulfilled: "They divided my garments among themselves and cast lots for my clothing"* (Psalm 22:18)

cross either strapped to His outstretched arms or resting on His shoulder Jesus collapsed from sheer exhaustion. He could not continue. Therefore, a man named Simon from Cyrene (a country in northern Africa, today called Libya) was picked from the crowd to finish the task of bearing Christ's cross. The precise identity of this man is unknown, though many suppose him to have been a Jew, especially since we know there was a synagogue in Cyrene (Acts 2:10; 6:9).

The term "Golgotha" means "skull" ("Calvary," from the Latin, also means "skull"). There have been three reasons offered for this title being given to the site where Jesus was crucified: (1) because it was the common location for crucifying criminals; (2) because skulls were once found there; and (3) because the figuration of the site itself resembles the shape of a skull. Possibly any combination of these options is the case. Maybe they are all true.

Today in Jerusalem there are two locations that are believed to be the actual sites of Jesus' cross and tomb—the Church of the Holy Sepulchre and the Garden Tomb.

2. *Rejected by Common People (27:39, 40)*

> **39Those who passed by hurled insults at him, shaking their heads 40and saying, "You who are going to destroy the temple and build it in three days, save yourself! Come down from the cross, if you are the Son of God!"**

Jesus was rejected by virtually everyone. Even the common people, those with whom He had achieved His greatest accomplishments, railed at Him with sarcasm. What a pitiful scene this is. The ones whom Jesus loved, served and came to save are shown here with their tongues both sharp and barbed. What an understatement it is to say that "Christ died for the ungodly" (Rom. 5:6). It is too tame a declaration to reveal its full meaning. How gracious and loving is our Lord, however, not to concencentrate on our innumerable flaws but to focus on Christ's redeeming love! Praise the Lord!

3. *Rejected by Religious People (27:41-43)*

> **41In the same way the chief priests, the teachers of the law and the elders mocked him. 42"He saved others," they said, "but he can't save himself! He's the king of Israel! Let him come down now from the cross, and we will believe in him. 43He trusts in God. Let God rescue him now if he wants him, for he said, 'I am the Son of God.' "**

If Jesus truly rescued others from death, surely He could deliver himself, or so reasoned the perverted minds of the religious leaders. They thought that if this were truly God's Son, then He would be rescued by God but because there was no such divine deliverance, then Jesus' claims were proved false. Tragically, the so-called spiritual leaders were incapable of detecting a divine proof when it was laid before them. They were as blind as a million midnights rolled into one moment. They were not qualified to make spiritual appraisals, especially regarding the death of Jesus on the cross. They were lost, horribly lost, in envy and self-righteousness (Matt. 27:18). Nothing they said made any sense at all.

4. *Rejected by Criminal People (27:44)*

44In the same way the robbers who were crucified with him also heaped insults on him.

Further verbal assaults were directed at Jesus by the two robbers with whom He was crucified. Each took a turn at mocking Him. Then something happened that Matthew does not record. One of these robbers detected that his language was altogether out of place. He suddenly realized that this one whom he had been ridiculing was indeed the prophesied Messiah (Luke 23:39-43)! His heart was pierced through with guilt. His insults were dramatically turned to inspiration, and he asked for what amounted to forgiveness and acceptance by Jesus. Here is a call for salvation in the final moments of life. Would Jesus receive him? Indeed, He would! In fact, that very day He would be welcomed into paradise with Christ.

We must witness to everyone, until their final breath is drawn. There is no one so wretched that Jesus will reject him, if he will but come to Him in a sorrowful spirit of repentance and faith. It is desirable for people to choose to follow Jesus soon after the moment of birth, but He will accept them even moments before death.

5. *Rejected by God (27:45-50)*

45From the sixth hour until the ninth hour darkness came over all land. 46About the ninth hour Jesus cried out in a loud voice, *"Eloi, Eloi,*[a] *lama sabachthani?"*—which means, "My God, my God, why have you forsaken me?"[b]

47When some of those standing there heard this, they said, "He's calling Elijah."

48Immediately one of them ran and got a sponge. He filled it with wine vinegar, put it on a stick, and offered it to Jesus to drink. 49But the rest said, "Leave him alone. Let's see if Elijah comes to save him."

50And when Jesus had cried out again in a loud voice, he gave up his spirit.

Finally, Jesus was even forsaken by God! There was nowhere that Jesus could turn for a word of encouragement. Neither Gentiles nor Jews wanted Him to live. Vicious verbal insults were hurled at Him from those beneath His cross, as well as those at His

---

a 46 Some manuscripts *Eli, Eli* *b 46* Psalm 22:1

THE SEVEN SAYINGS OF CHRIST ON THE CROSS

1. *Supplication:* "Father, forgive them, for they do not know what they are doing" (Luke 23:34).
2. *Salvation:* "I tell you the truth, today you will be with me in paradise" (Luke 23:43).
3. *Solicitation:* To his mother, "Dear woman, here is your son," and to the disciple, "Here is your mother" (John 19:26).
4. *Separation: "Eloi, Eloi, lama sabachthani"*—which means, "My God, My God, why have you forsaken me?" (Matt. 27:46).
5. *Sensation:* "I am thirsty" (John 19:28).
6. *Satisfaction:* "It is finished" (John 19:30).
7. *Summation:* "Father, into your hands I commit my spirit" (Luke 23:46).

side. And lastly, rejection came even from above. Jesus' death on the cross marked the darkest hour of human history.

What happened on the cross was carefully planned by God, though seeing its design at this precise moment was nearly impossible (Isa. 52:13-53:12; Acts 2:22-36; 4:23-28; Eph. 1:11). The cross was far more than a symbol of man's cruelty; it was also a symbol of God's bridge between heaven and earth. While Jesus hung on the cross, God was making reconciliation possible between himself and each person in the whole world for all of time. For upon Christ, the sinless one, were placed all the sins of each person ever born on this globe. Jesus paid for all of our sins—past, present and future. He died in our place so that we would never need to perish under the hand of God's wrath (Rom. 5; 2 Cor. 5). Today, if we will carry the cross, it will, in turn, carry us so that at the end of our lives we will enter heaven. We must see more than the hurt of Christ dying on the cross; we must primarily see the help Jesus provides for sinners through His substitutionary death on the cross. This divine perspective is imperative in order to properly understand the genuine meaning of the cross.

The events on the cross between nine o'clock until noon defy human comprehension. For three hours the sky gave forth no light as Jesus took all the sins of the whole world on His body (2 Cor. 5:21; Isa. 53:1-12). In some incomprehensible manner, Jesus tasted spiritual death for every man, woman, boy and girl who ever has or ever will live. In His body, where our sins lay, the wrath of God was satisfied, and justice was rendered for everyone at the cross. Now, no one ever needs to experience spiritual death, for Jesus paid this price in full. All that is left for us to do is receive it, personally (John 1:12; Rom. 10:9-13)!

6. *Rent Curtain (27:51a)*

51 At that moment the curtain of the temple was torn in two from top to bottom.

At the precise moment when Jesus finished His work on the cross, the veil in the Temple was torn in two by the hand of God, from top to bottom. There was no further need for this structure. Its purpose for existence had been fulfilled. The symbols it offered were now fully realized in Christ's substitutionary and atoning death. It was only a shadow of things to come; in Jesus the substance was revealed (see the entire book of Hebrews for details).

The veil in the Temple separated the people from God. Only the high priest was permitted entrance into this most holy of chambers. Once there, the high priest would sprinkle sacrificial blood upon the mercy seat as a symbol of God's acceptance of His people because of the substitutionary sacrifice. Now, Jesus, our high priest, has entered once and for all into God's presence with the supreme substitutionary sacrifice of himself. The sign of God's approval with this sacrifice is displayed in the severed curtain. No longer would there be any need for a high priest or animal sacrifices; for in Jesus every symbol of the Temple had been fulfilled.

7. *Resurrection from the Dead (27:51b-53)*

The earth shook and the rocks split. 52 The tombs broke open and the bodies of many holy people who had died were raised to life. 53 They came out of the tombs, and after Jesus' resurrection they went into the holy city and appeared to many people.

Few words are provided for us regarding this event—our comments shall be the same. It is not safe to speculate on this. There are only two things that ought to be stated: (1) The purpose of this event was to bring still further proof that Jesus was indeed the promised Messiah and the Son of God. (2) The result of this event was (and is) a sure confidence in the resurrection from the dead.

Although it is not stated, it is reasonable to assume that these persons possessed glorified bodies and went into heaven with Jesus, either prior to or at the time of His ascension.

8. *Revelation of Jesus' Uniqueness (27:54)*

54 When the centurion and those with him who were guarding Jesus saw the earthquake and all that had happened, they were terrified, and exclaimed, "Surely he was the Son[a] of God!"

How soon our doubts about Christ can be altered in a time of unusual crisis. The

[a] 54 Or *a son*

soldiers who but moments earlier had mocked Jesus are now in awe of Him. What happened to turn their hearts so suddenly? The answer is simple, yet profound—acts of nature, caused by the hand of God. When confronted with only words, our defenses may be strong, but who can fight the dark sky, the shaking earth or the splitting rocks? These men sensed that Jesus and the current acts of nature were directly associated with one another. And with a new-found faith they exclaimed their discovery for everyone near to hear.

Sometimes those to whom we witness give us no sign of interest whatever. Their ears are closed and their hearts are cold, like the soldiers' original condition. Even if this is our listeners' response, there is hope. Nature (directed by the hand of God) may yet speak to them. This voice often speaks much louder and more persuasively than human words. Let us trust God to speak to people, too. His actions are needed to convert a callous person.

9. *Response of Many Women (27:55, 56)*

55Many women were there, watching from a distance. They had followed Jesus from Galilee to care for his needs. 56Among them were Mary Magdalene, Mary the mother of James and Joseph, and the mother of Zebedee's sons.

Out of the many women who dared to watch the Crucifixion and death of Jesus, Matthew names but three (John adds a fourth name—Mary, the mother of Jesus—John 19:25-27). These were brave women. They were women who admired Jesus, and they would not cease their devotion to Him even in this darkest hour. They had followed and served Jesus in the good times; they now were found faithful to Him in bad times, too (Luke 8:1-3).

It is significant to note that women, not Jesus' male disciples, were at the Calvary scene. We only know that John stood at the foot of Jesus' cross (John 19:25-27). Perhaps there were others, but we cannot be certain. We are only certain that women and John were there. Let us applaud these loyal ladies for their matchless spirits of faith and service!

Jesus Is Buried (Matt. 27:57-66)

(cf. Mark 15:42-47; Luke 23:50-56 and John 19:38-42)

For portions of three days and three nights, the earth would serve as Jesus' home. His body would be removed from the cross, carefully washed (cf. Acts 9:37), anointed

(Mark 16:1), wrapped in linen garments with enclosed spices (John 19:40) and laid in a borrowed tomb (Matt. 27:57-60). The sequence seemed natural enough—Jesus was dead. But some were skeptical that this was the end. They expected trouble. And they were to receive more than they could have imagined.

I. *The Tomb (27:57-61)*

**57As evening approached, there came a rich man from Arimathea,
named Joseph, who had himself become a disciple of Jesus. 58Going to
Pilate, he asked for Jesus' body, and Pilate ordered that it be given to
him. 59Joseph took the body, wrapped it in a clean linen cloth, 60and
placed it in his own new tomb that he had cut out of the rock. He rolled a
big stone in front of the entrance to the tomb and went away. 61Mary
Magdalene and the other Mary were sitting there across from the tomb.**

Joseph from Arimathea. Joseph, a member of the Sanhedrin, was a secret disciple of Jesus (Luke 23:50; John 19:38). And though he followed Jesus at a distance, he was a good and righteous man, one who was waiting for the Kingdom of God (Luke 23:51). He did not wish to see Jesus die; and now he seeks to have His body so he might place it in his own newly purchased tomb.

The exact site of Arimathea is uncertain, although ancient Ramah, the birthplace of Samuel (1 Sam. 1:19), is a strong possibility. This town is situated about twenty miles northwest of Jerusalem.

He Asked for Jesus' Body. The Jewish officials wanted all three of these men killed and disposed of so they would present no ugly distraction in their Sabbath observances (such carnality—John 19:31-34). They sought to have their legs broken, so that they might die sooner. Jesus, however, had already died. His cruel and torturous treatment prior to the cross left Him without any strength whatever. Further, and probably more precisely, Jesus died so soon because His work was finished. He had completed God's call. It was time for the next phase in God's plans. So, Jesus died, and Joseph sought the right to claim His body for burial. According to Roman law, a crucified person could not be removed from a cross without first getting permission from the governor.

His Own New Tomb. Numerous tombs, especially among the wealthy, were actually carved out of rock walls. Inside these waterproof limestone caves ledges were made as resting places for corpses. There was room for a number of bodies in each tomb. Outside, a stone door would be rolled in place to cover the entrance and to protect it from hungry animals. In Jesus' case, a seal was also attached to this outer stone. The seal probably consisted of a cord which was extended across the stone, with a patch of clay at each end. Any tampering with the stone would easily break this seal.

The word "new" suggests that Joseph had just purchased the site, probably for the single purpose of providing a burial place for Jesus' body. It was not for himself, but for Jesus who was hanging on the cross.

II. *The Troops (27:62-66)*

62The next day, the one after Preparation Day, the chief priests and
the Pharisees went to Pilate. 63"Sir," they said, "we remember that while
he was still alive that deceiver said, 'After three days I will rise again.'
64So give the order for the tomb to be made secure until the third day.
Otherwise, his disciples may come and steal the body and tell the people
that he has been raised from the dead. This last deception will be worse
than the first."
65"Take a guard," Pilate answered. "Go, make the tomb as secure as
you know how." 66So they went and made the tomb secure by putting a
seal on the stone and posting the guard.

The Next Day. The first day of the week-long Passover Feast was called Preparation Day because everything was made ready on that day for the remainder of the week. This would have been Friday (we call it "Good Friday"). The "next day" would be Saturday, but it must be remembered that this day, according to Jewish reckoning, began immediately after sunset on Friday evening. The activities being discussed here, then, occurred just moments after Jesus' crucifixion and burial.

Go Make the Tomb Secure. The religious leaders were a determined lot. They would see their job through to the very end. They were afraid of the rumors regarding Jesus' resurrection, and they feared that Jesus' disciples might plot some hoax resurrection by stealing Jesus' body from the tomb. So, they sought the militia to guard the tomb from any attempted theft of the corpse. These added measures of precaution, however, only served to further validate the reality of Jesus' miraculous resurrection.

The role of Satan in all of this activity is plainly evident. He hated Jesus from the start. He wanted to see Him killed, and now he wanted to see to it that He stayed dead. But God always has a way of using the devil against his own evil purposes. Jesus' death had been a part of God's blueprints all along. His resurrection had been likewise. And Satan would not be able to stop it from happening. The greatest of all the miracles could not be prevented. Jesus had to rise from the dead; and God would see that it happened.

Jesus Rises from the Dead (Matt. 28:1-10)

(cf. Mark 16:1-8; Luke 24:1-11 and John 20:1-18)

"The Gospels do not explain the resurrection; the resurrection explains the Gospels" (John S. Whale).

Without the Resurrection there would be no Christianity. It is mentioned 104 times in the New Testament. Remove this event and Jesus would remain dead, the Bible would be a lie, and God would be a hoax. Through this event, however, the divine plan was fulfilled, giving strength and hope beyond description to us all.

Unlike all of the world's religions that stop at the grave, Christianity starts on the other side—with the Resurrection! Jesus did not enter this world so books might be written regarding His wisdom or love. He came to resurrect men from the dead, and to show them the passageway to heaven. He accomplished this feat through His very own resurrection.

I. *The Day of the Week (28:1)*

28 After the Sabbath, at dawn on the first day of the week, Mary Magdalene and the other Mary went to look at the tomb.

Jesus arose on the first day of the week—Sunday. Elsewhere this is called "the Lord's day" (Rev. 1:10). In the days before Christ's resurrection, believers assembled in the synagogue on Saturday—the Sabbath—for worship. But now they would meet on a new day—the Lord's day—in order to commemorate Christ's resurrection from the dead, as well as their own resurrection out of sin and eternal judgment (Acts 20:7; 1 Cor. 16:1, 2; Col. 2:16, 17).

II. *The Descent of the Angel (28:2-7)*

2There was a violent earthquake, for an angel of the Lord came down from heaven and, going to the tomb, rolled back the stone and sat on it. 3His appearance was like lightning, and his clothes were white as snow. 4The guards were so afraid of him that they shook and became like dead men.

5The angel said to the women, "Do not be afraid, for I know that you are looking for Jesus, who was crucified. 6He is not here; he has risen,

just as he said. Come and see the place where he lay. [7]Then go quickly and tell his disciples: 'He has risen from the dead and is going ahead of you into Galilee. There you will see him.' Now I have told you."

On this day several women journeyed to the tomb where Joseph had laid Jesus' body. They were not lightly shocked to be addressed by an angel, and to see the empty grave! But their fears were coupled with joy as they heard the angelic messenger announce, "He is risen!"

This is a tremendous scene. The women have come to a grave site, but it is not the end of things, as they might suspect; instead, it is just the beginning. The work has only begun. It is time to turn the hearts of Jesus' followers from bitter disappointment to utter ecstacy. The good news could not be better than what they heard today. He is risen! He is risen!

III. *The Delight of the Women (28:8-10)*

[8]So the women hurried away from the tomb, afraid yet filled with joy, and ran to tell his disciples. [9]Suddenly Jesus met them. "Greetings," he said. They came to him, clasped his feet and worshiped him. [10]Then Jesus said to them, "Do not be afraid. Go and tell my brothers to go to Galilee; there they will see me."

With haste, the women dashed off to tell the eleven disciples what had happened. But before they could reach their destination, Jesus appeared to them. Naturally, they could hardly believe what was happening to them. What excitement! They quickly fell upon their faces and hugged Jesus' feet in sheer awe. They believed the angel's words, and now they could see the proof for themselves.

We must never forget the women who were ever so true to Jesus. Their dedication was unsurpassed. These ladies displayed a triumphant faith and loyalty of the highest inspirational quality. Perhaps it is for this reason that Jesus chose to first reveal himself to them, and not to the eleven disciples.

The Resurrection Plot (Matt. 28:11-15)

The soldiers who guarded the grave site must have been terribly afraid when the dazzling white angel appeared before them. First their eyes were stunned; then their feet trembled as an earthquake shook the ground; and finally their ears vibrated as they heard the seal being broken and the stone being rolled away!

Immediately they ran to the chief priests to tell them what startling things had taken place. The leaders were perplexed, to say the least. What should they do? They decided to call in other religious leaders for their opinions. Finally they reached a decision—they would pay the soldiers to tell a lie. And that's precisely what they did. Regrettably, there are many, even in our own hour, who still believe the lies of these soldiers, and not the truth of Christ's very own disciples.

> **[11]While the women were on their way, some of the guards went into**
> **the city and reported to the chief priests everything that had happened.**
> **[12]When the chief priests had met with the elders and devised a plan,**
> **they gave the soldiers a large sum of money, [13]telling them, "You are to**
> **say, 'His disciples came during the night and stole him away while we**
> **were asleep.' [14]If this report gets to the governor, we will satisfy him**
> **and keep you out of trouble." [15]So the soldiers took the money and did as**
> **they were instructed. And this story has been widely circulated among**
> **the Jews to this very day.**

All the scheming and bribing could not conceal this truth. It could not be hidden or ignored. It was destined to be heard.

The reality of Christ's resurrection has marched triumphantly through the centuries and found a joyful response in each generation. Christ had won! The grave could not hold Him. Men and demons could not defeat Him, even after they had killed Him. He would rise. And His victory would transform millions, because the good news of the glorified Savior could not be stopped, not even by a tombstone!

The Great Commission (Matt. 28:16-20)

(cf. Mark 16:15-18)

The Great Commission is far more than a charge to make converts or to erect a church building. It is, instead, both a challenge and a command to win people to Christ and then to transform them into mature disciples who will joyfully and consistently walk a straight line with regard to God's will. This is the Great Commission—nothing more, nothing less and nothing else.

I. *Its Power (28:16-18)*

[16]Then the eleven disciples went to Galilee, to the mountain where Jesus had told them to go. [17]When they saw him, they worshiped him; but some doubted. [18]Then Jesus came to them and said, "All authority in heaven and on earth has been given to me.

Once Jesus was crucified, the disciples were crushed. No pain, sorrow or grief could match their desolation. Added to their trauma was the vexing mental torment of being terribly confused. Their dreams had been shattered. Their hopes had been turned to despair. And doubt was replacing faith in the life of some disciples.

How typical these responses are. When things do not proceed as we anticipate, we too often recoil or pout. We allow our circumstances to overwhelm us. We permit our eyes to be our guide, rather than the promises of Christ. This is precisely what happened to Jesus' disciples. Their hearts were grief-stricken and hopeless, because they were following their natural senses and not Christ's words to them. Jesus told them He would arise; they should have exercised more faith.

Then, just as dramatically as He had disappeared, Jesus suddenly appeared again with His disciples! The experience was almost too much for them to comprehend. Then Jesus began to teach them. His topic was "authority." Jesus wanted them to know that He was now the Commander-in-Chief of the universe. No one—in either heaven or earth—holds a higher position of authority. Nothing is outside of His immediate control. Satan cannot act without His approval. Governments (including the Jewish Sanhedrin) cannot make a single decision without His permission. There is not a single event that can occur apart from His direct consent. All authority now belongs to Him.

Certainly this teaching was designed to encourage the disciples. Their work was far from being over. Actually, their work was only about to begin. And Jesus wanted them to know that they could perform their work in the confidence that He would be in charge of every movement in heaven and earth.

There can be no accidents in all of life. Events are either ordered or permitted, for Jesus is in full control. He holds the reigns of total authority. That should give each one of us a mountain of peace and confidence. We are on the winning side. Our Lord is invincible.

II. *Its Points (28:19, 20)*

[19]Therefore go and make disciples of all nations, baptizing them in[a] the name of the Father and of the Son and of the Holy Spirit, [20]and teaching them to obey everything I have commanded you. And surely I will be with you always, to the very end of the age."

a 19 Or *into;* see Acts 8:16; 19:5; Romans 6:3; 1 Corinthians 1:13; 10:2 and Galatians 3:27.

What is the Great Commission? Simply stated, it means to make mature disciples of Christ by baptizing and teaching them. This is our first and greatest task, to "go . . . make . . . baptize . . . and teach."

Let us resolve to settle forever one matter regarding the nature of the Great Commission—making *converts to Christ* and making *disciples of Christ* are not the same things. This commission is far more embracing than merely winning lost souls; it includes teaching these new converts how to live the Christian life until they, too, are spontaneously fulfilling the Great Commission in their own daily lives!

One of the worst mistakes we can make is to abandon the last half of the Great Commission, the teaching half. The first part of the commission involves evangelism; the last half entails edification—*both are indispensable.*

Discipleship is the process of becoming all God intends for you to become. Evangelism opens the door. Edification crosses the threshold and aggressively enters the wide-open frontiers of Christian development and maturity.

And what is Jesus' promise to those who will fulfill this evangelism and edification commission? It is nothing less than His personal presence as we perform the tasks associated with the Great Commission. There may be many things we can do where the presence of Christ is not a reality; but you cannot ever seek to win the lost or to advance the status of the saved without a deep awareness that Jesus is with you. Will you accept the challenge and join the countless host of Christians who delight in fulfilling this Great Commission?

Introduction to the Gospel According to Mark

Date: Around A.D. 60

AUTHOR

In the history of the early church we read about Mark no less than eight times. He was the son of a wealthy woman named Mary, who opened her home to the Christian leaders in Jerusalem (Acts 12:12). He was also the cousin of Barnabas, a prominent leader in the first-century church (Col. 4:10).

As far as his own personal development is concerned, the picture is both bleak and bright. Initially, he traveled with Paul and Barnabas, serving as their aide (Acts 13:5; cf. 15:37). But at Perga he abandoned them and returned to Jerusalem (Acts 13:13). This departure caused Paul to reject him in a future journey, so Mark joined Barnabas in a separate ministry (Acts 15:39). Later, Mark proved to be quite reliable—enough for Paul to seek his company (2 Tim. 4:11; cf. Col. 4:10; Philem. 24).

Mark seems to have also worked closely with that great disciple of Christ, Peter (1 Pet. 5:13). It is from this association that his Gospel was probably put together.

AUDIENCE

It is quite clear that Mark wrote for Gentile readers, probably for the Romans in particular. This probability is chiefly based on the facts that he practically never refers to the Old Testament, and that he explains the meanings of Aramaic terms, which only the Jews would understand (5:41; 7:34).

AIM

While Matthew's Gospel presents Jesus as the Jew's Messiah, and Luke shows Him as the perfect man, and John proclaims Him as the divine Son, Mark describes Jesus as the lowly servant. The emphasis in Mark's account is not so much to present the teachings of Jesus as it is to display the works of Jesus (10:45). Here, Jesus is shown as a man of action, not just a good man with a knack for teaching. Mark is motivated by the fact that once you see Jesus at work, you too will seek to be His disciple.

ARRANGEMENT

The flow of Mark's Gospel is mainly chronological. Changes are presented abruptly, as Mark's slide-picture approach swiftly carries the reader from one scene to another. For instance, forty-two times he uses the word *euthus*, which is variously translated "at once" (1:18, 43), "without delay" (1:20), "immediately" (1:42), and so forth. The pace is rapid, and there is no formal outline structure for all of the movement. Perhaps it is best stated in four words: I. Preparation (1:1-13); II. Presentations (1:14-10:52); III. Problems (11:1-15:47); and IV. Power (16:1-20).

Special Note: Commentary notes for Mark's Gospel may be located in the corresponding sections of Matthew's Gospel, in cases where both books provide accounts of the same events. In instances where Matthew does not include events found in Mark's account, a separate exposition is provided in the commentary text related to the Gospel of Mark. Appropriate cross references in Luke's Gospel should also be read for a total picture of any account.

John the Baptist Prepares the Way (Mark 1:1-8)

(cf. Matt. 3:1-12; Luke 3:2-17 and John 1:6-8, 19-28)

Each of the Gospels bears a distinct starting point. Matthew takes us back to Abraham and to David. His intent is to show us Christ's legal right to the Messianic throne. Luke starts off with the birth narratives of John the Baptist and Jesus. His consuming motivation is to display the humanity of these impressive figures. John precedes each of these accounts by recording the eternal state of Jesus. His goal is to show forth Jesus' deity. Mark begins his Gospel account with the active ministry of John the Baptist, the forerunner of Jesus. His aim is to get his reader into the life and works of Jesus at the very beginning.

Characteristically, Mark is in a rush to introduce us to Jesus. Matthew uses 76 verses to introduce us to Christ's ministry; Luke uses 183 verses; John utilizes 51 verses; but Mark employs only 13 verses for this purpose. In Mark's Gospel, John the Baptist immediately announces the arrival of the Messiah, and then he introduces us to Him and His active ministry.

I. *Introduction (1:1)*

1 The beginning of the gospel about Jesus Christ, the Son of God.[a]

II. *The Messenger (1:2, 3)*

2 It is written in Isaiah the prophet:
"I will send my messenger ahead of you,
who will prepare your way"[b]
3 "a voice of one calling in the desert,
'Prepare the way for the Lord,
make straight paths for him.' "[c]

III. *The Message (1:4-8)*

4 And so John came, baptizing in the desert region and preaching a
baptism of repentance for the forgiveness of sins. 5 The whole Judean
countryside and all the people of Jerusalem went out to him. Confessing
their sins, they were baptized by him in the Jordan River. 6 John wore
clothing made of camel's hair, with a leather belt around his waist, and

---

a 1 Some manuscripts do not have *the Son of God.* *b 2* Mal. 3:1 *c 3* Isaiah 40:3

**he ate locusts and wild honey. 7And this was his message: "After me will
come one more powerful than I, the thongs of whose sandals I am not
worthy to stoop down and untie. 8I baptize you with[a] water, but he will
baptize you with the Holy Spirit."**

Jesus Is Baptized (Mark 1:9-11)

(cf. Matt. 3:13-17 and Luke 3:21, 22)

Baptism in the New Testament has three very interesting parallels in the Old Testament. First, baptism, as a symbol of allegiance, depicts the faithful pledge of those, like Abraham, who will resist their sinful ways in order to follow God (Col. 2:9-12). Second, baptism, as a symbol of judgment, pictures the wrath of God upon sinners and the escape of those, like Noah and his family, who put their trust in Him (1 Pet. 3:18-22). Third, baptism, as a symbol of entrance into God's Kingdom, displays the transition of those, like Moses and his followers, who left Egypt to enter the Promised Land of Canaan (1 Cor. 10:1-13).

In Jesus' baptism each of these three aspects is clearly displayed. First, Jesus offered himself to God's service as a sinless man. Second, Jesus willfully received God's wrath as our substitute. Third, Jesus bridged the gap (which sin created) between heaven and earth so that we might enter God's eternal Promised Land, the Kingdom of God.

Mark's account of Jesus' baptism is extremely brief, and this fits the author's fast-paced and abbreviated style. Still, we learn six things from this baptism: (1) the identity of Jesus' home—Nazareth of Galilee; (2) the person who baptized Jesus—his cousin, John; (3) the place where He was baptized—in the Jordan River, the lowest river in the earth (1,290 feet below sea level); (4) the mode of His baptism—immersion (He came up out of the water); (5) the source of His power—the dovelike Holy Spirit; and (6) the source of His confidence—the voice of God, the Father.

**9At that time Jesus came from Nazareth in Galilee and was baptized
by John in the Jordan. 10As Jesus was coming up out of the water, he
saw heaven being torn open and the Spirit descending on him like a
dove. 11And a voice came from heaven: "You are my Son, whom I love;
with you I am well pleased."**

[a] 8 Or *in*

Jesus Is Tempted (Mark 1:12, 13)

(cf. Matt. 4:1-11 and Luke 4:1-13)

Jesus, although He was totally divine, was equally human. This meant that He could be tempted just as much as every other human (Heb. 4:15). Jesus experienced hunger (Matt. 4:2), thirst (John 4:7; 19:28), weariness (John 4:6) and trials (Luke 22:44), as any other human being does. His deity would not make Him superhuman. Instead, Jesus had to face the same world each of us faces, and He had to live in it with the human limitations known to all of us. Certainly this fact makes the life of Christ all the more remarkable.

No one escapes temptations. They are common to life, rising from within and baited from without (James 1:13, 14). We can learn from this episode, however, the way of conquering such snares—by confessing God's Word as the standard and strength of our daily lives (read Matthew's account and Luke's account). The Word of God is the believer's best weapon against Satan (Eph. 6:10-18; James 4:7; Rev. 12:10, 11). If the devil had a single ambition, it would be to see God's children ignorant of the Word of God and lax in the use of the Bible.

This story is practical for other reason's too. Here we learn about the leading of the Holy Spirit, the strategies of Satan, the power of the confessed Word of God, the dangers of nature, and the ministry of angels.

> **12 At once the Spirit sent him out into the desert, 13 and he was in the**
> **desert forty days, being tempted by Satan. He was with the wild**
> **animals, and angels attended him.**

Jesus Preaches Good News (Mark 1:14, 15)

(cf. Matt. 4:12-17; Luke 4:14, 15 and John 4:43-45)

According to the book *Sharpening the Focus of the Church* by Gene Getz, a total of 184 specific communications between Jesus and others are recorded in the four Gospels. In analyzing these various conversations, Getz found that Jesus spent 32.5

percent of his time talking with individuals and 67.5 percent of his time working with groups. About 54 percent of these discussions reveal Jesus speaking with those who were definitely positive toward Him, while the remaining 46 percent of these dialogues center on His ministry to those who were either neutral or negative toward Him.

Based on this data, certain observations are clear. First, although Jesus spent much time with individuals, He seems to have devoted twice as much time to groups of two or more. Second, Jesus left no one out of His ministry—He devoted nearly half of His time to those who opposed, but apparently needed, His ministry.

At the heart of Jesus' communication was the preaching of the Kingdom of God. This is the good news about the existence of a nation where God serves as the only sovereign, and where each citizen joins together in following His legislation. It is an unmatched kingdom of righteousness, peace and joy (Rom. 14:17). But all who would enter it must first acknowledge their sins, turn from them, and put their trust in God.

**14After John was put in prison, Jesus went into Galilee, proclaiming
the good news of God. 15"The time has come," he said. "The kingdom of
God is near. Repent and believe the good news!"**

Jesus Calls Four Disciples (Mark 1:16-20)

(cf. Matt. 4:18-22 and Luke 5:1-11)

In this very brief scene we discover three important phases of the discipleship process.

First, Jesus said, "Follow me." In discipleship there is always one who leads and at least one other who follows. This is the first prerequisite to becoming a disciple—you must have someone to *follow*. If no following is involved, there can be no true discipleship. You can apply this fact to your own life; whose leadership are you following?

Second, Jesus said, "I will make you." There is something unfinished or incomplete initially with those who are called to be disciples. Converts need some shaping up; they need to be made ready for use. Unless there is a period of training, molding, fashioning and developing, there is no full discipleship.

Third, Jesus said that His finished product would be a "fisher of men." Jesus' disciples were to spend several years in the "following" and "making" stages of discipleship before they could be graduated to this final phase. Once they arrived at this stage, their mission would be to follow their Master's footsteps in making disciples, too. Their job would be to make other individuals into the kind of disciples they had become. We must remember that discipleship is never complete until those who are being trained are sent out to reproduce themselves (Matt. 28:19, 20).

I. *The Call of Simon and Andrew (1:16-18)*

16As Jesus walked beside the Sea of Galilee, he saw Simon and his
brother Andrew casting a net into the lake, for they were fishermen.
17"Come, follow me," Jesus said, "and I will make you fishers of men."
18At once they left their nets and followed him.

II. *The Call of James and John (1:19, 20)*

19When he had gone a little farther, he saw James son of Zebedee
and his brother John in a boat, preparing their nets. 20Without delay
he called them, and they left their father Zebedee in the boat with the
hired men and followed him.

Jesus Visits A Synagogue (Mark 1:21-28)

(cf. Luke 4:31-37)

Some fifty-six times in the New Testament we read of synagogues. There were scores of synagogues scattered within Jewish borders, and some elsewhere. Wherever Jews lived, at least one synagogue could be found (if there were ten or more Jewish males in a given area). In Jerusalem alone it has been estimated that there were as many as 480 separate synagogues.

The purpose for the existence of these synagogues is a fundamental one. They were centers for Jewish worship, the schools for young boys and the courts for handling minor civil disputes. Each synagogue was managed by a board of elders, with its chief elder presiding over its services. At his direction, any guest, like Jesus, could be given the opportunity to speak.

I. *His Authority As a Teacher (1:21, 22)*

21They went to Capernaum, and when the Sabbath came, Jesus went
into the synagogue and began to teach. 22The people were amazed at
his teaching, because he taught them as one who had authority, not as
the teachers of the law.

Jesus did not teach like His contemporaries. His speech was never shallow, insignificant, evasive, traditional or dull. Rather, Jesus was straightforward and profoundly practical. Additionally, Jesus' words always embraced eternal realities. He did not merely quote other rabbis and evaluate their opinions or discuss the traditions which had emerged over the years; instead, He plainly stated the very heart and will of God. His words decidedly possessed the clarion authority of heaven.

II. *His Authority As a Healer (1:23-28)*

[23]Just then a man in their synagogue who was possessed by an evil[a]
spirit cried out, [24]"What do you want with us, Jesus of Nazareth? Have you come to destroy us? I know who you are—the Holy One of God!"
[25]"Be quiet!" said Jesus sternly. "Come out of him!" [26]The evil spirit
shook the man violently and came out of him with a shriek.
[27]The people were all so amazed that they asked each other, "What is this? A new teaching—and with authority! He even gives orders to evil spirits and they obey him." [28]News about him spread quickly over the
whole region of Galilee.

Demonic activity is a prevalent theme in the New Testament. The subject of Satan and his demonic host appears nearly 175 times. At the time of Jesus' ministry on earth, the world believed very strongly in evil spirits. Demons were believed to be everywhere. It was in this context that Jesus established His authority as a healer of the demonized. Jesus would prove himself to be greater than the power of Satan.

While the audiences who heard Jesus were amazed by His teachings, they were even more astonished by His actions. Jesus confronted the unclean spirits, face to face, and sternly ordered their departure. Jesus would not tolerate any disruption by these spirits. He assumed command immediately. Certainly this dynamic presentation awoke a casual and traditional synagogue service. Jesus was in their midst, and in His presence everything would be (and is!) wonderfully different.

Other references to exorcisms in the Gospel according to Mark include the following: 1:32-34, 39; 3:11; 5:1-20; 7:24-30; 9:14-29; and 16:9.

a 23 Greek *unclean*; also in verses 26 and 27

Jesus Heals the Sick **(Mark 1:29-34)**

(cf. Matt. 8:14-17 and Luke 4:38-41)

Jesus' healing activities serve as an integral part of the gospel message. For instance, in Mark's Gospel eleven accounts of healing miracles are recorded: a leper (1:40-45), a paralyzed person (2:1-12), a man with a shriveled hand (3:1-5), many sick persons (3:10), a woman with a hemorrhage (5:24-34), a little girl who was imagined to be dead (5:21-23, 35-43), a few persons in Nazareth (6:5), scores along a seashore (6:53-56), a deaf and mute man (7:31-37), a blind man (8:22-26) and another blind person (10:46-52).

All of this evidence leads to the following conclusions: (1) Jesus possessed a healing gift from God; (2) Jesus expressed the heart's desire of God, including His wish to see people cured of their ailments; and (3) Jesus was never too busy or too theoretical to care for the needs of the common person.

Here we see Jesus interested in both friends and strangers. That makes Jesus the most powerful and practical figure of all time.

I. *Healing of Simon's Mother-in-Law (1:29-31)*

[29]As soon as they left the synagogue, they went with James and John
to the home of Simon and Andrew. [30]Simon's mother-in-law was in bed
with a fever, and they told Jesus about her. [31]So he went to her, took
her hand and helped her up. The fever left her and she began to wait
on them.

II. *Healing of Many Others (1:32-34)*

[32]That evening after sunset the people brought to Jesus all the sick
and demon-possessed. [33]The whole town gathered at the door, [34]and
Jesus healed many who had various diseases. He also drove out many
demons, but he would not let the demons speak because they knew who
he was.

Jesus Prays and Preaches (Mark 1:35-39)

(cf. Matt. 4:23-25 and Luke 4:42-44)

Mark's message is not given to us with bulky details. He deleted the fringe elements in order to be sure to emphasize the central core. It is as if Mark were handing us a series of very small diamonds—the general appearance of these gems may seem somewhat plain, but upon closer examination one discovers they possess a detailed beauty all their own.

Here are two very small jewels about Jesus' life. One focuses upon His private life of prayer; the other concentrates on His public life of power. In the former case we discover both when and where Jesus enjoyed praying. In the latter, the tirelessness, geography, strategy and authority of Jesus' ministry is unveiled.

I. *Jesus Prays (1:35-37)*

> **35Very early in the morning, while it was still dark, Jesus got up, left the house and went off to a solitary place, where he prayed. 36Simon and his companions went to look for him, 37and when they found him, they exclaimed: "Everyone is looking for you!"**

The praying habits of our Lord are a model for each one of us. He is seen praying at His baptism (Luke 3:21, 22), early in the morning (Mark 1:35), during the evening (Matt. 14:23), all night (Luke 6:12), before eating (Matt. 14:19; Luke 24:30), before great trials (Luke 22:39-46), and even while dying (Luke 23:34, 46).

II. *Jesus Preaches (1:38, 39)*

> **38Jesus replied, "Let us go somewhere else—to the nearby villages—so I can preach there also. That is why I have come." 39So he traveled throughout Galilee, preaching in their synagogues and driving out demons.**

Notice the emphasis of our Lord in this capsulized summary of His works in Galilee. Jesus plainly stated that He desired to "preach" the good news of salvation to these people. We know there were numerous miracles performed by Him at this time (v. 39b), but the emphasis of Christ was not upon the power of God which operated in His life. Rather, His interest was, as ours ought to be, upon bringing a saving faith to those who are perishing.

Jesus Heals a Leper (Mark 1:40-45)

(cf. Matt. 8:1-4 and Luke 5:12-16)

Leprosy was the most horrible disease of this time in history. It not only affected one's body, but even the clothes and homes of lepers were often contaminated by the terrible disease. Anyone who discovered he had this ailment was to make a full report to the priest immediately. Frequently the ill party, along with his family and household, would be quarantined (Lev. 13). This meant that a leper became an outcast of society as long as he was infected with the disease, often throughout the individual's lifetime.

Further, the leper was considered ceremonially unclean, and therefore unfit to worship in the house of God (Lev. 13:8, 11, 22, 44). Additionally, he was to keep his head bare, his clothes torn and his lips covered, so that everyone would immediately detect his condition and avoid him (Lev. 13:45). In fact, the leper was even to cry "Unclean!" whenever anyone approached him; this would assure that no contact would be made with the leper (Lev. 13:45). It is a wonderful scene, then, to picture Jesus actually talking with and even touching this spiritually hungry man.

How easy it is to skip over those members of our society who are unsightly, according to our standards. How much more enjoyable it seems to restrict ourselves only to those who are like ourselves. But Jesus came showing no partiality. From the highest to the lowest, He had something to offer everyone. This is the way Jesus operated. We can do no less.

I. *The Man and the Miracle (1:40-42)*

**40A man with leprosy[a] came to him and begged him on his knees, "If
you are willing, you can make me clean."**
**41Filled with compassion, Jesus reached out his hand and touched the
man. "I am willing," he said. "Be clean!" 42Immediately the leprosy left
him and he was cured.**

II. *The Message and the Mistake (1:43-45)*

**43Jesus sent him away at once with a strong warning: 44"See that you
don't tell this to anyone. But go, show yourself to the priest and offer the**

a 40 The Greek word was used for various diseases affecting the skin—not necessarily leprosy.

sacrifices that Moses commanded for your cleansing, as a testimony to them." [45]Instead he went out and began to talk freely, spreading the news. As a result, Jesus could no longer enter a town openly but stayed outside in lonely places. Yet the people still came to him from everywhere.

Jesus Heals a Paralytic (Mark 2:1-12)

(cf. Matt. 9:1-8 and Luke 5:17-26)

In the mind of many (if not most) Jews, there was a single cause behind all sickness—sin. According to this belief, if you were healthy, it meant you were righteous, but if you were ill, it meant you had to be living in sin (or possibly living in the effects of your parents' sins—John 9:1-3). Although Jesus never accepted this overly simplistic approach to diagnosing illnesses, this encounter did, nevertheless, provide a perfect setting to demonstrate His divine authority to forgive sins.

When Jesus announced that the paralytic was forgiven, He assumed a right that belongs only to God—the right to forgive a person of his or her sins. In order for Jesus to prove that He did in fact possess this profound authority, the sick man (who had presumably been forgiven) also had to be healed. (This was because in the Jewish order of things, the presence of sin meant the presence of sickness; therefore, the removal of sin would mean the disappearance of the sickness.) Without subscribing to their false notion, Jesus satisfied the natural curiosity of the Jews by healing the man of his paralysis.

What a remarkable Savior is Jesus, our Lord. He is always ready to forgive our sins and to bring a clear witness of His real identity to those who have doubts about Him. He will never disappoint anyone who approaches Him with an open-ended faith.

I. *The Man and the First Miracle (2:1-5)*

2 A few days later, when Jesus again entered Capernaum, the people heard that he had come home. [2]So many gathered that there was no room left, not even outside the door, and he preached the word to them.
[3]Some men came, bringing to him a paralytic, carried by four of them.
[4]Since they could not get him to Jesus because of the crowd, they made an opening in the roof above Jesus and, after digging through it, lowered the mat the paralyzed man was lying on. [5]When Jesus saw their faith, he said to the paralytic, "Son, your sins are forgiven."

II. *The Madness and the Second Miracle (2:6-12)*

**[6]Now some teachers of the law were sitting there, thinking to them-
selves, [7]"Why does this fellow talk like that? He's blaspheming! Who can
forgive sins but God alone?"**
**[8]Immediately Jesus knew in his spirit that this was what they were
thinking in their hearts, and he said to them, "Why are you thinking
these things? [9]Which is easier: to say to the paralytic, 'Your sins are
forgiven,' or to say, 'Get up, take your mat and walk'? [10]But that you may
know that the Son of Man has authority on earth to forgive sins. . . ." He
said to the paralytic, [11]"I tell you, get up, take your mat and go home."
[12]He got up, took his mat and walked out in full view of them all. This
amazed everyone and they praised God, saying, "We have never seen
anything like this!"**

Jesus Calls and Dines with Levi (Mark 2:13-17)

(cf. Matt. 9:9-13 and Luke 5:27-32)

In this warm, but controversial, scene we learn much about the nature of Jesus' work. From start to finish it was a ministry of grace.

Jesus concentrated His remedial efforts on those who possessed spiritual ailments; He did not attempt to convert the contemporary religious order. Jesus did not come to reform the hierarchy, but to replace it with the fulfillment of the Law and the Prophets (Matt. 5:17, 18). On the one hand, we see the humble and compassionate side of Jesus—He dined with sinners. On the other hand, we see more than a glimpse of Jesus' attitude toward the religious order of the day—He would have nothing to do with the self-righteous band.

Here, then, is a careful blend of grace and holiness. Jesus will help anyone, if that person will but receive His grace. But Jesus refused to assist anyone who believed himself to be without spiritual needs. This is still the case.

I. *The Calling (2:13, 14)*

**[13]Once again Jesus went out beside the lake. A large crowd came to
him, and he began to teach them. [14]As he walked along, he saw Levi son
of Alphaeus sitting at the tax collector's booth. "Follow me," Jesus told
him, and Levi got up and followed him.**

II. *The Dining (2:15-17)*

[15]While Jesus was having dinner at Levi's house, many tax collectors and "sinners" were eating with him and his disciples, for there were many who followed him. [16]When the teachers of the law who were Pharisees saw him eating with the "sinners" and tax collectors, they asked his disciples: "Why does he eat with tax collectors and 'sinners'?"
[17]On hearing this, Jesus said to them, "It is not the healthy who need a doctor, but the sick. I have not come to call the righteous, but sinners."

Facts About Fasting (Mark 2:18-22)

(cf. Matt. 9:14-17 and Luke 5:33-39)

Jesus' ministry would not fit into the same mold as that of the Pharisees or John. His works and words were unique. He would not follow the established trends; instead, He would create new ones for others to follow.

At times Jesus' answers must have seemed evasive, when in fact they were simply too deep for spiritually shallow persons to grasp. (Unfortunately, this frequently included Jesus' very own disciples.) The disciples of the Pharisees and of John were largely schooled in the physical aspects of God's promises. They saw things mostly in black-and-white terms. But Jesus enlarged greatly upon their narrow understandings by injecting radical truths which His audiences would only be able to grasp somewhere down the road.

This fact remains unaltered today. Jesus' message is still radical, when contrasted with mere formal religion. For Jesus, there is more than rules to follow (morality and ethics and discipline); there is also a relationship to enjoy (fellowship between God and man)!

I. *The Inquiry (2:18)*

[18]Now John's disciples and the Pharisees were fasting. Some people came and asked Jesus, "How is it that John's disciples and the disciples of the Pharisees are fasting, but yours are not?"

II. *The Information (2:19, 20)*

[19]Jesus answered, "How can the guests of the bridegroom fast while

**he is with them? They cannot, so long as they have him with them. [20]But
the time will come when the bridegroom will be taken from them, and
on that day they will fast.**

III. *The Illustration (2:21, 22)*

**[21]"No one sews a patch of unshrunk cloth on an old garment. If he
does, the new piece will pull away from the old, making the tear worse.
[22]And no one pours new wine into old wineskins. If he does, the wine will
burst the skins, and both the wine and the wineskins will be ruined. No,
he pours new wine into new wineskins."**

Lord of the Sabbath (Mark 2:23-28)

(cf. Matt. 12:1-8 and Luke 6:1-5)

This story exposes one of the supreme contrasts between the Pharisees and Jesus. The Pharisees were always bent on finding faults with people, while Jesus was always occupied with finding ways to bless people. The Pharisees were cold and negative; Jesus was warm and positive. The Pharisees were legalistic; Jesus was liberating. The Pharisees read only the surface of the Law; Jesus discerned the inner principle of the Law.

I. *The Immediate Problem (2:23, 24)*

**[23]One Sabbath Jesus was going through the grainfields, and as his
disciples walked along, they began to pick some heads of grain. [24]The
Pharisees said to him, "Look, why are they doing what is unlawful on
the Sabbath?"**

II. *The Past Picture (2:25, 26)*

**[25]He answered, "Have you never read what David did when he and
his companions were hungry and in need? [26]In the days of Abiathar the
high priest, he entered the house of God and ate the consecrated bread,
which is lawful only for priests to eat. And he also gave some to his
companions."**

III. *The Eternal Principle (2:27, 28)*

[27]Then he said to them, "The Sabbath was made for man, not man for the Sabbath. [28]So the Son of Man is Lord even of the Sabbath."

Jesus Heals on the Sabbath (Mark 3:1-6)

(cf. Matt. 12:9-14 and Luke 6:6-11)

The root term from which the word "Sabbath" is derived means "to cease from labor" or "to rest." On the seventh day, after six days of labor in creating the universe, God rested (Gen. 2:2). Here, then, is our pattern: we were made to work for six days and to rest for one. But what does it mean "to rest"?

The answer to this inquiry is a serious matter, especially when you consider the fact that the Lord stipulated to Moses that anyone breaking the appointed rest would either be "cut off from his people" or be "put to death" (Exod 31:12-17). Certain Jewish teachers eventually responded to this divine charge by creating a long series of minute details that were to be observed, presumably in order to keep the Sabbath day holy. Included in this list were numerous trivial matters, such as: you cannot engage in war on the Sabbath (so Israel's enemies, knowing this ruling, would attack and slaughter them on this day!); neither can you walk a distance greater than 606 feet (although the Jews devised unique methods for getting around this observance); and so forth.

These merely human traditions served to bind and blind the Jews from the genuine essence of the original law. In fact, the day which was designed for rest was becoming a day of such strict regulations that some doubtlessly thought of it as being more laborious than restful (Matt. 11:28-30).

Jesus was aware of the traditional spirit that was present in His audience. Still, there was a need, and this need, as far as Jesus was concerned, took precedence over the humanistic religion that had been devised by the Jews. Therefore, Jesus healed the man's shriveled hand, making it like new. The Pharisees hated Jesus all the more for this supposed violation of the sacred law, but He would have nothing to do with their petty stipulations. He came to bless people, and bless them He would.

I. *The Scene (3:1-3)*

3 Another time he went into the synagogue, and a man with a shriveled hand was there. [2]Some of them were looking for a reason to accuse Jesus, so they watched him closely to see if he would heal

**him on the Sabbath. [3]Jesus said to the man with the shriveled hand,
"Stand up in front of everyone."**

II. *The Silence (3:4)*

**[4]Then Jesus asked them, "Which is lawful on the Sabbath: to do good
or to do evil, to save life or to kill?" But they remained silent.**

III. *The Stubbornness (3:5, 6)*

**[5]He looked around at them in anger and, deeply distressed at their
stubborn hearts, said to the man, "Stretch out your hand." He stretched
it out, and his hand was completely restored. [6]Then the Pharisees went
out and began to plot with the Herodians how they might kill Jesus.**

Jesus Heals Many (Mark 3:7-12)

(cf. Matt. 12:15-21)

Jesus never gave up. When people intensely disliked His teachings, He kept on preaching God's good news. When people sought to terminate His works by plotting to kill Him, He never slackened His pace. Jesus would not concentrate on the stubborn and hateful members of His audiences; rather, He focused on those persons who would respond positively.

Here is an episode where Jesus withdrew from a horribly negative synagogue service but continued to serve God, despite formal resistance against Him. He would not be deterred. Wherever there are people, there is work; and wherever there is work to be done, Jesus will be busy.

If we will allow it to happen, people can get us down. We can sit and sulk in despair and become useless to anyone, or we can turn our attention toward God's great work and continue to press on. Jesus never wasted His time by pouting over those who opposed Him; instead, He continuously served all who would follow Him, and that kept Him extremely busy.

There will always be people who have needs and who will respond positively to the Christian message. We must find them and bring the fullness of Christ into their lives.

**[7]Jesus withdrew with his disciples to the lake, and a large crowd from
Galilee followed. [8]When they heard all he was doing, many people came**

to him from Judea, Jerusalem, Idumea, and the regions across the Jordan and around Tyre and Sidon. [9]Because of the crowd he told his disciples to have a small boat ready for him, to keep the people from crowding him. [10]For he had healed many, so that those with diseases were pushing forward to touch him. [11]Whenever the evil[a] spirits saw him, they fell down before him and cried out, "You are the Son of God." [12]But he gave them strict orders not to tell who he was.

Jesus Appoints Twelve Apostles (Mark 3:13-19)

(cf. Matt. 10:1-4 and Luke 6:12-16)

The New Testament mentions disciples of Moses (John 9:28), of the Pharisees (Matt. 22:16), of John the Baptist (Matt. 9:14) and of Jesus. Of Jesus' disciples, there are two basic categories: (1) the twelve whom He selected to be with Him in a special capacity (Matt. 10:1); and (2) all those who abide in His Word, which naturally includes present-day Christians (John 8:31; 13:35; 15:8; Acts 11:26).

Apostleship is an extension of discipleship. First, the twelve were to be trained as disciples (this term could be translated, "apprentices"). Then, after some extended period of equipping the disciples, they were to become apostles (a term which means "ones set forth by the Lord"). There are two categories of apostles: (1) the twelve whom the Lord Jesus selected (Matt. 10:1; Luke 22:30; Rev. 21:14); and (2) the men whom the Holy Spirit selected to fulfill this office in the early church (Acts 14:4, 14; Rom. 16:7; 1 Cor. 4:6-9).

I. *The Appointment (3:13-15)*

[13]Jesus went up into the hills and called to him those he wanted, and they came to him. [14]He appointed twelve—designating them apostles[b]—that they might be with him and that he might send them out to preach [15]and to have authority to drive out demons.

II. *The Appointed (3:16-19)*

[16]These are the twelve he appointed: Simon (to whom he gave the name Peter); [17]James son of Zebedee, and his brother John (to them he gave the name Boanerges, which means Sons of Thunder); [18]Andrew, Philip, Bartholomew, Matthew, Thomas, James son of Alphaeus, Thaddaeus, Simon the Zealot [19]and Judas Iscariot, who betrayed him.

a 11 Greek *unclean*; also in verse 30 *b 14* Some manuscripts do not have *designating them apostles.*

Jesus Is Misunderstood (Mark 3:20-25)

(cf. Matt. 12:24-37, 46-50 and Luke 8:19, 20; 11:14-23)

Jesus' ministry was as provocative as it was profound. Always in His audiences there were some who thought Him to be demonically empowered and others who considered Him to be divinely empowered. Those who held to this wide range of opinions included the common people, the high officials, and even His own family members. There was never any certainty of unity in the crowds who heard and saw Jesus.

Regrettably, today there are still teachers of the gospel of Jesus Christ who find themselves speaking to an audience with mixed reactions. In some instances, denominational officials (those from "Jerusalem") look down upon nontraditional ministries; in other cases, even family members attempt to persuade teachers away from their duty. Nevertheless, like Jesus, the devoted proclaimer of God's will knows from whom he has received his call and message. Further, he recognizes and rejoices in the fruit of his labors, that is, in the many new brothers and sisters he has gained through teaching God's transforming Word.

I. *The Accusations of His Family (3:20, 21)*

**20Then Jesus entered a house, and again a crowd gathered, so that he
and his disciples were not even able to eat. 21When his family heard
about this, they went to take charge of him, for they said, "He is out of his
mind."**

II. *The Accusations of His Foes (3:22)*

**22And the teachers of the law who came down from Jerusalem said,
"He is possessed by Beelzebub[a]! By the prince of demons he is driving
out demons."**

III. *The Answer for His Foes (3:23-30)*

**23So Jesus called them and spoke to them in parables: "How can Satan
drive out Satan? 24If a kingdom is divided against itself, that kingdom
cannot stand. 25If a house is divided against itself, that house cannot**

a 22 Greek *Beezeboul* or *Beelzeboul*

**stand. [26]And if Satan opposes himself and is divided, he cannot stand; his
end has come. [27]In fact, no one can enter a strong man's house and carry
off his possessions unless he first ties up the strong man. Then he can rob
his house. [28]I tell you the truth, all the sins and blasphemies of men will
be forgiven them. [29]But whoever blasphemes against the Holy Spirit
will never be forgiven; he is guilty of an eternal sin."**

[30]He said this because they were saying, "He has an evil spirit."

IV. *The Answer for His Family (3:31-35)*

**[31]Then Jesus' mother and brothers arrived. Standing outside, they sent
someone in to call him. [32]A crowd was sitting around him, and they told
him, "Your mother and brothers are outside looking for you."**

[33]"Who are my mother and my brothers?" he asked.

**[34]Then he looked at those seated in a circle around him and said,
"Here are my mother and my brothers! [35]Whoever does God's will is my
brother and sister and mother."**

The Parable of the Four Soils (Mark 4:1-20)

(cf. Matt. 13:1-23 and Luke 8:4-15)

In Mark's Gospel parables appear less frequently than they do in the Gospels of Matthew and Luke. Further, Mark includes only two parables that are not also found in the two other synoptic Gospels (4:26-29; 13:34, 35). Matthew, on the other hand, records eleven parables and Luke relates seventeen parables that are found only within their own writings.

In each of the synoptic Gospels this particular parable is always presented first. There are a number of good reasons why this parable heads the list: (1) it is probably the first detailed parable they ever heard Jesus teach; (2) it is an excellent introduction to the nature and purpose of parables, especially because of its parenthetical implications; and (3) it is the most revealing of all the parables with regard to how the Kingdom will shape up, who will oppose its appearance, how people will enter it presumptuously and then fall from it, and who will remain and bear fruit in it.

The central object in this parable is the "seed" (that is, the Word of God). Through this term Jesus shows us what responses God's Kingdom message will have, particularly as it relates to Satan, to the carefree hearer, to the casual responder, and to the committed laborer.

I. *The Information (4:1-9)*

**4 On another occasion Jesus began to teach by the lake. The crowd
that gathered around him was so large that he got into a boat
and sat in it out on the lake, while all the people were along the shore at
the water's edge. 2He taught them many things by parables, and in his
teaching said: 3"Listen! A farmer went out to sow his seed. 4As he was
scattering the seed, some fell along the path, and the birds came and ate
it up. 5Some fell on rocky places, where it did not have much soil. It
sprang up quickly, because the soil was shallow. 6But when the sun
came up, the plants were scorched, and they withered because they had
no root. 7Other seed fell among thorns, which grew up and choked the
plants, so that they did not bear grain. 8Still other seed fell on good soil. It
came up, grew and produced a crop, multiplying thirty, sixty, or even a
hundred times."**

9Then Jesus said, "He who has ears to hear, let him hear."

II. *The Implications (4:10-12)*

**10When he was alone, the Twelve and the others around him asked
him about the parables. 11He told them, "The secret of the kingdom of
God has been given to you. But to those on the outside everything is said
in parables 12so that,**

**" 'they may be ever seeing but never perceiving,
and ever hearing but never understanding;
otherwise they might turn and be forgiven!'[a]"**

III. *The Interpretation (4:13-20)*

**13Then Jesus said to them, "Don't you understand this parable? How
then will you understand any parable? 14The farmer sows the word.
15Some people are like seed along the path, where the word is sown. As
soon as they hear it, Satan comes and takes away the word that was
sown in them. 16Others, like seed sown on rocky places, hear the word
and at once receive it with joy. 17But since they have no root, they last
only a short time. When trouble or persecution comes because of the
word, they quickly fall away. 18Still others, like seed sown among**

---

a 12 Isaiah 6:9, 10

thorns, hear the word; [19]but the worries of this life, the deceitfulness of wealth and the desires for other things come in and choke the word, making it unfruitful. [20]Others, like seed sown on good soil, hear the word, accept it, and produce a crop—thirty, sixty or even a hundred times what was sown."

The Parable of the Lamp (Mark 4:21-23)

(cf. Matt. 5:15; 10:26 and Luke 8:16-18)

The term "lamp" might be more appropriately rendered "candle," since it actually refers to a small container of oil with a burning wick. Quite obviously you would not put a fire under a bowl (literally a peck measure) or flammable bedding (literally a mattress). Instead, these lamps belong on a stand, so their light will profit everyone. In like fashion, the Christian is not to conceal his faith, but to expose it to the view of everyone.

God does not impart His grace to us to amuse us or merely to satisfy any selfish ambitions. On the contrary, He dispenses His help so that after we have received it we might pass it along to others. We must learn the art of receiving things from God with both hands—one hand taking the blessings to ourselves, and the other hand sharing the same blessings freely.

[21]He said to them, "Do you bring in a lamp to put it under a bowl or a bed? Instead, don't you put it on its stand? [22]For whatever is hidden is meant to be disclosed, and whatever is concealed is meant to be brought out into the open. [23]If anyone has ears to hear, let him hear."

The Principle of Giving and Getting (Mark 4:24, 25)

(cf. Matt. 7:12 and 13:11, 12)

There are both productive and unproductive ways to use the grace extended to us from God. The productive approach is achieved by sharing what God gives to you. The more you give, the more you will be given in return. The opposite, however, is equally true. The more you cling to what you have, the more your possessions will slip through your fingers.

**[24]"Consider carefully what you hear," he continued. "With the measure
you use, it will be measured to you—and even more. [25]Whoever has will
be given more; whoever does not have, even what he has will be taken
from him."**

The Parable of Growing Seeds (Mark 4:26-29)

Inside this brief story are several big lessons. First, we see that the growth of the Kingdom is beyond human control. We drop the seeds here and there, but their taking root and growing is wholly outside our control. This is God's work. Second, we discover that just as in the farmer's field there is an appointed time for reaping the harvest, so there is an appointed time in God's Kingdom for gathering in His fruit. Someday, possibly very soon, God will say the time is ripe; it is harvest time! Naturally, this refers to the Second Coming of Jesus Christ (Rev. 19).

**[26]He also said, "This is what the kingdom of God is like. A man scatters
seed on the ground. [27]Night and day, whether he sleeps or gets up, the
seed sprouts and grows, though he does not know how. [28]All by itself the
soil produces grain—first the stalk, then the head, then the full kernel in
the head. [29]As soon as the grain is ripe, he puts the sickle to it, because
the harvest has come."**

The Parable of the Mustard Seed (Mark 4:30-34)

(cf. Matt. 13:31, 32 and Luke 13:18, 19)

Now Jesus tells the story of how the mustard seed must be buried (or planted) in the ground, out of human sight, before it can be resurrected in a new and expanded form of life. Out of this chamber of death, the earth, would rise the biggest of all the garden plants.

In like manner, before Jesus could become the Lord of the Resurrection, He would need to die and be buried. His body would have to be placed in the ground, out of human view. Then, from death itself, He would have to ascend and become the head of God's universal Kingdom.

How unimpressed the religious officials were by the Kingdom Jesus announced. They mocked Jesus and His tiny band of unschooled disciples. They were such a small group of men. Equally insignificant were the origins of the early church in a single upper room. But from this nearly microscopic start a worldwide faith of monumental importance has developed! So it is with the mustard seed and its resultant plant.

30Again he said, "What shall we say the kingdom of God is like, or what
parable shall we use to describe it? 31It is like a mustard seed, which is
the smallest seed you plant in the ground. 32Yet when planted, it grows
and becomes the largest of all garden plants, with such big branches
that the birds of the air can perch in its shade."
33With many similar parables Jesus spoke the word to them, as much
as they could understand. 34He did not say anything to them without
using a parable. But when he was alone with his own disciples, he
explained everything.

Jesus Quiets a Storm (Mark 4:35-41)

(cf. Matt. 8:18, 23-27 and Luke 8:22-25)

This is the second of six times when it is recorded that Jesus withdrew from His audience (cf. 3:7ff.; 6:30ff.; 7:24ff.; 8:1ff.; 8:27ff.). He was completely exhausted. In fact, His weariness was so great that He actually slept soundly during the worst storm His disciples ever encountered on the Sea of Galilee. Let us learn several lessons from this brief episode: (1) Jesus was totally human. Although He was the God-man, His deity never entered into and took control of the human side of his existence. Here we see Jesus thoroughly drained of strength. (2) Jesus was extremely limited. Today Jesus is at work around the world through His mystical body, the Church. But when Jesus lived in Israel, He was confined to laboring in only one spot at a time. That meant He constantly expended all of His energy in order to get His work accomplished. (3) Jesus was in control of every situation. Despite the fact that Jesus was often exhausted, He always responded with words of faith and continued to conquer every obstacle before Him.

I. *The Fear of the Disciples (4:35-38)*

35That day when evening came, he said to his disciples, "Let us go over
to the other side." 36Leaving the crowd behind, they took him along, just

as he was, in the boat. There were also other boats with him. 37 A furious squall came up, and the waves broke over the boat, so that it was nearly swamped. 38 Jesus was in the stern, sleeping on a cushion. The disciples woke him and said to him, "Teacher, don't you care if we drown?"

II. *The Faith of Jesus (4:39, 40)*

39 He got up, rebuked the wind and said to the waves, "Quiet! Be still!" Then the wind died down and it was completely calm.

40 He said to his disciples, "Why are you so afraid? Do you still have no faith?"

III. *The Fluster of the Disciples (4:41)*

41 They were terrified and asked each other, "Who is this? Even the wind and the waves obey him!"

Jesus Heals a Demonized Man (Mark 5:1-20)

(cf. Matt. 8:28-34 and Luke 8:26-39)

In Matthew's account two men are mentioned; Mark describes only one man. Perhaps Mark refers only to the one with whom Jesus spoke. Regardless of the exact cause for this omission, nothing is missing in Mark's account about these matters: the terrible results created by demonization; the terrific results created by deliverance; and the tragic results created by the deaths of the swine.

I. *The Encounter (5:1-5)*

5 They went across the lake to the region of the Gerasenes.[a] 2 When Jesus got out of the boat, a man with an evil[b] spirit came from the tombs to meet him. 3 This man lived in the tombs, and no one could bind him any more, not even with a chain. 4 For he had often been chained hand and foot, but he tore the chains apart and broke the irons on his feet. No one was strong enough to subdue him. 5 Night and day among the tombs and in the hills he would cry out and cut himself with stones.

a 1 Some manuscripts *Gadarenes*; other manuscripts *Gergesenes* b 2 Greek *unclean*; also in verses 8 and 13

II. *The Exchange (5:6-10)*

[6]When he saw Jesus from a distance, he ran and fell on his knees in front of him. [7]He shouted at the top of his voice, "What do you want with me, Jesus, Son of the Most High God? Swear to God that you won't torture me!" [8]For Jesus was saying to him, "Come out of this man, you evil spirit!"

[9]Then Jesus asked him, "What is your name?"

"My name is Legion," he replied, "for we are many." [10]And he begged Jesus again and again not to send them out of the area.

III. *The Exorcism (5:11-13)*

[11]A large herd of pigs was feeding on the nearby hillside. [12]The demons begged Jesus, "Send us among the pigs; allow us to go into them." [13]He gave them permission, and the evil spirits came out and went into the pigs. The herd, about two thousand in number, rushed down the steep bank into the lake and were drowned.

IV. *The Excitement (5:14-17)*

[14]Those tending the pigs ran off and reported this in the town and countryside, and the people went out to see what had happened. [15]When they came to Jesus, they saw the man who had been possessed by the legion of demons, sitting there, dressed and in his right mind; and they were afraid. [16]Those who had seen it told the people what had happened to the demon-possessed man—and told about the pigs as well. [17]Then the people began to plead with Jesus to leave their region.

V. *The Evangelism (5:18-20)*

[18]As Jesus was getting into the boat, the man who had been demon-possessed begged to go with him. [19]Jesus did not let him, but said, "Go home to your family and tell them how much the Lord has done for you, and how he has had mercy on you." [20]So the man went away and began to tell in the Decapolis[a] how much Jesus had done for him. And all the people were amazed.

a 20 That is, the Ten Cities

Jesus Heals a Girl and a Woman (Mark 5:21-43)

(cf. Matt. 9:18-26 and Luke 8:40-56)

Crowds. Great crowds. Everywhere there were people. Sixteen times Mark mentions the large number of people who seemed to relentlessly smother Jesus with their needs (2:13; 3:7-9, 20, 32; 4:1, 36; 5:21; 7:33; 8:1, 2; 9:14, 17; 14:43; 15:8). There was no escape. Crossing the sea to a new shore would mean other multitudes would be waiting for Him.

In this story Jesus was embraced by another crowd of desperate people. One person requested Jesus' miraculous help; another was content to merely touch His garments. Both were helped.

Here we discover the fact that in the midst of multitudes Jesus always managed to see the individual. His service was never general, but always specific. Jesus had time for the interruption, the single party, and the personal hurts of everyday people like you and me.

I. *The Information (5:21-24)*

21When Jesus had again crossed over by boat to the other side of the
lake, a large crowd gathered around him. While he was by the lake,
22one of the synagogue rulers, named Jairus, came there. Seeing Jesus,
he fell at his feet 23and pleaded earnestly with him, "My little daughter
is dying. Please come and put your hands on her so that she will be
healed and live." 24So Jesus went with him.
A large crowd followed and pressed around him.

II. *The Interruption (5:25-34)*

25And a woman was there who had been subject to bleeding for twelve
years. 26She had suffered a great deal under the care of many doctors
and had spent all she had, yet instead of getting better she grew worse.
27When she heard about Jesus, she came up behind him in the crowd
and touched his cloak, 28because she thought, "If I just touch his clothes,
I will be healed." 29Immediately her bleeding stopped and she felt in her
body that she was freed from her suffering.

30At once Jesus realized that power had gone out from him. He turned
around in the crowd and asked, "Who touched my clothes?"
31"You see the people crowding against you," his disciples answered,
"and yet you can ask, 'Who touched me?' "
32But Jesus kept looking around to see who had done it. 33Then the
woman, knowing what had happened to her, came and fell at his feet
and, trembling with fear, told him the whole truth. 34He said to her,
"Daughter, your faith has healed you. Go in peace and be freed from
your suffering."

III. *The Incomprehension (5:35-43)*

35While Jesus was still speaking, some men came from the house of
Jairus, the synagogue ruler. "Your daughter is dead," they said. "Why
bother the teacher any more?"
36Ignoring what they said, Jesus told the synagogue ruler, "Don't be
afraid; just believe."
37He did not let anyone follow him except Peter, James and John the
brother of James. 38When they came to the home of the synagogue ruler,
Jesus saw a commotion, with people crying and wailing loudly. 39He
went in and said to them, "Why all this commotion and wailing? The
child is not dead but asleep." 40But they laughed at him.
After he put them all out, he took the child's father and mother and
the disciples who were with him, and went in where the child was. 41He
took her by the hand and said to her, *"Talitha koum!"* (which means,
"Little girl, I say to you, get up!"). 42Immediately the girl stood up and
walked around (she was twelve years old). At this they were completely
astonished. 43He gave strict orders not to let anyone know about this,
and told them to give her something to eat.

Jesus Goes Home (Mark 6:1-6)

(cf. Matt. 13:53-58 and Luke 4:16-30)

There is no disappointment like the disappointment that comes from being turned aside by those you know the best. Jesus learned here that regardless of the fame He had received away from home, in His own town He was still just "the carpenter . . .

Mary's son." It was difficult for the people to be objective about such a familiar figure.

Faith often grows best when planted by unfamiliar hands in foreign soil. Jesus learned this fact, and when He did, He soon moved on to work in new sites. In like fashion, we cannot measure our effectiveness by the results we receive at home. The seeds we plant may be perfect enough; it may not be the seed's fault if there is a failure to produce fruit, but often the soil is to blame. We must learn, then, to plant the bulk of our seeds of faith, finances and service where they will have the best chance to succeed.

I. *The Resistance of the People (6:1-3)*

**6 Jesus left there and went to his home town, accompanied by his
disciples. 2When the Sabbath came, he began to teach in the synagogue, and many who heard him were amazed.**

**"Where did this man get these things?" they asked. "What's this wisdom
that has been given him, that he even does miracles! 3Isn't this the carpenter? Isn't this Mary's son and the brother of James, Joses, Judas and Simon? Aren't his sisters here with us?" And they took offense at him.**

II. *The Response of Jesus (6:4-6)*

**4Jesus said to them, "Only in his home town, among his relatives and in
his own house is a prophet without honor." 5He could not do any miracles
there, except lay his hands on a few sick people and heal them. 6And he
was amazed at their lack of faith.**

Then Jesus went around teaching from village to village.

The Twelve Are Sent Out (Mark 6:7-13)

(cf. Matt. 10:1-15 and Luke 9:1-6)

Jesus never waited for the populace to come streaming to His door; instead, He actively and systematically went to them. We can learn at least five vital truths from this strategy to apply to our lives: (1) Jesus always took the initiative in introducing people to the good news—we, too, must take the first step in communicating the gospel message to the non-Christian. (2) Jesus enlisted others in His evangelistic campaigns—in like fashion we must not go it alone. (3) Jesus used His volunteers in teams of two.

(This tactic gave each worker an opportunity to be used while drawing encouragement from the presence of the other team member. Also, the smallness of the number enabled the twelve to cover more territory and be less intimidating in their presentations.) We ought to follow the same approach, for the same reasons. (4) Jesus empowered His workers—nothing is less effective than a powerless presentation of the gospel. We must also receive Christ's anointing. (5) Jesus instructed His workers (they would go forth prepared). We must know what we are to do before we can ever begin; preparation is a must.

I. *The Commission (6:7)*

7Calling the Twelve to him, he sent them out two by two and gave them authority over evil[a] spirits.

II. *The Commandments (6:8-11)*

8These were his instructions: "Take nothing for the journey except a
staff—no bread, no bag, no money in your belts. 9Wear sandals but not
an extra tunic. 10Whenever you enter a house, stay there until you leave
that town. 11And if any place will not welcome you or listen to you, shake
the dust off your feet when you leave, as a testimony against them."

III. *The Consummation (6:12, 13)*

12They went out and preached that people should repent. 13They drove
out many demons and anointed many sick people with oil and healed
them.

John the Baptist Is Beheaded (Mark 6:14-29)

(cf. Matt. 14:1-12 and Luke 9:7-9)

In all, there are five different Herods discussed in the New Testament. This particular one, addressed as "King Herod" and "Antipas," is the son of Herod the Great and Malthace. He is the most written about of all the Herods in the Scriptures.

Assuming command of Galilee and Perea in 4 B.C., this Herod ruled until A.D. 39. His career was distinguished with the building of new cities, like Tiberias, his capital. But his rule was also badly marred by his inability to control his impulses. In a

[a] 7 Greek *unclean*

moment of passion he devised a successful plan to marry his brother's wife, Herodias. In a later thoughtless moment he promised Herodias's daughter anything, up to half his kingdom. The result of this decision cost John his life. In another hasty moment Antipas remarked that he would like to kill Jesus (Luke 13:31-33). When given that opportunity, however, his cowardice was shown by his merely mocking Jesus (Luke 23:6-12). Jesus would not give to him, the killer of God's prophet, so much as a single word.

Finally, in A.D. 39, Antipas, through the promptings of his nagging wife, went to Rome to seek a higher title. He did not expect the resulting decision, however; for his ambition caused him to be banished from the country until his death.

Below is the account of a weak man in a strong office. His crime was thoughtless, though his conscience would never permit him to stop thinking about the immaturity of his lust-centered decision.

I. *Herod's Conscience (6:14-16)*

14King Herod heard about this, for Jesus' name had become well-
known. Some were saying,[a] "John the Baptist has been raised from the
dead, and that is why miraculous powers are at work in him."
15Others said, "He is Elijah."
And still others claimed, "He is a prophet, like one of the prophets of
long ago."
16But when Herod heard this, he said, "John, the man I beheaded, has
been raised from the dead!"

II. *Herod's Carnality (6:17-20)*

17For Herod himself had given orders to have John arrested, and he
had him bound and put in prison. He did this because of Herodias, his
brother Philip's wife, whom he had married. 18For John had been say-
ing to Herod, "It is not lawful for you to have your brother's wife." 19So
Herodias nursed a grudge against John and wanted to kill him. But she
was not able to, 20because Herod feared John and protected him, know-
ing him to be a righteous and holy man. When Herod heard John, he
was greatly puzzled[b]; yet he liked to listen to him.

III. *Herod's Craziness (6:21-29)*

21Finally the opportune time came. On his birthday Herod gave a
banquet for his high officials and military commanders and the leading
men of Galilee. 22When the daughter of Herodias came in and danced,
she pleased Herod and his dinner guests.

a 14 Some early manuscripts *He was saying* *b 20* Some early manuscripts *he did many things*

The king said to the girl, "Ask me for anything you want, and I'll give it to you." [23]And he promised her with an oath, "Whatever you ask I will give you, up to half my kingdom."

[24]She went out and said to her mother, "What shall I ask for?"

"The head of John the Baptist," she answered.

[25]At once the girl hurried in to the king with the request: "I want you to give me right now the head of John the Baptist on a platter."

[26]The king was greatly distressed, but because of his oaths and his dinner guests, he did not want to refuse her. [27]So he immediately sent an executioner with orders to bring John's head. The man went, beheaded John in the prison, [28]and brought back his head on a platter. He presented it to the girl, and she gave it to her mother. [29]On hearing of this, John's disciples came and took his body and laid it in a tomb.

Jesus Feeds the Five Thousand (Mark 6:30-44)

(cf. Matt. 14:14-21; Luke 9:10-17 and John 6:1-13)

Jesus filled His life with work, and He filled His work with life. There was no trace of laziness in Jesus or in His disciples. They were all workers. This is a primary ingredient in their fruitfulness. You cannot expect to reap bountifully if you do not sow abundantly.

There is no aspect of life so rewarding as the selfless labors performed in Jesus' name. They revitalize the soul and renew the body. They awaken our whole being with expectancy and joy. Still, work is work, and labors done in Jesus' name are as demanding as any work anywhere. So, we must rest awhile, like the disciples. Balancing perspiration with relaxation is needed by each one of us.

We see here that people's needs are not subject to a schedule. They do not conveniently pop up between nine and five on weekdays. Rather, they come at all times and at all places. Even as Jesus' disciples, we too must be prepared to serve people in the instant of their need, and not just in the season of our convenience. Let us remember that seeming interruptions may be actually opportunities in disguise, as displayed in this most astonishing miracle.

I. *A Need for Rest (6:30, 31)*

[30]The apostles gathered around Jesus and reported to him all they had done and taught. [31]Then, because so many people were coming and

going that they did not even have a chance to eat, he said to them, "Come with me by yourselves to a quiet place and get some rest."

II. *A Need for Restoration (6:32-34)*

32So they went away by themselves in a boat to a solitary place. 33But
many who saw them leaving recognized them and ran on foot from all
the towns and got there ahead of them. 34When Jesus landed and saw a
large crowd, he had compassion on them, because they were like sheep without a shepherd. So he began teaching them many things.

III. *A Need for Refreshment (6:35-44)*

35By this time it was late in the day, so his disciples came to him. "This
is a remote place," they said, "and it's already very late. 36Send the
people away so they can go to the surrounding countryside and villages and buy themselves something to eat."

37But he answered, "You give them something to eat."

They said to him, "That would take eight months of a man's wages[a]! Are we to go and spend that much on bread and give it to them to eat?"

38"How many loaves do you have?" he asked. "Go and see."

When they found out, they said, "Five—and two fish."

39Then Jesus directed them to have all the people sit down in groups
on the green grass. 40So they sat down in groups of hundreds and fifties.
41Taking the five loaves and the two fish and looking up to heaven, he
gave thanks and broke the loaves. Then he gave them to his disciples
to set before the people. He also divided the two fish among them all.
42They all ate and were satisfied, 43and the disciples picked up twelve
basketfuls of broken pieces of bread and fish. 44The number of the men
who had eaten was five thousand.

Jesus Walks on Water (Mark 6:45-56)

(cf. Matt. 14:22-32 and John 6:15-21)

This brief story captures the essence of Jesus' entire ministry and life. His dependence upon God, His instruction of the disciples and His meaningful involvement with

a 37 Greek *take two hundred denarii*

people are three of the chief distinguishing marks of Jesus Christ. He was intensely spiritual, yet eminently practical. His special powers never overlooked human needs.

I. *Jesus Hears God (6:45)*

[45]Immediately Jesus made his disciples get into the boat and go on ahead of him to Bethsaida, while he dismissed the crowd.

II. *Jesus Helps Disciples (6:46-52)*

[46]After leaving them, he went into the hills to pray.
[47]When evening came, the boat was in the middle of the lake, and he
was alone on land. [48]He saw the disciples straining at the oars, because
the wind was against them. About the fourth watch of the night he went
out to them, walking on the lake. He was about to pass by them, [49]but
when they saw him walking on the lake, they thought he was a ghost.
They cried out, [50]because they all saw him and were terrified.
Immediately he spoke to them and said, "Take courage! It is I. Don't
be afraid." [51]Then he climbed into the boat with them, and the wind died
down. They were completely amazed, [52]for they had not understood
about the loaves; their hearts were hardened.

III. *Jesus Heals People (6:53-56)*

[53]When they had crossed over, they landed at Gennesaret and an-
chored there. [54]As soon as they got out of the boat, people recognized
Jesus. [55]They ran throughout that whole region and carried the sick on
mats to wherever they heard he was. [56]And everywhere he went—into
villages, towns or countryside—they placed the sick in the marketplaces.
They begged him to let them touch even the edge of his cloak, and all
who touched him were healed.

The Danger of Bad Traditions (Mark 7:1-23)

(cf. Matt. 15:1-20)

The term "tradition" means "that which is handed down from one person to another, especially teachings." Orthodox Christians, for instance, believe in a sacred tradition—we accept the Scriptures (both Old and New Testaments) as being accurately handed down from one generation to another. Unfortunately, there is a subtle danger in this passing-along process, and that danger involves affixing something that is merely man-made to that which is God-made.

It is these additions to (or as often as not, these subtractions from) the Word of God that get us into all sorts of problems. By the time of Jesus' day the sacred Word of the Lord (the Old Testament) had been all but obscured by the human traditions that evolved around it.

There is a natural tendency in man to become sidetracked by some superficial aspect of the faith, instead of steadfastly adhering to the faith itself (this character trait, by the way, has been repeatedly used by Satan to his evil advantage). Our five senses take control of us from time to time, and when they do, the rituals, the ceremonies, the human traditions, the edifices, the "sacred" furniture and the religious symbols become more real than the One whom each of these items is intended to reveal. Each of us ought to quiz ourselves regularly to see just how attached we have become to man-created methods, teachings and traditions. We may not see any need to change anything for the moment, but we must always remember that someday God may call us to let go of some of these items.

I. *Challenge of the Pharisees (7:1-5)*

**7 The Pharisees and some of the teachers of the law who had come
from Jerusalem gathered around Jesus and 2saw some of his disciples eating food with "unclean"—that is, ceremonially unwashed—
hands. 3(The Pharisees and all the Jews do not eat unless they give their
hands a ceremonial washing, holding to the tradition of the elders.
4When they come from the marketplace they do not eat unless they
wash. And they observe many other traditions, such as the washing of
cups, pitchers and kettles.[a])**

**5So the Pharisees and teachers of the law asked Jesus, "Why don't your
disciples live according to the tradition of the elders instead of eating
their food with 'unclean' hands?"**

II. *Charge of Jesus (7:6-16)*

**6He replied, "Isaiah was right when he prophesied about you hypo-
crites; as it is written:**

" 'These people honor me with their lips,
but their hearts are far from me.
7They worship me in vain;
their teachings are but rules taught by men.'[b]

[a] 4 Some early manuscripts *pitchers, kettles and dining couches* [b] 6, 7 Isaiah 29:13

[8]You have let go of the commands of God and are holding on to the traditions of men."

[9]And he said to them: "You have a fine way of setting aside the commands of God in order to observe[a] your own traditions! [10]For Moses said, 'Honor your father and mother,'[b] and, 'Anyone who curses his father or mother must be put to death.'[c] [11]But you say that if a man says to his father or mother: 'Whatever help you might otherwise have received from me is Corban' (that is, a gift devoted to God), [12]then you no longer let him do anything for his father or mother. [13]Thus you nullify the word of God by your tradition that you have handed down. And you do many things like that."

[14]Again Jesus called the crowd to him and said, "Listen to me, everyone, and understand this. [15]Nothing outside a man can make him 'unclean' by going into him. Rather, it is what comes out of a man that makes him 'unclean.'[d]"

III. *Conversation with Disciples (7:17-23)*

[17]After he had left the crowd and entered the house, his disciples asked him about this parable. [18]"Are you so dull?" he asked. "Don't you see that nothing that enters a man from the outside can make him 'unclean'? [19]For it doesn't go into his heart but into his stomach, and then out of his body." (In saying this, Jesus declared all foods "clean.")

[20]He went on: "What comes out of a man is what makes him 'unclean.' [21]For from within, out of men's hearts, come evil thoughts, sexual immorality, theft, murder, adultery, [22]greed, malice, deceit, lewdness, envy, slander, arrogance and folly. [23]All these evils come from inside and make a man 'unclean.'"

The Syrophoenician Woman **(Mark 7:24-30)**

(cf. Matt. 15:21-28)

Mark is not specific about the exact location of this event. He only states that Jesus traveled to the vicinity of Tyre (a city located along the Mediterranean coast, in the

a 9 Some manuscripts *set up* *b 10* Exodus 20:12; Deut. 5:16 *c 10* Exodus 21:17; Lev. 20:9 *d 15* Some early manuscripts *'unclean.' [16]If anyone has ears to hear, let him hear*

Roman province of Syria). The purpose for selecting this location is more revealing than the place itself. Jesus sought to be alone. He wanted some peace and quiet. He desired to escape the constant demands presented by the crowds who so frequently required His full attention.

The need to be away from people for a while so you can return to them more powerfully is a vital element in effective ministry. No one, including the impeccable and anointed Jesus, is made only to give. There is a limit to everyone's resources, and when these supplies become thin, we must seek to restore them. We must learn that feeding ourselves, where no one can disturb us, is an imperative in Christian service.

It is difficult to conceal famous persons from the public eye, however. This was especially true of Jesus. His fame saturated Judea and Galilee; even in Gentile territories people had heard of this most remarkable man. And when a Greek woman learned that this famous personage was in her vicinity, she would have no rest until her need, too, was miraculously satisfied by Him.

24 Jesus left that place and went to the vicinity of Tyre.[a] He entered a
house and did not want anyone to know it; yet he could not keep his
presence secret. 25 In fact, as soon as she heard about him, a woman
whose little daughter was possessed by an evil[b] spirit came and fell at his
feet. 26 The woman was a Greek, born in Syrian Phoenicia. She begged
Jesus to drive the demon out of her daughter.
27 "First let the children eat all they want," he told her, "for it is not
right to take the children's bread and toss it to their dogs."
28 "Yes, Lord," she replied, "but even the dogs under the table eat the
children's crumbs."
29 Then he told her, "For such a reply, you may go; the demon has left
your daughter."
30 She went home and found her child lying on the bed, and the demon
gone.

A Deaf and Mute Man Is Healed (Mark 7:31-37)

(cf. Matt. 15:29-31)

The second recorded miracle in Jesus' Gentile travels occurred in the region of Decapolis. The designation means "ten cities," and it refers to a league of Greek cities which united for mutual defense purposes. With the exception of Scythopolis, each of

[a] 24 Many early manuscripts *Tyre and Sidon*   [b] 25 Greek *unclean*

the other nine cities (including Pella, Dion, Gerasa, Philadelphia, Gadara, Raphana, Kanatha, Hippos and Damascus) was located east of the Jordan River.

Five things captivate our interest as we read the details of this healing. First, wherever Jesus went, there were crowds who believed in His miraculous powers. Second, Jesus always satisfied the desires of His petitioners. Third, Jesus never made a show of His spiritual gifts. Fourth, Jesus always ministered on a personal plane, giving individual attention to each concern. Fifth, Jesus was not interested in gaining any fame; He wanted men and women to reverence God.

I. *A Public Meeting (7:31, 32)*

**31Then Jesus left the vicinity of Tyre and went through Sidon, down to
the Sea of Galilee and into the region of the Decapolis.[a] 32There some
people brought a man to him who was deaf and could hardly talk, and
they begged him to place his hand on the man.**

II. *A Private Ministry (7:33-35)*

**33After he took him aside, away from the crowd, Jesus put his fingers
into the man's ears. Then he spit and touched the man's tongue. 34He
looked up to heaven and with a deep sigh said to him, "*Ephphatha!*"
(which means, "Be opened!"). 35At this, the man's ears were opened, his
tongue was loosened and he began to speak plainly.**

III. *A Personal Message (7:36, 37)*

**36Jesus commanded them not to tell anyone. But the more he did so,
the more they kept talking about it. 37People were overwhelmed with
amazement. "He has done everything well," they said. "He even makes
the deaf hear and the dumb speak."**

Feeding the Four Thousand (Mark 8:1-10)

(cf. Matt. 15:32-39)

If you ever engage yourself in the ministry of meeting the needs of people, you will discover that new difficulties will invariably emerge to take a seat beside old problems. But this is precisely the soil God uses to resurrect a miracle. Our problems are God's

a 31 That is, the Ten Cities

opportunities to show us His compassion and strength. Once we make our move to serve people, we can expect new troubles, but we also can anticipate new triumphs. It is practically a pattern without an exception: service, snares, success.

The disciples had to learn this principle. With the grand blessings of the long teachings from Jesus came inevitable problems concerning the feeding of this large audience. The disciples were perplexed, not knowing how to remedy the problem. But Jesus resolved their dilemma by demonstrating another profound spiritual truth—little is much, when God is in it. With just seven loaves and a few small fish, a large crowd was fed. God specializes in things thought to be impossible. Someone has wisely observed that when you rely upon human resources, you get what people can offer, but when you rely upon prayer, you get what God can offer.

I. *The Compassion of Jesus (8:1-3)*

8 During those days another large crowd gathered. Since they had
nothing to eat, Jesus called his disciples to him and said, 2“I have
compassion for these people; they have already been with me three days
and have nothing to eat. 3If I send them home hungry, they will collapse
on the way, because some of them have come a long distance.”

II. *The Concern of the Disciples (8:4)*

4His disciples answered, “But where in this remote place can anyone
get enough bread to feed them?”

III. *The Commandment of Jesus (8:5-10)*

5“How many loaves do you have?” Jesus asked.
“Seven,” they replied.
6He told the crowd to sit down on the ground. When he had taken the
seven loaves and given thanks, he broke them and gave them to his dis-
ciples to set before the people, and they did so. 7They had a few small fish
as well; he gave thanks for them also and told the disciples to distribute
them. 8The people ate and were satisfied. Afterward the disciples
picked up seven basketfuls of broken pieces that were left over. 9About
four thousand men were present. And having sent them away, 10he got
into the boat with his disciples and went to the region of Dalmanutha.

The Evil Side of Signs (Mark 8:11-13)

(cf. Matt. 16:1-4)

Asking for a "sign" is the same as asking for a miracle. It was believed (and to some degree correctly) that anyone claiming to be the Messiah should have miraculous proofs for such declarations. A sign, therefore, would theoretically authenticate the messenger as truly having been sent by God. But Jesus was not interested in entertaining or performing for the satisfaction of already hardened hearts.

Jesus *did*, however, perform signs when the context was more conducive to spiritual results. In fact, He believed that some people would not come to have any saving faith without the appearance of these authenticating miracles (John 4:48). But when hardened hearts seek a sign, just to amuse their own carnal appetites, then Jesus has no time for such a useless display of His spiritual endowments.

11The Pharisees came and began to question Jesus. To test him, they asked him for a sign from heaven. 12He sighed deeply and said, "Why does this generation ask for a miraculous sign? I tell you the truth, no sign will be given to it." 13Then he left them, got back into the boat and crossed to the other side.

The Yeast of Evil Persons (Mark 8:14-21)

(cf. Matt. 16:5-12)

Yeast (or fermented dough/leaven) is frequently mentioned in the Scriptures to illustrate the rapid-spreading ability of evil. Paul, for instance, states that "A little yeast works through a whole batch of dough. [Therefore] get rid of the old yeast that you may be a new batch without yeast" (1 Cor. 5:6, 7). In other words, if a small amount of evil is permitted to exist, it will soon become a large amount of evil. We must, then, get rid of all the evil that is present.

The particular sources for corruption mentioned here by Jesus are: (1) the yeast of the Pharisees and (2) the yeast of Herod. These two parties possessed a poison that was to be strictly guarded against.

Jesus' referral to the yeast of the Pharisees seems to focus upon their constant seeking for further proofs (or signs) from Jesus. They were critical, doubtful and destructive in their encounters with people. Their words and attitudes were harmful, because they so often conflicted with Jesus' teachings. So, Jesus issued a warning to His disciples to be on their guard when they were around these men.

The yeast of Herod (called "that fox" by Jesus, because he was a crafty coward—Luke 13:32), was to be found in his impulsive immaturity and in his inordinate desire to see signs (Luke 23:8).

14The disciples had forgotten to bring bread, except for one loaf they
had with them in the boat. 15"Be careful," Jesus warned them. "Watch
out for the yeast of the Pharisees and that of Herod."
16They discussed this with one another and said, "It is because we have
no bread."
17Aware of their discussion, Jesus asked them: "Why are you talking
about having no bread? Do you still not see or understand? Are your
hearts hardened? 18Do you have eyes but fail to see, and ears but fail to
hear? And don't you remember? 19When I broke the five loaves for the
five thousand, how many basketfuls of pieces did you pick up?"
"Twelve," they replied.
20"And when I broke the seven loaves for the four thousand, how many
basketfuls of pieces did you pick up?"
They answered, "Seven."
21He said to them, "Do you still not understand?"

Blindness Is Cured (Mark 8:22-26)

It seems safe to assume that this man was born blind. He had heard voices, smelled flowers and touched many different objects, but he had never seen any of them. His eyes were closed to a complex world of countless colors and shapes. But Jesus would change all of that for him. He would restore his vision, gradually and privately.

How considerate the Lord is of our particular situations and personalities. He sees our multiple weaknesses, and He deals with us on a very individualized basis. It could also be that Jesus used this particular approach in order to gradually enlarge the man's faith for his healing.

**22 They came to Bethsaida, and some people brought a blind man and
begged Jesus to touch him. 23 He took the blind man by the hand and led
him outside the village. When he had spit on the man's eyes and put his
hands on him, Jesus asked, "Do you see anything?"**
**24 He looked up and said, "I see people; they look like trees walking
around."**
**25 Once more Jesus put his hands on the man's eyes. Then his eyes were
opened, his sight was restored, and he saw everything clearly. 26 Jesus
sent him home, saying, "Don't go into the village.[a]"**

Peter's Confession of Christ (Mark 8:27-30)

(cf. Matt. 16:13-20 and Luke 9:18-21)

The words "Christ" (Greek) and "Messiah" (Hebrew) mean "anointed" or "set apart" by God. In the Old Testament, only prophets, priests and kings received this special qualifying touch from the Lord. From the prophecies regarding the Messiah, it is evident that this unique person would function in each one of these three significant capacities (see comments on Matt. 1:1-17 to learn how Jesus fulfills these three roles as the Christ).

The teaching of the coming of the Christ is the single most important theme of the Old Testament Scriptures. For the Jew, the hope of the Messiah's appearance was his constant desire. Here is a capsulized look at the biblical teaching regarding the coming Christ.

1. Elijah would return to pave the road for the appearing of the Messiah (Mal. 4:5).
2. The Messiah would appear and overpower Satan and his diabolic host (Isa. 24:21, 22).
3. The Messiah would suffer and die for the sins of everyone (Isa. 53).
4. There would be a period of unparalleled tribulation (Dan. 12:1).
5. The Messiah would be an all-powerful king, uprooting the nations that harassed Israel (Ps. 9:8; 96:13; 98:9; Isa. 2:2).
6. There would be a great resurrection of all who had died. The wicked would receive their due punishment, and the righteous would be given their proper rewards (Dan. 12:2, 3).
7. With the Messiah on the throne, the saints would have dominion over the whole earth (Dan. 7:27). Eventually, even death would be consumed (Isa. 25:8). The arrival

[a] 26 Some manuscripts *Don't go and tell anyone in the village*

of the Messiah would mean nothing less than the bursting forth of a new heaven and earth for everyone (Isa. 65:17; 66:22). Righteousness would now reign forever.

The above points, as abbreviated as they are, make it plain that the prophets' hopes for the future are intricately complex and distinctly prolonged. Unfortunately, the thoroughness of the Scriptures is often generalized into only one or two points. This happened in Jesus' day. Many Jews were only looking for a military Messiah, a political ruler who would deliver Israel from her earthly enemies (Luke 1:67-74 with John 6:15). It was this narrow interpretation of the Messiah that caused Jesus frequently to tell His followers to keep His identity a secret (Matt. 16:20; etc.). While Jesus desired to keep His identity clear, He also sought to keep it free from abuse through misinterpretation.

27 Jesus and his disciples went on to the villages around Caesarea Philippi. On the way he asked them, "Who do people say I am?"
28 They replied, "Some say John the Baptist; others say Elijah; and still others, one of the prophets."
29 "But what about you?" he asked. "Who do you say I am?"
Peter answered, "You are the Christ.[a]"
30 Jesus warned them not to tell anyone about him.

Jesus Predicts His Own Death (Mark 8:31-33)

(cf. Matt. 16:21-23 and Luke 9:21, 22)

Some sixty-five times the Gospel writers address Jesus as the "Son of man." It is the most common of all his titles (except "Christ"). There are no less than three ways in which this designation is used: (1) His role as a servant of all humans—Luke 9:58; 19:10; (2) His role as a suffering servant—Mark 8:31; 9:31; and (3) His role as a glorified king—Mark 8:38; 14:62. It is the second usage which Jesus employs here. Peter, however, only considers Jesus in terms of the third category. His shallowness in understanding this (which he himself created by being unteachable) caused him no small degree of embarrassment when the Lord rebuked him for not receiving God's total revealed will.

31 He then began to teach them that the Son of Man must suffer many things and be rejected by the elders, chief priests and teachers of the law, and that he must be killed and after three days rise again. 32 He

a 29 Or *Messiah*. "The Christ" (Greek) and "the Messiah" (Hebrew) both mean "the Anointed One."

spoke plainly about this, and Peter took him aside and began to rebuke him.

[33]But when Jesus turned and looked at his disciples, he rebuked Peter. "Out of my sight, Satan!" he said. "You do not have in mind the things of God, but the things of men."

Call to Discipleship (Mark 8:34-9:1)

(cf. Matt. 16:24-28 and Luke 9:23-27)

Jesus requires His followers to deny themselves. This is more than denying ourselves a few luxuries now and then. Self-denial refers to a deliberate readjusting of our priorities, combined with a disciplined approach to life.

Additionally, Jesus requires His followers to carry their own cross (not His). This cruel device of execution symbolized the result of taking a course of action not acceptable to the society at large. Stated slightly differently, those who would follow Christ were to be prepared to face whatever consequences the Christian life would bring to them. The cross referred to here is not some personal weakness or irritation, but it is strictly the persecution you can expect to receive because of choosing a Christ-centered life style.

Only those who have sacrificed self for the life of Christ know the full meaning of a truly rewarding life. The self-centered approach to life is profitless, both temporally and eternally. Abundant possessions may make us appear to be rich now, but this is only a subtle illusion.

I. *The Single Way (8:34)*

[34]Then he called the crowd to him along with his disciples and said: "If anyone would come after me, he must deny himself and take up his cross and follow me.

II. *The Several Warnings (8:35-38)*

[35]For whoever wants to save his life[a] will lose it, but whoever loses his life
for me and for the gospel will save it. [36]What good is it for a man to gain
the whole world, yet forfeit his soul? [37]Or what can a man give in
exchange for his soul? [38]If anyone is ashamed of me and my words in

[a] *35* The Greek word means either *life* or *soul*; also in verse 36.

this adulterous and sinful generation, the Son of Man will be ashamed of him when he comes in his Father's glory with the holy angels."

III. *The Special Witness (9:1)*

9 And he said to them, "I tell you the truth, some who are standing here will not taste death before they see the kingdom of God come with power."

Jesus Is Transfigured (Mark 9:2-13)

(cf. Matt. 17:1-8 and Luke 9:28-36)

The Transfiguration was probably the clearest proof any disciple could desire to have to attest to Jesus' fulfillment of all the Messianic expectations. Indeed, this man was, and is, the divine Son of God. But the Transfiguration meant more than this, especially to Jesus.

Here Jesus meets with Moses and Elijah (respectively representing the Law and the Prophets). They prepare Jesus for the soon-to-occur events by discussing His upcoming death, burial and resurrection in Jerusalem. Here, too, Jesus will again hear the voice of God confirm His soon-to-be-finished mission upon Calvary. These encounters are certain to yield a positive impact on Christ's heart and mind.

I. *Ascending the Mountain (9:2, 3)*

**2After six days Jesus took Peter, James and John with him and led
them up a high mountain, where they were all alone. There he was
transfigured before them. 3His clothes became dazzling white, whiter
than anyone in the world could bleach them.**

II. *Encamping on the Mountain (9:4-8)*

**4And there appeared before them Elijah and Moses, who were talking
with Jesus.**

**5Peter said to Jesus, "Rabbi, it is good for us to be here. Let us put up
three shelters—one for you, one for Moses and one for Elijah." 6(He did
not know what to say, they were so frightened.)**

7Then a cloud appeared and enveloped them, and a voice came from

the cloud: "This is my Son, whom I love. Listen to him!"
[8]Suddenly, when they looked around, they no longer saw anyone with
them except Jesus.

III. *Descending the Mountain (9:9-13)*

[9]As they were coming down the mountain, Jesus gave them orders not
to tell anyone what they had seen until the Son of Man had risen from
the dead. [10]They kept the matter to themselves, discussing what "rising
from the dead" meant.
[11]And they asked him, "Why do the teachers of the law say that Elijah
must come first?"
[12]Jesus replied, "To be sure, Elijah does come first, and restores all
things. Why then is it written that the Son of Man must suffer much and
be rejected? [13]But I tell you, Elijah has come, and they have done to him
everything they wished, just as it is written about him."

An Epileptic Boy Is Healed (Mark 9:14-29)

(cf. Matt. 17:14-21 and Luke 9:37-43)

In this scene we capture a rare moment of irritation in Jesus. He had come down from the mountaintop with an inspiring encounter with God and two heavenly saints. He had learned of His soon-to-be-accomplished mission in Jerusalem. He had been exposed to an indescribable experience of sheer glory. Now, however, Jesus was suddenly made aware of the ministry which must yet be fulfilled before His appointment with the cross.

It was a disappointing moment—the teachers of the Law were arguing with the disciples; the disciples were impotent to handle the situation; the crowd was passively watching the developing events; and the father of the boy seemed to be totally beside himself over what he should do to help his son. So, Jesus issued a mild rebuke to all at hand. Then He proceeded to heal the boy of his demonic aggravation.

How easily we can see ourselves in this story. We can identify with the helpless disciples or with the distraught father. Or we can remember when God granted us a moment of glorious ecstacy, only to bring us face to face with practical needs the next moment. Each of us is meant to enjoy the mountain peak for a season, but eventually we must all come down the slopes to live in a world of hurting people, including a sizable body of hurting believers, as this story reveals.

I. *The Report (9:14-18)*

[14]When they came to the other disciples, they saw a large crowd around them and the teachers of the law arguing with them. [15]As soon as all the people saw Jesus, they were overwhelmed with wonder and ran to greet him.

[16]"What are you arguing with them about?" he asked.

[17]A man in the crowd answered, "Teacher, I brought you my son, who is possessed by a spirit that has robbed him of speech. [18]Whenever it seizes him, it throws him to the ground. He foams at the mouth, gnashes his teeth and becomes rigid. I asked your disciples to drive out the spirit, but they could not."

II. *The Rebuke (9:19)*

[19]"O unbelieving generation," Jesus replied, "how long shall I stay with you? How long shall I put up with you? Bring the boy to me."

III. *The Result (9:20-27)*

[20]So they brought him. When the spirit saw Jesus, it immediately threw the boy into a convulsion. He fell to the ground and rolled around, foaming at the mouth.

[21]Jesus asked the boy's father, "How long has he been like this?"

"From childhood," he answered. [22]"It has often thrown him into fire or water to kill him. But if you can do anything, take pity on us and help us."

[23]" 'If you can'?" said Jesus. "Everything is possible for him who believes."

[24]Immediately the boy's father exclaimed, "I do believe; help me overcome my unbelief!"

[25]When Jesus saw that a crowd was running to the scene, he rebuked the evil[a] spirit. "You deaf and dumb spirit," he said, "I command you, come out of him and never enter him again."

[26]The spirit shrieked, convulsed him violently and came out. The boy looked so much like a corpse that many said, "He's dead." [27]But Jesus took him by the hand and lifted him to his feet, and he stood up.

IV. *The Reason (9:28, 29)*

[28]After Jesus had gone indoors, his disciples asked him privately, "Why couldn't we drive it out?"

[29]He replied, "This kind can come out only by prayer.[b]"

a 25 Greek *unclean* *b 29* Some manuscripts *prayer and fasting*

Jesus Foretells His Death Again (9:30-32)

(cf. Matt. 17:22, 23 and Luke 9:43-45)

Jesus had endeavored to be alone with His disciples before, but now there was an atmosphere of urgency about His desired solitude. Into their hands would rest the responsibility of carrying out Jesus' works. He, therefore, must have time to discuss future events with them privately. He must prepare them for the worst shock of their lives. He must equip them to face events that would contradict their own desires and deviate sharply from what they had been taught about the role of the Messiah. He must get alone with them and get them ready for Jerusalem.

> **30They left that place and passed through Galilee. Jesus did not want**
> **anyone to know where they were, 31because he was teaching his**
> **disciples. He said to them, "The Son of Man is going to be betrayed into**
> **the hands of men. They will kill him, and after three days he will rise."**
> **32But they did not understand what he meant and were afraid to ask**
> **him about it.**

Who Is the Greatest? (Mark 9:33-50)

(cf. Matt. 18:1-9 and Luke 9:46-48)

People have always struggled for greatness, to be one rung higher on the ladder of success than someone else. The disciples were no exception to this ambition. They were jealous men. As a group they felt they had the only corner of God's blessing (thus excluding themselves from all others—the haves and the have-nots). As individuals they competed with one another for a self-concocted position of superiority over one another. But Jesus demonstrated the true meaning of being great by picking up a little child and giving him His personal attention. It is not how high we ascend that makes us great, but true greatness is marked by how low we will condescend in order to help people.

I. *The Standard for Greatness (9:33-37)*

[33]They came to Capernaum. When he was in the house, he asked them, "What were you arguing about on the road?" [34]But they kept quiet because on the way they had argued about who was the greatest.

[35]Sitting down, Jesus called the Twelve and said, "If anyone wants to be first, he must be the very last, and the servant of all."

[36]He took a little child and had him stand among them. Taking him in his arms, he said to them, [37]"Whoever welcomes one of these little children in my name welcomes me; and whoever welcomes me does not welcome me but the one who sent me."

II. *The Struggle for Greatness (9:38-50)*

1. *Outside Factors (9:38-41)*

[38]"Teacher," said John, "we saw a man driving out demons in your name and we told him to stop, because he was not one of us."

[39]"Do not stop him," Jesus said. "No one who does a miracle in my name can in the next moment say anything bad about me, [40]for whoever is not against us is for us. [41]I tell you the truth, anyone who gives you a cup of water in my name because you belong to Christ will certainly not lose his reward.

2. *Inside Factors (9:42-50)*

[42]"And if anyone causes one of these little ones who believe in me to sin, it would be better for him to be thrown into the sea with a large millstone tied around his neck. [43]If your hand causes you to sin, cut it off. It is better for you to enter life maimed than with two hands to go into hell, where the fire never goes out.[a] [45]And if your foot causes you to sin, cut it off. It is better for you to enter life crippled than to have two feet and be thrown into hell.[b] [47]And if your eye causes you to sin, pluck it out. It is better for you to enter the kingdom of God with one eye than to have two eyes and be thrown into hell, [48]where

" 'their worm does not die,
and the fire is not quenched.'[c]

[49]Everyone will be salted with fire.

[50]"Salt is good, but if it loses its saltiness, how can you make it salty again? Have salt in yourselves, and be at peace with each other."

---

a 43 Some manuscripts *out, [44]where/'their worm does not die,/and the fire is not quenched'* *b 45* Some manuscripts *hell, [46]where/'their worm does not die,/and the fire is not quenched'* *c 48* Isaiah 66:24

Jesus Discusses Divorce (Mark 10:1-12)

(cf. Matt. 19:1-12)

Considerable confusion has arisen as a result of misunderstanding Jesus' words about divorce. The principal cause for this disturbance is due to the fact that many persons have read into Jesus' statements a number of things that He did *not* say.

Consider these two primary examples: First, Jesus did *not* say that *every* divorce was absolutely forbidden. Second, Jesus did *not* say that *every* remarriage with a divorced person was an act of adultery.

What, then, *did* Jesus say about marriage and divorce? Three matters should be noted: (1) Jesus accepted God's original (and present) plan for marriage, which anticipates no separation. (2) Jesus never condemned Moses' right to grant a bill of divorce. He, instead, rebuked the hard hearts of those who thought divorce was necessary because it satisfied their carnal lusts. (3) According to Jesus, divorced people—the type Moses encountered—who remarry out of lust are guilty of adultery. Their reason for divorce is inadequate.

The only satisfactory conclusions that can be drawn from this passage are that Jesus supports marriage until the death of a mate and condemns premature separation because of hardened hearts. Remarriage after this latter condition is equivalent to adultery. There is obviously no thought of repentance in these persons. (In order to get the full picture of the marriage-divorce situation we must read other passages, along with this one—cf. Matt. 19:1-12 and 1 Cor. 7.)

I. *The Setting (10:1, 2)*

10 Jesus then left that place and went into the region of Judea and across the Jordan. Again crowds of people came to him, and as was his custom, he taught them.

2Some Pharisees came and tested him by asking, "Is it lawful for a man to divorce his wife?"

II. *The Scripture (10:3-9)*

3"What did Moses command you?" he replied.

4They said, "Moses permitted a man to write a certificate of divorce and send her away."

**[5]"It was because your hearts were hard that Moses wrote you this
law," Jesus replied. [6]"But at the beginning of creation God 'made them
male and female.'[a] [7]'For this reason a man will leave his father and
mother and be united to his wife,[b] [8]and the two will become one flesh.'[c]
So they are no longer two, but one. [9]Therefore what God has joined
together, let man not separate."**

III. *The Severity (10:10-12)*

**[10]When they were in the house again, the disciples asked Jesus about
this. [11]He answered, "Anyone who divorces his wife and marries another
woman commits adultery against her. [12]And if she divorces her husband
and marries another man, she commits adultery."**

Jesus Blesses the Children (Mark 10:13-16)

(cf. Matt. 19:13-15 and Luke 18:15-17)

Most of us recognize today, unlike the early disciples, that Jesus' ministry was not for adults only. He loved children, too. And He managed to find time to bless them (that is, to speak with them and to pray for them). Children can love Jesus, and we must be diligent to introduce them to Him.

Earlier Jesus taught His disciples that if they were ever to become great, they must receive these little ones with love (Mark 9:33ff.). They understood Jesus, but understanding something with the mind and applying it with the will and heart are not the same things, as we so clearly see here.

Our discipleship with Christ today involves much more than knowledge and assent; it equally entails obedience to these insights. We cannot ever be more mature than what the fruit of our actions reveals.

**[13]People were bringing little children to Jesus to have him touch them,
but the disciples rebuked them. [14]When Jesus saw this, he was indignant.
He said to them, "Let the little children come to me, and do not hinder
them, for the kingdom of God belongs to such as these. [15]I tell you the
truth, anyone who will not receive the kingdom of God like a little child
will never enter it." [16]And he took the children in his arms, put his hands
on them and blessed them.**

---

a 6 Gen. 1:27 *b 7* Some early manuscripts do not have *and be united to his wife.* *c 8* Gen. 2:24

The Rich Young Man (Mark 10:17-31)

(cf. Matt. 19:16-30 and Luke 18:18-30)

This is a sober story. Here we find that the sincerity and purity of a person are insufficient to save him. We may come to Christ morally blameless in the eyes of men, but this supposed goodness does not necessarily imply any acceptance on Christ's part. He looks beyond our words and actions. He finds the central throne in our lives and asks us to surrender it. All the good deeds in the world can save no one. Christ wants our wills more than He wants our works. We must surrender our innermost love and follow Christ with a single-hearted loyalty.

There are many who think of themselves as being acceptable to God because of their generally "good" characters and their good works. These are not a sufficient gauge, however, for measuring our acceptance with God and Christ. Until there is a surrender of our lives to the Lordship of Christ, there can be no adoption into God's Kingdom. In other words, no one can stretch out his hands to receive Christ and also keep those hands full of earthly loves.

I. *Dialogue with the Man (10:17-22)*

17 As Jesus started on his way, a man ran up to him and fell on his knees before him. "Good teacher," he asked, "what must I do to inherit eternal life?"

18 "Why do you call me good?" Jesus answered. "No one is good—except God alone. 19 You know the commandments: 'Do not murder, do not commit adultery, do not steal, do not give false testimony, do not defraud, honor your father and mother.'[a]"

20 "Teacher," he declared, "all these I have kept since I was a boy."

21 Jesus looked at him and loved him. "One thing you lack," he said. "Go, sell everything you have and give to the poor, and you will have treasure in heaven. Then come, follow me."

22 At this the man's face fell. He went away sad, because he had great wealth.

II. *Dialogue with the Disciples (10:23-31)*

23 Jesus looked around and said to his disciples, "How hard it is for the rich to enter the kingdom of God!"

---

a 19 Exodus 20:12-16; Deut. 5:16-20

**24The disciples were amazed at his words. But Jesus said again, "Chil-
dren, how hard it is[a] to enter the kingdom of God! 25It is easier for a camel
to go through the eye of a needle than for a rich man to enter the kingdom
of God."**
**26The disciples were even more amazed, and said to each other, "Who
then can be saved?"**
**27Jesus looked at them and said, "With man this is impossible, but not
with God; all things are possible with God."**
28Peter said to him, "We have left everything to follow you!"
**29"I tell you the truth," Jesus replied, "no one who has left home or
brothers or sisters or mother or father or children or fields for me and
the gospel 30will fail to receive a hundred times as much in this present
age (homes, brothers, sisters, mothers, children and fields—and with
them, persecutions) and in the age to come, eternal life. 31But many who
are first will be last, and the last first."**

Jesus Again Predicts His Death (Mark 10:32-34)

(cf. Matt. 20:17-19 and Luke 18:31-34)

How often Jesus told His disciples of the events He would face in Jerusalem. Important matters must be stressed again and again. They must be lodged deeply so that they will not topple over when jarred. The disciples would face the test of their lives at Jerusalem. So, Jesus prepared them in advance for this terrible shock. They had to be forewarned. They had to be grounded in God's prophetic Word.

Several practical principles may be derived from this scene. First, there is no virtue in concealing the inevitable from anyone. People must be told the truth. Second, there is the necessity for repetition of important matters. It must not be assumed that people understand us or that they have received a certain truth just because we spoke of it once. We must tell it again and again, until it actually sinks in. Third, knowledge of future events is invaluable for developing a secure footing. We, too, must be intimately acquainted with God's Word for the future.

**32They were on their way up to Jerusalem, with Jesus leading the
way, and the disciples were astonished, while those who followed were
afraid. Again he took the Twelve aside and told them what was going to
happen to him. 33"We are going up to Jerusalem," he said, "and the Son**

a 24 Some manuscripts *is for those who trust in riches*

of Man will be betrayed to the chief priests and teachers of the law. They will condemn him to death and will hand him over to the Gentiles,
34who will mock him and spit on him, flog him and kill him. Three days later he will rise."

James and John: Status Seekers (Mark 10:35-45)

(cf. Matt. 20:20-28)

This is the second time that Jesus addressed the subject of status seeking (Mark 9:33-50). In His first discourse He illustrated greatness by embracing a small child and giving sincere attention to that child. In this, His second discussion, He illustrated greatness by spotlighting the role of a servant—a role which Jesus considers to be truly great. Greatness is not measured by how many persons serve you, but by how many persons you serve.

I. *The Request (10:35-37)*

35Then James and John, the sons of Zebedee, came to him. "Teacher," they said, "we want you to do for us whatever we ask."
36"What do you want me to do for you?" he asked.
37They replied, "Let one of us sit at your right and the other at your left in your glory."

II. *The Response (10:38-40)*

38"You don't know what you are asking," Jesus said. "Can you drink the cup I drink or be baptized with the baptism I am baptized with?"
39"We can," they answered.
Jesus said to them, "You will drink the cup I drink and be baptized with the baptism I am baptized with,
40but to sit at my right or left is not for me to grant. These places belong to those for whom they have been prepared."

III. *The Repercussions (10:41-45)*

41When the ten heard about this, they became indignant with James and John.
42Jesus called them together and said, "You know that those

who are regarded as rulers of the Gentiles lord it over them, and their high
officials exercise authority over them. 43Not so with you. Instead, whoever
wants to become great among you must be your servant, 44and whoever
wants to be first must be slave of all. 45For even the Son of Man did not
come to be served, but to serve, and to give his life as a ransom for many."

Bartimaeus Receives His Sight (Mark 10:46-52)

(cf. Matt. 20:29-34 and Luke 18:35-43)

Bartimaeus is an excellent example of a person who lived with a firm grip on faith. The obstacles he overcame were enormous. There was his natural handicap of blindness, but his condition did not dull his keen faith in Jesus Christ. Also, there was the social handicap of his having been rejected, even by Christ's very own disciples. Still, Bartimaeus pressed on with a determined faith that Jesus would help him. He never gave up.

Naturally, his perseverance was worth the cost. Jesus honored his aggressive and steadfast faith with a miracle. We must never forget such inspirational testimonies like these. No matter how hopeless we may feel, there is always someone who has gone through more severe trials than us—truimphantly. We can do the same as Bartimaeus, simply calling out to Jesus and not ceasing our confession of faith.

I. *The Request (10:46, 47)*

46Then they came to Jericho. As Jesus and his disciples, together with
a large crowd, were leaving the city, a blind man, Bartimaeus (that is,
the Son of Timaeus), was sitting by the roadside begging. 47When he
heard that it was Jesus of Nazareth, he began to shout, "Jesus, Son of
David, have mercy on me!"

II. *The Rebuke (10:48)*

48Many rebuked him and told him to be quiet, but he shouted all the
more, "Son of David, have mercy on me!"

III. *The Restoration (10:49-52)*

49Jesus stopped and said, "Call him."
So they called to the blind man, "Cheer up! On your feet! He's calling
you."

50Throwing his cloak aside, he jumped to his feet and came to Jesus.
51"What do you want me to do for you?" Jesus asked him.
The blind man said, "Rabbi, I want to see."
52"Go," said Jesus, "your faith has healed you." Immediately he received his sight and followed Jesus along the road.

The King's Entrance (Mark 11:1-11)

(cf. Matt. 21:1-11; Luke 19:29-44 and John 12:12-19)

The Triumphant Entry began at a site that rings with memorable events—the Mount of Olives. It is here that Jesus delivered His most devastating prophecy against the nation of Israel (Matt. 24:1ff.). It is here that Jesus prayed His three long and intense petitions before being betrayed (Matt. 26:30ff.). It is here that Jesus spoke His departing message and then ascended into heaven (Acts 1:6ff.). And it is here where Jesus will visibly return in His second coming to earth (Zech. 14:4).

In Scripture mountains are sometimes used as symbols of personal difficulties (Isa. 40:4; Zech. 4:7; Matt. 17:20) and desolate judgments (Isa. 41:15; 42:15; Mal. 1:3). From the mountain called Olivet (which is actually a small chain of mountains with four peaks) Jesus faced the strongest tests of His life, and it was there that He presented Israel with her most overwhelming prophetic judgments.

On this day, however, Jesus, like Moses who had descended the mountain of God before Him, will offer Israel the promises of the Kingdom of God. And, as in the earlier period, there will be shouts of jubilation at the start, but apostasy and rebellion in the end.

The depth of Israel's imminent judgment (A.D. 70) can only be contrasted with the height of her present divine offer—God's King, the prophesied Christ. Israel tasted God's very best offer in Jesus; in their rejection of Him they must taste His very worst sentence.

I. *Preparation (11:1-7)*

11 As they approached Jerusalem and came to Bethphage and Bethany at the Mount of Olives, Jesus sent two of his disciples,
2saying to them, "Go to the village ahead of you, and just as you enter it, you will find a colt tied there, which no one has ever ridden. Untie it and bring it here. 3If anyone asks you, 'Why are you doing this?' tell him, 'The Lord needs it and will send it back here shortly.' "

[4]They went and found a colt outside in the street, tied at a doorway. As they untied it, [5]some people standing there asked, "What are you doing, untying that colt?" [6]They answered as Jesus had told them to, and the people let them go. [7]When they brought the colt to Jesus and threw their cloaks over it, he sat on it.

II. *Presentation (11:8-11)*

[8]Many people spread their cloaks on the road, while others spread branches they had cut in the fields. [9]Those who went ahead and those who followed shouted,

"Hosanna![a]"
"Blessed is he who comes in the name of the Lord!"[b]
[10]"Blessed is the coming kingdom of our father David!"
"Hosanna in the highest!"

[11]Jesus entered Jerusalem and went to the temple. He looked around at everything, but since it was already late, he went out to Bethany with the Twelve.

Jesus Curses the Fig Tree (Mark 11:12-14)

(cf. Matt. 21:18, 19; 23:37-39)

When you superficially examine Jesus' reaction to this fig tree, it seems peculiar. It is odd to see Jesus cursing a tree. No one stands in front of a tree, gives it a stern stare, and then curses it—but Jesus did. And almost immediately the tree withered to death! What an astonishing account this is.

A closer examination of the episode, however, reveals a parallel situation and a prophetic curse. This tree reminded Jesus of the barrenness of Israel. Her leaves were full, but her productivity was an empty disgrace. The tree, like the nation of promise, was void of fruit. Israel was spiritually barren, when she should have been abounding with the fruit of godly obedience to Jesus' message. For this reason, Jesus cursed the fruitless tree, even as He would judge the carnal nation of Israel for her dearth of spiritual fruit.

[12]The next day as they were leaving Bethany, Jesus was hungry.
[13]Seeing in the distance a fig tree in leaf, he went to find out if it had any

a 9 A Hebrew expression meaning "Save!" which became an exclamation of praise; also in verse 10 b 9 Psalm 118:25, 26

fruit. When he reached it, he found nothing but leaves, because it was not the season for figs. [14]Then he said to the tree, "May no one ever eat fruit from you again." And his disciples heard him say it.

Jesus Cleanses the Temple (Mark 11:15-19)

(cf. Matt. 21:12-17; Luke 19:45-48 and John 2:13-22)

The Temple was designed by God to be a place where He and people (Jews and Gentiles) could meet for formal worship. It was to be a place of prayer and instruction. But the nonspiritual hierarchy had turned the Temple into a profit-making business. The spiritual aspects of the structure had been obscured and choked lifeless by many humanly instituted practices. It was a shame to see such an exquisite facility dominated by greedy wolves wearing sheep's clothing!

Jesus was justly enraged. So here, in the Temple (His Father's house), we see His only manifestation of physical aggression. Jesus would not lift a hand to overthrow the Roman military occupation of Israel, but He would exert every muscle to cast out the man-made religious tyranny that kept God's people from the truth about His love and forgiveness. Nothing angered Jesus more than false religion that bore God's name. He would expose it. He would attempt to remove it. And He would work to convert those who were ensnared by its subtle, yet lethal, teachings. Can *we* do anything less in our own day when the so-called "God" of liberalism is keeping hearts from the message of the true and full gospel of Jesus Christ?

I. *The Action (11:15-17)*

[15]On reaching Jerusalem, Jesus entered the temple area and began driving out those who were buying and selling there. He overturned the tables of the money changers and the benches of those selling doves,
[16]and would not allow anyone to carry merchandise through the temple
courts. [17]And as he taught them, he said, "Is it not written:

" 'My house will be called
a house of prayer for all nations'[a]?

But you have made it 'a den of robbers.'[b]"

[a] 17 Isaiah 56:7 [b] 17 Jer. 7:11

II. *The Reaction (11:18, 19)*

18The chief priests and the teachers of the law heard this and began looking for a way to kill him, for they feared him, because the whole crowd was amazed at his teaching.

19When evening came, they[a] went out of the city.

Faith Moves Mountains (Mark 11:20-26)

(cf. Matt. 21:20-22)

There are many lessons to be gleaned from Jesus' teaching on faith, but one item of paramount importance is His call to a spoken faith. Real faith does more than believe in the heart; it also speaks with the mouth an unwavering positive confidence in God's practical powers. There is always something verbal about genuine faith.

Jesus taught the disciples never to underestimate the power of spoken faith. Often it is our words, our daily speech, which either hinder or altogether prevent the removal of obstructing mountains which are before us. If we are going to learn how to pray in faith, we must first learn how to guard our speech from all forms of negative communication. All complaining must cease; every anxiety must be replaced with confidence in God's ability to resolve our every problem. Our speech must reveal an attitude of expectancy—both in prayer and outside of prayer. Faith, then, is more than the language of prayer; it should be the vocabulary of every hour.

20In the morning, as they went along, they saw the fig tree withered
from the roots. 21Peter remembered and said to Jesus, "Rabbi, look! The
fig tree you cursed has withered!"
22"Have[b] faith in God," Jesus answered. 23"I tell you the truth, if anyone
says to this mountain, 'Go, throw yourself into the sea,' and does not
doubt in his heart but believes that what he says will happen, it will be
done for him. 24Therefore I tell you, whatever you ask for in prayer,
believe that you have received it, and it will be yours. 25And when you
stand praying, if you hold anything against anyone, forgive him, so that
your Father in heaven may forgive you your sins.[c]"

a 19 Some early manuscripts *he* *b 22* Some early manuscripts *If you have* *c 25* Some manuscripts *sins. 26But if you do not forgive, neither will your Father who is in heaven forgive your sins.*

Jesus' Authority Is Questioned (Mark 11:27-33)

(cf. Matt. 21:23-27 and Luke 20:1-8)

There are two types of persons who expressed an interest in Jesus. The first kind was sincere; the second was sinister. Jesus met His share of both types. The good persons in Jesus' audience came with problems, wanting help for themselves or others. The bad persons in Jesus' audience came with questions, wanting to hurt Jesus. In the present episode we see a clear example of the latter kind of persons.

The mastery with which Jesus handled His critics is extraordinary. He outwitted them every time. His challengers would often find themselves caught in their own traps.

There is no need for any of us to go out of our way to trip a carnal person; we must use wisdom instead to let them trip themselves. Returning evil for evil will accomplish nothing constructive, but making a person live in his own self-erected evil is advantageous.

I. *The Charge (11:27, 28)*

27They arrived again in Jerusalem, and while Jesus was walking in the temple courts, the chief priests, the teachers of the law and the elders came to him. 28"By what authority are you doing these things?" they asked. "And who gave you authority to do this?"

II. *The Challenge (11:29, 30)*

29Jesus replied, "I will ask you one question. Answer me, and I will tell you by what authority I am doing these things. 30John's baptism—was it from heaven, or from men? Tell me!"

III. *The Culmination (11:31-33)*

31They discussed it among themselves and said, "If we say, 'From heaven,' he will ask, 'Then why didn't you believe him?' 32But if we say, 'From men'. . . ." (They feared the people, for everyone held that John really was a prophet.)

33So they answered Jesus, "We don't know."

Jesus said, "Neither will I tell you by what authority I am doing these things."

The Parable of the Land Owner (Mark 12:1-12)

(cf. Matt. 21:33-46 and Luke 20:9-19)

There is much to see in this parable about God: (1) He is committed to an earthly project; (2) He has provided everything that is necessary for the project to succeed; (3) He has entrusted the project to certain workmen; (4) He expects to make a return on the project; (5) He is extremely patient when this return is withheld; (6) He is hopeful that His Son will be able to turn the hearts of the evil workmen; and (7) He will have to take His project out of the hands of the original workers and give it to others.

There are also several important matters to see in this parable about the people to whom God has revealed and entrusted things: (1) the price of opportunity is responsibility; and (2) the price of not being responsible is loss of opportunity through divine judgment.

I. *His Rights (12:1, 2)*

12 He then began to speak to them in parables: "A man planted a vineyard. He put a wall around it, dug a pit for the winepress and built a watchtower. Then he rented the vineyard to some farmers and went away on a journey. 2At harvest time he sent a servant to the tenants to collect from them some of the fruit of the vineyard.

II. *His Resistance (12:3-8)*

3But they seized him, beat him and sent him away empty-handed. 4Then he sent another servant to them; they struck this man on the head and treated him shamefully. 5He sent still another, and that one they killed. He sent many others; some of them they beat, others they killed.

6"He had one left to send, a son, whom he loved. He sent him last of all, saying, 'They will respect my son.'

7"But the tenants said to one another, 'This is the heir. Come, let's kill him, and the inheritance will be ours.' 8So they took him and killed him, and threw him out of the vineyard.

III. *His Recompense (12:9-11)*

9"What then will the owner of the vineyard do? He will come and kill

those tenants and give the vineyard to others. [10]Haven't you read this scripture:

" 'The stone the builders rejected
has become the capstone[a];
[11]the Lord has done this,
and it is marvelous in our eyes'[b]?"

IV. *The Result (12:12)*

[12]Then they looked for a way to arrest him because they knew he had spoken the parable against them. But they were afraid of the crowd; so they left him and went away.

Should We Pay Taxes? (Mark 12:13-17)

(cf. Matt. 22:15-22 and Luke 20:20-26)

Crafty—that's the chief trait of Satan and his disciples. Naturally, Satan's disciples included certain ones among the Pharisees and Herodians. They were tricky, disguising their real motives behind the camouflage of pious-sounding words and important questions.

With all of the craftiness they could muster, they attempted to trick Jesus. Their trap was supposedly foolproof—any answer would discredit Jesus, according to their scheme. But Jesus easily confounded them with a single sentence!

I. *The Trap (12:13-15a)*

[13]Later they sent some of the Pharisees and Herodians to Jesus to catch him in his words. [14]They came to him and said, "Teacher, we know you are a man of integrity. You aren't swayed by men, because you pay no attention to who they are; but you teach the way of God in accordance with the truth. Is it right to pay taxes to Caesar or not? [15]Should we pay or shouldn't we?"

II. *The Truth (12:15-17)*

But Jesus knew their hypocrisy. "Why are you trying to trap me?" he

a 10 Or *cornerstone* *b 11* Psalm 118:22, 23

asked. "Bring me a denarius and let me look at it." [16]They brought the coin, and he asked them, "Whose portrait is this? And whose inscription?"

"Caesar's," they replied.

[17]Then Jesus said to them, "Give to Caesar what is Caesar's and to God what is God's."

And they were amazed at him.

No Marriage in Heaven (Mark 12:18-27)

(cf. Matt. 22:23-33 and Luke 20:27-38)

Nothing positive is ever said about the Sadducees in the Scriptures. They were a small but tightly knit religious body in Jerusalem which only appealed to the well-to-do. Generally speaking, they were powerful in civil matters, proud in character, judgmental in disposition and liberal in theology (they rejected more of the Old Testament than they accepted). They also were Jesus' critics, but He had an answer for them, too. Jesus always had an answer, and He still does.

I. *The Trap (12:18-23)*

[18]Then the Sadducees, who say there is no resurrection, came to him
with a question. [19]"Teacher," they said, "Moses wrote for us that if a
man's brother dies and leaves a wife but no children, the man must
marry the widow and have children for his brother. [20]Now there were
seven brothers. The first one married and died without leaving any
children. [21]The second one married the widow, but he also died, leaving
no child. It was the same with the third. [22]In fact, none of the seven left
any children. Last of all, the woman died too. [23]At the resurrection[a]
whose wife will she be, since the seven were married to her?"

II. *The Truth (12:24-27)*

[24]Jesus replied, "Are you not in error because you do not know the
Scriptures or the power of God? [25]When the dead rise, they will neither
marry nor be given in marriage; they will be like the angels in heaven.
[26]Now about the dead rising—have you not read in the book of Moses, in
the account of the bush, how God said to him, 'I am the God of Abraham,
the God of Isaac, and the God of Jacob'[b]? [27]He is not the God of the dead,
but of the living. You are badly mistaken!"

---

a 23 Some manuscripts *resurrection, when men rise from the dead* *b 26* Exodus 3:6

The Greatest Commandments (Mark 12:28-34)

(cf. Matt. 22:34-40)

There are many peripheral (or nonessential) questions we can ask Jesus, like the ones the Pharisees and Sadducees asked. But learning the proper answer to these inquiries will help us very little in advancing our spiritual status. There is another brand of question, however, that strikes at the core of things. Here is an example of such a question; in fact, this is the most important inquiry we can ever make.

The tragedy in this story is revealed by the fact that it is possible for us to detect a good answer to a spiritual question without personally applying its message to our lives. Knowledge of the truth makes us close to the Kingdom of God, but it is appropriating that knowledge that will actually cause us to enter in. Many fine persons live close to salvation, but they remain just far enough away to be spiritually lost.

I. *The Trap (12:28)*

28One of the teachers of the law came and heard them debating. Noticing that Jesus had given them a good answer, he asked him, "Of all the commandments, which is the most important?"

II. *The Truth (12:29-31)*

29"The most important one," answered Jesus, "is this: 'Hear, O Israel, the Lord our God, the Lord is one.[a] 30Love the Lord your God with all your heart and with all your soul and with all your mind and with all your strength.'[b] 31The second is this: 'Love your neighbor as yourself.'[c] There is no commandment greater than these."

III. *The Talk (12:32-34)*

32"Well said, teacher," the man replied. "You are right in saying that God is one and there is no other but him. 33To love him with all your heart, with all your understanding and with all your strength, and to love your neighbor as yourself is more important than all burnt offerings and sacrifices."

34When Jesus saw that he had answered wisely, he said to him, "You are not far from the kingdom of God." And from then on no one dared ask him any more questions.

---

a 29 Or *the Lord our God is one Lord* *b 30* Deut. 6:4, 5 *c 31* Lev. 19:18

Jesus Stumps the Teachers (Mark 12:35-37)

(cf. Matt. 22:41-46 and Luke 20:41-44)

Here Jesus confounded those who so persistently sought and failed to confound Him. He did this by asking them a question which focused on Ps. 110:1 and the coming Christ. According to David, the Christ would be both his son and his Lord. Jesus simply asked His inquirers how this could be the case. Naturally, they had no explanation. Jesus, however, held the answer in His two natures. In His humanity, He is a descendant (or son) of David; in His deity, He is the Son of God. Therefore, David can call Jesus both his "son" and his "Lord."

35While Jesus was teaching in the temple courts, he asked, "How is it
that the teachers of the law say that the Christ[a] is the son of David?
36David himself, speaking by the Holy Spirit, declared:

" 'The Lord said to my Lord:
"Sit at my right hand
until I put your enemies
under your feet." '[b]

37David himself calls him 'Lord.' How then can he be his son?"
The large crowd listened to him with delight.

Jesus Exposes the Teachers (Mark 12:38-40)

(cf. Matt. 23:1-36 and Luke 20:45-47)

In six brief phrases Jesus warned His hearers against the evil practices of certain so-called teachers of the Law. First, they showed off their flowing robes—attracting attention to themselves. Second, they liked being greeted in the marketplaces—wallowing in pride as they would be addressed with such titles as "Rabbi," which means "great teacher." Third, they occupied the important seats in the synagogue—this was a bench that faced the worshiping congregation. Fourth, they sought places

a 35 Or *Messiah* *b 36* Psalm 110:1

of honor at banquets, because being seated closest to the host indicated honor. Fifth, they took over widows' houses by persuading them that no higher service could be rendered in God's service than to give money (much money) to these special teachers of God's laws. Sixth, they put on an act of spirituality by praying long prayers—in the open for everyone to hear and see.

Our Lord hates an artificial and pretentious faith. Whenever we feel it is necessary to be noticed for anything we have done, we had better check out our relationship with Christ.

> **38As he taught, Jesus said, "Watch out for the teachers of the law. They like to walk around in flowing robes and be greeted in the marketplaces,
> 39and have the most important seats in the synagogues and the places of honor at banquets. 40They devour widows' houses and for a show make lengthy prayers. Such men will be punished most severely."**

The Widow's Small Coins (Mark 12:41-44)

The Temple was an impressive structure. This building, often called Herod's temple because he both authorized its construction and assisted greatly in the financing of its erection, was supposedly built by 10,000 skilled men over a period of eighty-five years (19 B.C. to A.D. 66). A thousand wagons were used to haul supplies. Its size was incredible—over 100,000 square feet, with one wall rising some 450 feet into the sky. Its beauty was absolutely matchless—utilizing massive amounts of polished marble and gold. But despite all the glitter, Jesus was most impressed with the people inside this edifice, especially with a poor widow.

I. *The Picture (12:41, 42)*

> **41Jesus sat down opposite the place where the offerings were put and watched the crowd putting their money into the temple treasury. Many rich people threw in large amounts. 42But a poor widow came and put in two very small copper coins,[a] worth only a fraction of a penny.[b]**

In the Court of the Women thirteen collection boxes were placed, in the shape of a trumpet. The collections for each box had a designated purpose in the overall maintenance of the Temple. Apparently it was not uncommon to see sizable contributions placed into these depositories, but Jesus' eye caught the gift of a poor widow. The

[a] 42 Greek *two lepta* [b] 42 Greek *kodrantes*

earthly amount of her gift has been valued as low as one-sixteenth of a cent for each coin; but in heaven, her gift was measured to be thousands of times more valuable than this.

II. *The Principle (12:43, 44)*

43Calling his disciples to him, Jesus said, "I tell you the truth, this poor widow has put more into the treasury than all the others. 44They all gave out of their wealth; but she, out of her poverty, put in everything—all she had to live on."

Life is full of rewarding illustrations to strengthen our faith, if we will keep our eyes on the right things. Jesus saw the tremendous demonstration of faith and loyalty in this woman, and He was not about to let His disciples escape the grandest beauty of the temple—the sincere worshipers it housed.

There is a further lesson here—a lesson in giving. It was not how much the people gave that impressed Jesus. Instead, it was how much the people kept back for themselves that He noticed. This widow left herself empty-handed. She held on only to the Lord she obviously adored. She doubtlessly trusted Him to supply her needs. What an inspiring faith!

The End of the Age (Mark 13:1-27)

(cf. Matt. 24:1-31 and Luke 21:1-28)

Prophecy is one of the most fascinating topics to be studied in all of the Scriptures. It is also the most detailed and difficult to interpret. Biblical scholars hold to a wide range of views regarding future events. In the text before us there are a number of different views that have captured the attention of various commentators. Some see this passage as dealing with only the period surrounding the A.D. 70 destruction of Jerusalem. Others see here only a reference to the Second Coming of Christ. Still others view these passages as possessing elements of both periods (this is the author's view).

I. *Signs (13:1-8)*

13 As he was leaving the temple, one of his disciples said to him, "Look, Teacher! What massive stones! What magnificent buildings!"

2“Do you see all these great buildings?” replied Jesus. “Not one stone here will be left on another; every one will be thrown down.”

3As Jesus was sitting on the Mount of Olives opposite the temple, Peter, James, John and Andrew asked him privately, 4“Tell us, when will these things happen? And what will be the sign that they are all about to be fulfilled?”

5Jesus said to them: “Watch out that no one deceives you. 6Many will come in my name, claiming, ‘I am he,’ and will deceive many. 7When you hear of wars and rumors of wars, do not be alarmed. Such things must happen, but the end is still to come. 8Nation will rise against nation, and kingdom against kingdom. There will be earthquakes in various places, and famines. These are the beginning of birth pains.

How much the disciples were like us. They were easily impressed by the splendor of a man-made creation. But Jesus had to warn them that such colossal buildings would soon crumble. Because of the resistance of the Jewish people to God’s will, they would be judged for their sins. Jesus, then, prepared His disciples for this devastating occurrence by forewarning them of the signs that will precede Jerusalem’s doom—false Christs, rumors of wars, actual wars, earthquakes and famines.

II. *Survival (13:9-13)*

9“You must be on your guard. You will be handed over to the local councils and flogged in the synagogues. On account of me you will stand before governors and kings as witnesses to them. 10And the gospel must first be preached to all nations. 11Whenever you are arrested and brought to trial, do not worry beforehand about what to say. Just say whatever is given you at the time, for it is not you speaking, but the Holy Spirit.

12“Brother will betray brother to death, and a father his child. Children will rebel against their parents and have them put to death. 13All men will hate you because of me, but he who stands firm to the end will be saved.

The period of tribulation which the disciples must pass through would be most severe, so Jesus counseled them to be on guard at all times. He further announced to them that they would face persecutors, but they were not to worry, because the Holy Spirit would equip them with what they were to say and do. In the midst of turmoil and chaos, the disciples of Jesus (which certainly encompassed more than just the eleven to whom Jesus now spoke) would not need to worry. The signs of the times would be bad, but the strength of the Holy Spirit would be far greater. This is a promise for all believers (1 Cor. 10:31)!

The "local councils" referred to here exercised a sizable degree of authority over the Jewish people. There were two types of councils in Jesus' day. The supreme council resided in Jerusalem and was called the Sanhedrin. This was the highest Jewish authority. But below this top level there were many lesser councils. Usually one council resided in each community where ten or more Jews lived.

These councils would act as courts to judge various civil disputes and even criminal cases. The meeting place for these proceedings was a separate room adjoining the synagogue. The decisions of these councils could be quite severe. They held the right to excommunicate and to discipline by scourging (2 Cor. 11:24). There were, presumably, 168 offenses for which scourging was to be the sentence.

III. *Sacrilege (13:14-23)*

14“When you see ‘the abomination that causes desolation’[a] standing
where it[b] does not belong—let the reader understand—then let those
who are in Judea flee to the mountains. 15Let no one on the roof of his
house go down or enter the house to take anything out. 16Let no one in
the field go back to get his cloak. 17How dreadful it will be in those days
for pregnant women and nursing mothers! 18Pray that this will not take
place in winter, 19because those will be days of distress unequaled from
the beginning, when God created the world, until now—and never to be
equaled again. 20If the Lord had not cut short those days, no one would
survive. But for the sake of the elect, whom he has chosen, he has short-
ened them. 21At that time if anyone says to you, ‘Look, here is the Christ[c]!’
or, ‘Look, there he is!’ do not believe it. 22For false Christs and false
prophets will appear and perform signs and miracles to deceive the
elect—if that were possible. 23So be on your guard; I have told you every-
thing ahead of time.

In the section of this discussion entitled "Sign" (13:1-8), the underlying theme is largely impersonal—the focus is upon the geography and politics of Israel and the nations around her. In the section entitled "Survival" (13:9-13), the supporting theme is largely personal—the focus is upon the Christian, especially the Christian Jew. Now, in this section entitled "Sacrilege" our attention is drawn to the city of Jerusalem, where Israel is given her final countdown. Here geography, politics and personal features are all blended together into a most regrettable prophetic account. Observe the four major thoughts of this episode.

a 14 Daniel 9:27; 11:31; 12:11 *b 14* Or *he;* also in verse 29 *c 21* Or *Messiah*

First, there is the abomination of desolation. This phrase is taken from Dan. 9:27, and it refers to some appalling sacrilege (or gross disrespect) for the Temple in Jerusalem (Matt. 24:15; Luke 21:20). In all probability its immediate fulfillment occurred when the Roman soldiers utterly destroyed the temple site in A.D. 70. Its ultimate fulfillment will occur when the antichrist enters Jerusalem's rebuilt temple and demands worship (2 Thess. 2:1-12; Rev. 13).

Second, there is the warning to flee. At the first glimpse of the Roman legions the occupants of the city are strongly instructed to leave the city with great speed. In fact, the believers are urged to pray that this event would not occur in the winter season, since this would slow down their time of departure.

Third, there is the severity of the upcoming doom. There will never again be such a horrible day in Israel's history (assuming a double fulfillment for this passage, the horrors of A.D. 70 are to be seen again in the days immediately prior to the Second Coming of Christ). In fact, the days will be so marred with killings and calamities that if the Lord would not (or does not) intervene, there will be no survivors at all.

Fourth, there is the repeated admonition to watch out for false Christs and false prophets. In times of turmoil people are extremely vulnerable to spiritual deception. They were (and we are) to be on guard to be certain that nothing is accepted as truth which does not conform to the teachings of the Bible.

IV. *Second Coming (13:24-27)*

24"But in those days, following that distress,

" 'the sun will be darkened,
and the moon will not give its light;
25the stars will fall from the sky,
and the heavenly bodies will be shaken.'[a]

26"At that time men will see the Son of Man coming in clouds with
great power and glory. 27And he will send his angels and gather his
elect from the four winds, from the ends of the earth to the ends of the
heavens.

With this panoramic presentation we see a mysterious blending of the events surrounding Jerusalem's destruction in A.D. 70 and her yet-to-be fulfilled destiny at the return of Jesus Christ to reign on this earth.

Be certain to read Matthew 24 and Luke 21 for other specific comments on this important prophecy.

important prophecy.

a 25 Isaiah 13:10; 34:4

The Parable of the Fig Tree (Mark 13:28-31)

(cf. Matt. 24:32-35 and Luke 21:29-33)

The Second Coming of Christ will not just suddenly occur without warning. The generation which is so fortunate to experience this event will be given a vast number of signs to make sense out of the chaos that will be rampant in the earth. Those with sound biblical (especially prophetic) teaching and spiritual eyesight will properly discern the signs of the times and ascertain that the Lord's return is very near.

28"Now learn this lesson from the fig tree: As soon as its twigs get
tender and its leaves come out, you know that summer is near. 29Even so,
when you see these things happening, you know that it is near, right at
the door. 30I tell you the truth, this generation[a] will certainly not pass
away until all these things have happened. 31Heaven and earth will pass
away, but my words will never pass away.

Be Ready (Mark 13:32-37)

(cf. Matt. 24:36-51 and Luke 21:34-36)

It is from this passage, and similar ones, that many people have drawn the conclusion that Jesus Christ could return at any possible moment. Naturally this assumes that no unfulfilled prophecy stands between the present hour and Jesus' return. But this assumption (often called the doctrine of imminence) must be reconciled with these considerations:

1. Jesus told His disciples that numerous signs must be fulfilled before He would return (Mark 13:1-29).

2. Jesus, aware that His disciples believed the Kingdom of God was soon to appear, told them a parable specifically designed to rid them of the notion of an any-instant Second Coming (or rapture) (Luke 19:11-27).

3. Jesus predicted Peter's death; certainly Peter could not have taught the doctrine of imminence, since he knew that at least his own death must precede this event (John 21:18, 19).

a 30 Or *race*

4. Peter preached that Jesus must remain in heaven until God's perfect timing arrives; which implies delay (Acts 3:21).

5. Paul taught that certain events (to this very day yet unfulfilled) must precede the rapture of the saints (2 Thess. 2:1-3).

6. Paul further taught that the day of the Lord will *not* come as a thief in the night to the spiritually enlightened; prophetic signs will prepare the way for this blessed event (1 Thess. 5:1-6).

While the early disciples were exhorted to watch the signs and to be ready spiritually for Christ's return, they were not told that His coming could be in the next second, the next week, the next month, or even in the next year. Such promises (or threats!) are unwarranted.

32"No one knows about that day or hour, not even the angels in heaven, nor the Son, but only the Father. 33Be on guard! Be alert[a]! You do not know when that time will come. 34It's like a man going away: He leaves his house in charge of his servants, each with his assigned task, and tells the one at the door to keep watch.

35"Therefore keep watch because you do not know when the owner of the house will come back—whether in the evening, or at midnight, or when the rooster crows, or at dawn. 36If he comes suddenly, do not let him find you sleeping. 37What I say to you, I say to everyone: 'Watch!' "

The Plot to Kill Jesus (Mark 14:1, 2)

(cf. Matt. 26:1-5 and Luke 22:1-6)

The greatest of all the feasts was Passover. Participation in this annual festival was compulsory according to the biblical Law (Exod. 23:14-19). It has been estimated that over 100,000 Jews would make this ordained trip to Jerusalem in order to celebrate Passover.

The Feast of Unleavened Bread was merely an extension of Passover. For seven days everyone would eat unleavened bread, and they would do no work on the first or final day of this week.

The spirit of the people ran high in Jerusalem during this season. So, the Jews sought for a way to dispose of Jesus without evoking a riot from the high-strung people.

14 Now the Passover and the Feast of Unleavened Bread were only two days away, and the chief priests and the teachers of the law were looking for some sly way to arrest Jesus and kill him. 2"But not during the Feast," they said, "or the people may riot."

a 33 Some manuscripts *alert and pray*

Jesus Is Anointed by Mary (Mark 14:3-9)

(cf. Matt. 26:6-13 and John 12:1-8)

Little did this woman realize that her generous display of affection for Jesus would draw such a heated reaction. She only sought to be kind and to show forth her appreciation for Jesus. With perfume costing nearly a year's pay, she anointed the Lord, not leaving even a drop for herself. Some of the disciples ridiculed her for such an extravagant and emotional ceremony, but Jesus commended the woman for this gracious act. Further, He stated that she had prepared His body for burial (it was an Eastern custom to bathe and anoint dead bodies with perfume before burial).

3While he was in Bethany, reclining at the table in the home of a man known as Simon the Leper, a woman came with an alabaster jar of very expensive perfume, made of pure nard. She broke the jar and poured the perfume on his head.

4Some of those present were saying indignantly to one another, "Why this waste of perfume? 5It could have been sold for more than a year's wages[a] and the money given to the poor." And they rebuked her harshly.

6"Leave her alone," said Jesus. "Why are you bothering her? She has done a beautiful thing to me. 7The poor you will always have with you, and you can help them any time you want. But you will not always have me. 8She did what she could. She poured perfume on my body beforehand to prepare for my burial. 9I tell you the truth, wherever the gospel is preached throughout the world, what she has done will also be told, in memory of her."

Judas Agrees to Betray Jesus (Mark 14:10, 11)

(cf. Matt. 26:14-16)

Sometimes we hear people say, "He's a Judas," implying that such a party was once loyal to someone but is now a traitor. It is a most despicable title.

a 5 Greek *than three hundred denarii*

Are there any "Judas" types among us today? Regrettably, there are numerous persons who will fall away from their walks with Jesus. In fact, biblical prophecy indicates that during the last days of the church age there will be more apostasy than in any other period (Matt. 24:9, 10; 2 Thess. 2:1-3; 1 Tim. 4:1ff.; 2 Tim. 3:1ff.; 4:1-5).

10Then Judas Iscariot, one of the Twelve, went to the chief priests to betray Jesus to them. 11They were delighted to hear this and promised to give him money. So he watched for an opportunity to hand him over.

The Passover Meal Is Eaten (Mark 14:12-25)

(cf. Matt. 26:17-29; Luke 22:7-23 and John 13:1-30)

The greatest celebration in the Christian Church is inaugurated on this emotionally charged Thursday night in an upper room of someone's home in Jerusalem—it is the Lord's Supper. In the Old Testament dispensation it was Passover that the Jews annually observed, remembering how the Lord had delivered them out of Pharaoh's hand and the land of Egypt. On this evening, however, the Passover meal would be forever superseded by the Lord's Supper, where we would remember how Jesus delivered us out of Satan's hand and the snares of this world through His atoning death on the cross. In Jesus, then, is the ultimate spiritual fulfillment of the Passover (1 Cor. 5:7).

I. *Preparations (14:12-16)*

12On the first day of the Feast of Unleavened Bread, when it was customary to sacrifice the Passover lamb, Jesus' disciples asked him, "Where do you want us to go and make preparations for you to eat the Passover?"

13So he sent two of his disciples, telling them, "Go into the city, and a man carrying a jar of water will meet you. Follow him. 14Say to the owner of the house he enters, 'The Teacher asks: Where is my guest room, where I may eat the Passover with my disciples?' 15He will show you a large upper room, furnished and ready. Make preparations for us there."

16The disciples left, went into the city and found things just as Jesus had told them. So they prepared the Passover.

II. *Proclamations (14:17-21)*

[17]When evening came, Jesus arrived with the Twelve. [18]While they were reclining at the table eating, he said, "I tell you the truth, one of you will betray me—one who is eating with me."

[19]They were saddened, and one by one they said to him, "Surely not I?"

[20]"It is one of the Twelve," he replied, "one who dips bread into the bowl with me. [21]The Son of Man will go just as it is written about him. But woe to that man who betrays the Son of Man! It would be better for him if he had not been born."

III. *Presentations (14:22-25)*

[22]While they were eating, Jesus took bread, gave thanks and broke it, and gave it to his disciples, saying, "Take it; this is my body."

[23]Then he took the cup, gave thanks and offered it to them, and they all drank from it.

[24]"This is my blood of the[a] covenant, which is poured out for many," he said to them. [25]"I tell you the truth, I will not drink again of the fruit of the vine until that day when I drink it anew in the kingdom of God."

Jesus Predicts the Disciples' Departure (Mark 14:26-31)

(cf. Matt. 26:31-35 and Luke 22:31-34)

Prophetic foresight is a valuable experience, but not always a comforting gift. Jesus could foresee the fleeing of all His disciples at His most crucial hour. Further, He could envision the triple denial of Peter's lips. It was a most distasteful vision, yet it was a necessary picture for Jesus.

We must sometimes be faced with the stark facts of human reality before we can face life realistically and responsibly. People *do* fail us. There *are* disappointments in life. And we must not attempt to cover up these facts. As long as people are people, there will be times of weakness, failure and disappointment.

Still, despite the agony of defeat, there is the promise of Jesus to go ahead of these failing men and to meet them down the road later, after their carnal retreat. He will not give up on them (or us!). Though His followers would turn away from Him for a season, He would not abandon them for this temporary lapse into sin. He loved them (and us!) to the very end.

---

a 24 Some manuscripts *the new*

26When they had sung a hymn, they went out to the Mount of Olives.
27"You will all fall away," Jesus told them, "for it is written:

" 'I will strike the shepherd,
and the sheep will be scattered.'[a]

28But after I have risen, I will go ahead of you into Galilee."
29Peter declared, "Even if all fall away, I will not."
30"I tell you the truth," Jesus answered, "today—yes, tonight—before
the rooster crows twice[b] you yourself will disown me three times."
31But Peter insisted emphatically, "Even if I have to die with you, I
will never disown you." And all the others said the same.

Gethsemane (Mark 14:32-42)

(cf. Matt. 26:36-46 and Luke 22:39-46)

Jesus chose to die when He could have chosen to live (John 10:11-18). No one coerced Jesus. He served as our substitute solely because He loved us.

Even love, however, has its agony. It is not always a pleasurable experience or a costless enterprise to do God's will or to help people. Sometimes the most penetrating trials of them all come in the service of love. Jesus offers clear proof of this fact.

32They went to a place called Gethsemane, and Jesus said to his
disciples, "Sit here while I pray." 33He took Peter, James and John along
with him, and he began to be deeply distressed and troubled. 34"My soul
is overwhelmed with sorrow to the point of death," he said to them. "Stay
here and keep watch."
35Going a little farther, he fell to the ground and prayed that if
possible the hour might pass from him. 36"*Abba*,[c] Father," he said,
"everything is possible for you. Take this cup from me. Yet not what I
will, but what you will."
37Then he returned to his disciples and found them sleeping. "Simon,"
he said to Peter, "are you asleep? Could you not keep watch for one
hour? 38Watch and pray so that you will not fall into temptation. The
spirit is willing, but the body is weak."
39Once more he went away and prayed the same thing. 40When he came

a 27 Zech. 13:7 b 30 Some early manuscripts do not have *twice*. c 36 Aramaic for *Father*

back, he again found them sleeping, because their eyes were heavy. They did not know what to say to him.
41Returning the third time, he said to them, "Are you still sleeping and resting? Enough! The hour has come. Look, the Son of Man is betrayed into the hands of sinners. 42Rise! Let us go! Here comes my betrayer!"

Jesus Is Betrayed (Mark 14:43-52)

(cf. Matt. 26:47-56; Luke 22:47-53 and John 18:1-11)

In this short account of Jesus' arrest we are left awestruck at how completely submissive and confident he was in God's Word. The test before Him, as terrible as it was, only drew this composed response: "the Scriptures must be fulfilled" (v. 49). What an amazing effect God's Word can produce in those who are yielded unreservedly to its promises. There is never a test so great that the Scriptures are not greater still.

I. *The Arrangement of Judas (14:43-46)*

43Just as he was speaking, Judas, one of the Twelve, appeared. With him was a crowd armed with swords and clubs, sent from the chief priests, the teachers of the law, and the elders.
44Now the betrayer had arranged a signal with them: "The one I kiss is the man; arrest him and lead him away under guard." 45Going at once to Jesus, Judas said, "Rabbi!" and kissed him. 46The men seized Jesus and arrested him.

II. *The Anger of Peter (14:47)*

47Then one of those standing near drew his sword and struck the servant of the high priest, cutting off his ear.

III. *The Address of Jesus (14:48-50)*

48"Am I leading a rebellion," said Jesus, "that you have come out with swords and clubs to capture me? 49Every day I was with you, teaching in the temple courts, and you did not arrest me. But the Scriptures must be fulfilled." 50Then everyone deserted him and fled.

IV. *The Action of Mark (14:51, 52)*

[51]A young man, wearing nothing but a linen garment, was following Jesus. When they seized him, [52]he fled naked, leaving his garment behind.

In this account we are given a peculiar record of a young man who escaped being captured, but lost his garment and fled naked. What an odd bit of information this story gives us. Why is it reported only in Mark's Gospel? What significance does it possess?

There is evidence that indicates that this person was none other than Mark, the author of this Gospel. Mark's home was in Jerusalem. In fact, it was his mother who had opened her home to the early church (Acts 12:12). This house may have been the central meeting place for the original church leaders, since no other residence is mentioned and because the leaders are seen praying here. It has also been conjectured that Jesus may have eaten the Last Supper here, and that the disciples were here praying in the upper room on the day of Pentecost (Acts 1-2). It is logical (though not necessary) to assume that Mark followed Jesus and His disciples from his home to the garden of Gethsemane. It is even possible that he alone witnessed the agony of Jesus during His three fervent prayers—how else would he know the precise details of these painstaking hours, since Jesus' own disciples slept through the whole ordeal?

Jesus Goes to Court (Mark 14:53-65)

(cf. Matt. 26:57-68 and John 18:12-14, 19-24)

How swiftly Jesus was whisked into the court chamber and given an illegal trial. His accusers searched almost frantically for those who would accuse Him of some evil. They were even content to hear lies and contradictory charges. Finally, Jesus was faced squarely and asked if He was the Christ, Israel's King. Without any hesitation, Jesus calmly retorted, "I am." That is all they wanted to hear. From their point of view, this was an act of blasphemy worthy of the death penalty. The meeting was adjourned immediately, but not before they could vent their irritation by cruelly mocking and beating Jesus.

[53]They took Jesus to the high priest, and all the chief priests, elders and teachers of the law came together. [54]Peter followed him at a distance, right into the courtyard of the high priest. There he sat with the guards and warmed himself at the fire.

[55]The chief priests and the whole Sanhedrin were looking for evidence against Jesus so that they could put him to death, but they did not find any. [56]Many testified falsely against him, but their statements did not agree.

[57]Then some stood up and gave this false testimony against him: [58]"We heard him say, 'I will destroy this man-made temple and in three days will build another, not made by man.' " [59]Yet even then their testimony did not agree.

[60]Then the high priest stood up before them and asked Jesus, "Are you not going to answer? What is this testimony that these men are bringing against you?" [61]But Jesus remained silent and gave no answer.

Again the high priest asked him, "Are you the Christ,[a] the Son of the Blessed One?"

[62]"I am," said Jesus. "And you will see the Son of Man sitting at the right hand of the Mighty One and coming on the clouds of heaven."

[63]The high priest tore his clothes. "Why do we need any more witnesses?" he asked. [64]"You have heard the blasphemy. What do you think?"

They all condemned him as worthy of death. [65]Then some began to spit at him; they blindfolded him, struck him with their fists, and said, "Prophesy!" And the guards took him and beat him.

Peter Denies Christ (Mark 14:66-72)

(cf. Matt. 26:69-75; Luke 22:55-62 and John 18:15-18, 25-27)

There are two matters preserved in this record that we must never forget. First, notice how suddenly and thoroughly a disciple of Christ can fall away from obedience. There is no believer, no matter how holy he may seem to be, who is not capable of the worst kind of sin. Second, notice how sorrowful this disciple was after he completed his sin. Nothing in all of life is so crushing as personal sin.

[66]While Peter was below in the courtyard, one of the servant girls of the high priest came by. [67]When she saw Peter warming himself, she looked closely at him.

"You also were with that Nazarene, Jesus," she said.

[68]But he denied it. "I don't know or understand what you're talking about," he said, and went out into the entryway.[b]

---

a 61 Or *Messiah* *b 68* Some early manuscripts *entryway and the rooster crowed*

**69When the servant girl saw him there, she said again to those
standing around, "This fellow is one of them." 70Again he denied it.
After a little while, those standing near said to Peter, "Surely you are
one of them, for you are a Galilean."
71He began to call down curses on himself, and he swore to them, "I
don't know this man you're talking about."
72Immediately the rooster crowed the second time.[a] Then Peter
remembered the word Jesus had spoken to him: "Before the rooster
crows twice[b] you will disown me three times." And he broke down and
wept.**

Jesus Stands Before Pilate (Mark 15:1-15)

(cf. Matt. 27:11-26; Luke 23:3-25 and John 18:28-40)

Pontius Pilate was well-acquainted with the men who brought Jesus to him. As procurator of Judea he appointed the high priest (who also headed the Jewish Supreme Court, called the Sanhedrin) and oversaw the use of the temple finances. He was familiar with their scheming ways. And he could easily see through their accusations and demands. But in the end Pilate proved to be no more righteous or capable of enforcing justice than the leaders of the Jewish council beneath his authority. The man was a coward, catering to public pressure. He may have washed his hands clean, but his soul took on its darkest stain in the hour he consented to Jesus' crucifixion.

I. *Pilate's Impression (15:1-5)*

**15 Very early in the morning, the chief priests, with the elders, the
teachers of the law and the whole Sanhedrin, reached a
decision. They bound Jesus, led him away and handed him over to
Pilate.
2"Are you the king of the Jews?" asked Pilate.
"Yes, it is as you say," Jesus replied.
3The chief priests accused him of many things. 4So again Pilate asked
him, "Aren't you going to answer? See how many things they are
accusing you of."
5But Jesus still made no reply, and Pilate was amazed.**

---

a 72 Some early manuscripts do not have *the second time*. b 72 Some early manuscripts do not have *twice*.

II. *Pilate's Intention (15:6-14)*

[6]Now it was the custom at the Feast to release a prisoner whom the
people requested. [7]A man called Barabbas was in prison with the
insurrectionists who had committed murder in the uprising. [8]The
crowd came up and asked Pilate to do for them what he usually did.
[9]"Do you want me to release to you the king of the Jews?" asked Pilate,
[10]knowing it was out of envy that the chief priests had handed Jesus
over to him. [11]But the chief priests stirred up the crowd to have Pilate
release Barabbas instead.
[12]"What shall I do, then, with the one you call the king of the Jews?"
Pilate asked them.
[13]"Crucify him!" they shouted.
[14]"Why? What crime has he committed?" asked Pilate.
But they shouted all the louder, "Crucify him!"

III. *Pilate's Intimidation (15:15)*

[15]Wanting to satisfy the crowd, Pilate released Barabbas to them. He had Jesus flogged, and handed him over to be crucified.

Jesus Is Crucified (Mark 15:16-41)

(cf. Matt. 27:27-50; Luke 23:44-49 and John 19:2, 3, 18-37)

Crucifixion was Rome's method for executing non-Roman criminals, particularly those guilty of robbery, rioting or treason. The purpose for this form of death is clear—torture the victim for his offense, shame him publicly, and use him as an example for anyone else who might be thinking of committing a similar crime.

There were various types of crosses used for crucifying someone (see picture below). The style of cross used for Christ was either the first one or the third one shown below, since an inscription was written and placed above His head (Luke 23:38).

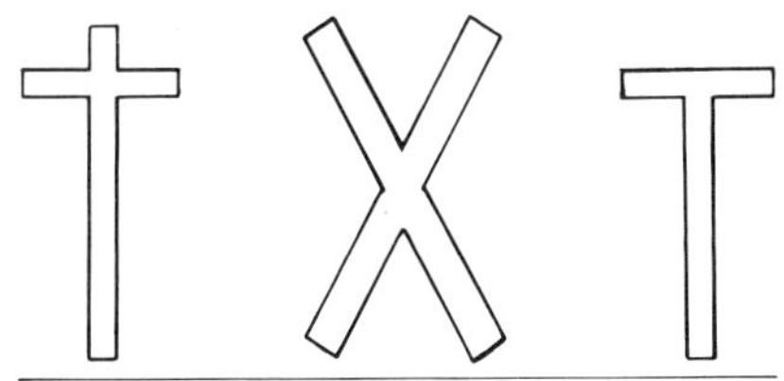

While the cross was as cruel as it was severe, its real ugliness resided in the fact that the victim would frequently suffer for days before hunger, thirst, muscle cramps, fatigue and exposure to the elements of nature would take their fatal toll. Doubtlessly Jesus' early death on the cross was due to His brutal flogging just moments earlier.

I. *The Mockery (15:16-20)*

**16The soldiers led Jesus away into the palace (that is, the Praetorium)
and called together the whole company of soldiers. 17They put a purple
robe on him, then wove a crown of thorns and set it on him. 18And they
began to call out to him, "Hail, King of the Jews!" 19Again and again they
struck him on the head with a staff and spit on him. Falling on their
knees, they worshiped him. 20And when they had mocked him, they took
off the purple robe and put his own clothes on him. Then they led him
out to crucify him.**

II. *The Misery (15:21-28)*

**21A certain man from Cyrene, Simon, the father of Alexander and
Rufus, was passing by on his way in from the country, and they forced
him to carry the cross. 22They brought Jesus to the place called Golgotha
(which means The Place of the Skull). 23Then they offered him wine
mixed with myrrh, but he did not take it. 24And they crucified him.
Dividing up his clothes, they cast lots to see what each would get.**

**25It was the third hour when they crucified him. 26The written notice
of the charge against him read: THE KING OF THE JEWS. 27They crucified
two robbers with him, one on his right and one on his left.[a]**

III. *The Misrepresentation (15:29-32)*

**29Those who passed by hurled insults at him, shaking their heads and
saying, "So! You who are going to destroy the temple and build it in three
days, 30come down from the cross and save yourself!"**

**31In the same way the chief priests and the teachers of the law mocked
him among themselves. "He saved others," they said, "but he can't save
himself! 32Let this Christ,[b] this King of Israel, come down now from the
cross, that we may see and believe." Those crucified with him also
heaped insults on him.**

[a] Some manuscripts *left* 28and the scripture was fulfilled which says, "He was counted with the lawless ones" (Isa. 53:12)   [b] 32 Or *Messiah*

IV. *The Mission (15:33-39)*

**33At the sixth hour darkness came over the whole land until the ninth
hour. 34And at the ninth hour Jesus cried out in a loud voice, *"Eloi, Eloi,
lama sabachthani?"*—which means, "My God, my God, why have you
forsaken me?"**
**35When some of those standing near heard this, they said, "Listen, he's
calling Elijah."**
**36One man ran, filled a sponge with wine vinegar, put it on a stick, and
offered it to Jesus to drink. "Leave him alone now. Let's see if Elijah
comes to take him down," he said.**
37With a loud cry, Jesus breathed his last.
**38The curtain of the temple was torn in two from top to bottom. 39And
when the centurion, who stood there in front of Jesus, heard his cry
and[b] saw how he died, he said, "Surely this man was the Son[c] of God!"**

V. *The Ministers (15:40, 41)*

**40Some women were watching from a distance. Among them were
Mary Magdalene, Mary the mother of James the younger and of Joses,
and Salome. 41In Galilee these women had followed him and cared for
his needs. Many other women who had come up with him to Jerusalem
were also there.**

Jesus Is Buried (Mark 15:42-47)

(cf. Matt. 27:57-61; Luke 23:50-56 and John 19:38-42)

It was 3:00 P.M., only three hours before the Sabbath day (which started, according to our reckoning of time, at 6:00 P.M. on Fridays). So Joseph had to act quickly if he was to get Jesus' body and provide Him with a respectable burial. Otherwise, Jesus' body, like the crucified bodies of criminals, would be removed from the cross and left on the surface of the ground for the dogs and vultures to consume (perhaps this explains the meaning behind the designation, "place of the skull" where Jesus was crucified).

**42It was Preparation Day (that is, the day before the Sabbath). So as
evening approached, 43Joseph of Arimathea, a prominent member of**

a 34 Psalm 22:1 *b 39* Some manuscripts do not have *heard his cry and.* *c 39* Or *a son*

**the Council, who was himself waiting for the kingdom of God, went
boldly to Pilate and asked for Jesus' body. 44Pilate was surprised to hear
that he was already dead. Summoning the centurion, he asked him if
Jesus had already died. 45When he learned from the centurion that it
was so, he gave the body to Joseph. 46So Joseph bought some linen cloth,
took down the body, wrapped it in the linen, and placed it in a tomb cut
out of rock. Then he rolled a stone against the entrance of the tomb.
47Mary Magdalene and Mary the mother of Joses saw where he was laid.**

The Resurrection (Mark 16:1-8)

(cf. Matt. 28:1-10; Luke 24:1-11 and John 20:1-18)

The Resurrection is foundational to the Christian faith. It is the resurrection of Jesus which guarantees our own resurrection (2 Cor. 4:14; 1 Thess. 4:14). Without His resurrection there can be no hope of heaven for anyone; neither can there be any confidence in God's Word. The entirety of God's Word rests on this single event (1 Cor. 15:14, 17). It is little wonder, then, that Christians wholeheartedly endorse this event.

I. *The Day of the Week (16:1, 2)*

**16 When the Sabbath was over, Mary Magdalene, Mary the mother
of James, and Salome bought spices so that they might go to
anoint Jesus' body. 2Very early on the first day of the week, just after
sunrise, they were on their way to the tomb**

II. *The Dilemma of the Women (16:3, 4)*

**3and they asked each other, "Who will roll the stone away from the
entrance of the tomb?"
4But when they looked up, they saw that the stone, which was very
large, had been rolled away.**

III. *The Discourse of the Angel (16:5-8)*

**5As they entered the tomb, they saw a young man dressed in a white
robe sitting on the right side, and they were alarmed.
6"Don't be alarmed," he said. "You are looking for Jesus the Nazarene,**

who was crucified. He has risen! He is not here. See the place where they laid him. [7]But go, tell his disciples and Peter, 'He is going ahead of you into Galilee. There you will see him, just as he told you.' "

[8]Trembling and bewildered, the women went out and fled from the tomb. They said nothing to anyone, because they were afraid.

The Appearances of Jesus (Mark 16:9-18)

(cf. Luke 24:13-49 and John 20:11-18)

The first problem needing consideration here is the very entrance of these verses in the text at all. The New International Version makes the point that these verses are not found in the most reliable early manuscripts. Then, if this be the case, where did these words come from?

There is divided opinion here. Some teachers content themselves with accepting this passage as being from the pen of Mark. They base their claims on the fact that these words are found in numerous manuscripts, some as early as the late second century. Other teachers doubt that the passage was written by Mark, because of its noticeable absence in so many other ancient manuscripts. Additionally, it is noted by various Greek scholars that the transition between verse eight and verse nine is awkward; plus, they say that the vocabulary and style in the questioned verses seem to be non-Markan in flavor. These teachers contend that either Mark was unable to finish his Gospel or that the final part was somehow lost, and that this new conclusion was inserted by those who later copied the text.

Regardless of the particular position you may prefer, there is no debate over the fact that the data presented does generally align itself with the close of the other Gospel writings and the subsequent testimony of the book of Acts. There is no information presented here that cannot be found elsewhere in the New Testament. Therefore, there is no need to fear teaching its contents.

I. *The Appearance to Mary (16:9-11)*

[9]When Jesus rose early on the first day of the week, he appeared first to Mary Magdalene, out of whom he had driven seven demons. [10]She went and told those who had been with him and who were mourning and weeping. [11]When they heard that Jesus was alive and that she had seen him, they did not believe it.

There are two points that require our earnest attention here. First, notice that Jesus showed himself to a faithful female disciple before He ever appeared to His male disciples. We must both recognize and appreciate the loyalty and works of Christ's numerous female followers. Second, notice that the disciples of Jesus doubt Mary's testimony. How regrettable it is when we permit our prejudice and our emotions to dominate our faith. We can miss a great deal when these are in the forefront of our lives.

II. *The Appearance to the Two Disciples (16:12, 13)*

[12]Afterward Jesus appeared in a different form to two of them while
they were walking in the country. [13]These returned and reported it to
the rest; but they did not believe them either.

Jesus' famous walk on the Emmaus road is discussed in Luke 24:13-35.

III. *The Appearance to the Eleven Disciples (16:14-18)*

[14]Later Jesus appeared to the Eleven as they were eating; he rebuked
them for their lack of faith and their stubborn refusal to believe those
who had seen him after he had risen.
[15]He said to them, "Go into all the world and preach the good news to
all creation. [16]Whoever believes and is baptized will be saved, but
whoever does not believe will be condemned. [17]And these signs will
accompany those who believe: In my name they will drive out demons;
they will speak in new tongues; [18]They will pick up snakes with their
hands; and when they drink deadly poison, it will not hurt them at all;
they will place their hands on sick people, and they will get well."

When Jesus joins the eleven disciples, there are two matters of business to discuss.

First, He chides them for their doubts and refusal to believe the testimony of those who had previously seen Him. These words may also need to find a proper place in our hearts, especially as we listen to the supernatural accounts of our brothers and sisters in the body of Christ today.

Second, Jesus charged His disciples to go into all the world, preaching the gospel and baptizing the converts. The further details in this charge have been misunderstood by certain sincere Christians. The abuse of this passage has caused some people to contend that only those persons who defy snakes, drink poison, cure the sick and speak in tongues are really saved. But this certainly is *not* the case. Instead, Jesus is simply declaring that all of these events would occur to some (not all!) of His disciples; and they did—read the book of Acts for a fulfillment of each one of these points.

The Ascension of Jesus (Mark 16:19, 20)

(cf. Matt. 28:18-20; Luke 24:50-52 and Acts 1:6-11)

Possibly the most wonderful (as well as the most mysterious) aspect of the Ascension is found in the fact that Jesus is still here, working through the Holy Spirit with those who submit to His Lordship. His presence is with each one who loves Him and who seeks to follow Him in fulfilling the Great Commission.

19 After the Lord Jesus had spoken to them, he was taken up into
heaven and he sat at the right hand of God. 20 Then the disciples went out
and preached everywhere, and the Lord worked with them and con-
firmed his word by the signs that accompanied it.

Introduction to the Gospel According to Luke

Date: Around A.D. 60

Author:

Luke is mentioned by name only three times in the New Testament (Col. 4:14; 2 Tim. 4:11; Philem. 24), but his infrequent appearances are no indication of his absence. Actually, while Luke was a physician by trade, he was a longtime traveling companion of Paul by choice (Acts 16:10-17; 20:5-15; 21:1-18; 27:1-28:16). In fact, he may have been one of Paul's earliest converts from Antioch.

In addition to this Gospel, Luke is also responsible for writing the ever-popular book of Acts.

Luke, like today's authors, never walked with Jesus. Instead, he learned about the life of Christ through sermons, writings about Him, and conversations held with those who were closest to Him. There is something encouraging about these facts. Perhaps Jesus states it best when he told Thomas, "Blessed are those who have not seen and yet have believed" (John 20:29).

Audience:

This Gospel was intended to reach the hands of a man called "Theophilus" (1:3). We know nothing about this person. Some suppose he was a Gentile, since his name is Greek. Others add to this by stating that he might have been a high official in the Roman government because Luke addressed him as being "most excellent" (1:3). Still others believe Theophilus was not a person at all, but a general designation for all "lovers of God," since this is the meaning of the word/name (*theo* means "God"; *phileo* means "to love"). Perhaps each idea suggested here holds a measure of truth.

While Luke may have had only Theophilus—one man—in mind as he wrote, his gospel message is certainly universal. More than any other Gospel writer, Luke makes it clear that God's plan for salvation is for Gentiles, too (2:14, 32; 3:4-6; 24:47).

Aim:

There can be no guessing about Luke's aim for his writing. He desires earnestly to provide ample data concerning the ministry of Christ so that Theophilus might know—with certainty—the things he has been taught up to this point. In other words, Luke's goal is to establish his reader in the Christian faith (1:3, 4). It is a perfect catechism for new disciples.

Arrangement:

Luke's account of the life of Jesus Christ is certainly no dull repetition of Matthew's account or Mark's writings. Instead, his inclusion of much new data, along with a forceful writing style, makes this Gospel both brilliantly refreshing and rewarding. So far as arrangement is concerned, Luke'a ambition was to write an "orderly account" (1:3). He seems to have meant a somewhat chronological and topical orderliness.

There are four principal sections in this book: (Introduction 1:1-4); I. The Savior's Maturing Years (1:5-4:13); II. The Savior's Ministry in Galilee (4:14-9:50); III. The Savior's Ministry from Galilee to Jerusalem (9:51-19:27); IV. The Savior's Ministry in Jerusalem (19:28-24:53).

Special Note: Commentary notes for Luke's Gospel may be located in the appropriate sections of Matthew's or Mark's Gospels, where these books provide reports of the same events. In instances where Matthew or Mark do not include a matter found in Luke's account, a separate commentary is provided in Luke's text.

Luke's Introduction (Luke 1:1-4)

(cf. Acts 1:1ff.)

This Gospel is no carbon copy of previous writings. Luke's message is uniquely fresh, attractive and compelling. In this Gospel we see words and scenes that are not recorded in any other book. Luke, for instance, tells us about the parents of John the Baptist, the two encounters with the angel Gabriel, the visit of Mary and Elizabeth, the birth of John the Baptist, the prophecy of Zechariah and other special events.

In these opening lines Luke introduces us to his delightful tasks—the putting together of another Gospel. Here we discover his exacting approach to his labor, the pupil to whom he writes and the purpose for this writing.

I. *Previous Gospels (1:1, 2)*

1 Many have undertaken to draw up an account of the things that have been fulfilled[a] among us, 2just as they were handed down to us by those who from the first were eyewitnesses and servants of the word.

During the period in which Luke wrote, and for hundreds of years to follow, the majority of those who became Christians never saw a single copy of any Gospel. These persons were obliged to rely on the testimony of "eyewitnesses" and "servants of the Word" (or preachers). Many, nevertheless, had undertaken to compile an account of Jesus' works and words. Luke was one of those men. And apparently he had at his disposal a number of other similar documents. It is possible that the Gospels of Matthew and Mark served as his primary sources.

II. *Present Gospel (1:3, 4)*

3Therefore, since I myself have carefully investigated everything from the beginning, it seemed good also to me to write an orderly account for you, most excellent Theophilus, 4so that you may know the certainty of the things you have been taught.

Four things can be stated regarding the compiling and writing of the Gospel according to Luke. First, the *search*—Luke carefully investigated every available detail from the beginning of Jesus' ministry. Second, the *system*—Luke wrote an orderly (largely chronological) account of Jesus' life. Third, the *student*—Luke addressed his work to Theophilus (see introduction of this Gospel for details). Fourth, the *scheme*—Luke's intention was to expose the unquestioned truth about Jesus to his friend so that he might possess assurance in his faith.

---

a 1 Or *been surely believed*

The Parents of John the Baptist (Luke 1:5-25)

The previous Gospel writers were content merely to introduce John as the baptizer; but Luke, the physician, takes us to John's parents and shows us the miraculous nature of his conception. The birth of John was special. He, like Jesus who followed him, was a unique gift from God.

I. *The Couple (1:5-7)*

> **5In the time of Herod king of Judea there was a priest named Zechariah, who belonged to the priestly division of Abijah; his wife Elizabeth was also a descendant of Aaron. 6Both of them were upright in the sight of God, observing all the Lord's commandments and regulations blamelessly. 7But they had no children, because Elizabeth was barren; and they were both well along in years.**

The prophets Isaiah and Malachi foretold the coming of the Messiah, but they also stated that His arrival would be preceded by someone who would pave the way for the Messiah's appearance (Isa. 40:3-5; Mal. 3:1; 4:5). It was the destiny of Zechariah and Elizabeth to be the proud parents of this prophesied man. Let us observe four matters about them.

1. *The period in which they lived.* John's parents lived during the cloudy days of the reign of Herod the Great (40-4 B.C.). Herod was an industrious man—maintaining peace in Palestine for Rome and supervising lavish building projects in Rome's honor. But the favor of the Jewish people was never granted to him. His Edomite background, his merciless treatment of the people and his erection of temples to foreign gods made him a dark figure in the history of Palestine. His order to have all male infants killed, aged two and under, in and around Bethlehem, is but one illustration of Herod's sick character (Matt. 2:16-18).

2. *The positions of Zechariah and Elizabeth.* Elizabeth was born into a priest's home, and she married Zechariah, a priest in the division of Abijah. A priest had to be a descendant of Aaron. In Jesus' day there may have been as many as 20,000 priests. They were separated into twenty-four divisions, with Abijah being eighth on the roster. For one week, twice a year, each division would serve in the Temple at Jerusalem. For the remainder of the year they lived at home and assumed a normal occupation.

3. *The purity of Zechariah and Elizabeth.* Zechariah and Elizabeth were "upright" and "blameless" people. To be upright (or righteous) means to stand approved in God's sight, both externally in behavior and internally in motives. To be blameless means to stand with unquestioned faithfulness in the sight of men. John, the son of a priest, would learn the meaning of godly living throughout his life at home.

4. *The problem of Zechariah and Elizabeth.* They were barren, and they were old. In the thinking of the Jews, this condition would have been due to the commission of a serious sin. Parents were intended to have children; not to have offspring was considered disgraceful (1:25). Understandably, Zechariah and Elizabeth wanted a son.

II. *The Confrontation (1:8-23)*

**8Once when Zechariah's division was on duty and he was serving as
priest before God, 9he was chosen by lot, according to the custom of the
priesthood, to go into the temple of the Lord and burn incense. 10And
when the time for the burning of incense came, all the assembled
worshipers were praying outside.**

**11Then an angel of the Lord appeared to him, standing at the right
side of the altar of incense. 12When Zechariah saw him, he was startled
and was gripped with fear. 13But the angel said to him: "Do not be
afraid, Zechariah; your prayer has been heard. Your wife Elizabeth
will bear you a son, and you are to give him the name John. 14He will be a
joy and delight to you, and many will rejoice because of his birth, 15for
he will be great in the sight of the Lord. He is never to take wine or other
fermented drink, and he will be filled with the Holy Spirit even from
birth.[a] 16Many of the people of Israel will he bring back to the Lord
their God. 17And he will go on before the Lord, in the spirit and power
of Elijah, to turn the hearts of the fathers to their children and the
disobedient to the wisdom of the righteous—to make ready a people
prepared for the Lord."**

**18Zechariah asked the angel, "How can I be sure of this? I am an old
man and my wife is well along in years."**

**19The angel answered, "I am Gabriel. I stand in the presence of God,
and I have been sent to speak to you and to tell you this good news. 20And
now you will be silent and not able to speak until the day this happens,
because you did not believe my words, which will come true at their
proper time."**

21Meanwhile, the people were waiting for Zechariah and wondering

a 15 Or *from his mother's womb*

why he stayed so long in the temple. 22When he came out, he could not speak to them. They realized he had seen a vision in the temple, for he kept making signs to them but remained unable to speak.
23When his time of service was completed, he returned home.

Chosen by Lot. Through the casting of lots (probably the placing of colored stones, or stones with symbols on them, into a jar and shaking them until one of the stones fell out) Zechariah was chosen to enter the holy place of the Temple and to burn incense. This practice, which was performed twice a day, was considered to be a most honored task. No priest would be allowed to do this more than once in his lifetime.

An Angel of the Lord. In the holy place of the Temple, when he was by himself, Zechariah was confronted by Gabriel. "Your prayer has been heard." What ecstasy! The name Zechariah means "the Lord remembers." The Lord had neither forgotten His promises to Israel nor the prayer of Zechariah and Elizabeth for a son. This promised son would bless both a nation and a family.

Give Him the Name John. The name the angel announced for the coming baby was "John," meaning "the Lord is gracious," or "the gracious gift of God." The significance of this name may be seen in both God's giving Zechariah a son in his old age, and in His giving Israel a prophet, after nearly 400 years of prophetic silence.

Nine things are said here about this son: (1) He will bring joy to his parents. (2) Many will rejoice because of his birth and work. (3) He will be great in God's sight. (4) He will never drink intoxicating beverages. (5) He will know the Spirit's filling from his birth onward. (6) He will convert many of his brethren. (7) He will operate in the spirit and power of Elijah. (8) He will restore the brokenness of many homes. (9) He will prepare people to meet the Lord Jesus Christ.

Can I Be Sure? Here we see the all-too-common reaction of even sincere Christians when they are confronted with the supernatural—Zechariah doubted. He looked at the circumstances, could not believe his eyes or ears and then asked for additional proofs. We can learn a lesson here. When God makes His will plain, there is no need for a confirmation. Otherwise, the consequences of such a doubting attitude may prove as shocking to us as they did to Zechariah. He was speechless—for nine months!

III. *The Conception (1:24, 25)*

24After this his wife Elizabeth became pregnant and for five months remained in seclusion. 25"The Lord has done this for me," she said. "In these days he has shown his favor and taken away my disgrace among the people."

Naturally, Elizabeth was elated. The social stigma associated with her childless condition would now be removed. She would devote the next five months to private prayer, worship and meditation for her miracle. (It ought to be stressed that this world could use far more mothers who possess a similar disposition to pray over their children.)

The Mother of Jesus (Luke 1:26-38)

Here is a fabulous story; it's actually too exciting to capture the full impact in printed form. Mary is about to conceive God's only Son! You must ask God for a revelation of the atmosphere that surrounded this thrilling experience in order to appreciate its supernatural and utterly unique qualities.

I. *The Commission (1:26, 27)*

26In the sixth month, God sent the angel Gabriel to Nazareth, a town in
Galilee, 27to a virgin pledged to be married to a man named Joseph, a
descendant of David. The virgin's name was Mary.

Once again Gabriel was sent by God to deliver a message. This time the recipient would be a virgin girl named Mary who lived in the insignificant town of Nazareth. It was not to the capital city or to some princess that this divine spotlight came, but to a young teen-ager (who was probably about fourteen years old) who lived in what we might call "the middle of nowhere" (Matt. 1:18-25).

How clearly we see here that God's ways are not our ways—His methods are past finding out (Isa. 55:8-9). We must not lean upon our own understanding when we walk in the Spirit; instead, we must always be open, teachable and ready whenever God speaks.

II. *The Communication (1:28-37)*

28The angel went to her and said, "Greetings, you who are highly
favored! The Lord is with you."
29Mary was greatly troubled at his words and wondered what kind of
greeting this might be. 30But the angel said to her, "Do not be afraid,
Mary, you have found favor with God. 31You will be with child and give
birth to a son, and you are to give him the name Jesus. 32He will be great
and will be called the Son of the Most High. The Lord God will give him

the throne of his father David, [33]and he will reign over the house of
Jacob forever; his kingdom will never end."
[34]"How will this be," Mary asked the angel, "since I am a virgin?"
[35]The angel answered, "The Holy Spirit will come upon you, and the
power of the Most High will overshadow you. So the holy one to be born
will be called[a] the Son of God. [36]Even Elizabeth your relative is going to
have a child in her old age, and she who was said to be barren is in her
sixth month. [37]For nothing is impossible with God."

The first words spoken by Gabriel are noteworthy. He indicated to Mary the distinctively rare honor she had been shown by God. Too many Christians have overlooked this point. In attempting to place Mary beside all other believers (Luke 8:19-21; 11:27, 28), we may have neglected to appreciate her wonderfully humble spirit and abundantly strong faith. There is a model here of worship and obedience from which we can each profit.

The next words spoken to Mary by the angel were even more astonishing. It was the formal announcement of the role she would play in bringing the Messiah into the world. Four matters are stated here regarding this prophesied figure: (1) He will be great; (2) He will be called the Son of the Most High; (3) He will be given David's throne; and (4) He will reign forever. Quite naturally, Mary was perplexed, wondering how all of this could possibly happen. But she was assured that God is big enough to manage easily these apparent impossibilities.

III. *The Consignment (1:38)*

[38]"I am the Lord's servant," Mary answered. "May it be to me as you
have said." Then the angel left her.

Mary's response to the angel ought to be memorized by every Christian. She said, "I am the Lord's servant. May it be to me as you have spoken." This is no lighthearted surrender to God's will. She calls herself a "servant"—which could easily be translated "slave girl." This term connotes Mary's complete submission to God's plans. Imagine how difficult a matter this would have been. Becoming a mother before marriage was certain to bring public disgrace and deep personal pain. Yet Mary consigned herself to obedience—without any regard to its inevitable consequences. Indeed, Mary's faith was a radiant example of a living trust in a miraculous God.

It should be noted here that doing God's will is not always easy or void of public misinterpretation. God cannot use someone who is merely casual in his faith or governed by the opinions of the populace.

---

a 35 Or *So the child to be born will be called holy,*

Mary Visits Elizabeth (Luke 1:39-56)

It is so easy to read the Bible for its content and miss the spirit that accompanies the content. We must remember that spiritual facts do not rest on emotionless hooks. Rather, they are intimately attached to real people, like you and me. Here, then, is an episode that is abundant in content but also equally rich in its emotion-charged atmosphere.

I. *The Joy of Elizabeth (1:39-45)*

39 At that time Mary got ready and hurried to a town in the hill country
of Judah, 40 where she entered Zechariah's home and greeted Elizabeth.
41 When Elizabeth heard Mary's greeting, the baby leaped in her womb,
and Elizabeth was filled with the Holy Spirit. 42 In a loud voice she
exclaimed: "Blessed are you among women, and blessed is the child you
will bear! 43 But why am I so favored, that the mother of my Lord should
come to me? 44 As soon as the sound of your greeting reached my ears,
the baby in my womb leaped for joy. 45 Blessed is she who has believed
that what the Lord has said to her will be accomplished!"

Immediately upon hearing Mary's greeting three things happened to Elizabeth: (1) She felt her baby leap in her womb; (2) she was filled with the Holy Spirit; and (3) she prophesied in a loud voice.

These are two exceptional mothers, but one wonders what might have been our response at a scene such as this one. We might have branded the whole event as being too emotional. Or, we might have spurned the prophetic blessing as being too sensational. Regardless of our theoretical reactions, the experience was valid, and we are left to rejoice as we observe their joy.

The content of Elizabeth's prophecy was forthrightly Christ-centered. She boldly addressed Mary's yet unborn child as her personal Lord. Then, in the manner of the future duty of her own son, Elizabeth retired to the background and gave to Jesus her fullest devotion. What a remarkable scene!

II. *The Joy of Mary (1:46-55)*

46 And Mary said:

"My soul praises the Lord

47 and my spirit rejoices in God my Savior,
48for he has been mindful
of the humble state of his servant.
From now on all generations will call me blessed,
49 for the Mighty One has done great things for me—
holy is his name.
50His mercy extends to those who fear him,
from generation to generation.
51He has performed mighty deeds with his arm;
he has scattered those who are proud in their
inmost thoughts.
52He has brought down rulers from their thrones
but has lifted up the humble.
53He has filled the hungry with good things
but has sent the rich away empty.
54He has helped his servant Israel,
remembering to be merciful
55to Abraham and his descendants forever,
even as he said to our fathers."

Mary was no less jubilant. Instantly, after Elizabeth finished her short but enthusiastic prophecy, Mary rejoiced in overflowing praise for the Lord's manner of dealing righteously with people—blessing those who fear Him and humbling those who resist Him. She was particularly excited by the fact that her Savior had selected her to be the recipient of His special works. Finally, she reveled in God's faithfulness to help Israel.

This is a remarkable offering of praise, especially from the lips of a teen-ager. Mary was, unquestionably, a mature and spiritual woman.

III. *The Journey Home (1:56)*

56Mary stayed with Elizabeth for about three months and then returned home.

After three months of visiting, sharing the news of what God was doing and praising Him with Elizabeth, Mary went home.

Is it not possible that Elizabeth and Mary also spent their time in isolation because they wanted to solidify their experience before releasing it to the general public? They would not hastily rush out and announce their supernatural experiences. Instead, they would wait upon God for the personal fulfillment of His miracle upon their behalf before telling others. In other words, before telling people about their miracle, they would carry the proof with them as a confirmation of their testimony.

Can there be a wise piece of counsel in this for us too? Presumptuous declarations of faith help no one. Genuine miracles are not any less spectacular once they have been confirmed. Let us be certain before we make ignorant (though sincere) boasts.

The Birth of John the Baptist (Luke 1:57-66)

When Elizabeth gave birth to John, these things happened within eight days: (1) Friends joined them in celebrating the joyful birth; (2) John was circumcised; (3) John was named according to the directions of Gabriel; (4) Zechariah's ability to speak was restored; (5) Zechariah was filled with the Holy Spirit, and he prophesied about his son, the coming Messiah, and the nation of Israel; and (6) the people who witnessed all of these events went forth and told the details to everyone. For the next thirty years Israel would speculate about these reports and anticipate the soon arrival of God's Messiah.

I. *The Childbearing (1:57, 58)*

57When it was time for Elizabeth to have her baby, she gave birth to a
son. 58Her neighbors and relatives heard that the Lord had shown her
great mercy, and they shared her joy.

There is a wonderful bursting forth of joy in this scene. Before the pregnancy, Elizabeth felt only guilt and shame for not having borne children (1:25). But now her relatives and neighbors shared her victory. Her years of disappointment were now behind her. All Elizabeth could see was the fulfillment of God's promise and the answer to her earnest prayers. Her heart was full and overflowing.

II. *The Circumcision and Cognomen (1:59-66)*

59On the eighth day they came to circumcise the child, and they were
going to name him after his father Zechariah, 60but his mother spoke up
and said, "No! He is to be called John."

61They said to her, "There is no one among your relatives who has that
name."

62Then they made signs to his father, to find out what he would like to
name the child. 63He asked for a writing tablet, and to everyone's aston-
ishment he wrote, "His name is John." 64Immediately his mouth was

opened and his tongue was loosed, and he began to speak, praising God. [65]The neighbors were all filled with awe, and throughout the hill country of Judea people were talking about all these things. [66]Everyone who heard this wondered about it, asking, "What then is this child going to be?" For the Lord's hand was with him.

They Came to Circumcise the Child. The laws of the Old Testament required all male babies to be circumcised (Gen. 17:11, 12; Exod. 12:48; Lev. 12:3). By the time of the New Testament all these children were circumcised either at the Temple in Jerusalem or at the local synagogue. The chief value of this action was spiritual, since it symbolized God's redemptive covenant with His people. It also was to serve as a perpetual reminder of the holy life style the individual was to maintain, otherwise the outward symbol would be meaningless (Lev. 26:41; Deut. 10:16; Jer. 4:4).

He Is to Be Called John. Greek parents named their sons on the seventh day after birth. The Romans named their children on the ninth day. The Jews named their boys on the eighth day.

The Jews usually affixed some significance to names. Often a name contained a meaning that expressed the wishes of the parents for their child and/or for Israel. The desired character or work of each child would be expressed in his name. Also, by this period, it was not uncommon to give children the name of a parent or of an ancestor—this was expected in this case, but Zechariah and Elizabeth had other plans. God had given them this son, and He had selected his name. He would be called "John," meaning "the Lord is gracious" or "the gracious gift of God" (see notes on 1:5-25).

With this act of naming the child, Zechariah was released from his muteness. There is a lesson for us in this event. We must learn that if holy men like Zechariah are not beyond rebuke or refinement, then neither can we expect to be beyond divine discipline (Heb. 12:5ff.). Further, let us observe that there is always an end to chastisement, once the lesson is learned and doubts are replaced with faithful obedience.

The Prophecy of Zechariah (Luke 1:67-80)

These inspiring words have been called the last prophecy of the Old Testament and the first prophecy of the New Testament—at the same time. This portion of the Gospel—the ministry of John—rightly serves as the hinge that connects the two great testaments (Matt. 11:11-13; Luke 16:16).

I. *Promises for National Salvation (1:67-75)*

67His father Zechariah was filled with the Holy Spirit and prophesied:

68"Praise be to the Lord, the God of Israel,
because he has come and has redeemed his people.
69He has raised up a horn[a] of salvation for us
in the house of his servant David
70(as he said through his holy prophets of long ago),
71salvation from our enemies
and from the hand of all who hate us—
72to show mercy to our fathers
and to remember his holy covenant,
73 the oath he swore to our father Abraham:
74to rescue us from the hand of our enemies,
and to enable us to serve him without fear
75 in holiness and righteousness before him all our days.

Deeply imbedded in the heart of every faithful Jew was the intense desire to see his tiny state forever delivered from national foes. For nearly six hundred years Israel had been subjected to Gentile dominion—first, by Babylon (606-537 B.C.); second, by the Medes and Persians (537-331 B.C.); third, by the Greeks (331-166 B.C.); and now by the Romans (63 B.C. to Zechariah's time). For years their prayer sounded the same—"Rescue us from the hands of our enemies, and enable us to serve you without fear." The prolonged wait for the fulfillment of this petition, like the agonizing years of Elizabeth's barrenness, was now seemingly becoming a wonderful reality.

II. *Promises for Personal Salvation (1:76-79)*

76And you, my child, will be called a prophet of the
Most High;
for you will go on before the Lord to prepare the way
for him,
77to give his people the knowledge of salvation
through the forgiveness of their sins,
78because of the tender mercy of our God,
by which the rising sun will come to us from heaven
79to shine on those living in darkness
and in the shadow of death,
to guide our feet into the path of peace."

---

a 69 *Horn* here symbolizes strength.

Zechariah now revealed the divinely ordered mission of his new son—he would be a prophet, proclaiming the message of personal salvation from the consequences brought about by sin.

National promises are fine, but if they do not filter down to an individual and spiritual level, they will not come into fulfillment. Here is a message that far too many Jews deliberately overlooked. They sought a deliverance from the sinners who controlled them nationally but not a deliverance from the sins that controlled them personally. It was this oversight that kept the national promises from becoming a first-century reality. Israel was to learn that the personal has precedent over the national; that the spiritual has priority over the physical (Matt. 21:43-44; Rom. 9-11).

III. *Privacy of John (1:80)*

80 And the child grew and became strong in spirit; and he lived in the desert until he appeared publicly to Israel.

There is certainly a great deal of good that can be spoken on behalf of public religious training, but this can never be a replacement for the instruction that comes privately, while in the desert (Matt. 4:1-11; Gal. 1:11-18). It seems that those who best know these hot, dry and isolated experiences are God's choicest vessels for service. This is John's testimony.

Jesus Is Born (Luke 2:1-7)

(cf. Matt. 1:18-25; John 1:14)

The birth of a child, though it is precious, is not unique. Children are born in every city of the world every day of the year. Why, then, is such attention displayed over this particular birth? It is because this is the birth of God's only Son!

There is no other birth narrative like this one. It stands alone in all of time, for this baby has a virgin for His mother and God for His Father!

I. *The Census (2:1-3)*

2 In those days Caesar Augustus issued a decree that a census should be taken of the entire Roman world. 2 (This was the first census that took place while Quirinius was governor of Syria.) 3 And everyone went to his own town to register.

Caesar Augustus, who reigned from 30 B.C. to A.D. 14, ordered a census to be taken throughout his empire. The chief purpose for this decree was to determine taxation for the subjects of Rome. The registration included one's name and occupation and the names of living relatives.

II. *The Cities (2:4)*

4So Joseph also went up from the town of Nazareth in Galilee to Judea, to Bethlehem the town of David, because he belonged to the house and line of David.

The little town of Bethlehem rested six miles south of Jerusalem. It was commonly called "the city of David," because it was here that David had been born (1 Sam. 17:12, 15). Out of this city was to come Israel's greatest king of the past—David—and Israel's greatest King of all ages—Jesus. Today this city is called Beth-Lahm, and it has about 8,000 residents.

Nazareth was located about eighty miles north of Bethlehem. This distance, coupled with Mary's condition and the relatively poor modes of transportation, probably made the five-to-six-day journey quite uncomfortable. Still, it was in God's prophesied plans for the birth to occur just as it happened (Mic. 5:2).

III. *The Child (2:5-7)*

5He went there to register with Mary, who was pledged to be married to him and was expecting a child. 6While they were there, the time came for the baby to be born, 7and she gave birth to her firstborn, a son. She wrapped him in cloths and placed him in a manger, because there was no room for them in the inn.

There is something irritating in this passage. The inconsiderate attitudes of the people about Mary's condition strike a note of pity and disgust. One is only left to wonder how different it would have been if we were there observing the plight of these strangers. Would *we* have taken them in, sacrificing our comforts for mere strangers?

There is also something warm in this story. The amazing lowliness of our Lord and the joy of His parents must touch us. This first Christmas has left an indelible mark of peace and hope for all of mankind. Each year our hearts are drawn away from the hustle and bustle to remember this tremendous night when our Lord and Savior was born.

A Manger. A manger is a feeding-trough for animals. According to the early church fathers, Jesus is believed to have been born in a cave which served as a stall for animals. If this is the case, the manger would probably have been a cut-out section in a wall of the cave where food would be stored for animals to eat from.

In about A.D. 330 Constantine erected a church at the supposed site of this cave. Later, about A.D. 550, Justinian rebuilt the church, and today this structure (called "The Church of the Nativity") still stands as a memorial to Jesus' birth.

The Inn. There is no adequate English term to describe this inn. It was not a hotel, as we use that term. Instead, it was simply a shelter for animals and strangers who came to a community where they knew no one. Travelers were expected to carry their own bedding, cooking utensils, food (such as bread, cheese, figs and olives) and all other necessities. The inn would provide protection from the elements, nothing more. But because of the requirement to register, the unusually high number of people coming to Bethlehem filled all available space. Joseph and Mary had to find their shelter elsewhere.

The Angels Visit the Shepherds (Luke 2:8-14)

Here we see a few shepherds of Bethlehem meeting the Shepherd of all the ages (John 10:14; Heb. 13:20). It is an unexpected meeting. One would imagine that the Christ child should first be hailed by men of regal attire and priestly robes, but instead, he is greeted by common shepherds of the field.

Can anyone doubt the humble character of our Lord? Can anyone see even the smallest particle of selfish interest in Him? Can anyone fathom the depths of His love for us? Naturally, the answer is a resounding "No" to each of these inquiries. There is none like Him—none!

8 And there were shepherds living out in the fields nearby, keeping
watch over their flocks at night. 9 An angel of the Lord appeared to them,
and the glory of the Lord shone around them, and they were terrified.
10 But the angel said to them, "Do not be afraid. I bring you good news of
great joy that will be for all the people. 11 Today in the town of David a
Savior has been born to you; he is Christ[a] the Lord. 12 This will be a sign
to you: You will find a baby wrapped in cloths and lying in a manger."
13 Suddenly a great company of the heavenly host appeared with the
angel, praising God and saying,

14 "Glory to God in the highest,
and on earth peace to men on whom his favor rests."

---

a 11 Or *Messiah.* "The Christ" (Greek) and "the Messiah" (Hebrew) both mean "the Anointed One"; also in verse 26.

There are no less than three points that must be observed here.

First, consider the shepherds. These were ordinary men. They had no status, no wealth and no education. Still, it was to them that the good news first came. It has been suggested by some writers, and probably correctly, that these men were responsible for handling the sheep used in the Temple sacrifices in nearby Jerusalem. How appropriate, then, that they should first see God's great lamb who would be sacrificed for the sins of the world (John 1:29).

Second, consider the angels. The involvement of angels with people is a repeated testimony of the Scriptures. They assist in the reign of the nations (Dan. 10:12, 13; 10:20-11:1); they execute God's plans in the earth (Acts 12:21-23); and they serve those who are the heirs of salvation (Heb. 1:14). There is virtually nothing God does in which He does not make use of His angels. Here, we witness them testifying with great joy of the Messiah's birth. Doubtlessly, angels still serve an integral (though usually secretive) part in introducing us to Christ, our Savior.

Third, consider the message of the angels. The New International Version brings a vastly different rendering to the angelic announcement than does the King James Version of the Bible. The new rendering is correct. The birth of the Lord means peace on earth, but only for those "on whom his favor rests." Indeed, the Savior's birth is a meaningless gesture by the appraisal of many persons. But for those people who receive Jesus as their personal Savior and Lord, they find the peace that can only come from the favor or grace of God.

The Shepherds Visit Jesus (Luke 2:15-20)

It must have seemed strange, on the one hand, to see the glory of the Lord, and on the other hand, to see the pathetic crib for the newborn Savior. What a dramatic contrast!

Often God deals with us in opposite extremes. One moment we are on the mountain's peak; the next instant we are in the valley's lowest basin. Both experiences are ordered from God. We must learn to see Him and to trust Him in every circumstance life offers.

> **15When the angels had left them and gone into heaven, the shepherds said to one another, "Let's go to Bethlehem and see this thing that has happened, which the Lord has told us about."**
>
> **16So they hurried off and found Mary and Joseph, and the baby, who**
> **was lying in the manger. 17When they had seen him, they spread the**

word concerning what had been told them about this child, [18]and all
who heard it were amazed at what the shepherds said to them. [19]But
Mary treasured up all these things and pondered them in her heart.
[20]The shepherds returned, glorifying and praising God for all the
things they had heard and seen, which were just as they had been told.

Without hesitation the shepherds followed the directions of the angels, and without delay they confidently declared both the glory and the humiliation they saw. Mary, however, stored up these experiences, only to reflect upon them again and again. Her heart and mind were certainly full of excitement and possibilities, but her tongue would remain silent. She would let others pass along the story of her son. It would be inappropriate for her to boast in such a way. She would allow God to work out His timing and method for the disclosure of her special son. What patience! What maturity!

Jesus' Circumcision, Naming and Dedication (Luke 2:21-24)

Whenever a baby was born in Jewish society, a fairly routine procedure was followed: (1) The baby would first be washed. (2) The child would then be rubbed with salt, probably because it was considered to be a disinfectant and skin conditioner. (3) Next, the baby would be wrapped in swaddling clothes (strips of cloth) from its waist to its feet—to prevent bruising. (4) The baby, during the early Old Testament period, was then named on the day of its birth, though by the New Testament period this naming was delayed to the day of circumcision—the eighth day.

After the birth process, the mother was considered unclean because it was believed she had been contaminated by the discharges connected with her delivery. This condition was to last seven days if the baby was a boy, or fourteen days if the child was a girl (Lev. 12). After this period, a mother would bathe and then offer a sacrifice. Finally, if the baby was a firstborn son, he would be dedicated to God (that is, given to God for His own purposes).

In the following narrative we see the four major elements associated with the birth of a firstborn son—circumcision, naming, sacrifice for cleansing and dedication.

I. *Jesus Is Circumcised and Named (2:21)*

[21]On the eighth day, when it was time to circumcise him, he was named Jesus, the name the angel had given him before he had been conceived.

Circumcision is the act of cutting off the male's foreskin (Lev. 12:3). This was a sign (like baptism today—Col. 2:8-15) of the relationship that was to be shared between its recipient and God (Gen. 17:10-14). The bearer of the sign was to live a holy life as a member of the covenant community, Israel. For further comments on the act of circumcision and on Jesus' name see Matt. 1:1, 21 and Luke 1:59-61.

II. *Jesus Is Dedicated (2:22-24)*

22When the time of their purification according to the Law of Moses had been completed, Joseph and Mary took him to Jerusalem to present him to the Lord 23(as it is written in the Law of the Lord, "Every firstborn male is to be consecrated to the Lord"[a]), 24and to offer a sacrifice in keeping with what is said in the Law of the Lord: "a pair of doves or two young pigeons."[b]

According to the laws written by Moses, the firstborn son of every parent was to be given back to God (Exod. 13:2). Additionally, the law stated that a woman was to purify herself after childbirth by presenting an offering to God (Lev. 12:1-8). Let's observe several important matters that will result in our edification.

First, the piety of Jesus' parents is shown here. They were delighted to surrender Him over to God. They would hold no claims upon Him. He would be raised as the Lord's Son. They were merely custodians of His care. How desperately and deeply this practice needs to invade our own homes.

Second, the poverty of Jesus' parents is shown here. They were poor people. The law stipulated that a lamb was to be offered for purification, but if the family did not possess the funds for this animal, then pigeons or doves would suffice. Mary offered the latter. Her home knew no wealth. Jesus would be raised in a poor man's home, wear a poor man's clothes and eat a poor man's food. But these adversities would not stunt Jesus in any way. Rather, they would serve to intensify His awareness of the true feelings and needs of people. What condescension!

Simeon Sees the Lord's Christ (Luke 2:25-35)

We know nothing about Simeon beyond this single account. What we learn about him here, however, is most impressive. He is spiritual (v. 25a), Spirit-anointed (v. 25b), Spirit-taught (v. 26) and Spirit-led (v. 27).

Simeon's message comes to us in two parts: (1) the public words spoken to the Lord

a 23 Exodus 13:2, 12 *b 24* Lev. 12:8

(vv. 29-32) and (2) the private words spoken to Mary (vv. 34, 35). The former address is praise-centered, emphasizing the role of Jesus as the Savior of all men, including Gentiles. The latter address is piercing, emphasizing the role of Jesus as the great divider of people.

I. *The Man (2:25-27)*

25Now there was a man in Jerusalem called Simeon, who was righteous and devout. He was waiting for the consolation of Israel, and the Holy Spirit was upon him. 26It had been revealed to him by the Holy Spirit that he would not die before he had seen the Lord's Christ. 27Moved by the Spirit, he went into the temple courts. When the parents brought in the child Jesus to do for him what the custom of the Law required,

There Was a Man: Israel, as a whole, and Jerusalem in particular, had been absorbed by a subtle form of self-righteousness. The height of this carnality was to be found in the Temple itself. But it is also here that we meet a reverent man who walked with God.

God always has men who will hear and follow His voice. A quick glance at the Jewish state in the first century will reveal many problems, but a more penetrating scrutiny will also expose some saintly jewels. We must remember that God's people are everywhere, and they cannot be hidden.

The Consolation of Israel. This is another way of saying, "salvation from our enemies" (Luke 1:71) or "the redemption of Jerusalem" (Luke 2:38). The Jews sought political freedom. They looked for a thorough and final deliverance from all Gentile tyranny. Through the appearance of "the Lord's Christ" this was to occur.

The Lord's Christ. The Greek term "Christ" (or its Hebrew equivalent—"Messiah") means "anointed, set apart and divinely qualified." According to the prophetic expectations, He was to be the highest of all the previous prophets, priests and kings (see notes on Matt. 1:1).

II. *The Message (2:28-35)*

28Simeon took him in his arms and praised God, saying:

29"Sovereign Lord, as you have promised,
you now dismiss[a] your servant in peace.
30For my eyes have seen your salvation,
31 which you have prepared in the sight of all people,
32a light for revelation to the Gentiles
and for glory to your people Israel."

---

[a] 29 Or *promised,/now dismiss*

**[33]The child's father and mother marveled at what was said about him.
[34]Then Simeon blessed them and said to Mary, his mother: "This child is destined to cause the falling and rising of many in Israel, and to be a sign that will be spoken against, [35]so that the thoughts of many hearts will be revealed. And a sword will pierce your own soul too."**

The nature of Simeon's public praise focuses on the unique identity of Jesus—in Him is God's salvation. But for Simeon (and characteristically for Luke's Gospel) this salvation is envisioned as touching the Gentiles, too. The Lord's Christ will bring a universal consolation.

The nature of Simeon's private comments to Mary are of a peculiarly negative nature. While this child will be a light for the whole world, He will also cause some to stumble and fall—namely, the proud, self-righteous and unteachable. Further, He will be a sign (or divine proof) of God's interest in Israel; still, many people will resist His ministry. And, in doing so, they will reveal the real nature of their carnal hearts. Finally, Mary too will suffer because of Jesus' ministry, especially in the hour of His crucifixion.

Anna Sees Jesus (Luke 2:36-39)

Only Luke records this touching story. Here we read about an eighty-four-year-old woman named Anna. In this brief account we learn of her widowhood, her work in the Temple and her words of witness. The devotion of this woman to God and her denial of self is a precious scene of profound inspiration.

[36]There was also a prophetess, Anna, the daughter of Phanuel, of the tribe of Asher. She was very old; she had lived with her husband seven years after her marriage, [37]and then was a widow until she was eighty-four.[a] She never left the temple but worshiped night and day, fasting and praying. [38]Coming up to them at that very moment, she gave thanks to God and spoke about the child to all who were looking forward to the redemption of Jerusalem.

[39]When Joseph and Mary had done everything required by the Law of the Lord, they returned to Galilee to their own town of Nazareth.

A Prophetess. Anna joins a very small company of ladies who knew this title. Only four women are identified as prophetesses in the entire Old Testament: Miriam

a 37 Or *widow for eighty-four years*

(Exod. 15:20), Deborah (Judg. 4:4), Huldah (2 Kings 22:14) and Noadiah (Neh. 6:14). It was Anna's divinely ordained duty to tell people God's will throughout the Temple in Jerusalem.

Just as surely as God has men who will serve Him faithfully in the midst of corruption (like Simeon—Luke 2:25-35), so, too, He has women who are equally devoted and gifted (like Anna). God has His witnesses everywhere. And they will not be silent.

She Never Left the Temple. The temple was a massive structure—over 100,000 square feet. It was common for hundreds of persons to mingle, meditate, be taught and discuss spiritual matters in this house of God. Without a doubt, many of these persons would meet Anna and hear her proclaim God's will, especially about the birth of the Messiah. Certainly this straightforward and enthusiastic witness added to the positive responsiveness Jesus received.

The Redemption of Jerusalem. See notes on Luke 2:25-35—"The Consolation of Israel."

Jesus Grows Up to Young Adulthood (Luke 2:40)

In a single verse we read of the transition of Jesus from babyhood to near-adulthood (or age twelve). Because of the extreme brevity of the text we are left with virtually no information about these formative years. The account tells us only that Jesus grew physically, intellectually and spiritually. Read Matt. 3:13-17 for other specific details.

40 And the child grew and became strong; he was filled with wisdom, and the grace of God was upon him.

Although the Scriptures are mostly silent regarding Jesus' early years, we are, nevertheless, capable of painting a fairly detailed and colorful picture of life in Nazareth from the historical information we possess in sources other than the New Testament.

1. *Jesus' Country.* Jesus lived in the land of Palestine, which became divided into territories after the death of Herod the Great. There were numerous borders over which Roman officials were given positions of authority. The two principal areas of interest to the Gospel writers were Galilee and Judea. See the map on page 40.

Jesus was raised in the territory of Galilee. The Jews who lived there were generally less intense about the traditions that so strongly controlled the hierarchy of Jerusalem in Judea. As a result, they were looked down upon by the Judeans because the Galileans did not legalistically adhere to these oral interpretations of the Law. The Galileans were also belittled for their speech accent, colloquialisms and informal manners. The social prejudice that existed between these two territories aroused considerable distaste for one another.

2. *Jesus' Town.* Nazareth was situated on the east and southeast sections of a hillside, about midway between the Mediterranean Sea and the Sea of Galilee. From these hills Jesus could enjoy a view of the plains and snowcapped Mount Hermon in the North, the Mediterranean Sea and Mount Carmel in the West, a forest and the Sea of Galilee in the East and the Plain of Esdraelon in the South. In Jesus' day Nazareth was a small town, with only one spring. Today, however, it boasts a population of over 30,000 residents.

3. *Jesus' House.* The houses of Nazareth were mostly constructed from the white limestone that came from nearby quarries. It is believed that the vast majority of this town's citizens were of a lower middle-class status. Jesus probably lived in a square house with a single door. The floor would have either been dirt or dirt covered with tiles. His bed would have been made by spreading a mat on the floor. The flat roof would have been used on hot summer days as a place for fellowship and entertaining guests.

4. *Jesus' Education.* Jesus' informal learning was done at home. Here His parents instructed Him in the writings of the Old Testament. This began at about the age of three. Much attention was placed on memorization. Jesus expanded His insights as He joined His family in the weekly Sabbath services and at the annual feasts (the latter were designed to visualize the story of Israel's divinely ordered relationship with God). Finally, Jesus learned from the example of his godly parents.

Jesus' formal training took place in the synagogue, between 10:00 A.M. and 3:00 P.M. There, he would sit cross-legged on the floor. From the ages of about five to ten, all Jewish boys were taught to read and write, using the Old Testament as their text. They would start in the books of Moses (probably the book of Leviticus because of its practical and significant contents), proceed to the Prophets and finish in the poetic literature. At the age of ten the boys would begin their study of the oral traditions (or interpretations that developed around the Old Testament writings). These studies often lasted for five years.

The Boy Jesus Amazes the Teachers (Luke 2:41-52)

When God reveals something, we ought to declare it; but when He conceals something, we ought to keep silent. The thirty years of silence in Jesus' life at Nazareth were only broken once—for a brief scene of Jesus' visit to Jerusalem at the age of twelve.

The causes that may be offered for the absence of any other information regarding Jesus' past are debated. Perhaps the best answer is that God wants us to concentrate on Jesus' ministering, not on His maturing. Nothing else is so important as the work Jesus performed in order to secure our salvation. This fact must never be obscured by any other aspect of His life or mission.

I. *The Custom (2:41, 42)*

**41Every year his parents went to Jerusalem for the Feast of the Pass-
over. 42When he was twelve years old, they went up to the Feast, according to the custom.**

The Law of Moses stipulated that every Jew was to go to Jerusalem three times each year and celebrate a particular feast (Exod. 23:17; Deut. 16:16). By this time, however, 1,500 years later, it was the custom of most Jews who lived any distance from Jerusalem to come but once a year—to the Passover celebration.

Observe the unity between Mary and Joseph in their worship. For them the house of God and its services were a family affair. It was not necessary for both of them to make this expensive and toilsome twelve-day round trip, but their mutual commitments would have it no other way. Such an attitude is a model for all Christian couples.

For comments on the Passover see Matt. 26:1-5, 17-30.

II. *The Check (2:43-46)*

**43After the Feast was over, while his parents were returning home, the
boy Jesus stayed behind in Jerusalem, but they were unaware of it.
44Thinking he was in their company, they traveled on for a day. Then
they began looking for him among their relatives and friends. 45When
they did not find him, they went back to Jerusalem to look for him.
46After three days they found him in the temple courts, sitting among
the teachers, listening to them and asking them questions.**

Thousands of persons traveled to Jerusalem to celebrate Passover. After the seven-day feast was finished, the crowds would start their journeys home. It was not uncommon for groups of people to travel together. Usually the women and little children, because they walked more slowly than the men, would leave Jerusalem first. Later in the day, the men and older children would depart. In the evening the men would join their families. It is from this natural setting that Joseph probably thought Mary had taken Jesus with her when she left town, and that Mary figured Jesus would come with Joseph. That evening they discovered their lack of communication.

Now they had to retrace their steps and begin a painstaking search for a young boy in a large city. The searching would last for three long days.

III. *The Conversations (2:47-50)*

> **47Everyone who heard him was amazed at his understanding and his
> answers. 48When his parents saw him, they were astonished. His mother
> said to him, "Son, why have you treated us like this? Your father and I
> have been anxiously searching for you."**
>
> **49"Why were you searching for me?" he asked. "Didn't you know I had
> to be in my Father's house?" 50But they did not understand what he was
> saying to them.**

They Found Him. It was a common practice for the scholars of the Law to hold informal classes in the courts of the Temple. They would discuss topics among themselves in the open air, allowing questions to be asked of them from their audience. Often these scholars would, in turn, ask questions for their inquirers to answer. It is here that Jesus demonstrated His rich insights into God's Word. This does not imply that Jesus was actually correcting the teachers with His own views, but He was revealing His exceptional knowledge.

My Father's House. These are the very first words we hear from the lips of Jesus. Three matters ought to be seen here.

1. Jesus expressed surprise that Joseph and Mary had not known where they could find Him. He had meant them no inconvenience. He simply had thought they knew where He was all this time. (Parenthetically, it is interesting to note Jesus' remarkable self-composure. The temporary absence of His parents did not ruffle Him at all.)

2. Jesus announced that God was in fact His Father. Mary had just called Joseph His Father, but Jesus (without any tone of rebuke) stated that His real Father is God. Exactly when this realization came to Jesus is not known, though it was clear that at the young age of twelve, He knew about His uniqueness.

3. Jesus gave a short preview here that He was destined to be intimately involved in God's house.

IV. *The Compliance and Coming of Age (2:51, 52)*

[51]Then he went down to Nazareth with them and was obedient to them. But his mother treasured all these things in her heart. [52]And Jesus grew in wisdom and stature, and in favor with God and men.

What an inspiring relationship Jesus had with His parents, the community in which He lived and with God. He was obedient to His parents. Before His community and God, He grew in favor. We must never forget that the Christian life is more than a relationship with God alone; it also embraces those at home, work and play.

John the Baptist Prepares the Way (Luke 3:1-20)

(cf. Matt. 3:1-12; Mark 1:1-8; John 1:6-8, 15-37)

The Messiah did not blaze a path from heaven to earth, leaving everyone awestruck. No, He came much more subtly. He came as a baby, and then He was introduced only after He had become a mature man.

God knows we need to be made ready for spiritual experiences. The soil of our hearts needs to be prepared before God's seeds can bear their intended fruit. In like manner, before Christ would be able to arrive, He had to be properly introduced first. The job of introducing Him fell to a man named John.

I. *The Politicians and Priests (3:1, 2)*

3 In the fifteenth year of the reign of Tiberius Caesar—when Pontius Pilate was governor of Judea, Herod tetrarch of Galilee, his brother Philip tetrarch of Iturea and Traconitis, and Lysanias tetrarch of Abilene— [2]during the high priesthood of Annas and Caiaphas, the word of God came to John son of Zechariah in the desert.

Luke provides his readers with as much information as possible, and because of this, we are able to know the precise time of the beginnings of the ministries of John and Jesus. First he outlines the people in political office (v. 1), then he names the people in the high priest's office (v. 2).

Tiberius (or Caesar) was emperor of the Roman Empire from August 19, A.D. 14 until he died in A.D. 37 (although he retired from an active role in government in A.D. 26). The fifteenth year of his reign, according to monarchial reckoning procedures, would have started in either September or October of A.D. 27. Pontius Pilate was procurator (or governor of the region) of Judea from A.D. 26 to 36. Herod (also called Antipas), a son of Herod the Great, was tetrarch (a ruler of a fourth part of a region) of Galilee and Perea from 4 B.C. to A.D. 39. Philip, another son of Herod the Great, was tetrarch of Iturea and Traconitis from 4 B.C. to A.D. 34. Lysanias, a son of Ptolemy, served a short reign over Abilene from around A.D. 26 to 28.

Annas was high priest from approximately A.D. 6 to 15, when he was officially replaced by Caiaphas, his son-in-law. Caiaphas held this title from about A.D. 15 to 36. Apparently these men co-served in the position of high priest during the period of the New Testament Gospels.

With all of this chronological information it seems safe to state that John the Baptist started his ministry around A.D. 26 or 27. This means his work of preparing the way for the coming Christ must have lasted only one year (or less).

II. *The Proclamation of Repentance (3:3-14)*

3He went into all the country around the Jordan, preaching a baptism
of repentance for the forgiveness of sins. 4As is written in the book of the
words of Isaiah the prophet:

"A voice of one calling in the desert,
'Prepare the way for the Lord,
make straight paths for him.
5Every valley shall be filled in,
every mountain and hill made low.
The crooked roads shall become straight,
the rough ways smooth.
6And all mankind will see God's salvation.' "[a]

7John said to the crowds coming out to be baptized by him, "You brood
of vipers! Who warned you to flee from the coming wrath? 8Produce
fruit in keeping with repentance. And do not begin to say to yourselves,
'We have Abraham as our father.' For I tell you that out of these stones
God can raise up children for Abraham. 9The ax is already at the root of
the trees, and every tree that does not produce good fruit will be cut
down and thrown into the fire."
10"What should we do then?" the crowd asked.
11John answered, "The man with two tunics should share with him
who has none, and the one who has food should do the same."
12Tax collectors also came to be baptized. "Teacher," they asked, "what
should we do?"

a 6 Isaiah 40:3-5

[13]"Don't collect any more than you are required to," he told them.
[14]Then some soldiers asked him, "And what should we do?"
He replied, "Don't extort money and don't accuse people falsely—be content with your pay."

There was nothing soft about this man—neither in his appearance nor in his speech. He would call those who were insincere a "brood of vipers" (poisonous snakes). And for each angle individuals used in attempting to justify themselves, John had a stunning rebuke. He called people to repent, and he expected to see proof of that repentance in those whom he baptized.

III. *The Proclamation of Jesus' Coming (3:15-18)*

[15]The people were waiting expectantly and were all wondering in their hearts if John might possibly be the Christ.[a] [16]John answered them all, "I baptize you with[b] water. But one more powerful than I will come, the thongs of whose sandals I am not worthy to untie. He will baptize you with the Holy Spirit and with fire. [17]His winnowing fork is in his hand to clear his threshing floor and to gather the wheat into his barn, but he will burn up the chaff with unquenchable fire." [18]And with many other words John exhorted the people and preached the good news to them.

John's powerful and persuasive preaching attracted some speculation that he might be the long-awaited Christ. He assured his listeners, however, that his works were merely symbols in relationship to the works of the coming Messiah. He told them that when this figure would appear, He would baptize the faithful ones in the Holy Spirit and burn up the rest in an everlasting fire. (See a special study on this subject at the end of Matt. 3:12.)

IV. *The Proclamation of Herod's Sin (3:19, 20)*

[19]But when John rebuked Herod the tetrarch because of Herodias, his brother's wife, and all the other evil things he had done, [20]Herod added this to them all: He locked John up in prison.

John's voice never evaded controversial issues or prominent personalities. He faithfully sounded forth a clear message and standard for righteous living. No one was exempt from these realistic guidelines, including the highest members of society. John would not make Herod an exception. He would call out his sin, and expect a formal repentance. As a result, John received a prison sentence that ultimately led to his execution. Nonetheless, the voice of those, like John, who do not compromise God's message for the audience to whom they speak is a beautiful testimony.

---

a 15 Or *Messiah* *b 16* Or *in*

Jesus Is Baptized (Luke 3:21, 22)

(cf. Matt. 3:13-17; Mark 1:9-11; John 1:31-34)

John baptized many hundreds of persons before Jesus arrived to be baptized by him. The atmosphere in Palestine was ripe with expectancy. John's works and words were exceptionally productive, especially with the common folks. Now it was time to baptize his greatest candidate, Jesus.

Jesus did not need to be baptized by John. He had no sin to remove. Still, Jesus would, from the very start, identify with the sins of people. As our substitute, He would taste the totality of our unrighteousness.

**21When all the people were being baptized, Jesus was baptized too.
And as he was praying, heaven was opened 22and the Holy Spirit
descended on him in bodily form like a dove. And a voice came from heaven:
"You are my Son, whom I love; with you I am well pleased."**

The Roots of Jesus (Luke 3:23-38)

(cf. Matt. 1:1-17)

Here is a listing of seventy-five names, the bulk of which appear only here. Most of these persons are completely unknown to us. Their occupations and conduct are never revealed. Still, in God's plans, they served an important role. When the final word has been spoken about fruitfulness, it won't be how much biography we left behind us that will merit any rewards, but how faithfully we pursued God's will to the full on a day-to-day basis.

**23Now Jesus himself was about thirty years old when he began his
ministry. He was the son, so it was thought, of Joseph,**

**the son of Heli, 24the son of Matthat,
the son of Levi, the son of Melki,
the son of Jannai, the son of Joseph,**

25the son of Mattathias, the son of Amos,
the son of Nahum, the son of Esli,
the son of Naggai, 26the son of Maath,
the son of Mattathias, the son of Semein,
the son of Josech, the son of Joda,
27The son of Joanan, the son of Rhesa,
the son of Zerubbabel, the son of Shealtiel,
the son of Neri, 28the son of Melki,
the son of Addi, the son of Cosam,
the son of Elmadam, the son of Er,
29the son of Joshua, the son of Eliezer,
the son of Jorim, the son of Matthat,
the son of Levi, 30the son of Simeon,
the son of Judah, the son of Joseph,
the son of Jonam, the son of Eliakim,
31the son of Melea, the son of Menna,
the son of Mattatha, the son of Nathan,
the son of David, 32the son of Jesse,
the son of Obed, the son of Boaz,
the son of Salmon,[a] the son of Nahshon,
33the son of Amminadab, the son of Ram,[b]
the son of Hezron, the son of Perez,
the son of Judah, 34the son of Jacob,
the son of Isaac, the son of Abraham,
the son of Terah, the son of Nahor,
35the son of Serug, the son of Reu,
the son of Peleg, the son of Eber,
the son of Shelah, 36the son of Cainan,
the son of Arphaxad, the son of Shem,
the son of Noah, the son of Lamech,
37the son of Methuselah, the son of Enoch,
the son of Jared, the son of Mahalaleel,
the son of Cainan, 38the son of Enos,
the son of Seth, the son of Adam,
the son of God.

a 32 Some early manuscripts *Sala*   *b 33* Some manuscripts *Amminadab, the son of Admin, the son of Arni*; other manuscripts vary widely.

Jesus Is Tempted (Luke 4:1-13)

(cf. Matt. 4:1-11; Mark 1:12, 13)

We must never overlook the humanity of our Lord. Jesus was affected by thirst (John 4:7), weariness (John 4:6), hunger (Matt. 4:2), sorrow (John 11:35) and anguish (Luke 22:44) as much as anyone who ever lived. Jesus was tempted at all points, like each of us (Heb. 4:14-16).

Also, we must never overlook the works of our adversary, the devil. This evil, fallen angel is always busy with schemes to trap God's children and to hinder their spiritual progress (Gen. 3:1-6; Acts 5:1-11; 2 Cor. 2:11; Eph. 6:10-18; 2 Tim. 2:26; 2 Pet. 5:8).

I. *The First Temptation (4:1-4)*

4 Jesus, full of the Holy Spirit, returned from the Jordan and was led
by the Spirit in the desert, [2]where for forty days he was tempted by
the devil. He ate nothing during those days, and at the end of them he
was hungry.
[3]The devil said to him, "If you are the Son of God, tell this stone to
become bread."
[4]Jesus answered, "It is written: 'Man does not live on bread alone.'[a] "

This temptation was against Jesus' physical body. How frequently Satan's primary target is our body. While God works principally with our innermost beings—our spirits—Satan reverses the order of attack and concentrates on our outermost beings—our bodies. Doubtlessly Satan reasoned that Adam and Eve fell through this source of temptation (along with many others—Ezek. 16:49; Matt. 24:37-39; Luke 21:34; Phil. 3:19) and that Jesus might yield in the same way. But Jesus would be a far greater opponent than His predecessors had been. This line of attack would be in vain.

II. *The Second Temptation (4:5-8)*

[5]The devil led him up to a high place and showed him in an instant all
the kingdoms of the world. [6]And he said to him, "I will give you all their
authority and splendor, for it has been given to me, and I can give it to
anyone I want to. [7]So if you worship me, it will all be yours."

---

a 4 Deut. 8:3

8Jesus answered, "It is written: 'Worship the Lord your God and serve him only.'[a] "

The devil follows the old motto, "If at first you don't succeed, try, try again." He never gives up. The nature of this trial was centered in distorting God's call for Jesus' life. Jesus came as the King of God's Kingdom, but Satan now offered Him a kingdom of His own, with deceptive tinsel and glitter. Which would he take—the one costing Him His physical life (the cross—God's choice), or the one affecting His spiritual life (Satan's choice)? Jesus resolutely selects God's will.

III. *The Third Temptation (4:9-13)*

9The devil led him to Jerusalem and had him stand on the highest point of the temple. "If you are the Son of God," he said, "throw yourself down from here. 10For it is written:

" 'He will command his angels concerning you
to guard you carefully;
11they will lift you up in their hands,
so that you will not strike your foot against a stone.'[b] "

12Jesus answered, "It says: 'Do not put the Lord your God to the test.'[c] "
13When the devil had finished all this tempting, he left him until an opportune time.

Lastly, according to Luke's arrangement, Satan devised a tricky situation where the credibility of God and His Word would seem to fall flat. But Jesus saw through this illegitimate challenge. You don't put God up to silly tests to prove His interest in you. So, for the third time, Jesus set Satan straight by quoting God's Word in its intended context.

Jesus Is Rejected at Nazareth (Luke 4:14-30)

(cf. Mark 4:12-17; Matt. 1:14, 15; and John 4:43-45)

It is a disappointment when you tell God's will to those you know best, those who presumably are spiritual, but who respond in a most unfavorable manner. Our Lord was raised in Nazareth. He was a respected member of the community (Luke 2:52).

a 8 Deut. 6:13 *b 11* Psalm 91:11, 12 *c 12* Deut. 6:16

Still, He would be soundly turned against for this single speech.

People are not always predictable. Even church people have been known to do the unexpected. They sit, and they listen. But sometimes they will rise up in revolt if something doesn't go according to their line of thinking—even if that something is for their own good. Carnality has not escaped the Church, as Jesus learns here.

There is another side to this story, a side that must have the preeminence. Here we discover the five-fold preaching mission of Jesus (vv. 18, 19). Further, we learn that Jesus' powerful delivery would be due to the work of the Holy Spirit. Jesus would not be great in himself; instead, He would be made great by the power of the Spirit.

I. *The Return of Jesus (4:14, 15)*

> **14Jesus returned to Galilee in the power of the Spirit, and news about him spread through the whole countryside. 15He taught in their synagogues, and everyone praised him.**

Jesus emerged a stronger man after His encounter with and defeat of the devil. We must learn a lesson from this example. God will send us no test without also providing the ingredients to make us better, stronger, and more productive people as a direct result of that trial.

Remember, it is only after this ordeal that Jesus started His ministry. Only at this point—after His baptism, Spirit-anointing, confirmation by God and tests from Satan—did Jesus start His work. Timing plays an important role in effective Christian service. We must not rush out to do God's will. Instead, we must wait, grow up and be empowered from heaven. Also, we must defeat Satan in our own lives before we can expect to be effective in helping others find victory for themselves.

II. *The Reading of Jesus (4:16-22)*

> **16He went to Nazareth, where he had been brought up, and on the Sabbath day he went into the synagogue, as was his custom. And he stood up to read. 17The scroll of the prophet Isaiah was handed to him. Unrolling it, he found the place where it is written:**
>
> **18"The Spirit of the Lord is on me,**
> **because he has anointed me**
> **to preach good news to the poor.**
> **He has sent me to proclaim freedom for the prisoners**
> **and recovery of sight for the blind,**
> **to release the oppressed,**

[19]to proclaim the year of the Lord's favor."[a]

[20]Then he rolled up the scroll, gave it back to the attendant and sat down. The eyes of everyone in the synagogue were fastened on him, [21]and he began by saying to them, "Today this scripture is fulfilled in your hearing."

[22]All spoke well of him and were amazed at the gracious words that came from his lips. "Isn't this Joseph's son?" they asked.

It was customary for guests of the synagogue (especially rabbis) to be extended an opportunity to participate in the service. Jesus was offered this privilege. So, He rose to read from the writing of Isaiah. This selection may have followed the natural sequence of reading through the Prophets as a part of the weekly traditional reading. The selection could not have been more appropriate (Isa. 61:1, 2). God had opened a perfect door for Jesus to explain His ministry. There are no less than two major points to be made from this prophetic text.

First, Jesus would accomplish His works by the Holy Spirit. Without this anointing He would have been a powerless man, incapable of a single spiritual victory. But through the Holy Spirit, the very works of God would be accomplished.

Second, Jesus would have a five fold preaching ministry. He would:

1. preach the good news to the poor
2. proclaim freedom to the prisoners
3. give sight to the blind
4. release the oppressed
5. proclaim the year of God's favor

While Jesus engaged heavily in the physical dimensions of people's lives (such as healing their ailments), His key interest was in their spiritual lives. Here the gospel of salvation would deliver them from the bondage, blindness and oppression caused by sin. Jesus came to rescue people from the penalty and power of sin. This is vividly displayed in these five points.

The final words of Isaiah's prophecy announce the start of a new era—the year of God's favor. The arrival of Jesus ushered in a new age. Through Him would come a penetrating and thorough victory over the consequences brought on by sin.

It must have been an awesome, though difficult, thing to hear Jesus announce that He was the one of whom Isaiah wrote. Skepticism was immediate. You can well imagine the conflict that would naturally arise as a result of such a bold declaration. Jesus did not flinch; but the people twisted and turned until their anger could not be contained. An explosion was inevitable.

---

a 19 Isaiah 61:1, 2

III. *The Rebuke from Jesus (4:23-27)*

**[23]Jesus said to them, "Surely you will quote this proverb to me:
'Physician, heal yourself! Do here in your home town what we have
heard that you did in Capernaum.' "
[24]"I tell you the truth," he continued, "no prophet is accepted in his
home town. [25]I assure you that there were many widows in Israel in
Elijah's time, when the sky was shut for three and a half years and there
was a severe famine throughout the land. [26]Yet Elijah was not sent to
any of them, but to a widow in Zarephath in the region of Sidon. [27]And
there were many in Israel with leprosy[a] in the time of Elisha the
prophet, yet not one of them was cleansed—only Naaman the Syrian."**

At the start, the members in the synagogue were delighted with Jesus' gracious speech. His words were compelling. Then, as quickly as they had seemingly appreciated His words, they turned and became outraged by them.

When Jesus announced the fulfillment of Isaiah's prophecy, the people were joyful, but uncommitted. However, the longer they thought about the matter, the more impractical such an interpretation became in their reasonings. Finally, Jesus set forth a straightforward rebuke by reminding them of how this same attitude existed in Elijah's time, and that because of it, God went to a Gentile to bless her (1 Kings 17-18). In other words, Jesus identified His audience with those doubt-filled Jews of Elijah's day. These Nazarenes were not a bit different from those carnal Jews who lived long ago.

Jesus recognizes a critical and negative spirit when it exists in our hearts. There is no room for such a disposition among God's people. We must not repeat the errors of doubt of previous generations. Jesus has a message of power and deliverance for us, and we must believe it.

IV. *The Repercussion (4:28-30)*

**[28]All the people in the synagogue were furious when they heard this.
[29]They got up, drove him out of the town, and took him to the brow of the
hill on which the town was built, in order to throw him down the cliff.
[30]But he walked right through the crowd and went on his way.**

Jesus' statements dug too deeply into the hearts of these callous people. They were furious. In fact, they sought to kill this offensive (toe-stepping) preacher. Unteachable people never want to hear the truth. They don't want to change. They are content just to be themselves. But Jesus will not permit them to think their opinionated views are acceptable to God.

a 27 The Greek word was used for various diseases affecting the skin—not necessarily leprosy.

Also observe how Jesus passed through this mob and escaped what would appear to be a certain death. Let us register this point deeply within our hearts. Death is not in man's hands. No one can kill or be killed apart from God's ultimate (or sovereign) control (Exod. 21:13; Ps. 135:8; Isa. 25:8; Rev. 1:18). God (or Christ) alone determines the time of our departures.

Jesus Enters a Synagogue in Capernaum (Luke 4:31-37)

(cf. Mark 1:21-28)

Jesus' ministry always attracted attention, because it was founded on a unique base of authority. Jesus never quoted some famous scholar in order to prove himself. Instead, He simply declared God's will—period. His words possessed an unusual punch. No wonder the people raised their eyebrows and listened attentively at His powerful messages.

Jesus did much more than teach with authority. He also practiced His authority, especially over the kingdom of Satan. He did this by expelling (or commanding the departure of) demons from people's bodies.

In the following account we have a presentation of Jesus' superior authority. It can be heard, and it can be seen.

I. *Jesus' Authority Is Heard (4:31, 32)*

**31Then he went down to Capernaum, a town in Galilee, and on the
Sabbath began to teach the people. 32They were amazed at his teaching,
because his message had authority.**

II. *Jesus' Authority Is Seen (4:33-37)*

**33In the synagogue there was a man possessed by a demon, an evil[a] spirit.
He cried out at the top of his voice, 34"Ha! What do you want with us,
Jesus of Nazareth? Have you come to destroy us? I know who you
are—the Holy One of God!"**

**35"Be quiet!" Jesus said sternly. "Come out of him!" Then the demon
threw the man down before them all and came out without injuring
him.**

36All the people were amazed and said to each other, "What is this

a 33 Greek *unclean*; also in verse 36

teaching? With authority and power he gives orders to evil spirits and they come out!"
[37]And the news about him spread throughout the surrounding area.

First, Jesus took the matter of demonization as a real (and not an imagined) problem. Second, He never backed away from the persons in whom demons resided. Third, Jesus recognized that the demons were under His authority and that not one of them could order Him around. Fourth, He exorcised demons from people's bodies with an authoritative command, not a timid prayer.

This same power has been entrusted to each believer today, too (Mark 16:18; Eph. 6:10-18; James 4:7). Let us use this power over our arch-foe and set our loved ones free!

Jesus Heals Many (Luke 4:38-41)

(cf. Matt. 8:14-17 and Mark 1:29-34)

One of the paramount aims of each Gospel writer is to establish the unique character of Jesus. Luke successfully handled this goal. In the foregoing passages Jesus has been seen as the awaited Messiah, the conquerer of Satan, the reader of minds and the greatest of all the teachers. Now He is proudly displayed as the healer of sickness. Indeed, there never was (or will be!) another person like Jesus.

This is the first of a dozen healing miracles recorded by Luke. The following healings are located in Luke's Gospel:

1.	Fever	4:38,39
2.	Leprosy	5:12-16
3.	Paralysis	5:17-26
4.	Shriveled hand	6:6-11
5.	Death bed suffering	7:1-10
6.	Apparently fatal sickness	8:40-56
7.	Hemorrhage	8:43-48
8.	Epilepsy	9:37-43
9.	Crippled condition	13:10-21
10.	Leprosy	17:11-19
11.	Blindness	18:35-43
12.	Cut-off ear	22:50,51

I. *Peter's Mother-In-Law Is Healed (4:38, 39)*

[38]Jesus left the synagogue and went to the home of Simon. Now Simon's mother-in-law was suffering from a high fever, and they asked

Jesus to help her. [39]So he bent over her and rebuked the fever, and it left her. She got up at once and began to wait on them.

II. *Many Others Are Healed (4:40, 41)*

[40]When the sun was setting, the people brought to Jesus all who had various kinds of sickness, and laying his hands on each one, he healed them. [41]Moreover, demons came out of many people, shouting, "You are the Son of God!" But he rebuked them and would not allow them to speak, because they knew he was the Christ.[a]

Jesus Expands His Ministry (Luke 4:42-44)

(cf. Mark 1:35-39)

Preaching was one of Jesus' chief tools (if not His principal one) for reaching people's consciences. It does not require much to move a teachable person toward God. The truth, spoken with authority and love, is often all that is necessary.

[42]At daybreak Jesus went out to a solitary place. The people were looking for him and when they came to where he was, they tried to keep him from leaving them. [43]But he said, "I must preach the good news of the kingdom of God to the other towns also, because that is why I was sent." [44]And he kept on preaching in the synagogues of Judea.[b]

Jesus Calls First Disciples (Luke 5:1-11)

(cf. Matt. 4:18-22 and Mark 1:16-20)

The fact that Jesus attracted such large crowds to hear Him teach the Word of God may indicate the prevalence of both spiritual barrenness and spiritual hunger. The common Jew seemed to have held great expectations in regard to the promises of the Old Testament, but on the whole their level of scriptural knowledge was shallow. They must be taught. Some would need to start from the beginning; others would

[a] 41 Or *Messiah* [b] 44 Or *the land of the Jews*; some manuscripts *Galilee*

need to correct wrong notions about God's will; and a few would find their convictions being confirmed as Jesus taught.

I. *The Crowd of People (5:1-3)*

**5 One day as Jesus was standing by the Lake of Gennesaret,[a] with the
people crowding around him and listening to the word of God, [2]he
saw at the water's edge two boats, left there by the fishermen, who were
washing their nets. [3]He got into one of the boats, the one belonging to
Simon, and asked him to put out a little from shore. Then he sat down
and taught the people from the boat.**

II. *The Catch of Fish (5:4-7)*

**[4]When he had finished speaking, he said to Simon, "Put out into deep
water, and let down[b] the nets for a catch."**

**[5]Simon answered, "Master, we've worked hard all night and haven't
caught anything. But because you say so, I will let down the nets."**

**[6]When they had done so, they caught such a large number of fish that
their nets began to break. [7]So they signaled their partners in the other
boat to come and help them, and they came and filled both boats so full
that they began to sink.**

Fishing with nets was a nighttime art. Jesus' request to drop nets now was impractical, according to the natural order of things. Nevertheless, Simon obeyed—out of courtesy, not expectation. When the nets became so full that they nearly broke from the weight of the catch, it became apparent, especially to Peter, that Jesus was more than lucky in His suggestion to drop the nets, Peter now knew positively that Jesus was unique. In fact, he even felt uneasy or unworthy in Jesus' presence.

III. *The Call of Jesus (5:8-11)*

**[8]When Simon Peter saw this, he fell at Jesus' knees and said, "Go away
from me, Lord; I am a sinful man!" [9]For he and all his companions were
astonished at the catch of fish they had taken, [10]and so were James and
John, the sons of Zebedee, Simon's partners.**

**Then Jesus said to Simon, "Don't be afraid; from now on you will catch
men." [11]So they pulled their boats up on shore, left everything and
followed him.**

After the miraculous catch of fish, Peter was thoroughly pierced through by a sense of his own inadequacies. No doubt he had seen other miracles of Jesus before this one,

---

a 1 That is, Sea of Galilee *b 4* The Greek verb is plural.

but now he was personally on the receiving end of a supernatural experience, and that makes a great deal of difference. He could not even stand to his feet because there was such awe in his heart for Jesus. It is with this event that Peter and his companions knew it was time to abandon the trade of casting nets for fish and to start casting nets for men's souls.

Jesus Heals a Leper (Luke 5:12-16)

(cf. Matt. 8:1-4 and Mark 1:40-45)

Leprosy was the most dreaded disease of the biblical world. Its toll affected every dimension of life—physical, psychological, social, domestic, vocational and spiritual. The leper in this story was so shamed by his condition that he buried his welted face in the ground before begging for Jesus' assistance.

The incredible love and healing power of our Lord is displayed here. Lepers were outcastes. Untouchables. But Jesus stretched forth His hand to touch him. And in that instant a miracle occurred. The leprosy left!

I. *The Man and the Miracle (5:12, 13)*

[12]While Jesus was in one of the towns, a man came along who was covered with leprosy.[a] When he saw Jesus, he fell with his face to the ground and begged him, "Lord, if you are willing, you can make me clean."

[13]Jesus reached out his hand and touched the man. "I am willing," he said. "Be clean!" And immediately the leprosy left him.

II. *The Message and the Mistake (5:14, 15)*

[14]Then Jesus ordered him, "Don't tell anyone, but go, show yourself to the priest and offer the sacrifices that Moses commanded for your cleansing, as a testimony to them."

[15]Yet the news about him spread all the more, so that crowds of people came to hear him and to be healed of their sicknesses.

III. *The Meditation of Jesus (5:16)*

[16]But Jesus often withdrew to lonely places and prayed.

---

a 12 The Greek word was used for various diseases affecting the skin—not neccessarily leprosy.

Of the four Gospel writers, Luke is apparently the most impressed by Jesus' frequent retreats in order to pray (3:21, 22; 4:1-14; 6:12, 13; 9:28, 29; 22:31, 32, 39-44). It would be difficult to overstress the importance of divine fellowship. Jesus considered vertical communion a vital and vibrant aspect of His daily life. Most certainly we, too, ought to make regular retreats into seclusion for uninterrupted periods of meaningful prayer.

Jesus Heals a Paralytic (Luke 5:17-26)

(cf. Matt. 9:1-8 and Mark 2:1-12)

There are no less than six matters in this episode that deserve our attention. First, we see that Jesus' fame reached every town—both large and small—in all of Palestine. His reputation attracted both the high and the low members of society (v. 17). Second, we notice that Jesus was powerless to heal anyone on His own initiative (v. 17b). It was the power of the Holy Spirit working in His life that performed these miracles. Further, there is the clear deduction from this fact that this power was not always present, indicating the sovereign control God exercised over the healing-gift Jesus possessed. Third, we are moved by the profound example of determined faith in the friends of the paralytic (vv. 18, 19). Our approach to Jesus is not always without complications, though no obstacles are too large for anyone with a relentless faith. Fourth, we learn that Jesus is qualified to forgive all of our sins (v. 20). Fifth, we discover that there will always be those who oppose Jesus' bold declarations (v. 21). Lastly, we learn that Jesus has an answer for every problem. He cannot be trapped or found mistaken (vv. 22ff.).

I. *The Man and the First Miracle (5:17-20)*

**17One day as he was teaching, Pharisees and teachers of the law, who
had come from every village of Galilee and from Judea and Jerusalem,
were sitting there. And the power of the Lord was present for him to
heal the sick. 18Some men came carrying a paralytic on a mat and tried
to take him into the house to lay him before Jesus. 19When they could not
find a way to do this because of the crowd, they went up on the roof and
lowered him on his mat through the tiles into the middle of the crowd,
right in front of Jesus.**

20When Jesus saw their faith, he said, "Friend, your sins are forgiven."

II. *The Madness and the Second Miracle (5:21-26)*

21The Pharisees and the teachers of the law began thinking to themselves, "Who is this fellow who speaks blasphemy? Who can forgive sins but God alone?"

22Jesus knew what they were thinking and asked, "Why are you thinking these things in your hearts? 23Which is easier: to say, 'Your sins are forgiven,' or to say, 'Get up and walk'? 24But that you may know that the Son of Man has authority on earth to forgive sins. . . ." He said to the paralyzed man, "I tell you, get up, take your mat and go home." 25Immediately he stood up in front of them, took what he had been lying on and went home praising God. 26Everyone was amazed and gave praise to God. They were filled with awe and said, "We have seen remarkable things today."

Jesus Calls and Dines with Levi (Luke 5:27-32)

(cf. Matt. 9:9-13 and Mark 2:14-17)

There were high ranks and low ranks among the tax collectors. The higher officials oversaw the collection. Most of these administrators lived in Rome. The next rank down included men who went out into the various regions of Roman control and recruited local residents to collect the taxes. These tax collectors were considered traitors by most Jews. Levi (or Matthew), one of Jesus' disciples, was a tax collector.

I. *The Calling (5:27, 28)*

27After this, Jesus went out and saw a tax collector by the name of Levi sitting at his tax booth. "Follow me," Jesus said to him, 28and Levi got up, left everything and followed him.

II. *The Dining (5:29-32)*

29Then Levi held a great banquet for Jesus at his house, and a large crowd of tax collectors and others were eating with them. 30But the Pharisees and the teachers of the law who belonged to their sect complained to his disciples, "Why do you eat and drink with tax collectors and 'sinners'?"

31Jesus answered them, "It is not the healthy who need a doctor, but the sick. 32I have not come to call the righteous, but sinners to repentance."

Facts About Fasting (Luke 5:33-39)

(cf. Matt. 9:14-17 and Mark 2:18-22)

We notice several interesting points in this brief encounter between the disciples of John and the disciples of Jesus.

One, we see that there will always be differences of opinion, even among those who hold to the same major convictions. John's disciples and Jesus' disciples had much in common; still there were some disagreements between them. These dissimilarities, however, did not divide them, although the areas of disagreement did distinguish them.

Two, we observe that there will always be major differences between popular religious convictions and Jesus' radical message. These differences spell out a definite separation between a man-made religion and a God-created relationship.

I. *The Inquiry (5:33)*

33They said to him, "John's disciples often fast and pray, and so do the disciples of the Pharisees, but yours go on eating and drinking."

II. *The Information (5:34)*

34Jesus answered, "Can you make the guests of the bridegroom fast while he is with them?

III. *The Illustrations (5:35-39)*

35But the time will come when the bridegroom will be taken from them; in those days they will fast."

36He told them this parable: "No one tears a patch from a new garment and sews it on an old one. If he does, he will have torn the new garment, and the patch from the new will not match the old.
37And no one pours new wine into old wineskins. If he does, the new wine will burst the skins, the wine will run out and the wineskins will be ruined.
38No, new wine must be poured into new wineskins.
39And no one after drinking old wine wants the new, for he says, 'The old is better.' "

Lord of the Sabbath **(Luke 6:1-5)**

(cf. Matt. 12:1-8 and Mark 2:23-28)

The sabbath day (from Friday's sunset to Saturday's sunset), as important as it was, was never intended to regulate our every action, but to provide us with an opportunity to rest. The Pharisees, however, turned this period into a day of numerous external restrictions. The genuine meaning of the day was all but covered over by the many legalistic demands they required of each other. Jesus would not submit to these profitless rulings.

Here, too, we see the first indication of the fading of the command to keep the Sabbath as prescribed by the Old Testament. Jesus announced His supremacy over this day. And from the day of Jesus' resurrection (Sunday—"the first day of the week"/"the Lord's Day"—Acts 20:7; 1 Cor. 16:2; Rev. 1:10) until this present hour, it is the conviction of most Christians that this former sabbath was but "a shadow of the things that were to come . . . in Christ" and therefore is not binding for the believer today (Col. 2:16, 17).

I. *The Immediate Problem (6:1, 2)*

6 One Sabbath Jesus was going through the grainfields, and his disciples began to pick some heads of grain, rub them in their hands and eat the kernels. 2Some of the Pharisees asked, "Why are you doing what is unlawful on the Sabbath?"

II. *The Past Picture (6:3, 4)*

3Jesus answered them, "Have you never read what David did when he and his companions were hungry? 4He entered the house of God, and taking the consecrated bread, he ate what is lawful only for priests to eat. And he also gave some to his companions."

III. *The Eternal Principle (6:5)*

5Then Jesus said to them, "The Son of Man is Lord of the Sabbath."

Jesus Heals on the Sabbath (Luke 6:6-11)

(cf. Matt. 12:9-14 and Mark 3:1-6)

When people are caught up in legalistic bondage, they view everything as a matter of life and death. The breaking of the smallest ruling, according to their perverted logic, spells out a lethal offense. There is very little room for grace in their ironclad system of dos and don'ts.

Jesus was acutely aware of this rigid and unmerciful attitude. And He would not approve of their ridiculous rules. Collision was inevitable.

According to Jesus it is always right to do good—at any place and at any time. God did not make people for the Sabbath; instead, He made the Sabbath for people. This day, of all the days in the week, should be utilized to help alleviate the hurts of people. Jesus would heal on this day as on other days.

I. *The Picture (6:6-8)*

**[6]On another Sabbath he went into the synagogue and was teaching,
and a man was there whose right hand was shriveled. [7]The Pharisees
and the teachers of the law were looking for a reason to accuse Jesus, so
they watched him closely to see if he would heal on the Sabbath. [8]But
Jesus knew what they were thinking and said to the man with the
shriveled hand, "Get up and stand in front of everyone." So he got up
and stood there.**

II. *The Problem (6:9)*

**[9]Then Jesus said to them, "I ask you, which is lawful on the Sabbath: to
do good or to do evil, to save life or to destroy it?"**

III. *The Products (6:10, 11)*

**[10]He looked around at them all, and then said to the man, "Stretch out
your hand." He did so, and his hand was completely restored. [11]But they
were furious and began to discuss with one another what they might do
to Jesus.**

Jesus Chooses Twelve Apostles (Luke 6:12-16)

(cf. Mark 3:13-19)

Here we see Jesus selecting twelve men from among His many followers to be His closest disciples—men who would be with Him full-time. Observe that before this selection occurred there was preparation—Jesus prayed to know the names of those whom God wanted to be at His side. Further observe that after the selection occurred there was a responsibility—Jesus made them apostles. There is an orderliness in all of this—a design, a plan. The future of Christianity would rest on those twelve men.

12One of those days Jesus went out into the hills to pray, and spent the
night praying to God. 13When morning came, he called his disciples to
him and chose twelve of them, whom he also designated apostles:
14Simon (whom he named Peter), his brother Andrew, James, John,
Philip, Bartholomew, 15Matthew, Thomas, James son of Alphaeus,
Simon who was called the Zealot, 16Judas son of James, and Judas
Iscariot, who became a traitor.

The Sermon on the Mount (Luke 6:17-49)

(cf. Matt. 5-7)

Below is a greatly abbreviated version of Jesus' wonderful Sermon on the Mount. After spending a night on some mountaintop, Jesus called His twelve disciples to himself. Together, they began the journey down the slope until Jesus spotted a level place along the mountainside. Here He stopped His descent and began to minister to the crowd which had come to Him from all over the region. First, He healed the sick; then, He taught the people.

I. *His Works of Healing (6:17-19)*

17He went down with them and stood on a level place. A large crowd
of his disciples was there and a great number of people from all over

Judea, from Jerusalem, and from the seacoast of Tyre and Sidon, [18]who had come to hear him and to be healed of their diseases. Those troubled by evil[a] spirits were cured, [19]and the people all tried to touch him, because power was coming from him and healing them all.

Jesus healed hundreds of people during His short, three-year campaign. God's power worked through Him in an unprecedented manner. But why would Jesus be enabled to heal so many sick persons? Was there a deeper significance to these healings than the physical benefit? What were these miracles designed to teach the recipients or the ones who saw these supernatural occurrences?

No less than five reasons might be offered to explain Jesus' healing miracles:

1. They marked a fulfillment of Messianic prophecies (Isa. 42:1-4, with Matt. 12:15-21; Isa. 53:4, with Matt. 8:17).
2. They proved that Jesus could forgive people of all their sins (Luke 5:24).
3. They displayed evidence that God was at work in Jesus (John 9:3; Acts 2:22). These miracles were God's authentication of Jesus' ministry. His words were proven correct by His works.
4. They glorified God (John 11:4).
5. They caused people to put their faith in Jesus as the Christ and to be saved (John 20:30, 31).

II. *His Words of Blessing (6:20-23)*

[20]Looking at his disciples, he said:

"Blessed are you who are poor,
for yours is the kingdom of God.
[21]Blessed are you who hunger now,
for you will be satisfied.
Blessed are you who weep now,
for you will laugh.
[22]Blessed are you when men hate you,
when they exclude you and insult you
and reject your name as evil,
because of the Son of Man.

[23]Rejoice in that day and leap for joy, because great is your reward in heaven. For that is how their fathers treated the prophets.

Four sets of people are seen here as being blessed: (1) the poor, (2) the hungry, (3) the weeping and (4) the persecuted. It is evident that these conditions in themselves do not yield blessedness. Rather, it is those who know these experiences and remain faithful

---

a 18 Greek *unclean*

to God that will receive the truly blessed life. Such persons should take comfort in the fact that the prophets before them underwent these same afflictions, yet their reward is great in heaven. Today our life is filled with a mixture of joyful and tearful experiences; but tomorrow, in God's presence, there will be only sustained joy.

III. *His Words of Woe (6:24-26)*

> **24"But woe to you who are rich,**
> **for you have already received your comfort.**
> **25Woe to you who are well fed now,**
> **for you will go hungry.**
> **Woe to you who laugh now,**
> **for you will mourn and weep.**
> **26Woe to you when all men speak well of you,**
> **for that is how their fathers treated the false prophets.**

In direct contrast to the four declarations of blessings above, we now see four pronouncements of woe for these parties: (1) the rich, (2) the well-fed, (3) the mockers and (4) the well-spoken-of. Jesus warns that you cannot trust your present circumstances for determining your future state. It may well be that the very opposite of what we see occurring today will be happening in the not-so-distant future.

IV. *His Words of Love (6:27-36)*

> **27"But I tell you who hear me: Love your enemies, do good to those who**
> **hate you, 28bless those who curse you, pray for those who mistreat you.**
> **29If someone strikes you on one cheek, turn to him the other also. If**
> **someone takes your cloak, do not stop him from taking your tunic.**
> **30Give to everyone who asks you, and if anyone takes what belongs to**
> **you, do not demand it back. 31Do to others as you would have them do to**
> **you.**
> **32"If you love those who love you, what credit is that to you? Even**
> **'sinners' love those who love them. 33And if you do good to those who are**
> **good to you, what credit is that to you? Even 'sinners' do that. 34And if**
> **you lend to those from whom you expect repayment, what credit is that**
> **to you? Even 'sinners' lend to 'sinners,' expecting to be repaid in full.**
> **35But love your enemies, do good to them, and lend to them without**
> **expecting to get anything back. Then your reward will be great, and**
> **you will be sons of the Most High, because he is kind to the ungrateful**
> **and wicked. 36Be merciful, just as your Father is merciful.**

As members of the royal kingdom we are to imitate the traits found in our King. Jesus makes it clear that the chief characteristic of God, and therefore the chief characteristic of God's people, is love and mercy. Genuine love and mercy will result in prayer, good deeds, giving blessings to people, lending goods, and going the second mile when asked to help someone. This is the golden rule for Christian life—treating others the same way you yourself want to be treated. Unless we behave in this fashion we prove ourselves to be no different from sinners.

V. *His Words of Judging (6:37-45)*

**37"Do not judge, and you will not be judged. Do not condemn, and you
will not be condemned. Forgive, and you will be forgiven. 38Give, and it
will be given to you. A good measure, pressed down, shaken together
and running over, will be poured into your lap. For with the measure
you use, it will be measured to you."**
**39He also told them this parable: "Can a blind man lead a blind man?
Will they not both fall into a pit? 40A student is not above his teacher, but
everyone who is fully trained will be like his teacher.**
**41"Why do you look at the speck of sawdust in your brother's eye and
pay no attention to the plank in your own eye? 42How can you say to your
brother, 'Brother, let me take the speck out of your eye,' when you
yourself fail to see the plank in your own eye? You hypocrite, first take
the plank out of your eye, and then you will see clearly to remove the
speck from your brother's eye.**
**43"No good tree bears bad fruit, nor does a bad tree bear good fruit.
44Each tree is recognized by its own fruit. People do not pick figs from
thornbushes, or grapes from briers. 45The good man brings good things
out of the good stored up in his heart, and the evil man brings evil things
out of the evil stored up in his heart. For out of the overflow of his heart
his mouth speaks.**

This section is a logical continuation of the above point. In the former passages we are taught the positive things we are to do for people. In this passage we are instructed about the negative things that we are not to do to people. For specific comments on these words, see Matt. 7:1-6.

VI. *His Words of Admonition (6:46-49)*

**46"Why do you call me, 'Lord, Lord,' and do not do what I say? 47I will
show you what he is like who comes to me and hears my words and puts
them into practice. 48He is like a man building a house, who dug down**

deep and laid the foundation on rock. When a flood came, the torrent struck that house but could not shake it, because it was well built. [49]But the one who hears my words and does not put them into practice is like a man who built a house on the ground without a foundation. The moment the torrent struck that house, it collapsed and its destruction was complete."

Jesus recognized that there were some persons in His audience who merely listened with no intent of applying what they heard, while others thoroughly sought to put His words into practice. The former persons, says Jesus, will fall apart when tests come, but the latter persons will hold fast in even the worst tempests. Trials will strike everyone—Christians and non-Christians alike—but only the believer who has applied Jesus' words has the resources to withstand any attack. The contrasting testimony of people in the world and those in the Church proves this point each day.

Jesus Heals a Centurion's Servant (Luke 7:1-10)

(cf. Matt. 8:5-13)

The quality of this centurion's character commands our attention: (1) He was considerate—his heart was touched by the physical needs of another; (2) he was generous—his finances were used to erect a synagogue where God's Word could be taught; (3) he was humble—his unworthiness compelled him to send others to speak to Christ in his behalf; and (4) he was full of faith—his confidence in Christ's power to heal his slave was unwavering.

I. *The Exhortation (7:1-5)*

7 When Jesus had finished saying all this in the hearing of the people,
he entered Capernaum. [2]There a centurion's servant, whom his
master valued highly, was sick and about to die. [3]The centurion heard
of Jesus and sent some elders of the Jews to him, asking him to come and
heal his servant. [4]When they came to Jesus, they pleaded earnestly with
him, "This man deserves to have you do this, [5]because he loves our nation
and has built our synagogue."

II. *The Explanation (7:6-8)*

[6]So Jesus went with them.

He was not far from the house when the centurion sent friends to say

to him: "Lord, don't trouble yourself, for I do not deserve to have you
come under my roof. [7]That is why I did not even consider myself worthy
to come to you. But say the word, and my servant will be healed. [8]For I
myself am a man under authority, with soldiers under me. I tell this one,
'Go,' and he goes; and that one, 'Come,' and he comes. I say to my servant,
'Do this,' and he does it."

III. *The Exclamation (7:9, 10)*

[9]When Jesus heard this, he was amazed at him, and turning to the
crowd following him, he said, "I tell you, I have not found such great
faith even in Israel." [10]Then the men who had been sent returned to the
house and found the servant well.

Jesus Raises the Dead (Luke 7:11-17)

Here is a picture of passion, power and praise. First, there is the mourning over the death of an only son. Second, there is the miracle of the dead man's resurrection. Third, there is the marveling of everyone who witnesses this incredible scene.

I. *The Mourning (7:11-13)*

[11]Soon afterward, Jesus went to a town called Nain, and his disciples
and a large crowd went along with him. [12]As he approached the town
gate, a dead person was being carried out—the only son of his mother,
and she was a widow. And a large crowd from the town was with her.
[13]When the Lord saw her, his heart went out to her and he said, "Don't
cry."

A Town Called Nain. This small town, located several miles south of Nazareth, is mentioned only in this passage of the Bible. Today there is a small chapel in this village that commemorates Jesus' raising this young man from the dead.

A Dead Person Was Being Carried Out. There were usually no grave sites located inside eastern cities. So, it was the custom for the body to be placed in a cloth-covered coffin and carried by several teams of men. Often professional mourners (usually several women) and musicians were hired to follow the body to the place of burial—this act presumably assured a full and proper ceremony. These paid mourners would set the pace for showing grief by beating their chests, pulling their hair and making honorable statements. There was plenty of weeping and wailing, too. Out in front of this procession of mourners would be the nearest of kin—in this case it was the widowed mother.

It was this setting that moved Jesus to greet the mourning mother and to stop the traditional ceremony. The sorrowing was about to be reversed. And the professional mourners would be left to find another sorrowing family.

She Was a Widow. No greater sorrow can happen than to lose one's family. This grieving mother had previously seen her husband die; now her only son was gone, too.

Jesus' words to her were, "Don't cry." This admonition must have seemed a bit out of place. And if Jesus were anyone other than God's Son, these words would have been inappropriate. But Jesus was certain that God had something for this woman that would turn her sorrow into ecstasy.

II. *The Miracle (7:14, 15)*

> **14Then he went up and touched the coffin, and those carrying it stood**
> **still. He said, "Young man, I say to you, get up!" 15The dead man sat up**
> **and began to talk, and Jesus gave him back to his mother.**

This restoration miracle, like each of Jesus' miracles, possesses a deeper significance than what we can see on the surface. Here is a scene that offers confidence for our hope in the Resurrection. Death cannot hold its subjects in the presence of Jesus. Through Him a resurrection to life will come (John 11:25ff.; 1 Cor. 15).

III. *The Marvel (7:16, 17)*

> **16They were all filled with awe and praised God. "A great prophet**
> **has appeared among us," they said. "God has come to help his people."**
> **17This news about Jesus spread throughout Judea[a] and the surrounding**
> **country.**

Notice the effects this miracle had on those who witnessed it. They were filled with awe. They praised God. They glorified God and His Prophet, Jesus. And they spread this good news everywhere. Who can dare to belittle the supernatural—either as it has been demonstrated in the past or during the present hour? The never-changing power and compassion of Jesus are truths to get excited about!

---

a 17 Or *the land of the Jews*

John the Baptist's Final Inquiry (Luke 7:18-23)

(cf. Matt. 11:1-16)

The perplexity which confronted John is not at all unlike the confusion that occasionally strikes each believer. John expected a sudden spiritual and political reversal in Palestine, but things did not progress as he had anticipated. So, he sent several of his disciples to get the answers he needed.

For us, too, things do not always go as planned. We are sometimes left only with question marks. And like John, we must unashamedly ask Jesus for some answers.

Jesus did not disappoint John, and neither will He disappoint us. There *is* an answer for our inquiries, although that answer might not always be the one we anticipate.

I. *The Perplexity (7:18-20)*

18John's disciples told him about all these things. Calling two of them,
19he sent them to the Lord to ask, "Are you the one who was to come, or should we expect someone else?"
20When the men came to Jesus, they said, "John the Baptist sent us to you to ask, 'Are you the one who was to come, or should we expect someone else?' "

II. *The Power (7:21-23)*

21At that very time Jesus cured many who had diseases, sicknesses and evil spirits, and gave sight to many who were blind.
22So he replied to the messengers, "Go back and report to John what you have seen and heard: The blind receive sight, the lame walk, those who have leprosy[a] are cured, the deaf hear, the dead are raised, and the good news is preached to the poor.
23Blessed is the man who does not fall away on account of me."

a 22 The Greek word was used for various diseases affecting the skin—not necessarily leprosy.

Jesus Talks About John (Luke 7:24-35)

(cf. Matt. 11:7-19)

Jesus could not speak highly enough of John, His cousin. Jesus said that John was a prophet—the greatest one who ever lived. He was a man of unswayed convictions. Further, he was a man of humble means, the man about whom Malachi prophesied (Mal. 3:1). Despite all these wonderful words of praise, any person who lives during the Kingdom era was (and is!) more fortunate than John. It is a great privilege to live in the New Testament period. John served as the hinge between the old dispensation and the new era. Now, in this day, all the hopes of the past are being fulfilled in the person of Jesus Christ. Through Him all of the shadows are turning into their intended substance.

The people to whom Jesus spoke, however, were not impressed by these facts. Their hearts were practically dead—responding neither to joyful music nor to a funeral hymn. Instead, they were always critical and belligerent. If they had any opinions to offer, they were certain to be negative ones.

I. *The Prophet (7:24-28)*

**24 After John's messengers left, Jesus began to speak to the crowd
about John: "What did you go out into the desert to see? A reed swayed
by the wind? 25 If not, what did you go out to see? A man dressed in fine
clothes? No, those who wear expensive clothes and indulge in luxury
are in palaces. 26 But what did you go out to see? A prophet? Yes, I tell
you, and more than a prophet. 27 This is the one about whom it is written:**

" 'I will send my messenger ahead of you,
who will prepare your way before you.'[a]

**28 I tell you, among those born of women there is no one greater than
John; yet the one who is least in the kingdom of God is greater than he."**

II. *The People (7:29-35)*

**29 (All the people, even the tax collectors, when they heard Jesus'
words, acknowledged that God's way was right, because they had been**

a 27 Mal. 3:1

baptized by John. [30]But the Pharisees and experts in the law rejected God's purpose for themselves, because they had not been baptized by John.)

[31]"To what, then, can I compare the people of this generation? What are they like? [32]They are like children sitting in the marketplace and calling out to each other:

" 'We played the flute for you,
and you did not dance;
we sang a dirge,
and you did not cry.'

[33]For John the Baptist came neither eating bread nor drinking wine, and you say, 'He has a demon.' [34]The Son of Man came eating and drinking, and you say, 'Here is a glutton and a drunkard, a friend of tax collectors and "sinners." ' [35]But wisdom is proved right by all her children."

Jesus Eats with a Pharisee (Luke 7:36-50)

Some people understand so little about the teaching of grace. They miss seeing their own level of guilt before God, and they miss seeing their own judgmental attitude toward others.

Here is the story of a man—a highly religious man—who entertained Christ in his own home but failed to grasp the principle of grace, even when it was displayed before his own eyes. Here is also the story of a woman—a sinful woman—who could not help but express her admiration for the grace that God extended through His Son, Jesus.

I. *The Pharisee (7:36)*

[36]Now one of the Pharisees invited Jesus to have dinner with him, so he went to the Pharisee's house and reclined at the table.

We know virtually nothing about this Pharisee named Simon. The story, however, causes us to view his character negatively. There is no evidence of faith in Simon's words nor love in his works. Perhaps Simon was merely curious, seeking a closer look at this famous man from Nazareth.

It is certain Jesus knew the motives and the spiritual shallowness that lay behind Simon's invitation. Jesus did not see an eager heart ready for spiritual rebirth. But He could see an invitation to join sinners at a meal. Here was an opportunity to tell the story of God's grace. Jesus would never bypass chances like this.

II. *The Penitent (7:37, 38)*

[37]When a woman who had lived a sinful life in that town learned that Jesus was eating at the Pharisee's house, she brought an alabaster jar of perfume, [38]and as she stood behind him at his feet weeping, she began to wet his feet with her tears. Then she wiped them with her hair, kissed them and poured perfume on them.

In the Eastern world it was customary to eat in a reclining position, either resting comfortably on the left arm (allowing freedom of movement to eat with the right hand) or to lie chest downward.

This notoriously sinful woman had a rare appreciation for Jesus. She discovered the deepest need of her life through Him—her need for forgiveness. So, with a bold display of her love, she entered this Pharisee's home without any invitation; then she anointed Jesus' feet with her own tears, drying them with her hair. Surely these actions revealed a transformation—a spiritual rebirth—on the part of this woman.

Simon, however, refused to see this transformation. His eyes only perceived the past scars that, to him, made this person unholy.

III. *The Parable (7:39-43)*

[39]When the Pharisee who had invited him saw this, he said to himself, "If this man were a prophet, he would know who is touching him and what kind of woman she is—that she is a sinner."

[40]Jesus answered him, "Simon, I have something to tell you."

"Tell me, teacher," he said.

[41]"Two men owed money to a certain moneylender. One owed him five hundred denarii,[a] and the other fifty. [42]Neither of them had the money to pay him back, so he canceled the debts of both. Now which of them will love him more?"

[43]Simon replied, "I suppose the one who had the bigger debt canceled."

"You have judged correctly," Jesus said.

Jesus discerned what was taking place in Simon's thoughts. He saw through the man. So, Jesus offered a simple parable in relation to the nature and effects of God's grace to demonstrate what had happened. Unfortunately, like too many religious persons, Simon was capable of answering the question correctly, but was incapable of drawing from his knowledge any personal or practical application.

---

a 41 A denarius was a coin worth about a day's wages.

IV. *The Pardon (7:44-50)*

[44]Then he turned toward the woman and said to Simon, "Do you see this woman? I came into your house. You did not give me any water for my feet, but she wet my feet with her tears and wiped them with her hair. [45]You did not give me a kiss, but this woman, from the time I entered, has not stopped kissing my feet. [46]You did not put oil on my head, but she has poured perfume on my feet. [47]Therefore, I tell you, her many sins have been forgiven—for she loved much. But he who has been forgiven little loves little."

[48]Then Jesus said to her, "Your sins are forgiven."

[49]The other guests began to say among themselves, "Who is this who even forgives sins?"

[50]Jesus said to the woman, "Your faith has saved you; go in peace."

There is no room for any doubts about the repentance of this woman—at least not in the mind of Jesus. This woman manifested her abundant faith and love by her actions—actions which Simon himself, if he had a similar faith and love, would have demonstrated as a customary courtesy.

Several practical matters deserve our attention here: (1) Observe that religious (though non-Christian) persons can express an openness to Christ without being committed to Him personally. (2) Observe that religious (though non-Christian) persons can understand natural matters, but they cannot make the shift from the physical world to the spiritual one. (3) Observe that truly repentant persons, like this woman, will prove their conversion to Christ by showing forth an affection and gratitude toward Him.

Women Support Jesus' Ministry (Luke 8:1-3)

In this passage we find an inspirational balance between the ministry of the Blesser (Jesus) and those who are the blessed. On the one hand, we see Jesus tirelessly giving of himself so that every possible person might know the good news God has for them. On the other hand, we see the selfless response of those who receive Jesus' works and words—they follow Him and support His ministry to the limit of their resources.

8 After this, Jesus traveled about from one town and village to another, proclaiming the good news of the kingdom of God. The Twelve were with him, [2]and also some women who had been cured of evil spirits and diseases: Mary (called Magdalene) from whom seven demons had

come out; [3]Joanna the wife of Cuza, the manager of Herod's household; Susanna; and many others. These women were helping to support them out of their own means.

Several important points may be made from this story. First, we learn that despite our Lord's powers, He still had need of the most elementary essentials. Man cannot live on miracles alone; there must also be provisions that come from a very natural base. Second, we discover that transformed women were largely responsible for providing the material needs of Jesus' ministry. Third, we know that at least one of these women (Mary, called Magdalene) served Him even through the hour of His death—an action which Jesus' male disciples failed to perform (Luke 23:49ff.; John 19:25ff.). It is quite an honor for women to note that not once, in any of the four Gospels, is it reported that a woman ever showed opposition to Jesus' mission.

The Parable of the Four Soils (Luke 8:4-15)

(cf. Matt. 13:1-23 and Mark 4:1-20)

This is one of the most loved and frequently quoted stories of Jesus. It is a simple message taken from the world of agriculture, but its truths are applicable for all people the world over.

There are several lessons to be learned from this parable. First, we see the Word of God—acting as a seed, it can grow in our lives and produce a wonderful fruit. Second, we notice the devil—one who can remove the Word of God from us, if it is not properly understood (this underscores the need for a strong, systematic teaching ministry in the local church). Third, we observe the shallowness of some who profess a Christian faith—they have no root. Fourth, we perceive the natural enemies of God's Word—worry, riches and pleasures. Fifth, we see the qualification for bearing spiritual fruit—a noble, good and persevering heart. Sixth, we understand that only one out of four who hear God's Word retain it to the extent that they are truly saved—the remainder may profess faith, but they do not possess it.

I. *The Information (8:4-8)*

[4]While a large crowd was gathering and people were coming to Jesus
from town after town, he told this parable: [5]"A farmer went out to sow
his seed. As he was scattering the seed, some fell along the path; it was

trampled on, and the birds of the air ate it up. [6]Some fell on rock, and
when it came up, the plants withered because they had no moisture.
[7]Other seed fell among thorns, which grew up with it and choked the
plants. [8]Still other seed fell on good soil. It came up and yielded a crop, a
hundred times more than was sown."

When he said this, he called out, "He who has ears to hear, let him hear."

II. *The Implications (8:9, 10)*

[9]His disciples asked him what this parable meant. [10]He said, "The
knowledge of the secrets of the kingdom of God has been given to you,
but to others I speak in parables, so that,

" 'though seeing, they may not see;
though hearing, they may not understand.'[a]

III. *The Interpretation (8:11-15)*

[11]"This is the meaning of the parable: The seed is the word of God.
[12]Those along the path are the ones who hear, and then the devil comes
and takes away the word from their hearts, so that they cannot believe
and be saved. [13]Those on the rock are the ones who receive the word
with joy when they hear it, but they have no root. They believe for a
while, but in the time of testing they fall away. [14]The seed that fell among
thorns stands for those who hear, but as they go on their way they are
choked by life's worries, riches and pleasures, and they do not mature.
[15]But the seed on good soil stands for those with a noble and good heart,
who hear the word, retain it, and by persevering produce a crop.

The Parable of the Lamp (Luke 8:16-18)

(cf. Matt. 5:14-16; Mark 4:21-25 and Luke 11:33-36)

The Christian faith, though intensely personal, is not a private matter. Christians are to be as noticeable as bright lights in dark places.

Nothing can be concealed forever. Eventually everything will be exposed. We can hide some things from some people, but we can never keep anything from God's view.

a 10 Isaiah 6:9

In view of this fact, we ought to listen attentively to Jesus' words and follow them to the letter. In the end, we will be glad we paid attention, for everyone who heeds His voice will be granted more and more blessings, while the persons who fail to listen, will fall lower and lower into barrenness.

[16]"No one lights a lamp and hides it in a jar or puts it under a bed.
Instead, he puts it on a stand, so that those who come in can see the light.
[17]For there is nothing hidden that will not be disclosed, and nothing
concealed that will not be known or brought out into the open.
[18]Therefore consider carefully how you listen. Whoever has will be
given more; whoever does not have, even what he thinks he has will be
taken from him."

Jesus' Original and New Family (Luke 8:19-21)

(cf. Matt. 12:46-50 and Mark 3:31-35)

Sometimes it is those who are nearest to us who unintentionally attempt hindering God's will for our lives. And numerous persons have yielded to the sincere, but misguided, voices of their families. Home, as important as it is—even to God—cannot replace the priority God has placed on His Kingdom for our lives. Above all else, the Kingdom is to be number one in our lives. Jesus knew this, and He would not fall to the undiscerning concern of His family.

[19]Now Jesus' mother and brothers came to see him, but they were not
able to get near him because of the crowd. [20]Someone told him, "Your
mother and brothers are standing outside, wanting to see you."
[21]He replied, "My mother and brothers are those who hear God's
word and put it into practice."

Jesus Quiets a Storm (Luke 8:22-25)

(cf. Matt. 8:23-27 and Mark 4:35-41)

There are five things in this story that call for our attention. First, there is the humanity of Jesus. He was so wearied by His work that He was able to sleep in a storm-tossed boat—how much Jesus is like us. Second, there is the fear of the disciples. Their eyes were fixed solely on the problem at hand, and not on the possibility that God might grant them a miracle in the hour of their need. So, they reported their plight to Jesus; they did not expect, however, any miraculous results. How often we are like these disciples. Third, there is the power of Christ which is displayed over the (Satanic?) forces of nature. Jesus will take nothing for granted; instead, he would call upon God's power for every need He encountered. Fourth, there is the rebuke from Jesus because His disciples walked by sight and not by faith. Fifth, there is the amazement of the disciples. They could not believe what they had just seen—and that, naturally, accounted for their lack of success in handling the matter in the first place.

[22]One day Jesus said to his disciples, "Let's go over to the other side of
the lake." So they got into a boat and set out. [23]As they sailed, he fell
asleep. A squall came down on the lake, so that the boat was being swamped, and they were in great danger.

[24]The disciples went and woke him, saying, "Master, Master, we're going to drown!"

He got up and rebuked the wind and the raging waters; the storm
subsided, and all was calm. [25]"Where is your faith?" he asked his disciples.

In fear and amazement they asked one another, "Who is this? He commands even the winds and the water, and they obey him."

Jesus Heals a Demonized Man (Luke 8:26-39)

(cf. Matt. 8:28-34 and Mark 5:1-20)

Jesus is able to transform the worst life and make it wonderful. Here we see the pitiful extent to which Satan goes to destroy his subjects. But here we also see the power of Christ to restore that which Satan has abused. And in the sidelines, as is so typical, we notice some people who have negative reactions to Jesus' cure.

I. *The Encounter (8:26, 27)*

**26They sailed to the region of the Gerasenes,[a] which is across the lake
from Galilee. 27When Jesus stepped ashore, he was met by a demon-
possessed man from the town. For a long time this man had not worn
clothes or lived in a house, but had lived in the tombs.**

II. *The Exchange (8:28-30)*

**28When he saw Jesus, he cried out and fell at his feet, shouting at the top
of his voice, "What do you want with me, Jesus, Son of the Most High
God? I beg you, don't torture me!" 29For Jesus had commanded the evil[b]
spirit to come out of the man. Many times it had seized him, and though
he was chained hand and foot and kept under guard, he had broken his
chains and had been driven by the demon into solitary places.
30Jesus asked him, "What is your name?"
"Legion," he replied, because many demons had gone into him.**

III. *The Exorcism (8:31-33)*

**31And they begged him repeatedly not to order them to go into the
Abyss.
32A large herd of pigs was feeding there on the hillside. The demons
begged Jesus to let them go into them, and he gave them permission.
33When the demons came out of the man, they went into the pigs, and the
herd rushed down the steep bank into the lake and was drowned.**

IV. *The Excitement (8:34-37)*

34When those tending the pigs saw what had happened, they ran off

---

a 26 Some manuscripts *Gadarenes;* other manuscripts *Gergesenes;* also in verse 37 b 29 Greek *unclean*

and reported this in the town and countryside, [35]and the people went out to see what had happened. When they came to Jesus, they found the man from whom the demons had gone out, sitting at Jesus' feet, dressed and in his right mind; and they were afraid. [36]Those who had seen it told the people how the demon-possessed man had been cured. [37]Then all the people of the region of the Gerasenes asked Jesus to leave them, because they were overcome with fear. So he got into the boat and left.

V. *The Evangelism (8:38, 39)*

[38]The man from whom the demons had gone out begged to go with him, but Jesus sent him away, saying, [39]"Return home and tell how much God has done for you." So the man went away and told all over town how much Jesus had done for him.

Jesus Heals a Girl and a Woman (Luke 8:40-56)

(cf. Matt. 9:18-26 and Mark 5:21-43)

What an incredible amount of sickness and suffering were brought into this world when Adam and Eve resisted God's will and were sentenced (along with all their descendants) to live in a cursed earth (Gen. 3:15ff.; Rom. 8:19-22). Everywhere there are persons with hurts and sorrows.

Yet it is here—in the midst of personal anguish—that Christ performed His finest works. If there were no tests, there would be no development of character. If there were no trials, there would be no miracles to receive from the hand of God. But there are troubles—and plenty of them for each of us. And until Jesus returns to recreate this world, they will continue to exist. It is our duty (and privilege!) then, to learn to trust Christ for the strength we need in order to live in this world triumphantly and optimistically.

Below is the story of two persons who needed help. They were godly persons, and they were hurting persons. Each sought the assistance of Jesus, and each was abundantly rewarded for having faith.

I. *The Information (8:40-42a)*

[40]Now when Jesus returned, a crowd welcomed him, for they were all expecting him. [41]Just then a man named Jairus, a ruler of the

synagogue, came and fell at Jesus' feet, pleading with him to come to his house [42]because his only daughter, a girl of about twelve, was dying.

II. *The Interruption (8:42b-48)*

As Jesus was on his way, the crowds almost crushed him. [43]And a woman was there who had been subject to bleeding for twelve years,[a] but no one could heal her. [44]She came up behind him and touched the edge of his cloak, and immediately her bleeding stopped.

[45]"Who touched me?" Jesus asked.

When they all denied it, Peter said, "Master, the people are crowding and pressing against you."

[46]But Jesus said, "Someone touched me; I know that power has gone out from me."

[47]Then the woman, seeing that she could not go unnoticed, came trembling and fell at his feet. In the presence of all the people, she told why she had touched him and how she had been instantly healed. [48]Then he said to her, "Daughter, your faith has healed you. Go in peace."

III. *The Incomprehension (8:49-56)*

[49]While Jesus was still speaking, someone came from the house of Jairus, the synagogue ruler. "Your daughter is dead," he said. "Don't bother the teacher any more."

[50]Hearing this, Jesus said to Jairus, "Don't be afraid; just believe, and she will be healed."

[51]When he arrived at the house of Jairus, he did not let anyone go in with him except Peter, John and James, and the child's father and mother. [52]Meanwhile, all the people were wailing and mourning for her. "Stop wailing," Jesus said. "She is not dead but asleep."

[53]They laughed at him, knowing that she was dead. [54]But he took her by the hand and said, "My child, get up!" [55]Her spirit returned, and at once she stood up. Then Jesus told them to give her something to eat. [56]Her parents were astonished, but he ordered them not to tell anyone what had happened.

---

a 43 Many manuscripts *years, and she had spent all she had on doctors*

Jesus Sends Out the Twelve (Luke 9:1-6)

(cf. Matt. 10:1-15 and Mark 6:7-13)

The time had arrived. The twelve whom Jesus chose to be His closest companions must now be sent out. They had been schooled; now it was time for them to apply their learning to their very own mission. Up to this point, they had followed Jesus. Today they would go forth without Him. They were ready to assume the role of leaders.

There are three matters in this commission that require individual attention.

First, there is the issuance of power over Satan and sickness. The fact that this miraculous ministry continued throughout the entire period of the New Testament (and beyond) is undeniable. But it must also be remembered that the bestowal of these gifts upon the twelve apostles was not intended to represent a power that all believers could exercise at will (cf. Acts 4:33; 5:12). The ministry of these men was decidedly unique.

Second, there is the charge to preach about God's Kingdom. There was much misunderstanding regarding God's plans. Most of the people felt God would march His army throughout Palestine and restore political freedom to the Jews. Instead, the disciples were instructed to preach a deliverance from the penalty and power caused by the enemy of sin.

Third, there is the element of provisions. The disciples had seen God provide for each need of Jesus; now they were to trust Him to meet their own needs. They were to take no money, only a message. If the people to whom they preached accepted them, then their needs would be met through them, but if their audience became critical, then they were to leave the very dust behind. In either case, God would provide what was needed. The disciples were to learn to live by faith, not by sight.

**9 When Jesus had called the Twelve together, he gave them power
and authority to drive out all demons and to cure diseases, [2]and he
sent them out to preach the kingdom of God and to heal the sick. [3]He told
them: "Take nothing for the journey—no staff, no bag, no bread, no
money, no extra tunic. [4]Whatever house you enter, stay there until you
leave that town. [5]If people do not welcome you, shake the dust off your
feet when you leave their town, as a testimony against them." [6]So they
set out and went from village to village, preaching the gospel and
healing people everywhere.**

Herod's Conscience (Luke 9:7-9)

(cf. Matt. 14:1-12 and Mark 6:14-29)

Herod was nagged by a piercing problem—his conscience wouldn't allow him to rest after killing God's prophet John. His dilemma was one of confusion: who was this new man of miracles called Jesus? Herod's desire was based on convenience: he wanted to meet this mysterious person, but on his own terms. Jesus, however, had no time for this callous and carnal ruler. He would have to live in his own self-made condition of guilt.

**7Now Herod the tetrarch heard about all that was going on. And he
was perplexed, because some were saying that John had been raised
from the dead, 8others that Elijah had appeared, and still others that
one of the prophets of long ago had come back to life. 9But Herod said, "I
beheaded John. Who, then, is this I hear such things about?" And he
tried to see him.**

Jesus Feeds the Five Thousand (Luke 9:10-17)

(cf. Matt. 14:13-21; Mark 6:30-44 and John 6:1-15)

Whenever the Lord sends you somewhere, you will come back with a story to tell. The disciples had plenty to report after their mission, so Jesus thought that a brief retreat to Bethsaida (a small community with plenty of wilderness area for quiet reflection and meditation) would be in order. This would provide them with the rest and reorientation they needed after such a tour of ministry.

Jesus' intentions, however, were not immediately fulfilled. There were people who learned of His whereabouts, and they would settle for nothing short of meeting Him personally and requesting His help. As a result of their determination, Jesus was again confronted with hurting and poorly taught people. Jesus never tired of caring for people. The retreat would have to be delayed until He had taught and healed these people, too.

We are creatures of constant need. Even in the presence of Jesus we find ourselves inadequate to provide for our own essentials, like food and lodging. Additionally, we are apt to conclude, along with the disciples, that natural problems require natural remedies. But Jesus demonstrated a better approach to problem solving. Miracles know no boundaries either in their type or degree. God's power and desire to help us is limitless. Therefore, let us seek Him with the confidence that every matter touching us has a profound remedy waiting to be sent from heaven.

10When the apostles returned, they reported to Jesus what they had
done. Then he took them with him and they withdrew by themselves to a
town called Bethsaida, 11but the crowds learned about it and followed
him. He welcomed them and spoke to them about the kingdom of God,
and healed those who needed healing.
12Late in the afternoon the Twelve came to him and said, "Send the
crowd away so they can go to the surrounding villages and countryside
and find food and lodging, because we are in a remote place here."
13He replied, "You give them something to eat."
They answered, "We have only five loaves of bread and two fish—
unless we go and buy food for all this crowd." 14(About five thousand
men were there.)
But he said to his disciples, "Have them sit down in groups of about
fifty each." 15The disciples did so, and everybody sat down. 16Taking the
five loaves and the two fish and looking up to heaven, he gave thanks
and broke them. Then he gave them to the disciples to set before the
people. 17They all ate and were satisfied, and the disciples picked up
twelve basketfuls of broken pieces that were left over.

Peter's Confession of Christ (Luke 9:18-22)

(cf. Matt. 16:13-21; Mark 8:27-32 and John 6:66-69)

The identity of Jesus was not clear to the masses of people who became acquainted with Him. The reason for this is twofold. First, Jesus never made it a priority to broadcast His identity. Second, the people's understanding of biblical prophecy was so narrow (politically oriented) that it never crossed their minds that the Messiah might first seek to deliver Israel from her greatest enemy—sin. It is precisely their lack of biblical insight that kept Jesus from proclaiming His Christhood.

Peter, however, knew Jesus' identity because God the Father revealed it to him (Matt. 16:17). Jesus was (and is) the "Christ." This term means "anointed one." The Scriptures use the term to designate the one person whom God would anoint to be His special Prophet (Deut. 18:15), Priest (Ps. 110:4) and King (Ps. 2:6).

By looking back in time it is easy to understand these truths. But had we lived in Jesus' day, our minds, too, would have been perplexed at the differences between what we had been taught and what we were seeing and hearing from Jesus. It is this natural confusion that caused Jesus to charge His disciples to keep the matter of His Messiahship a sealed matter, at least for a period of time.

I. *The Opinion of the Crowds (9:18, 19)*

[18]Once when Jesus was praying in private and his disciples were with
him, he asked them, "Who do the crowds say I am?"
[19]They replied, "Some say John the Baptist; others say Elijah; and still
others, that one of the prophets of long ago has come back to life."

II. *The Opinion of Peter (9:20-22)*

[20]"But what about you?" he asked. "Who do you say I am?"
Peter answered, "The Christ[a] of God."
[21]Jesus strictly warned them not to tell this to anyone. [22]And he said,
"The Son of Man must suffer many things and be rejected by the elders,
chief priests and teachers of the law, and he must be killed and on the
third day be raised to life."

The Test of Discipleship (Luke 9:23-27)

(cf. Matt. 16:22-28 and Mark 8:32-38)

There is always the matter of "if" in discipleship. Twice Jesus said that the door was open for people to follow Him, but each time He qualified the terms by which people would be approved.

Placed between these two "if" qualifiers are two threats and two promises. Here is the judgment for not meeting the conditions; here also is the reward for paying the price Jesus requires for becoming one of His disciples.

[23]"Then he said to them all: "If anyone would come after me, he must
deny himself and take up his cross daily and follow me. [24]For whoever

a 20 Or *Messiah*

wants to save his life will lose it, but whoever loses his life for me will save it. [25]What good is it for a man to gain the whole world, and yet lose or forfeit his very self? [26]If anyone is ashamed of me and my words, the Son of Man will be ashamed of him when he comes in his glory and in the glory of the Father and of the holy angels. [27]I tell you the truth, some who are standing here will not taste death before they see the kingdom of God."

Jesus is not seeking out fine, moral people who are willing to forsake a few hours each week for His Church. Instead, He is in search of those persons who will cheerfully yield to Him their entire lives in unconditional surrender.

The first discovery every disciple must make, if he is to follow Jesus, is that his greatest hindrance to spiritual progress is *self-will.* A disciple's most dreaded and violent foe is not Satan, not antagonistic people and not besetting circumstances, but self-will.

In order for discipleship to take root and produce fruit, self-will must be dealt with consciously, constantly and completely. It is impossible to follow both Christ and self. Self-will must be crucified, buried and left in the grave.

It must be grasped at the outset that denial of self and self-denial are not equivalent. Self-denial is only a sacrifice of certain luxuries. It may include the giving up of certain foods, pleasures, activities and habits; but denial of self is far more personal and exacting.

When Jesus speaks of the denial of self, He is calling for a complete abandonment of self-will. This is the sacrifice of all personal claims to every form of independence and selfishness. Every thought, word and deed must now be brought into subjection to Christ (2 Cor. 10:3-5; 1 John 3:18). All devotion to possessions and love for praise must be deliberately and definitely forsaken. Denial of self has pleasure only in the performance of God's will—everything else is superficial and unrewarding.

Thomas á Kempis has correctly written, "Jesus has many lovers of His Kingdom, but few bearers of the cross. All are disposed to rejoice with Him, but few to suffer for His sake." The call to discipleship is the call to death—the death of self-will.

Finally, a word should be said about duration. Commitment to Christ is never a once-for-all settlement. Bearing the cross is by no means a "one-shot" experience. Quite the contrary. Bearing the cross is a daily exercise; it is a moment-by-moment discipline that has no end. It is to be worn in the morning and the evening, at work and at home, in school and in play, in public and in private, in speech and in deed, in thought and in dress. In short, the cross is God's perennial tool for refining disciples. It is never to be abandoned and never to be hidden!

The Transfiguration (Luke 9:28-36)

(cf. Matt. 17:1-13 and Mark 9:2-13)

Sensing the tremendous weight of what awaited Him in Jerusalem, Jesus retired to an isolated site for a period of intense prayer. How desperately Jesus needed God's help in order to accomplish His plans. We must never overlook the reliance Jesus displayed upon God, for in this fact lies the key ingredient to His powerful works and words.

In the midst of this prayer retreat two amazing events occurred: (1) Jesus was transfigured—that is, His entire countenance was charged with brilliantly radiant glory; (2) Moses and Elijah (respectively representing the Law and the Prophets) came to discuss with Jesus the details of His approaching crucifixion and resurrection.

The aim behind this spectacular experience seems to be twofold. First, it would prepare Jesus to endure the shame of the cross (Heb. 12:2). Second, it would equip the disciples to face the death of the Messiah (2 Pet. 1:16-18).

I. *The Transfiguration of Jesus (9:28, 29)*

**28 About eight days after Jesus said this, he took Peter, John and James
with him and went up onto a mountain to pray. 29 As he was praying, the
appearance of his face changed, and his clothes became as bright as a
flash of lightning.**

II. *The Talk of Moses and Elijah (9:30, 31)*

**30 Two men, Moses and Elijah, 31 appeared in glorious splendor, talking
with Jesus. They spoke about his departure, which he was about to
bring to fulfillment at Jerusalem.**

III. *The Talk of Peter (9:32, 33)*

**32 Peter and his companions were very sleepy, but when they became
fully awake, they saw his glory and the two men standing with him. 33 As
the men were leaving Jesus, Peter said to him, "Master, it is good for us
to be here. Let us put up three shelters—one for you, one for Moses and
one for Elijah." (He did not know what he was saying.)**

IV. *The Talk of God the Father (9:34-36)*

**34While he was speaking, a cloud appeared and enveloped them, and
they were afraid as they entered the cloud. 35A voice came from the
cloud, saying, "This is my Son, whom I have chosen; listen to him."
36When the voice had spoken, they found that Jesus was alone. The
disciples kept this to themselves, and told no one at that time what they
had seen.**

An Epileptic Is Healed (Luke 9:37-45)

(cf. Matt. 17:14-23 and Mark 9:14-32)

No one ever wants to leave a mountaintop experience, but life in the real world is more than one blessing after another. There are needs, too, that require our attention. Jesus had no more than set foot into the crowds than someone wanted His attention and help. A man cried out desperately for a miracle in behalf of his son, while the befuddled disciples looked on to see what their Master would do in the hour of their impotence.

What a grim scene this is, especially when held in contrast to the exhilarating moment Jesus knew only moments earlier. And what a rare moment of disgust do we see here in Jesus. His heart is broken by the lack of faith among the people in general, and among His disciples in particular. Also, His heart is angered by the outright perversion among all of them.

It is a real test of patience and love for Jesus. But in the end He sees and heals the troubled boy. Jesus will not permit personal hurts to hinder His ministry. He came to strengthen the weak, and He would do just that.

I. *The Report (9:37-40)*

**37The next day, when they came down from the mountain, a large
crowd met him. 38A man in the crowd called out, "Teacher, I beg you to
look at my son, for he is my only child. 39A spirit seizes him and he
suddenly screams; it throws him into convulsions so that he foams at the
mouth. It scarcely ever leaves him and is destroying him. 40I begged
your disciples to drive it out, but they could not."**

II. *The Rebuke (9:41)*

[41]"O unbelieving and perverse generation," Jesus replied, "how long shall I stay with you and put up with you? Bring your son here."

III. *The Result (9:42)*

[42]Even while the boy was coming, the demon threw him to the ground in a convulsion. But Jesus rebuked the evil[a] spirit, healed the boy and gave him back to his father.

IV. *The Reminder (9:43-45)*

[43]And they were all amazed at the greatness of God.
While everyone was marveling at all that Jesus did, he said to his disciples, [44]"Listen carefully to what I am about to tell you: The Son of Man is going to be betrayed into the hands of men." [45]But they did not understand what this meant. It was hidden from them, so that they did not grasp it, and they were afraid to ask him about it.

Who Is the Greatest? (Luke 9:46-50)

(cf. Matt. 18:1-5 and Mark 9:33-41)

Competition may have its place in sports, but it has no place in the Kingdom of God. Thoughts of being greater (or more important) than someone else will not be tolerated.

It isn't how prominent you may be that really counts, but how humble your service is toward the insignificant folks of this world. Jesus' gauge for measuring greatness is not the same as the world's gauge for this measurement. Greatness takes on a whole new meaning in the Kingdom.

I. *Jesus' Illustration (9:46-48)*

[46]An argument started among the disciples as to which of them would be the greatest. [47]Jesus, knowing their thoughts, took a little child and had him stand beside him. [48]Then he said to them, "Whoever welcomes this little child in my name welcomes me; and whoever welcomes me welcomes the one who sent me. For he who is least among you all—he is the greatest."

---

a 42 Greek *unclean*

II. *John's Insistence (9:49, 50)*

[49]"Master," said John, "we saw a man driving out demons in your name and we tried to stop him, because he is not one of us."

[50]"Do not stop him," Jesus said, "for whoever is not against you is for you."

Samaritans Do Not Welcome Jesus (Luke 9:51-56)

This brief account introduces a powerful section in Luke's Gospel. From Luke 9:51 to 19:44 we are provided with the details of Jesus' final journey to Jerusalem. The bulk of this information is found in no other Gospel. Therefore, in certain respects, it serves as Luke's most significant contribution to our story of Jesus.

[51]As the time approached for him to be taken up to heaven, Jesus
resolutely set out for Jerusalem, [52]and he sent messengers on ahead.
They went into a Samaritan village to get things ready for him, [53]but the
people there did not welcome him, because he was heading for Jeru-
salem. [54]When the disciples James and John saw this, they asked, "Lord,
do you want us to call fire down from heaven to destroy them[a]?" [55]But
Jesus turned and rebuked them, [56]and[b] they went to another village.

In order to make the journey from Galilee (in the north) to Judea (in the south) as direct and short as possible, Jesus selected a road that cuts through Samaritan territory. The Samaritans, however, were not inclined to honor Jesus' travel plans. That is, they (probably) refused lodging for Him and His disciples. The cause for this opposition was due to the fact that they knew Jesus was headed for the Temple of Jerusalem.

According to the Samaritans the holiest place of worship was Mount Gerizim; therefore, they resisted those Jews who arrogantly insisted that only Jerusalem could serve as the center for worship. Once James and John, "the Sons of Thunder" (Mark 3:17), learned of their reaction, they quickly sought Jesus' favor to consume them on the spot with a holy fire! Jesus, however, rebuked them for their impulsive and intense bigotry. He came to save the world, not to devour it and leave everyone in ashes who opposed Him for the moment. There were other routes to Jerusalem, and He would take one of them.

Sometimes our so-called righteous indignation is a covering for a more carnal trait known as prejudice. We must not be quick to judge others when they do not see things as we see them; instead, we must seek ways to avoid trouble in order to achieve the higher good.

---

a 54 Some manuscripts *them, even as Elijah did* *b 55, 56* Some manuscripts *them. And he said, "You do not know what kind of spirit you are of, for the Son of Man did not come to destroy men's lives, but to save them." [56]And*

***Some Ground Rules for Following Jesus* (Luke 9:57-62)**

(cf. Matt. 8:18-22)

No less than sixteen times in the Gospels do we hear Jesus saying, "Follow me" (Matt. 4:19; 8:22; 9:9; 16:24; 19:21; Mark 2:14; 8:34; 10:21; Luke 5:27; 9:23, 59; 18:22; John 1:43; 12:26; 21:19, 22). There is no higher honor bestowed upon mortals than to be invited to follow the Son of God!

Becoming a disciple of Jesus Christ is the most serious and sober affair in all the world. There are no demands so taxing, nor any rewards so glorious!

Not everyone, however, equally comprehends the implications involved in this call from Jesus. Some persons are too quick to respond, others are too slow, and still others suffer from indecision. In the following text we see each of these all-too-common reactions.

I. *The First Candidate (9:57, 58)*

57As they were walking along the road, a man said to him, "I will follow you wherever you go."

58Jesus replied, "Foxes have holes and birds of the air have nests, but the Son of Man has no place to lay his head."

Discipleship entails much more than good teachings and marvelous miracles. Following Jesus is not only enjoyment without exhausting trials. Warm feelings at the outset may soon give way to cold facts. We must be prepared for these moments from the start. No one can erect a structure without first counting the cost, and neither can anyone become a full-fledged disciple who has not also first counted the price he must pay for following Jesus. We must think our commitment through—from beginning to end—before we make any hasty and ill-planned decisions. Discipleship involves a careful blend of mountain peaks and dark valleys. We must see both before we hurriedly run off to join Jesus wherever He goes.

II. *The Second Candidate (9:59, 60)*

59He said to another man, "Follow me."
But the man replied, "Lord, first let me go and bury my father."
60Jesus said to him, "Let the dead bury their own dead, but you go and proclaim the kingdom of God."

Here is a man of excuses. How sad it is that some people try putting off following Jesus. Benjamin Franklin once said, "He that is good at making excuses is seldom good at anything else." This is too true of many would-be disciples. Satan cares little how spiritual our intentions may be, so long as they are projected for a fulfillment at some time in the future. (See other notes in Matthew's Gospel.)

III. *The Third Candidate (9:61, 62)*

> [61]**Still another said, "I will follow you, Lord; but first let me go back and say good-by to my family."**
> [62]**Jesus replied, "No one who puts his hand to the plow and looks back is fit for service in the kingdom of God."**

This final candidate suffers from what could be called spiritual seasickness. First he looks forward, then he looks backward; to and fro he spins his head. Such a person has no stability because he has no roots; he hops around too much to grow up into a fruitful disciple. Jesus rebuked this type of person for inconsistency.

Jesus will not compromise His call to discipleship. Certainly much harm has come to the Church because it has not maintained these identical standards.

Accepting overly anxious volunteers, overlooking carnal hesitators and receiving inconsistent workers into prominent positions has greatly grieved the plans of God for His glorious Body, the Church. These snares are treacherous, and we must beware of each of them.

The Mission of the Seventy-Two (Luke 10:1-24)

It is now the third year of Jesus' ministry. The time available to Him is very brief. There is much yet to be done, but so precious little time remains to see it accomplished. Therefore, Jesus enlisted sixty additional disciples to go ahead of Him to prepare the way for His entrance into these final communities.

The majority of this ministry would be conducted on the west bank of the Jordan. Jesus previously devoted himself to the Judeans, the Galileans and the Samaritans. Now He would concentrate on the neglected towns in the territories of Decapolis and Perea.

I. *They Go Forth (10:1-16)*

10 After this the Lord appointed seventy-two[a] others and sent them two by two ahead of him to every town and place where he was about to go. [2]He told them, "The harvest is plentiful, but the workers are few. Ask the Lord of the harvest, therefore, to send out workers into his harvest field. [3]Go! I am sending you out like lambs among wolves. [4]Do not take a purse or bag or sandals; and do not greet anyone on the road.

[5]"When you enter a house, first say, 'Peace to this house.' [6]If a man of peace is there, your peace will rest on him; if not, it will return to you. [7]Stay in that house, eating and drinking whatever they give you, for the worker deserves his wages. Do not move around from house to house.

[8]"When you enter a town and are welcomed, eat what is set before you. [9]Heal the sick who are there and tell them, 'The kingdom of God is near you.' [10]But when you enter a town and are not welcomed, go into its streets and say, [11]'Even the dust of your town that sticks to our feet we wipe off against you. Yet be sure of this: The kingdom of God is near.' [12]I tell you, it will be more bearable on that day for Sodom than for that town.

[13]"Woe to you, Korazin! Woe to you, Bethsaida! For if the miracles that were performed in you had been performed in Tyre and Sidon, they would have repented long ago, sitting in sackcloth and ashes. [14]But it will be more bearable for Tyre and Sidon at the judgment than for you. [15]And you, Capernaum, will you be lifted up to the skies? No, you will go down to the depths.[b]

[16]"He who listens to you listens to me; he who rejects you rejects me; but he who rejects me rejects him who sent me."

Jesus' instructions for the thirty-six pairs were straightforward. Here is a ten-point analysis of Jesus' words. Each disciple is to do the following things:

1. Pray (v. 2). The work before them would be greater than the number of workers. They would have to go with the prayer that God would raise up still more workers to accomplish the monumental task of advancing God's Kingdom throughout the whole world.
2. Discern (v. 3). The work before them would be greater than their natural abilities. They would have to be wise, cautious, and tactful.
3. Trust (v. 4a). The work before them would be greater than their financial resources. They would have to live by faith in God's faithfulness. They could not be governed by their senses, but by the promises of Christ.
4. Hurry (v. 4b). The work before them would call for a greater degree of haste than

a 1 Some manuscripts *seventy;* also in verse 17 *b 15* Greek *Hades*

normal manners would dictate. They would have to utilize each moment to its fullest potential. There was not a single minute to waste.

5. Stay (vv. 5-8). The work before them would be deserving of their support. They would have to receive the hospitality that would be offered to them with a spirit of grace and appreciation. They were not to move around from house to house, but to settle down and accomplish the mission for which they were sent forth.

6. Heal (v. 9). The work before them would include miraculous proofs that God's Kingdom had in fact invaded their territory.

7. Rebuke (vv. 10-11a). The work before them would be uncompromising. They would tell the gospel message the way it is and let people decide for themselves how they wanted to respond. If the response would be negative, however, the disciples were to remove even the slightest remains of any contact with them.

8. Believe (v. 11b). The work before them would be carried out in a manner that would be both positive and penetrating. They would have to be convinced of their message themselves, and out of this clear conviction their message would be proclaimed.

9. Remember (vv. 12-15). The work before them would carry a weighty responsibility. Their witness would make their audiences accountable.

10. Understand (v. 16). The work before them would be equivalent to the work of Jesus himself. Their acceptance would mean the acceptance of Jesus; their rejection would mean the rejection of Jesus. And the rejection of Jesus would mean the discarding of God. Therefore, the disciples were to carry a weighty authority in their witness to these cities. (Also read Matt. 10:1-45 for comments.)

II. *They Come Back (10:17-24)*

17The seventy-two returned with joy and said, "Lord, even the demons submit to us in your name."

18He replied, "I saw Satan fall like lightning from heaven. 19I have given you authority to trample on snakes and scorpions and to overcome all the power of the enemy; nothing will harm you. 20However, do not rejoice that the spirits submit to you, but rejoice that your names are written in heaven."

21At that time Jesus, full of joy through the Holy Spirit, said, "I praise you, Father, Lord of heaven and earth, because you have hidden these things from the wise and learned, and revealed them to little children. Yes, Father, for this was your good pleasure.

22"All things have been committed to me by my Father. No one knows who the Son is except the Father, and no one knows who the Father is except the Son and those to whom the Son chooses to reveal him."

[23]Then he turned to his disciples and said privately, "Blessed are the eyes that see what you see. [24]For I tell you that many prophets and kings wanted to see what you see but did not see it, and to hear what you hear but did not hear it."

The mission was a remarkable success, and the disciples returned with joyful stories to tell Jesus. They were especially excited at how even the demons retreated because of the authority Jesus had given the disciples through His name. Jesus concurred that, indeed, Satan's power in the towns where they ministered had been overthrown, almost as if Satan had himself fallen from heaven with a swift and unexpected blow. (This scene, however, is not to be confused with the future fall of Satan as revealed in Revelation 12. The figure of speech used here is figurative, not literal.)

After hearing the stories the disciples so eagerly told, Jesus then put everything back into focus. Miracles are a wonderful part of God's will, but the greatest miracle of them all—and the source for our deepest joy—is the miracle that our names can be written in heaven's book of salvation (Exod. 32:32; Rev. 3:5; 20:11-15). Power over Satan is fine; but finding peace with God is what life is all about.

Next, Jesus burst forth with joyful praise. He could not contain His delight over how God had worked such astonishing signs through such unlikely persons. He further rejoiced in the fact that those arrogant persons who thought they knew something had been left empty-handed.

Finally, there was a profound disclosure regarding the nature of God's revelation. First, He said that no one truly understands the nature and mission of Jesus except God the Father (and, of course, those to whom the Father extends this revelation—Matt. 16:17; John 6:65). Second, our Lord stated that no one knows the Father, except those who understand Jesus. And third, Jesus told His companions how fortunate they were to live in the days when He walked on the earth and revealed God's Kingdom to them, for the desire of the ages was being fulfilled in their very own lifetimes.

The Parable of the Neighborly Samaritan (Luke 10:25-37)

Frequently Jesus found himself confronted with someone who sought to trap Him in some point of His teaching (Matt. 21:23; 22:15, 23, 34; etc.). His critics reasoned that their knowledge would prove adequate to corner Jesus. But, as ought to be expected, the professional critic always ended up being openly embarrassed.

If it were not for these subtly barbed confrontations with Jesus, we would have missed much of His brilliance. Wisdom displays itself best in settings of ignorance. Such was the case here. A so-called expert in the Mosaic Law had attempted to disprove Jesus' superiority, but Jesus ably demonstrated that He is in fact the master teacher of all time.

I. *The First Question by the Expert (10:25-28)*

25On one occasion an expert in the law stood up to test Jesus.
"Teacher," he asked, "what must I do to inherit eternal life?"
26"What is written in the Law?" he replied. "How do you read it?"
27He answered: " 'Love the Lord your God with all your heart and
with all your soul and with all your strength and with all your mind'[a];
and, 'Love your neighbor as yourself.'[b]"
28"You have answered correctly," Jesus replied. "Do this and you will
live."

First, observe the content of the question. This is the most essential inquiry anyone can ask. Each of us should know the answer, for herein lies the sole key to the doorway of heaven.

Second, observe the context of the question. The one who asked for an answer was not sincere. His heart was proud, and his speech was deliberately deceptive. How tragic it is that people will play verbal games with a topic that involves their own eternal destinies.

Third, observe the reaction of Jesus. He told the inquirer to answer his own question. This is a masterful strategy. When persons are insincere in their probings, we ought to call them to commit themselves; this causes them to fall into their own traps.

Fourth, observe the response of the expert. He answers correctly—the essence of the whole law can be summed up in the two-sided commandment to love God and your neighbor (Lev. 19:18; Deut. 6:5; Gal. 5:14). Unfortunately, like far too many persons today, this man could provide a satisfactory answer with his mouth but he did not apply its truth to his own life. This is certainly our greatest downfall—to know what is right and best, but not to do it.

II. *The Second Question by the Expert (10:29-37)*

29But he wanted to justify himself, so he asked Jesus, "And who is my
neighbor?"
30In reply Jesus said: "A man was going down from Jerusalem to
Jericho, when he fell into the hands of robbers. They stripped him of his

a 27 Deut. 6:5 *b 27* Lev. 19:18

clothes, beat him and went away, leaving him half dead. 31A priest
happened to be going down the same road, and when he saw the man,
he passed by on the other side. 32So too, a Levite, when he came to the
place and saw him, passed by on the other side. 33But a Samaritan, as he
traveled, came where the man was; and when he saw him, he took pity
on him. 34He went to him and bandaged his wounds, pouring on oil and
wine. Then he put the man on his own donkey, took him to an inn and
took care of him. 35The next day he took out two silver coins[a] and gave
them to the innkeeper. 'Look after him,' he said, 'and when I return, I
will reimburse you for any extra expense you may have.'

36"Which of these three do you think was a neighbor to the man who
fell into the hands of robbers?"

37The expert in the law replied, "The one who had mercy on him."

Jesus told him, "Go and do likewise."

Since the expert felt insulted by Jesus' last statement, he continued the dialogue, hoping to save face, but in the end he only managed to draw himself more deeply into disgrace. His inquiry focused on the identity of our "neighbor."

The popular Jewish teaching was to "love your neighbor and hate your enemies" (Matt. 5:43). By this standard the Jew should love other Jews, but he should hate everyone else. This statement was clearly the product of strong Jewish prejudices. Jesus would discard such a narrow-minded interpretation of the term "neighbor."

Four matters capture our attention in this famous parable: (1) We notice how rare it is to discover persons who truly love their neighbors, even among top religious officials; (2) we notice that our neighbor is anyone who crosses our path; (3) we notice that love for a neighbor is demonstrated by meeting that person's needs; and (4) we notice that the most unlikely persons are capable of showing neighborly love—a fact that ought to prevent us from making judgmental generalizations about any group of persons.

This story must have burned the cocky scholar, because he, like most Jews, disliked the Samaritans. The illustration was impeccable, striking at the root of the man's prejudice. If the lawyer wanted to be saved, then he was required to put love for everyone into practice.

---

a 35 Greek *two denarii*

Jesus Visits Martha and Mary (Luke 10:38-42)

How easily our hearts can shift from being enthralled with the *Lord* of the work to being entangled with the *work* of the Lord. No finer illustration can be seen than the one provided for us here. There is a time for attending to the ordinary duties of life. But, too, there is a time when these tasks must be set aside for a higher duty. And taking time to hear from Jesus is the highest duty assigned to any human.

> **38As Jesus and his disciples were on their way, he came to a village**
> **where a woman named Martha opened her home to him. 39She had a**
> **sister called Mary, who sat at the Lord's feet listening to what he said.**
> **40But Martha was distracted by all the preparations that had to be**
> **made. She came to him and asked, "Lord, don't you care that my sister**
> **has left me to do the work by myself? Tell her to help me!"**
> **41"Martha, Martha," the Lord answered, "you are worried and upset**
> **about many things, 42but only one thing is needed.[a] Mary has chosen**
> **what is better, and it will not be taken away from her."**

Martha Was Distracted. Martha could not see the Lord because all of her unfinished works stood in the way, blocking her vision. Mary could not see the unfinished works because her Lord stood before her eyes. There is a lesson of priorities and values for each one of us in this rich episode.

How easily our attention can be given over to physical ambitions (rather than spiritual ones). In one moment our eyes are upon Christ; in the next instant our minds are distracted and drawn away to other concerns. We have each experienced the same distractions encountered here by Martha. Let us, then, learn how to avoid these pitfalls in the future.

Lord, Don't You Care? Invariably when you are sidetracked by nonessential matters, you will wonder why the Lord is not concerned about your state of affairs. Martha, however, learned that the troubles she stumbled over were of her own making. She permitted her priorities to become unbalanced, and irritation was the inevitable result.

Only One Thing Is Needed. This profound line ought to be memorized by every Christian. Its implications ought to be carefully pondered. And its excellence ought to saturate our beings entirely, much like a blotter soaks up ink into its fibers. We desperately need to devote our full attention to such striking and practical words as these from the lips of Jesus, our Lord.

---

a 42 Some manuscripts *but few things are needed—or only one*

The Model Prayer (Luke 11:1-4)

(cf. Matt. 6:9-13)

Prayer is powerful because God is powerful. Prayer changes things because God changes things. Prayer works because God works. There is no shortage to the value of prayer because there is no shortage to the value of knowing God.

I. *The Petition (11:1)*

11 One day Jesus was praying in a certain place. When he finished, one of his disciples said to him, "Lord, teach us to pray, just as John taught his disciples."

We teach no lessons so clearly as the ones people see us live. Jesus' prayer life was an inspiration to this unnamed disciple. This man wanted more than a secondhand joy in his walk with God; he sought Jesus to teach him how this profound dialogue with God could become his very own experience, too.

This is the type of question Jesus delights to answer. It is not theoretical or hypothetical, but it is an intensely practical concern.

II. *The Pattern (11:2-4)*

2He said to them, "When you pray, say:

" 'Father,[a]
hallowed be your name,
your kingdom come.[b]
3Give us each day our daily bread.
4Forgive us our sins,
for we also forgive everyone who sins against us.[c]
And lead us not into temptation.[d] ' "

There are five main parts to this prayer:

1. "Father, hallowed be your name"—Adoration
2. "Your kingdom come"—Intercession
3. "Give us . . . our daily bread"—Physical Petition

a 2 Some manuscripts *Our Father in heaven*　b 2 Some manuscripts *come. May your will be done on earth as it is in heaven.*
c 4 Greek *everyone who is indebted to us*　d 4 Some manuscripts *temptation but deliver us from the evil one*

4. "Forgive us our sins"—Spiritual Petition
5. "Lead us not into temptation"—Spiritual Protection

There is a subtle power in these words. They are packed with a calm expectation. The words are simple and common; yet they are equally penetrating and practical.

The Parable of the Persistent Friend (Luke 11:5-13)

(cf. Matt. 7:7-11)

While the preceding verses (vv. 2-4) teach that prayer is guided by principles, these verses teach that prayer is productive through perseverance. It is through "faith and patience [that we] inherit what has been promised" (Heb. 6:12). Only the person who has learned to aggressively exercise his faith in patience will receive the best that God offers.

I. *Jesus Tells a Parable (11:5-8)*

> **5Then he said to them, "Suppose one of you has a friend, and he goes to**
> **him at midnight and says, 'Friend, lend me three loaves of bread,**
> **6because a friend of mine on a journey has come to me, and I have**
> **nothing to set before him.'**
> **7"Then the one inside answers, 'Don't bother me. The door is already**
> **locked, and my children are with me in bed. I can't get up and give you**
> **anything.' 8I tell you, though he will not get up and give him the bread**
> **because he is his friend, yet because of the man's persistence he will get**
> **up and give him as much as he needs.**

Our friends are not always immediately responsive to our requests or needs. They sometimes hesitate; they sometimes resist. But in the end, if we will not take no for an answer, our friends will come through for us.

II. *Jesus Applies the Parable (11:9-13)*

> **9"So I say to you: Ask and it will be given to you; seek and you will find;**
> **knock and the door will be opened to you. 10For everyone who asks**
> **receives; he who seeks finds; and to him who knocks, the door will be**
> **opened.**

[11]"Which of you fathers, if your son asks for[a] a fish, will give him a snake instead? [12]Or if he asks for an egg, will give him a scorpion? [13]If you then, though you are evil, know how to give good gifts to your children, how much more will your Father in heaven give the Holy Spirit to those who ask him!"

Jesus makes two applications from His parable: (1) If we can ask a friend for the things we need, we can also ask God for the things we need; and (2) if a friend will give us good things upon our request, how much more will our perfectly loving heavenly Father give good things to those who ask Him. In fact, He is willing to give each seeker the very best gift of heaven—the Holy Spirit (Acts 2:38; 8:20; 10:45; 11:17).

The Holy Spirit was not an available gift upon request prior to Jesus' coming. Before this time the Spirit was "with" people, but now (and especially from the day of Pentecost forward) He would be "in" each one who prayed for this experience (John 14:17).

The central intent of this passage is to teach us the extent to which our Father is concerned about each matter in our lives. He will withhold no good thing from those who seek Him in a sincere and patient faith. Such promises are deserving of our most concentrated meditations.

Jesus and Beelzebub (Luke 11:14-28)

(cf. Matt. 12:22-32, 43-45 and Mark 3:22-30)

Aristotle and Plato (famous Greek philosophers of the fourth century before Christ) believed in attendant spirits, which they deemed as being good. Socrates felt his spirit would warn him whenever he was about to make a wrong decision.

The Greek word employed for these spirits is *daimon* (or demon). It comes from a root word meaning "to know." So, the demons were believed to be intelligent spirits who helped people. The New Testament, however, calls them evil spirits, followers of Satan.

A demon is a spirit (Luke 10:17, 20). They have no flesh or bones (Luke 24:39). Yet they are capable of manifesting all the characteristics of a full personality. They can speak (Mark 1:24, 34), hear (Mark 5:6-10), feel (Mark 5:7, 12; James 2:19), make decisions (Jude 6), distinguish between the saved and lost people of the earth (Rev. 9:4) and submit to higher authorities (Mark 1:34; 3:22). We should never consider a demon as some blank, impersonal force. They are not things, but persons of a different order from humans. They are a unique "race" of their own.

a 11 Some manuscripts *for bread, will give him a stone; or if he asks for*

The prince (or ruler) of the demons is Beelzebub (which is another name for Satan). Under his leadership demons go about to fulfill his plans. Jesus, on the other hand, is their archenemy. Jesus (and each Christian) has a higher authority than both Satan and his companions. And as each opportunity becomes available, Jesus will exercise this authority to spoil Satan's plans and replace them with God's will. The following account amply demonstrates this point.

I. *The Exorcism (11:14-16)*

**14Jesus was driving out a demon that was mute. When the demon left,
the man who had been dumb spoke, and the crowd was amazed. 15But
some of them said, "By Beelzebub,[a] the prince of demons, he is driving
out demons." 16Others tested him by asking for a sign from heaven.**

II. *The Explanation (11:17-26)*

**17Jesus knew their thoughts and said to them: "Any kingdom divided
against itself will be ruined, and a house divided against itself will fall. 18If
Satan is divided against himself, how can his kingdom stand? I say this
because you claim that I drive out demons by Beelzebub. 19Now if I drive
out demons by Beelzebub, by whom do your followers drive them out? So
then, they will be your judges. 20But if I drive out demons by the finger of
God, then the kingdom of God has come to you.**

**21"When a strong man, fully armed, guards his own house, his
possessions are safe. 22But when someone stronger attacks and over-
powers him, he takes away the armor in which the man trusted and
divides up the spoils.**

**23"He who is not with me is against me, and he who does not gather
with me, scatters.**

**24"When an evil[b] spirit comes out of a man, it goes through arid places
seeking rest and does not find it. Then it says, 'I will return to the house I
left.' 25When it arrives, it finds the house swept clean and put in order.
26Then it goes and takes seven other spirits more wicked than itself, and
they go in and live there. And the final condition of that man is worse
than the first."**

III. *The Exclamation (11:27, 28)*

**27As Jesus was saying these things, a woman in the crowd called out,
"Blessed is the mother who gave you birth and nursed you."**

**28He replied, "Blessed rather are those who hear the word of God and
obey it."**

---

a 15 Greek *Beezeboul* or *Beelzeboul*; also in verses 18 and 19 *b 24* Greek *unclean*

As this woman listened and as her joy grew, she finally could contain it no longer. She had to shout out how blessed (or happy) the mother of Jesus must be with her son.

Unfortunately the New International Version translates Jesus' response as a negative contrast to what the woman said. It is acceptable, however, to translate the particle (here rendered "rather") as a positive affirmation (like, "Yes, but especially"). In other words, it is doubtful that Jesus denied this woman's remarks; instead, He sought to widen the base for those who can be equally (or even more fully) blessed. Naturally, this blessedness is the inheritance of everyone who hears and heeds God's Word.

The Sign of Jonah (Luke 11:29-32)

(cf. Matt. 12:38-42)

The greatest light ever sent from heaven came in the life of Jesus Christ. Still, many of those who saw Him had serious doubts. They witnessed His miracles; they listened to His messages. But they remained unmoved. They always wanted more proofs.

Some people will never be satisfied with God's signs (or proofs). They will insist upon still further evidences. But God will draw the line with such persons, for if they will not believe what He has already shown them, neither will they believe if they see more signs.

29 As the crowds increased, Jesus said, "This is a wicked generation. It asks for a miraculous sign, but none will be given it except the sign of Jonah. 30 For as Jonah was a sign to the Ninevites, so also will the Son of Man be to this generation. 31 The Queen of the South will rise at the judgment with the men of this generation and condemn them, for she came from the ends of the earth to listen to Solomon's wisdom, and now one[a] greater than Solomon is here. 32 The men of Nineveh will stand up at the judgment with this generation and condemn it, for they repented at the preaching of Jonah, and now one greater than Jonah is here.

a 31 Or *something;* also in verse 32

The Parable of the Lamp (Luke 11:33-36)

(cf. Matt. 5:14-16; 6:22, 23; Mark 4:21, 22 and Luke 8:16-18)

The placement of this parable is significant. It comes after statements regarding "a wicked generation" that always seeks more proofs. Obviously these persons were guilty of shutting their eyes to the Light—Jesus. Therefore, their bodies were full of darkness. Jesus, however, exhorted them to receive this light and to let it fill every room of their lives.

**[33]"No one lights a lamp and puts it in a place where it will be hidden,
or under a bowl. Instead he puts it on its stand, so that those who come in
may see the light. [34]Your eye is the lamp of your body. When your eyes
are good, your whole body also is full of light. But when they are bad,
your body also is full of darkness. [35]See to it, then, that the light within
you is not darkness. [36]Therefore, if your whole body is full of light, and
no part of it dark, it will be completely lighted, as when the light of a
lamp shines on you."**

Jesus Rebukes the Pharisees (Luke 11:37-54)

(cf. Matt. 15:1-19; 23:1-39; Mark 12:38-40 and Luke 20:45-47)

The Pharisees taught that no one could be saved, except those who maintained the strictest adherence to the Old Testament laws and their subsequent, minute interpretations. Literally hundreds of insignificant matters now overshadowed the original laws from God. As a result, the Pharisees failed to represent the true religion God ordained. In fact, despite all of their religious fervor, they had actually become a cult! And Jesus boldly told them just that!

"You insult us," they said. But Jesus responded, in effect, by saying that they had disgraced themselves. The truth about their spiritual emptiness could not be hidden, and therefore it could not go unchecked. This was Jesus' attitude and approach; certainly this, too, speaks to the frame of mind we should have about such matters.

I. *The Setting for the Six Woes (11:37-41)*

[37]When Jesus had finished speaking, a Pharisee invited him to eat with him; so he went in and reclined at the table. [38]But the Pharisee, noticing that Jesus did not first wash before the meal, was surprised.

[39]Then the Lord said to him, “Now then, you Pharisees clean the outside of the cup and dish, but inside you are full of greed and wickedness. [40]You foolish people! Did not the one who made the outside make the inside also? [41]But give what is inside ⌊the dish⌋[a] to the poor, and everything will be clean for you.

II. *The First Woe (11:42)*

[42]“Woe to you Pharisees, because you give God a tenth of your mint, rue and all other kinds of garden herbs, but you neglect justice and the love of God. You should have practiced the latter without leaving the former undone.

III. *The Second Woe (11:43)*

[43]“Woe to you Pharisees, because you love the most important seats in the synagogues and greetings in the marketplaces.

IV. *The Third Woe (11:44)*

[44]“Woe to you, because you are like unmarked graves, which men walk over without knowing it.”

V. *The Fourth Woe (11:45, 46)*

[45]One of the experts in the law answered him, “Teacher, when you say these things, you insult us also.”

[46]Jesus replied, “And you experts in the law, woe to you, because you load people down with burdens they can hardly carry, and you yourselves will not lift one finger to help them.

VI. *The Fifth Woe (11:47-51)*

[47]“Woe to you, because you build tombs for the prophets, and it was your forefathers who killed them. [48]So you testify that you approve of what your forefathers did; they killed the prophets, and you build their tombs. [49]Because of this, God in his wisdom said, ‘I will send them proph-

---

a 41 Or *what you have*

ets and apostles, some of whom they will kill and others they will perse-
cute.' [50]Therefore this generation will be held responsible for the blood
of all the prophets that has been shed since the beginning of the world,
[51]from the blood of Abel to the blood of Zechariah, who was killed
between the altar and the sanctuary. Yes, I tell you, this generation will
be held responsible for it all.

VII. *The Sixth Woe (11:52)*

[52]"Woe to you experts in the law, because you have taken away the key to knowledge. You yourselves have not entered, and you have hindered those who were entering."

VIII. *The Plotting After the Six Woes (11:53, 54)*

[53]When Jesus left there, the Pharisees and the teachers of the law be-
gan to oppose him fiercely and to besiege him with questions, [54]waiting
to catch him in something he might say.

Jesus Warns His Disciples (Luke 12:1-12)

(cf. Matt. 10:16-33; 16:5-12)

It is unfortunate that a new chapter division starts here. The story that began in Luke 11:37 does not really conclude until Luke 13:10. We must occasionally remind ourselves that the original text (the one penned by Luke) possessed no chapters or verses. The helpful, but imperfect, device of textual divisions was developed during the thirteenth century. Therefore, it is always wise, regardless of where you may begin a reading of the Scriptures, to note what precedes and what follows a particular passage.

At the close of chapter 11 Jesus was speaking directly to the Pharisees and so-called experts in the Mosaic writings (Genesis-Deuteronomy). His speech was uncompromisingly critical. In this passage, however, Jesus was speaking directly to His disciples, although he talked to them about the hypocritical religious leaders (and apparently he did so in the hearing of the leaders!).

The things Jesus said here, He had said before. Comments, then, may be found at the appropriate references in Matthew's Gospel.

I. *Warnings Against the Pharisees (12:1-3)*

12 Meanwhile, when a crowd of many thousands had gathered, so that they were trampling on one another, Jesus began to speak first to his disciples, saying: "Be on your guard against the yeast of the Pharisees, which is hypocrisy. [2]There is nothing concealed that will not be disclosed, or hidden that will not be made known. [3]What you have said in the dark will be heard in the daylight, and what you have whispered in the ear in the inner rooms will be proclaimed from the housetops.

See Matt. 10:26, 27 and 16:5-12 for comments.

II. *Warnings Against Fearing Men (12:4-7)*

[4]"I tell you, my friends, do not be afraid of those who kill the body and after that can do no more. [5]But I will show you whom you should fear: Fear him who, after the killing of the body, has power to throw you into hell. Yes, I tell you, fear him. [6]Are not five sparrows sold for two pennies[a]? Yet not one of them is forgotten by God. [7]Indeed, the very hairs of your head are all numbered. Don't be afraid; you are worth more than many sparrows.

See Matt. 10:28-31 for comments.

III. *Warnings Against Disowning Jesus (12:8, 9)*

[8]"I tell you, whoever acknowledges me before men, the Son of Man will also acknowledge him before the angels of God. [9]But he who disowns me before men will be disowned before the angels of God.

See Matt. 10:32, 33 for comments.

IV. *Warnings Against Blaspheming the Holy Spirit (12:10)*

[10]And everyone who speaks a word against the Son of Man will be forgiven, but anyone who blasphemes against the Holy Spirit will not be forgiven.

See Matt. 12:22-37 for comments.

V. *Warnings Against Self-Defense (12:11, 12)*

[11]"When you are brought before synagogues, rulers and authorities, do not worry about how you will defend yourselves or what you will say, [12]for the Holy Spirit will teach you at that time what you should say."

See Matt. 10:16-20 for comments.

a 6 Greek *two assaria*

The Parable of the Rich Fool (Luke 12:13-21)

The setting of this story is quite revealing. Jesus had just completed instructing His disciples, in the hearing of everyone, to keep their minds and hearts centered on spiritual priorities. Immediately upon the completion of Jesus' instruction, someone in the crowd spoke up and requested a most self-centered and nonspiritual petition.

In the midst of the most spiritual atmosphere someone will always be mentally distracted from the immediate surroundings. Their self-consuming interests are so strong that everything else passes by them without notice. And when they open their mouths to speak, they expose their shameful carnal condition.

Still, Jesus is able to use even these situations to instruct everyone. He took this greedy request and turned it into a spiritual lesson.

I. *The Problem of the Man (12:13-15)*

> **13Someone in the crowd said to him, "Teacher, tell my brother to divide the inheritance with me."**
>
> **14Jesus replied, "Man, who appointed me a judge or an arbiter between you?" 15Then he said to them, "Watch out! Be on your guard against all kinds of greed; a man's life does not consist in the abundance of his possessions."**

Jesus' twofold response to this man is revealing. First, He told the man that He is not a judge; that is, civil concerns should be brought to and handled by the local authorities. Jesus would not be sidetracked in His mission to deal with people's deepest need: spiritual conversion. Second, Jesus warned the man to guard his heart from a spirit of greed. Even if this man had been treated unjustly in the settlement of some estate, his far more serious trouble resided in his own attitude toward temporal things in general. The abundant life Jesus offers does not necessitate having possessions in order to experience it to the fullest possible degree.

II. *The Parable of Jesus (12:16-21)*

> **16And he told them this parable: "The ground of a certain rich man produced a good crop. 17He thought to himself, 'What shall I do? I have no place to store my crops.'**
>
> **18"Then he said, 'This is what I'll do. I will tear down my barns and**

build bigger ones, and there I will store all my grain and my goods.
[19]And I'll say to myself, "You have plenty of good things laid up for many years. Take life easy; eat, drink and be merry." '

[20]"But God said to him, 'You fool! This very night your life will be demanded from you. Then who will get what you have prepared for yourself?'

[21]"This is how it will be with anyone who stores up things for himself but is not rich toward God."

There are several far-reaching principles in this parable that can touch each one of us: (1) Our futures are unpredictable. No one can say what tomorrow holds or when he will do this or do that (James 4:13-17). (2) Those who only labor to be rich in earthly goods are foolish persons. They are too short-sighted and self-centered to discern the importance of being rich in spiritual matters. Wise persons, then, are those who live one day at a time, and do those things that are rewarding, both temporally and eternally.

Promises for Kingdom Seekers (Luke 12:22-34)

(cf. Matt. 6:19-34)

How different this world would be if everyone saw things from a divine perspective. Immediately all worrying would cease, and all greed would vanish forever.

Interestingly, Jesus' remarks about worry and greed were not addressed to the world at large, but to His very own disciples. It is these followers of Jesus (like us, today) who need to hear the exhortation to cease worrying about daily needs.

Jesus' comments were both positive and negative. On the positive side of things, He called His disciples to consider the unmatched value of the human body and life itself. Human life merits, by virtue of its creation, a higher service than that given to an anxious spirit about physical needs. Further, He reminded them of how the birds and flowers are watched over by the care of God, and how much more God will protect them who are made in His image. On the negative side, Jesus reminded them that worrying will not produce a single productive thing. He also informed them that it is only the pagans (those who are spiritually dead) who crave for physical things.

In summation, Jesus stated that if His disciples (both then and today) will seek

God's Kingdom (that is, seek the fulfillment of God's will in their own lives and in this world—Matt. 6:10), then God will see to it that they have everything they need. In fact, Jesus exhorted them to give to the poor from their substance, and to line their wallets with spiritual riches.

I. *Exhortations Not to Worry (12:22-31)*

**22Then Jesus said to his disciples: "Therefore I tell you, do not worry
about your life, what you will eat; or about your body, what you will
wear. 23Life is more than food, and the body more than clothes. 24Con-
sider the ravens: They do not sow or reap, they have no storeroom or
barn; yet God feeds them. And how much more valuable you are than
birds! 25Who of you by worrying can add a single hour to his life[a]?
26Since you cannot do this very little thing, why do you worry about the
rest?**

**27"Consider how the lilies grow. They do not labor or spin. Yet I tell
you, not even Solomon in all his splendor was dressed like one of these.
28If that is how God clothes the grass of the field, which is here today,
and tomorrow is thrown into the fire, how much more will he clothe
you, O you of little faith! 29And do not set your heart on what you will eat
or drink; do not worry about it. 30For the pagan world runs after all
such things, and your Father knows that you need them. 31But seek his
kingdom, and these things will be given to you as well.**

II. *Exhortations to Help the Poor (12:32-34)*

**32"Do not be afraid, little flock, for your Father has been pleased
to give you the kingdom. 33Sell your possessions and give to the poor.
Provide purses for yourselves that will not wear out, a treasure in heaven
that will not be exhausted, where no thief comes near and no moth
destroys. 34For where your treasure is, there your heart will be also.**

Anyone seeking the Kingdom is certain to find it, and to receive its three crown jewels—personal righteousness, peace and joy (Rom. 14:17). Since these gifts are priceless, and since nothing can even compare to their unsurpassing value, our affection for physical things ought to hold little space in our hearts or hands. Indeed, rather than clinging to this world's goods, we ought to be ready to part with them in order to relieve the burdens of those less fortunate than ourselves.

This passage, however, is *not* teaching that every follower of Christ is to sell every article he owns and give it away to the poor. Instead, Jesus is encouraging a walk of faith—not anxiety—with regard to personal possessions. He seeks to create in His

a 25 Or *single cubit to his height*

disciples a generous spirit that is both sensitive and responsive to people's needs.

The fact that Jesus was not commanding His disciples to sell everything is proven in at least these two ways: (1) If those with goods sold everything they had and gave it to the poor, then they in turn would become poor and need the relief of others. This hardly makes sense. (2) There is nothing wrong with having an abundance of earthly things; it is only wrong to desire these things above spiritual matters and/or to hold on to them with a greedy fist (1 Tim. 6:6-10, 17-19).

Being Ready When the Master Returns (Luke 12:35-48)

(cf. Matt. 24:42-51 and Mark 13:32-37)

It should be remembered that this teaching is but one piece from a broader speech that actually began in Luke 11:37. In the foregoing verses Jesus had rebuked a greedy man for being overly preoccupied with temporal matters (12:13-21). Next, He instructed His own disciples not to worry about their physical needs—God would take care of them (12:22-34). Now, Jesus advised His audience to keep their eyes on heaven, and to be ready for the coming of the Son of Man (that is, Jesus in His Second Coming—Matt. 16:27, 28; 24:26-31; 25:31; etc.).

I. *Be Watching (12:35-40)*

**35"Be dressed ready for service and keep your lamps burning, 36like
men waiting for their master to return from a wedding banquet, so that
when he comes and knocks they can immediately open the door for him.
37It will be good for those servants whose master finds them watching
when he comes. I tell you the truth, he will dress himself to serve, will
have them recline at the table and will come and wait on them. 38It will
be good for those servants whose master finds them ready, even if he
comes in the second or third watch of the night. 39But understand this:
If the owner of the house had known at what hour the thief was coming,
he would not have let his house be broken into. 40You also must be ready,
because the Son of Man will come at an hour when you do not expect
him."**

The man of the world is always looking down at the earth, seeking to receive some reward for his labors; the man of the Church is always looking up at heaven expecting to receive the reward of the ages—the coming of the Son of Man, who will rule the earth in perfect justice (Dan. 7:13, 14).

The essence of Jesus' instruction here centers in the necessity to be prepared for His return—whenever it might occur (see note on Matt. 24:42-44). In His absence (after His ascension) there will be no time for laxness. Indeed, whenever the moment of His second coming occurs, His followers are to be prepared to greet Him as ready servants. Interestingly, while Jesus told His followers to be ready servants, He announced that the Son of Man himself will be ready to serve them, too! See Matt. 25:1-13 for other specific comments.

II. *Be Working (12:41-48)*

41Peter asked, "Lord, are you telling this parable to us, or to everyone?"
42The Lord answered, "Who then is the faithful and wise manager,
whom the master puts in charge of his servants to give them their food
allowance at the proper time? 43It will be good for that servant whom
the master finds doing so when he returns. 44I tell you the truth, he will
put him in charge of all his possessions. 45But suppose the servant says to
himself, 'My master is taking a long time in coming,' and he then begins
to beat the menservants and womenservants and to eat and drink and
get drunk. 46The master of that servant will come on a day when he does
not expect him and at an hour he is not aware of. He will cut him to
pieces and assign him a place with the unbelievers.
47"That servant who knows his master's will and does not get ready or
does not do what his master wants will be beaten with many blows. 48But
the one who does not know and does things deserving punishment will
be beaten with few blows. From everyone who has been given much,
much will be demanded; and from the one who has been entrusted with
much, much more will be asked.

Inside this parable are several practical matters that affect every disciple who waits for Jesus' second coming: (1) Waiting for Jesus' return does not, in any degree, imply that we ought to become idle in the meantime. Rather, our number of works ought not to be reduced at all. Neither must the quality of these labors be cheapened a single bit. (2) Those who grow weary in waiting for Jesus' return will also grow slack in their spiritual conduct. Undeniably, there is a direct link between what we believe about the future and the way we live today. Anyone losing sight of Jesus' return will not be ready for His coming, and he will be assigned a judgment with all the other unbelievers. See Matt. 25:14-30 for specific comments.

In concluding this teaching, Jesus announced the methods that will be used on the day of judgment. First, we see that it will be a judgment based upon opportunity and responsibility—not everyone will stand before the Son of Man having equally shared in the same spiritual privileges or having equally responded to this light. Second, we notice that there will be degrees of punishment for the wicked—not everyone who is lost will suffer as intensely as other lost persons. Also read these passages: Matt. 10:15; 11:22-24 and Rev. 20:11-15.

The Consequences of Jesus' Coming (Luke 12:49-53)

(cf. Matt. 10:34-36 and Mark 13:12)

Every Jew who followed the Scriptures awaited a day when the Messiah would come and judge the world with a holy fire (Mal. 3:1-3; 4:1; Matt. 3:11, 12). For this purpose Jesus came into the world, and how He longed to rid the earth of all its vices! Yet, He must first be submerged in the agonies of bearing everyone's sins on the cross. But even immediately after that it will not be the appointed hour for the judgment of fire—this will only occur at His second coming (2 Thess. 1:6-9). In the meantime, many persons will become His loyal followers, while numerous others, in the same household, will bitterly oppose His very name. See Matt. 10:34-36 and Mark 13:12 for specific comments on these words.

**[49]"I have come to bring fire on the earth, and how I wish it were
already kindled! [50]But I have a baptism to undergo, and how distressed
I am until it is completed! [51]Do you think I came to bring peace on earth?
No, I tell you, but division. [52]From now on there will be five in one
family divided against each other, three against two and two against
three. [53]They will be divided, father against son and son against father, mother
against daughter and daughter against mother, mother-in-law against
daughter-in-law and daughter-in-law against mother-in-law."**

The Signs of the Times (Luke 12:54-59)

These few verses, when left to themselves, seem to be a bit out of place. Their relationship to each other appears to be disassociated, at least at first. But the longer you look at the overall context (starting at 11:37), the more sensible these verses become in this setting.

First, Jesus rebuked His hearers for their lack of spiritual perception (vv. 54-56). Just moments earlier He had encouraged them to be watching and working for the unknown hour of the coming of the Son of Man, but they apparently paid little attention to His counsel. Although these people would follow the signs of the sky, they would not bring themselves to follow the signs of the approaching Kingdom of God, as displayed in the ministry of Jesus Christ. See Matt. 16:2, 3 for other comments.

Second, Jesus charged His audience to listen and to decide for themselves about the reality of His statements (vv. 57-59). He then told them that if they had wronged their adversaries, they should settle things soon, or else they would certainly pay the fullest degree for their offenses. In like manner, they ought to rectify their callous condition with reference to God and His Kingdom by heeding the advice of His Son, Jesus. Also read Matt. 5:25, 26 for comments.

I. *Sure Signs in the Sky (12:54-56)*

**54He said to the crowd: "When you see a cloud rising in the west,
immediately you say, 'It's going to rain,' and it does. 55And when the
south wind blows, you say, 'It's going to be hot,' and it is. 56Hypocrites!
You know how to interpret the appearance of the earth and the sky.
How is it that you don't know how to interpret this present time?**

II. *Sure Signs in the Court (12:57-59)*

**57"Why don't you judge for yourselves what is right? 58As you are
going with your adversary to the magistrate, try hard to be reconciled
to him on the way, or he may drag you off to the judge, and the judge
turn you over to the officer, and the officer throw you into prison. 59I tell
you, you will not get out until you have paid the last penny.[a]"**

---

a 59 Greek *lepton*

Repent or Perish (Luke 13:1-9)

The Jews had a peculiar knack for finding some association between bad events and personal sin. They were of the opinion that nothing harmful ever happened to true followers of God (Job 4:7; John 9:1, 2). Unfortunately, this false notion, under various modifications, still exists today.

Jesus, on the other hand, rejects this overly simplistic explanation of cause and effect. While sin may be at the root of some of our troubles (John 5:14), it can never be said that adversity is always the byproduct of personal sin (2 Tim. 3:10-12; 1 Pet. 4:19).

I. *God Requires Repentance (13:1-5)*

13 Now there were some present at that time who told Jesus about
the Galileans whose blood Pilate had mixed with their sacrifices.
2Jesus answered, "Do you think that these Galileans were worse sinners
than all the other Galileans because they suffered this way? 3I tell you,
no! But unless you repent, you too will all perish. 4Or those eighteen who
died when the tower in Siloam fell on them—do you think they were
more guilty than all the others living in Jerusalem? 5I tell you, no! But
unless you repent, you too will all perish."

The precise context for this particular episode is missing. It would appear that at least some in Jesus' audience were becoming concerned that He was saying things that were too severe against them. So, in defense, they raised the matter of how certain Galileans were killed in the midst of their moments of worship. Surely, they reasoned, such tragedies demonstrated that the Galileans, and not themselves, were the ones who were deserving of such harsh words. Jesus, however, retorted by saying that each one who hears Him needs to repent, or else their final destinies will be no less devastating than the destinies of those whom they cited as being so evil.

There are several significant points to be made from this brief account: (1) We discover how easily people shift guilt and judgment to others, rather than making a personal application for themselves. (2) We discover that Jesus requires repentance of everyone—without any exceptions. God shows no favoritism toward anyone. (3) We discover the consequences of a self-justifying spirit—perishing in hell.

II. *God Requires Fruit (13:6-9)*

**6Then he told this parable: "A man had a fig tree, planted in his vine-
yard, and he went to look for fruit on it, but did not find any. 7So he said
to the man who took care of the vineyard, 'For three years now I've
been coming to look for fruit on this fig tree and haven't found any. Cut
it down! Why should it use up the soil?'**
**8" 'Sir,' the man replied, 'leave it alone for one more year, and I'll dig
around it and fertilize it. 9If it bears fruit next year, fine! If not, then cut
it down.' "**

If this parable teaches us anything about salvation, it is that you cannot profess one thing, live another thing and expect to escape judgment. God requires spiritual fruit (that is, obedience) from each of His children.

If this parable teaches us anything about grace, it is that God always provides ample opportunities for us to get our lives organized and lined up with His will.

If this parable teaches us anything about judgment, it is that there is no escape for those who fail to produce spiritual fruit. They will all be cut down and thrown into the fires of divine judgment (John 15:1-6).

Jesus Heals on the Sabbath (Luke 13:10-17)

Wherever you find Jesus, you also find plenty of excitement. In this particular story the excitement occurred during a synagogue service. In only a matter of moments the whole assembly was in an uproar. Some were angered; others were blessed. These consequences pretty much describe the usual mixed response Jesus received from His audiences.

I. *The Restoration of the Woman (13:10-13)*

**10On a Sabbath Jesus was teaching in one of the synagogues, 11and a
woman was there who had been crippled by a spirit for eighteen years.
She was bent over and could not straighten up at all. 12When Jesus saw
her, he called her forward and said to her, "Woman, you are set free
from your infirmity." 13Then he put his hands on her, and immediately
she straightened up and praised God.**

II. *The Rebuttal of the Synagogue Ruler (13:14)*

14Indignant because Jesus had healed on the Sabbath, the synagogue ruler said to the people, "There are six days for work. So come and be healed on those days, not on the Sabbath."

III. *The Response of Jesus and the People (13:15-17)*

**15The Lord answered him, "You hypocrites! Doesn't each of you on the
Sabbath untie his ox or donkey from the stall and lead it out to give it
water? 16Then should not this woman, a daughter of Abraham, whom
Satan has kept bound for eighteen long years, be set free on the
Sabbath day from what bound her?"**
**17When he said this, all his opponents were humiliated, but the people
were delighted with all the wonderful things he was doing.**

Let us learn something here about the compassion and power of Jesus. First, He spotted a crippled woman—Jesus always sees those who hurt. Second, He invited this afflicted woman to stand at His side—Jesus wants to be close to those who suffer. Third, He spoke words of faith to the woman—Jesus will never be the author of doubts or fears. Fourth, He touched her—Jesus, by the power of the Holy Spirit, will make her well. Fifth, He broke the strongly held traditions without so much as a single flinch—Jesus is governed by divine love, not legalistic, man-made laws.

Let us learn something here about the condition of this woman. First, we cannot mistake her genuine faith—she was a child of Abraham. Second, we cannot mistake her prolonged need—she was bound by Satan (a proof that Satan can afflict believers, although believers can resist this afflicting work of Satan). Third, we cannot mistake her obedient faith—she came forward for her healing.

Let us learn something here about the synagogue and its ruler. First, notice the disposition of this chief elder—he was angered by a healing miracle that should have caused him to be jubilant (a situation that is not altogether foreign to some of today's miracles). Second, notice the doctrine of this chief elder—he was more bound by the deadly traditions of his professed faith than the woman was bound by Satan (spiritual bondage is always worse than the bondage of physical afflictions). Third, notice the deficiency of the synagogue—for eighteen years this woman had (probably) attended these services, but she never received the miracle that was available to her.

Let us learn something here about the people. They rejoiced. How often the common people will follow Jesus, if they are only given the opportunity to know Him.

The Parables of the Mustard Seed and the Yeast (Luke 13:18-21)

(cf. Matt. 13:31-33 and Mark 4:30-32)

In the mind of the Jews, the Kingdom of God would appear suddenly and be in its final political form. In the mind of Jesus, however, the Kingdom would appear gradually and be spiritual in form.

Those who sought a release from the Romans were keenly disappointed in Jesus' words concerning the Kingdom. But those who sought a release from the consequences brought by sin were pleased indeed!

18Then Jesus asked, "What is the kingdom of God like? What shall I
compare it to? 19It is like a mustard seed, which a man took and planted
in his garden. It grew, became a tree, and the birds of the air perched in
its branches."
20Again he asked, "What shall I compare the kingdom of God to? 21It is
like yeast that a woman took and mixed into a large amount[a] of flour
until it worked all through the dough."

Few Will Be Saved (Luke 13:22-30)

As Jesus was preaching, "Repent or perish" (Luke 13:1-9), it crossed the mind of one of His listeners that if this is the condition for becoming saved, there must be few who will truly experience salvation. So, he voiced his concern. Jesus' response confirmed this man's assumption—indeed, only a small number will be qualified to enjoy the Kingdom of God.

I. *A Simple Question (13:22-23a)*

22Then Jesus went through the towns and villages, teaching as he
made his way to Jerusalem. 23Someone asked him, "Lord, are only a few
people going to be saved?"

a 21 Greek *three satas* (probably about ½ bushel or 22 liters)

Numerous Jews felt that they, and they alone, were going to be saved. The Gentiles, according to the Jewish way of thinking, were only fit to serve God as fuel for maintaining the fires of hell.

This nationalistic (or exclusive) approach to salvation is by no means foreign to our very day. There are groups, with millions of members, who contend that only a membership in their association will assure one of salvation. Certainly such narrow-minded thinkers need to hear Jesus' rebuke concerning this self-righteous kind of reasoning.

II. *A Shocking Answer (13:23b-30)*

**He said to them, 24"Make every effort to enter through the narrow
door, because many, I tell you, will try to enter and will not be able to.
25Once the owner of the house gets up and closes the door, you will stand
outside knocking and pleading, 'Sir, open the door for us.'**

"But he will answer, 'I don't know you or where you come from.'

**26"Then you will say, 'We ate and drank with you, and you taught in
our streets.'**

**27"But he will reply, 'I don't know you or where you come from. Away
from me, all you evildoers!'**

**28"There will be weeping there, and gnashing of teeth, when you see
Abraham, Isaac and Jacob and all the prophets in the kingdom of God,
but you yourselves thrown out. 29People will come from east and west
and north and south, and will take their places at the feast in the
kingdom of God. 30Indeed there are those who are last who will be first,
and first who will be last."**

Jesus' answer must have shocked those who proudly contended that they were saved because they were religious or because they were a part of some special group. Note these five penetrating statements.

First, Jesus taught that entrance into the Kingdom is not automatic for anyone, but instead it is something everyone must work to achieve. Only the diligent seeker has any hope of being saved. The casual inquirer and the lukewarm believer will be left outside to weep over their lack of diligence (Matt. 7:13, 14; Rev. 3:14-22).

Second, Jesus taught that many persons will want to be, and even try to be, saved but they will fall short. This is not a frightening statement to the eager Christian, for he possesses a resolute assurance of his salvation (John 3:16-21; Rom. 8:1-39; 1 John 5:13). However, it is a sober warning to anyone seeking to be saved on his own terms—with or without Christ (Rom. 10:1-3). Such persons are trying to enter into

God's Kingdom, but they are utilizing illegal methods of entry (John 10:1-10). They will not be saved.

Third, Jesus taught that someday the door to the Kingdom will be closed. The sealing of this door will certainly occur for many persons at the moment of Jesus' Second Coming. But it will also be closed to us personally upon the instant of our deaths, if we have not been saved prior to this final hour. There will be no further opportunities after we die (Luke 16:19-31).

Fourth, Jesus taught that many persons will be surprised to discover that they did not make it into the Kingdom. These persons will cry out about how they were so close to Him (physically), though Jesus will tell them how far they actually were from Him (spiritually).

Fifth, Jesus taught that many persons would be saved outside the body of Israel. In fact, He even declared that those who, to the natural eye, would be the last to enter the Kingdom will actually be the first to diligently enter it, while those who, to the natural eye, would be the first to enter the Kingdom will actually be the last ones to actively pursue it.

Jesus' Burden for Jerusalem (Luke 13:31-35)

(cf. Matt. 23:37-39)

It is an odd thing to imagine that anyone would desire to kill Jesus, the Son of God. But we must remember that in this world there are numerous sons and daughters of Satan who possess little interest in doing God's will (1 John 3:8-10, with Eph. 2:1-3). They are spiritually bankrupt. Such persons, when the circumstances are right, will not hesitate to express their resistance to Jesus as a personal Lord or Savior.

Jesus, on the other hand, came for the express purpose of rescuing each one of us from Satan's clasp. He was aware of the risks involved in such an operation, and He knew the consequences that awaited Him. Still, He willfully entered the shadow of death in order that we might have the opportunity to know God personally and to live with Him forever.

I. *Jesus' Rebuke for Herod (13:31-33)*

31At that time some Pharisees came to Jesus and said to him, "Leave this place and go somewhere else. Herod wants to kill you."
32He replied, "Go tell that fox, 'I will drive out demons and heal people

today and tomorrow, and on the third day I will reach my goal.' [33]In any case, I must keep going today and tomorrow and the next day—for surely no prophet can die outside Jerusalem!

Pharisees Came to Jesus. On the surface it would seem that the Pharisees here are expressing a concern for Jesus' safety. But this conclusion is far from convincing. In the first place, it would be the only evidence in the Gospels of such an interest on the part of the Pharisees. In the second place, the fact that Herod informed the Pharisees of his schemes sounds suspicious. In the third place, Jesus informed the Pharisees to tell the crafty fox, Herod, that his idle threats and schemes would not alter His plans in the slightest degree.

It appears to be more reasonable to conclude that both Herod and the Pharisees wanted Jesus to hurriedly finish His works in the regions of Galilee and Perea. Herod's conscience was getting the best of him; after killing John the Baptist, he feared that Jesus was actually John, resurrected from the dead (Luke 9:7-9). The Pharisees, on the other hand, felt helpless to hinder Jesus outside of their headquarters in Jerusalem; so, naturally, they sought to speed Him along on His journey to this capital city.

On the Third Day I Will Reach My Goal. Jesus refused to be intimidated by anyone. He would not change His schedule in order to accommodate the wishes of carnal men. Instead, He would fulfill God's will, day by day. How calm, yet resolute, was (and is) Jesus.

No Prophet Can Die Outside Jerusalem. Jerusalem, the place known as "the holy city" (Matt. 27:53), is also known as the city that killed God's prophets (Luke 13:34). What a contrast! In the city with the greatest privileges and potential resided the worst offenders of God's grace.

An abundance of revelation is no guarantee that those having access to it will take advantage of this opportunity. People may hear God's call countless times, but until they themselves repent and receive Jesus as Lord, they are as lost as (even more lost than—Matt. 11:20-24) those far less privileged.

II. *Jesus' Regrets for Jerusalem (13:34-35)*

[34]"O Jerusalem, Jerusalem, you who kill the prophets and stone those sent to you, how often I have longed to gather your children together, as a hen gathers her chicks under her wings, but you were not willing! [35]Look, your house is left to you desolate. I tell you, you will not see me again until you say, 'Blessed is he who comes in the name of the Lord.'[a] "

---

[a] *35* Psalm 118:26

How Often I Longed. . . But. Jesus was neither unwilling nor unable to transform all of Israel, and Jerusalem in particular. The snag rested solely with the stubborn wills of numerous Jews. They refused to submit to His authority, and as a direct result they would bring upon themselves a horrible calamity.

Your House Is Left Desolate. Sin will always produce negative consequences. The graver the rebellion, the greater the judgment. Repeatedly Israel resisted God's voices. Unflinchingly Israel rejected God's miraculous signs. Sadistically they killed God's messengers. Now, the end of God's patience was at hand. The apostasy could continue no longer without a divine reprisal. God would send in Roman troops to level the land and to kill thousands of its self-righteous citizens.

The day of God's special dealings with Israel was coming to a rapid close. After the Day of Pentecost the Jews were offered one final chance to receive God's gracious offer of salvation, but again they stubbornly refused to accept it. By approximately A.D. 40 God's spotlight of attention had shifted to the Gentile people (Acts 13:46; Rom. 9-11). By the fall of A.D. 70 Jerusalem was in utter ruins (see Luke 21 for details).

Blessed Is He Who Comes. For the present hour (or dispensation) it is the Gentile who calls Jesus the Blessed One. The focal point of God's redemptive dealings now rests upon these non-Jewish people (Acts 13:46; Rom. 9-11). In the future, however, the Jews will turn to the Son of God, Jesus, and will confess Him as their personal Savior and Lord. They have not fallen away forever. At the moment of Jesus' return, the Holy Spirit will renew His convicting and converting works with them (Zech. 12:10-13:1; Rom. 11:25-32). And these labors will culminate in the salvation of many Jews.

Jesus Dines at a Pharisee's Home (Luke 14:1-24)

In this somewhat lengthy section on Jesus' dining with a prominent Pharisee, we discover that He took full advantage of each opportunity to teach important spiritual truths to them. Jesus never had anything good to say about the Pharisees. Still, this never caused Him to snub them with a retaliating or sarcastic spirit. Rather, He welcomed each opening to witness, and He entered into these situations with the disposition of a humble, yet uncompromising, moral instructor.

In the scene before us Jesus keenly observes four opportunities where He can instruct those present about God's moral (or righteous) standards. Naturally, Jesus' observations are as practical and penetrating in our own day as they were then.

I. *The Problem of the Man with Dropsy (14:1-6)*

14 One Sabbath, when Jesus went to eat in the house of a prominent Pharisee, he was being carefully watched. [2]There in front of him was a man suffering from dropsy. [3]Jesus asked the Pharisees and experts in the law, "Is it lawful to heal on the Sabbath or not?" [4]But they remained silent. So taking hold of the man, he healed him and sent him away.

[5]Then he asked them, "If one of you has a son[a] or an ox that falls into a well on the Sabbath day, will you not immediately pull him out?" [6]And they had nothing to say.

First, observe the day of the week. It was the Sabbath. On this day, more than any other, the Jews gave special attention to God. For some, especially for the Pharisees, this was a day full of restrictions. All work on this day was to be suspended.

Second, observe the place where Jesus ate. It was in the home of a highly esteemed Pharisee. Without a doubt the motives for Jesus being invited to this residence are in question, for from the moment He entered the premises He was carefully watched.

Third, observe the man with dropsy. He seemed to be so out of place in this formal setting (vv. 12-14). It is proper to assume that this person was deliberately selected to be there—in front of Jesus—just for the purpose of seeing whether or not Jesus would break the Sabbath law (the Pharisees considered healing someone on the Sabbath to be a violation of the commandment to rest on this day).

Fourth, observe Jesus' response. He healed the man; then He disgraced the guests for their theological inconsistency. The Pharisees felt it was permissible to help a son or an ox on the Sabbath, but for some reason it was wrong to help an ill person on this day. Clearly this was a glaring error in both judgment and love. Jesus would not permit such a distorted interpretation of the Sabbath to go unchecked.

No single person or group of persons is beyond correction. While it is not the Christian's duty to walk about with a judgmental attitude (Matt. 7:1ff.), neither is it proper for him to ignore evil practices (especially among believers—Matt. 18:15-18; Luke 17:3; Gal. 6:1; 2 Thess. 3:6-14 and so forth). Christians have the responsibility to expose wrongs and to work to remedy acts of carnality (Matt. 5:13-16; Eph. 5:11ff.).

II. *The Parable of Selecting a Seat (14:7-11)*

[7]When he noticed how the guests picked the places of honor at the table, he told them this parable: [8]"When someone invites you to a wedding feast, do not take the place of honor, for a person more distinguished than you may have been invited. [9]If so, the host who invited both of you

---

a 5 Some manuscripts *donkey*

will come and say to you, 'Give this man your seat.' Then, humiliated,
you will have to take the least important place. [10]But when you are
invited, take the lowest place, so that when your host comes, he will say
to you, 'Friend, move up to a better place.' Then you will be honored in
the presence of all your fellow guests. [11]For everyone who exalts
himself will be humbled, and he who humbles himself will be exalted."

The guests who were invited to this distinguished Pharisee's home apparently thought of themselves as being significant, too. And, according to the custom of the day, the more significance you had, the closer you were to be seated to the host (particularly on his right side). Since no one was assigned to particular seats, each guest was left to decide for himself where he ought to sit. As might be expected, there was a rush for the more prominent seats of honor.

Jesus, the man with a word for every occasion, could not permit this situation to go without a comment. So, He told them a parable that possessed this punch line: those who flock to the front for attention will be placed in the back, while those who humbly remain in the back will be brought to the front.

We do not need to elevate ourselves. At the proper place, and in the proper time, God will see to our promotions. It is pride, envy and greed that crave attention. Persons with these character traits cannot be counted among those to whom God will bestow His honor.

III. *The Picture of a Rewarding Dinner (14:12-14)*

[12]Then Jesus said to his host, "When you give a luncheon or dinner, do
not invite your friends, your brothers or relatives, or your rich
neighbors; if you do, they may invite you back and so you will be repaid.
[13]But when you give a banquet, invite the poor, the crippled, the lame,
the blind, [14]and you will be blessed. Although they cannot repay you,
you will be repaid at the resurrection of the righteous."

Just as the guests at this meal sought to be honored by seating themselves in the more notable settings, so it would appear that the host himself served the meal with less than pure motives. Sometimes we invite special people to join us at a meal because we want to show off something or because we want to generate some self-elevating effect. Such seems to be the case here.

This host gave generously to his guests, but he knew this gesture would be returned in like measure. In the end, each member of the party would have received and given an equal share. This type of giving is really not giving at all. Instead, it is merely exchanging the same for the same.

Jesus encourages the host (and us, too) to give a meal to those who cannot return the same favor. This act of kindness would display the maximum in hosting skills; plus, it would yield the highest returns, for God himself will reward this kind of hosting (this reward will be bestowed at the resurrection of the righteous, which is at the time of the second coming of Jesus Christ).

IV. *The Parable of a Great Banquet (14:15-24)*

15When one of those at the table with him heard this, he said to Jesus, "Blessed is the man who will eat at the feast in the kingdom of God."

16Jesus replied: "A certain man was preparing a great banquet and invited many guests. 17At the time of the banquet he sent his servant to tell those who had been invited, 'Come, for everything is now ready.'

18"But they all alike began to make excuses. The first said, 'I have just bought a field, and I must go and see it. Please excuse me.'

19"Another said, 'I have just bought five yoke of oxen, and I'm on my way to try them out. Please excuse me.'

20"Still another said, 'I just got married, so I can't come.'

21"The servant came back and reported this to his master. Then the owner of the house became angry and ordered his servant, 'Go out quickly into the streets and alleys of the town and bring in the poor, the crippled, the blind and the lame.'

22" 'Sir,' the servant said, 'what you ordered has been done, but there is still room.'

23"Then the master told his servant, 'Go out to the roads and country lanes and make them come in, so that my house will be full. 24I tell you, not one of those men who were invited will get a taste of my banquet.' "

Often Jesus would color a strong rebuke with a subtle story, but He would never cover up His penetrating point in the process. Here Jesus leveled a serious charge against the Jews (and probably the Pharisees in particular). They oftentimes had received God's invitation to join Him at His great banquet, when the righteous would be resurrected (Rev. 19:1ff.). But again and again they refused to take up His offer, which is here proven in their critical attitudes toward Jesus, God's Son. As a result, God would extend this invitation to others, to those who seemed the least fit for such an honor (Matt. 21:42-44; 22:1-14).

The Cost of Discipleship (Luke 14:25-35)

If someone thinks there are no costs associated with being a disciple of Christ, that person needs to read these verses. Jesus states that the most costly thing a person can do is become one of His disciples. Therefore, no one should entertain the prospects of discipleship unadvisedly.

I. *The Domestic Cost of Discipleship (14:25, 26)*

25Large crowds were traveling with Jesus, and turning to them he
said: 26"If anyone comes to me and does not hate his father and mother, his wife and children, his brothers and sisters—yes, even his own life—he cannot be my disciple.

The first toll for becoming a disciple of Jesus will be paid at home. No one can follow the orders of Jesus and also heed nonspiritual voices at home. We must choose whom we will honor—Christ or family. See other comments at Matt. 10:34-37.

II. *The Personal Cost of Discipleship (14:27)*

27And anyone who does not carry his cross and follow me cannot be my
disciple.

The cross was not merely a symbol in Jesus' day—it was a horrible reality. Anyone found carrying a cross was carrying the instrument with which he would be put to death. In like manner, anyone who wishes to follow Jesus must be prepared to surrender his life for the sake of the gospel message. See Matt. 10:38 and Luke 9:23, 24 for other remarks.

III. *Counting the Cost of Discipleship Beforehand (14:28-33)*

28"Suppose one of you wants to build a tower. Will he not first sit down
and estimate the cost to see if he has enough money to complete it? 29For
if he lays the foundation and is not able to finish it, everyone who sees it
will ridicule him, 30saying, 'This fellow began to build and was not able
to finish.'
31"Or suppose a king is about to go to war against another king. Will

he not first sit down and consider whether he is able with ten thousand men to oppose the one coming against him with twenty thousand? [32]If he is not able, he will send a delegation while the other is still a long way off and will ask for terms of peace. [33]In the same way, any of you who does not give up everything he has cannot be my disciple.

Here are two illustrations depicting the necessity to plan ahead and to make a knowledgeable decision based upon the facts. Should a builder or a king fail to count the costs before he undertakes a certain project, then everyone will make fun of him for his poor foresight.

Likewise, prospective disciples need to understand, from start to finish, that Jesus requires our total lives. This fact does not imply that Christians are merely puppets in Christ's hand. Rather, by surrendering our wills to Christ, He is enabled to use us for His glory, and He is further capable of blessing us by working all things together for our own good (Rom. 8:28). There is no other relationship possible on this earth that can yield such positive fruits as can the one where Christ and His disciples are mutually committed one to another.

IV. *The Consequences of Not Counting the Cost (14:34, 35)*

[34]"Salt is good, but if it loses its saltiness, how can it be made salty again? [35]It is fit neither for the soil nor for the manure pile; it is thrown out.

"He who has ears to hear, let him hear."

Salt is only good as long as it retains its saltiness. If this is ever lost, the salt becomes useless. The same truth fits every disciple of Jesus. When Christians count the cost and pay the price for following Jesus, their saltiness (or effectiveness) remains intact, but if they fail to count the cost or pay the price of obedience to God's will, they become useless in accomplishing His plans. See Matt. 5:13 for other notes.

The Parable of the Lost Sheep (Luke 15:1-7)

This parable finds a warm reception in everyone's heart. The compassion and intimacy with which our Lord fulfilled His mission are so vividly displayed in this story that we are moved by its tenderness. Somehow, each one of us senses it is us whom the Lord came to find. And we are left with a feeling of sheer gratitude for His personal interest in us.

I. *The Problem (15:1, 2)*

15 Now the tax collectors and "sinners" were all gathering around to hear him. [2]But the Pharisees and the teachers of the law muttered, "This man welcomes sinners and eats with them."

Those persons who were neglected by the Jewish society were never neglected by Jesus. His interest in people would exclude no one—the good or the bad, the educated or the ignorant, the rich or the poor, the healthy or the sick. Jesus had a place in His heart for everyone.

It was this open-armed approach of Jesus that got Him in trouble with the folded-armed religious leaders. While Jesus was eager to embrace others, these persons were content to embrace only themselves.

II. *The Parable (15:3-7)*

[3]Then Jesus told them this parable: [4]"Suppose one of you has a hundred sheep and loses one of them. Does he not leave the ninety-nine in the open country and go after the lost sheep until he finds it? [5]And when he finds it, he joyfully puts it on his shoulders [6]and goes home. Then he calls his friends and neighbors together and says, 'Rejoice with me; I have found my lost sheep.' [7]I tell you that in the same way there is more rejoicing in heaven over one sinner who repents than over ninety-nine righteous persons who do not need to repent.

This is the first in a chain of three "lost" parables. First, there is the lost sheep (vv. 3-7); second, there is the lost coin (vv. 8-10); and third, there is the lost son (vv. 11-32).

Interestingly, in each succeeding parable the value of the lost object is increased. This orderliness is certainly deliberate. Jesus' aim was to show His critical spectators how they themselves rejoiced over the recovery of ordinary objects (like sheep and coins). How much more ought they to rejoice over the recovery of a lost person. In other words, if humans rejoice when they find their lost objects or children, and if heaven rejoices over the repentance of spiritually lost sinners, then these so-called religious leaders ought to rejoice too at the fruit Jesus was gaining among the tax collectors and sinners.

Another interesting, though somewhat subtle, point in this parable can be found in its conclusion. Jesus stated that heaven (probably a reference to God, Jesus, the angels and the redeemed in heaven) rejoices over the sinner who repents, but not over the ninety-nine (self-) righteous persons (like the Pharisees and other teachers) who do not need to repent (that is, in their own opinion—Matt. 3:7ff.; 9:10-13).

The word "more" (in v. 7) is not in the original Greek text. Its presence tends to obscure the intended meaning of Jesus' words. Further, also in verse 7, it would be a better translation to supply the word "rather" before the word "than," and thereby convey the real punch in Jesus' parable. (Thus the verse would read, ". . . there is rejoicing in heaven over one sinner who repents, rather than over ninety-nine righteous persons who do not need to repent.")

The Parable of the Lost Coin (Luke 15:8-10)

This parable, like the one preceding it and the one following it, tells about the earnest search for a significant lost object, and the joy that is expressed and felt upon finding it. In like fashion, the angels in heaven are jubilant over the recovery of each formerly lost sinner.

> **8"Or suppose a woman has ten silver coins[a] and loses one. Does she not**
> **light a lamp, sweep the house and search carefully until she finds it?**
> **9And when she finds it, she calls her friends and neighbors together and**
> **says, 'Rejoice with me; I have found my lost coin.' 10In the same way, I**
> **tell you, there is rejoicing in the presence of the angels of God over one**
> **sinner who repents."**

There are some historical insights that can provide considerable vividness and drama to this scene. First, a silver coin represented a day's wages. To lose such a valuable possession must have made the woman feel most tense and anxious, especially since most Jews needed every available coin. Second, if the woman inadvertently dropped the coin on the floor of her home, it could be a difficult task to discover it. Floors were made of dirt, sometimes covered with either tiles or dried reeds. To further complicate the situation, her home might only have one door and one small window to let in the light to aid her in her search. Third, the chief identifying mark that distinguished the married women in Israel was a headdress made of ten silver coins. This adornment (a part of which may be referred to here) would have had the same effect as losing a woman's wedding ring today. The loss of such an object certainly would have produced much heartache.

What a joy, then, must have been felt in spotting the lost coin! And, in like manner, what a joy there is in heaven when the angels spot a sinner turning to God!

---

a 8 Greek *ten drachmas*, each worth about a day's wages

The Parable of the Lost Son (Luke 15:11-32)

This is the third, and final member, in the "lost" parable series. In the first parable, one out of one hundred sheep was lost (vv. 1-7); in the second parable, one out of ten coins was lost (vv. 8-10); now, we read about the loss of one of two sons.

Also in each of these parables is the joyful recovery of what was lost (the sheep, the coin and the son). And, finally—stated in the first two parables and assumed in the third—Jesus paralleled the delight that accompanies these discoveries with the happiness that is created in heaven when an erring person turns from his sins to serve God. It is as if a person who wandered away from heaven has returned home!

I. *The Division of the Property (15:11, 12)*

> **11Jesus continued: "There was a man who had two sons. 12The younger one said to his father, 'Father, give me my share of the estate.' So he divided his property between them.**

The Jews practiced two customs with regard to settling estates in this period. The first option, and the more common option of the two, was to divide the property of the father through a written will. Once the father died, the possessions would be separated according to the terms of the will, the firstborn son would receive twice as much as any of the other sons (Deut. 21:15-17). The second option was actually to transfer the possessions of the father to the children prior to his death. It was this latter alternative that the younger son in this parable insisted upon and received.

II. *The Destitution of the Lost Son (15:13-16)*

> **13"Not long after that, the younger son got together all he had, set off for a distant country and there squandered his wealth in wild living. 14After he had spent everything, there was a severe famine in that whole country, and he began to be in need. 15So he went and hired himself out to a citizen of that country, who sent him to his fields to feed pigs. 16He longed to fill his stomach with the pods that the pigs were eating, but no one gave him anything.**

Sometimes people, especially some younger people, have to learn about the facts of life the hard way. They are headstrong and unteachable. They believe they are smarter than their parents, but they can convince only themselves of this notion. Here is a case in point.

When words avail nothing in communicating with our children, then experience must become their teacher. Despite the heartache of the situation, a wise and loving parent must be willing to permit his child to learn the lessons of life on his own. (It seems only right to assume that this son had passed the age of accountability, and therefore, was legally permitted to make this self-managed journey.)

The son decided that the farther he could get away from home, the better; so, he traveled to a "distant" land. Once there (like so many other persons have dreamed), he did whatever he wanted to do. He was free to do as he pleased. And, as is practically always the case, the free-living son soon discovered that his fantasies were not everything he had envisioned them to be. Actually, in a short span of time he became destitute, even to the point of hiring himself out to feed unclean swine (Lev. 11:7).

III. *The Decision of the Lost Son (15:17-19)*

17"When he came to his senses, he said, 'How many of my father's hired men have food to spare, and here I am starving to death! 18I will set out and go back to my father and say to him: Father, I have sinned against heaven and against you. 19I am no longer worthy to be called your son; make me like one of your hired men.'

When seeds fall on hardened soil, there will be no harvest, because the seeds cannot grow in this environment. But when the soil is broken, the seeds can enter their earthen nest and bring forth an abundant crop. The same principles may be applied to a person's heart and mind. Whenever someone is unteachable, God's words will produce no profitable results in his life; but whenever someone opens up to God's will, then His words will yield their intended results.

IV. *The Delight of the Father (15:20-24)*

20So he got up and went to his father.

"But while he was still a long way off, his father saw him and was filled with compassion for him; he ran to his son, threw his arms around him and kissed him.

21"The son said to him, 'Father, I have sinned against heaven and against you. I am no longer worthy to be called your son.[a]'

22"But the father said to his servants, 'Quick! Bring the best robe and put it on him. Put a ring on his finger and sandals on his feet. 23Bring the fattened calf and kill it. Let's have a feast and celebrate. 24For this son of mine was dead and is alive again; he was lost and is found.' So they began to celebrate.

---

a 21 Some early manuscripts *son. Make me like one of your hired men.*

Notice that eight things are said about this father, who represents God in this parable: (1) The father saw his son even when he was still a great distance away—God's loving eyes never leave us. (2) The father was filled with compassion as he saw his son returning home—it is God's love, and not His wrath, that greets us as we turn to Him. (3) The father ran to his son and greeted him with a deeply emotional affection—God will always come to us with a joyful spirit, if we will but turn to Him. (4) The father treated his son as though he were completely ignorant of his son's folly—God utterly forgives us when we confess our sins to Him. (5) The father put his best robe on his son, as a symbol of his restored honor—God, too, gives worth and dignity to each one who comes to Him. (6) The father put a ring on his son's finger, as a symbol of his restored authority—God grants all spiritual authority to each of His repentant children. (7) The father put shoes on his feet, as a symbol of sonship (only the slaves went barefooted)—God makes us more than servants when we come to Him; He also makes us His very own children. (8) The father celebrated the occasion with a special feast—God, too, and all of heaven with Him, celebrate our conversion (Luke 15:7, 10)!

V. *The Disgust of the Other Son (15:25-32)*

25"Meanwhile, the older son was in the field. When he came near the
house, he heard music and dancing. 26So he called one of the servants
and asked him what was going on. 27'Your brother has come,' he
replied, 'and your father has killed the fattened calf because he has him
back safe and sound.'

28"The older brother became angry and refused to go in. So his father
went out and pleaded with him. 29But he answered his father, 'Look! All
these years I've been slaving for you and never disobeyed your orders.
Yet you never gave me even a young goat so I could celebrate with my
friends. 30But when this son of yours who has squandered your property
with prostitutes comes home, you kill the fattened calf for him!'

31" 'My son,' the father said, 'you are always with me, and everything
I have is yours. 32But we had to celebrate and be glad, because this
brother of yours was dead and is alive again; he was lost and is found.' "

Spiritual victories are not equally enjoyed by everyone. What may delight one person may irritate another. Naturally, those persons who are not truly interested in the well-being of others will not rejoice over their repentance.

Jesus makes it clear that the critical Pharisees (and other like-minded religious officials) were identical to this older brother. They were like him because they refused to rejoice in the repentance of tax collectors and sinners (Luke 15:1, 2).

The Parable of the Dishonest Manager (Luke 16:1-15)

Upon a first or second reading, this parable sounds altogether unlike anything Jesus might have said. But, as we shall see, Jesus used His words in the most clever way to communicate some stinging truths.

I. *The Parable Is Delivered (16:1-8a)*

16 Jesus told his disciples: "There was a rich man whose manager
was accused of wasting his possessions. [2]So he called him in and
asked him, 'What is this I hear about you? Give an account of your management, because you cannot be manager any longer.'
[3]"The manager said to himself, 'What shall I do now? My master is taking away my job. I'm not strong enough to dig, and I'm ashamed to
beg— [4]I know what I'll do so that, when I lose my job here, people will welcome me into their houses.'
[5]"So he called in each one of his master's debtors. He asked the first, 'How much do you owe my master?'
[6]" 'Eight hundred gallons[a] of olive oil,' he replied.
"The manager told him, 'Take your bill, sit down quickly, and make it four hundred.'
[7]"Then he asked the second, 'And how much do you owe?'
" 'A thousand bushels[b] of wheat,' he replied.
"He told him, 'Take your bill and make it eight hundred.'
[8]"The master commended the dishonest manager because he had acted shrewdly.

In Palestine it was not uncommon for a master (or landlord) to rent out his property to a number of tenants, and then to hire a manager to oversee the affairs of his farm. Among other things, it was the manager's responsibility to keep accurate records of all the transactions between the tenants and the owner.

In this particular parable we discover that the manager of the property was guilty of shortchanging the master of his just income. For this action the manager was called to give an accounting of his dealings. Further, he was relieved of his responsibilities. But before he departed, he was quick to further juggle the books in an attempt to assure his own future security.

---

a 6 Greek *one hundred batous* (probably about 3 kiloliters) *b 7* Greek *one hundred korous* (probably about 35 kiloliters)

The manager reasoned that by reducing the actual bills of the owner's creditors he could accomplish two feats: (1) He could gain their financial favor once he was publicly removed from his position, and (2) he could, if necessary, use the falsified billings as a type of blackmail in order to keep his financial security a firm reality. In short, the manager was quite shrewd in protecting his own interests.

II. *The Parable Is Explained to the Disciples (16:8b-13)*

For the people of this world are more shrewd in dealing with their own kind than are the people of the light. [9]I tell you, use worldly wealth to gain friends for yourselves, so that when it is gone, you will be welcomed into eternal dwellings.

[10]"Whoever can be trusted with very little can also be trusted with much, and whoever is dishonest with very little will also be dishonest with much. [11]So if you have not been trustworthy in handling worldly wealth, who will trust you with true riches? [12]And if you have not been trustworthy with someone else's property, who will give you property of your own?

[13]"No servant can serve two masters. Either he will hate the one and love the other, or he will be devoted to the one and despise the other. You cannot serve both God and Money."

There are four points that Jesus derived from this parable that can profit His disciples (which, in this case, probably refers to the larger circle of learners who listened to Him teach).

First, He remarked how much more clever the people of the world are in accomplishing their self-centered ambitions than are the people of the light (Christians) in accomplishing their spiritual goals (v. 8b). In other words, if Jesus' disciples would be as resourceful and creative in their works as the world is in their works, they would experience much more success.

Second, Jesus advised His followers to use their money to win new converts, so they would be warmly welcomed into God's eternal home (even as the shrewd manager used his resources to gain friends and be welcomed into their homes—v. 9).

Third, Jesus stated that the true test of our character is revealed in how we manage the little duties given to us (vv. 10-12). If a person is faithful in small things, he will be equally faithful in larger things. Naturally, the opposite is also just as true. If a person is unfaithful in small things, he will be equally unfair in bigger things.

Fourth, Jesus makes it plain that no one can be truly faithful to both God and Money (v. 13). In the mind of Jesus, a servant can only possess one devotion, and in order for that devotion to be true, it must be full time (twenty-four hours per day, seven days per week). No one can be a part-time Christian. It is either a total surrender of the whole life, or it is no surrender at all (also see comments at Matt. 6:19-34).

III. *The Parable Is Explained to the Pharisees (16:14, 15)*

[14]The Pharisees, who loved money, heard all this and were sneering at Jesus. [15]He said to them, "You are the ones who justify yourselves in the eyes of men, but God knows your hearts. What is highly valued among men is detestable in God's sight.

God's measurement of things and peoples' measurement of things do not always coincide. This was especially true among the Pharisees. They did not serve God; they served money. While their exterior lives revealed a supposed devotion to God, their inner hearts revealed a love for riches. The things these persons highly valued God hated because of their temporal and selfish features.

Kingdom and Divorce Principles (Luke 16:16-18)

(cf. Matt. 5:18, 32; 11:11-15; 19:1-12)

Jesus discussions on the Kingdom and on divorce have been discussed at length earlier. See the above references for pertinent comments.

I. *The Kingdom (16:16, 17)*

[16]"The Law and the Prophets were proclaimed until John. Since that time, the good news of the kingdom of God is being preached, and everyone is forcing his way into it. [17]It is easier for heaven and earth to disappear than for the least stroke of a pen to drop out of the Law.

II. *Divorce (16:18)*

[18]"Anyone who divorces his wife and marries another woman commits adultery, and the man who marries a divorced woman commits adultery.

The Rich Man and Lazarus (Luke 16:19-31)

It has been suggested by some writers that this story is not a parabolic teaching but a real case history of what happened to two literal persons. Other scholars contend that this story, like the preceding four stories (15:1-16:8a), is definitely a parable. Regardless of the actual classification of this episode, the realities of the story are equally true in either case. Here is a clear picture of the inequities that exist in our present society, and the ultimate justice that will be rendered upon our deaths.

I. *The Rich Man and Lazarus Before Death (16:19-21)*

19"There was a rich man who was dressed in purple and fine linen and
lived in luxury every day. 20At his gate was laid a beggar named
Lazarus, covered with sores 21and longing to eat what fell from the rich
man's table. Even the dogs came and licked his sores.

Here are two sharply contrasting pictures of how some people live. The first person was covered with fine linen (made from a rare species of flax) and expensive purple robes. Further, he enjoyed the benefits of his wealth on a daily basis. There was nothing he wanted that he did not already possess. The second person was covered with welts and sores. Further, he suffered from the lowest level of poverty. He did not possess the things he needed.

II. *The Rich Man and Lazarus After Death (16:22-31)*

22"The time came when the beggar died and the angels carried him
to Abraham's side. The rich man also died and was buried. 23In hell,[a]
where he was in torment, he looked up and saw Abraham far away,
with Lazarus by his side. 24So he called to him, 'Father Abraham, have
pity on me and send Lazarus to dip the tip of his finger in water and cool
my tongue, because I am in agony in this fire.'
25"But Abraham replied, 'Son, remember that in your lifetime you
received your good things, while Lazarus received bad things, but now
he is comforted here and you are in agony. 26And besides all this,
between us and you a great chasm has been fixed, so that those who
want to go from here to you cannot, nor can anyone cross over from
there to us.'

a 23 Greek *Hades*

27"He answered, 'Then I beg you, father, send Lazarus to my father's house, 28for I have five brothers. Let him warn them, so that they will not also come to this place of torment.'

29"Abraham replied, 'They have Moses and the Prophets; let them listen to them.'

30" 'No, father Abraham,' he said, 'but if someone from the dead goes to them, they will repent.'

31"He said to him, 'If they do not listen to Moses and the Prophets, they will not be convinced even if someone rises from the dead.' "

Here are two sharply contrasting pictures of how some people die. The one man went to Abraham's side, while the other went to hell (literally, hades—see Matt. 25:31-46 for a special study on the doctrine of "Hell").

There are three images presented here that depict the state of those who die as believers: (1) The believer is carried by the angels, at the precise moment of death, into a place of conscious existence. Death is not the end of life, but the start of a new life in another world. (2) The believer is comforted in his new life. The environment and persons surrounding the believer in this new life make it a perfect paradise. (3) The believer is permanently separated from the nonbeliever. His destiny of bliss is forever sealed. (For notes on "Abraham's side" see Matt. 25:31-46.)

We see here that earthly appearances do not always carry over into eternal destinies. The man who held no riches in his hand before his death now holds incalculable riches, while the man who selfishly possessed untold wealth in his hand before his death now possesses inexpressible poverty.

Interestingly, the name of the poor man is "Lazarus." This name means "God is my help." While the reality of this name may have escaped people's notice when he lived on earth, the substance of its reality could be denied by no one after his death. We must not evaluate persons by their possessions or positions in life, but by their disposition towards God and Christ.

There are four other images presented here, depicting the state of those who die as nonbelievers: (1) The nonbeliever, at the precise moment of his death, is taken to hades, a place of conscious existence and torment. (2) The nonbeliever can remember his past life of self-centeredness. (3) The nonbeliever is assigned a place of torment from which he cannot ever escape. (4) The nonbeliever possesses a burden for those who, like himself, are spiritually lost. There is a burden in hades to see families and friends (still alive on the earth) saved in order to escape the anguish that will ultimately accompany all foolish and nonrepentant living.

Finally, Abraham told the rich man how ineffective miracles are to convert the lost person if he will not believe God's Word in the first place. God has supplied everything that is necessary to keep people out of hades and hell. But if they reject what is available to them, surely the addition of more evidence will secure no other results. (The truth of this statement needs to penetrate those sign-centered ministries that always insist upon outward manifestations or miracles from God.)

Special Study: Parables—How to Understand Them

A parable is a story, and its message is designed to teach some practical truth. Some people call parables earthly stories with heavenly meanings. In brief, parables are stories from everyday life that hold a message of eternal significance. Jesus, more than anyone else, utilized the parabolic method of teaching (see the chart on page 154 for a listing of His parables).

Whenever you read a parable, the three following points ought to be kept in clear focus.

1. *Generally, there is but one main point in each parable.* Look for the central lesson. Seek to know the primary purpose that lies behind the story. Some interpreters have strained to find a revelation in every single object or movement of every parable, but this exercise is both unnecessary and misleading. Don't overwork the parable's message. Look for the obvious truths, and not for so-called deep or mystical meanings.

2. *Look for the interpretation from the one who tells the parable.* Some of the parables are explained for us (for instance, see Matt. 13:1-23). In these cases it is virtually impossible to miss the intended point of the parable. If, however, the storyteller does not supply a commentary on his parable, then read the verses before and after the parable, or the whole chapter. This broader context will provide the light needed in order to properly interpret the parable's central thrust.

3. *Be certain that the conclusions you draw from each parable are in harmony with the clearly stated (nonparabolic) teachings of Scripture.* This should be an obvious rule, but sometimes it is not followed. When any interpreter of a parable strains to find more in the story than is actually intended, then there is always the danger that he will contradict some established truth of the Bible. For instance, some persons have concluded from the parable of the rich fool (Luke 12:16-21) that it is sinful to be rich, or even to own anything that belongs to this world. Such a conclusion, however, violates other clear statements from the Scriptures, and it ought to be rejected as an erroneous interpretation (1 Tim. 6:10, 17-19). The best interpreter of the Scriptures are the Scriptures themselves. The message of a parable will not contradict other Scriptures. The Bible does not contradict itself.

Four Important Lessons (Luke 17:1-10)

(cf. Matt. 17:20; 18:6, 7, 21, 22; 21:21)

The setting for these words is uncertain. Whether they were spoken by Jesus immediately after the parable of the rich man and Lazarus (16:19-31), or whether they occurred at another period (or at several other periods) is unimportant. What counts is this: Jesus wants His disciples to get a firm hold on the important lessons involving these four matters—sin, forgiveness, faith and duty.

I. *Sin (17:1-3a)*

17 Jesus said to his disciples: "Things that cause people to sin are bound to come, but woe to that person through whom they come.
[2]It would be better for him to be thrown into the sea with a millstone tied around his neck than for him to cause one of these little ones to sin. [3]So watch yourselves.

No one can separate himself from every temptation that is present in this world. We will all be tempted, but how serious an offense it is to be the source responsible for even one of these temptations. It is bad enough to sin, but to lead others into sin is doubly bad. Such persons will receive a far more serious judgment from God. See Matt. 18:6, 7 for further comments.

II. *Forgiveness (17:3b, 4)*

"If your brother sins, rebuke him, and if he repents, forgive him. [4]If he sins against you seven times in a day, and seven times comes back to you and says, 'I repent,' forgive him."

There are two important lessons here that must not be missed. The first matter involves the issue of rebuking (or reprimanding) your Christian brother or sister when he or she sins. While it is not our task to be self-appointed critics, neither are we to ignore the unrepentant sins that are committed by fellow believers. According to this verse, which states our duty in the most clear terms, we are responsible to bring correction whenever someone is caught up in sin (Matt. 18:15-18; 1 Cor. 5; Gal. 6:1; 2 Thess. 3:6-15; and so forth).

The second matter involves the issue of forgiveness. Before we are quick to forgive everyone of all their sins, let us remind ourselves of the fact that in order for forgiveness to be extended, there must first be some evidence of repentance. This verse plainly states, through the use of two "if" clauses, that forgiveness is conditioned by an action of repentance. If there is no turning away from sin, then there can be no forgiveness offered.

Those who teach an unqualified forgiveness commit a grave injustice to God's righteous judgments. Certainly God does not forgive us apart from our repentance; neither, then, can we forgive others without this same seal. Otherwise, we will find ourselves forgiving people of sins that God himself has not forgiven (and we are not at liberty to extend a grace that God does not first extend).

Certainly, if there is even a trace of repentance, we are to be quick to forgive. And this forgiving attitude is not to know any limitations of the number of times it can be offered. See Matt. 6:14, 15 and 18:15-20 for other comments.

III. *Faith (17:5, 6)*

5The apostles said to the Lord, "Increase our faith!"
6He replied, "If you have faith as small as a mustard seed, you can say to this mulberry tree, 'Be uprooted and planted in the sea,' and it will obey you.

For comments on these words see Matt. 17:20; 21:21 and Mark 11:22-24.

IV. *Duty (17:7-10)*

7"Suppose one of you had a servant plowing or looking after the sheep.
Would he say to the servant when he comes in from the field, 'Come
along now and sit down to eat'? 8Would he not rather say, 'Prepare my
supper, get yourself ready and wait on me while I eat and drink; after
that you may eat and drink'? 9Would he thank the servant because he
did what he was told to do? 10So you also, when you have done
everything you were told to do, should say, 'We are unworthy servants;
we have only done our duty.' "

No one can look at his works and demand a reward from God. Our very best works represent only our duty to God, the loving Master of our lives. When we labor simply for what we hope to receive in return for our services, we labor in vain. At best we are unworthy of God's grace, though we know that He will be generous with everyone who has been faithful in serving Him (Matt. 5:12; 10:41, 42; Luke 6:35; 1 Cor. 3:10-15; 1 Tim. 5:18; Rev. 22:12).

Jesus Heals Ten Lepers (Luke 17:11-19)

When Jesus was prevented from passing through Samaria on His final journey to Jerusalem (Luke 9:51ff.), He took a route to the East, beyond the Jordan and in the territory of Perea (see the map on page 40). It is in this region, where Jesus was inconvenienced, that God set the stage for another miracle.

I. *The Call of the Ten Lepers (17:11-13)*

[11]Now on his way to Jerusalem, Jesus traveled along the border between Samaria and Galilee. [12]As he was going into a village, ten men who had leprosy[a] met him. They stood at a distance [13]and called out in a loud voice, "Jesus, Master, have pity on us!"

II. *The Council of Jesus (17:14)*

[14]When he saw them, he said, "Go, show yourselves to the priests." And as they went, they were cleansed.

III. *The Considerate Attitude of the Samaritan Leper (17:15-19)*

[15]One of them, when he saw he was healed, came back, praising God in a loud voice. [16]He threw himself at Jesus' feet and thanked him—and he was a Samaritan.

[17]Jesus asked, "Were not all ten cleansed? Where are the other nine? [18]Was no one found to return and give praise to God except this foreigner?" [19]Then he said to him, "Rise and go; your faith has made you well."

Five things strike us in this story: (1) The lepers, from a respectful distance (since any contact with a leper rendered one ceremonially unclean), called out to Jesus for help. (2) Jesus was willing to heal all of them, but He wanted them to fulfill God's will regarding the cure of leprosy, so they could be restored to their families and communities with ease. (3) They were not healed as Jesus spoke, but only as they responded in obedience and faith to His words. (4) Just one of the healed lepers had sufficient respect to come back to Jesus and to thank Him for his healing. (5) Jesus

a 12 The Greek word was used for various diseases affecting the skin—not necessarily leprosy.

expressed disappointment over the absence of gratitude in the other nine men who were healed. They, too, should have returned and expressed their gratefulness.

After carefully reading this account and noting these five observations, the practical applications are obvious. Consult Matt. 8:1-4; Mark 1:40-45 and Luke 5:12-14 for other comments related to Jesus' healing of leprosy.

The Coming and Climax of the Kingdom (Luke 17:20-37)

(cf. Matt. 24:23-28, 37-41 and Mark 13:15-18, 21)

In Jesus' discussion of the Kingdom here, there are no less than two different time references in His mind. First, when talking with the Pharisees, Jesus explained that the coming of the Kingdom would not be visible. Second, when talking with the disciples, Jesus explained that the climax of the Kingdom will be both visible and dynamic. Let us consider these two discussions.

I. *Jesus Explains the Kingdom's Coming (17:20, 21)*

20Once, having been asked by the Pharisees when the kingdom of God would come, Jesus replied, "The kingdom of God does not come visibly,
21nor will people say, 'Here it is,' or 'There it is,' because the kingdom of God is within[a] you."

The Pharisees, like most of the Jews in this period, figured that God's Kingdom would come to earth like lightning and thunder. They anticipated much commotion; they even expected all the nations of the earth to be defeated by God's mighty host. There would be nothing secretive or casual when God's Kingdom would come to Israel—or so many persons reasoned.

Jesus' teaching on the entrance of God's Kingdom differed radically from these common expectations. Rather than being nationalistic and militaristic, Jesus announced that the Kingdom was already present—within those persons who obeyed God's will. Consult Matt. 4:17 for detailed remarks.

II. *Jesus Explains the Kingdom's Climax (17:22-37)*

1. *The Day of the Son of Man (17:22-25)*

22Then he said to his disciples, "The time is coming when you will long to see one of the days of the Son of Man, but you will not see it. 23Men will

a 21 Or *among*

tell you, 'There he is!' or 'Here he is!' Do not go running off after them.
[24]For the Son of Man in his day[a] will be like the lightning, which flashes
and lights up the sky from one end to the other. [25]But first he must suffer
many things and be rejected by this generation.

Jesus shifted His attention to His disciples and to the climax of our present era, when He, as the Son of Man, will return like lightning. It is as if this latter group of people were told the end of the story because they had already received its beginning by becoming members of God's Kingdom, while the Pharisees, on the other hand, were not told about this climax of the Kingdom because they had yet to grasp its meaning.

The climax of the Kingdom would be off in the unknown distant future (Matt. 24:36). The disciples, said Jesus, would not see this event, so they need not rush here and there to see the Son of Man after His crucifixion (or more precisely, His ascension). Such rumors of His presence would be false, and the disciples should not waste their time trying to find Him.

Certainly statements like these ought to make us rethink currently popular teachings that Jesus could return at any possible second. This is not a doctrine that the apostles taught, and there is little (if any) evidence to support the notion that we, in this present hour, can make such bold and precise declarations, either.

2. *The Days of Noah (17:26, 27)*

[26]"Just as it was in the days of Noah, so also will it be in the days of the
Son of Man. [27]People were eating, drinking, marrying and being given
in marriage up to the day Noah entered the ark. Then the flood came
and destroyed them all.

See Matt. 24:36-39 for comments.

3. *The Days of Lot (17:28, 29)*

[28]"It was the same in the days of Lot. People were eating and drinking,
buying and selling, planting and building. [29]But the day Lot left Sodom,
fire and sulfur rained down from heaven and destroyed them all.

The days of Lot, like the days of Noah, were filled with self-centered living. None of the items mentioned here by Jesus is a sin in itself, but when these items occupy the sole attention of one's life, then spiritual priorities or preparedness are bound to be absent. It is this preoccupation with temporal and earthly affairs that Jesus warns against.

There is another significant note in this warning that ought to interest everyone who speculates about the timing of the rapture of the Church (1 Thess. 4:13-18). Jesus

a 24 Some manuscripts do not have *in his day.*

stated that the very day when Lot was rescued from Sodom, judgment fell from heaven. Supporters of the pretribulational or midtribulational rapture (that is, those who believe that the rapture of the Church will occur *before* or in the *middle of* the tribulation period) should carefully notice the absence of any delay between Lot's departure and the city's extermination, especially since Jesus stated that "It will be just like this on the day the Son of Man is revealed" (v. 30).

4. *The Day of the Son of Man (17:30-37)*

30"It will be just like this on the day the Son of Man is revealed. 31On
that day no one who is on the roof of his house, with his goods inside,
should go down to get them. Likewise, no one in the field should go
back for anything. 32Remember Lot's wife! 33Whoever tries to keep his
life will lose it, and whoever loses his life will preserve it. 34I tell you,
on that night two people will be in one bed; one will be taken and the
other left. 35Two women will be grinding grain together; one will be
taken and the other left.[a]"
37"Where, Lord?" they asked.
He replied, "Where there is a dead body, there the vultures will gather."

When the Son of Man comes (in both A.D. 70 and at Jesus' second coming), it will be too late to look back, as Lot's wife demonstrated (Gen. 19:17, 26). See Matt. 24:1-3, 40-44 for specific comments.

Finally, the disciples asked, "Where will the unrighteous be taken and judged?" Jesus' reply was not specific; His comments only concerned their physical judgment. He said that we will know where they are by the sight of the devouring vultures (Rev. 19:11-21).

The Parable of the Persistent Woman (Luke 18:1-8)

In this parable Jesus compared the widow to the poor and suffering people of Israel who were being robbed of justice in the courts by crooked Roman judges. Also, in this parable Jesus contrasted the delinquent judge with the punctual Judge of all men, God.

---

a 35 Some manuscripts *left.* *36Two men will be in the field; one will be taken and the other left.*

I. *The Parable (18:1-5)*

18 Then Jesus told his disciples a parable to show them that they should always pray and not give up. 2He said: "In a certain town there was a judge who neither feared God nor cared about men. 3And there was a widow in that town who kept coming to him with the plea, 'Grant me justice against my adversary.'

4"For some time he refused. But finally he said to himself, 'Even though I don't fear God or care about men, 5yet because this widow keeps bothering me, I will see that she gets justice, so that she won't eventually wear me out with her coming!' "

II. *The Principle (18:6-8)*

6And the Lord said, "Listen to what the unjust judge says. 7And will not God bring about justice for his chosen ones, who cry out to him day and night? Will he keep putting them off? 8I tell you, he will see that they get justice, and quickly. However, when the Son of Man comes, will he find faith on the earth?"

There are two important matters to note in this parable: (1) If this insignificant woman could win her case in an unjust court by being persistent, how much more will the children of God receive justice from Him when the Son of Man (Jesus) comes (back) to earth! The main aim of the story is to assure believers that, despite the current conditions of inequity, there is coming a day when God will pay everyone his due reward—good or bad. While justice may not be fulfilled now, immediately upon the descent of the Son of Man it will be realized to the maximum extent. Therefore, believers ought not to give up. God will never let them down. (2) Jesus expressed concern over the spiritual state of the believers who will be present when He returns to earth. He does not state that they will be completely without faith, but He does question whether they will have the kind of persevering faith that was present in this determined woman of the parable. Last-day prophecies indicate that there will be many converts just prior to Jesus' return (Rev. 7:9-17), but also there will be a great deal of weak faith among many so-called believers (2 Tim. 3:1ff.) or no faith at all (2 Thess. 2:1-3; 1 Tim. 4:1ff.).

The Parable of the Pharisee and the Tax Collector (Luke 18:9-14)

In the preceding parable Jesus encouraged His followers to pray with perseverance; in the present parable He exhorted them to pray with purity.

I. *The Parable's Intent (18:9)*

9To some who were confident of their own righteousness and looked down on everybody else, Jesus told this parable:

While Jesus frequently directed His messages in such a manner that the convicted would be made comfortable, He also often spoke in a manner so that the comfortable would be convicted. Here is an illustration of this latter case.

Jesus resented the self-righteous attitudes of the Pharisees. He despised their hypocrisy. And He was quick to expose their spiritual bankruptcy.

II. *The Parable Itself (18:10-13)*

10"Two men went up to the temple to pray, one a Pharisee and the other a tax collector. 11The Pharisee stood up and prayed about[a] himself: 'God, I thank you that I am not like all other men—robbers, evildoers, adulterers—or even like this tax collector. 12I fast twice a week and give a tenth of all I get.'

13"But the tax collector stood at a distance. He would not even look up to heaven, but beat his breast and said, 'God, have mercy on me, a sinner.'

God does not hear every prayer that is directed to Him. Some people, like this Pharisee, only pray about (or to) themselves. All of this sort of praying is useless, because God refuses to hear words that are spoken to Him by the proud or self-justifying (2 Chron. 7:14, 15; Zech. 7:12, 13; Matt. 6:14, 15; John 15:7).

III. *The Parable's Interpretation (18:14)*

14"I tell you that this man, rather than the other, went home justified before God. For everyone who exalts himself will be humbled, and he who humbles himself will be exalted."

---

a 11 Or *to*

Those who come into God's presence with an erect stature will be brought to their knees, but those who come before Him with a humble posture will be elevated to their feet. You can enter God's presence empty-handed and leave full of His blessings, but you cannot come to Him being full of yourself and then expect to leave any other way.

Jesus Touches the Babies and Children (Luke 18:15-17)

(cf. Matt. 19:13-15 and Mark 10:13-16)

One of the strongest interests of parents is to see their children grow up into mature adults. And it isn't long before many parents discover that their longing is as complicated as it is intense. Therefore, all mature or sensitive parents want their children to meet Jesus, to love Him and to serve Him. In this scene we find parents taking their children to Jesus so He might touch them and pray for God's blessing to rest upon them.

15People were also bringing babies to Jesus to have him touch them.
When the disciples saw this, they rebuked them. 16But Jesus called the
children to him and said, "Let the little children come to me, and do not
hinder them, for the kingdom of God belongs to such as these. 17I tell you
the truth, anyone who will not receive the kingdom of God like a little
child will never enter it."

The Rich Young Man (Luke 18:18-30)

(cf. Matt. 19:16-30 and Mark 10:17-31)

The Holy Spirit saw fit to impress this story upon each of the synoptic Gospel writers—Matthew, Mark and Luke. Therefore, it is imperative for us to allow the truths of this episode to permeate our entire being.

There are few persons in this world who are truly interested in being saved. They will die being spiritually lost (Matt. 7:13, 14). There are other persons in this world who would like to be saved, but they cannot manage to separate themselves from the snare of some all-embracing sin—unfortunately, they, too, will die being spiritually lost (Luke 13:22-24). Below is the account of a would-be Christian.

I. *Jesus' Dialogue with the Rich Man (18:18-25)*

**[18]A certain ruler asked him, "Good teacher, what must I do to inherit
eternal life?"
[19]"Why do you call me good?" Jesus answered. "No one is good—except
God alone. [20]You know the commandments: 'Do not commit adultery, do
not murder, do not steal, do not give false testimony, honor your father
and mother.'[a]"
[21]"All these I have kept since I was a boy," he said.
[22]When Jesus heard this, he said to him, "You still lack one thing. Sell
everything you have and give to the poor, and you will have treasure in
heaven. Then come, follow me."
[23]When he heard this, he became very sad, because he was a man of
great wealth. [24]Jesus looked at him and said, "How hard it is for the rich
to enter the kingdom of God! [25]Indeed, it is easier for a camel to go
through the eye of a needle than for a rich man to enter the kingdom
of God."**

II. *Jesus' Dialogue with the Disciples (18:26-30)*

**[26]Those who heard this asked, "Who then can be saved?"
[27]Jesus replied, "What is impossible with men is possible with God."
[28]Peter said to him, "We have left all we had to follow you!"
[29]"I tell you the truth," Jesus said to them, "no one who has left home or
wife or brothers or parents or children for the sake of the kingdom of
God [30]will fail to receive many times as much in this age and, in the age
to come, eternal life."**

Jesus Predicts His Death (Luke 18:31-34)

(cf. Matt. 20:17-19 and Mark 10:32-34)

This is not the first time, but at least the fourth time, when Jesus discussed His upcoming death with His disciples (Matt. 16:21ff.; 17:9ff.; 17:22ff.). And, again, the disciples were perplexed. The meaning of Jesus' words eluded them, probably because what He said did not coincide with their own understanding of the role of the Messiah; neither could they imagine that such a wonderful figure as Jesus would be killed, even

a 20 Exodus 20:12-16; Deut. 5:16-20

by cruel men. Naturally, these words, though not understood at that particular hour, would be remembered and deeply appreciated after Jesus' resurrection.

**[31]Jesus took the Twelve aside and told them, "We are going up to
Jerusalem, and everything that is written by the prophets about the Son
of Man will be fulfilled. [32]He will be handed over to the Gentiles. They
will mock him, insult him, spit on him, flog him and kill him. [33]On the
third day he will rise again."**

**[34]The disciples did not understand any of this. Its meaning was hidden
from them, and they did not know what he was talking about.**

Jesus Heals a Blind Man (Luke 18:35-43)

(cf. Matt. 20:29-34 and Mark 10:46-52)

Never cease praying for your miracle until you get a word from Jesus. Don't permit your circumstances to hinder you. Don't let people stop you. Stay with it, like this blind man who faced each of his rugged obstacles with a persevering faith. Jesus honors this kind of diligent faith.

**[35]As Jesus approached Jericho, a blind man was sitting by the road-
side begging. [36]When he heard the crowd going by, he asked what was
happening. [37]They told him, "Jesus of Nazareth is passing by."**

[38]He called out, "Jesus, Son of David, have mercy on me!"

**[39]Those who led the way rebuked him and told him to be quiet, but he
shouted all the more, "Son of David, have mercy on me!"**

**[40]Jesus stopped and ordered the man to be brought to him. When he
came near, Jesus asked him, [41]"What do you want me to do for you?"**

"Lord, I want to see," he replied.

**[42]Jesus said to him, "Receive your sight; your faith has healed you."
[43]Immediately he received his sight and followed Jesus, praising God.
When all the people saw it, they also praised God.**

Zacchaeus Is Saved (Luke 19:1-10)

This potent little story, like the one preceding it (18:35-43), occurred in Jericho. In the first episode we read how a poor beggar became a disciple of Jesus; in the second account we see how a rich tax collector became a disciple of Jesus.

Christ bridges the gap between heaven and earth for everyone. No matter what our stations in life may be, Jesus is able to perform a saving miracle in our behalf.

I. *The Curiosity of Zacchaeus (19:1-4)*

**19 Jesus entered Jericho and was passing through. [2]A man was
there by the name of Zacchaeus; he was a chief tax collector and
was wealthy. [3]He wanted to see who Jesus was, but being a short man
he could not, because of the crowd. [4]So he ran ahead and climbed a
sycamore-fig tree to see him, since Jesus was coming that way.**

Jericho was one of the most beautiful and wealthy cities in Palestine. Its rose gardens, dates and balsam groves made her fame known everywhere. Naturally, in such a setting it would be a prosperous occupation to collect taxes.

But we see another side to this story. Despite the pleasant surroundings and his wealthy position, Zacchaeus was an unfulfilled man. Something was missing. He wanted more out of life than mere things. Therefore, he earnestly sought to meet this famous spiritual leader, Jesus.

II. *The Calling of Zacchaeus (19:5-7)*

**[5]When Jesus reached the spot, he looked up and said to him, "Zacchaeus,
come down immediately. I must stay at your house today." [6]So he came
down at once and welcomed him gladly.**

**[7]All the people saw this and began to mutter, "He has gone to be the
guest of a 'sinner.' "**

Jesus took an interest in everyone, especially in those whom society at large rejected. There was (and is) no one whom Jesus does not love or cannot save. No one!

III. *The Conversion of Zacchaeus (19:8-10)*

**[8]But Zacchaeus stood up and said to the Lord, "Look, Lord! Here and
now I give half of my possessions to the poor, and if I have cheated**

anybody out of anything, I will pay back four times the amount."
[9]Jesus said to him, "Today salvation has come to this house, because
this man, too, is a son of Abraham. [10]For the Son of Man came to seek and
to save what was lost."

The fruit of salvation, like the fruit from a tree, is certain to be plainly visible. No person can truly be saved who does not behave in a saved manner (Matt. 7:15-20). The first (and the continuing) proof of conversion is a changed life (1 John 3:9). If there is no outward evidence, then there is (in all probability) no possession of a genuine salvation.

The Parable of the Man Who Became King (Luke 19:11-27)

(cf. Matt. 25:14-30)

This parable, though not identical with the parable of the talents, is so similar to it that the comments pertaining to the earlier parable ought to be read carefully with this one (Matt. 25.14-30).

Several matters should capture our attention in this parable.

First, we should note the cause for telling the parable. Some of the people who were with Jesus thought the Kingdom of God would suddenly appear, possibly the moment He entered the city of Jerusalem. Their minds were fixed on seeing a dynamic and climactic entrance of God's Kingdom among the Jews. They envisioned the utter restoration of the nation of Israel, especially in regard to delivering them from their political enemies. But this narrow interpretation of the Kingdom was both out of balance in its theology and premature in its timing. So, Jesus admonished them to be patient and faithful. Someday God's Kingdom will indeed visit men in its judgmental aspects, but this would not occur in the immediate future of the members of His audience.

In our very own day this same essential attitude of an any-instant appearance of the Kingdom is popularly endorsed. The exhortations from this parable, however, direct us away from this view and on to a thought pattern that centers on spiritual preparedness.

Second, we see two opposite responses from the people to the appointment of this king—one group is negative; the other group is positive. Surely Jesus was telling His hearers that those who would follow Him represented the positive group of servants, while those who opposed Him represented the negative group who resisted the coronation of the king.

Third, we see two opposite responses from the returning king. He will greatly reward his faithful servants; and he will severely punish his unfaithful resisters (which includes both the obvious sinner and the not-so-obvious sinner).

The message of this parable ought to have a sobering effect on each one of us, for surely we see here the inevitable consequences that will befall everyone at the second coming of Jesus Christ.

I. *The Purpose for the Parable (19:11)*

11While they were listening to this, he went on to tell them a parable, because he was near Jerusalem and the people thought that the kingdom of God was going to appear at once.

II. *The Parable (19:12-27)*

A. *The Command of the Future King (19:12, 13)*

12He said: "A man of noble birth went to a distant country to have himself appointed king and then to return. 13So he called ten of his servants and gave them ten minas.[a] 'Put this money to work,' he said, 'until I come back.'

B. *The Response of the Servants (19:14)*

14"But his subjects hated him and sent a delegation after him to say, 'We don't want this man to be our king.'

C. *The Recompense of the King (19:15-27)*

15"He was made king, however, and returned home. Then he sent for the servants to whom he had given the money, in order to find out what they had gained with it.

16"The first one came and said, 'Sir, your mina has earned ten more.'

17" 'Well done, my good servant!' his master replied. 'Because you have been trustworthy in a very small matter, take charge of ten cities.'

18"The second came and said, 'Sir, your mina has earned five more.'

19"His master answered, 'You take charge of five cities.'

20"Then another servant came and said, 'Sir, here is your mina; I have kept it laid away in a piece of cloth. 21I was afraid of you, because you are a hard man. You take out what you did not put in and reap what you did not sow.'

22"His master replied, 'I will judge you by your own words, you wicked servant! You knew, did you, that I am a hard man, taking out

a 13 A mina was about three months' wages.

**what I did not put in, and reaping what I did not sow? 23Why then didn't
you put my money on deposit, so that when I came back, I could have
collected it with interest?'**

**24"Then he said to those standing by, 'Take his mina away from him
and give it to the one who has ten minas.'**

25" 'Sir,' they said, 'he already has ten!'

**26"He replied, 'I tell you that to everyone who has, more will be given,
but as for the one who has nothing, even what he has will be taken away.
27But those enemies of mine who did not want me to be king over them—
bring them here and kill them in front of me.' "**

The Triumphal Entry (Luke 19:28-44)

(cf. Matt. 21:1-11; Mark 11:1-11 and John 12:12-19)

It was Palm Sunday—less than a week from the hour in which Jesus would be crucified.

Everyone should have understood the significance of His unique entry into Jerusalem. Jesus was fulfilling Zechariah's prophecy about the Messiah's entrance into the holy city, but because of the callousness of the people's hearts (particularly the hearts of the religious leaders), many persons were blind to this prophetic fulfillment (Zech. 9:9).

Jesus offered God's peace to Jerusalem—spiritual peace—but she would have little to do with it. As a result, she must ultimately taste God's judgment (which occurred in A.D. 70—see details in Luke 21).

I. *The Preparation (19:28-34)*

**28After Jesus had said this, he went on ahead, going up to Jerusalem.
29As he approached Bethphage and Bethany at the hill called the Mount
of Olives, he sent two of his disciples, saying to them, 30"Go to the village
ahead of you, and as you enter it, you will find a colt tied there, which no
one has ever ridden. Untie it and bring it here. 31If anyone asks you,
'Why are you untying it?' tell him, 'The Lord needs it.' "**

**32Those who were sent ahead went and found it just as he had told
them. 33As they were untying the colt, its owners asked them, "Why are
you untying the colt?"**

34They replied, "The Lord needs it."

II. *The Presentation (19:35-38)*

[35]They brought it to Jesus, threw their cloaks on the colt and put Jesus
on it. [36]As he went along, people spread their cloaks on the road.
[37]When he came near the place where the road goes down the Mount
of Olives, the whole crowd of disciples began joyfully to praise God in loud voices for all the miracles they had seen:

[38]"Blessed is the king who comes in the name of the Lord!"[a]

"Peace in heaven and glory in the highest!"

III. *The Problem (19:39, 40)*

[39]Some of the Pharisees in the crowd said to Jesus, "Teacher, rebuke your disciples!"
[40]"I tell you," he replied, "if they keep quiet, the stones will cry out."

IV. *The Prophecy (19:41-44)*

[41]As he approached Jerusalem and saw the city, he wept over it [42]and
said, "If you, even you, had only known on this day what would bring
you peace—but now it is hidden from your eyes. [43]The days will come
upon you when your enemies will build an embankment against you
and encircle you and hem you in on every side. [44]They will dash you to
the ground, you and the children within your walls. They will not leave one stone on another, because you did not recognize the time of God's coming to you."

Jesus at the Temple (Luke 19:45-48)

(cf. Matt. 21:12-17 and Mark 11:15-19)

On Sunday Jesus made His triumphal entry into Jerusalem. Once inside the city, He began to heal sick persons in the crowds and to teach everyone. (Be certain to see the chart at Matt. 21:1-11 for the details regarding Jesus' final week.)

On Monday Jesus took aim at the corrupt practices that were occurring in the Temple. In a rare burst of anger, He swept the Temple clean of its profiteering practices. Then, He continued where He left off Sunday evening—healing and teaching.

a 38 Psalm 118:26

On Tuesday Jesus brought more teachings in the Temple, but by now it was clear that the core of Judaism was incorrigible, depraved beyond repair. While many of the common persons heard Him gladly, many others (especially among the leaders) sought to take His life at a convenient moment.

All of this reveals how unworthy Israel was to receive God's King. Instead, they were only worthy of a Judge.

I. *The Actions of Jesus (19:45, 46)*

**45Then he entered the temple area and began driving out those who
were selling. 46"It is written," he said to them, "'My house will be a house
of prayer'[a]; but you have made it 'a den of robbers.'[b]"**

II. *The Reactions of the Leaders (19:47, 48)*

**47Every day he was teaching at the temple. But the chief priests, the
teachers of the law and the leaders among the people were trying to kill
him. 48Yet they could not find any way to do it, because all the people
hung on his words.**

Jesus' Authority Is Challenged (Luke 20:1-8)

(cf. Matt. 21:23-27 and Mark 11:27-33)

In this twentieth chapter Jesus is challenged three times: first, by the chief priests, teachers and elders (20:1-8); second, by certain spies who are sent out by His first challengers (20:20-26); and third by the Sadducees (20:27-40). It is clear that in Jerusalem, at the very heart of the Jewish faith, Jesus would not be welcome.

Unfortunately, there are "Christian" churches today where the Christ of the Gospels is not welcome. He is a stranger to its services. His absolute authority as the resurrected God-Man is repudiated, being reduced to a mere model of ideal humanity. Unfortunately, the scene at Jerusalem has its parallels in many other sites, too.

I. *The Challenge (20:1, 2)*

**20 One day as he was teaching the people in the temple courts and
preaching the gospel, the chief priests and the teachers of the
law, together with the elders, came up to him. 2"Tell us by what**

[a] 46 Isaiah 56:7 [b] 46 Jer. 7:11

authority you are doing these things," they said. "Who gave you this authority?"

II. *The Counterchallenge (20:3-8)*

3He replied, "I will also ask you a question. Tell me, 4John's baptism—
was it from heaven, or from men?"

5They discussed it among themselves and said, "If we say, 'From
heaven,' he will ask, 'Why didn't you believe him?' 6But if we say, 'From
men,' all the people will stone us, because they are persuaded that John was a prophet."

7So they answered, "We don't know where it was from."

8Jesus said, "Neither will I tell you by what authority I am doing these things."

The Parable of the Landowner (Luke 20:9-19)

(cf. Matt. 21:33-46 and Mark 12:1-12)

It is a serious matter to resist the truth, for some day it will return to condemn you.

Jesus' critics took the lead role in challenging His authority; now He would expose their empty-handed faith.

I. *The Parable Is Told (20:9-16a)*

9He went on to tell the people this parable: "A man planted a vineyard,
rented it to some farmers and went away for a long time. 10At harvest
time he sent a servant to the tenants so they would give him some of the
fruit of the vineyard. But the tenants beat him and sent him away
empty-handed. 11He sent another servant, but that one also they beat
and treated shamefully and sent away empty-handed. 12He sent still a
third, and they wounded him and threw him out.

13"Then the owner of the vineyard said, 'What shall I do? I will send my son, whom I love; perhaps they will respect him.'

14"But when the tenants saw him, they talked the matter over. 'This is
the heir,' they said. 'Let's kill him, and the inheritance will be ours.' 15So
they threw him out of the vineyard and killed him.

"What then will the owner of the vineyard do to them? [16]He will come and kill those tenants and give the vineyard to others."

II. *The Parable Is Applied (20:16b-19)*

When the people heard this, they said, "May this never be!"
[17]Jesus looked directly at them and asked, "Then what is the meaning of that which is written:

" 'The stone the builders rejected
has become the capstone[a,b]'?

[18]Everyone who falls on that stone will be broken to pieces, but he on whom it falls will be crushed."
[19]The teachers of the law and the chief priests looked for a way to arrest him immediately, because they knew he had spoken this parable against them. But they were afraid of the people.

Should We Pay Taxes? (Luke 20:20-26)

(cf. Matt. 22:15-22 and Mark 12:13-17)

The natural man often fails to learn from his mistakes. If he cannot succeed in his schemes through one process, then he will attempt another process. Here we see the continued determination of carnal persons to discredit Jesus. Earlier they had failed in direct confrontation; now they would try a subtle and flattering tactic.

How little interest there is in Jesus among those who are spiritually lost. They resent Him, resist Him, repudiate Him and attempt to reduce Him, while all the time they claim to recognize Him as being unique. Without a doubt this brief scene is as alive today as it was nearly 2,000 years ago.

I. *The Anticipated Trap (20:20-22)*

[20]Keeping a close watch on him, they sent spies, who pretended to be honest. They hoped to catch Jesus in something he said so that they might hand him over to the power and authority of the governor. [21]So the spies questioned him: "Teacher, we know that you speak and teach what is right, and that you do not show partiality but teach the way of

a 17 Or *cornerstone* *b 17* Psalm 118:22

God in accordance with the truth. [22]Is it right for us to pay taxes to Caesar or not?"

II. *The Actual Truth (20:23-26)*

[23]He saw through their duplicity and said to them, [24]"Show me a denarius. Whose portrait and inscription are on it?"

[25]"Caesar's," they replied.

He said to them, "Then give to Caesar what is Caesar's, and to God what is God's."

[26]They were unable to trap him in what he had said there in public. And astonished by his answer, they became silent.

No Marriage in Heaven (Luke 20:27-40)

(cf. Matt. 22:23-33 and Mark 12:18-27)

The final group to test Jesus in this chapter is the Sadducees. They represent Israel's elite class, but for all of their social status, they possessed very little spiritual understanding.

According to the Sadducees, when you die, you cease to exist. There is no life beyond the grave. The Sadducees taught that both the body and the soul die together. Therefore, the very notion of any resurrection was preposterous to them. Still, they confronted Jesus with their hypothetical situation in hopes of exposing some flaw in His credibility as a teacher. If this could be accomplished, then they could satisfy their contention that this man was no prophet or Messiah, but a mere pest who was upsetting their traditions.

I. *The Anticipated Trap (20:27-33)*

[27]Some of the Sadducees, who say there is no resurrection, came to Jesus with a question. [28]"Teacher," they said, "Moses wrote for us that if a man's brother dies and leaves a wife but no children, the man must marry the widow and have children for his brother. [29]Now there were seven brothers. The first one married a woman and died childless. [30]The second [31]and then the third married her, and in the same way the seven died, leaving no children. [32]Finally, the woman died too. [33]Now then, at the resurrection whose wife will she be, since the seven were married to her?"

II. *The Actual Truth (20:34-40)*

**34Jesus replied, "The people of this age marry and are given in
marriage. 35But those who are considered worthy of taking part in that
age and in the resurrection from the dead will neither marry nor be
given in marriage, 36and they can no longer die; for they are like the
angels. They are God's children, since they are children of the resurrection. 37But in the account of the bush, even Moses showed that the dead
rise, for he calls the Lord 'the God of Abraham, and the God of Isaac,
and the God of Jacob.'[a] 38He is not the God of the dead, but of the living,
for to him all are alive."**

**39Some of the teachers of the law responded, "Well said, teacher!"
40And no one dared to ask him any more questions.**

Jesus Stumps His Critics (Luke 20:41-44)

(cf. Matt. 22:41 46 and Mark 12:35-37)

Jesus' critics thought they understood the Scriptures, so they were quick to use these writings against Him. But Jesus' knowledge of the Old Testament was far greater than theirs. Another proof of this fact was displayed here, when Jesus asked them to explain the meaning of Ps. 110:1. As could be expected, they were again left without any sensible response to Jesus' statements.

**41Then Jesus said to them, "How is it that they say the Christ[b] is the Son
of David? 42David himself declares in the Book of Psalms:**

**" 'The Lord said to my Lord:
"Sit at my right hand
43until I make your enemies
a footstool for your feet." '[c]**

44David calls him 'Lord.' How then can he be his son?"

---

a 37 Exodus 3:6 b 41 Or *Messiah* c 43 Psalm 110:1

Jesus Warns His Disciples (Luke 20:45-47)

(cf. Matt. 23:1-39 and Mark 12:38-40)

One of Jesus' aims while He taught was to destroy people's faith—that is, their improper faith in the integrity of pseudo-followers of God. A person's faith is closely aligned to the leaders of the faith itself; therefore, it is only sensible that when a leader is in error then those believing in such persons are equally in a state of deception. Such a lethal faith needs to be exposed, as Jesus does here.

45While all the people were listening, Jesus said to his disciples,
46"Beware of the teachers of the law. They like to walk around in
flowing robes and love to be greeted in the marketplaces and have the most important seats in the synagogues and the places of honor at
banquets. 47They devour widows' houses and for a show make lengthy
prayers. Such men will be punished most severely."

The Widow's Small Coins (Luke 21:1-4)

(cf. Mark 12:41-44)

George Mueller once said, "God judges what we give by what we keep." This has to be true. A hundred-dollar gift from a millionaire is not nearly so meaningful as a dollar gift from a poor person.

If there will be room for regret in heaven, it will not be because we sacrificed so much to Christ, but rather that we did not sacrifice more. When the time comes for us to die, we will only possess that which we gave away for the good of others and for the glory of God. In this short story we see a woman who is poor in physical things but profoundly rich in spiritual wealth.

21 As he looked up, Jesus saw the rich putting their gifts into the
temple treasury. 2He also saw a poor widow put in two very
small copper coins.[a] 3"I tell you the truth," he said, "this poor widow has

a 2 Greek *two lepta*

put in more than all the others. [4]All these people gave their gifts out of their wealth; but she out of her poverty put in all she had to live on."

The Coming of the Son of Man (Luke 21:5-28)

(cf. Matt. 24:1-31 and Mark 13:1-27)

In order to understand Jesus' prophecy in this chapter, it is imperative that you read the parallel passages (cited above), along with the comments on those Scriptures. Only after this reading will you be prepared to investigate Luke's account.

Commentators have expressed different interpretations on this discourse by Jesus (see the appropriate chart in the discussion found in Matthew's text). It may not be possible to find a final word that satisfies everyone, but the following two major observations should pose no problems, while providing some necessary insights: (1) In Matthew and Mark the overall context appears to be global in its dimensions, although Jerusalem-centered statements are plainly evident. (2) In Luke the overall context is Jerusalem-centered, although the global aspects are also clearly detected. In other words, while each of the Gospel writers record Jesus' prophecy, the first two (Matthew and Mark) see His words from a vantage point far above the earth, while the third one (Luke), sees the bulk of the episode from inside the walls of Jerusalem.

See the chart entitled "Jesus' Olivet Discourse" for a comparative analysis of this prophecy from the pens of the three synoptic Gospel writers.

I. *First Cycle of Signs: Global Chaos (21:5-11)*

**[5]Some of his disciples were remarking about how the temple was
adorned with beautiful stones and with gifts dedicated to God. But
Jesus said, [6]"As for what you see here, the time will come when not one
stone will be left on another; every one of them will be thrown down."
[7]"Teacher," they asked, "when will these things happen? And what
will be the sign that they are about to take place?"
[8]He replied: "Watch out that you are not deceived. For many will
come in my name, claiming, 'I am he,' and, 'The time is near.' Do not
follow them. [9]When you hear of wars and revolutions, do not be
frightened. These things must happen first, but the end will not come
right away."**

[10]**Then he said to them: "Nation will rise against nation, and kingdom against kingdom. [11]There will be great earthquakes, famines and pestilences in various places, and fearful events and great signs from heaven.**

The most splendid labor of Herod the Great was the complete rebuilding of Jerusalem's Temple. This massive and elaborate structure was begun in 19 B.C. and not completed until A.D. 64 (only six short years before its utter destruction).

JESUS' OLIVET DISCOURSE

The Prophecy	Matthew 24	Mark 13	Luke 21
First Cycle of Signs *Center of focus is global chaos*	False christs—vv. 5, 23, 24 Wars—v. 6 Rumors of wars—v. 6 Nations/kingdoms against nations/kingdoms—v. 7 Famines—v. 7 Earthquakes—v. 7	False christs—vv. 5, 6 Wars—v. 7 Rumors of wars—v. 7 Nations/kingdoms against nations/ kingdoms—v. 8 Famines—v. 8 Earthquakes—v. 8	False christs—v. 8 Revolutions—v. 9 Rumors of wars—v. 9 Nations/kingdoms against nations/kingdoms—v. 10 Famines—v. 11 Earthquakes—v. 11 Pestilence—v. 11 Fearful events—v. 11 Signs from heaven—v. 11
Second Cycle of Signs *Center of focus is Christians' persecution*	Persecution—vv. 9, 10 Apostasy—v. 10 False prophets—vv. 11, 24 Wickedness—v. 12 Gospel in whole world—v. 14	Persecution—vv. 9, 12, 13 Gospel in whole world—v. 10 Protection—vv. 11, 13	Persecution—vv. 12, 13, 16, 17 Protection—vv. 14, 15, 18, 19
Third Cycle of signs *Center of focus is Jerusalem's desolation*	Abomination of desolation—v. 15 Flee—vv. 16-20 Great distress—vv. 21-22 Deception—v. 26 Vultures gather—v.28	Abomination of desolation—v. 14 Flee—vv. 14-18 Unequalled distress—vv. 19, 20 Deception—vv. 21, 22	Jerusalem surrounded by armies—v. 20 Flee—v. 21 Time of prophesied punishment—vv. 22, 23 Times of the Gentiles—v. 24
Final Sequence of Signs *Center of focus is Son of Man's return*	Sun darkened—v. 29 Moon dimmed—v. 29 Stars fall—v. 29 Heavens shaken—v. 29 Signs in sky—v. 30 All nations mourn—v. 30 Coming in clouds—v. 30 Elect gathered—v. 31 Trumpet—v. 31	Sun darkened—v. 24 Moon dimmed—v. 24 Stars fall—v. 25 Heavens shaken—v. 25 Coming in clouds—v. 26 Elect gathered—v. 27	Signs in sun, moon and stars —v. 25 Anguish and perplexity among the nations—v. 25 Men faint from fear—v. 26 Coming in clouds—v. 27 Redemption draws near—v. 28

Ten thousand workers were employed for the project. A thousand wagons were used to haul the materials for construction. The edifice rested on nearly thirty-five acres of land. Its walls rose as high as 450 feet into the blue skies. Gold lavishly covered many of the Temple's articles. Solid marble columns adorned entrances and halls. Precious stones were embedded in carefully prepared fittings. It was, without a doubt, an incredibly breathtaking sight (see Matt. 21:12-17 for a floor plan of the Temple).

While the disciples marveled at the splendor of the Temple, Jesus prophesied the most severe judgment imaginable upon the structure. Further, He predicted a chain of other judgments, both national and natural in identity, that would precede the Temple's ruin.

II. *Second Cycle of Signs: Christian Persecution (21:12-19)*

12"But before all this, they will lay hands on you and persecute you.
They will deliver you to synagogues and prisons, and you will be
brought before kings and governors, and all on account of my name.
13This will result in your being witnesses to them. 14But make up your
mind not to worry beforehand how you will defend yourselves. 15For I
will give you words and wisdom that none of your adversaries will be
able to resist or contradict. 16You will be betrayed by parents, brothers,
relatives and friends, and they will put some of you to death. 17All men
will hate you because of me. 18But not a hair of your head will perish.
19By standing firm you will save yourselves.

Before Jerusalem would fall, however, and before these national and natural signs would appear, Jesus warned that His disciples would be certain to experience persecution. They (along with their converts) will be hated and persecuted, and some will even die as martyrs for their faith. Still, they are comforted with Jesus' promise that they will be given the help that is needed to face such difficult trials. In fact, He even stated that if they will remain faithful to the end, they will not only be saved from the penalty of hell, but even every hair on their head will escape this judgment (which seems to be a figurative way of expressing how God will watch over His own children, seeing to it that nothing happens to them apart from His presence and provisions—see Matt. 10:21, 22, 28-31).

III. *Third Cycle of Signs: Jerusalem's Desolation (21:20-24)*

20"When you see Jerusalem surrounded by armies, you will know that
its desolation is near. 21Then let those who are in Judea flee to the

mountains, let those in the city get out, and let those in the country not
enter the city. [22]For this is the time of punishment in fulfillment of all
that has been written. [23]How dreadful it will be in those days for
pregnant women and nursing mothers! There will be great distress
in the land and wrath against this people. [24]They will fall by the
sword and will be taken as prisoners to all the nations. Jerusalem will be
trampled on by the Gentiles until the times of the Gentiles are fulfilled.

The words of this prophecy ring with grief for the occupants of Jerusalem. Her destruction is certain; and her desolation will be complete. In about forty years (or A.D. 70) this prophecy will find its fulfillment. Below are comments on the most significant phrases used in this particular section of the prediction.

Its Desolation Is Near: Both Matthew and Mark refer to this portion of Jesus' prophecy as "the abomination of desolation," which was prophesied to occur by the prophet Daniel (Dan. 9:26, 27). This is a highly technical section in Daniel's writing (see detailed comments in the author's book, *Armageddon 198?*, Plainfield, N.J.: Haven Books, 1980, pp. 209-28). Luke reduces the complexities of these words to one central theme—the destruction of Jerusalem in A.D. 70.

In the year A.D. 66 the Jews revolted against Rome and attempted to gain their independence. Vespasian was sent from Rome to put down the rebellion through mass murders. And until the emperor's death in A.D. 69, he slaughtered the occupants of numerous Jewish cities. In A.D. 69, Vespasian left for Rome to become its emperor, but he left his son, Titus, to finish the task of squashing the Jewish revolt. While the actual siege against Jerusalem lasted only 134 days, the repulsive details of this dreadful period are staggering.

The military occupants within Jerusalem—a number recorded as being between 23,000 and 24,000—were divided into three self-centered factions, each holding a certain section of the city, and occasionally fighting one another. Under Titus there were 54,000 legionnaires, along with archers and horsemen—an army twice the size of Jerusalem's militia.

Famine within the walled city was inevitable. The stench of dead bodies became so great that 600,000 corpses are said to have been thrown over the walls. In the peak of destitution, children were even eaten for survival. Finally, in A.D. 70, General Titus's men overran the city, slaughtering people indiscriminately and burning the city. In total, some 1,100,000 people supposedly died in the siege. Another 97,000 were taken captives, while a few were allowed to go free.

These figures are taken from the first-century historian Josephus. They are highly exaggerated. More realistic figures estimate that there may have been a maximum of

70,000 persons inside Jerusalem at the time of the siege. Still, many of them faced the agonies described above.

Flee to the Mountains. This gloomy forecast was not delivered without some notes of hope. That is, for those persons who took Jesus' words seriously, there would be the opportunity to avoid Jerusalem's blackest hour, but they must act quickly. According to the writings of Eusebius (c. A.D. 265-339) and Epiphanius (c. A.D. 315-403) there were many Christians who hurriedly departed from Jerusalem when they learned of the approaching Roman armies. They, then, traveled northeast to the city of Pella, where they took refuge.

Fulfillment of All That Has Been Written. Many of the Old Testament prophets spoke harsh words against sinning Jews, warning them about the consequences of their evil practices (Lev. 26:14-33; Deut. 28:15-68; 29:19-28; Dan. 9:26, 27; and so forth). Now, after repeated declarations, this judgment would occur. This particular fulfillment, however, does not imply that all of God's judgments for the Jew or for Jerusalem were consummated in A.D. 70. Indeed, there are other judgmental prophecies against the Jews and against Jerusalem that are yet to be fulfilled (Dan. 12:1; Zech. 14:1, 2; Mal. 4:1; Rev. 6-19). The prophecy before us merely implies that Jerusalem will receive a full measure of punishment in accordance with the numerous prophetic warnings given to her during her long history.

The Times of the Gentiles. According to Jesus' words, the "times of the Gentiles" will possess three principal marks: (1) the fall of Jerusalem to Gentiles; (2) the scattering of the Jews into Gentile territory; and (3) the submission of Jerusalem to Gentile domination. The record of history dramatically confirms this consuming prediction. Below is a brief sketch of Jerusalem's dominance by Gentile powers since A.D. 70.

70-131	Desolation
131-312	Rebuilt—called Aelia Capitalina
312-395	Name of Jerusalem restored under Constantine
395-614	Greek control
614-969	Persian control
969-1077	Egyptian control
1077-1517	Crusader/Arab control mixed
1517-1917	Ottoman Empire control
1917-1947	British control
May 14, 1948	Independent nation
June 1967	Jerusalem under Israel's control

Jesus provided no starting date for "the times of the Gentiles." He only indicated that defeat, dominion and dispersion were to be Jerusalem's lot until God would bring the Gentile dispensation to a climax. The most common date suggested for the start of this era is 606 B.C., when Jerusalem fell under the control of the Babylonian Empire. With the exception of one brief period, Jerusalem lived under Gentile rule from that date until Jesus gave this prediction. While this somewhat insignificant starting date is debated by scholars, the concluding date for the "times of the Gentiles" is even more controversial. Some see the conclusion of this prophecy as having occurred on May 14, 1948, when Israel officially became a nation. Others see the fulfillment as having occurred on June 10, 1967, when Israel regained possession of of old Jerusalem in the Six-Day War. Still other commentators, like myself, view the end of the Gentile dispensation as coming with the descent of Jesus Christ at His second coming. Regardless of the exact times, between these two events Israel was to suffer terribly, as certainly she has done. For further comments on the destiny of Israel, see the author's book, *Armageddon 198?*, (Plainfield, N.J.: Haven Books, 1980).

IV. *Final Sequence of Signs: Son of Man Comes (21:25-28)*

25"There will be signs in the sun, moon and stars. On the earth, nations will be in anguish and perplexity at the roaring and tossing of the sea.
26Men will faint from terror, apprehensive of what is coming on the world, for the heavenly bodies will be shaken. 27At that time they will see the Son of Man coming in a cloud with power and great glory.
28When these things begin to take place, stand up and lift up your heads, because your redemption is drawing near."

Here we see a far-distant prophecy. The previous cycle of signs concluded with a prophecy that was to cross many centuries ("the times of the Gentiles"—v. 24). Now, at the climax of these "times," is the appearance of Jesus, coming down out of heaven as the Son of Man (Dan. 7:13, 14).

Based upon the signs found in this passage (and on prophecies for the same period, located elsewhere—Luke 21:34-36; 2 Thess. 2:1-12; Rev. 6-19), it is clear that the same general anguish Jerusalem experienced in A.D. 70 will now be felt by the world at large just prior to Christ's return. The times will be so terrible that people will actually faint as a result of the world's condition.

The signs in the heavenly bodies seem to be both literal (Rev. 8:12; 9:1-12; 16:8, 9) and symbolic (probably referring to the fall of demonic powers—Job 38:7; Rev. 12:1-10). The signs in the earth, symbolized as the roaring sea (a common symbol for Gentile nations—Isa. 17:12, 13; 57:20; Dan. 7:3, 17; Rev. 13:1, 2, 11; 17:1, 15), probably has reference to the social, political and economic chaos that will be rampant in the earth during the last days before Jesus returns.

Despite the natural tendency to be fearful about these matters, Jesus exhorts this second-coming generation to stand to its feet and to look up into the sky, for their redemption (or deliverance) is very near. The Christian need not be consumed by the depressing conditions of the last days, for he knows not only what the future holds, but he also knows the One who holds the future!

The Parable of the Fig Tree (Luke 21:29-33)

(cf. Matt. 24:32-35 and Mark 13:28-31)

Luke is a bit more precise in his recording of this parable than are Matthew and Mark. While these latter authors require a double fulfillment in order to exhaust the full meaning of their choice of words, Luke's words only need a single fulfillment.

According to Luke's orderly arrangement of this prophecy, there are four progressive stages of events in Jesus' prediction: (1) there will be persecution of believers; (2) there will be national and natural chaos; (3) there will be the destruction of Jerusalem—followed by the Jewish dispersion during the centuries known as the "times of the Gentiles"; and (4) there will be the coming of the Kingdom of God. Therefore, when Luke writes that "this generation [or race] will certainly not pass away until all these things have happened," he has the Jewish *race* in mind, those who must face the brunt of these prophetic words. (Be certain to read the comments in Matthew for other important insights.)

29He told them this parable: "Look at the fig tree and all the trees.
30When they sprout leaves, you can see for yourselves and know that
summer is near. 31Even so, when you see these things happening, you
know that the kingdom of God is near.
32"I tell you the truth, this generation[a] will certainly not pass away
until all these things have happened. 33Heaven and earth will pass
away, but my words will never pass away.

a 32 Or *race*

Jesus Cautions His Followers (Luke 21:34-38)

These words are intimately tied to the previous prophecies regarding the coming of the Kingdom of God. It is in this light that Jesus warns His followers to "be careful."

**34"Be careful, or your hearts will be weighed down with dissipation, drunkenness and the anxieties of life, and that day will close on you unexpectedly like a trap.
35For it will come upon all those who live on the face of the whole earth.
36Be always on the watch, and pray that you may be able to escape all that is about to happen, and that you may be able to stand before the Son of Man."**

**37Each day Jesus was teaching at the temple, and each evening he went out to spend the night on the hill called the Mount of Olives,
38and all the people came early in the morning to hear him at the temple.**

Let us notice three things about Jesus' words: (1) We learn here that unless we prepare for the coming of God's Kingdom, we will surely miss its benefits altogether. (2) We learn here that the coming of the Kingdom will affect everyone living on the whole earth. (3) We learn here that through watchfulness (or living with spiritual discernment) and prayer, we can escape the divine judgments associated with the coming of the Kingdom, and thereby be able to stand safely before the Son of Man.

Some persons have used these verses, especially verse 36, as a proof of a pretribulational rapture of the Church. Such interpreters contend that believers will "escape" the trials of the Great Tribulation. But such reasoning faces the following problems: (1) The immediate context (v. 34ff.) does not describe the Great Tribulation but "that day"—which is a designation for the coming Kingdom of God. (2) The broader context (v. 25ff.) reaffirms the same fact that the discussion focuses on divine judgments, not human ones. (3) Those who escape this judgment are able to stand erect (or without any guilt) before the Son of Man. Certainly escaping human judgments (such as those in the Great Tribulation) will qualify no one to stand in Jesus' presence; although those escaping God's judgments at the Second Coming will qualify to be counted among those who stand before Jesus (Matt. 25:1-46).

The Plot Against Jesus **(Luke 22:1-6)**

(cf. Matt. 26:1-5, 14-16; Mark 14:1, 2, 10, 11 and John 11:45-53)

If a person is not open to Jesus, he is open to Satan. It is just that simple.

Judas acted like he was open to Jesus. No doubt he convinced those about him that he was open to Jesus. But the fact is, in his heart, Judas was closed to Jesus. Though he was a disciple of Jesus externally, he was a disciple of Satan internally.

22 Now the Feast of Unleavened Bread, called the Passover, was
approaching, [2]and the chief priests and the teachers of the law
were looking for some way to get rid of Jesus, for they were afraid of the
people. [3]Then Satan entered Judas, called Iscariot, one of the Twelve.
[4]And Judas went to the chief priests and the officers of the temple guard
and discussed with them how he might betray Jesus. [5]They were de-
lighted and agreed to give him money. [6]He consented, and watched for
an opportunity to hand Jesus over to them when no crowd was present.

The Last Supper **(Luke 22:7-23)**

(cf. Matt. 26:17-30; Mark 14:12-25 and John 13:1-20)

During the Old Testament dispensation God instituted various feasts and ceremonies in order to display the spiritual realities vividly. On this night, Jesus, along with His disciples, celebrated one of those symbolic feasts—the Feast of Unleavened Bread (or the Passover). This ancient ordinance pictured in a physical way what was to ultimately become a spiritual reality through the sacrifice of the Messiah. In Jesus, then, is the fulfillment of this annual feast. Through His body and blood we receive God's eternal forgiveness!

I. *Preparations (22:7-13)*

[7]Then came the day of Unleavened Bread on which the Passover lamb
had to be sacrificed. [8]Jesus sent Peter and John, saying, "Go and make
preparations for us to eat the Passover."

**9"Where do you want us to prepare for it?" they asked.
10He replied, "As you enter the city, a man carrying a jar of water will
meet you. Follow him to the house that he enters, 11and say to the owner
of the house, 'The Teacher asks: Where is the guest room, where I may
eat the Passover with my disciples?' 12He will show you a large upper
room, all furnished. Make preparations there."
13They left and found things just as Jesus had told them. So they prepared the Passover.**

II. *Proclamations (22:14-23)*

**14When the hour came, Jesus and his apostles reclined at the table.
15And he said to them, "I have eagerly desired to eat this Passover with
you before I suffer. 16For I tell you, I will not eat it again until it finds
fulfillment in the kingdom of God."
17After taking the cup, he gave thanks and said, "Take this and divide
it among you. 18For I tell you I will not drink again of the fruit of the vine
until the kingdom of God comes."
19And he took bread, gave thanks and broke it, and gave it to them,
saying, "This is my body given for you; do this in remembrance of me."
20In the same way, after the supper he took the cup, saying, "This cup
is the new covenant in my blood, which is poured out for you. 21But the
hand of him who is going to betray me is with mine on the table. 22The
Son of Man will go as it has been decreed, but woe to that man who
betrays him." 23They began to question among themselves which of
them it might be who would do this.**

The Meaning of True Greatness (Luke 22:24-30)

Jesus' disciples seem to be incurably ambitious. At least two times prior to this episode in the upper room Jesus discussed the meaning of true greatness with them, but they found it easy to slip back into their old ways (Matt. 18:1-5; 20:24-28; Mark 9:33-37; 10:41-45; Luke 9:46-48). So, Jesus, ever so patiently, instructed them again about how they ought to behave before one another.

**24Also a dispute arose among them as to which of them was considered
to be greatest. 25Jesus said to them, "The kings of the Gentiles lord it**

**over them; and those who exercise authority over them call themselves
Benefactors. [26]But you are not to be like that. Instead, the greatest
among you should be like the youngest, and the one who rules like the
one who serves. [27]For who is greater, the one who is at the table or the
one who serves? Is it not the one who is at the table? But I am among you
as one who serves. [28]You are those who have stood by me in my trials.
[29]And I confer on you a kingdom, just as my Father conferred one on
me, [30]so that you may eat and drink at my table in my kingdom and sit on
thrones, judging the twelve tribes of Israel.**

First, notice how Jesus used this carnal ambition of the disciples to illustrate the fact that their disposition was no different from the character of the self-centered kings among the Gentiles. These men of God were acting like men of the world (cf. 1 Cor. 3:1-3). Unfortunately, this scene is all too common among the saints—both of the past and of the present. Therefore, we should frequently remind ourselves that our mission is not to become great ourselves, but to make others great for God's service.

Second, notice Jesus' definition for true greatness. According to Him, the greatest of all persons is the one who serves others. How different this is from the world's greedy and status-seeking orientation. In the Kingdom of God the lowest are actually the tallest. Therefore, on the day of the believers' judgment it will not be the number of works or the kind of works that will impress God to reward us, but it will be the quality of our disposition that went into the performance of these works (compare and contrast Matt. 7:21-23 with 1 Cor. 3:10-15).

Third, notice the ultimate purpose for Jesus' rebuke of the disciples. It is their destiny to rule over Israel; therefore, they must learn the marks that accompany spiritual leadership. The time of this judging (or more precisely, this ruling) of Israel is not stated here, though it is not difficult to discern that Jesus has the time of His return to earth in view. When He comes again—to sit on His glorious throne (Matt. 25:31ff.)—He will rule the whole earth in righteousness. Those serving Him in the highest positions during this new era will also sit on thrones (Rev. 20:4-6). Here we see that the twelve disciples (minus Judas, who was later replaced—Acts 2) will exercise authority over the restored nation of Israel. Elsewhere we see that faithful Gentile Christians will be given rule over their own cities and lands during this millennial reign of Christ (Rev. 2:26, 27; 3:21).

Jesus Prays for Peter (Luke 22:31-34)

(cf. Matt. 26:31-35; Mark 14:26-31 and John 13:36-38)

There are some weighty lessons in this story that no one can afford to miss.

First, we see both the desire and the limitations of Satan. His intent is to sift (that is, to separate or to scatter) all of the disciples (the word "you" in verse 31 is plural), but he cannot touch God's holy children without first securing His permission (Job 1-2). This fact remains true to this very day.

Second, we see that Jesus prays when He learns of this soon-coming attack upon His disciples, but observe these three interesting facts about this prayer: (a) Although all twelve disciples will be tested, Jesus only prayed for Peter in this particular instance (the "you" in verse 32 is singular). The cause for this singling out of Peter is probably due to the fact that he was the recognized leader of the twelve. This test would strengthen him personally and further solidify his leadership role among the other disciples. (b) Jesus did not resist Satan in His prayer; instead, it is evident that this testing was in harmony with God's will, so He prayed for the key figure in the trial, that he would not utterly despair. (c) Jesus recognized that Satan would get the upper hand of the situation, at least for a while, but in the end He knew that Peter would come around and be stronger because of the ordeal.

From all of this information we ought to learn to assess matters carefully before settling on any immature judgment. Trials, even trials from Satan, are not always out of God's will (Job 1-2; 2 Cor. 12:1-10). Neither is a temporary setback (or sin!) always counterproductive, for God specializes in working "all" things together for good to those who love Him (Rom. 8:28)! We must never overlook the marvelous nature and works of God's grace.

31"Simon, Simon, Satan has asked to sift you[a] as wheat. 32But I have prayed for you, Simon, that your faith may not fail. And when you have turned back, strengthen your brothers."

33But he replied, "Lord, I am ready to go with you to prison and to death."

34Jesus answered, "I tell you, Peter, before the rooster crows today, you will deny three times that you know me."

---

a 31 The Greek is plural.

A Purse, Bag and Sword (Luke 22:35-38)

In a matter of just several hours the disciples of Jesus would see their Master betrayed and arrested. But before this would occur, Jesus laid out some rules for them that are practically the opposite of a former command He gave them.

In the former order, the disciples were to travel by faith alone; Jesus, and others, would provide for their necessities (Matt. 10:9ff.). Now, however, He tells them to carry a purse for money, a bag for material needs and a sword for protection (possibly against animals or thieves). Why did Jesus change these orders? Because life would be different without His physical presence among the disciples. The circumstances would be different; therefore, the rules must change. These men had to be told to prepare for Jesus' absence.

35Then Jesus asked them, "When I sent you without purse, bag or sandals, did you lack anything?"

"Nothing," they answered.

36He said to them, "But now if you have a purse, take it, and also a bag; and if you don't have a sword, sell your cloak and buy one. 37It is written:
'And he was numbered with the transgressors'[a]; and I tell you that this must be fulfilled in me. Yes, what is written about me is reaching its fulfillment."

38The disciples said, "See, Lord, here are two swords."

"That is enough," he replied.

These words must be understood without any exaggeration. Certainly Jesus would (and will) continue to meet the needs of all His disciples (Phil. 4:19), but it cannot be said that the lives of the disciples—after Jesus' death—were (or are) the same as they were during that past period when they walked at His side; and neither will it be the same as during that future period when His followers will join Him in His glorious second coming. These two periods (when Jesus walked among men and when He will return to this earth a second time) are events without parallel in God's calendar. We, today, like the disciples after Jesus' death, live between these two points. We do not live in a valley of defeat (certainly not!), but we do live in a lower level of divine supply than was experienced or will be experienced in these two peaks.

Therefore, while we trust our Lord supremely, we still must act responsibly and

---

a 37 Isaiah 53:12

sensibly in this world. We are to have purses (wallets? a savings plan?) for money, bags (homes?) for our material needs and a sword (a gun? insurance?) for our protection. During this dispensation in God's economy, having such possessions is not unspiritual, but sound management in handling what God has entrusted to our care.

Faith in heavenly provisions does not exempt us from earthly responsibilities or realities. Christians pray for God to meet their needs, then they go to work. Christians pray for safety as they travel; but they always have a spare tire in the trunk of the car. Christians trust God for the miracles they need; still we use common sense. This is not a demonstration of a lack of faith but of practical principles for saints who still live in this Satan-governed world.

Jesus Prays on the Mount of Olives (Luke 22:39-46)

(cf. Matt. 26:36-46 and Mark 14:32-42)

This mount, looking more like a ridge, runs along the east side of Jerusalem. At its peak it is 100 feet higher than the city. The best view of Jerusalem can seen from this location. No doubt from this site Jesus often lifted His eyes with tears as he looked across the city that was so callous to spiritual matters (Luke 19:41-44). On this night, His final one before the crucifixion, He would pray earnestly about the works He must accomplish as the Savior of the world.

Only Luke informs us about the angel that aided Jesus as He prayed. The nature of the need and the specific assistance provided are not mentioned. Some people believe the angel's help was solely physical; others believe it was emotional; still others think the angel may have overcome demons that were attacking Jesus. Perhaps any or all of these views are correct.

39Jesus went out as usual to the Mount of Olives, and his disciples
followed him. 40On reaching the place, he said to them, "Pray that you
will not fall into temptation." 41He withdrew about a stone's throw
beyond them, knelt down and prayed, 42"Father, if you are willing, take
this cup from me; yet not my will, but yours be done." 43An angel from
heaven appeared to him and strengthened him. 44And being in anguish,
he prayed more earnestly, and his sweat was like drops of blood falling
to the ground.[a]

45When he rose from prayer and went back to the disciples, he found
them asleep, exhausted from sorrow. 46"Why are you sleeping?" he
asked them. "Get up and pray so that you will not fall into temptation."

---

a 44 Some early manuscripts do not have verses 43 and 44.

Jesus Is Arrested (Luke 22:47-53)

(cf. Matt. 26:47-56; Mark 14:43-50 and John 18:1-11)

It was a common gesture for a disciple of a rabbi to greet his teacher with a kiss. In this action he displayed his respect and confidence in the man. Judas, however, reversed this courtesy and turned it into an abominable thing—a sign for betrayal.

Certainly this episode demonstrates the terrible extent to which some supposed followers of Christ (some "Christians") are actually separated from Him. Some who profess a love for Christ and seemingly display an affection for Him are not always revealing their inner convictions. It is never enough to merely give lip service to Christ. We must love Him with all of our heart, soul, mind and strength.

I. *The Arrangement of Judas (22:47, 48)*

47While he was still speaking a crowd came up, and the man who was called Judas, one of the Twelve, was leading them. He approached Jesus to kiss him, 48but Jesus asked him, "Judas, are you betraying the Son of Man with a kiss?"

II. *The Action of the Disciples (22:49, 50)*

49When Jesus' followers saw what was going to happen, they said, "Lord, should we strike with our swords?" 50And one of them struck the servant of the high priest, cutting off his right ear.

III. *The Address of Jesus (22:51-53)*

51But Jesus answered, "No more of this!" And he touched the man's ear and healed him.

52Then Jesus said to the chief priests, the officers of the temple guard, and the elders, who had come for him, "Am I leading a rebellion, that you have come with swords and clubs? 53Every day I was with you in the temple courts, and you did not lay a hand on me. But this is your hour—when darkness reigns."

Peter Denies Christ (Luke 22:54-62)

(cf. Matt. 26:58, 69-75; Mark 14:54, 66-72 and John 18:15-18, 25-27)

In the story before this one we saw to what degree a person can appear to be a true disciple, when all the while he is actually filled with Satan (Luke 22:3). In this episode we discover to what degree a true disciple can be sifted by Satan (Luke 22:31).

It is a sad story. Jesus was arrested, and all of the disciples scattered—all except two (Peter and an unnamed disciple—John 18:15). These two men followed Jesus and the captors back into the city. They kept a secretive distance, but before long Peter was detected as being one of Jesus' disciples, and then he started his chain of denials.

It is a hope-filled story. Though Peter failed miserably, he did not end his life in defeat. He was quick to sense his guilt and to repent tearfully of his errors. Surely God can use such a man as this. It is not the mighty men God chooses, but the broken ones.

I. *The First Denial (22:54-57)*

54Then seizing him, they led him away and took him into the house of the high priest. Peter followed at a distance. 55But when they had kindled a fire in the middle of the courtyard and had sat down together, Peter sat down with them. 56A servant girl saw him seated there in the firelight. She looked closely at him and said, "This man was with him."
57But he denied it. "Woman, I don't know him," he said.

II. *The Second Denial (22:58)*

58A little later someone else saw him and said, "You also are one of them."
"Man, I am not!" Peter replied.

III. *The Third Denial (22:59-62)*

59About an hour later another asserted, "Certainly this fellow was with him, for he is a Galilean."
60Peter replied, "Man, I don't know what you're talking about!" Just as he was speaking, the rooster crowed. 61The Lord turned and looked

straight at Peter. Then Peter remembered the word the Lord had spoken to him: "Before the rooster crows today, you will disown me three times." 62And he went outside and wept bitterly.

The Soldiers Beat Jesus (Luke 22:63-65)

(cf. Matt. 26:67, 68 and Mark 14:65)

Luke bypasses the illegal trial that followed Jesus' arrest (Matt. 26:57-66); instead, he immediately shows us the cruel manner of Jesus' treatment. With a vicious and sadistic disposition, the soldiers began a ruthless persecution that would not be quenched until Jesus was crucified.

There is no limit to the depravity of people—including religious people—who refuse to submit to Christ. They will beat the very One who came to bless them.

**63The men who were guarding Jesus began mocking and beating
him. 64They blindfolded him and demanded, "Prophesy! Who hit you?"
65And they said many other insulting things to him.**

Jesus Is Condemned by the Council (Luke 22:66-71a)

(cf. Matt. 27:1, 2 and Mark 15:1)

The Council (or Sanhedrin) represents the highest power in the Jewish judicial system. Their decisions were final. It is before this panel of judges that Jesus now stood.

The Council was composed of seventy men from three classes of people: (1) the priests (probably twenty-four members), (2) the elders (also probably twenty-four members), and (3) the scribes (probably twenty-two members). The majority of these persons were also members of the Sadducee party.

In order to become a member of the Council (at least in theory), you had to be blameless before men, middle-aged, a scholar, wealthy, a father and accepted by the Council president. Unfortunately, when theory gives way to reality, there is often a massive gulf between the two. Such was the case during the New Testament period.

The official meeting place for conducting the business of the Council was in the Temple (or more specifically, in the Hall of Squares—called this because the floor here was made of hewn square stones. It was located in the middle of the southern portion of the Temple courts).

It was customary for the Council to meet daily, except on the Sabbath and during festivals. They would sit in a semicircle (so they could see each other). The High Priest was situated at the center of the half-circle, while the other members were arranged according to their age (the older members being closer to the High Priest). Only twenty-three members needed to be present in order to conduct business. And in matters of voting, the younger men voted first, casting their vote one after another until the oldest member present voted.

The Council presumably worked on the theory that the accused party was always innocent until proven to be guilty. In fact, it was to be the Council's aim to do everything possible to prove the innocence of the convicted party. This ideal philosophy, however, never appeared in the trial of Jesus.

66At daybreak the council of the elders of the people, both the chief
priests and teachers of the law, met together, and Jesus was led before
them. 67"If you are the Christ,[a]" they said, "tell us."
Jesus answered, "If I tell you, you will not believe me, 68and if I asked
you, you would not answer. 69But from now on, the Son of Man will be
seated at the right hand of the mighty God."
70They all asked, "Are you then the Son of God?"
He replied, "You are right in saying I am."
71Then they said, "Why do we need any more testimony? We have
heard it from his own lips."

Jesus Stands Before Pilate and Herod (Luke 23:1-25)

(cf. Matt. 27:11-26; Mark 15:1-15 and John 18:28-40)

When a person's mind is made up, even the truth is useless. It is a terrible thing to be close-minded, for such a person separates himself from the facts that can save his life.

The leading Jews closed their ears to God's Word; Pilate closed his ears to justice; and Herod closed his ears to morality. Each of these persons, because of their close-mindedness, would be responsible for Jesus' physical death.

a 67 Or *Messiah*

I. *Jesus Stands Before Pilate (23:1-7)*

**23 Then the whole assembly rose and led him off to Pilate. 2And
they began to accuse him, saying, "We have found this man
subverting our nation. He opposes payment of taxes to Caesar and
claims to be Christ,[a] a king."
3So Pilate asked Jesus, "Are you the king of the Jews?"
"Yes, it is as you say," Jesus replied.
4Then Pilate announced to the chief priests and the crowd, "I find no
basis for a charge against this man."
5But they insisted, "He stirs up the people all over Judea[b] by his
teaching. He started in Galilee and has come all the way here."
6On hearing this, Pilate asked if the man was a Galilean. 7When he
learned that Jesus was under Herod's jurisdiction, he sent him to
Herod, who was also in Jerusalem at that time.**

II. *Jesus Stands Before Herod (23:8-12)*

**8When Herod saw Jesus, he was greatly pleased, because for a long
time he had been wanting to see him. From what he had heard about
him, he hoped to see him perform some miracle. 9He plied him with
many questions, but Jesus gave him no answer. 10The chief priests and
the teachers of the law were standing there, vehemently accusing him.
11Then Herod and his soldiers ridiculed and mocked him. Dressing him
in an elegant robe, they sent him back to Pilate. 12That day Herod and
Pilate became friends—before this they had been enemies.**

III. *Jesus Again Stands Before Pilate (23:13-25)*

**13Pilate called together the chief priests, the rulers and the people,
14and said to them, "You brought me this man as one who was inciting
the people to rebellion. I have examined him in your presence and have
found no basis for your charges against him. 15Neither has Herod, for he
sent him back to us; as you can see, he has done nothing to deserve death.
16Therefore, I will punish him and then release him.[c]"
18With one voice they cried out, "Away with this man! Release
Barabbas to us!" 19(Barabbas had been thrown into prison for an
insurrection in the city, and for murder.)
20Wanting to release Jesus, Pilate appealed to them again. 21But they
kept shouting, "Crucify him! Crucify him!"
22For the third time he spoke to them: "Why? What crime has this man**

---

a 2 Or *Messiah;* also in verses 35 and 39 *b 5* Or *over the land of the Jews* *c 16* Some manuscripts *him.* *17Now he was obliged to release one man to them at the Feast.*

commited? I have found in him no grounds for the death penalty. Therefore I will have him punished and then release him."

23But with loud shouts they insistently demanded that he be
crucified, and their shouts prevailed. 24So Pilate decided to grant
their demand. 25He released the man who had been thrown into
prison for insurrection and murder, the one they asked for, and
surrendered Jesus to their will.

Jesus Is Crucified (Luke 23:26-49)

(cf. Matt. 27:26-56; Mark 15:16-41 and John 19:17-37)

This is the ugliest moment in all of human history. The second member of the triune Godhead became a man, and now men would kill Him! It is unthinkable. It is incomprehensible. Still, it happened.

This is the brightest moment in all of human history, too. The second member of the Godhead was now satisfying God's just demands for the penalty of everyone's sins. In Jesus' death is the hope of the world. Here we witness the building of a highway between heaven and earth—paved with the cross of Calvary (Rom. 5:12-21; Eph. 2:1-22).

I. *The Trail to Calvary (23:26-31)*

A. *Simon Carries Jesus' Cross (23:26)*

26As they led him away, they seized Simon from Cyrene, who was on his way in from the country, and put the cross on him and made him carry it behind Jesus.

B. *Women Mourn Over Jesus (23:27-31)*

27A large number of people followed him, including women who
mourned and wailed for him. 28Jesus turned and said to them, "Daugh-
ters of Jerusalem, do not weep for me; weep for yourselves and for your
children. 29For the time will come when you will say, 'Blessed are the
barren women, the wombs that never bore and the breasts that never
nursed!' 30Then

" 'they will say to the mountains, "Fall on us!"
and to the hills, "Cover us!" '[a]

[31]For if men do these things when the tree is green, what will happen when it is dry?"

Although these women grieved over the plight of Jesus, He took the time in this cruel march to inform them to grieve instead for a far greater disaster that was soon to happen. Because of the callousness of Israel, God would raise up an enemy to utterly desolate her land. The fulfillment of these predictive words came in A.D. 69 and 70, when 50,000 Roman soldiers completely destroyed and scattered the entire Jewish nation (Matt. 24; Mark 13; Luke 21).

II. *The Trials at Calvary (23:32-49)*

A. *The Crucifixion (23:32-34)*

[32]Two other men, both criminals, were also led out with him to be executed. [33]When they came to the place called The Skull, there they crucified him, along with the criminals—one on his right, the other on his left. [34]Jesus said, "Father, forgive them, for they do not know what they are doing."[b] And they divided up his clothes by casting lots.

B. *The Response of the People and Rulers (23:35)*

[35]The people stood watching, and the rulers even sneered at him. They said, "He saved others; let him save himself if he is the Christ of God, the Chosen One."

C. *The Response of the Soldiers (23:36-38)*

[36]The soldiers also came up and mocked him. They offered him wine vinegar [37]and said, "If you are the king of the Jews, save yourself."

[38]There was a written notice above him, which read: THIS IS THE KING OF THE JEWS.

D. *The Response of the Criminals (23:39-43)*

[39]One of the criminals who hung there hurled insults at him: "Aren't you the Christ? Save yourself and us!"

a 30 Hosea 10:8 *b 34* Some early manuscripts do not have this sentence.

40But the other criminal rebuked him. "Don't you fear God," he said,
"since you are under the same sentence? 41We are punished justly, for
we are getting what our deeds deserve. But this man has done nothing
wrong."
42Then he said, "Jesus, remember me when you come into your king-
dom."
43Jesus answered him, "I tell you the truth, today you will be with me
in paradise."

E. *The Response of God (23:44-46)*

44It was now about the sixth hour, and darkness came over the whole
land until the ninth hour, 45for the sun stopped shining. And the curtain
of the temple was torn in two. 46Jesus called out with a loud voice,
"Father, into your hands I commit my spirit." When he had said this, he
breathed his last.

F. *The Response of the Centurion (23:47)*

47The centurion, seeing what had happened, praised God and said,
"Surely this was a righteous man."

G. *The Response of Those Who Loved Him (23:48, 49)*

48When all the people who had gathered to witness this sight saw what
took place, they beat their breasts and went away. 49But all those who
knew him, including the women who had followed him from Galilee,
stood at a distance, watching these things.

Jesus Is Buried (Luke 23:50-56)

(cf. Matt. 27:57-66; Mark 15:42-47 and John 19:38-42)

Before us are two touching scenes. First, we see Joseph, a man who defended Jesus before the Council (or Sanhedrin), and who now does everything within his power to provide Jesus with a decent burial. Second, we see a group of women who also want to make Jesus' burial proper, but because of the nearness of the start of the Sabbath (6:00 P.M. Friday), and because of their deep respect for God's laws, they are unable to complete their work at that time, though they will be at Jesus' tomb with the burial spices the instant the Sabbath is over.

I. *Joseph's Concern (23:50-54)*

**[50]Now there was a man named Joseph, a member of the Council, a
good and upright man, [51]who had not consented to their decision and
action. He came from the Judean town of Arimathea and he was waiting
for the kingdom of God. [52]Going to Pilate, he asked for Jesus' body.
[53]Then he took it down, wrapped it in linen cloth and placed it in a
tomb cut in the rock, one in which no one had yet been laid. [54]It was
Preparation Day, and the Sabbath was about to begin.**

II. *The Women's Concern (23:55, 56)*

**[55]The women who had come with Jesus from Galilee followed Joseph
and saw the tomb and how his body was laid in it. [56]Then they went home
and prepared spices and perfumes. But they rested on the Sabbath in
obedience to the commandment.**

Jesus Rises from the Dead (Luke 24:1-12)

(cf. Matt. 28:1-10; Mark 16:1-8 and John 20:1-18)

The miraculous is unbelievable for some, and nearly unbelievable for many others. Even those who followed Jesus found it difficult, at times, to accept the possibility that a miracle would occur, especially regarding His resurrection.

The faithful women who came to the tomb early Sunday morning were not truly full of faith. They came with spices to anoint a dead body, not to witness a resurrection.

Probably all of the disciples considered the report of the Resurrection of Jesus too fanatical to be taken seriously. The dash of Peter and another disciple to the tomb may have been sparked more by curiosity than by faith (Luke 24:12; John 20:3-9).

The news of the Resurrection was seemingly too good to be true. It was more than anyone could hope for. Therefore, it was doubted.

How much some of us are like these men and women. We believe, but only in a qualified measure; we believe until we hear about the miraculous, and then we stop believing. But there is room for the miraculous in our faith. The Resurrection of Christ is a literal reality, and we must accept it if we are to be saved (Rom. 10:9, 10). Indeed, the very heart of the gospel of Jesus Christ is found in this glorious event (1 Cor. 15:1ff.).

I. *The Women Visit the Tomb (24:1-8)*

**24 On the first day of the week, very early in the morning, the
women took the spices they had prepared and went to the tomb.
2They found the stone rolled away from the tomb, 3but when they
entered, they did not find the body of the Lord Jesus. 4While they
were wondering about this, suddenly two men in clothes that gleamed
like lightning stood beside them. 5In their fright the women bowed
down with their faces to the ground, but the men said to them, "Why
do you look for the living among the dead? 6He is not here; he has
risen! Remember how he told you, while he was still with you in
Galilee: 7'The Son of Man must be delivered into the hands of sinful
men, be crucified and on the third day be raised again.' " 8Then they
remembered his words.**

II. *Peter Visits the Tomb (24:9-12)*

**9When they came back from the tomb, they told all these things to the
Eleven and to all the others. 10It was Mary Magdalene, Joanna, Mary
the mother of James, and the others with them who told this to the
apostles. 11But they did not believe the women, because their words
seemed to them like nonsense. 12Peter, however, got up and ran to the
tomb. Bending over, he saw the strips of linen lying by themselves, and
he went away, wondering to himself what had happened.**

Jesus Meets Two Disciples on the Way to Emmaus (Luke 24:13-35)

There are some compelling points in this story that must not be overlooked: (1) Notice how downcast our lives are without any hope in the Resurrection of Christ. (2) Notice how an inadequate knowledge of the Scriptures will yield bewilderment and depression. (3) Notice how Jesus uses the Scriptures (rather than a miraculous sign) to validate His own resurrection—during this dispensation of God's dealings with people it is the written Word that has priority. (4) Notice the result of assurance in Jesus' resurrection—jubilation and testifying on the Lord's behalf.

I. *The Regret of the Disciples (24:13-24)*

13Now that same day two of them were going to a village called
Emmaus, about seven miles[a] from Jerusalem. 14They were talking with
each other about everything that had happened. 15As they talked and
discussed these things with each other, Jesus himself came up and
walked along with them; 16but they were kept from recognizing him.
17He asked them, "What are you discussing together as you walk
along?"
They stood still, their faces downcast. 18One of them, named Cleopas,
asked him, "Are you the only one living in Jerusalem who doesn't know
the things that have happened there in these days?"
19"What things?" he asked.
"About Jesus of Nazareth," they replied. "He was a prophet, powerful
in word and deed before God and all the people. 20The chief priests and
our rulers handed him over to be sentenced to death, and they crucified
him; 21but we had hoped that he was the one who was going to redeem
Israel. And what is more, it is the third day since all this took place. 22In
addition, some of our women amazed us. They went to the tomb early
this morning 23but didn't find his body. They came and told us that they
had seen a vision of angels, who said he was alive. 24Then some of our
companions went to the tomb and found it just as the women had said,
but him they did not see."

Jesus had more disciples than the twelve. Many believed in Him. Here are two such examples. Apparently these men traveled from their home in Emmaus when they learned of Jesus' experiences in Jerusalem. They wanted to be near Him in these final hours. After His death they remained in Jerusalem until Sunday. They heard the reports of His resurrection from the women, and they listened to the testimony of Peter, but somehow it was all too incredible to accept. So they decided to journey home, with confusion and disappointment in their hearts.

As they traveled, Jesus joined them, though His identity was withheld from them. The method of the concealment is not important (Mark says He appeared "in a different form"—16:12). It is important, however, to understand why the secrecy was employed at all. The least complicated reason, and probably the most accurate, is that Jesus wanted the disciples, like all of those who will place their trust in Him, to put their confidence in the credibility of the Scriptures. The Jews, on the whole, were notorious for seeking signs (1 Cor. 1:22ff.), but Jesus wanted them to trust God's Word rather than to demand signs for proof.

There seems to be a significant shift in our focus here. Originally Jesus stressed the

a 13 Greek *sixty stadia* (about 11 kilometers)

importance of placing confidence in himself, while now He stressed the worth of placing confidence in the Scriptures that discuss His prophesied role. In other words, Jesus would not be with His disciples, after His resurrection or ascension, in the same manner that He was with them prior to these events. Therefore, a new period and a new relationship is developing between Jesus and His disciples. Jesus, then, is preparing them for the transition that must occur. Once they walked with the living Word; now they must walk with the written Word. Both would be in agreement, and both would be effectual, but the written Word was now to become the source of each disciple's convictions and confidence.

II. *The Reasonings of Jesus (24:25-27)*

25He said to them, "How foolish you are, and how slow of heart to
believe all that the prophets have spoken! 26Did not the Christ[a] have to
suffer these things and then enter his glory?" 27And beginning with
Moses and all the Prophets, he explained to them what was said in all the
Scriptures concerning himself.

All sixty-six books of the Bible, either explicitly or implicitly, reveal Christ. "Abraham rejoiced at the thought of seeing my day," said Jesus (John 8:56). "Moses . . . wrote of me" declares the Lord (John 5:46). "These are the Scriptures," says Jesus, "that testify about me" (John 5:39).

God wrote a book to reveal Christ. The highest interest of heaven is to exalt Jesus Christ and to reveal Him to the world. The Bible, then, is primarily a book about God and His Son, Jesus (Gen. 3:15; 49:10; Deut. 18:15; Ps. 2:1, 2; 22:1-22; Isa. 7:14; 9:1, 2, 6, 7; 49:6; Dan. 9:24-27; Mic. 5:2; Zech. 9:9; Mal. 3:1; 4:1 and so forth).

III. *The Revelation of the Disciples (24:28-32)*

28As they approached the village to which they were going, Jesus
acted as if he were going farther. 29But they urged him strongly, "Stay
with us, for it is nearly evening; the day is almost over." So he went in to
stay with them.

30When he was at the table with them, he took bread, gave thanks,
broke it and began to give it to them. 31Then their eyes were opened and
they recognized him, and he disappeared from their sight. 32They asked
each other, "Were not our hearts burning within us while he talked with
us on the road and opened the Scriptures to us?"

a 26 Or *Messiah;* also in verse 46

IV. *The Report of the Disciples (24:33-35)*

33They got up and returned at once to Jerusalem. There they found the Eleven and those with them, assembled together 34and saying, "It is true! The Lord has risen and has appeared to Simon." 35Then the two told what had happened on the way, and how Jesus was recognized by them when he broke the bread.

Jesus Appears to the Disciples (Luke 24:36-49)

(cf. Mark 16:14 and John 20:19-23)

The extremes to which the disciples' emotions must have been stretched on this first Easter Sunday requires our attention. First, their hearts were at the lowest possible ebb. Their Master was dead, and this day, the third one after His crucifixion, seemed to seal that fact once and for all. Next, there was the nearly hysterical report from the women, who claimed to have seen angels, an empty tomb and the resurrected Jesus. Following this, Peter verified the women's testimony regarding the empty tomb, though they did not believe the absence of Jesus' body from the tomb necessarily implied a resurrection. Finally, the Lord himself appeared before them!

The essence of Jesus' moments among His disciples is designed to accomplish three things: (1) He came to bring peace to their troubled and shocked hearts; (2) He came to bring proofs (both physical and scriptural) for their perplexed minds; and (3) He came to bring promises for their unclear futures.

I. *Peace for Troubled Hearts (24:36)*

36While they were still talking about this, Jesus himself stood among them and said to them, "Peace be with you."

II. *Proofs for Perplexed Minds (24:37-48)*

37They were startled and frightened, thinking they saw a ghost. 38He said to them, "Why are you troubled, and why do doubts rise in your minds? 39Look at my hands and my feet. It is I myself! Touch me and see; a ghost does not have flesh and bones, as you see I have."

40When he had said this, he showed them his hands and feet. 41And while they still did not believe it because of joy and amazement, he

**asked them, "Do you have anything here to eat?" 42They gave him a
piece of broiled fish, 43and he took it and ate it in their presence.
44He said to them, "This is what I told you while I was still with you:
Everything must be fulfilled that is written about me in the Law of
Moses, the Prophets and the Psalms."
45Then he opened their minds so they could understand the Scriptures.
46He told them, "This is what is written: The Christ will suffer and rise
from the dead on the third day, 47and repentance and forgiveness of sins
will be preached in his name to all nations, beginning at Jerusalem.
48You are witnesses of these things.**

III. *Promises for Unclear Futures (24:49)*

**49I am going to send you what my Father has promised; but stay in the
city until you have been clothed with power from on high."**

Jesus' Ascension (Luke 24:50-53)

(cf. Mark 16:19, 20 and Acts 1:9-11)

There is a separation of forty days between verses 49 and 50. During this period Jesus appeared numerous times to His followers. (See the chart entitled, "Jesus' Post-Resurrection Appearances.") He also taught His disciples at these times (Acts 1:1-8).

Now comes Jesus' ascension. He will not appear to people in bodily form again until His second coming. From this hour forward the works of God will rest in the hands of Jesus' loyal followers.

One might expect the final departure of Jesus to be a tearful experience, but, instead, the disciples were full of joy and praise. This was not the end, and they knew it. Indeed, this was but the beginning. They had a mission to perform. People must be rescued from the judgment of hell, and they must be about this task. But first they must wait for the appointed time to commence this mission—the day of Pentecost. On this day Jerusalem would be full of people to hear them speak about Jesus; also on this day they would be filled with the Holy Spirit to enable them to make their speech both clear and forceful!

**50When he had led them out to the vicinity of Bethany, he lifted up his
hands and blessed them. 51While he was blessing them, he left them and**

was taken up into heaven. [52]Then they worshiped him and returned to Jerusalem with great joy. [53]And they stayed continually at the temple, praising God.

JESUS' POST-RESURRECTION APPEARANCES

1. To Mary Magdalene—Mark 16:9-11
2. To the other Mary—Matt. 28:1-10
3. To Peter—Luke 24:34; 1 Cor. 15:5
4. To the two disciples on the Emmaus road—Mark 16:12, 13; Luke 24:13-35
5. To ten disciples in the upper room—Mark 16:14; Luke 24:36-43; John 20:19-24
6. To the eleven disciples in the upper room—John 20:26-29
7. To seven disciples by the Sea of Galilee—John 21:1-23
8. To the five hundred—1 Cor. 15:6
9. To James, the Lord's brother—1 Cor. 15:7
10. To the eleven disciples on a mountain in Galilee—Matt. 28:16-20; Mark 16:15-18
11. To the eleven disciples on the Mount of Olives—Luke 24:44-53; Acts 1:9-11

SELECTED BIBLIOGRAPHY

Commentaries

Barclay, William. *The Gospel of Matthew.* Philadelphia: The Westminster Press, 1957.

_______. *The Gospel of Mark.* Philadelphia: The Westminster Press, 1954.

_______. *The Gospel of Luke.* Philadelphia: The Westminster Press, 1953.

Geldenhuys, J. Norval. *Commentary on the Gospel of Luke.* Grand Rapids: Wm. B. Eerdmans Publishing Company, 1951.

Hendriksen, William. *New Testament Commentary: Exposition of the Gospel According to Matthew.* Grand Rapids: Baker Book House, 1973.

_______. *New Testament Commentary: Exposition of the Gospel According to Mark.* Grand Rapids: Baker Book House, 1975.

_______. *New Testament Commentary: Exposition of the Gospel According to Luke.* Grand Rapids: Baker Book House, 1978.

Henry, Matthew. *Matthew Henry's Commentary on the Whole Bible,* vol. 3. Grand Rapids: Guardian Press, 1976.

Lane, William L. *The Gospel According to Mark.* Grand Rapids: Wm. B. Eerdmans Publishing Company, 1974.

Morgan, G. Campbell. *The Gospel According to Mark.* Old Tappan: Fleming H. Revell, 1927.

Ryle, John Charles. *Expository Thoughts on the Gospels.* 8 vols. Cambridge: James Clark and Co.

Reference Works

Buttrick, George A., and Crim, Keith R., eds. *The Interpreter's Dictionary of the Bible.* 4 vol. Nashville: Abington Press, 1962.

Douglas, J. D. *The New Bible Dictionary.* Grand Rapids: Wm. B. Erdmans Publishing Company, 1962.

Edersheim, Alfred. *Sketches of Jewish Social Life in the Days of Christ.* Grand Rapids: Wm. B. Eerdmans Publishing Company, 1970.

Freeman, James M. *Manners and Customs of the Bible.* Plainfield: Logos, 1972, Reprint.

Hackett, H.B., ed. *Smith's Dictionary of the Bible.* 4 vol. Grand Rapids: Baker Book House, 1971. Reprint.

Harrison, Everett F., ed. *Baker's Dictionary of Theology.* Grand Rapids: Baker Book House, 1960.

M'Clintock, John, and Strong, James. *Cyclopedia of Biblical, Theological and Ecclesiastical Literature.* 10 vols. New York: Arno Press, 1969.

Miller, Madeleine S., and Miller, J. Lane. *Harper's Encyclopedia of Bible Life.* San Francisco: Harper and Row, 1978. Reprint.

Pfeiffer, Charles F. *The Biblical World.* Grand Rapids: Baker Book House, 1966.

Pfeiffer, Charles F., and Vos, Howard F. *The Wycliffe Historical Geography of Bible Lands.* Chicago: Moody Press, 1967.

Shepherd, J.W. *The Christ of the Gospels.* Grand Rapids: Wm. B. Eerdmans Publishing Company, 1939.

Tenney, Merrill C. *The Zondervan Pictorial Encyclopedia of the Bible.* 4 vols. Grand Rapids: Zondervan Publishing House, 1975.

This is the first volume in a series of continuing volumes. We will be pleased to send you information on succeeding works.

Please write to:

Logos Commentary 2
Box 191
Plainfield, NJ 07061
USA

notes

notes

notes

notes

notes

notes

notes

notes

notes

notes

notes

notes